GENDER AND ADDICTIONS

LIBRARY OF SUBSTANCE ABUSE AND ADDICTION TREATMENT

A Series of Books Edited By
Jerome David Levin, Ph.D.

Substance abuse and addiction are the third most common cause of mortality in the United States. They are among the most prevalent mental illnesses, not only in the United States, but throughout the world. They are also notoriously difficult to treat. Mental health professionals see few patients whose lives or illnesses have not been profoundly affected by their own use or that of their families or peers. Addiction is not peripheral but central to the human condition and research into it is illuminating our understanding of self.

The *Library of Substance Abuse and Addiction Treatment* is dedicated to providing mental health professionals with the tools they need to treat these scourges—tools ranging from scientific knowledge to clinical technique. Nonideological, it is equally open to behavioral, cognitive, disease model, psychodynamic, and least harm perspectives. An overdetermined disorder affecting millions of people requires multiple viewpoints if it is to be successfully treated. The *Library* provides those multiple perspectives for clinicians, students, and laypeople as articulated by the most insightful workers in the field. Practical, utilitarian, scholarly, and state-of-the-art, these books are addressed to all who wish to deepen their understanding of and increase their clinical efficacy in treating addiction.

Family Therapy of the Addictions
Jerome D. Levin

Primer of Treating Substance Abusers
Jerome D. Levin

Treatment of Alcoholism and Other Addictions: *A Self-Psychology Approach*
Jerome D. Levin

Recovery from Alcoholism:
Beyond Your Wildest Dreams
Jerome D. Levin

Couple and Family Therapy of Addiction
Jerome D. Levin

The Dynamics and Treatment of Alcoholism: *Essential Papers*
Jerome D. Levin and Ronna Weiss, Editors

Gender and Addictions:
Men and Women in Treatment
S. Lala Ashenberg Straussner
and Elizabeth Zelvin, Editors

Psychodynamics of Drug Dependence
Jack D. Blaine and
Demetrios A. Julius, Editors

The Hidden Dimension
Leon Wurmser

Substance Abusing High Achievers:
Addiction as an Equal Opportunity Destroyer
Abraham J. Twerski

Creating the Capacity for Attachment:
Treating Addictions and the Alienated Self
Karen B. Walant

Psychotherapy of Cocaine Addiction:
Entering the Interpersonal World of the Cocaine Addict
David Mark and Jeffrey Faude

GENDER AND ADDICTIONS

Men and Women
in Treatment

EDITED BY

Shulamith Lala Ashenberg Straussner, DSW, CAS
Elizabeth Zelvin, MSW, ACSW, CASAC

JASON ARONSON INC.
Northvale, New Jersey
London

This book was set in 10 pt. Veljovic by Alpha Graphics of Pittsfield, New Hampshire and printed and bound by Book-mart Press, Inc. of North Bergen, New Jersey.

Copyright © 1997 by Jason Aronson Inc.

10 9 8 7 6 5 4 3 2 1

Library of Congress Cataloging-in-Publication Data
Gender and addictions : men and women in treatment / edited by
  Shulamith Lala Ashenberg Straussner, Elizabeth Zelvin.
      p.   cm.—(Jerome D. Levin series)
  Includes bibliographical references and index.
  ISBN 0-7657-0070-0 (alk. paper)
  1. Substance abuse—Sex differences.   2. Compulsive behavior—Sex
differences.   3. Substance abuse—Treatment.   4. Compulsive
behavior—Treatment.   5. Sex differences (Psychology)   6. Women—
Substance use.   7. Men—Substance use.   8. Recovering addicts.
  I. Straussner, Shulamith Lala Ashenberg.   II. Zelvin, Elizabeth.
  III. Series.
  [DNLM: 1. Substance Dependence—therapy.   2. Sex Factors.
  3. Psychotherapy—methods. WM 270 G324 1997]
  RC564.G3727   1997
  616.86'0082—dc21
  DNLM/DLC
  for Library of Congress   97-5148

Printed in the United States of America on acid-free paper. Jason Aronson Inc. offers books and cassettes. For information and catalog write to Jason Aronson Inc., 230 Livingston Street, Northvale, New Jersey 07647-1731. Or visit our website: http://www.aronson.com

CONTENTS

Preface and Acknowledgments   **xi**

Part I:
Overview of Gender Issues in
Addiction Treatment   **1**

1   Gender and Substance Abuse   **3**
    Shulamith Lala Ashenberg Straussner, DSW, CAS

Part II:
Women's Issues in Addiction Treatment   **29**

2   Applying Relational Theory to
    Addiction Treatment   **31**
    Diane B. Byington, PhD

3   Codependency Issues of
    Substance-Abusing Women   **47**
    Elizabeth Zelvin, ACSW, CASAC

4   Women, Addiction, and Sexuality   **71**
    Stephanie S. Covington, PhD, LCSW

5   Substance-Abusing Women and
    Sexual Abuse   **97**
    Rita Teusch, PhD

6   Parenting Issues for Substance-
    Abusing Women   **123**
    Nancy J. Smyth, PhD, CSW, CASAC
    Brenda A. Miller, PhD

7   High-Achieving Women: Issues in
    Addiction and Recovery   **151**
    Betsy Robin Spiegel, MSW, ACSW
    Donna Demetri Friedman, MSW, MA

8   Lesbian Women and Substance Abuse   **167**
    Eloise Rathbone-McCuan, PhD, MSW
    Diana L. Stokke, MSW, CSW, CASAC

9   The Impact of AIDS on the Lives of Women   **197**
    Ellen Grace Friedman, MSW, CASAC

10 Women with Depression and Substance Abuse Problems   **223**
Carolyn Morell, PhD

11 Substance-Abusing Women and Eating Disorders   **243**
Katherine van Wormer, PhD, MSSW
Emily Askew, MA

12 Overcoming Sexism in AA: How Women Cope   **263**
Margaret Coker, MSW, ACSW

Part III: Men's Issues in Addiction Treatment   **283**

13 Psychodynamic Perspectives on Substance-Abusing Men   **285**
Jerome D. Levin, PhD

14 Incorporating Men's Values into Substance
Abuse Treatment   **311**
Jeffrey Zeth, MSW, CASAC

15 Alcoholic Fathers and Substance-Abusing Sons   **333**
Paul Mulinski, PhD

16 Sexual Dependence among Recovering
Substance-Abusing Men   **359**
Douglas K. Braun-Harvey, MA

17 Recovery Issues of Substance-Abusing Gay Men   **385**
Douglas J. Warn, MSW, CSW

18 Substance-Abusing Male Executives   **411**
Mark Cohen, DSW, MPH

19 Assessment and Treatment of Male Substance Abusers
with Learning Disabilities and Attention-Deficit/
Hyperactivity Disorder   **427**
Christianne De Witt-Downey, MA
Karen Spinelli-Falberg, MSW, CSW

20 Hispanic Substance-Abusing Men and Machismo   **451**
Elisa Valladares Goldberg, ACSW, CASAC

21 Men and Gambling   **469**
Rick LairRobinson, MSW

Index   **493**

CONTRIBUTORS

Emily Askew, MA
Group and Family Therapist
Choices, Covenant Hospital
Waterloo, Iowa

Douglas K. Braun-Harvey, MA
Director, The Sexual Dependency Institute
San Diego, California

Diane B. Byington, PhD
Associate Professor, Graduate School of Social Work
University of Denver
Denver, Colorado

Mark Cohen, DSW, MPH
Partner, Harris, Rothenberg, International
New York, New York

Margaret Coker, MSW, ACSW
Department of Social Work, Albany Medical Center
    Hospital
Clinical Instructor, Albany Medical College
Albany, New York

Stephanie S. Covington, PhD, LCSW
Co-director, Institute for Relational Development
La Jolla, California

Christianne De Witt-Downey, MA
Albert Einstein College of Medicine
Division of Substance Abuse
Bronx, New York

Donna Demetri Friedman, MSW, MA
Clinical Social Worker/Psychotherapist
Riverdale Mental Health Center
Bronx, New York

Ellen Grace Friedman, MSW, CASAC
Associate Director, Supportive Services Methadone
    Maintenance Treatment Program
Beth Israel Medical Center, New York, New York
Associate Adjunct Professor
New York University Ehrenkranz School of Social
    Work
New York, New York

Elisa Valladares Goldberg, ACSW, CASAC
Coordinator, Satellite Clinic at Holland House
Outpatient Department, Project Renewal
New York, New York

Rick LairRobinson, MSW
Southwest State University
Department of Social Sciences, Social Work Program
Marshall, Minnesota

Jerome D. Levin, PhD
Director, Alcohol Counseling Program
New School for Social Research
New York, New York

Brenda A. Miller, PhD
Deputy Director, Research Institute on Addiction
Buffalo, New York

Carolyn Morell, PhD
Assistant Professor
Social Work Program, Niagara University
Niagara University, New York

Paul Mulinski, PhD
Assistant Chief of Staff
VA Connecticut Healthcare System
West Haven, Connecticut
Assistant Clinical Professor of Psychiatry
Yale University School of Medicine
New Haven, Connecticut

Eloise Rathbone-McCuan, PhD, MSW
Associate Chief of Social Work for Research & Planning
Colmery-O'Neil Veterans Administration Medical Center
Topeka, Kansas

Nancy J. Smyth, PhD, CSW
Assistant Professor
University of Buffalo School of Social Work, SUNY
Buffalo, New York

Betsy Robin Spiegel, MSW, ACSW
Private Practice
New York, New York

Karen Spinelli-Falberg, MSW, CSW
Albert Einstein College of Medicine
Division of Substance Abuse
Bronx, New York

Diana L. Stokke, MSW, CSW, CASAC
Case Manager, Hope Case Management Services
Psychotherapist, New Hope Guild
Brooklyn, New York

Shulamith Lala Ashenberg Straussner, DSW, CAS
Associate Professor and Coordinator, Post-Master's Program in the
    Treatment of Alcohol and Drug Abusing Clients
New York University Ehrenkranz School of Social Work
New York, New York

Rita Teusch, PhD
Private Practice, Cambridge and Wellesley, Massachusetts
Formerly, Director, Eating Disorders and Dual Diagnosis, Women's
    Program
Charles River Hospital
Wellesley, Massachusetts

Katherine van Wormer, PhD, MSSW
Associate Professor of Social Work, University of Northern Iowa
Cedar Falls, Iowa

Douglas J. Warn, MSW, CSW
Project Renewal Social Worker, Outpatient Department
New York, New York

Elizabeth Zelvin, ACSW, CASAC
Program Director, Outpatient Department
Project Renewal
New York, New York

Jeffrey Zeth, MSW, CASAC
Chemical Dependency Specialist
Hazelden New York
New York, New York

PREFACE
AND
ACKNOWLEDGMENTS

This book was first conceived as part of a larger work focusing on treatment implications related to diversity among substance-abusing clients and exploring such areas as gender, ethnicity, and life cycle issues. It soon became apparent that, on the one hand, each of these three areas covered an enormous number of subcategories and variables and, on the other, not only substance abuse or chemical dependency but process addictions and compulsive behaviors as well must be considered for an adequate exploration of the issues. This book on gender and addictions is the first result of these conclusions.

As clinicians and trainers of clinicians, we were determined to produce a work that connected theory with good clinical practice. We know that clinicians today, whether they are psychiatrists, psychologists, social workers, nurses, or counselors, work with clients with multiple diagnoses and that the simplistic approaches of the past are no longer viable. In order to make a significant difference in the recovery of individual clients, effective treatment must move beyond gender sensitivity to gender competence.

While historically, substance abuse research and treatment were based mostly on male models, in reviewing the literature and seeking contributors for this book, we found that currently to express an interest in *gender* is usually assumed to mean that one is concerned with *women*. The idea that men too are a "gender," and that their addiction patterns and treatment needs must be reexamined in the light of postfeminist and men's movement consciousness as well as the rapid growth of scientific knowledge in the 1990s, has barely been explored. It was much easier to find contributors for that portion of our book addressing women's issues than to solicit authors who could consider the impact of male gender on addictions in a reflective way.

Certain themes emerged as we began to compile our topics. In the women's section, the most important of these, unquestionably, is the relational model of women's psychological development formulated over the past twenty years by such theorists as Miller, Chodorow, and Gilligan. This long overdue illumination of how women function, with its emphasis on connection and relationship, as opposed to the Freudian-based, male-oriented models of development focusing on separation and individuation, provides the underpinning for many valuable insights about the nature of female addictions and the framing of the recovery process. In the men's section, traditional male roles, values, and concerns are both confirmed and reconsidered in explorations of psychodynamics and men's movement trends; issues of power, control, and dependency; and socially condoned male activities and values such as gambling and machismo. Other themes that emerged in the process of putting together a coherent work were the interrelationship of substance and process addictions, the importance of sexuality and gender identity, and the profound impact of familial substance abuse on both men and women.

We have tried to address as many as possible of the most significant areas of male and female differences. However, this is by no means an exhaustive work. Time limitation necessitated the omission of planned chapters addressing addiction issues among elderly men and women and the impact of gender and racism on substance-abusing black men.

We would like to thank our contributors, who cooperated diligently and patiently through many delays and revisions and provided a rich stew of scholarship, observation, clinical experience, and fresh thinking. Liz also would like to thank Project Renewal, which has supported her professional ventures far beyond her "day job," while Lala would like to thank Dean Thomas Meenaghan and the many colleagues at New York University Ehrenkranz School of Social Work who offered encouragement and support, Drs. Jerome Levin and Jeffrey Seinfeld for linking us with Dr. Jason Aronson, and Nancy Chow who helped with last minute copying and mailing and all the little details leading to the production of a manuscript with so many contributors. Finally, we want to thank our families, particularly our husbands Joel Straussner and Brian Daly, who lovingly tolerate life with "women who do too much."

S. Lala Ashenberg Straussner
Elizabeth Zelvin
New York, New York
August 1997

I

Overview of Gender Issues in Addiction Treatment

Gender and Substance Abuse

Shulamith Lala Ashenberg Straussner

1

Why can't a woman be more like a man?

—Henry Higgins in *My Fair Lady*

One problem in talking about difference and the consequent theorizing of "difference" lies in the readiness with which difference becomes deviance and deviance becomes sin. . . .

—Carol Gilligan 1993

As numerous writers, philosophers, psychologists, and other mental health professionals have recognized over the years, men and women are different. Such real, or even presumed gender differences, whether or not they are perceived as deficits, have implications for clinical practice:

> Increasingly we recognize that gender has pervasive and fundamental consequences for every aspect of life. Around the globe, gender is assumed to reflect not only anatomy, but personal competence as well. Gender dictates the paycheck, occupational opportunity, and status. And of course, gender and gender differences affect the way in which worker and client interact with and perceive each other. [Davis and Proctor 1989, p. 124]

Gender and gender differences are important variables in both clinical treatment in general and substance abuse treatment in particular. Gender plays a role in differential use of various substances by men and women, in their physiological reactions to the substances, in familial and societal reactions to their problems, in their help-seeking behavior, and in their interactions with clinicians. It also plays a role in the counter-transference reactions of treatment providers. This chapter provides a brief overview of the concept of gender and focuses on the differences in psychopathology between men and women and in their use and abuse of various substances. Treatment implications for clinicians treating substance-abusing men and women are discussed.

THE CONCEPT OF GENDER AND GENDER IDENTIFICATION

There is no generally accepted definition of the concept of gender. It is often used interchangeably with the term *sex* (Maccoby 1988). Nonetheless, a growing number of theorists, researchers, and clinicians view the concept of *sex* as focusing on biological differences between men and women, whereas *gender* is seen as describing those male and female traits and behaviors that are culturally defined as appropriate for that sex (Unger 1979).

Gender is not only a constellation of individual dynamics. It is also a social category that generates certain social beliefs and expectations about behavior. These beliefs and expectations are introjected by individuals and, for better or worse, become part of their self-identity as men and women. Consequently, when a clinician sees a client he or she needs to be sensitive to the biological characteristics of the client, to the client's sense of his or her own gender identity, and to societal expectations or reactions to the client's gender. For example, a pregnant woman coming to a treatment facility with a recent history of cocaine abuse is dealing not only with the biological changes related to her pregnancy and to her drug abuse. She is also dealing with societal views—and her own intro- jects—about women, women who are pregnant, and pregnant women who abuse drugs. It is this multilayered context that makes gender such an important, yet often neglected, treatment variable.

GENDER-RELATED DIFFERENCES

The numerous differences between boys/men and girls/women have been attributed variously to biochemical, physiological, psychological, familial, sociocultural, and economic factors with each perspective hav- ing tremendous implications for the understanding and treatment of men and women. This section will discuss only a few of these theories, em- phasizing the major psychological and social dynamics related to gender differences.

Freudian Theory of Gender Differences

Despite numerous criticisms, Freud's psychoanalytic theory of personal- ity development and psychopathology (Brenner 1973, Freud 1925) re- mains an important component in the training of many clinicians. Freud emphasized the role of instinctual drives and the child's perception of anatomical differences between the sexes in personality formation. Ac- cording to Freud, it is during the phallic stage of psychosexual develop- ment—between the ages of 3 and 6—that the development of boys and girls diverges. During this stage a child first becomes aware that boys and men have penises and girls and women do not. This realization leads to "penis envy" in girls and "castration anxiety" in boys. It is during this phase also that children become sexually attracted to the parent of the oppo- site sex and develop hostility for the same-sex parent. The healthy reso- lution of these incestuous desires—the Oedipus complex for boys and the Electra complex for girls—is through identification with the same-sex parent. However,

> the different courses followed by boys and girls in forming and resolv- ing the Oedipus complex have far-reaching consequences in Freudian theory for the development of psychological gender differences. Among males, the result of resolution is masculine identification, contempt for

or fear of women, and a strong superego. Among females, the upshot of the complex is feminine identification, a sense of inferiority, contempt for other women, a tendency toward jealousy, a rejection of clitoral sexuality, masochism, a wish for a child, an obsession with sexual attractiveness and a weaker superego. [Lips 1993, p. 42]

According to some critics, the classical Freudian view of gender development implied that

accepting the feminine role would always mean settling for inferior status and opportunities, and women who were not able to reconcile themselves to this status were candidates for therapy because they had not accepted their femininity. . . . Freud's theory also held stringent and inflexible standards for the development of masculinity. For boys to develop normally, they must experience severe anxiety during early childhood and develop hatred for their father. This trauma should lead boys to identify with their father and to experience the advantages of the male role through becoming like him. Boys who do not make a sufficiently complete break with their mother were not likely to become fully masculine and to remain somewhat feminine and thus experience the problems that society accords to nonmasculine men. [Brannon 1996, p. 7]

Although some of Freud's female followers, such as Klein (1932) and Horney (1926), proposed a less phallocentric view of development and emphasized the importance for personality development of a child's pre-oedipal relationship with the mother, the classical Freudian view of femininity and masculinity has played a crucial role in prevailing views of mental health problems and treatment approaches over the years. It was only after the 1960s, as a consequence of the growing feminist movement, that a different perspective on gender development, particularly on women's development, became more widely accepted.

Feminist Views of Gender Development

Feminist theorists and researchers, reacting to what they perceived as a male-centered bias in the existing theories of gender development, began exploring a different conceptualization of gender differences. Building on the work of Horney (1926), Chodorow (1974) hypothesized that gender differences result from a child's attempt to separate from his or her mother. Contrary to Freud, who emphasized the difficulties faced by girls in forming a positive gender identity, Chodorow viewed boys as needing to struggle to separate in order to form a masculine identity. This process includes a rejection of female values and all that is feminine, including intense interest and skills in relationships. For girls, however, feminine identity "comes to define itself in relation and connection to other people" (Chodorow 1974, p. 43). Gender identity formation is thus an outcome of different processes in boys and girls: whereas boys need to separate and individuate in order to form a masculine identity, girls form their identity through attachment.

Chodorow's theory influenced Gilligan (1982) to reexamine the moral model of development formulated by Kohlberg (1981), who classified the more frequent emphasis on human relationships of females as indicating a lower level of moral development than the common emphasis of males on the principles of justice. Gilligan's research confirmed that men and women differ in their moral focus: whereas men's moral judgments reflect separation, individuation, and justice, women's emphasize attachment, caring, and a balancing of conflicting responsibilities. However, such differences indicate the different developmental paths and social reinforcement of behavioral choices of men and women, rather than women's inferiority. Moreover, according to Gilligan, women's greater concern with human relationships and feelings may indicate a higher level of moral development than men's focus on an abstract notion of justice.

While more recent studies (Gilligan et al. 1988) indicate that the moral development of adults does not differ very dramatically between the sexes, research findings continue to indicate that the focus on attachment and caring for others is more common for women than men. Moreover, Gilligan's research confirmed Chodorow's (1978) views regarding the crucial, yet different, role of dependency and interpersonal relationship in men and women: "It appears that men and women may experience attachment and separation in different ways and that each sex perceives a danger which the other does not see—men in connection, women in separation" (Gilligan 1982, p. 42). As will be discussed later, such differences may play an important role in the dynamics of substance abuse among men and women.

The body of work done at the Robert S. and Grace W. Stone Center for Developmental Services and Studies at Wellesley College, established in 1981, has further increased the theoretical and research foci on the different developmental pathways of men and women in general and on the *relational model of self* in particular. As elaborated in the following chapters, the self-in-relation theory focuses on the need for connection rather than viewing separation and individuation as the ultimate goal of healthy human development (Jordan et al. 1990).

Current Research on Gender Differences

The last twenty years have seen a tremendous increase in gender-focused research. Some of the studies point to innate biological differences between men and women in such areas as aggression and physical vulnerability, emphasizing that males are both more aggressive (Goleman 1990) and more vulnerable biologically than females—particularly at the beginning and the end of the life span (Jacklin 1989).

Other theorists and researchers focus on psychological and social dynamics. They believe that gender differences reflect not just innate or instinctual drives and abilities but social reinforcement of certain behavioral choices:

> Social expectations push each (gender) toward different options and thus toward different lives. These choices are more important than ability in determining what happens in people's lives. The gender differences that exist in education, employment, family life, relationships, sexuality, emotionality, health-related behaviors, body image, and behavior problems reflect these different choices and the expectations that foster them. . . . Indeed the differences in choices may promote the idea that greater differences exist than research has confirmed. Women choose different educational experiences and careers than men. Women are more likely to put their family before their career, whereas careers are the primary focus of many men's lives. Men tend to choose an activity-based style of forming close relationships, whereas women choose to establish intimacy through emotional sharing. Men also choose a riskier lifestyle than women, and their decreased life expectancy reflects those choices. [Brannon 1996, pp. 465–469]

Cross-cultural anthropological studies point to the importance of interactive social dynamics in gender differences. An analysis of children's development in eleven different cultures (Whiting and Edwards 1988) concluded that gender differences are the result of social interactions: "The individuals we interact with, if they are infants, peers, or individuals older than we are, elicit particular behaviors from us . . . in many cultures, but not all, young girls are given child-care responsibilities, whereas young boys are not. As a function of those responsibilities, girls are more likely to become nurturant" (Jacklin 1989, p. 131). This perspective has implications for our understanding of the process of initiation into substance use as well as the important role of the company we keep in eliciting and reinforcing drug-free and pro-social behavior during recovery.

Other research studies found gender differences in attribution, or the way men and women define cause and effect. Girls and women tend to attribute failure to their own lack of ability, while boys and men tend to attribute failure to the difficulty of the task or to the evaluator's assessment of their task performance. In short, girls blame themselves, while boys externalize their failures (Dweck et al. 1978). Once again, this gender difference has treatment implications.

Recent research and popular literature has focused on differences in communication patterns between men and women (Tannen 1990). Such communication differences have been attributed to distinct differences in socialization of men and women resulting in "distinct female and male subcultures" (De Lange 1995, p. 76). According to De Lange (1995):

> When men and women listen, they use different behaviors and may, in fact, listen for different things. Men tend to listen for the bottom line, for some action to be taken or decision to be made; women tend to listen for details to fill in the full picture. Men use less eye contact and head nods; women ask more questions and tend to work at maintaining the communication. . . . Research has found that men generally talk more than women and interrupt more. Women tend to engage in more self-disclosure, display more empathetic behaviors, and be more adept at decoding and translating nonverbal behavior into meaningful messages. [p. 75]

Different communication patterns between men and women are particularly noticeable in group settings. In general, studies indicate that mixed-gender groups benefit men, while all-female groups are most beneficial to women (Lex 1996). Studies of small group dynamics found that "men tend to be more competitive and women more cooperative. Males are said to have an exploitative behavioral style and females to have an accommodative style; the latter results in more favorable outcomes for group members" (Davis and Proctor 1989, p. 248). Since much of substance abuse treatment is provided in group settings, these findings need to be kept in mind.

Numerous ongoing gender-focused research studies in the fields of biochemistry, psychology, sociology, cultural anthropology, ethnology, and psychotherapy are constantly adding to our knowledge regarding the biopsychosocial differences and similarities between men and women. As more data become available, such knowledge will have an increasing impact on our understanding of substance-abusing men and women and treatment approaches with them.

GENDER-RELATED EMOTIONAL PROBLEMS

There are significant gender differences in the prevalence and manifestation of various mental health or emotional problems. Epidemiological and clinical studies point to gender differences in psychopathology: Women are more likely to suffer from major depression and dysthymia, panic attacks, phobic reactions, eating disorders, sexual dysfunctions, somatization disorders, and borderline personality disorders. Men, on the other hand, are much more likely to be diagnosed with antisocial personality, hyperactivity and attention-deficit disorders, paraphilia, pathological gambling, and substance-related disorders. They are also more likely to commit suicide (Kaplan et al. 1994, Raymond 1991).

As Brannon (1996) pointed out, manifestation of psychopathology tends to occur along gender stereotypical lines:

> The categories of psychopathology more common among women are an exaggeration of the elements of the feminine gender role—dependent (dependent personality disorder), passive (major depression), self-sacrificing (self-defeating personality disorder), fearful (agoraphobia), and emotional (histrionic personality disorder). Men experience psychopathology that seems to be an exaggeration of the elements of the masculine gender role—irresponsible, untruthful, and violent (antisocial personality disorder), recklessness (psychoactive substance abuse disorder), and inappropriately sexual (paraphilias). [p. 467]

Such gender differences are confirmed by the findings in a recent study comparing men and women seeking outpatient mental health services in a rural community in New England (O'Hare 1995). According to the author,

> women reported significantly higher ratings on depression, anxiety, anger or hostility, conflict with others, loneliness, sexual abuse, trouble sleeping, trouble with appetite or eating, poor concentration, marital or couples problems, problems with children and being affected by another's substance use [while] (m)en reported significantly higher ratings on problems with job or school, alcohol or drugs, legal problems, problems in the community, and need for dental care. [O'Hare 1995, p. 209]

Even when men and women report similar problems such as depression, the manifestations or ways of expressing or dealing with these problems differ: Depressed women display greater indecisiveness and self-dislike, lack of confidence, apathy, and sensitivity to criticism, while depressed men display decreased social interest, problems with memory and concentration, sleep disturbance, tension, and a sense of failure (Hammen and Padesky 1977, Podesky and Hammen 1981). Moreover, the etiology of such a diagnostic category as posttraumatic stress disorder differs for men and women: the most common precipitating traumatic event for men is combat experience, while the trauma for women is most commonly assault or rape (Kaplan et al. 1994). Regardless of the diagnosis, women are more likely to blame themselves for their problems, while men are more likely to blame others or external circumstances. Such gender differences need to be taken into account during assessment and treatment of all clients.

Not only do men and women differ in predisposition to mental ill-ness and attribution of their problems but also in clinicians' perceptions of their mental health. As the classic study by Broverman and colleagues (1970) showed, clinically trained psychologists, psychiatrists, and social workers had a concept of a normal, healthy man that was the same as their concept of a normal, healthy adult, while their views of what con-stituted a normal, healthy woman differed from their views of a normal, healthy adult. The researchers concluded that a double standard existed: the standard for adult mental health was male, while socially desirable feminine traits were viewed as inappropriate for adult mental health. While this double standard appears to have changed to some degree since 1970, the potential for clinician bias based on a client's gender may still be operating and needs to be addressed during clinical training and supervision.

Help-Seeking Behavior

In general, women appear more likely than men to seek mental health services, and this is particularly true for community mental health set-tings (Russo and Sobel 1981)."Asking for help, displaying emotions, and expressing distress are more consistent with women's traditional roles. . . . Men, on the other hand, are often expected to be strong. Asking for help has been equated with weakness, and therefore may be avoided by men. Men often prefer to 'tough out' their problems, rather than seeking professional help" (Davis and Proctor 1989, p. 142). Such patterns may not apply to substance abuse settings, which historically have been under-utilized by women (Weisner and Schmidt 1992).

SUBSTANCE ABUSE AND GENDER

Gender plays a significant and complex role in the use of and reactions to various substances. Studies indicate that substance-abusing men and women differ on numerous variables including etiological, physiological, psychological, sociological, and familial factors. While extensive litera-ture exploring the differences between alcohol-abusing men and women can be found (e.g., Beckman 1976, Blume 1986, Sandmaier 1980, Strauss-ner 1985, Wilsnack et al. 1994), studies focusing on gender differences in relation to other substances are still limited (Griffin et al. 1989, Lex 1995, Pape 1993). This section explores substance abuse issues as they relate to gender.

Epidemiological Differences

Due to the nature of drug use surveys in the United States, it is difficult to obtain data that is clinically useful. National epidemiological surveys focus on frequency of use (lifetime, monthly, weekly, etc.) and do not provide information on the biopsychosocial consequences of substance use required in order to diagnose substance abuse and dependence (Straussner 1993). Nonetheless, epidemiological surveys do indicate that men and women differ in their use of various substances. (See Table 1-1.)

According to the latest prevalence surveys from the National Institute on Drug Abuse (NIDA), men are almost three times as likely to drink alcohol or to smoke marijuana on a weekly basis than women (NIDA 1992). In other surveys, men report greater average alcohol consumption and more alcohol-related problems than women (Wilsnack and Wilsnack 1991). However, when the lower average consumption by women is controlled for, some researchers find "comparable levels of alcohol-related problems in both male and female drinkers" (Helzer and Pryzbeck 1988, p. 220).

National surveys also indicate that men are more likely than women to smoke cigarettes, to use opiates, particularly heroin, and inhalants, and to report more severe problems with cocaine. Women, on the other hand, report more severe problems with amphetamines and tranquilizers (Kaplan et al. 1994, NIDA 1992). As summarized by Kaufman (1994):

> Men use more alcohol, marijuana, heroin, cocaine, hallucinogens and inhalants. Women use more legal drugs, most of which are prescribed by male physicians to keep them calm (passive and depressed); they

TABLE 1-1: Prevalence estimates for alcohol, cocaine, and marijuana: frequency of use within past year (1992) by gender for total U.S. population

Substance	Gender	At least once (%)	12 or more times (%)	Once a week or more (%)
Alcohol	Combined	64.7	37.5	20.3
	Male	69.5	48.6	29.7
	Female	60.2	27.2	11.5
Cocaine	Combined	2.4	0.7	0.3
	Male	3.2	0.9	0.4
	Female	1.7	0.6	0.3
Marijuana	Combined	8.5	4.2	2.5
	Male	10.8	5.7	3.5
	Female	6.3	2.8	1.6

Adapted from National Institute on Drug Abuse 1993.

may also turn to stimulants or illegal drugs such as cocaine and amphetamines to lose weight or overcome depression. Recently, there has been an increase in the use of illicit drugs by women, as this pattern has become more ego-syntonic with being female. [p. 30]

The increase in illicit drug use by women is confirmed by the 1992 National Client Data System survey findings (cited in Kaufman 1994). According to this survey, the primary drugs abused by females admitted to substance abuse treatment facilities during 1992 were (in descending order): alcohol, cocaine (including crack), heroin, cannabis, amphetamines and other stimulants, and tranquilizers and sedatives/hypnotics.

Gender and Dual Diagnosis

According to research studies, men who abuse alcohol and other drugs are significantly more likely to be dually diagnosed (also referred to as having comorbid or co-occurring disorders) with such severe mental illnesses as schizophrenia and bipolar disorder than women (Alexander 1996, Kaplan et al. 1994). Substance-abusing men also are more likely to have coexisting antisocial and narcissistic personality disorders, attention-deficit/hyperactivity disorder, and impulse disorders such as compulsive gambling. Substance-abusing women, on the other hand, are more likely to be dually diagnosed with major depression, panic disorder, an eating disorder, particularly bulimia, and borderline personality disorder.

It may be difficult to separate which diagnosis is primary. Psychiatric illness may lead to substance abuse or substance abuse may be a factor in the onset of psychiatric illness. Studies of alcoholics point to the likelihood of depression as secondary to alcoholism in men and primary in women (Helzer and Pryzbeck 1988). Studies of mainly male cocaine abusers indicate that alcohol abuse as well as mood disorders are more likely to follow the onset of cocaine-related disorders, whereas anxiety, antisocial personality, and attention-deficit/hyperactivity disorders tend to precede the development of cocaine-related disorders (Kaplan et al. 1994). While research data are lacking, it is likely that among women depression, borderline personality, eating disorders, and posttraumatic stress disorder related to sexual abuse precede their substance abuse, while anxiety and sleep disorders are often the result of substance abuse.

Regardless of which disorder is primary, all co-occurring disorders need to be identified and treated in order to minimize relapse and maximize the quality of life for clients. The question of which disorder is addressed first becomes an important clinical decision during the treatment process. In general, the problem of highest crisis potential needs to be addressed first. For most substance-abusing men and women, the most immediate, and often most life-threatening, issue is their abuse of alcohol and other drugs. By helping men and women recover from substance abuse, the clinician will provide them with the wherewithal to address and cope better with all their other disorders and life problems (Straussner 1996).

Etiological Differences

Research findings indicate that different factors influence the use of substances for men and women. While genetic studies of drug abusers are lacking, studies have repeatedly demonstrated a genetic component in the development of alcoholism in men (Cloninger et al. 1981, Svikis et al. 1994). This is particularly apparent among the subgroup of men, referred to as *essential* or Type II alcoholics, who show an earlier onset and greater severity of problems related to their drinking (Cloninger 1983). While the role of genes in the development of alcoholism among women is less clear, alcoholic women have been shown to be more likely than men to come from alcoholic families.

> While most of the focus in literature has been on the high rates of alcoholism among the fathers of alcoholic women, researchers have also noted higher rates of alcoholism in the mothers and siblings of alcoholic women, as well as generally higher rates of mental illness in their families of origin and more disruptive early family life than that experienced by men. [Straussner 1985, p. 63]

Various studies of alcohol, marijuana, and heroin users indicate that men's use appears to be influenced by the availability of substances and extra-familial forces, such as school, poverty, and peer group context, whereas women's use is more likely to be a reaction to an unhappy family situation, including exposure to sexual, physical, or emotional abuse in childhood, poor self-esteem, and interpersonal influences of male partners (Alexander 1996, Binion 1982, Lex 1995, Straussner 1985). Such a "partner effect" may reflect the previously discussed women's focus on relationships and is likely to be related to women's codependency issues. (See Chapter 3 for further discussion of codependency in women.)

A male counterpart to women's codependency dynamics has been proposed by Kipnis (1991). According to Kipnis, men have been socialized to take care of women ("men who give too much"), and thus their self-worth is based on their success as providers rather than on who they are as individuals. This dynamic may account for the increase of substance abuse among men who become unemployed (Straussner 1994), and particularly among men, such as Hispanics and the more recent

Russian Jewish immigrants, whose cultural values emphasize their role as providers.

Additional psychodynamics cited in the literature as related to substance abuse among men include the following: (1) unresolved dependency needs and a need for bonding with other men. These repressed feelings are allowed expression under the influence of such substances as alcohol; (2) mastery over unacceptable aggressive impulses, particularly common among heroin and marijuana users; and (3) increased sense of power, commonly seen among alcohol and cocaine-abusing men (McClelland et al. 1982, Van Wormer 1989). (For fuller discussion of these issues, see Chapters 13, 14, and 15.)

Both men and women use substances as a way of dealing with conflicts around sexuality. According to Bepko and Krestan (1985), the abuse of alcohol (and by extension, other substances) may be an effort to deal with the tension between sexual feelings and gender role expectations: "Drinking may function to permit a male dependency and emotional intensity while it may allow a woman to be competent, powerful and aggressive" (p. 52).

Biophysiological Differences

Men and women appear to have different biophysiological reactions to substances, particularly alcohol. Women experience the adverse physiological effects of drinking on the liver, cardiovascular, and gastrointestinal systems more quickly and at lower drinking rates than men—a phenomenon referred to as "the telescoping effect" (Alexander 1996, National Institute on Alcohol Abuse and Alcoholism 1990, Straussner 1985). Consequently, they are at higher risk than their male counterparts for rapid development of liver disease and for death due to cirrhosis (NIAAA 1990).

Although data are limited, studies of cocaine abusers also indicate that women become addicted more rapidly than men (Lex 1995). Moreover, since many drug-abusing women tend to support themselves through prostitution or to exchange drugs for sex, they have a high rate of sexually transmitted diseases. Consequently, substance-abusing women experience numerous health and reproductive consequences not experienced by men. These include pelvic inflammatory disease, amenorrhea, ectopic pregnancies, and spontaneous second trimester abortions (Lex 1995). Women also need to deal with the consequences of the detrimental impact of their substance use on their unborn and newborn children, such as fetal alcohol syndrome or having babies born addicted to crack or heroin (Pape 1993, Straussner 1989). While there are some indications of increased infertility among heroin- and alcohol-abusing women (NIAAA

1990), clinical experience suggests that women abusing crack cocaine appear not only to be more sexually active but also to have both increased fertility rates and premature births, resulting in more children within a shorter time frame.

While substance use plays a role in the spread of the human immunodeficiency virus (HIV) infection among both men and women, the link between HIV/AIDS (acquired immunodeficiency syndrome) and drug use is greater for women: "Nearly 70 percent of AIDS cases among women are related to their use of injecting drugs or to having sex with an injecting drug user" (Leshner n.d., p. 50). Moreover, AIDS appears to progress differently in men and women. Women are likely to die more rapidly than men once diagnosed with HIV infection. This finding may reflect the fact that women enter treatment at much later stages of infection than men (Alexander 1996, Leshner n.d).

Hormones also appear to play a role in substance use, which may impact disproportionately on women. Studies indicate that depressive episodes and periods of emotional lability, leading to a potential increase in substance use as well as potential relapse, come at times of low estrogen secretion. Such dynamics affect women of varying ages, because levels of estrogen have been found to be particularly low during premenstrual, postpartum, and menopausal phases of the life cycle (McMichael 1996).

Hormone levels may also relate to substance abuse in men. It is known that aggression is correlated with the male sex hormone testosterone (Goleman 1990), and studies of children indicate that aggressive young boys are more likely to experiment with and abuse drugs as teens (Leshner n.d).

Psychosocial and Familial Consequences of Substance Abuse

In her research on gender differences in psychosocial problems associated with alcohol and other drug use, Robbins (1989) found that men and women have different deviant behavior styles, or what she termed *styles of pathology*. In line with the gender differences in psychiatric diagnosis, substance-abusing women report greater depression, anxiety, and guilt than men, whereas men are more likely to report substance-related belligerence, employment problems, and legal problems.

Age appears to be an important variable in the psychosocial and familial dynamics of male and female substance abusers. Younger substance-abusing women are more likely to come from substance-abusing and dysfunctional families, to have been sexually or physically abused both as children and as adults, to be primary caretakers of children, and to have more housing and legal problems and fewer vocational skills than substance-abusing men or older women (Morgan and Kinney 1996). They are also more likely to be involved with a substance-dependent partner than men or older women (Miller et al. 1989).

On the other hand, clinical observation suggests that younger substance-abusing men, particularly those in inner city communities, are more likely than older men to have a criminal record, to be sexually involved with more women, to have more children by more women, and to be dually diagnosed. They are also less likely to be legally employed or to keep a job once employed. The latter may be partly due to an increase in workplace drug testing. Moreover, unlike drug-abusing and particularly alcoholic men in previous generations, young substance-abusing men today are less likely to have a stable relationship with a nonsubstance-abusing woman (Straussner 1994). They are also likely to have few substance-free male role models and to be functionally fatherless. As Dore (1994) has pointed out: "Younger men are exposed more to women, to the media, and to peer groups than they are to healthy masculine models. . . . In the absence of fatherly guidance, young men often turn to drugs or gangs as a way to enter manhood. In the absence of healthy rituals for initiating boys into manhood, self-destructive behavior tends to emerge" (p. 245).

Referrals for Treatment

The majority of both male and female clients in substance abuse settings today come to treatment through involuntary referral, although some individuals, particularly middle-class women, may attend twelve–step programs on a voluntary basis. Men are more likely to be referred for substance abuse treatment through the legal system or by employee assistance programs than women (Straussner 1988), while women are more likely to be referred around child-related issues. Despite a "200 percent increase in the women's prison population in the past 8 years . . . , prisons for men are more likely to have medical services, substance abuse treatment and other support services than are those for women" (Center for Substance Abuse Treatment 1994, p. 113).

In general, substance-abusing women are more likely than men to seek help from their primary care physician or to go for counseling in a mental health or family agency. Consequently, they are less likely to obtain treatment for their abuse of substances. This is especially true of women suffering from dual diagnosis. For example, when Ms. P., a 39-year-old, recently divorced woman sought mental health services at a local community agency, she was readily diagnosed as suffering with anxiety disorder and dysphoria. Her daily use of alcohol, while noted on the intake form, was ignored during both the diagnostic assessment and the early phases of treatment. It was only after her hospitalization following a car accident, four months after beginning treatment, that the full extent of her alcohol dependence and abuse of prescription medications was recognized and addressed.

Recovery and Relapse

While studies of treatment outcomes by gender are still limited and often contradictory, it appears that men and women show different patterns of recovery and may have different treatment needs. Based on the patterns of treatment of fifty alcoholic housewives (Straussner et al. 1980), the author hypothesized that "just as the progression of alcoholism in women may differ from that in men, so may the process of recovery. . . . It may be that women abstain for longer periods before 'slipping'—but are then more likely than men to seek professional help once they do" (Straussner 1985, p. 69), thereby appearing to have a higher relapse rate. Sokolow and colleagues (1980) found that alcoholic women had a higher abstinence rate if treated in a medically oriented alcoholism facility, whereas men did better in a peer group-oriented facility. A more recent study of hospitalized cocaine abusers found that men's improvement was more rapid and steady compared to that of women, whose recovery was slower and who had more residual problems after treatment (Griffin et al. 1989). The authors hypothesized that this may be related to women's greater incidence of clinical depression and more severe subjective distress during early abstinence.

In line with the relational theory, according to which men perceive danger in connection while women experience it in separation (Gilligan 1982), the author's clinical experience indicates that men are more likely to relapse during "happy connecting" occasions such as family reunions, engagements, marriages, and childbirth, while women are more likely to relapse in reaction to interpersonal loss such as death or separation.

GENDER-SENSITIVE ASSESSMENT AND TREATMENT

Despite the increasing literature on the treatment needs of women, treatment models and approaches have historically been based on men's addictions (Alexander 1996). Good and colleagues (1990) have suggested five principles of gender-aware therapy. According to these principles, all treatment should:

1. Include the concept of gender as an integral aspect of work with all clients.
2. Consider problems within their societal context.
3. Actively seek to change gender injustice experienced by men and women.
4. Emphasize development of collaborative therapeutic relationships.
5. Respect clients' freedom to choose.

Applying the first principle to substance-abuse assessment, clinicians should avoid using any instruments and assessment tools, such as the Michigan Alcoholism Screening Test (MAST), that have been normed only on one sex. Moreover, clinicians need to take into account gender differences regarding physiological reactions and co-occurring disorders. The assessment process must include gender-sensitive questions. For example, questions regarding history of sexual and physical abuse, physical and gynecological problems, depression and suicidal gestures, eating disorders, recent losses, as well as history of depression and mental illness in the family of origin, sources of supply of substances, and the use of substances by a spouse or partner are particularly salient for women, while questions regarding hyperactivity and school problems, work history, recent emotional connections, and gambling and legal problems are important areas in assessing men.

During the treatment process, clinicians "need to be vigilant about the sensitivity of the entire treatment program to gender differences, the consequences of stereotyped roles, and the implications of status differences between men and women" (Kaufman 1994, p. 45). The gender difference in attribution, whereby women are more likely to blame themselves for their problems while men are more likely to blame others or external circumstances, needs to be taken into account and addressed in treatment. Individual and group sessions need to focus on helping women to become more assertive, while encouraging men to address appropriately "the four core emotions that men seem to have significant difficulty dealing with: grief, anger, fear, and shame" (Dore 1994, p. 244). In group treatment, given the disparity in men's and women's expressive and relational skills, "group leaders must attempt to sustain the expressive functions of females in mixed groups and males in all-male groups" (Davis and Proctor 1989, p. 248).

Since both men and women are frequently involved with substance-abusing partners and often have children, family involvement, including treatment of children, needs to be encouraged whenever possible (Straussner 1994). Both men and women may need to learn appropriate parenting skills. Besides diminishing the likelihood of the children becoming substance abusers, such interventions serve as corrective experiences for recovering men and women who, themselves inadequately parented as children, need to re-parent themselves in order to heal fully (Benedek 1970, Olson 1984).

Dealing with substance-abusing men and women within a societal context, clinicians need to explore what it means for a given client to be a man or a woman with a diagnosis of alcohol or drug abuse or dependence. While both men and women are stigmatized for their substance abuse disorders, women face additional stigma in their failed roles as partners and mothers, while men are further stigmatized in their failed role as breadwinners. Clinicians need to be sensitive to the impact on self-image of male clients who are mandated for treatment by an employee assistance program or the criminal justice system, and on the self-image of female clients whose children are placed in foster care. Moreover, in light of the large number of clients in methadone maintenance treatment programs, it is important to explore the implications for both men and women of the dependency inherent in such treatment approaches. Lastly, clinicians need to explore the impact of limited income opportunities and lack of housing options on women living with an abusive or addicted partner and on men residing with their enabling mothers.

Given the large number of gay men and lesbians with substance abuse problems, clinicians need to be sensitive to the double stigma of being a substance abuser and homosexual in a homophobic society. While many of the dynamics and issues of gay men and lesbian women differ, there may be value to putting them in a co-ed group in which a more or less equal number of men and women can address their own internalized homophobia as well as the obstacles that they may encounter during early recovery. Clinicians also need to monitor their own stereotypes regarding homosexuals and their own homophobic reactions. (For further discussion see Chapters 8 and 17.)

The third principle that Good and his colleagues (1990) suggested moves beyond the treatment setting and encourages clinicians to become aware of, and actively attempt to eliminate, the gender-related injustices resulting from differential social, economic, and legal sequelae of alcohol and drug abuse, such as the increasing penalization of substance-abusing pregnant women. It also implies the need for further research and challenging of the injustices that are inherent in the process of criminalization of drugs. For instance, in order to support their habits and their families, men sell drugs while women sell themselves. Such impact is particularly devastating on low-income minority communities, since substance-abusing men of color are greatly overrepresented in the prison population, while women of color are overrepresented among women giving birth to drug-addicted babies (Center for Substance Abuse Treatment 1994, NIDA 1992).

The fourth principle urges therapists to form a collaborative relationship with clients and become their partners in recovery. While originating in the feminist vision that values a nonhierarchical, nonauthoritative, collective, and cooperative style of work (Van Den Bergh 1991), the collaborative treatment relationship also has been shown to be highly valuable in working with men. It has been particularly effective in problem-solving short-term treatment with involuntary clients (Walter and Peller 1992).

The fifth principle, freedom to choose, advocates clients' freedom to choose any combination of traditional and nontraditional gender roles that will enhance their lives regardless of societal gender norms or "political correctness." Client preferences in treatment provider's gender must also be considered. Such choice recognizes the value of positive gender role models for substance abusers whose families and peer groups are frequently dysfunctional.

Countertransference Issues

Male and female clinicians inevitably bring with them their own gender role socialization. Thus, it is not surprising to find that research studies indicate that client's gender often triggers assumptions, expectations, and interpersonal responses from clinicians that may impede the therapeutic alliance and the client's recovery (Davis and Proctor 1989). Moreover, the gender of the clinician evokes transferential reactions from clients, inducing additional countertransferential reactions from clinicians. Consequently, clinicians must be constantly attuned to their countertransferential reactions to their male and female clients.

Clinicians working with substance-abusing men and women need to guard against induced countertransference in which they become either the punishers or the rescuers of clients. Those working with female substance-abusing clients need to avoid telling them what to do and reinforcing their learned helplessness and dependency on others. They also need to avoid assuming the role of abusers and further victimizing their female clients. Clinicians working with men may need to learn how to tolerate the rejection inherent in trying to be helpful to males who have been socialized to equate help seeking with weakness and who initially may prefer an action-oriented style of communicating to focusing on their feelings.

CONCLUSION

There is no question that gender plays an important role in the abuse of alcohol and other drugs and impacts on the treatment and recovery process. Consequently, gender-specific and gender-sensitive assessment and treatment are essential components of good clinical practice. It is crucial that all clinicians become sensitive to gender effects on human development, to their own gender development and expectations, and most importantly, to the impact of gender on the lives and needs of their male and female clients.

REFERENCES

Alexander, M. J. (1996). Women and co-occurring addictive and mental disorders: an emerging profile of vulnerability. *American Journal of Orthopsychiatry* 66(1):61–70.

Beckman, L. J. (1976). Alcoholism problems and women: an overview. *Alcoholism Problems in Women and Children*, ed. M. Greenblatt and M. A. Schuckit, pp. 65–96. New York: Grune & Stratton.

Benedek, T. (1970). Parenthood as a developmental process. In *Parenthood: Its Psychology and Psychopathology*, ed. T. Benedek and E. J. Anthony, pp. 124–131. New York: Little, Brown & Co.

Bepko, C., and Krestan, J. A. (1985). *The Responsibility Trap: A Blueprint for Treating the Alcoholic Family*. New York: Macmillan.

Binion, V. J. (1982). Sex differences in socialization and family dynamics of female and male heroin users. *Journal of Social Issues* 38(2):43–57.

Blume, S. B. (1986). Women and alcohol: a review. *Journal of the American Medical Association* 256:1467–1470.

Brannon, L. (1996). *Gender: Psychological Perspectives*. Boston: Allyn & Bacon.

Brenner, C. (1973). *An Elementary Textbook of Psychoanalysis*. New York: Anchor Books.

Broverman, I., Broverman, D., Clarkson, E., et al. (1970). Sex-role stereotypes and clinical judgment of mental health. *Journal of Consulting and Clinical Psychology* 34:1–7.

Center for Substance Abuse Treatment. (1994). *Practical Approaches in the Treatment of Women Who Abuse Alcohol and Other Drugs*. Rockville, MD: U.S. Department of Health and Human Services.

Chodorow, N. (1974). Family structure and feminine personality. In *Woman, Culture and Society*, ed. M. Z. Rosaldo and L. Lamphere, pp. 40–57. Stanford, CA: Stanford University Press.

—— (1978). *The Reproduction of Mothering: Psychoanalysis and the Sociology of Gender*. Berkeley: University of California Press.

Cloninger, C. R. (1983). Genetic and environmental factors in the development of alcoholism. *Journal of Psychiatric Treatment and Evaluation* 5:487–496.

Cloninger, C. R., Bohman, M., and Sigvardsson, S. (1981). Inheritance of alcohol abuse: cross-fostering analysis of adopted men. *Archives of General Psychiatry* 38:861–868.

Davis, L. E., and Proctor, E. K. (1989). *Race, Gender & Class*. Englewood Cliffs, NJ: Prentice Hall.

De Lange, J. (1995). Gender and communication in social work education: a cross-cultural perpective. *Journal of Social Work Education* 31(1):75–81.

Dore, J. (1994). A model of time-limited group therapy for men: its use with recovering addicts. *Group* 18(4):243–258.

Dweck, C. S., Davidson, W., Nelson, S., and Enna, B. (1978). Sex differences in learned helplessness: the contingencies of evaluated feedback in the classroom and experimental analysis. *Developmental Psychology* 14:268–276.

Freud, S. (1925). Some psychical consequences of the anatomical distinction between the sexes. *Standard Edition* 19:241–260.

Gilligan, C. (1982). *In a Different Voice: Psychological Theory and Women's Development*. Cambridge, MA: Harvard University Press, 1993.

Gilligan, C., Ward, J., and Taylor, J., with Bardiga, B., eds. (1983). *Mapping the Moral Domain: A Contribution of Women's Thinking to Psychological Theory and Education*. Cambridge, MA: Harvard University Press.

Goleman, D. (1990). Aggression in men: hormone levels are a key. *New York Times*, July 17, p. C1.

Good, C., Gilbert, L., and Scher, M. (1990). Gender aware therapy: a synthesis of feminist therapy and knowledge about gender. *Journal of Counseling and Development* 68:376–380.

Griffin, M. L., Weiss, R. D., Mirin, S. M., and Lange, U. (1989). A comparison of male and female cocaine abusers. *Archives of General Psychiatry* 46(2):122–126.

Hammen, C. L., and Padesky, C. A. (1977). Sex differences in the expression of depressive responses on the Beck Depression Inventory. *Journal of Abnormal Psychology* 86:609–614.

Helzer, J. F., and Pryzbeck, T. R. (1988). The co-occurrence of alcoholism and other psychiatric disorders in the general population and its impact on treatment. *Journal of Studies on Alcohol* 49:219–224.

Horney, K. (1926). The flight from womanhood. In *Psychoanalysis and Women*, ed. J. B. Miller, pp. 5–20. Baltimore, MD: Penguin, 1973.

Jacklin, C. N. (1989). Female and male: issues of gender. *American Psychologist* 44(2):127–133.

Jordan, J., Kaplan, A., Miller, J. B., et al. (1990). *Women's Growth in Connection.* New York: Guilford.

Kaplan, H. I., Sadock, B. J., and Grebb, J. A. (1994). *Kaplan and Sadock's Synopsis of Psychiatry,* 7th Edition. Baltimore, MD: Williams & Wilkins.

Kaufman, E. (1994). Psychotherapy of Addicted Persons. New York: Guilford.

Kipnis, A. R. (1991). *Knights without Armor: A Practical Guide for Men in Quest of Masculine Soul.* Los Angeles: Jeremy P. Tarcher.

Klein, M. (1932). *The Psychoanalysis of Children.* New York: Grove, 1960.

Kohlberg, L. (1981). *The Philosophy of Moral Development.* San Francisco: Harper & Row.

Leshner, A. (n.d). Filling the gender gap in drug abuse research. NIDA handout.

Lex, B. W. (1995). Alcohol and other psychoactive substance dependence in women and men. In *Gender and Psychopathology,* ed. M. V. Seeman, pp. 311–357. Washington, DC: American Psychiatric Press.

Lips, H. J. (1993). *Sex & Gender: An Introduction,* 2nd ed. Mountain View, CA: Mayfield.

Macobby, E. (1988). Gender as a social category. *Developmental Psychology* 24:755–765.

McClelland, D., Davis, W., Kalin, R., and Wanner, E. (1982). *The Drinking Man.* New York: Free Press.

McMichael, C. (1996). Women's susceptibility to relapse is affected by estrogen levels. *Employee Assistance* 8(7):13.

Miller, B. A., Downs, W. R., and Gondoli, D. M. (1989). Spousal violence among alcoholic women as compared to a random household sample of women. *Journal of Studies on Alcohol* 50:533–540.

Morgan, S. M., and Kinney, J. (1996). Women. In *Clinical Manual of Substance Abuse,* ed. J. Kinney, 2nd ed., pp. 318–332. St. Louis, MO: Moseby.

National Institute on Alcohol Abuse and Alcoholism. (1990). Alcohol and women. *Alcohol Alert* 10, 290:1–4.

National Institute on Drug Abuse (1992). National Pregnancy and Health Survey. Handout.

O'Hare, T. (1995). Mental health problems and alcohol abuse: co-occurrence and gender differences. *Health & Social Work* 20(3):207–214.

Olson, M. (1984). Parenthood and the transformation of narcissism. In *Parenthood: A Psychodynamic Perspective,* ed. R. S. Cohen, B. J. Cohler, and S. H. Weissman, pp. 297–317. New York: Guilford.

Padesky, C. A., and Hammen, C. L. (1981). Sex differences in depressive symptom expression and help-seeking among college students. *Sex Roles* 7(3):892–905.

Pape, P. A. (1993). Issues in assessment and intervention with alcohol- and drug-abusing women. In *Clinical Work with Substance-Abusing Clients*, ed. S. L. A. Straussner, pp. 251–269. New York: Guilford.

Raymond, C. (1991). Recognition of the gender differences in mental illness and its treatment prompts a call for more health research on problems specific to women. *The Chronicle of Higher Education*, June 12, p. 5.

Robbins, C. (1989). Sex differences in psychosocial consequences of alcohol and drug abuse. *Journal of Health and Social Behavior* 30:117–130.

Russo, N. F., and Sobel, S. (1981). Sex differences in the utilization of mental health services. *Professional Psychology* 12(1):7–19.

Sandmaier, M. (1980). *The Invisible Alcoholics: Women and Alcohol Abuse in America*. New York: McGraw-Hill.

Sokolow, L., Welte, J., Hynes, G., and Lyons, J. (1980). Treatment-related differences between female and male alcoholics. *Journal of Addictions and Health* 1:42–56.

Straussner, S. L. A. (1985). Alcoholism in women: current knowledge and implications for treatment. In *Psychosocial Issues in the Treatment of Alcoholism*, ed. D. Cook, S. Straussner, and C. Fewell, pp. 61–77. New York: Haworth.

—— (1988). A comparative analysis of in-house and contractual EAPs. In *Evaluation of Employee Assistance Programs*, ed. M. Feit and M. Holosko, pp. 43–56. New York: Haworth.

—— (1989). Assessment and intervention with maltreating parents who are drug and alcohol abusers. In *Clinical Social Work with Maltreated Children and Their Families: An Introduction to Practice*, ed. S. Ehrenkranz et al., pp. 149–177. New York: New York University Press.

—— (1993). Assessment and treatment of clients with alcohol and other drug abuse problems: an overview. In *Clinical Work with Substance Abusing Clients*, pp. 3–30. New York: Guilford.

—— (1994). The impact of alcohol and other drugs on the American family. *Drug and Alcohol Review* 13:393–399.

—— (1996). The chicken or the egg dilemma in treating substance abusing clients. *Met Chapter Forum of New York State Society of Clinical Social Work* 7(1):4–6.

Straussner, S. L. A., Straussner, J., Kitman, C., and Demos, E. (1980). The alcoholic housewife: a psychosocial analysis. *Focus on Women* 1(1):15–32.

Svikis, D. S., Velez, M., and Pickens, R. W. (1994). Genetic aspects of alcohol use and alcoholism in women. *Alcohol Health & Research World* 18(3):192–196.

Tannen, D. (1990). *You Just Don't Understand: Women and Men in Conversation*. New York: William Morrow.

Unger, R. K. (1979). Toward a redefinition of sex and gender. *American Psychologist* 34:1085–1094.

Van Den Bergh, N., ed. (1991). Having bitten the apple: a feminist perspective on addictions. In *Feminist Perspectives on Addictions*, pp. 3–30. New York: Springer.

Van Wormer, K. (1989). The male-specific group in alcoholism treatment. *Small Group Behavior* 20(2):228–242.

Walter, J., and Peller, J. (1992). *Becoming Solution Focused in Brief Treatment*. New York: Brunner/Mazel.

Weisner, C., and Schmidt, L. (1992). Gender disparities in treatment for alcohol problems. *Journal of the American Medical Association* 268:1872–1876.

Whiting, B. B., and Edwards, C. P. (1988). *Children of Different Worlds: The Formation of Social Behavior*. Cambridge, MA: Harvard University Press.

Wilsnack, S. C., and Wilsnack, R. W. (1991). Epidemiology of women's drinking. *Journal of Substance Abuse Treatment* 3:133–157.

Wilsnack, S. C., Wilsnack, R. W., and Hiller-Sturmhofel, S. (1994). How women drink: epidemiology of women's drinking and problem drinking. *Alcohol Health and Research World* 18(3):173–181.

II

*Women's
Issues
in
Addiction
Treatment*

2

Applying
Relational
Theory
to
Addiction
Treatment

Diane B. Byington

Many people at the end of the twentieth century are isolated, contradicting our innate need for connection and community. Models of development that stress the need for individuation, differentiation, and autonomy are increasingly being recognized as inappropriate and unfulfilling for women and to some extent also for men. In spite of numerous cultural messages attempting to convince women that autonomy and individuation are the highest states of development, women consistently turn to relationships for their sense of self. Although often not stressed in male models of development, the ability to form and sustain a variety of interpersonal relationships is considered to be a major component of healthy human development, and newer developmental theories are beginning to balance this component alongside that of autonomy. Relational, or self-in-relation, theory focuses on the importance of relationships, particularly for women, and examines how these are enacted throughout women's lives.

The importance of relationships in addiction, especially for women, has only recently begun to be explored. Relational theory can be extended to support the hypothesis that addiction represents, at least in part, a misplaced striving for connection. This chapter examines the various relational aspects of addictions for women, reviews relational theory and applies it to women and addictions, and suggests treatment interventions based on the relational approach.

WOMEN, RELATIONSHIPS, AND ADDICTION

Interpersonal relationships are always problematic when accompanied by addiction. It is difficult, however, to determine a direction of causality to this association. It may be impossible to unravel which comes first. The following six points, although not comprehensive, illustrate how integral relationships are in women's addictions.

1. *Women are often introduced to alcohol and drugs through a close romantic relationship.* Initially, many women become involved with drugs in service to an interpersonal relationship (Waldorf et al. 1991). In other words, they care less about the drug than about pleasing the person with whom they are romantically involved. Consequently, in order to recover, or remain drug free, women may have to terminate the romantic relationship.

2. *Addicted women are more likely than men to be diagnosed with underlying emotional problems, and both problems may be associated with difficult*

relationships. The most frequent mental health diagnosis for addicted women is depression (Turnbull and Gomberg 1988), which has been found to be closely associated with isolation (Belle 1982). In addition, Straussner and colleagues (1980) have shown that alcoholic housewives exhibit distinctive MMPI profiles as compared with nonalcoholic women, indicating that alcoholic women attribute their drinking to the behavior of their loved ones.

3. *Women's addiction is often associated with prior or current relationship violence or boundary violation.* Research studies of women in treatment for addiction find alarmingly high rates of childhood sexual abuse (Rohsenow et al. 1988), as well as higher rates of sexual assault (Klassen and Wilsnack 1986) and family violence (Gorney 1989) compared to men or nonaddicted women.

4. *Addictions and parenting are closely and conflictually associated for women.* Many women seek treatment or at least attempt to reduce their drug intake when they are pregnant (Rosenbaum and Murphy 1990). Moreover, since children of addicted mothers are often removed from their custody, the potential of regaining custody is a strong motivator toward recovery. On the other hand, addicted mothers are constantly confronted with their guilt for not being perfect, pushing them further into their addiction (Black and Mayer 1980, Corrigan 1980).

5. *Women are the fastest-growing group to be diagnosed with HIV/AIDS, and this is closely associated with relationships.* Women are more likely to be infected with HIV through sexual relationships with infected men than from sharing needles (Kelly 1994). Moreover, women with few economic options may trade sex for drugs or may be reluctant to insist that their sex partner wear a condom (Fullilove et al. 1990). Furthermore, women are more likely to take care of other family members with the disease and neglect their own care, resulting in quicker AIDS-related death rates than those found in men (Amaro 1995).

6. *Women receive less social support than men for recovery.* Women are less likely to be emotionally supported and encouraged during their recovery process by their families than men. For example, although most wives remain married to alcoholic men, most husbands divorce alcoholic women (Johnson et al. 1990, Schilit and Gomberg 1987).

RELATIONAL THEORY

Relational, or self-in-relation, theory was originally developed by theorists at the Stone Center of Wellesley College in the 1980s. Its primary assumption is that connecting with others is a basic human need, and that this need is particularly strong in women (Jordan et al. 1991). The developmental framework for the theoretical model is based on the work of Miller (1976), Gilligan (1982), and Chodorow (1978), among others. Briefly, it states that all people have a need for connection with others as well as for differentiation from others and that these are enacted differently by gender, with females being much more attuned to connection than males.

Theoretically, girls perceive themselves to be more similar than different to their earliest maternal caretakers, so they do not have to differentiate from their mothers in order to continue to develop their identities. This is in contrast to boys, who must develop an identity that is different from the mother's in order to continue their development. Thus, women's psychological growth and development occur through adding to rather than separating from relationships. Consequently, defining themselves as similar to others through relationships is fundamental to women's identities.

One component of relationships is achieving a sense of connection with others. A *connection* can be regarded as an interaction that engenders a sense of being in tune with self and others, of being understood and valued. Growth-enhancing relationships facilitate more and stronger connections as they develop. Of course, relationships also involve disconnections, when the people involved feel their separateness and distance from each other. Growth-enhancing relationships have the ability to allow disconnections which, with effort on everyone's part, may be turned into connections.

Relationships are defined here as interactions over time that can be assumed to occur with some regularity. All interactions are not assumed to be connections, and all relationships are certainly not growth-enhancing. At least two kinds of interpersonal relationships can be distinguished, close and functional, although others may also exist (Gilmour and Duck 1986). *Close* relationships (Kelley et al. 1983) are ongoing interactions between people who care about and mutually influence each other, while *functional* relationships are oriented to achieving a certain goal.

We have close relationships with, for example, our families, friends, and romantic partners. We have functional relationships with our hair stylists, teachers, and so on. We may have both types of relationships with people with whom we work; the relationship may be considered close while we are working together but may actually be based on function and not continue after one person leaves the work environment.

APPLICATION OF RELATIONAL THEORY TO ADDICTIONS

It has been suggested (Byington 1993) that people not only have relationships with other people but that they may also have a relationship with an object or experience. Addiction develops when a relationship with a drug, including alcohol, food, gambling, or another person treated as an object, is pursued and believed by these individuals to be essential to their life, despite continuing negative consequences, and is considered to be at least as important as relationships with other people. For example, many smokers deny the health hazards of cigarettes in spite of hacking coughs or other physical problems and may even curtail relationships with family members or friends who object to their smoking. The relationship with the cigarettes is at least as important to the smoker as relationships with other people and continues despite numerous negative consequences.

The essence of addiction, in this model, lies in troubled relationships rather than in internal or disease processes. The relationship with the drug is presumed by the individual to be a close one, as with best friends, but is actually functional, providing to the person a feeling of well-being or a "high." However, addiction is only associated with, not caused by, the drug involved. The person is addicted to the consciousness-changing experience, or "high," that is achieved through the drug (Weil 1986). Although the addicted person believes that this experience can only be achieved through the drug, in actuality it can be generated through a variety of methods and comes from within the person rather than outside. This reality is extremely difficult to accept if it has only been experienced in association with drugs. After physical addiction (tolerance) develops, continued drug use may be more associated with fear of withdrawal than the desire to maintain the "high," which has become elusive. Addicted persons realize at some level that they are not in control of the relationship with the drug but, rather, act in service to it.

Healthy interpersonal relationships involve some degree of mutuality, with both people contributing to the interactions and building of the relationship. Relationships with drugs are not mutual, no matter how much the drug is anthropomorphized or valued. The drug cannot "give back" to the individual, although this is not recognized by the addicted persons, who regard the drug as essential to their well-being and even existence. It is the nature of addictive relationships to increase in importance until they eventually usurp most of a person's relationship time and energy.

Not everyone who uses drugs becomes addicted. Why some people develop an addictive relationship with a drug and others do not is probably more reflective of the characteristics of the person (including that person's genetics) and the setting than the nature of the drug (Bratter and Forrest 1985). The relational approach suggests that individuals are most vulnerable to developing an addiction when a problem or gap exists in one or more areas of interpersonal relationships, which is then filled by the relationship with the drug. The problem or gap may take many forms. For example, it could be associated with a lack of experience with fulfilling interpersonal relationships, loss of a significant other, ongoing problems in close relationships, negative past experiences that lead to mistrust in current relationships, or an environment in which relationships with drugs are "safer" emotionally than investing in people.

The mix of relationships for any woman is called her relational field. One way of depicting a person's overall relational field is through the use of relational maps (McAuliffe and McAuliffe 1992). Relationships that are more important are depicted as larger and closer to the person than those that are less important. Healthy, nonaddicted people have a variety of growth-enhancing interpersonal relationships, whereas addicted individuals have their strongest relationship with their drug of choice and weaker relationships with other people.

First, every woman has a relationship with herself, whether or not she is involved in any other relationship. For healthy individuals, this relationship is positive and involves self-care and self-empathy; addicted people have a shame-filled, negative relationship with themselves (Mason 1991). Healthy women also have relationships with family, friends, romantic partners, co-workers, and others. They may have a spiritual relationship with a Higher Power, as well as significant relationships with special pets or plants. Many people have relationships with objects, such as a house or car, or with experiences, such as running, gambling, or work. All of these relationships, however, are balanced, with each receiving relatively equal energy and attention over a period of time. Healthy people's relational maps include a variety of relationships, but the strongest ones are interpersonal relationships. If one relationship drops out, others are available to fill the gap.

The relational map for a typical healthy woman, such as Ann, is exemplified in Figure 2–1. Ann has numerous relationships, and these are all nicely balanced. Figure 2–2 reflects Ann's restricted range of relationships after she has developed an addiction to alcohol. She has a limited number of interpersonal relationships, and her closest relationship is with the bottle. Note that the former relationship with John, her husband, is no longer in her relational field after addiction.

Relationships are extremely important for women, and relationships with drugs are initally seductive and less stressful than interpersonal relationships, which may be troubled. Unfortunately, as the drug relationship becomes addictive, the initial pleasant connections become more difficult to attain and more effort goes into regaining them. Other types of relationships weaken as the relationship with the drug strengthens. The addicted person is searching for connections, albeit in an ultimately self-destructive fashion.

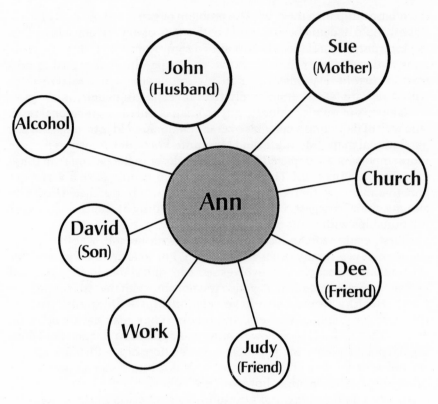

FIGURE 2-1: Relational Map: Healthy Person

ROLE OF RELATIONSHIPS IN HEALING

Since relationships are important for women, and addictions are bound up with relationships, they can be an important motivator for healing. Women have major but usually unacknowledged strengths in regard to relationships that can be drawn upon in treatment.

First, women are dedicated and tenacious in maintaining relationships. For example, many women will stay with abusive men and, in spite of all evidence to the contrary, hope and believe that the relationship will change. Some of them even develop a relationship with drugs in order to remain in the abusive interpersonal relationship. That innate optimism and tenacity are major strengths that can be used to help women turn their self-destructive addictive relationships into healthy interpersonal ones.

Second, women's sense of identity is largely derived and defined through relationships. Rather than viewing this as a deficit and attempting to eliminate it, we can draw upon this relational self for healing. Addicted women have substituted a relationship with a drug for healthy interpersonal relationships, and this reflects an underlying but misdirected need for connection. This need can be acknowledged and rechanneled for healing.

Relationships with children and significant others can be used to support healing. Women want to be good mothers. Because addicted

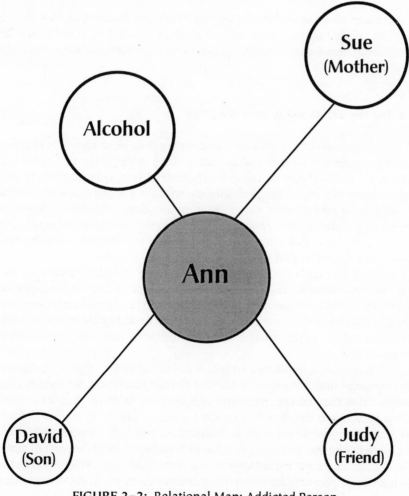

FIGURE 2–2: Relational Map: Addicted Person

women usually have difficulty with their mothering role, this results in guilt, which reinforces their sense of unworthiness and leads them to lean even more heavily on the relationship with the drug. Such desire to be a good parent can be invoked to help women succeed in treatment. In the best of conditions, women would have a strong sense of self and feel worthy of succeeding for themselves, but until that confidence develops, healing can be motivated by the desire to do things for other people that women might not initially do for themselves.

TREATMENT APPROACHES

Treatment techniques can be devised that are focused on developing healthy relationships. These techniques may be used as adjuncts to more traditional forms of treatment. Suggestions for treatment are in four general areas.

Ending the Relationship with the Drug

First and foremost, the *relationship with the drug must end*. It is theoretically possible for a relationship with a drug to decrease in importance for an individual, just as some interpersonal love relationships evolve from lovers to friends, but probably not without a lengthy transition time in which no relationship exists. Ending an addictive relationship is an incredibly difficult task, especially given women's dedication to relationships in general, and may take quite a while to complete, but the relationship must be ended in order for healing to commence.

It may be helpful to initiate this process by assisting clients in making two relational maps, one representing the time before the addictive relationship and the second depicting the time just before entering treatment. As seen in the case of Ann, these will probably show a restriction of other relationships as the relationship with the drug increased in importance.

If addiction is explained in relational terms rather than as a disease, the message that is transmitted is that change can occur. Women need to believe that they can be in control of their lives, because they have traditionally been so much out of control. Assuring them that they are sick and not responsible for their behavior does not help women to feel and be more in control; it merely reinforces their belief that someone or something else has more control over their lives than they. Women are used to feeling responsible for everything around them while at the same time feeling unable to control any of it. The relational model of addiction is simple to understand and to explain, and through it women can reframe their experiences away from badness or sickness to understand them as misplaced efforts to connect.

In addition, women need to understand the general process of how relationships end. Ending an addictive relationship with a drug is at least as difficult and painful as ending any other love relationship. It can be a slow process with much ambivalence until and even after the final decision is reached and action taken.

Any time a relationship ends, it must be grieved. Humans have a need to understand why and how events occur, especially endings. In the process of making meaning out of painful situations or transitions, we naturally move through the stages of grief. The first stage of grief is denial (Kübler-Ross 1969), and we know that addicts deny the strength of their addiction in the face of overwhelming evidence to the contrary. Denial will probably need to be addressed in treatment for quite a while, especially if the client relapses in an attempt to continue the drug relationship. When relapses occur, explaining them through the relational approach might make them more understandable and less shame producing. Conceptualizing relapse as an unsuccessful attempt to deny the strength of an addictive relationship honors the woman's efforts to control her life and encourages more productive attempts at developing relationships.

Grief is an all-consuming experience and must not be trivialized. After a woman has ended an addictive relationship, she can expect to experience the physical effects of withdrawal as well as the physical and emotional effects of grief. These are normal stages of recovery. Grief takes time and a great deal of energy, but it does abate in time, and the person can and will recover.

Two Gestalt-type therapeutic techniques to assist grieving have been suggested by Duffy (1992). Since the relationship with the drug substituted for interpersonal relationships, the suggestion might be made to the woman to give the drug a name and talk to it. In addition, she might write or compose some sort of eulogy to the addictive relationship in deference to the finality of its ending.

Building Healthy Relationships

As the grief begins to subside, the client can be supported in developing new, healthy relationships to fill the gap left by the addictive relationship. Relational maps can be drawn and examined regularly as part of the healing process to examine where gaps continue to exist and where progress has been made. Women with a variety of roles are less prone to developing addictions (Wilsnack and Cheloha 1987), and this translates in the relational model into having a variety of interpersonal relationships. Clients can draw a best-case scenario relational map and plan for how to get from where they are to where they want to be.

People who are involved in addictive relationships are assumed to have other problematic relationships, and most have very few relationships of any kind by the time they enter treatment. Addicts frequently refer to their drug of choice as their "best friend." Addictions are so disastrous to interpersonal relationships that the drug may indeed be the addict's only remaining "friend" or source of companionship. Since women define themselves primarily in terms of their relationships, they are likely to accept even poor relationships in lieu of no relationships at all. Relationship training can be very helpful in helping women to understand why they choose the relationships they do and how to recognize and foster healthy relationships. Women who have been involved in exploitive relationships throughout their lives have "de-selfed" themselves (Lerner 1985), or given more of themselves away than they would prefer. They need to learn how to recognize when a relationship is not mutual and be supported in even minimal efforts to make positive changes.

Supportive relationships among women in treatment can be facilitated by involving them in women-only groups. These groups can explore commonalities in experiences and help women put a voice to their experiences. Since many women have been sexually or physically abused by men, women-only groups can provide a safe haven to explore their experiences away from potential abusers. One of the results of victimization is a difficulty in establishing trust (Russell and Wilsnack 1991), and many women have never developed trusting relationships with other women. Building healthy relationships with group members is another possible outcome of the group. Women can also be encouraged to attend self-help groups. Although the value of twelve–step programs for women has been criticized (see Kasl 1992 and Coker's chapter in this book), women's meetings of 12-step programs or Women for Sobriety may be especially helpful.

Of course, women will continue with their lives while they are in treatment. This may include romantic involvements. Most treatment programs, for good reasons, discourage romantic involvements until clients have been drug-free for some lengthy period of time in the interest of supporting their own self-care. Many of these involvements are not healthy for either party and retard recovery. If these can be reframed, however, as attempts to establish connections in a positive manner, these relationships can be discussed openly in treatment, rather than hidden, and can be considered to be relationship practice.

Practicing Relationship Skills

Recovering women need practice in all types of relationships. This includes developing friends of both sexes, possibly rethinking or reconstructing a romantic involvement, attempting to repair disconnections with family and friends, and practice in self-empathy and valuing self. Significant others can be brought into the treatment process by including them in relationship training sessions, couples and family counseling, and education groups on the relational model. Parent education can be offered to women who are pregnant or already parents, and children can be taught to understand their mother's experiences.

Women's relationship to creativity and productivity should also be explored. Vocational testing and training can help women find meaningful work to provide them a decent standard of living as well as foster pride in achievement. A focus on encouraging creativity in all of its many aspects can balance an extreme dependence on relationships for life's rewards (Bepko and Krestan 1993). Social action may be a satisfying experience for women who have previously felt incapable of making changes in their lives and in the outer world.

Relationship practice can include visualization of successful recovery and healing of relationships. Visualization can be used to identify potential blocks and areas of anxiety before they must be confronted in reality. Staff should model positive relationships, both in their relationships with clients and with each other. Disagreements among staff are not necessarily negative, because staff can model remaining with a disconnection until it is resolved and turned into a connection.

The client–counselor relationship is an extremely important area for relationship practice. Many issues can be resolved through a corrective therapeutic relationship in which the client gains experience in trusting, being valued, and feeling understood.

Strengthening Relationship with Self, Society, and Universe

Possibly most important to consider, women need to be encouraged to examine their relationship with themselves. Addicted people have major disconnections between the parts of themselves that need to be discovered and reconnections made. However, they need to be allowed to choose the extent of this exploration and the timing, especially if sexual abuse is involved (Barrett and Trepper 1991). Regardless of the form or extent of this exploration, some level of insight into feelings and behavior should be encouraged.

Women may also benefit by an understanding of feminism and the overall negative effects of patriarchy and sexism on both women and men and society in general (Bepko 1989). An exploration of these issues can empower women to initiate more balanced, equal relationships in their own relational fields and in the larger society. Similarly, understanding how sexism interacts with racism, homophobia, and other attempts to discriminate against particular groups can assist women in understanding the larger context of addictions and in taking action against prejudice and discrimination.

Finally, clients should be encouraged to explore their understanding of their place in the universe and to formulate their own spirituality. Whether or not clients are interested in organized religion, they can learn to accept, to quote from Desiderata, the anonymous stonecarving found in Old Saint Paul's Church in Baltimore and dated 1692, that "you are a child of the universe, no less than the trees and the stars; you have a right to be here."

CONCLUSION

It is an extremely sad situation when a woman's "best friend" is her drug of choice. Addiction is, at least in part, associated with isolation and poor interpersonal relationships, which can result in a person developing a primary relationship with a drug that gives temporary relief from pain and loneliness. Relationships are only one aspect of addiction, but they are very important, especially for women, and have largely been ignored in traditional forms of treatment.

The relational model recognizes the need for connection that is common to all humanity and utilizes it in the service of healing from addiction. The need to feel connected to others is universal, and assisting addicted women to connect in healthy ways with other people can enhance their overall treatment process. A focus on relationships can offer a positive direction to the healing effort that may continue to provide benefits throughout a recovering person's lifetime.

REFERENCES

Amaro, H. (1995). Love, sex, and power: considering women's realities in HIV prevention. *American Psychologist* 50:437–447.

Barrett, M. J., and Trepper, T. S. (1991). Treating women drug abusers who were victims of childhood sexual abuse. In *Feminism and Addiction,* ed. C. Bepko, pp. 127–146. New York: Haworth.

Belle, D. (1982). *Lives in Stress: Women and Depression.* Beverly Hills, CA: Sage.

Bepko, C. (1989). Disorders of power, women and addiction in families. In *Women in Families: A Framework for Family Therapy,* ed. M. McGoldrick, C. Anderson, and F. Walsh, pp. 406–426. New York: Norton.

Bepko, C., and Krestan, J. (1993). *Singing at the Top of Our Lungs: Women, Love, and Creativity.* New York: HarperPerennial.

Black, R., and Mayer, J. (1980). Parents with special problems: alcoholism and opiate addiction. *Child Abuse and Neglect* 4:45–54.

Bratter, T. E., and Forrest, G. G. (1985). *Alcoholism and Substance Abuse: Strategies for Clinical Intervention.* New York: Free Press.

Byington, D. B. (1993). Love and drugs: a relational approach to addiction. Unpublished manuscript.

Chodorow, N. (1978). *The Reproduction of Mothering.* Berkeley: University of California Press.

Corrigan, E. M. (1980). *Alcoholic Women in Treatment.* New York: Oxford University Press.

Duffy, T. K. (1992). Psychodrama in beginning recovery: an illustration of goals and methods. *Journal of Psychoactive Drugs* 21:97–105.

Fullilove, M. T., Fullilove, R. E., Haynes, K., and Gross, S. (1990). Black women and AIDS prevention: a view towards understanding the gender rules. *Journal of Sex Research* 27:47–64.

Gilligan, C. (1982). *In a Different Voice: Psychological Theory and Women's Development.* Cambridge: Harvard University Press.

Gilmour, R., and Duck, S., eds. (1986). *The Emerging Field of Personal Relationships.* Hillsdale, NJ: Lawrence Erlbaum.

Gorney, B. (1989). Domestic violence and chemical dependency: dual problems, dual interventions. *Journal of Psychoactive Drugs* 21:229–237.

Johnson, N. P., Robbins, K. H., Hornung, C. A., and Gallman, H. S. (1990). Characteristics of women alcoholics. *Substance Abuse* 11:23–29.

Jordan, J. V., Kaplan, A. G., Miller, J. B., et al. (1991). *Women's Growth in Connection: Writings from the Stone Center.* New York: Guilford.

Kasl, C. D. (1992). *Many Roads, One Journey: Moving Beyond the Twelve Steps.* New York: HarperPerennial.

Kelley, H. H., Berscheid, E. S., Christensen, A., et al., eds. (1983). *Close Relationships.* New York: W. H. Freeman.

Kelly, A. M. (1994). Human immunodeficiency virus: current trends in assessment, diagnosis, and treatment. *Journal of Intravenous Nursing* 17:83–92.

Klassen, A. D., and Wilsnack, S. C. (1986). Sexual experiences and drinking among women in a U.S. national survey. *Archives of Sexual Behavior* 15:363–392.

Kübler-Ross, E. (1969). *On Death and Dying*. New York: Macmillan.

Lerner, H. G. (1985). *The Dance of Anger*. New York: Harper & Row.

Mason, M. (1991). Women and shame: kin and culture. In *Feminism and Addiction*, ed. C. Bepko, pp. 175–194. New York: Haworth.

McAuliffe, M. B., and McAuliffe, R. M. (1992). *Patient Workbook: A Guide for Exploring Love Relationships to Mood Altering Chemicals*. Dubuque, IA: Kendall/Hunt.

Miller, J. B. (1976). *Toward a New Psychology of Women*. Boston: Beacon.

Rohsenow, D. J., Corbette, R., and Devine, D. (1988). Molested as children: A hidden contribution to substance abuse? *Journal of Substance Abuse Treatment* 5:13–18.

Rosenbaum, M., and Murphy, S. (1990). Women and addiction: process, treatment, and outcome. In *The Collection and Interpretation of Data from Hidden Populations*, ed. E. Y. Lambert, pp. 120–127. (NIDA Research Monograph 98.) Washington, DC: US Government Printing Office.

Russell, S. A., and Wilsnack, S. (1991). Adult survivors of childhood sexual abuse: substance abuse and other consequences. In *Alcohol and Drugs Are Women's Issues*, vol. 1, ed. P. Roth, pp. 61–70. Metuchen, NJ: Women's Action Alliance.

Schilit, R., and Gomberg, E. L. (1987). Social support structures for women in treatment for alcoholism. *Health- Society-Work* 12:187–195.

Straussner, S. L. A., Kitman, C., Straussner, J., and Demos, E. S. (1980). The alcoholic housewife. *Focus on Women: Journal of Addictions and Health* 1:15–26.

Turnbull, J. E., and Gomberg, E. S. L. (1988). Structure of depression in alcoholic women. *Journal of Studies on Alcohol* 51:148–155.

Waldorf, D., Reinarman, C., and Murphy, S. (1991). *Cocaine Changes: The Experience of Using and Quitting*. Philadelphia: Temple University Press.

Weil, A. (1986). *The Natural Mind*. Boston: Houghton Mifflin.

Wilsnack, R. W., and Cheloha, R. (1987). Women's roles and problem drinking across the lifespan. *Social Problems* 34:231–248.

Codependency Issues of Substance-Abusing Women

Elizabeth Zelvin

3

In the past twenty years, a growing body of literature and clinical experience has indicated that alcoholism and drug abuse in women differ from these addictions in men, and there has been increasing acknowledgment that gender-specific substance abuse treatment for women may be a more effective response to their needs than the traditional male models. It is possible that a key difference between addicted men and women is the prevalence in women of what has been termed codependency. This concept has been variously defined as *addiction* to, or enmeshment with, a chemically dependent person; membership in an alcoholic or otherwise dysfunctional family of origin; and most broadly, the way people, especially women, who in our culture are socialized to expect external sources of fulfillment, tend to seek their identity and self-worth outside the self. The traditional and still persistent socialization of women to be nurturant on the one hand and dependent on the other is particularly compatible with a maladaptive codependency.

It is frequently assumed that codependents and addicts are two mutually exclusive and even inimical groups of people. This chapter will demonstrate that codependency issues of rescue, control, excessive caretaking, extreme dependence, and pathological approval seeking, along with low self-esteem, poor boundaries, and undeveloped sense of self are common dynamics in substance-abusing women and have a significant impact on their treatment. Codependency in substance-abusing women makes it more difficult to overcome denial, access treatment, get clean and sober, stay chemical free, and achieve an optimal quality of life in recovery. Thus, while in traditional treatment "other" problems are left "on the shelf" until sobriety is firmly established, addicted women's codependency issues must be integrated into their treatment, or stable sobriety may never be achieved.

CODEPENDENCY

The term *codependency* has evolved greatly since its introduction in the 1970s, has been the subject of considerable controversy, and is still defined and used in a variety of ways.

Defining Codependency

While the word *codependent* was originally used to designate the enmeshed but not chemically dependent partner of an alcoholic or drug addict, current usage of the term is extremely broad. Efforts to define it have ranged from identifying it as a diagnosable personality disorder (Cermak 1984) to declaring it a societal ill afflicting 96 percent of the population (Schaef 1986). At a major conference on the subject, a group of leaders in the field stated that it "is a pattern of painful dependence upon compulsive behavior and on approval from others in the search for safety, self-worth, and identity. Recovery is possible" (Codependents Anonymous 1989). While this definition opposes the idea that codependency is as chronic and intractable as a classic personality disorder, it suggests that substance and process addictions such as alcoholism and compulsive gambling are no more than symptoms of codependency. A more precise definition is that codependency is "an exaggerated dependence upon a loved object or, by extension, external sources of fulfillment. It is characterized by incomplete development [of] or loss of identity, neglect of self, and low self-esteem" (Zelvin 1993, p. 201). Even more simply, we might define codependency as a problematic or maladaptive seeking of identity, self-worth, and fulfillment outside the self. Characteristic codependent behaviors include rescue and control, excessive caretaking, and approval seeking, particularly from unavailable or unresponsive objects, of whom substance abusers are a good example. It may be noted that in our society, caretaking, approval seeking, and what might be termed emotional rescuing have traditionally been considered acceptable, characteristic female behaviors, while controlling has been considered a negative trait for women.

Etiology

Codependency results from one or a combination of three major phenomena: a close relationship with an alcoholic or drug abuser, growing up in a dysfunctional family, and socialization in our culture with its emphasis on competition and material values and its myths and assumptions about gender roles, intimacy, and happiness.

In the alcoholic or chemically dependent relationship, traditionally conceptualized as a marriage between a substance-abusing man and a woman who is not addicted to chemicals, the wife or partner becomes increasingly preoccupied with the substance abuser's behavior and increasingly insecure about her own identity and value. She functions more and more rigidly and overresponsibly to compensate for the addict's decreasing ability to cope, while pursuing an ever more distant and emotionally unavailable partner.

In the alcoholic or chemically dependent dysfunctional family, in which the entire system is organized around the destructive focus of a parent's drinking or drug abuse, children learn early to suppress their own needs and feelings and to react to subtle cues related to the family symptom. If untreated, they carry into adult life maladaptive roles such as the rescuing and controlling "family hero" (Wegscheider 1981). They often repeat family patterns of caretaking, approval seeking, and over-responsibility as well as patterns of substance use and other compulsive behaviors.

One reason children may grow up to be both addicted and codependent is that they learn to abuse substances and sedate their pain by emulating the addicted parent, while at the same time they fail to learn the developmental tasks of boundary formation and self-soothing from an enmeshed and overresponsible codependent parent. Alternatively, the codependent parent may be so preoccupied with the chemical dependent's addiction and so out of control with his or her behavior and feelings that the children's needs go unmet. Consequently, the children may then grow into adults who are incapable of providing themselves with identity and self-esteem. Since women also learn codependent behaviors and attitudes in the socialization process, girls are particularly prone to this dual dynamic.

Women are socialized to be the custodians of family caretaking and intimate relationships. At the same time, a distorted view of the nature and perfectibility of such relationships is culturally reinforced through advertising, movies, television, novels, and popular songs. Covington and Surrey (1994) point out: "Historically, women have been assigned the task of fostering the psychological development of others, including men and children" (p. 337). Nelson-Zlupko and colleagues (1995) go further, stating: "Women who are repeatedly placed in positions of dependence on others for survival experience low self-esteem, lack of confidence in their ability to make decisions, and feel hopeless about the future. . . . In many ways, the drug-addicted woman reflects the dependence and oppression of all women in this society" (p. 48). Thus women's socialization can lead to both chemical dependency and codependency, two sides of the same coin.

How Women Are Socialized to Be Codependent

Nelson-Zlupko and colleagues (1995) pointed out that addicted women often have a history of overresponsibility in their families of origin and tend to carry primary responsibility for child care and the care of others in their families. Women's socialization to be loyal caretakers keeps them in prolonged relationships with alcoholics and addicts, in which the ten-

dency of the partners of chemical dependents to develop all the characteristics of codependency is allowed to flourish. Addicted women are frequently bound to addicted partners through the shared activity of chemical use, particularly when the use of chemicals accompanies sexual
activity. The emotional unavailability of partners who are habitually either high or preoccupied with chemicals accustoms women to relationships in which they pursue, merge, caretake, depend, and yearn without
receiving much in return in terms of intimacy or support.

Recent research indicates that many addicted women come from
families of origin in which there are other addicted family members
(Nelson-Zlupko et al. 1995). The substance abuse of parents and other
family members generates maladaptive coping strategies, thus creating
the prototypical dysfunctional family. The pattern is frequently intergenerational, with daughters of alcoholics, whether or not they abuse
substances themselves, learning codependent patterns of enabling, approval seeking, rescuing, and controlling behaviors, and reinforcing them
by marrying alcoholics and producing alcohol- or drug-addicted children.
Overresponsible behaviors can coexist with the impulsiveness, irrespon-
sibility, and acting out that characterize chemical dependents in individuals from such a background, while poorly developed boundaries are characteristic of both. To the extent that women model themselves on their
mothers, the codependent characteristics may be as deeply instilled in
addicted women as the use of chemicals as a coping mechanism.

Only in the postfeminist '90s has it been widely acknowledged that
personality development in women follows a unique course. Briefly,
because girls do not need to separate from their mothers in order to develop gender identity, they maintain a pattern that can emphasize connectedness rather than separation and individuation as they grow. This
allows them to develop the expressive and relational skills considered
characteristically female (Chodorow 1978, Gilligan 1982). Previously, the
typically female personality was considered a distortion or failure of the
more instrumental personality outlined by Erikson (1963), in which *industry* and *initiative* are key concepts on which the "normal" personality,
actually the typically male personality, is based. The new model of woman
as healthily gifted in connectedness and caring coexists with its subtle
distortion, woman as secondary to and incomplete without significant
others: notably, a male partner, children, and any family members such
as aging parents who may need her caretaking skills. In the mythology
of "romance," unrealistic expectations of love relationships are aroused
in both men and women, and an excessive, obsessive dependency and
fusion are confused with intimacy. Women in particular are taught that
this fusion is desirable and that they must nurture in order to control,

rescue, kiss, and change the frog into a prince who can meet their dependency needs. When a woman is seeking her prince in an alcoholic or addict, her dreams are especially unlikely to come true.

This societal expectation has been deeply internalized by today's women. The popular culture, in songs, television and movies, and a whole genre of fiction aimed primarily at women, still presents romantic love as a process of losing boundaries and merging identity on the basis of physical attraction and the projection of fantasies of perfection on the beloved. In other words, the popular notion of love resembles codependency rather than a healthy intimacy based on trust and communication between partners with secure identities. Furthermore, in the media, especially in advertising, the use of alcohol and tobacco is often depicted as an integral component of the romantic fantasy. Thus, for women, codependent relationships with substance abusers can easily develop in the guise of love and romance.

Critique of the Codependency Concept

The concept of codependency, while developed by professionals in the chemical dependency field, has always been largely in the province of the popular recovery movement rather than the scholarly community. Recently, articles in scholarly journals (Anderson 1994, Miller 1994) have begun to question the validity of the concept. Even in the recovery movement, some—perhaps "family heroes" themselves—have objected to defining the codependent's exaggerated ability to cope, take charge, and pursue perfection as maladaptive. Others have challenged the very existence of a phenomenon that claims, perhaps absurdly, to embrace most of the population. Scientists query the description of such a subjective and clearly nonphysical phenomenon as a disease. An important criticism from a feminist perspective is that the term may have the effect of pathologizing the characteristic traits of women and reinforcing their negative self-image. Some claim that the model blames the victim and concentrates on the internal sources of the woman's problem to such an extent that it ignores external or societal issues and prevents empowerment. The suggestion that codependency might be considered a personality disorder is seen as stigmatizing as well as disempowering. Calling codependency a personality disorder tends to deny the treatability of the disorder and to overlook the important point that it develops as a coping or survival mechanism in response to addiction, abuse, or similar dysfunction. Krestan and Bepko (1990) have suggested the term *overresponsibility* as a less pejorative alternative.

Usefulness of the Codependency Concept

In the face of these challenges, it is important to emphasize that the term codependency is a useful tool in illuminating and changing behaviors and ways of thinking that are *maladaptive.* Nurturing is admirable; rescue and caretaking to the point where the caretaker neglects self-care and the rescued lose the ability to be responsible for themselves is maladaptive. Responsiveness to the needs of others is admirable; excessive approval-seeking or "people-pleasing"—a key aspect of codependency that is not covered by the term *overresponsibility*—is maladaptive and disempowering. Critics of the idea of codependency as a disease demonstrate an inadequate understanding of how the disease model is most effectively used to promote recovery. Recovering addicts and codependents use the disease concept not to blame themselves, label themselves hopelessly "sick," or deny that there are external and even societal factors that contribute to their condition, but to help them discriminate between aspects of the situation that they can most readily change by their own efforts—their own behavior, attitudes, thoughts, and feelings—and those that either require concerted political effort or may prove futile attempts to control people, places, and things outside the self. If codependency is a disease, then, as the adherents of this view put it, recovery is possible. Similarly, the admission of powerlessness that is a prerequisite to the self-help model of recovery is far from disempowering. Covington (1994) stated:

> For women, recovery is about empowerment—finding and using our true inner power. It may seem contradictory to claim our power when we've just admitted our powerlessness, but actually we are made more powerful by this admission. . . . By admitting our powerlessness over our addiction, we are freeing ourselves to turn our attention to areas where we *do* have control. When we give up the struggle to control the things we can't control, we begin to discover our true source of power. [p. 12]

The Relational Voice in the Codependency Debate

Feminist theorists including Miller, Chodorow, and Gilligan have argued convincingly that while male psychological development focuses on the process of separation, women develop their identity through relationship and connections. Miller (1976) described the healthy relationship as one of mutuality and healthy interdependence and reframes women's participation in the development of others as an empowering expression of self. Chodorow (1978), while describing the psychodynamics of female development as relational due to a girl's continuing to identify with her mother, still stated that a girl "must be sufficiently differentiated to grow up and experience herself as a separate individual" (p. 177). Gilligan (1982) questioned the very concepts of independence and autonomy in human experience and "reframe(s) women's psychological development as centering on a struggle for connection rather than speaking about women . . . as having a problem in achieving separation" (p. xv).

Reexamining codependency in the light of this model, it becomes possible to see codependency in women not as a failure in separation, but as a series of misguided attempts at connection. It is not the fact that women tend to focus on relationships that is pathological, but rather the fact that the relationships that codependent women choose, with addicted, unavailable, or abusive objects, lack mutuality and fail to promote empowerment. It is also clear that gender-specific treatment for women's codependency, whether in the context of substance abuse treatment or not, can draw on the relational strengths that are a product not only of socialization but of female psychological development. Women's experience can be reframed as empowering, and they can be taught to form healthy, mutual, interdependent connections that support their sobriety and sense of self and enrich their lives.

GENDER-SPECIFIC ASPECTS OF SUBSTANCE ABUSE

The etiology, physiology, and progression of alcoholism and other chemical dependencies in women, as well as the behaviors of substance-abusing women, all differ from men's in ways that to some extent illuminate the integral relationship between women's codependency and their substance abuse. For example, women are more likely than men to come from alcoholic families (Pape 1993). Such women not only internalize the behaviors of substance-abusing role models but also practice codependent behaviors—rescue and control, caretaking, parentification—from early childhood.

> Jessica was an actress with a long history of alcoholism and drug abuse. She had seen both her parents drinking and engaging in sexual acting out and violence throughout her childhood. Jessica reported an early memory of sitting in a big chair, her feet stretched straight out before her—she believes she could not have been more than 18 months old—with her infant sister in her lap. Family anecdotes about how she always "took care of" her little sister were often repeated with approval. At the age of 11, she appeared in a Broadway play. She recalled that from this time on, she believed that it was her duty to be responsible for financially supporting her family.

Physiologically, women are affected by smaller amounts of alcohol or other drugs than men (Kolata 1990, Pape 1993). Consequently, in comparison to an alcoholic or drug-addicted male partner or family member, a woman's chemical intake may appear negligible and her substance abuse remain unidentified. Thus, whereas the man's role in the system is to be the "designated drunk" or addict who needs treatment, the woman remains the caretaker, enabler, codependent—even if she herself is chemically dependent.

The reasons for using chemicals may also be gender-specific. Women frequently begin using substances in attempts to "stay psychologically connected with someone who is using . . . to maintain relationships . . . (or) to try to alter themselves to fit the relationships available" (Covington and Surrey 1997, p. 8). What is basically a codependent behavior becomes a drug addiction that must either be treated as a primary disorder or run its destructive course.

Both drinking behavior and associated sexual behavior not only tend to differ but are evaluated differently for men and women in our society. "Passive or limited interest in both [alcohol and sex] are valued for women while almost the opposite is true for men" (Covington and Kohen 1984, p. 42). Drinking as a social activity or bonding ritual and expansive, sexually aggressive, or assertively self-protective behavior are not expected of women. Thus social mores reinforce the isolation of the substance-abusing woman in terms of female solidarity and her dependence on dysfunctional sexual relationships in which she frequently becomes the victim of physical and sexual abuse. Alcohol has been found to cause sexual dysfunction in women while allowing a subjective perception of increased sexual response. The same may be true of other drugs. This paradox fits neatly into the codependency concept, in which women wish to please their partners and assure themselves of their own worth through their sexual responsiveness but in fact are out of touch with their own sexual feelings, which may include decreased arousal and pleasure or inability to achieve orgasm (Covington and Kohen 1984).

Male and female addicts' behaviors in obtaining illegal drugs may also tend to differ. There is evidence that men characteristically engage in antisocial or criminal behaviors such as dealing, stealing, and violence (Forrest 1994), while women frequently engage in prostitution or exchange sexual favors for drugs. These behaviors reinforce women's codependency by decreasing their sense of self, reducing their worth in their own and society's eyes, placing them in a dependent position in which they may be dominated and abused, and destroying any chance they might otherwise have for emotional or financial autonomy.

HOW CODEPENDENCY AFFECTS SUBSTANCE ABUSE TREATMENT

Codependency can sabotage substance-abusing women's recovery at various points, from their ability to enter and engage in a treatment program to their achieving a satisfactory quality of life in long-term sobriety. Some women cannot establish abstinence because of their enmeshment in destructive relationships. Others relapse periodically because their external sources of identity and self-worth inevitably let them down.

Various characteristics of codependency must be specifically addressed during treatment. Poor boundaries lead to a tendency to form dysfunctional systems that replicate the family of origin. Excessive caretaking and enabling of fellow substance abusers and dependent family members or other loved ones take the focus off a woman's treatment and recovery. Maladaptive approval seeking may lead to behaviors ranging from continued drug use to insincere compliance in the treatment setting. The need for control may foster noncompliance with treatment and power struggles with helping professionals. Perfectionism fosters low self-esteem and may trigger relapse. And finally, the tendency to seek identity and worth outside the self not only leads the addicted woman to destructive relationships, but some corrective personality development must take place if the recovering woman, frequently without any history of emotional or economic autonomy, is to achieve the ability to know and love herself that is essential to her continued sobriety.

Overcoming Denial

Codependent women's tendency to cling to destructive relationships and their preoccupation with the needs and problems of others can reinforce their denial of their own substance abuse.

> Rochelle sought help for her husband, a lawyer who went on periodic drinking and spending sprees. She admitted to classic enabling behaviors such as drinking from his glass at dinner parties to reduce his intake of wine. It was only after a year as an "Al-Anon wife" that Rochelle, a nightclub entertainer, realized that "I never went on stage without a drink in my hand" and sought treatment for her own drinking problem.

In many alcoholic relationships, the male partner is the "designated drunk," his greater consumption of alcohol and more spectacular acting-out behavior overshadowing the woman's less obtrusive substance abuse. In addition, in a case like Rochelle's, the social acceptability of the wife's concern with her husband's behavior reinforces her denial of her own substance abuse.

Accessing and Staying in Treatment

Traditionally, when alcoholics or addicts have cited responsibilities and commitments in their daily lives as reasons that they cannot enter an inpatient program or attend an outpatient program regularly, these have been considered as excuses or resistances to treatment. Priority has been given to achieving sobriety, or as the "Big Book" of Alcoholics Anonymous (1976) puts it, alcoholics must be willing to go to any lengths, because the continued use of chemicals will eventually interfere with their ability to maintain their responsibilities and commitments anyway.

However, our society still places the role of family caretaker squarely on women's shoulders and has so far failed to provide adequate resources outside the family for the care of children, the elderly, and the disabled, especially those who lack the means to pay for services. When a woman states that she cannot attend a daily treatment program because she has no one with whom to leave her three preschool children or her demented and incontinent mother, she may be telling the simple truth. On the other hand, her inability to find a solution may indeed be a resistance, reflecting her ambivalence about sobriety. As a third alternative, her codependent belief that only she can or should play the caretaker role may prevent her from accepting substitutes such as another family member or a home attendant.

> Juana insisted that she could not possibly attend AA meetings and would not always be able to attend her five-day treatment program because of her housekeeping chores and need to care for her six children, whose ages ranged from 3 to 20. When asked why the older children could not take over some of these tasks, she stated that only she could perform them well enough.

This mother had to be helped to see that her overresponsible function was a codependent attitude that not only prevented her from getting the help she needed but denied the children the chance to develop their own sense of responsibility and independence. She needed to be shown how her excessive drinking had in fact interfered with her performing these tasks and would continue to do so unless she got the help she needed. Finally, she had to be persuaded that it would be possible for her to strike a balance between her admirable desire to care properly for her children and her home and the need to devote some of her time to her own recovery.

Sometimes the client's ambivalence to treatment may prevent her from accessing available resources, such as publicly funded homemaking services or a friend or relative who could provide child care. It is the worker's task to continue to confront the client's ambivalence and unwillingness to make efforts in her own behalf, rather than merely to solve the problem for her.

Unfortunately, many alcoholic and drug-addicted women come from families and environments in which everyone around them may also be drinking and drugging and thus may be unavailable or irresponsible caretakers. In order to be responsive to women's needs, programs treating chemically dependent women indeed should provide child care, or better yet, therapeutic interventions, since children are inevitably affected by a mother's alcoholism or other drug abuse. However, lack of funding, lack of specialized training, and the reluctance of institutions primarily serving adults to accept liability for children conspire to make the provision of such services the exception rather than the rule. Even a recent thrust toward funding some residential programs for women with their children is flawed by stipulations that only one child, or children under a certain age, be admitted with the mother, who may have several older children to care for as well. Ironically, it may be women mandated to treatment after their children have been removed from the home for abuse or neglect who have the easiest time accessing services they need to recover. At times, children may be returned to the mother prematurely, without regard to her possible ambivalence or lack of parenting skills. Because her new role limits her access to treatment, support may be withdrawn just when she needs it most, leaving the woman at high risk for relapse.

> Karen's children were placed in foster care and she was mandated to treatment. Motivated by the desire to get her children back, she attended regularly and achieved stable sobriety. However, once they were returned to her, her parenting responsibilities began to interfere with her attendance at the treatment program, and she reported feeling overwhelmed. Eventually she dropped out of treatment.

Achieving Abstinence

Frequently, for women, the pressures of codependency, such as the pain of relying on an unavailable partner or the projection onto a beloved other of unrealistic fantasies in which the codependent woman will be so well taken care of that she need not take any responsibility for herself, can play a major role in preventing the establishment of basic abstinence.

> Josie, a teacher, entered an outpatient program, reporting that she was unable to achieve more than a few days' abstinence at a time. She was living with a man who spent every Monday to Friday with her, but each weekend he would "borrow" money from her and leave for another city where he had a second girlfriend. Josie attributed her continued drinking to the stress of this situation, saying, "I know I should throw him out, but I'm so afraid of being alone." Antabuse was suggested as an interim measure to help her stabilize her sobriety, but she left the program before it could be implemented.

A codependent terror of abandonment kept this client in a state of constant anxiety that she needed alcohol to medicate. She, not the treatment staff, identified the destructive relationship as the source of the problem. However, even a gentle approach—suggesting that for the time being she might give up, not the man, but the coping mechanism, alcohol—made her bolt from treatment. For some codependent women, being alone—without someone to hold, without self, without an object for their fantasies or a chemical to blur the emptiness—is the worst fate that can befall them.

> Dale and Stella, two lesbian women living in a shelter, were mandated to treatment by a vocational program in which they were both enrolled. They had been getting high on crack together every two weeks, when Stella got her welfare check. Stella had a history of suicidal ideation, auditory hallucinations, and poor impulse control. She assured the outpatient program psychiatrist that she could make it through the weekend without using or acting out because, she said, "Dale will keep me straight." Meanwhile, Dale was telling the treatment staff, "I'll try to stay clean, but I won't lie to you, I really love crack." Neither woman succeeded in becoming engaged in treatment, and both continued to use crack.

Nontraditional relationships, like this lesbian couple's, are unfortunately not immune from the codependent assumptions of traditional socialization. Stella, the more needy partner, had a fantasy of being rescued from her addiction, while in fact Dale's preoccupation with getting high drew her further into the cycle of substance abuse. These two substance-abusing women had both internalized the fantasy of romantic love as a blurring of ego boundaries. Stella believed this meant that they could succeed in taking responsibility for each other's impulses. Dale was more realistic about her continued craving for crack but was in denial about the extent of Stella's psychological instability. As a result, both of them were more likely to sabotage each other's attempt to achieve abstinence than to support it.

Maintaining Sobriety

Even if a woman manages to achieve abstinence, approval-seeking attitudes, caretaking priorities, and destructive relationships can sabotage her sobriety at any time. Treatment for women involves constant reassessment and readjusting of the balance between addressing codependency issues as they threaten sobriety and deferring them in order to focus more directly on building skills to stabilize the sobriety and prevent relapse. Even a woman who has internalized and continues to use these skills can be derailed by inattention to or inability to address her codependency issues effectively.

> Hilda, a 63-year-old German-born woman, was an architect whose alcoholism had led to her spending two years on the street and eventually to being a halfway house resident in a slum area. She described her 17-year marriage to her publisher husband as "just two happy drunks together." Having inadvertently lost contact with him during her transfer from the hospital where she detoxed to the halfway house, she was preoccupied with rescuing him. She was unable to take any pleasure or pride in her own six months of sobriety, saying, "If I can't find him and get him sober too, I don't want to live."

Hilda's anhedonia and passive suicidality appeared to be related to her codependency rather than to the fact that she was newly sober. Her sobriety was in danger of being sabotaged by her codependent attitude, which was destroying her motivation for building a new life. In addition to assessing and, if necessary, medicating her depression, she needed to be helped to form ego boundaries so she could value her own sobriety and to "detach with love" so that she could accept a more realistic view of her husband's chances of recovery without losing hope for herself.

At its most extreme, codependency, like chemical dependency, can lead to tragedy. In one dramatic case, a woman with a history of prolonged sobriety, good knowledge of the disease process, and well-developed relapse prevention skills was destroyed by her inability to resist a codependent relationship. Her denial of the destructiveness of the relationship, evidenced by her returning to a man who had raped her so brutally she was hospitalized, led to denial of the unlikelihood of her remaining clean and sober in such a relationship.

Willa was a 42-year-old woman with a history of relationships with addicted men. She stated, "I'm more attracted to them because they need me," although she also admitted that the progression of her drinking and drugging had always been related to joining them in their chemical use and dealing with grief when they left or died. Willa had recently achieved a year of sobriety through attendance at an outpatient day program and extremely active participation in AA. A leader among the clients, she was known for sharing recovery wisdom, such as, "You can't be high and sober."

Willa had previously achieved almost ten years of sobriety and had even considered becoming a counselor. During her prior sobriety, she had met Jake at an AA meeting and began living with him. She described him as "very loving and a good provider" when sober. However, Jake resumed using cocaine after four years. Determined to remain in the relationship without losing her sobriety, Willa continued her involvement in AA, over his objections, for a year before she, too, returned to alcohol and other drugs. She eventually left the relationship and made several attempts to get sober again, but did not do so until an encounter with Jake ended in his raping her. Hospitalized with internal hemorrhaging, she got into detox and then into an outpatient treatment program.

Around the time she was celebrating one year of sobriety, Jake reappeared in her life. He had just had a baby with another woman, but courted Willa, telling her the other woman was "lazy," "not a good cook," and a poor caretaker to the baby. Strongly attracted in spite of their history, Willa declared she could "detach with love" by telling Jake he could see her only when he wasn't high and by continuing her outpatient treatment and AA involvement. Gradually, she became less involved in treatment and eventually stopped coming altogether. Fellow clients reported she was using cocaine and prostituting to obtain money for drugs.

On the day of the annual client graduation ceremony, Willa appeared at the alcohol treatment program looking emaciated and ill. She stated that she was scheduled to enter an inpatient drug treatment program in three days and that she had come to graduate. When told this was not possible, she was astonished, saying, "But I didn't drink!" She went away angry, and six months later, it was learned that she had died on the street.

This client had all the tools she needed to maintain abstinence from chemicals. It was codependency that killed her.

Quality of Recovery

Even if the persistence of codependency issues does not lead the client back to alcohol or other drugs, it can drastically affect those aspects of recovery that are often termed *emotional* and *spiritual*. The promise of recovery frequently includes a transformation that goes far beyond abstinence from chemicals to dramatic improvements in self-esteem, judgment, self-awareness, and other aspects of ego functioning, as well as in social and instrumental functioning. If codependency issues are not adequately addressed, the recovering woman's personal growth may be stunted.

> Deirdre was an alcoholic with ten years of sobriety. She was actively involved in AA and had good tools for relapse prevention. She had also been in treatment during much of her recovery. She had been involved for several years with a man who was actively addicted to drugs and had a history of violence and psychotic episodes. Deirdre had made several attempts to end the relationship, which she perceived as destructive, but was unable to follow through on self-protective actions such as seeking an order of protection or changing the locks on her apartment. She said, "I'm afraid he'll die if I don't take care of him."

Although Deirdre did not appear to be in danger of resuming her drinking, her emotional and spiritual health was sabotaged by her acutely codependent relationship, which kept her on a "roller coaster" of dangerous crises and reinforced a grandiose perception of herself as essential caretaker.

Codependent Behavior in the Treatment Setting

Codependent addicted women carry their tendencies to rescue, control, and caretake and their inability to maintain boundaries into the treatment setting, where these problems can adversely affect their treatment.

Melanie was a 24-year-old homeless woman whose alcoholism had progressed to a severe chronic stage. She had been thrown out of her parents' home, had a child in foster care, and was living on the street with a boyfriend who was also a chronic alcoholic. Melanie presented herself repeatedly at a local hospital requesting treatment. Each time, she was drunk and accompanied by her boyfriend. On several occasions, the couple left detox together prematurely, against medical advice. Not until her boyfriend died of his alcoholism did Melanie successfully complete detox and establish stable sobriety in a women's halfway house.

Friendship established within a women's treatment program can demonstrate aspects of both the relational strengths of recovering women and how their codependent enmeshment can take the focus off recovery.

Joyce and Annie came into outpatient treatment in a women's program at about the same time and quickly formed a close friendship. At times, the friendship reinforced the sobriety of both women, who attended AA meetings together and sometimes spent the weekend together at Annie's former rehab. However, sometimes Joyce claimed that she had to skip treatment to babysit for Annie, or Annie would explain she had missed a session to drive Joyce to a medical appointment. Episodes of relapse or acting out by one invariably precipitated a crisis in the other, and emotional upheavals in the friendship frequently took the focus off sobriety for both. The ups and downs of this volatile relationship also became a distracting focus for the other clients.

In some ways, this friendship was a demonstration of the recovery goal of learning to trust and socialize with other women, an important aspect of women's treatment with the underlying agenda of increasing the recovering woman's own sense of self-worth. On the other hand, the enmeshed quality of the relationship detracted on many occasions from the focus on treatment. The clients' codependent preoccupation with each other's issues and with the friendship itself sometimes detracted from their personal growth and, at worst, was a precipitating factor in relapse. The treatment community as a whole was also affected by the drama of these two strong personalities' interaction.

Clients who play caretaker or co-therapist in the group or treatment community are known to all clinicians. In the context of the codependency model, these behaviors can be seen as an aspect of "the disease," expectable in women who have learned through socialization and through participation in dysfunctional families and addicted relationships to derive whatever self-worth they may have from their value to others. However, such behaviors must be modified if the client is to achieve the autonomy, self-esteem, and internal focus needed for ongoing recovery. Caretaking and leadership in the group can be validated for their positive aspects, but their maladaptive and excessive aspects must not be allowed to interfere with the treatment process.

> Katherine, who was older than the other clients in a women's outpatient program and had a substantial work history as well as a prior period of long-term sobriety, became a "mother" to the group. When a fellow client who had relapsed phoned her repeatedly late at night while drunk, Katherine became overwhelmed and had to be helped to confront the relapsing woman and set limits on her availability.

INTEGRATIVE TREATMENT APPROACHES

Gender-specific treatment for women must maintain a constantly reassessed and carefully individualized balance between chemical dependency and codependency as its primary focus. It is essential to incorporate the codependency and "family disease" concepts into the presentation of chemical dependency from the beginning, rather than polarizing the concepts by presenting the codependent or enabler as a malignant "other" whose role is to threaten the addict's sobriety. Presenting codependency as a disease that is part of the disease of addiction gives women in very early sobriety a way to understand some of their counterproductive behavior through a model that they already understand with respect to their substance abuse. By identifying and joining with the idea of codependency as an aspect of "the disease," they are laying a foundation for incorporating firmer boundaries and healthier relationships into their recovery.

> A group of homeless women referred to outpatient treatment together from a women's shelter had difficulty working productively as a group because, either prior to getting sober or on first entering treatment, they had formed chaotic and dysfunctional relationships. Some were in lesbian relationships with each other or with women who were living in the shelter but not seeking sobriety; others had formed ties with male clients in the program. These impulsively formed and emotionally charged relationships, complicated by the presence of HIV in some of the participants, had a destabilizing effect on sobriety and repeatedly disrupted the work of the group. A decision to devote some group time to

psychoeducation on codependency helped the women begin to grapple with this aspect of their disorder.

While giving women "their own space" is an important aspect of gender-specific models of treatment, it can be complicated by the existence of same-sex love relationships, which introduce elements of sexuality and emotional lability into what is intended, through the absence of males, to be a "safe" environment. Furthermore, many heterosexual addicted women do not initially perceive an all-female environment as either safe or desirable. They frequently project their inability to love themselves onto their peers, claiming that they have never liked or never trusted other women, and may resist the suggestion that gender-specific treatment will meet their needs and allow them to be vulnerable and open. However, most can benefit from socializing with other women in a structured and nonsexual environment in which recovery is promoted and appropriate boundaries and communication encouraged. The remarkable capacity for connectedness that the relational theorists have observed enables recovering women to form a community and support each other effectively through all the risks and frustrations of early sobriety. They can mutually reinforce each other's growing self-esteem and help each other find alternatives to excessive caretaking and abusive relationships.

> Eileen, an alcoholic and daughter of an alcoholic, had been in individual treatment for several years without achieving stable sobriety. After prolonged resistance to group treatment and self-help, she agreed to try a women's day program. Within a year, she had achieved stable abstinence and was actively involved in both AA and social activities with her friends from the treatment program. She was also able to set limits, for the first time in many years, on her involvement as primary caregiver for her husband, a paraplegic who was hostile and embittered and who, in spite of his verbal abusiveness to her, had always refused to allow anyone else to care for him. Eileen eventually pursued vocational training, got a part-time job outside the home, and was able to let go of much of her own rage toward her husband.

Cognitive-behavioral methods of introducing women in early sobriety to the concepts of codependency and the family disease may include psychoeducation regarding the roles and rules of alcoholic or dysfunctional families and their effect on adult children. Later on in treatment, reparenting, through a combination of self-nurture and corrective experiences with helping professionals and supportive peers, may be an essential ingredient not only in learning appropriate parenting skills but also in reducing codependent attitudes and behaviors. Role models are helpful, not only in the form of professionals who are both nurturing and limit setting, but in the guise of twelve–step "double winner" sponsors who have successfully integrated the two aspects of recovery in Alcoholics Anonymous or Narcotics Anonymous and Al-Anon or Codependents Anonymous. The parenting curriculum in women's treatment must take into account the needs of the substance-abusing mother's "inner child."

> Caroline, an alcoholic woman in treatment, was constantly angry at her 7-year-old daughter, who failed to meet her inappropriately high expectations regarding the child's school performance and household tasks such as cleaning and doing the laundry. Exploration revealed that Caroline had married and become pregnant at the age of 16 as a means of escaping an abusive stepfather and felt deeply resentful that she had "never had a childhood."

Aspects of codependency in this client included perfectionism, need for control, and the inability to perceive a boundary between her daughter and herself. Not only was this damaging to the daughter's self-esteem, but it kept Caroline in a state of resentment and frustration that was detrimental to her continued sobriety and personal growth.

Transference and Countertransference

The people-pleasing or approval-seeking aspect of codependency can play itself out as false compliance with treatment and idealizing transference toward helping professionals. Clinicians, themselves at risk for codependent feelings of excessive gratification at successfully rescuing or inspiring the addict, must be continually attentive to their countertransference issues and maintain strong and clear professional boundaries.

> Alice, a counselor who was a recovering addict herself, reported in supervision that Jeanne, one of her clients, had said Alice was the only staff member she could trust. Alice believed that this demonstrated the success of her therapeutic relationship with Jeanne. When the client relapsed, Alice was devastated.

Overidentification with the client and unlimited helping are pitfalls for professionals, especially those who are also in recovery, because they must avoid both codependency and burnout even as they reinforce their own sobriety by helping others.

CONCLUSION

The concept of codependency is effective in addressing many of the gender-specific problems of substance-abusing women. It may be presented as an aspect of addiction with a progression similar to that of chemical dependency and an analogous opportunity for recovery. Codependency can result from relationships with substance abusers, childhood in a dysfunctional family, and socialization in a culture that emphasizes external sources of fulfillment and places the burden of caretaking on women. All of these dynamics are particularly relevant to chemically dependent women. Treatment approaches include psychoeducation that avoids polarizing chemical dependency and codependency and ongoing assessment on an individual basis so that destructive codependency issues can be addressed without sabotaging sobriety. Also essential are acknowledgment of women's interpersonal strengths, modeling of healthy boundaries and appropriate relationships, and reparenting of the addicted woman so that her inner child can be healed and she can achieve not only lasting sobriety but also identity, self-esteem, empowerment, and a satisfying quality of life.

REFERENCES

Alcoholics Anonymous (3rd ed.). (1976). New York: Alcoholics Anonymous World Services.

Anderson, S. C. (1994). A critical analysis of the concept of codependency. *Social Work* 39(6):677–685.

Cermak, T. L. (1984). Children of alcoholics and the case for a new diagnostic category of codependency. *Alcohol Health and Research World* 3(4):38–42.

Chodorow, N. (1978). *The Reproduction of Mothering.* Berkeley: University of California Press.

Codependents Anonymous (1989). First International Conference. Scottsdale, AZ. Personal communication.

Covington, S. S. (1994). *A Woman's Way Through the Twelve Steps.* Center City, MN: Hazelden.

Covington, S. S., and Kohen, J. (1984). Women, alcohol, and sexuality. *Advances in Alcohol and Substance Abuse* 4(1):41–56.

Covington, S. S., and Surrey, J. L. (1997). The relational model of women's psychological development: implications for substance abuse. In *Gender and Alcohol,* ed. S. Wilsnack and R. Wilsnack, pp. 335–351. Piscataway, NJ: Rutgers University.

Erikson, E. H. (1963). *Childhood and Society,* 2nd ed. New York: Norton.

Forrest, G. G. (1994). *Chemical Dependency and Antisocial Personality Disorder: Psychotherapy and Assessment Strategies.* New York: Haworth.

Gilligan, C. (1982). *In a Different Voice: Psychological Theory and Women's Development.* Cambridge, MA: Harvard University Press, 1993.

Kolata, G. (1990). Study tells why alcohol is greater risk to women. *The New York Times,* January 11.

Krestan, J., and Bepko, C. (1990). Codependency: the social reconstruction of female experience. *Smith College Studies in Social Work* 60:216–232.

Miller, J. B. (1976). *Toward a New Psychology of Women.* Boston: Beacon.

Miller, K. J. (1994). The co-dependency concept: does it offer a solution for the spouses of alcoholics? *Journal of Substance Abuse Treatment* 11(4):339–345.

Nelson-Zlupko, L., Kauffman, E., and Dore, M. M. (1995). Gender differences in drug addiction and treatment: implications for social work intervention with substance-abusing women. *Social Work* 40(1):45–54.

Pape, P. A. (1993). Issues in assessment and intervention with alcohol- and drug-abusing women. In *Clinical Work with Substance Abusing Clients,* ed. S. L. A. Straussner, pp. 251–269. New York: Guilford.

Schaef, A. W. (1986). *Co-Dependence: Misunderstood—Mistreated.* New York: Harper & Row.

Wegscheider, S. (1981). *Another Chance: Hope and Health for the Alcoholic Family.* Palo Alto, CA: Science and Behavior Books.

Zelvin, E. (1993). Partners of substance abusers. In *Clinical Work with Substance Abusing Clients,* ed. S. L. A. Straussner, pp. 196–213. New York: Guilford.

Women, Addiction, and Sexuality

4

Stephanie S. Covington

WOMEN, ADDICTION, AND SEXUALITY

Although research has been done on women and addiction since the 1970s, the subject of sexuality is still often neglected in both the research and treatment of chemically dependent females. Part of the reason for this omission in treatment programs is the lack of strong models that assist clinicians to honestly address and help heal sexual issues and concerns. This is unfortunate, because healing in the sexual/relational area is crucial to the whole process of recovery from addiction. According to noted sex therapist Helen Singer Kaplan (1974), healthy sexuality is integral to one's sense of self-worth. It represents the integration of biological, emotional, and social aspects of who one is and how one relates to others. Addiction is often defined as a physical, emotional, social, and spiritual disease. If we define healthy sexuality as the integration of all these aspects of the self, we can easily see why addiction can have an impact on every area of our sexuality. Therefore, addressing and healing all aspects of the sexual self is critical to a woman's recovery process. This chapter will present an overview of a model for the sexual recovery of addicted women that can be used by clinicians and other health care professionals, as well as by women themselves.

The neglect of much serious study in the field of addiction and female sexuality is surprising in light of the fact that for thousands of years human sexuality and the consumption of alcohol and other drugs have been closely linked in the mythos of many cultures. To the ancient Greeks, Bacchus, the god of wine, provoked licentiousness. When the ancient Hebrews became intoxicated at the foot of Mount Sinai, the Bible tells us that they lost all restraint and engaged in adultery. We can see a twentieth century version of these beliefs in the deliberate association of sexuality and some of the legal drugs (alcohol and tobacco) in advertising. There is also the belief that some illegal drugs, such as cocaine and marijuana, are aphrodisiacs, or sex-enhancing drugs. The myth propagated by contemporary advertisers is that beer, wine, and liquor promote sexual arousal, and that alcohol consumption is directly connected with sexual attractiveness, flirtation, dating, and romance. The underlying message is that drinking makes men more virile and women more sensual and available. The subtext of magazine and billboard ads, which portray attractive, smiling men and women in intimate poses, is that alcohol will not only enable a person to meet more beautiful and desirable partners but to have a more exciting and deeply satisfying sex life. The same images of independence, power, and sexual enhancement are also portrayed in cigarette ads. Even though alcohol and tobacco use are undergoing a slow decline in our culture, a considerable number of people still buy into the image of the desirable and sophisticated man or woman holding a drink or a cigarette. So great is the power of advertising to deny the negative effects of addiction and to present images of alcohol and cigarettes as normal, appropriate, and innocuous that very little is ever heard to counter the implied connection between sexuality and addictive substances (Kilbourne 1991).

Socialization of Men and Women

In spite of the glamorous magazine image of a woman in an evening gown holding a martini in one hand and touching the cheek of a man in a tuxedo with the other, the general societal perception of women who drink and use drugs is negative. The German philosopher Immanuel Kant could have been summing up contemporary attitudes when he wrote that women should avoid drunkenness because their privileged place in society was ensured only if they adhered to a higher moral code of behavior than men (quoted by Jellinek 1941). And little has changed from the days of Chaucer when it was believed that women who drank were inviting sexual assault: "A woman in her cups has no defence./As lechers know from long experience" (Chaucer, translated by Coghill 1951).

The boundaries of what is considered acceptable and unacceptable behavior for women and men begins with early childhood socialization. Whereas, traditionally, boys have been encouraged to be aggressive, physically combative, independent, nonemotional, and outwardly oriented, girls are more often taught to be passive, dependent, emotional, and oriented toward relationship. Much has been written in the last two decades about the limiting and negative effects of such socialization upon both men and women. Even though many parents are aware of these effects and try to raise their children along more flexible gender lines, the stereotypical standards of male/female behavior still prevail in the culture at large (Covington and Beckett 1988).

There is even less awareness of how these behavioral norms affect the healthy expression of male and female sexuality. In spite of the "sexual revolution" of the 1960s, men and women still have a separate sexual socialization that places gender roles above the spectrum of differences found among individual men and women. Men are taught to act knowledgeable about sex, comfortable with their bodies, and to touch themselves and their genitals unselfconsciously. One cannot even imagine female athletes engaging in the kind of nonchalant physical behavior that male athletes display on the playing field: adjusting their jock straps, scratching their chests, and patting each other playfully on the derriere (Covington 1991). As the sexual initiators, men are also expected to know all about sex before marriage (Harrison and Pennell 1989, Richmond-Abbot 1983).

Women, on the other hand, are discouraged from learning about sex, touching or thinking about their genitals, or being sexually assertive (Shaffer 1981). Many women cannot even speak about the sexual parts of their bodies without using euphemisms such as "down there," and many more have never even looked at their vaginas. Traditionally, the value of a virgin has been her inexperience and her trust in her husband to awaken her sexually. Whereas a sexually uninformed male may be ridiculed by his peers, a sexually experienced woman is at risk of being considered "wild" by hers.

Men are expected to be assertive in physical relationships, to seek out and choose a partner, initiate sexual behavior, produce an erection, and orchestrate the sexual encounter. The performance anxiety that results from these one-sided expectations is the primary cause of some male sexual dysfunction (Harrison and Pennell 1989).

Women, on the other hand, are socialized toward passivity in their intimate relationships and are expected to wait for another to approach them. Any sexual signaling a woman gives must be extremely subtle. When she is assertive, overtly signaling her sexual interest, she risks being branded as a "slut" or a "loose woman" and possibly even sexually abused. So much punishment and disdain is meted out to the sexually assertive woman in our society that many women are disconnected from their own sexual feelings. This situation is exacerbated by the expectation that women will orient their behavior outward toward the satisfaction of their partner. Many recovering women alcoholics and drug users have spent so many years focusing on the needs of their partners that they do not have any idea what would be sexually gratifying for them (Covington 1991). Even though, in the general population, only 30 percent of women report experiencing an orgasm during intercourse (Hite 1976), it is still the preferred sexual activity among men and for many is synonymous with "having sex."

Social Stereotypes of Women Who Drink and Use Drugs

This polarization of sexual roles is mirrored in society's beliefs about male and female drinking and drug use. Women who drink or use other drugs are perceived as being more eager for sex, more vulnerable to seduction, and less selective about partners (George et al. 1986, 1988). In light of this, the stigma against addicted women is often expressed in sexual terms, branding such women as promiscuous, loose, or "looking for it." Sexual terms are rarely used to describe addicted men (Covington 1993). Unlike drunken men, drunken women can never be perceived as just spending a pleasant night out on the town with "the boys."

Several studies by George and colleagues (1986, 1988) have documented the attitudes that contemporary society has toward women who drink. In one, ninety-six men were asked to watch videos of a woman drinking either beer or cola under a variety of conditions. Without exception, whenever the young woman was viewed as drinking alcohol she was rated higher by the viewers in terms of sexual responsiveness and promiscuity. The authors concluded: "These results imply that men view a woman's drunkenness as an exploitable weakness. In real-life dating situations, such a biased view of a drinking woman could support or even precipitate unwelcome sexual advances. Moreover, these perceptual biases could potentially play a mediating role in sexually violent acts that involve a drinking female victim" (George et al. 1986, p. 10).

In a study by Richardson and Campbell (1982), 187 male and female undergraduates were asked to evaluate four rape scenarios. In the first, the rapist was drunk; in the second, the victim was drunk. In the third scenario, both were intoxicated; and in the last, neither had been drinking. Both male and female students rated both the man and the woman as more accountable for the rape when drunk. Even when the rapist was not drunk, the victim was still considered more responsible than her attacker for the violence perpetrated against her if she herself was intoxicated at the time. The societal expectation that women are more eager for sex when drunk strongly suggests that women will suffer from more sexual and physical aggression when intoxicated and that the actions of the sexual aggressor will be more easily rationalized or excused at such times (Blume 1991).

Sexual Victimization of the Addicted Woman

The societal perceptions represented by these studies are reflected in the experiences of addicted women. A study of alcohol and sexuality (Covington and Kohen 1984) compared a group of alcoholic women—the majority of whom were poly-drug addicted and had a primary identity of "alcoholic"—with another sample of nonalcoholics. Although high rates of physical, emotional, and sexual abuse were reported by all women, addicted women consistently suffered greater levels of abuse in all of these areas. Seventy-one percent of the alcoholic women reported emotional abuse, including ridicule, degradation, harassment, jealous accusations, blame, yelling, lying, unfaithfulness, and the emotional withdrawal of their partner. Only 44 percent of nonalcoholic women experienced these behaviors (Covington 1986). Alcoholic women also experienced more physical abuse, 51 percent compared to 34 percent of the nonalcoholic women. This type of abuse included being hit with fists and/or objects, pulled by the hair, spanked, thrown, and slapped. Though all abuse is violent, the physical abuse against alcoholic women had a more brutal quality to it. Alcoholic women reported being beaten, given black eyes, forced to have unneeded surgery, held in arm locks and police holds, and purposely held under water until they had nearly drowned. Although all of the physical abusers were known by the women, 82 percent of the perpetrators of physical abuse against alcoholic women were male compared to 75 percent for nonalcoholic women (Covington 1986).

Seventy-four percent of alcoholic women reported experiencing some form of sexual abuse during their lifetime, compared to 50 percent of nonalcoholic women, a significant difference. Alcoholic women were also likely to experience the more extreme forms of sexual assault—rape, rather than attempted rape. One possible reason for this is that an intoxicated woman is not able to fight off her attacker or be as clear about her nonconsent as a nondrinking woman (Norris 1994). Only the alcoholic women reported sexual abuse with the same perpetrator extending for a period of ten years or more. In most cases, alcoholic women experience their first instance of abuse in childhood. One hundred percent of the alcoholic women who experienced sexual abuse (incest, childhood molestation, rape, or attempted rape) had been violated at least once by the age of 10, compared to 65 percent of the nonalcoholic women (Covington 1986). The high incidence of alcohol and substance abuse among survivors of physical or sexual abuse in childhood suggests that, in the absence of healthy parental relationships, women turn to addictive substances for support (Covington and Surrey 1996).

The great amount of abuse suffered by addicted women has a tragic impact upon their lives and a negative impact upon their ability to function sexually. In view of the high rates of abuse (Table 4–1), it is not surprising that addicted women have trouble trusting enough to express themselves sexually or to enjoy themselves in intimate relationships. When the majority of one's intimate relationships have been filled with violence, violation, and fear since childhood, it is nearly impossible to relax into the trust that an intimate sexual experience requires (Covington 1993).

The high correlation between addiction and abuse in women's lives makes it of paramount importance that both abuse and sexual issues be addressed during recovery. Treatment should be focused on assessing the history of abuse of addicted women, understanding their sexual dysfunctions, addressing their fears, helping them to develop the ability to trust,

TABLE 4-1: A Comparison of Abuse Reported by Alcoholic and Nonalcoholic Women

	Alcoholic	Nonalcoholic
Experienced emotional abuse	71%	44%
Experienced physical abuse	51%	34%
Experienced sexual abuse	74%	50%
Experienced sexual abuse before the age of 10 (of those sexually abused)	100%	65%

and *most important,* creating a *sense of safety* (Herman 1992). For women to be able to express their sexuality in fulfilling ways, they must first be able to begin healing their abusive pasts.

DISTORTION OF SEXUALITY

As previously mentioned, addiction is a physical, emotional, social, and spiritual disease. Sexuality also depends upon the healthy integration of all these aspects of the self. Therefore, we can see why addiction impacts upon every area of our sexuality.

The Physiological Effects of Addiction

Alcohol and other drugs interfere with sexual sensitivity and enjoyment in many ways. They disrupt the delicate balance of a woman's hormonal system, interfering with her body's proper emotional, reproductive, and physiological functions. Alcohol, as well as heroin and marijuana, act upon the body as depressants, decreasing sexual desire, and retarding blood congestion and swelling in the genitals and pelvic area, creating lessened sensation, numbness, or a sense of disconnection. Under such conditions, excitement to orgasm will take longer and require more pressure, if it can occur at all. Alcohol deadens sensory input, making women less sensitive to touch (Covington and Kohen 1984).

Clinical research in the last twenty years has shown that, although the consumption of alcohol and other drugs creates a greater desire for sex in the mind of the user (especially in those who use cocaine), heavy alcohol and drug users report a greater incidence of sexual dysfunction than do moderate or nonusers. In fact, Wilsnack and colleagues (1991) list sexual dysfunction as the best single predictor that a woman might be having chronic problems with alcohol. Although only 6 percent of women who use alcohol are heavy drinkers,[1] as opposed to 21 percent of men (Midanick and Clark 1992), studies have shown that the physiological consequences of women's alcohol abuse is greater than men's. At the same body weight, women reach higher blood concentration levels than men, and they may also develop liver disorders after shorter periods of use and lower levels of consumption (Wilsnack et al. 1994).

Types of sexual dysfunctions caused by addiction include lack of desire, arousal, lubrication, and orgasm; dyspareunia (painful intercourse); and vaginismus (vaginal spasms) (Covington and Kohen 1984). One study found that 69 percent of alcoholic women reported having experienced sexual dysfunction before addiction, 85 percent while addicted, and 74 percent suffered from continued sexual dysfunction during early recovery (Covington 1982). Table 4–2 (Covington and Kohen 1984) compares the sexual dysfunctions reported by alcoholic and nonalcoholic women.

Though healthy sexual functioning is clearly a problem for substance abusers during active drinking, drug use, and sobriety, this is the one area least likely to be mentioned by either the client or her family members during the initial assessment and subsequent treatment for chemical dependency. Unfortunately, few addiction recovery programs make any

TABLE 4–2: A Comparison of Sexual Dysfunctions Reported by Alcoholic and Nonalcoholic Women

	Alcoholic	*Nonalcoholic*
Lack of orgasm	64%	27%
Lack of sexual interest	64%	44%
Lack of sexual arousal or pleasure	61%	30%
Lack of lubrication	46%	24%
Painful intercourse	24%	9%
Muscular spasms (Vaginismus)	6%	—

---

1. The term *heavy drinking* is defined as taking two or more drinks each day. A standard drink is defined as 12 fluid ounces of beer, 5 fluid ounces of wine, or 1.5 fluid ounces of distilled spirits and contains about 0.5 fluid ounces of pure alcohol.

provision for helping clients reestablish healthy sexual function. Although recovering alcoholics report fewer sexual problems in sobriety than when they are drinking, they still admit to general dissatisfaction in their sexual lives (Covington and Kohen 1984). For these reasons, strong models are needed to help women to address and heal their sexuality during recovery.

The use of alcohol and other drugs during sexual intercourse also increases the risk of contracting sexually transmitted diseases, including the human immunodeficiency virus (HIV) that causes acquired immuno-deficiency syndrome (AIDS) (Norris 1994). As of this writing, women account for the highest percentage of new AIDS cases in the United States, either through heterosexual intercourse or the sharing of needles during drug use (Norris 1994). There are three primary reasons for this increase in female AIDS patients. When drunk or high, many women neglect to protect themselves by having their sexual partners use a condom during intercourse or making sure that they do not use a contaminated needle. Often women who are addicts find themselves in relationships with men who are chemically dependent themselves, therefore increasing the risk that their partner may be carrying HIV. The use of alcohol and drugs also weakens the immune system, making chemically dependent women more susceptible to infection (Covington and Surrey 1996).

Relational, Emotional, and Social Aspects of Addiction

Since recovery from addiction is about facilitating wholeness and balance, it is essential to have a theoretical understanding of women's psychologi-cal development, as well as a theoretical understanding of addiction. According to the self-in-relation model developed by the Stone Center, women develop through a process of relationship or connection (for more information on the relational model, see Chapter 2). Sexuality is at the core of the relational self (Covington and Surrey 1996), and many women use alcohol and drugs to establish and maintain intimate connections to others. The link between sexuality, relationships, and drugs often becomes established at an early age when girls are given their first alcohol and/or drugs by their boyfriends. Boys, on the other hand, are more likely to have their first alcohol or drug experience with their peers and to buy these substances on their own. Girls, therefore, are often romantically involved with their "supplier." This early association between substance abuse and love can often lead to using substances with chemically dependent part-ners in order to join them in their experience. As girls grow into woman-hood, they often continue to receive their drugs from their sexual partners, a strong factor influencing women's treatment and recovery (Freeman and Landesman 1992).

Studies of high school students have also shown that many girls have their first drinking experience and their first sexual encounter at the same time. In our society, alcohol is still the favorite drug of choice for seduction, and many still believe in its power as an aphrodisiac, despite physical evidence to the contrary (Kilbourne 1991). Men generally drink to feel more powerful and aggressive, while women drink to overcome shyness and to feel more "feminine" (Goodwin 1981, National Institute on Alcohol Abuse and Alcoholism 1986).

Also, women may trade sex for their drug of choice. This is a fairly common practice for women who are cocaine or crack-cocaine addicts. However, prostitution can take many forms in the lives of addicted women.

A MODEL FOR TREATMENT

Many women in recovery programs from alcoholism and other drugs express dissatisfaction with their sexuality. These perceptions are accompanied by feelings of inadequacy and the sense that they lack the understanding necessary to implement real changes in their emotional and sexual life. Even nonsubstance abusers have difficulty understanding what it means to be a sexual woman in our society. Honesty and openness about sex are not always supported by a woman's counselor, partner, or family while she is involved in a recovery program, and many counselors avoid any mention of sexuality in the early stages of treatment because the subject seems too complex to discuss.

It takes great courage for recovering women to explore their sexual and relational self, and counselors have an obligation to support them in their struggle for healing and growth, giving them hope and guidance. To aid counselors in their wish to help in these area, two models are outlined. The first is a four-level approach called the PLISSIT model developed by Annon (1975). The second, called the "Inner and Outer Journey," is described in *Awakening Your Sexuality* (Covington 1991).

The PLISSIT Model

P-LI-SS-IT is a four-level approach for addressing sexual problems based upon permission, limited information, specific suggestions, and intensive therapy. The first two levels can be handled by a counselor who has had some sexuality training and is comfortable about addressing these issues. The last two levels require special training in sex therapy.

Permission. Sometimes women in recovery just want to know that they are all right and that they are not the first person in the world to have their particular sexual difficulties. It is intensely reassuring to hear a counselor say that one's sexual concerns are not unusual (Annon 1975). This method of treatment is especially effective within a same-sex group setting. In this context, peer support can enable women to discuss issues such as where they received their sexual information, how little they know about their bodies, and how their early family experiences affected their sexuality. In such a setting many common issues will emerge, and women will feel less isolated.

Permission also works well in a one-on-one setting with a counselor. If a client says that she is afraid of having sex clean and sober, a counselor might reassure her that this is a common problem among most alcoholic/ addicted women who have had the majority of their sexual experiences while intoxicated or high. A counselor can also give a client permission to abstain from sexual activity if the client does not feel interest, a common experience in the early stages of recovery (Covington 1986, Kaplan 1979). Permission may also be given to engage in a wider variety of sexual behaviors or to abstain from a variety of behaviors.

Limited Information. In contrast with permission, which simply reassures the client that it is all right to continue whatever she has been doing, limited information goes one step further, providing her with specific factual information that directly relates to her experience (Annon 1975). For example, when a woman in the early stages of recovery expresses her concern that she can no longer masturbate to orgasm, her counselor might inform her that some women in her situation are able to achieve orgasm by means of a vibrator because of the level of consistent stimulation it provides. Subjects on which providing limited information is most helpful include: penetration during menstruation, breast size, genital shape and configuration, sexual frequency and performance, and oral-genital contact (Annon 1975).

Specific Suggestions. This level of help requires that a clinician have specific training in sexual counseling, which one member of a staff might be willing to acquire. For this treatment to be effective, a sexual history of the client should be taken, including a description of the current problem, its onset and course, past treatment and its results, and the client's expectations and goals for the present treatment.

Intensive Therapy. This level of treatment is useful for clients whose sexual problems have not responded to other forms of treatment. It begins with a sexual history and continues with long-term psychodynamically oriented therapy aimed at exploring and resolving problem areas.

The effective use of the PLISSIT model requires a commitment on the part of alcohol and drug recovery programs and counselors to extend their knowledge of sexuality and become comfortable with sex education in general, with the discussion of sexual difficulties, and with the use of explicit sexual terms.

The Inner and Outer Journey of Sexual Recovery

Whereas the PLISSIT model looks at general issues and levels of intervention, the *inner* and *outer journey* (Covington 1991) is a more comprehensive level of treatment based on women's experiences. When treating women in alcohol and drug recovery programs, counselors should be aware that recovery from addiction involves the healing and reintegration of both the inner and outer aspects of a woman's being. The *inner journey* has to do with a client's internal world, her thoughts, beliefs, and feelings about herself. The *outer journey* involves her exterior world, her relationships with others. The steps or tasks a client needs to accomplish while being guided through these two journeys are shown in Table 4–3.

TABLE 4–3: The Inner and Outer Journey of Sexual Recovery

The Steps of the Inner Journey

Recognizing the effects of female socialization on sexuality
Accepting one's body
Feeling good about one's genitals
Accepting sexual pleasure from oneself
Becoming aware of one's sexual feelings
Facing one's fears of being sexual while sober

The Steps of the Outer Journey

Exploring childhood and family sexual issues
Honestly naming the sexual events of one's personal past
Looking at one's sexual behaviors, including charting the sexual/chemical lifeline (See Figure 4–1)
Looking at one's selection of sexual partners and filling out the relationship chart (See Figure 4–2)
Learning to live in the present

The Inner Journey

Women seeking recovery from alcohol or drugs have reached the end of a long cycle of confusion, disempowerment, dependency, and isolation. After years or even decades of living with an addiction, their inner and outer lives are out of balance. They are probably out of touch with their feelings and unable to act on them, even if they knew what they were. An understanding and exploration of the following six key areas will help women to develop a stronger sense of what they want and need and who they are as feeling, sexual women.

Socialization. As we have previously seen, our culture gives women very clear messages about what is considered appropriate and inappropriate feminine behavior. Most women have learned to obey these rules, even though they may find them contrary to their own desires. Ironically, even women who have benefited from the "sexual revolution" and have learned how to be assertive and outspoken about their needs are still often unable to express what they really want sexually. It is as if the cultural message of the "good" passive woman and the "loose, wanton, and whorish" sexual woman is still operating on a deep level. Before a woman can feel fulfilled sexually, she must learn to accept this part of her nature and to communicate her needs to a partner. This is an area where a counselor can provide a supportive atmosphere for clients to begin to break free of the limitations and inauthentic messages of female socialization.

The Body. Most women, no matter how attractive, feel uncomfortable about some aspect of their body—their weight, their height, their hair color, the shape and size of their breasts, the amount of cellulite on their thighs—the list is endless. While actively involved in addiction, many women neglect, ignore, or cover up their bodies. Others become obsessed with having the "perfect" body, not from a sense of self-love, but solely to attract and please partners. All of these attitudes hinder a woman's ability to accept herself as she is.

When a woman becomes fixated upon improving or changing the shape of her body, she plays right into the addictive pattern. When women feel too "big" (i.e., too angry, sexual, passionate, powerful, or needy) or too "small" (i.e., too fearful, childlike, dependent, or vulnerable), they often use alcohol/drugs to regulate their size. This disconnection and disrespect women feel toward the natural size, shape, and variety of their personal body types is profoundly supported by our culture. This can be seen in the proliferation of self-help book authors and medical doctors who encourage women to change themselves to fit ideal societal images of weight and beauty. Sixty percent of psychoactive drugs, 71 percent of antidepressants, and 80 percent of amphetamines taken by women are prescribed by their doctors (Covington and Surrey 1997).

When a woman is so caught up with pursuing a physical ideal that she will relentlessly abuse her body with drugs to fit into that image, her whole sensitivity to her body, her feelings, and her deep levels of knowing will eventually be cut off. An important step in the recovery process is for women to learn to love, respect, and accept their bodies, whatever their form.

The Genitals. In our culture it is difficult even to find language that speaks positively about the female genitals. Many of the terms used— pussy, cunt, beaver, box, hole—create feelings of unease, embarrassment, and shame. Others, such as vulva, labia majora, vagina, and clitoris, sound too technically correct. Some women have tried to create language that celebrates the value and beauty of the female genitals, using words such as inner flute, labia flower, mound of Venus, or even the Sanskrit term *yoni*, a term associated with the erotic paintings of India. Whatever terminology a woman in recovery chooses to speak about this important part of her body, it is vital that she begin to feel comfortable with her genitals, learning to look at herself, accept herself, and discover what gives her pleasure.

Pleasure. Though many women have been conditioned to provide others with pleasure, giving it to themselves or accepting it from a partner is something that often needs to be learned. Women in our culture are seldom taught or encouraged to consider their own sexual needs, fantasies, or desires. To many, "having sex" does not include seeking their own gratification or having an orgasm, but making sure that their partner is satisfied.

An important first step in learning how to ask for and receive pleasure from another is to give pleasure to oneself. In the 1970s Hite (1976) queried 3,000 women and found that 82 percent masturbated compared to only 62 percent in Kinsey's study from the late '40s (Kinsey et al. 1953). Although the number of women who are learning to pleasure themselves is increasing, many still have ambiguous feelings about "sex with one." There are good reasons for this. Historically, women have received many negative messages about masturbation. We have been told that any sexual activity that does not relate to procreation is a sin, or that pleasuring ourselves will make us lose desire for partnered sex. Some religions even teach that masturbation is a carnal activity that debases a person. Another social view of masturbation is that it is only for women without partners, to be used as a last resort. When self-pleasuring is viewed in this light, it is likely to be accompanied by feelings of personal inadequacy and loneliness. The woman feels that she does not have what it takes to attract a partner.

In spite of the contradictory cultural messages women receive about masturbation, self-pleasuring is an important part of developing positive inner feelings. It teaches a woman to know her body, to learn about what she enjoys and does not enjoy. Masturbation is especially important for women recovering from substance abuse because it is a powerful tool to help them reconnect with their sexuality. Women who have been alcoholic or chemically dependent have depressed responses and limited physical sensation and need to get back in touch with what it feels like to experience sexual satisfaction. Women who have been sexually abused may associate sex with guilt, shame, or danger, or they may have difficulties trusting enough to enjoy sex with a partner. Masturbation can help these women to feel sexually safe again.

Sexual Feelings. Many women in our culture find it difficult to know when they are feeling sexual desire. Men see the beginning of their arousal in an erection, but for women the issue can be much more complex. In light of this difficulty, it is important for a woman in recovery to learn to talk about her sexual desires and needs apart from the context of her partner's.

Desire is traditionally defined as those specific feelings and sensations that create a state of receptivity and sexual excitement. Many women would not be able to recognize their own sexual activity in that definition because they almost never engage in sex to gratify personal desire. Many women use sex as a means to fulfill needs that have nothing to do with actual physical desire—affection, touching, comfort, physical release, and escape. During recovery, sexual exploration often involves the process of learning to separate sexual feeling from other types of feeling. Only when a women learns how to be in touch with her sexual desire can she begin to learn about her sexual self.

Sober Sex. As we have seen, alcohol and other drugs such as cocaine have long been considered as aphrodisiacs by our society. In a study done by Klassen and Wilsnack (1986), 60 percent of women drinkers said that they felt less sexually inhibited after drinking. This belief was most prevalent among the heaviest drinkers in the study. Leigh and Schafer (1993) found that, for both men and women, the likelihood of sex occurring on a given occasion was directly connected to the amount of alcohol consumed; and Temple and Leigh (1992) found that men and women were more likely to drink when with a new partner than they were with someone familiar. Another study (Covington and Kohen 1984) found that alcoholic women participated in a wider variety of sexual activities than did sober women. As we have seen, the advertising industry equates sex with alcohol and tobacco, and many adolescent girls have their first sexual experience under the influence of alcohol or some other drug.

All of these findings confirm that many women in recovery have had little sexual experience without the aid of some kind of addictive substance. This reliance on alcohol and drugs to relax them, and the conviction that these substances enhance sexual pleasure (contrary to actual physiological evidence), creates an aura of fear around the thought of having sex while clean and sober. This fear may occur on three levels. A woman who has never had sex sober may be fearful because she does not know what the experience will be like. A second concern is that sex will not be fun or satisfying in sobriety and that she has a lifetime of mediocre sex to look forward to. A third category is made up of women who are afraid to have sex at all, especially if they feared or avoided it when involved in addictive behavior.

An important thing to remember is that sexual responses are learned responses. Counselors can help clients to understand that any behavior that has been learned can also be unlearned with time, patience, and support. Clients need to discover the necessary conditions that will make them feel comfortable in a sexual encounter and to rediscover their own needs as they begin to understand their sexual feelings. It is important for women in recovery to acknowledge the inner life of feelings and for counselors to support them on this journey.

The Outer Journey

The strength, self-knowledge, and insights into her sexuality a woman gains from doing her inner work can be used to help her evaluate her sexual interactions and relationships, both past and present. It is not always easy to face up to the pain, guilt, or shame connected with memories of former sexual encounters. In spite of this, women must look at these experiences and patterns honestly because they can sabotage present relationships, make women fearful of intimacy, take away their hopes of ever having a fulfilling sexual life, and be a trigger for relapse. In assessing a client's outer relational dynamics, there are certain key areas to consider.

Childhood and Family Sexual Issues. One of the most important steps a woman in recovery must take is examining and appropriately labeling her past sexual experiences and patterns of relationship. At the core of this process is the family. Some of the family issues women must face and understand are sexual or emotional abuse, inappropriate emotional or sexual boundaries, and negative attitudes toward sexuality in general. Helping a client to think about her sexuality in early life and to keep a journal of her memories and experiences is a good way to begin.

Our basic ideas about sex are formed in early family encounters, and these attitudes stay with us throughout life. A counselor needs to help clients sift through these memories and beliefs to see which ones are useful to them as adults and which serve as a hindrance to the healthy expression of sexuality. Important questions are how the parents expressed affection to each other and the children, how the family spoke about someone who "had" to get married, and how the women in the family spoke about sex. If a woman's mother or aunts spoke about their husbands with disrespect or revulsion as wanting only "one thing," this will have colored the client's adult views of sexuality. If nothing at all was ever said about sex, this omission will also have had an impact upon the client.

Sexual boundaries are often unclear in a dysfunctional family, and it is not unusual for parents in such situations to be both overly rigid and intrusive at the same time. Teenagers may find that they have no privacy in the bathroom, yet their parents will make them adhere to an unrealistic set of regulations about dating. Parents may express shock at inadvertent nudity and act as if the body were something to be ashamed of, yet touch their children in inappropriate sexual ways. As a girl matures into womanhood, the effect of these contradictory messages can be devastating, creating confusion or emotional paralysis in sexual situations and predisposing her for fragmented ideas about sex and herself as a sexual being.

Honestly Naming the Past. One of the most crucial tasks of recovery from addiction is to name our past sexual experiences honestly. When exploring this difficult task, many women find that they have been minimizing the abusiveness of their adult sexual encounters. A woman who believed she was merely "having sex when I didn't want to" may discover that she was being forced to have sex against her will. Many women have shut out the awareness of the reality of their sexual experiences in order to survive. In order to recover and move beyond old behaviors, however, a woman must be able to tell the truth about where she has been.

The Sexual/Chemical Lifeline. A powerful tool for sorting out the truth about one's sexual past is the Sexual/Chemical Lifeline. As exemplified in Figure 4-1, by charting the development of her sexuality in tandem with her addiction, a woman can see how the two have become inter-

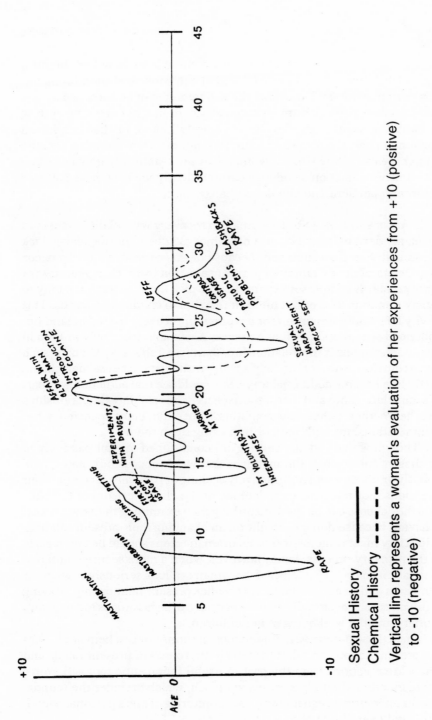

FIGURE 4–1: Sexual Chemical Lifeline

Sexual History ——
Chemical History ━ ━ ━ ━
Vertical line represents a woman's evaluation of her experiences from +10 (positive) to -10 (negative)

twined. This chart is crucial to helping a client learn how her chemical dependence has affected her past sexual behavior. A woman filling out this chart may remember events she had forgotten or be surprised at how painful some memories are. She may discover that her drinking or drug use and her sexual experiences are closely linked, or that her sexual encounters became more and more infrequent as her addiction became unmanageable. Only when a woman can see graphically how her sexuality and her addiction developed can she clearly see how these patterns are interdependent and choose to change them.

Partner Selection. Often a woman in recovery will relate to others in a codependent manner because of unmet childhood needs, abuse, lack of mutuality, and socialization. Because of this pattern, a woman needs to understand the dynamics of partner selection from the perspective of family systems and personal pain. People pick their partners not only to satisfy romantic desires but often in reaction to childhood wounds. This is why it is vitally important for a woman in recovery to understand her childhood sexual and familial patterns. A valuable tool that can help in this understanding is the Relationship Chart (see Table 4–4). Utilizing such a chart during treatment can help a woman understand her sexual/chemical lifeline in some additional ways. She could see that addiction was part of each relationship and that some aspects of her childhood relationships with her mother, father, and stepfather were either being repeated in her adult relationships with men or impacting upon them.

Though women in our culture are conditioned to wait passively to be chosen, the truth of the matter is that we *do* choose our mates, consciously or unconsciously, by actively seeking or passively accepting their attentions. For many women, looking at the characteristics of the partners they choose can be more disturbing than examining their own sexual behavior, because doing so might mean changing their present relationship. They must remember that no dramatic steps should be taken early in the recovery process. Later, however, when a more secure emotional foundation has been established, a woman can look seriously at whether her wants and needs are being met by her present relationship. Staying with a physically or sexually abusive partner can be hazardous to a woman's sobriety and the well-being of her children.

Once these patterns are understood, a counselor can help her look at her present actions and discern which are rooted in present needs and which are reactions from the past. A useful therapeutic tool is Bowen's intergenerational family systems approach, which provides the foundation for an improved ego identity, the monitoring of one's personal boundaries, and overall sexual functioning (Bowen 1974).

TABLE 4–4: Relationship Chart

	Mother	Father	Stepfather	Ex-Husband	Current Husband
CHARACTERISTICS OF PERSON	Passive Mental Illness Unavailable	Jovial Flirtatious Fun-loving Seductive	Mean Macho Critical	Passive Immature	Authoritarian Insecure Rigid Critical
CHARACTERISTICS OF RELATIONSHIP	Undependable Role Reversal Inconsistent	Unreliable Playful	Abusive Neglectful Fearful	Both too young to marry	Hostile
USE OF CHEMICALS/ ADDICTIVE BEHAVIORS	Abused prescription drugs	Abused alcohol	Used alcohol, marijuana	Alcohol Marijuana	Periodic overeater
SEXUAL QUALITIES OF RELATIONSHIP	No sex education No sense of mother as sexual person	Strong attachment Affectionate	Sex Abuser	Poor sex	Sex as obligation
SEXUAL LIKES AND DISLIKES IN RELATIONSHIP			Rage re: gang rape	Disliked sex with him	Dislikes husband masturbating w/pornography

Living in the Present. Living in the present with an awareness of what is going on in her life *right now* is essential to a woman's recovery from addiction. Most people spend much of their time either worrying and feeling about past mistakes and patterns or worrying about and planning for the future. When a woman thinks constantly about the past, she might live in fear that negative experiences will continue to happen to her. If she lives in the future, perhaps fantasizing that each new relationship will come to a depressing conclusion, she might become paralyzed, ending encounters before they even begin. Healthy sexuality can only take place in the present moment between two people who are really there for each other and for themselves. Reclaiming one's past does not mean reliving it. One can break old patterns by reconnecting with one's true self and being firmly grounded in the present.

Sexual Identity

A counselor must help a woman in recovery discover her true sexual identity. If substance abuse began during adolescence, the process of developing a sexual identity may have been interrupted. Some women use drugs to act out their erotic attachments and then feel "dead" sexually in recovery. Others may use drugs to numb themselves to their feelings for another woman. Once the addictive substance has been removed from a woman's life, the counselor can help her discover whether her identity is heterosexual, lesbian, or bisexual.

Support Groups

Women are more at ease when talking with other women about sexuality, and naming one's past may be facilitated by participation in a woman's support group or twelve-step program. When women discover that others have had similar experiences, they feel intense relief that they are not alone or crazy for having ambiguous or uncomfortable feelings about sex. Recovery groups can also remove the tremendous burden of individual responsibility that women often feel about their sexuality, allowing them to see that unhealthy ways of acting and relating are not part of their legacy as women.

CONCLUSION

The special needs of women, and particularly issues of sexuality in recovery, have not generally been met by existing substance abuse treatment programs. Sexuality is a fundamental aspect of being and, as such, is integral for women's physical, psychological, social, and spiritual healing. For full recovery to take place, a woman does not just stop drinking or using drugs, but heals her relationships with others because these form the framework of her life. Some of the steps that counselors can take to promote this healing and understanding are listed below:

1. Become aware of the interconnections between issues of chemical dependency, sexuality, and family relationships.
2. Incorporate sexual issues into individual counseling programs and into family treatment and group therapy sessions to enhance natural helping tendencies of family members and peers.
3. Become aware of one's own sexual attitudes and beliefs and the need to refrain from projecting them onto clients.
4. Create a referral network for sexual issues that go beyond each practitioner's level of experience based on the models presented in this chapter.
5. Become aware of the special sexual issues of women, including the influence of female sexual socialization and the extent of sexual abuse.
6. Create women's groups that provide a safe place for women to begin to explore the connections between their addictions, family relationships, sexual abuse, and sexuality.

The spontaneous recovery of sexual health is not assured by just being clean and sober. It is up to the clinicians to ensure that these issues are raised and that sexual issues are integrated into treatment programs. Women's groups can be vital to this process, enabling clients to begin to see other women as resources, thus enhancing their individual strengths and their family and peer support networks.

REFERENCES

Annon, J. (1975). The behavioral treatment of sexual problems: vol. I. *Brief Therapy*. New York: Harper & Row.

Blume, S. B. (1991). Sexuality and stigma: the alcoholic woman. *Alcohol and Sexuality*, U.S. Department of Commerce, National Technical Information Services. Washington, D.C.: CSR, Inc., p. 142.

Bowen, M. (1974). Alcoholism as viewed through family systems theory and family psychotherapy. *Annals of the New York Academy of Science* 233:115–122.

Carpenter, J. A., and Armenti, N. P. (1972). Some effects of ethanol on human sexual and aggressive behavior. In *The Biology of Alcoholism*

(Vol. 2): Physiology and Behavior, ed. B. Kissin and H. Belerter, p. 509. New York: Plenum.

Chaucer, G. (1951). *The Canterbury Tales*, Trans. N. H. Coghill. England: Penguin Classics.

Covington, S. S. (1982). Sexual experience, dysfunction, and abuse: a descriptive study of alcoholic and nonalcoholic women. Doctoral dissertation. Ann Arbor, MI: University Microfilm.

—— (1986). Facing the clinical challenges of women alcoholics' physical, emotional, and sexual abuse. *Focus on Family* 10:37–44.

—— (1991). *Awakening Your Sexuality: A Guide for Recovering Women and Their Partners*. San Francisco: HarperCollins.

—— (1993). Alcohol addiction and sexual dysfunction. In *Substance Abuse Treatment: A Family Systems Perspective*, ed. E. M. Freeman, pp. 189–216. London: Sage.

Covington, S. S., and Beckett, L. (1988). *Leaving the Enchanted Forest: The Path from Relationship Addiction to Intimacy*. San Francisco: Harper-Collins.

Covington, S. S., and Kohen, J. (1984). Women, alcohol, and sexuality. In *Advances in Alcohol and Substance Abuse* 4 (1):41–56.

Covington, S. S., and Surrey, J. L. (1997). The relational model of women's psychological development: implications for substance abuse. In *Gender and Alcohol*, ed. S. Wilsnack and R. Wilsnack, pp. 335–357. Piscataway, NJ: Rutgers University Press.

Freeman, E. M., and Landesman, T. (1992). Differential diagnosis and the least restrictive alcohol treatment. In *The Addiction Process: Effective Social Work Approaches*, ed. E. M. Freeman, pp. 27–42. New York: Longman.

George, W. H., Gournic, S. J., and McAfee, M. P. (1988). Perceptions of postdrinking female sexuality: effects of gender, beverage choice, and drink payment. *Journal of Applied Social Psychology* 18 (15):1295–1317.

George, W. H., Skinner, J. B., and Marlatt, G. A. (1986). Male perceptions of the drinking woman: is liquor quicker? Poster presented at the meeting of the Eastern Psychological Association, New York, April.

Goodwin, D. W. (1981). *Alcoholism: The Facts*. New York: Oxford University Press.

Harrison, D. F., and Pennell, C. R. (1989). Contemporary sex roles for adolescents: New options or confusion? *Journal of Social Work and Human Sexuality* 8:27–46.

Herman, J. L. (1992). *Trauma and Recovery*. New York: HarperCollins/ Basic Books.

Hite, S. (1976). *The Hite Report*. New York: Macmillan.

Jellinek, E.M. (1941). Immanuel Kant on drinking. *Quarterly Journal of Studies on Alcohol* 1:777–778.

Kaplan, H. S. (1974). *The New Sex Therapy: Active Treatment of Sexual Dysfunction.* New York: Brunner/Mazel.

—— (1979). *Disorders of Sexual Desire and Other New Concepts and Techniques in Sex Therapy.* New York: Simon & Schuster.

Kilbourne, J. (1991). The spirit of the czar: selling addictions to women. In *Alcohol and Drugs are Women's Issues,* vol. 1, ed. P. Roth, pp. 10–22. Metuchen, NJ, and London: Women's Action Alliance and The Scarecrow Press.

Kinsey, A. C., Pomeroy, W. B., Martin, C. E., and Gebhard, P. H. (1953). *Sexual Behavior in the Human Female.* Philadelphia: Saunders.

Klassen, A. D., and Wilsnack, S. C. (1986). Sexual experience and drinking among women in a U.S. national survey. *Archives of Sexual Behavior* 15(5):363–392.

Leigh, B. C., and Schafer, J. C. (1993). Heavy drinking occasions and the occurrence of sexual activity. *Psychology of Addictive Behaviors* 7(3): 197–200.

Midanick, L. T., and Clark, W. B. (1992). *The demographic distribution of U.S. drinking patterns in 1990: description of trends from 1984.* Paper presented at the 120th Annual Meeting, American Public Health Association, Washington, DC, November.

National Institute on Alcohol Abuse and Alcoholism. (1986). *Women and alcohol: health-related issues.* (Research Monograph 16, DHHS Publication No. ADM 86–1139.) Washington, DC: Government Printing Office.

Norris, J. (1994). Alcohol and female sexuality: a look at expectancies and risks. *Alcohol World* 18(3):200.

Richardson, D., and Campbell, D. L. (1982). The effect of alcohol on attributions of blame for rape. *Personality and Social Psychology Bulletin* 8(3):468–476.

Richmond-Abbot, M. (1983). *Masculine and Feminine Sex Roles Over the Life Cycle.* Reading, MA: Addison-Wesley.

Schaffer, K. (1981). *Sex Roles and Human Behavior.* Cambridge, MA: Winthrop.

Temple, M. T., and Leigh, B. C. (1992). Alcohol consumption and unsafe sexual behavior in discrete events. *Journal of Sex Research* 29(2): 207–219.

Wilsnack, S. C., Klassen, A. D., Schur, B. E., and Wilsnack, R. (1991). Predicting onset and chronicity of women's problem drinking: a five-year longitudinal analysis. *American Journal of Public Health* 81(3): 305–318.

Wilsnack, S. C., Wilsnack, R. W., and Hiller-Sturmhofel, S. (1994). How women drink: epidemiology of women's drinking and problem drinking. *Alcohol World* 18(3):173–181.

Substance-Abusing Women and Sexual Abuse

R i t a   T e u s c h

5

In the past two decades we have become alerted to the fact that the experience of sexual abuse is quite common in women. Herman's (1981) review of the literature suggests that between one-fifth and one-third of all women have experienced some form of childhood sexual encounter with an adult male. Similarly, Russel (1986) reported that in a random sample of over 900 women, one in four had been raped and one in three had been sexually abused in childhood.

Various short- and longer-term sequelae of sexual abuse have been identified. Data from psychiatric hospitals have revealed that 50–60 percent of inpatients and 40–60 percent of psychiatric outpatients report childhood histories of sexual or physical abuse or both (Bryer et al. 1987, Carmen et al. 1984, Jacobson 1989). Several studies of women in substance abuse treatment report that up to 75 percent have a history of physical or sexual abuse (Bollerud 1990, Forth-Finegan 1991, Rohsenow et al. 1988, Yandow 1989). Incest and rape are frequently cited as precipitating events for alcohol and drug use among women (Volpe and Hamilton 1982–1983).

Some clients with a sexual abuse history do well in substance abuse treatment with a primary focus on their sobriety. After obtaining a solid period of sobriety, they go on and work through the feelings and memories stemming from their sexual abuse. However, many sexually abused women are not able to put their emotional troubles aside while attempting to get clean and sober. Their trauma-related emotions are too intense and their substance abuse is intricately connected with feelings stemming from their sexual abuse. Such women require an integrated treatment approach in which their substance abuse and sexual abuse issues are seen as interrelated and mutually reinforcing (Bepko and Krestan 1985, Beschner et al. 1982, Turner and Colao 1985, Zankowski 1987).

This chapter describes the short- and longer-term sequelae of sexual abuse and the functions that alcohol and drugs often serve for the sexually abused woman. Issues crucial in the assessment of sexual abuse among substance-abusing women are highlighted, and indicators of a possible sexual abuse history are outlined. Short- and longer-term treatment goals, typical therapeutic challenges, and effective interventions are delineated.

ACUTE AND LONG-TERM SEQUELAE OF SEXUAL ABUSE

The sequelae of sexual abuse are manifold and not always easily diagnosable. Gelinas (1983) stressed that many women with sexual abuse present for treatment with a "disguised presentation" such as "characterological depression with complications and with atypical and dissociative elements" (Gelinas 1983, p. 326). Symptoms such as low self-esteem, difficulties in relationships, depression, anxiety, panic attacks, suicidal feelings, and eating disorders, in addition to substance abuse, are common presenting problems. Turner and Colao (1985) identified issues related to secrecy, betrayal, guilt, shame, and anger at mothers for not being protected as central issues for women with a history of sexual abuse.

It is generally helpful to distinguish between acute reactions to the traumatic sexual experience and the longer-term sequelae that tend to involve changes in the person's character (Gelinas 1983). Acute effects of sexual traumatization may fit the diagnosis of posttraumatic stress disorder (PTSD) and be characterized by recurrent and intrusive distressing recollections of the traumatic event, including images, thoughts, and perceptions (*DSM-IV* 1994). The woman may have distressing dreams of the abusive experience and relive the trauma through dissociative flashback episodes and frightening hallucinations. She may repress the trauma or avoid thoughts, feelings, or activities associated with the trauma and thus have a restricted range of affect or generalized numbing. She may believe she has a short future and may not expect to have a normal life span or a career, to marry, or have children. Physiological effects of trauma include increased arousal that can be manifested in difficulties falling asleep, irritability and outbursts of anger, difficulties concentrating, hypervigilance, and an exaggerated startle response. In women with sexual abuse who repressed their trauma for many years and only recover memories of childhood sexual abuse as adults, the revival and recollection of the traumatic experience can be so intense that diagnostic criteria for posttraumatic stress disorder are fulfilled.

The longer-term effects of sexual traumatization are less clearly subsumed under a single diagnostic heading. They tend to vary with the severity and duration of the abuse, the age of onset, and other variables such as the relationship of the survivor to the perpetrator, the family's reaction to the abuse, and other stressors in the woman's life (Herman 1992, Kluft 1992). The most salient feature of chronic traumatization is often some kind of dissociative disorder that tends to involve a disruption of consciousness, memory, identity, or perception of the environment.

It is commonly assumed that an early onset of abuse in combination with severe violence perpetrated by a closely related individual, as is the case in incest, increases the danger of a personality fragmentation in the survivor. Dissociative identity disorder (formerly known as multiple personality disorder) presents the extreme form of dissociation. This disorder is characterized by the presence of two or more distinct identities or personality states, each with its own relatively enduring pattern of perceiving, relating to, and thinking about the environment and the self. These personality states recurrently take control of the individual's behavior, and depending on the personality state, the individual may be unable to recall important personal information (*DSM-IV* 1994). Other dissociative disorders are: dissociative amnesia, generally characterized by an inability to recall past traumatic information; dissociative fugue, which involves the sudden travel away from one's home and the assumption of a new identity while forgetting one's former identity; and depersonalization disorder, characterized by a persistent or recurrent feeling of being detached from one's own mental processes or body, with reality testing generally intact (*DSM-IV* 1994).

THE ABUSE OF SUBSTANCES TO COPE WITH SEXUAL ABUSE SEQUELAE

Women who suffer from posttraumatic stress disorder due to sexual trauma frequently use alcohol and drugs to reestablish emotional control or to numb the physiological sequelae of their trauma (Khantzian et al. 1990). They may also resort to alcohol and/or drugs to continue to be able to function in an intimate relationship or to numb themselves to the pain resulting from a current physically or emotionally abusive relationship. The above is exemplified by Ann, a 30-year-old divorced white woman with two young children who was sexually abused by her stepfather from ages 7 till 11.

> I began to use cocaine regularly when I realized that it relaxed me. Since I began to face my memories of the sexual abuse, I've had great difficulties sleeping. I'm afraid to go to sleep because I know I'll have nightmares of the abuse. During the day I may suddenly have a body memory or go into a flashback, which is totally embarrassing. I've withdrawn from my friends because I never know when I'll have a flashback or dissociate. Cocaine has given me this warm and comfortable feeling that I never thought I would have again. I tried to cut down because I knew it was addictive. At night I smoked marijuana because it helped me sleep. I guess I needed the drugs to feel normal. I was tired of being constantly afraid of everything. I wasn't doing it to get high. I wanted to be able to be calm enough to go to the grocery store, to take care of my kids, and to be with my husband. Also I didn't feel that I deserved a loving relationship. My husband was abusive, but I couldn't leave him. The drugs helped me to numb the pain when he beat me, and it helped with the frustration.

Some women alcoholics and addicts recover childhood sexual abuse memories only after they have achieved a stable sobriety. Upon reconstruction of their histories, it becomes evident that they unconsciously warded off overwhelming thoughts and effects stemming from their childhood sexual abuse through the use of alcohol and drugs. Some of these women numbed themselves with drugs or alcohol for years, while others used drugs or alcohol more intermittently. In either case, the involvement with drugs or alcohol left no psychological space for the reemergence of traumatic memories, as can be seen in the comments made by Lea, a 25-year-old single black woman with a history of paternal incest from ages 6 to 12.

> During all these years when I was drinking or doing drugs I didn't feel anything. I was just going through the motions, almost as if I was dead. I did not care about anything, and I engaged in many dangerous activities that could've killed me. I was totally numb. When I drank or took drugs, at least I knew that I was still alive. When I hurt myself, at least I knew why I was in pain, and I felt that my pain made sense. After I attempted to become clean and sober two years ago, I began to recover memories of sexual abuse. I had many relapses in the past two years. I just couldn't get used to the idea that I had become an alcoholic and addict and that I had been sexually abused, but I guess now I feel at least I have an explanation for why I acted this way all these years. I know now that I was trying to run away from the incest. I just wasn't ready to face it until now.

ASSESSMENT OF SEXUAL TRAUMA IN SUBSTANCE-ABUSING WOMEN

Assessing sexual trauma in substance-abusing women is a complicated task for two reasons. First, as indicated previously, sexual abuse sequelae can appear either as acute symptomatology such as in PTSD or in a "disguised presentation" (Gelinas 1983). Second, manifestations of sexual abuse sequelae may be similar to symptomatology of alcohol or drug abuse (i.e. denial, depression, anxiety, panic attacks, social isolation, shame, guilt, flashbacks, auditory hallucinations, blackouts, seizures, physiological symptoms such as frequent headaches, sleep problems, hypervigilance, etc.). This overlap makes a differential diagnosis difficult. A reliable differential diagnosis that does not only take into account the immediate effects of drug and alcohol abuse but also the more long-term physiological and neurological effects may require anywhere from three months to a year of sobriety.

THE ASSESSMENT INTERVIEW

The assessment of sexual abuse commonly requires more than one interview. During the assessment process it is crucial to allow the client to disclose her thoughts and feelings at her own pace. Too many questions too quickly tend to make a sexually abused woman feel out of control and are often experienced as another boundary violation. Besides helping the client talk about her sexual trauma, the interviewer also needs to help the client become aware of her feelings and reactions and to increase her sense of control and responsibility.

Women with histories of sexual abuse generally feel ambivalent about revealing their thoughts and feelings about the abuse, their experiences of dissociation, and their attempts at coping through the use of drugs or alcohol. Many survivors of sexual abuse were told by their perpetrators that "bad things" will happen to them if they tell their stories. Consequently, a therapist's matter-of-fact attitude combined with an explicit statement of understanding and acceptance is necessary whenever sexual abuse is suspected. For example:

> Some people who have issues with alcohol and drugs also have a history of sexual trauma which often causes certain symptoms, feelings, and behaviors in the person that may seem kind of weird, but they are in fact normal consequences of sexual abuse. If you think that you may have experienced sexual abuse or think that you suffer from symptoms, feelings, thoughts, or behaviors that you don't fully understand, perhaps you could tell me about them so that we can learn to understand them together. I understand that this may be difficult to talk about, and I want you to tell me only what you feel comfortable telling. At some point I may want to ask you some specific questions to be sure that I don't miss any important part of your experience, but you should always feel free to say that you don't feel comfortable answering a particular question.

Such a statement invites the client to speak about her experiences, but it also states explicitly that she has the control about what she wants to reveal. This is very important, because one wants to avoid the retraumatization of the client by pushing her into revealing what she does not feel comfortable revealing. It is generally advised to ask as many open-ended questions as possible while watching for the specific feelings, experiences, and behaviors that are typically seen in women with sexual abuse (and which are outlined below). Once the client experiences the clinician as accepting and knowledgeable, specific follow-up questions and education about certain aspects of sexual trauma and the symptoms of posttraumatic stress disorder are usually welcomed.

Most substance-abusing women experience talking about their sexual abuse as a great relief. Some clients, however, may react with shame and fear and shut down their emotions after revealing their secret. It is helpful for the clinician to acknowledge the client's reaction and tell her that "this often happens because you may have some shame and fears about disclosing your abuse. Maybe we can talk about how it feels to talk about the abuse." Such an empathic response indicates respect for the client's own process and makes her feel understood.

Given the nature of the traumatic material, it is likely that the client will feel overwhelmed during the initial stages of disclosure. An inpatient setting where she can be kept safe and learn about her tolerance for affect may be necessary at this stage. Frequently, the interrelationship between substance abuse and sexual abuse becomes apparent to the client as she feels an urge to drink or use drugs when talking about traumatic memories. Repeatedly drawing the client's attention to this interrelationship helps her begin to realize that becoming clean and sober is a prerequisite to doing recovery work from sexual trauma. It is helpful to ask the client to think about how she can handle her affect without acting on it. If a client feels pressure to reveal all her sexual abuse memories, the clinician needs to explore why she may be feeling pressure to proceed so fast. The client may feel that if she discloses a lot fast, she will get better more quickly. She needs to learn that her recovery will take time and that her first task is to learn about her emotions, how talking about certain topics will make her feel, and how she can keep herself safe and sober as she is going through her recovery from both substance abuse and sexual abuse.

In the recent trauma literature there is an ongoing debate regarding the accuracy of memories of childhood abuse recovered by adults after considerable delay. The false-memory advocates believe that false memories are easy to create and warn that patients who falsely come to believe that they were abused may cut off relationships with or sue family members (Loftus 1993, Ofshe and Watters 1993). This point of view has been rejected by a growing number of researchers on memory and clinicians stating that these findings are based on normal memory research rather than research on traumatic memory (Horowitz and Reidbord 1992). For a thorough discussion of this controversy the reader is referred to Brown (1995). Brown concludes from his extensive review of the literature that false beliefs about abuse can occur under very specific conditions. Even then, "these conditions are more the exception than the rule" (Brown

1995, p. 9). Memory confabulation in therapy can be significantly reduced when therapists are aware of their own bias about the possibility of trauma, are more egalitarian than authoritarian, seek outside consultation when treating a difficult client, work with the sexually abused client on safety, stabilization, and coping enhancement, and allow clients as much freedom as possible in their own recall rather than using a structured inquiry. Clearly, the use of hypnotic techniques to recover repressed memories, which is not even discussed in this chapter, should be left to a clinician specifically trained in hypnotherapy.

INDICATORS OF A POSSIBLE SEXUAL ABUSE HISTORY

The following symptoms describe affects, behaviors, and experiences that are typically seen in women with sexual trauma. While a specific client may not show all of these symptoms, the presence of any of these should alert the clinician to a possible history of sexual abuse.

Posttraumatic Stress Disorder

The client may suffer from intrusive traumatic memories or recurrent obsessive thoughts that she may have been sexually abused even though she does not have specific memories. She may have flashbacks of abuse and remember a past event so vividly that she feels she is reliving it. She may have nightmares or other sleep disturbances, panic attacks, painful body memories, concentration problems, exaggerated startle response, hypervigilance, fear, or inability to relax. She may avoid situations with certain people, such as her parents, grandparents, uncles, gynecologists, people in authority, or sexual situations that may serve as potential triggers of abuse memories.

Dissociation

A sexually abused woman may have dissociative episodes and not remember important events in her life such as her graduation or her wedding. She may lose time driving her car, in conversations, at work, or when just at home by herself. She may find herself in unfamiliar places at times when she is not drinking. She may find objects around her house that she does not remember buying. She may have been approached by people who call her by a different name, or by people who say they know her but whom she does not recognize.

Depersonalization

Some women experience episodes of depersonalization (i.e. persistent or recurrent experiences of feeling detached from their own mental processes or body). They describe feeling as if they were an outside observer of their own mental processes or as if they are living in a dream or fog. A sexually abused woman may be able to ignore physical pain or experience a sense of confusion about herself and events in her life (i.e. she may not be sure whether a thing that she remembers really happened or whether she just dreamt it).

Depression

A woman with a history of sexual abuse may suffer from chronic depressive feelings or feelings of hopelessness, be preoccupied with suicidal thoughts, or have a history of suicidal gestures. She may report feelings of powerlessness, intense guilt and shame, poor self-esteem, and anxiety. She may suffer from numerous somatic complaints, such as frequent tiredness, headaches, abdominal and pelvic pain, ringing in her ears, tingling or numbness in her fingers, chronic lack of appetite, difficulties swallowing food, or frequent nausea.

Sexuality

Some sexually abused women have a history of prostitution or promiscuity. Others may be currently suffering from difficulties with sexual contact or orgasmic dysfunction, or they may avoid the topic of sexuality or sexual practices altogether. Many feel confused about their sexual feelings or experience sexual feelings when they do not want to have them.

Impulsivity

Women with histories of sexual abuse may engage in impulsive behaviors such as compulsive gambling, shopping, stealing, overeating, purging, or drinking and drugging. Some may have frequent episodes of self-injury, such as auto accidents, falling down the stairs, or frequent gynecological operations. Others may live in fear that they may sexually abuse their own child.

Dysfunctional Relationships

Sexually abused women are likely to have a history of dysfunctional relationships or currently be involved in an abusive relationship. Many are adult children of alcoholics and have a history of being a parentified child, which impacts on their ability to form satisfactory relationships in adulthood.

ASSESSMENT OF SUBSTANCE ABUSE IN WOMEN WITH SEXUAL ABUSE

The assessment of substance abuse in women with sexual abuse follows the general principles of assessing substance abuse in other populations. For a review of substance abuse assessment, the reader is referred to Straussner (1993). However, it is important to keep the dynamics of traumatization in mind, especially the woman's fear of losing control, her sense of powerlessness, which may manifest itself as a strong need to be in control, and her fear of revictimization.

When the sexually abused client realizes that she has developed an addiction and that her "coping strategy" of using substances is no longer working to regulate her emotions, she often feels very frightened and that she is a failure. This fear and shame reaction may further intensify her addiction as she tries to convince herself that she still has some control. If the client is dealing with acute PTSD symptoms, the realization that she is doubly out of control may be quite traumatic and needs to be carefully processed with her. How does she feel about having two out-of-control problems now (her PTSD symptoms and her addiction)?

The client will need time to acknowledge both her problems. She may need a period of forced abstinence in an inpatient setting combined with a trial of antidepressant or neuroleptic medications. As pointed out earlier, it is nearly impossible to make a differential diagnosis at this point. If a client views her addiction as a coping strategy rather than a disease, a thorough exploration of how she feels about giving up her coping strategy is crucial. Some women may prefer to view themselves as psychiatric patients rather than feeling stigmatized by a diagnosis of substance abuse. Some clients may even harbor the fantasy that their problems with alcohol or drugs would be resolved if they could just recover a certain memory. While such thinking indicates denial, it is helpful to respond to the wishful aspect of this statement by saying, "I can understand your wish to want to recover from just one problem and not two," and then commenting on the fact that alcohol and drug abuse tends to develop a dynamic of its own and needs to be addressed specifically in order for her to recover.

If the client's perpetrator or other significant people in her life were substance abusers, a woman may have difficulty accepting her substance abuse diagnosis because she cannot face being "like" her perpetrator. It is important to appreciate the fear and shame around this issue while at the same time reinforcing reality. Even if she has the same substance abuse problem as her perpetrator, she is not like that person. This obvious fact sometimes needs to be stated overtly, because the substance-abusing woman may not be consciously aware that this is her reason for her denial of her addiction. Her often unconscious identification with the perpetrator may make the distinction difficult.

A crucial aspect of assessment is to ascertain whether substance abuse initially was directly connected with sexual abuse. Drugs and alcohol may have been given to the woman by her perpetrator to numb and sedate her. If this occurred, a careful exploration of the circumstances is indicated: How frequently did this happen? What were her feelings and thoughts when she was given drugs or alcohol? What did she actually receive— shots? oral administration of drugs? Was she physically forced to take them? Was the perpetrator intoxicated or high when doing this? Does she sometimes think about this connection when she drinks alcohol or takes drugs now? How does she feel about disclosing this?

THE FUNCTIONS OF SUBSTANCE ABUSE FOR SEXUALLY ABUSED WOMEN

An important part of the recovery process for the sexually abused woman is to become fully aware of the functions alcohol and drugs have served for her. Once she is able to identify the benefits she has gained from substances, she can begin to work on alternative coping strategies. Three functions of alcohol and drug abuse for women with sexual abuse seem to be common: (1) numbing and self-soothing, (2) self-harm, and (3) dissociation.

Numbing and Self-Soothing

While some sexually abused women manage to numb their feelings completely, others live with feelings ranging from constant mild dysphoria and anxiety to extremes of depression, panic, helplessness, fury, and despair. Herman (1992) pointed out that trauma survivors tend to employ what she calls "pathological soothing mechanisms" (p. 109), which can include self-injury, compulsive spending, gambling, sexual behavior, compulsive risk-taking, bingeing, or purging, as well as the use of psychoactive drugs or alcohol. While these behaviors cause the woman significant pain, they also allow her temporarily to soothe herself or numb her feelings altogether.

It is crucial to identify the recent as well as the earlier precipitants of the woman's substance use and how her use is or was related to either acute or chronic sequelae of trauma. What was the context of her most recent pattern of use? How is it different from her substance use in the past? Did she have thoughts of the sexual abuse or contact with the perpetrator before using? Were there specific traumatic memories? Did she have sleep problems and medicate herself with alcohol or drugs or both? Did she feel hopeless and was she hoping the alcohol or drugs would kill her? Did she feel the need to numb an abusive relationship? Did she drink or drug to be able to have sex? Did she drink or drug so that she did not feel emotional pain, anger, frustration, or physical pain from cutting herself? Did she drink or drug to quiet the voices from the dissociated parts of herself?

Self-Harm

Women with histories of sexual abuse often abuse substances as a more or less deliberate way of self-harm, which, in turn, is frequently an expression of the woman's underlying feelings of depression and hopelessness and her passive suicidal tendencies, for example, "I don't really care if I die from alcohol poisoning because I want to die anyway, but I feel afraid to commit suicide more actively." Such underlying suicidal intent (as well as the denial of the fact that she is in fact killing herself actively with alcohol or other drugs) must be brought into the woman's awareness so that she can begin to explore the reasons for her suicidal feelings. These often stem from feelings and fantasies surrounding the sexual abuse. She may feel that she should have died during the abuse, that she does not deserve to live because she is so bad, or that the abuse has damaged her forever so that there is nothing to look forward to in life. A woman who felt that her life was in danger during the sexual abuse will often live with a sense that her premature death is inevitable. Such a client may make repeated serious suicide attempts to take control over her profound fear of dying. By helping her see that her present wish/fear of dying is actually a repetition of a real traumatic experience in the past, intense suicidality can often be alleviated and worked through.

Some sexually abused clients engage in physical self-harm. Such behavior allows the woman to focus on the pain that she has inflicted on herself and therefore is within her control, in contrast to experiencing diffuse anxiety and tension or feelings of anger, rage, and hurt related to sexual abuse memories. Self-harm may also be the woman's way of turning anger or rage against herself, because she may feel too frightened to experience those feelings toward her perpetrator who tends to remain very powerful in the unconscious mind. When the therapist is able to empathically acknowledge the woman's wish to hurt herself, the door is opened to exploring the meaning of such behavior: Is it an effort to soothe profound feelings of pain? Is this her way of expressing anger and rage toward herself for "allowing" the abuse to happen? Is it anger that is really meant to be directed at the perpetrator? Could it be an expression of her fantasies of revenge, or all of these at various times?

It is important to explore the relationship between alcohol and drug abuse and self-harm. Was drinking and drugging ever part of a suicide attempt? An overdose? A factor in seeking help in the emergency room or being hospitalized? A self-mutilation episode? The therapist also needs to explore whether the client has ever been raped or assaulted when drinking or drugging. Does she have any medical problems that get worse as a result of her substance abuse? Do drinking and drugging affect her taking any prescribed medication? This is important because not taking proper care of a medical condition is often a disguised form of self-harm.

Dissociation

Dissociation is a frequent response to trauma-related anxiety. The client may protect herself from unbearable affect or memories by inducing an altered state of consciousness or a trance state (Herman 1992). Janet (1929) described dissociation as a mechanism for coping with traumatic events in which memories for highly emotionally arousing experiences are not encoded as narrative memory, but as traumatic memories. Traumatic memories or "subconscious fixed ideas" are split off from conscious perception, thus helping the individual adapt to psychological trauma. When a client begins to become aware of memories of sexual abuse, she often does so in a dissociative state that feels quite involuntary. Consequently, she may feel ashamed and afraid of what happens to her without her knowledge.

Dissociation may be exacerbated when a client is under the influence of drugs or alcohol. A careful differential diagnosis between substance induced blackouts and dissociative episodes needs to be established. In some cases, both phenomena may be present and may reinforce each other. A client may have a particular theory about her dissociation, preferring to see it either as a substance-related blackout or as a psychological sequela to sexual trauma. The clinician needs to keep an open mind and carefully establish the facts by obtaining answers to such questions as: Does she often find herself drunk/drugged and does not recall how it happened? Does she dissociate without any drug/alcohol use? If she has dissociative identity (multiple personality) disorder, who does the drinking in her system? Who sabotages sobriety or getting clean?

TREATMENT OF SUBSTANCE-ABUSING WOMEN WITH SEXUAL ABUSE: INITIAL STABILIZATION

The initial treatment goals for women with sexual abuse aim at stabilizing the client. Specifically, treatment is directed at enabling the client to maintain safety and empowering her to regain a measure of emotional and behavioral control that will allow her to function in her life and work productively in therapy. Achieving sobriety is a necessary part of this. In the process of reaching these initial treatment goals, the client will gain increasing self-esteem and self-confidence as she becomes better able to handle her emotions and implement alternative coping strategies.

The specific treatment goals during this phase include: (1) developing a therapeutic alliance, (2) maintaining safety, (3) educating the client about the impact of sexual trauma and substance abuse, and (4) titrating recovery from sexual abuse and substance abuse.

Developing a Therapeutic Alliance

Sexual traumatization results in severely impaired self-esteem and difficulties in relatedness. If the client has suffered severe and chronic abuse, the establishment of a therapeutic alliance may be very difficult because she will have little capacity to trust other people. She may try to rupture the therapeutic relationship repeatedly to prevent becoming dependent on the therapist. Even to accept a suggestion and follow it may be associated with unbearable fear. In such cases it may take a year or much longer before a solid therapeutic alliance is established. The therapist's task initially is to listen to what is most important to the client. Repeatedly validating the client's feelings and planting the seed that her substance abuse may be related to her sexual abuse helps the client feel less guilty and self-blaming and more understood. If a client cannot control her self-destructive impulses or her use of alcohol and drugs, hospitalization is indicated. Such a recommendation is usually experienced as an act of caring even though the client may initially resist it.

Maintaining Safety

Many clients benefit from a brief or more extended period of hospitalization or repeated brief hospitalizations, because suicidal impulses and actions or toxicity from alcohol or drug abuse are quite common. While the hospital can provide initial stabilization, the bulk of the extended stabilization work usually takes place in outpatient treatment.

Many women with sexual abuse tend to prefer to work with a female therapist, especially if their perpetrator was male. However, others may prefer a male therapist, feeling that they have been betrayed or not protected by the significant women in their lives. If possible, the client's own preference in regard to the sex of her therapist should be honored. Only when the client begins to feel truly safe in her relationship with her therapist and is able to use him or her as a source of soothing and comfort do safety issues gradually become less prominent.

Just as the therapist pays careful attention to the client's internal impulses to hurt herself, he or she needs to be attentive to the client's relational situation and its potential dangers. Many sexually abused women tend to become involved in abusive relationships because they did not reliably experience that their attempts to protect their boundaries were respected. Consequently, they may not feel deserving of a healthy relationship. If the client is in a relationship that is harmful to her, she may need the therapist's help to leave it. It is unlikely that she will be able to achieve a stable sobriety until she is in a safe living situation. A recent study found that being in an unsupportive relationship is a major cause of relapse for women (Ravndal and Vaglum 1994). The sexually abused woman may need repeated reassurance that she deserves a life free of abuse and pain. Living in pain may have become a way of life for the client who may feel too guilty or too powerless to work toward a better life without the therapist's encouragement to do so.

The survivor of sexual abuse will invariably test her therapist to see if he or she indeed cares, that is, will the therapist react to her self-harm, take it seriously, and take steps to protect her. In some therapists this "testing" elicits strong countertransference feelings. Such a client may be experienced as manipulative or provocative. While such a client is indeed a challenge to every therapist, it is important to understand that this testing behavior is a normal sequela of trauma, that is, the client needs to experience in her current relationships that she is deserving of protection. In this sense, relapses into self-harm, including substance abuse, are to be expected as part of the recovery work. The therapist must be prepared to discuss any subtle signs of potential self-harm vigorously and directly. Sometimes the client may not even be consciously aware that what she is about to do will be harmful because she has internalized the aggressive attitude toward her that she felt from her perpetrator. Now she relentlessly attacks herself verbally and/or behaviorally, and it feels completely ego-syntonic. The therapist needs to help such a client become aware of this particular trauma sequela by repeatedly interpreting the client's attacks against herself. If the therapist does not address unsafe behaviors, the client will feel that she is again in an unsafe situation where dangerous behaviors go unnoticed. Such a repetition of earlier failures to be protected will reduce her trust in the therapist. While the therapist will want to make it clear that an important goal of therapy is to decrease and ultimately overcome the client's tendency to harm herself, the therapist also must avoid being judgmental when self-harm or relapses occur.

Safety maintenance presents a challenge in clients suffering from dissociative disorders. The establishment of safety with the dominant personality will only be the first step. As more personality states emerge, they will eventually need to learn to make a commitment to keeping the whole person safe. (For a detailed discussion of treatment of dissociative identity disorder, see Bernstein and Putnam 1986, Kluft 1992, Putnam 1989, and Sakheim et al. 1988.) As a general rule, the task is to map out the client's system of personalities in as much detail as possible and to begin to form a therapeutic alliance with each of them so that they can begin to work towards keeping the client safe. Helping the client develop co-consciousness by helping her various personality states communicate and develop empathy for each other's needs is an important piece of therapeutic work. The woman often strongly rejects the angry, rageful part of her personality. Clients tend to feel afraid and ashamed of that part of themselves. If the therapist can accept and welcome the anger and rage and explain these feelings as normal sequelae of trauma, the client will eventually become more accepting of this part of herself.

Educating about the Impact of Sexual Trauma and Substance Abuse

Providing the client with a cognitive understanding of sexual trauma and the nature of posttraumatic stress disorder is reassuring and validating. Helping the client to understand that she suffers from affect and memories that are indeed overwhelming reduces her shame about her alcohol and drug abuse. At the same time, explaining to her that she suffers from flashbacks or dissociation, or is hearing voices from dissociated parts of herself rather than going crazy, will bring the client great relief. Understanding that hyperarousal, impulses to hurt herself, and difficulties with trust are normal for someone with her condition reduces the client's feelings of shame about these behaviors. Similarly, the client needs education regarding substance abuse, for example, blackouts, increased anxiety, depression, and physiological reactions to various substances.

It is also helpful to explain the process of recovery from both substance abuse and sexual trauma. Many clients feel hopeless and overwhelmed and cannot imagine that recovery is possible. Telling the client that she will recover but that it will take time and a lot of work is reassuring. This form of psychoeducation is best viewed as an ongoing task in the recovery process rather than information to be given in the form of a "lecture." It is most effectively communicated at the point when the client indicates a lack of knowledge about addictions or trauma or voices shame, self-blame, guilt, or despair about her sexual abuse or addiction.

Titrating Recovery from Substance Abuse and Sexual Abuse

As the sexually abused woman stops drinking or drugging, she often experiences increasing anxiety, depression, suicidal feelings, and panic attacks. Her nightmares and flashbacks may become more intense as she no longer numbs herself. At this point she needs reassurance that she will be able to get through this initial phase in her recovery. She also needs help to put her nightmares and flashbacks into words so that she can learn to tolerate and work through the accompanying affect. Relapses in this phase are extremely common and need to be anticipated with the client.

In addition to experiencing feelings directly related to trauma, the client may also have to deal with feelings of social isolation, fears of making changes in her life, and fears of getting better. The therapist needs to help her identify these feelings and connect them to her urges to relapse. Continuous cravings for her drug of choice need to be discussed and precipitants to these cravings understood so that she gradually will have less of a need to act on impulse, as can be seen in the following case example:

> Susan is a 38-year-old married Caucasian woman who was sexually abused from ages 7 till 14 by her older brother and as an adult by her gynecologist. As in many dysfunctional families, the experience of her sexual abuse was denied by her family. Susan had been suicidal for several months and made several serious suicide attempts that involved overdosing on drugs and alcohol. An important factor contributing to Susan's self-destructiveness was her identification with her older drug-addicted brother who was

her perpetrator. Susan was first hospitalized after a suicide attempt that involved a serious overdose with sleeping pills and alcohol.

Following her discharge from the hospital, she continued in individual psychotherapy. It became evident that Susan had been sexually abused as a child and adolescent and also had an addiction to over-the-counter sleeping medications in addition to abusing alcohol. For the first year the therapist focused on helping her attain sobriety by encouraging her to go to AA meetings, contracting with her about not drinking and drugging, and providing education about the relationship between substance abuse and sexual abuse.

When she was free of alcohol and drugs for about three months, Susan began to panic at the realization that she had suicidal feelings, even though she had talked about being suicidal many times before. However, now that she was sober, it was as if she felt her suicidal feelings for the first time and also felt a healthy fear of them for the first time. She began to discuss her suicidal thoughts as well as her overwhelming cravings for sleeping pills, which she used to take "to numb out." She talked in detail about how close she came on several occasions to buying them.

Gradually Susan realized that what precipitated both her suicidal feelings and her cravings was the feeling that she was "invisible" to her family of origin and that no one cared to notice her pain. Every time Susan had contact with a family member who blatantly ignored her difficulties, she felt overwhelming anger, and her immediate impulse was to want to buy sleeping pills and alcohol and kill herself. Susan gradually became able to express her feelings of hurt, anger and disappointment in words. At that point she stopped feeling suicidal or resorting to sleeping pills and alcohol.

COMMON ISSUES DURING THE RECOVERY PROCESS

The recovery process is necessarily destabilizing as it upsets the homeostasis that has been established. Consequently, it is to be expected that as the client makes changes toward a healthy life, she will also be confronted with mounting anxiety and other symptoms such as shifting of addictions. Furthermore, difficulties accepting therapeutic support frequently become a major obstacle to recovery and need to be carefully addressed and, where relevant, related to the woman's fear of revictimization as well as shame and discomfort about acute PTSD symptomatology.

Shifting Addictions

Sexually abused women quite commonly shift addictions during the process of recovery. The original addiction has served an important psychological purpose, that is, to provide soothing and to ward off overwhelming affect. Thus, even if a client makes a serious effort to stop a particular addiction, she may not be ready emotionally to give up addictions or compulsions altogether until she has become able to internalize the capacity to soothe herself. The therapist must be vigilant about newly developing addictive behaviors. For example, a client who has stopped drinking and drugging may begin to show symptoms of an eating disorder (i.e., anorexia nervosa or anorexic-like behavior, bulimia, or compulsive overeating). Or she may begin compulsive shoplifting, spending, cutting herself, or compulsive sexual behavior. For some clients the idea of suicide may become an obsession, particularly for those with a family history of any obsessions or compulsions. The therapist needs to recognize these dynamics and point them out to the client as soon as the new behavior makes its appearance. In healthier clients such an interpretation may be sufficient to prevent an escalation of the new addiction. However, in more severe cases the new problem may need specific treatment. Many clients think that they are failures if they develop yet another addiction. They need to be reminded that recovery does not proceed without complications and that they need to learn to be patient with themselves.

Difficulties Using Twelve-Step Programs

Another issue in the recovery process often arises from the client's fear and hesitancy to accept support. The sexually abused woman may be reluctant to get involved in self-help groups. She may have an intense need to feel in control that often masks her fear of showing vulnerability or relying on others for support because of the danger of revictimization. Those fears must be accepted, respected, and carefully explored in the hope that eventually she will feel safe enough and motivated to get a sponsor or build connections with other people. Depending on the degree of psychological damage from the sexual abuse, some clients may need to rebuild their trust in people by first developing a trusting relationship with one person (perhaps an individual therapist) before they become ready to trust others.

Acute PTSD symptoms present a further challenge during the recovery process. The client may be reluctant to sit in meetings for fear that she might suffer a flashback or a panic attack. The sexually abused client may be triggered into a flashback by many different stimuli, such as being in a room full of people where she may feel trapped, hearing the name of a particular brand of alcohol, seeing the color red, and so forth. It is helpful to explore her triggers and to discuss various options in handling them. Perhaps she can go to a meeting with a friend or select a small group or a women's meeting.

A client with dissociative identity disorder with child personalities who are too afraid to go to meetings may need help with reassuring "her children." She may need to accept that she has to take baby steps in her recovery, such as allowing herself to sit in the back of a meeting near the door for five minutes, rather than expecting herself to stay for a whole meeting.

Sometimes the client may have an unrealistic expectation of what twelve-step groups may provide for her. Some clients may reject twelve-step groups because they feel that they cannot talk about their sexual abuse experiences in meetings. Recommending and helping her find a small discussion meeting or a women's meeting is often helpful. Clients also may benefit from hearing that it may not be wise to discuss their problems in all contexts but to learn to set boundaries and to use meetings in the way they can best be used, that is, to stay clean and sober. Some clients have reported good experiences with Survivors of Incest Anonymous (SIA). Hocking (1994) does not recommend this form of self-help for clients with dissociative identity disorder, who may find that leaderless meetings evoke intense and overstimulating emotions. A client who continues to reject twelve-step groups may benefit from a leader-led support group where she can learn to trust and rely on someone outside of herself.

Use of Medication

Many women with sexual abuse need to be treated with medications in order to relieve overwhelming symptoms of acute depression, anxiety, panic, and sleep problems or symptoms such as hearing voices from dissociated parts of themselves. The issue of taking medication can be conflictual for the sexually abused client, and she needs the opportunity to discuss her fears around taking medication and to explore the particular psychological meaning this step holds for her. Helping the client to realize that she has two coexisting disorders and that both need to be treated can be helpful. Also, reminding her that Alcoholics Anonymous or similar recovery groups urge their members to consult physicians for conditions other than chemical dependency can be helpful. It is important to

refer clients to physicians or psychiatrists who are sensitive and knowledgeable about the possibility for these clients to abuse any medication.

Reenactment of Abusive Situations

Clients with a history of sexual abuse will have the tendency to set up an
adversarial situation with their therapist. The more severe the abuse, the
stronger the client's pull to reenact an abusive situation and make the
therapist into the abuser. Such a reenactment is difficult for client and
therapist alike, because it often is not easily recognized as a reenactment.
Even if the experienced therapist recognizes it as such, the countertransferential feelings can range from confusion, anger, and rage to severe
guilt and shame or a wish to get rid of the client, and may be difficult to
handle. If the therapist recognizes what is happening, he or she can explain to the client that experiencing a crisis with the therapist is a common phenomenon in the treatment of trauma. Sometimes these client-
therapist impasses take the form of a struggle to be in control. Issues
around "the best way to recover" lend themselves to these dynamics. The
therapist needs to find a balance between suggesting what will be helpful to the client and respecting the client's views regarding her recovery.
In most cases the client should be encouraged to try it her way. If this is
not successful, it is important that she is not shamed by a subtle attitude
conveying, "I told you so." The sensitive therapist will say that it often
takes time to discover what works best and that the client may want to
try a different approach.

Reenactment of abusive dynamics often occurs around the issue of
attending twelve-step meetings. If too lenient, the therapist will be experienced as not really caring. If the therapist is too forceful, the client will
feel abused again. It is most helpful if the therapist shares with the client
how it feels to be in this dilemma. For example:

> We both know that whenever you attend meetings regularly, you feel a
> lot better. But since you have not been going, I wonder what that is all
> about. If I ignore that you have not been going, you feel that I don't really
> care about your getting better, but if I focus on it, you feel pushed. It
> makes me wonder whether there is a part of you that wants to be pushed
> or even forced to do something against your will. Maybe we can talk
> about how you see the situation.

Such a discussion may need to be repeated before the client can
address relational issues and feelings stemming from traumatization.
Such a direct discussion may also prevent a rupture in the therapeutic
relationship.

Another variant of abusive reenactments is the reenactment of sexual abuse. The woman with sexual abuse may have many conflicting feelings around sexuality, and she may be confused about how to express them. She may still feel unable to say no when she is faced with unwanted sexual contact because she has never worked through the original feelings of helplessness. Or, she does not feel that she has a right to say no. In identification with her perpetrator she may associate her sexuality with having power and thus employ it to gain power and control over other people, including her therapist. She may feel a strong need to please her therapist, and one way she knows how to please is with her sexuality. She may associate sexual contact with closeness and caring and thus try to provoke the therapist to get engaged in a sexualization of the therapeutic relationship. She may also feel ashamed of any sexual feelings that are likely to come up, especially in a more intensive individual therapy. Again, it is important for the therapist to be vigilant for these dynamics and to feel comfortable with them. The therapist needs to make it clear that all the client's feelings, including her sexual feelings, can be discussed and sorted out. However, the therapist must also be clear that there will be no acting on any sexual feelings. It is best to avoid what might seem like casual nonsexual contacts, such as hugs or holding hands. While these expressions of affection are often longed for by the client who has been sexually abused, they are often experienced as sexual violations. It is more helpful to help the client process her feelings of disappointment and anger when she does not get the wanted sexual contact.

LONGER-TERM TREATMENT GOALS

Longer-term treatment goals aim at consolidating the gains of the initial stabilization phase. Once stabilization of the client's emotions and sobriety is achieved, she is more ready to explore deep-seated feelings and memories related to past sexual traumatization. As this process gets under way the client is again confronted with mounting anxiety and becomes vulnerable to relapsing and resorting to old dysfunctional coping strategies. In many cases a regression is inevitable as the client reexperiences and then integrates her traumatic affect. The therapeutic approach during this time is the same as in the first phase of recovery work, that is, to address these issues as they come up. If interpretation of the situation is not sufficient, a specific verbal or written contract focusing on safety and avoiding relapse may be helpful until such time as the client feels able to manage these situations on her own. By constantly monitoring the client's feelings with regard to her trauma issues and how these affect her recovery from substance abuse, a relapse or a general worsening of the client's condition can be anticipated and perhaps prevented.

CONCLUSION

Many substance-abusing women with a history of sexual abuse benefit from a treatment approach that provides an integration of substance abuse treatment and recovery work from sexual traumatization. The focus is the client's distress from both her substance abuse and sexual abuse. While achieving sobriety is the manifest goal in the first phase of treatment, the client's difficulties with reaching this goal tend to be embedded in issues related to her sexual traumatization. The overwhelming affect that is the legacy of sexual traumatization makes healthy self-soothing a difficult task. Difficulties trusting others and self-destructive tendencies often need to be modified therapeutically before a stable sobriety becomes possible. The challenge for the therapist is to stay empathic with the client's efforts at recovery, no matter how small her progress may be initially. Working with sexually abused women who abuse drugs or alcohol is a challenging task because the treatment is often slow and frustrating and the feelings that are stirred up in both therapist and client can be painful and frightening. When the client eventually feels secure with her therapist and begins to understand the functions that substance abuse has served for her, she will gradually develop the capacity for recovery from both her sexual traumatization and her substance abuse.

REFERENCES

American Psychiatric Association. (1994). *Diagnostic and Statistical Manual of Mental Disorders*, 4th ed. Washington, DC: Author.

Bepko, C., and Krestan, J. (1985). *The Responsibility Trap: A Blueprint for Treating the Alcoholic Family*. New York: Free Press.

Bernstein, M. A., and Putnam, F. W. (1986). Development, reliability, and validity of a dissociation scale. *Journal of Nervous and Mental Disease* 174:727–735.

Beschner, G. M., Reed, B. G., and Mondanaro, J., eds. (1981). *Treatment Services for Drug Dependent Women*, vol. 1, pp. 1–24. Rockville, MD: National Institute on Drug Abuse.

Bollerud, K. (1990). A model for the treatment of trauma-related syndromes among chemically dependent inpatient women. *Journal of Substance Abuse Treatment* 7:83–87.

Briere, J. (1988). Long-term clinical correlates of childhood sexual victimization. *Annals of the New York Academy of Sciences* 528:327–334.

Brown, D. (1995). Pseudomemories: the standard of science and the standard of care in trauma treatment. *American Journal of Clinical Hypnosis* 37(3):1–24.

Bryer, J. B., Nelson, B. A., Miller, J. B., and Krol, P. A. (1987). Childhood sexual and physical abuse as factors in adult psychiatric illness. *American Journal of Psychiatry* 144:1426–1430.

Carmen, E. H., Rischer, P. P., and Mills, T. (1984). Victims of violence and psychiatric illness. *American Journal of Psychiatry* 141:378–383.

Forth-Finegan, J. (1991). Sugar and spice and everything nice: gender socialization and women's addiction—a literature review. In *Feminism and Addiction*, ed. C. Bepko, pp. 19–48. New York: Haworth.

Gelinas, D. J. (1983). The persisting negative effects of incest. *Psychiatry* 46:312–332.

Herman, J. (1981). *Father–Daughter Incest*. Cambridge, MA: Harvard University Press.

—— (1992). *Trauma and Recovery*. New York: Basic Books.

Hocking, S. J. (1994). *Someone I Know Has MPD: A Book for Significant Others, Family and Friends*. Rockville, MD: Launch Press.

Horowitz, M. J., and Reidbord, S. P. (1992). Memory, emotion, and response to trauma. In *The Handbook of Emotion and Memory: Research and Theory*, ed. S. Christianson, pp. 343–358. Hillsdale, NJ: Lawrence Erlbaum.

Jacobson, A. (1989). Physical and sexual assault histories among outpatients. *American Journal of Psychiatry* 146:755–758.

Janet, P. (1929). *The Major Symptoms of Hysteria*, 2nd ed. New York: Hafner.

Khantzian, E. J., Halliday, K. S., and McAuliffe, W. E. (1990). *Addiction and the Vulnerable Self*. New York: Guilford.

Kluft, R. P. (1992). *Incest-Related Syndromes of Adult Psychopathology*. Washington, DC: American Psychiatric Press.

Loftus, E. F. (1993). The reality of repressed memories. *American Psychologist* 48:518–537.

Ofshe, R., and Watters, E. (1993). Making monsters. *Society* 30:4–16.

Putnam, F. W. (1989). *Diagnosis and Treatment of Multiple Personality Disorder*. New York: Guilford.

Ravndal, E., and Vaglum, P. (1994). Treatment of female addicts: the importance of relationships to parents, partners and peers for treatment outcome. *International Journal of the Addictions* 29(1):115–125.

Rohsenow, D. J., Corbett, R., and Devine, D. (1988). Molested as children: A hidden contribution to substance abuse? *Journal of Substance Abuse Treatment* 5:13–15.

Russel, D. (1986). *The Secret Trauma: Incest in the Lives of Girls and Women.* New York: Basic Books.

Sakheim, D. K., Hess, E. P., and Chivas, A. (1988). General principles for short-term inpatient work with multiple personality disorder patients. *Psychotherapy* 25(1):117–124.

Straussner, S. L. A. (1993). Assessment and treatment of clients with alcohol and other drug problems: an overview. In *Clinical Work with Substance-Abusing Clients*, pp. 3–30. New York: Guilford.

Turner, S., and Colao, F. (1985). Alcoholism and sexual assault: a treatment approach for women, exploring both issues. In *Psychosocial Issues in the Treatment of Alcoholism*, ed. D. Cook, S. Straussner, and C. Fewell, pp. 91–116. Binghamton, NY: Haworth.

Volpe, J., and Hamilton, G. (1982–1983). How women recover: experience and research observations. *Alcohol Health and Research World* 7(2):28–39.

Yandow, V. (1989). Alcoholism in women. *Psychiatric Annals* 19:243–247.

Zankowski, G. L. (1987). Responsive programming: meeting the needs of chemically dependent women. *Alcoholism Treatment Quarterly* 4(4): 53–65.

Parenting Issues for Substance-Abusing Women

Nancy J. Smyth

Brenda A. Miller

6

Of the many issues confronting women with substance abuse problems, parenting is one that often evokes the strongest reactions, both for women and for society at large. American society still places motherhood on a pedestal; women who violate the expectations associated with motherhood continue to be viewed as deviant (Faludi 1991, Morell 1994). Specifically, substance-abusing mothers are often viewed as immoral because of the assumption that they are irresponsible and negligent toward their children, as well as sexually promiscuous (an assumption often made about all substance-abusing women) (Finkelstein 1994). These assumptions can then lead to the conclusion that all substance-abusing women are unfit mothers and deserve to lose their children. Such social attitudes often increase the shame and guilt experienced by these mothers, making it more difficult for them to address issues related to parenting and complicating their recovery (Finkelstein 1994, Reed 1985).

Research suggests that approximately three-quarters of the women in treatment are mothers (Beckman and Amaro 1986, Marsh and Miller 1985) and that many substance-abusing women have significant child-rearing responsibilities (Marsh and Miller 1985). Although pregnancy and substance abuse have received considerable attention, parenting among substance-abusing women has received surprisingly little focus among researchers and practitioners.

The purpose of this chapter is to review the issues that are relevant to practice with substance-abusing mothers. It presents the characteristics of addicted mothers in light of their impact on parenting and explores strategies to address parenting issues with these mothers.

CHARACTERISTICS OF SUBSTANCE-ABUSING MOTHERS

Prior to discussing the characteristics of substance-abusing mothers, it would be helpful to discuss the case of Anna, a mother who has a substance abuse problem. Anna's experiences will illustrate some of the concerns that can confront substance-abusing mothers.

Anna is a 32-year-old, divorced, European-American woman with five children, ages 14 years, 10, 5, 3, and 18 months. Anna's live-

The preparation of this chapter was supported, in part, by a grant from the National Institute on Alcohol Abuse and Alcoholism (Grant No. R01AAo7554).

in partner, Jack, age 40, is the father of her youngest child. Anna was physically abused by both her parents as a child. When she was 8, her parents divorced because of her father's drinking, and she has had minimal contact with her father since then. Her mother remarried when Anna was 10. Anna's stepfather sexually abused her from ages 10 to 14. Anna married and left home at age 17 and had two children; her husband left shortly after her second child was born. After their divorce he disappeared and stopped paying child support. Anna found a job as a cashier in a grocery store, using her mother for child care. Eventually, Anna met her second husband. After they were married, it became clear to her that he was alcoholic. He would become violent with her frequently, and she left him after he started to hurt her children. Upon leaving him, she then moved in with her mother, who was now divorced again. By this time Anna had four children. She also was drinking heavily and frequently. After a few weeks, Anna met Jack at a bar where he worked as a bartender. Several months after they met, Anna became pregnant with her youngest child, and she and her children moved in with him. Anna cut back on her drinking throughout her pregnancy. After she gave birth, she resumed her previous level of drinking and began to use the cocaine that Jack would bring home. Shortly after Jack was arrested for driving while intoxicated and began intensive outpatient alcohol treatment, Anna entered an addiction treatment program because of her concern about her own cocaine use. Anna and Jack are in different treatment programs; she chose one close to home and he entered one near his workplace.

Anna's case suggests some of the factors that may affect mothers with substance abuse problems. A wide range of issues can affect parenting for substance-abusing women. These may include victimization history; child maltreatment; parental substance abuse; mental health problems; low self-esteem and stigmatization; family system issues, including partner substance abuse; substance use during pregnancy; and social and economic resource deficits. A discussion of each of these concerns follows. Periodically, we will return to Anna to help elucidate some of these concerns.

The Impact of Mothers' Victimization on Their Parenting

Research studies have identified that a majority of women entering addiction treatment facilities report high rates of childhood physical and sexual abuse as well as adult victimization (Clayson et al. 1995, Miller et al. 1993).

Miller and colleagues (1993) found that 66 percent of women in alcohol treatment reported a history of childhood sexual abuse compared with 35 percent of women in a general population sample. Differences in childhood physical abuse rates were similar to those for sexual abuse, with 65 percent of women in alcoholism treatment reporting physical abuse by their mothers and 56 percent physical abuse by fathers, compared with 51 percent by mothers and 35 percent by fathers among women from the general population (Miller et al. 1993). Finally, researchers have identified that substance-abusing women have higher rates of partner violence (87 percent vs. 28 percent) than other women (Downs et al. 1993).

These findings paint a picture of pervasive and repeated violent victimization for many substance-abusing women. Past and current victimization experiences can affect a woman and her ability to parent effectively in several ways. At the most basic level, women who have experienced physical, emotional, and sexual abuse from parents grow up with poor models for effective parenting. As mothers, abused women may repeat patterns of violence and power they learned, or they may find it difficult to establish any limits on their children's behavior for fear of becoming like their abusive parents. Unless more appropriate models are acquired, these women will develop a distorted understanding of parenting. For instance, incest survivors from alcoholic families were found to be less consistent in their child rearing and to make fewer age-appropriate demands of their children than did both controls and adult children of alcoholics with no incest history (Cole et al. 1992). Another study found that women who had experienced paternal incest were more likely than women who had experienced childhood sexual abuse by unrelated men to use child-rearing strategies that emphasized "pushing a child toward autonomy" (Cole and Woolger 1989, p. 415) earlier in children's development. Furthermore, adults who have experienced violence in childhood have been found to be at higher risk than other adults of engaging in child abuse themselves (Miller et al. 1995, Starr et al. 1991). Even when women are determined not to repeat their own parents' behavior, they may not have a clear idea about what they should be doing instead.

Moreover, women who have been sexually victimized as children are frequently revictimized as adults (Beitchman et al. 1992, Wyatt et al. 1992). This pattern of revictimization may make it difficult for these women to protect their children. For example, if mothers develop relationships with abusive partners, not only are they in danger, but their children are in danger too. In their review of the long-term effects of child sexual abuse, Beitchman and colleagues (1992) have suggested several explanations for this pattern. One explanation is that victimized children may be forced out of the family into high-risk situations. A second is that the impact of childhood sexual abuse on self-esteem may make mothers conspicuous targets for sexually exploitive men who may also abuse their children. A third explanation is that women may idealize abusive men, seeking to reestablish the special relationship with their abusive father. Finally, women may have an impaired ability to identify correctly untrustworthy persons who may abuse their children (Beitchman et al. 1992).

The stress of living in an abusive situation as an adult may compromise a woman's ability to cope with the stress inherent in parenting, thereby placing her at higher risk of abusing her children. Research on mothers' alcohol problems and children's victimization found that women experiencing partner abuse were more likely to abuse their children than other women (Miller et al. 1995).

Past or current victimization history also increases the risk of psychiatric disorders. For example, Finkelhor and Browne (1988) found that women who experienced childhood sexual abuse were more likely to have psychiatric problems than women who did not report this experience. As will be discussed later, such psychiatric problems also can affect parenting.

> Even while in treatment, Jack would occasionally hit Anna. Several weeks ago, after the most recent incident, Anna left the house with her children and moved back in with her mother. While this is a physically safe environment, Anna's mother is very critical of her, and Anna feels very inadequate about herself in general and her parenting in particular. Like many adult survivors of abuse, Anna alternates between setting few limits with her children and setting rigid ones. When she has lost her temper she has hit them with a belt. She has not shared much specific information about her parenting (including the information that she has used a belt with her children) with treatment staff because of her fears that she will lose her children (she was informed about mandated child abuse reporting laws upon entering treatment, and several women in treatment with her have lost their children to foster care). For their part, treatment staff have inquired generally about her children but have not assessed Anna's parenting in depth, partly for fear they might scare her away from treatment (given that she is not mandated to treatment).
>
> In the past few months, Anna has had more difficulty with the children, something she has just started to share in her women's group. Her oldest child, Kevin, recently shoved her and threw a book at her when he was angry.On several occasions, she has discovered that Sarah, her 10 year old, lied to her for no apparent reason. In addition, Sarah's school performance has declined. Anna is afraid that her children are getting out of control, and

she feels overwhelmed as a parent and unable to handle them. Finally, Anna's mother has been willing to provide child care when Anna works but has been less consistent in doing so when Anna wants to leave the house for other reasons, including to attend treatment.

Child Maltreatment

As Anna's case suggests, substance-abusing mothers are at higher risk of abusing or neglecting their children than are other mothers. One study found that the existence of a current alcohol problem among mothers increased the likelihood of the women physically abusing their children, even when controlling for the incidence of physical abuse in their own childhood (Miller et al. 1995). Other research also has shown a relationship between women's substance abuse and their abuse of children. For instance, among women recruited from prenatal clinics of a large metropolitan hospital, those who had reported using cocaine or heroin during pregnancy had significantly higher scores on an inventory measuring child abuse potential than those from the general population (Black et al. 1994). Among children prenatally exposed to drugs, the rates of abuse are 2 to 3 times higher than those of the general population of children from the same geographic area (Jaudes et al. 1995). Another study found that 23 percent of infants prenatally exposed to cocaine had at least one episode of abuse, neglect, or sex abuse by 24 months of age (Wasserman and Leventhal 1993).

Children of substance-abusing parents also are at risk for neglect, since these parents tend to spend less time monitoring their children than do other parents (Miller et al. 1995). For example, a mother who is hung over or sick from partying the night before may not wake up in time to get her children off to school in the morning, leaving this responsibility to an older child. Further, an intoxicated mother will be less able to monitor her children's activities both in and outside the home. If she is bringing other drug users into the house, she may be less aware of their interactions with her children. If she is using drugs away from the home, she may lose track of time and leave her children unattended.

Parental Substance Abuse

In addition to high rates of family violence, substance-abusing women report higher rates of parental alcoholism than do other women (Binion 1979, Gomberg 1986, Miller et al. 1987, Straussner et al. 1980). Parental substance abuse may disrupt parent-child interactions (Seilhamer and Jacob 1990), which in turn may affect children's development. The relationship between parental substance abuse and child development is mitigated by a variety of influences, such as poverty, the nature of the parent's substance abuse, social support to the family, and the presence of other caregivers. The empirical literature suggests the impact of parental alcoholism on an individual is complex and may vary as a function of a wide range of factors, including the degree of family conflict and violence; the type, severity, and duration of drinking or drug use; the gender of the substance-abusing parent; the nature of the child's relationship with the nonsubstance-abusing parent and siblings; the degree to which the family is organized around the substance abuse; the child's temperament/constitution; the child's gender; and the child's perception about growing up in a substance-abusing home (Johnson and Rolf 1990). The clinical literature identifies specific roles children may assume to cope with parental addiction (Black 1982, Wegscheider 1981). While considered adaptive in childhood, these roles are thought to be maladaptive in adulthood (Black 1982, Wegscheider 1981).

As can be seen, women who grew up in substance-abusing families may have additional emotional and behavioral concerns as a result of their childhood experiences. In addition, they may lack knowledge of and experience with appropriate parenting, healthy parent–child interactions, and healthy family functioning. Finally, women whose parents continue to abuse substances may receive less social support from these parents than women without addicted parents. Addicted parents may be less likely to support their adult daughter's getting substance abuse treatment. They also may be less capable of providing consistent practical support in the form of child care, transportation, and financial assistance. As is discussed later, deficiencies in social and practical support can make accessing treatment as well as caring for children more difficult.

Mental Health Problems

Women with alcohol problems (in the general population) have a higher risk of psychiatric disorders than women without such problems (19 percent vs. 7 percent) (Helzer and Pryzbeck 1988); rates of coexisting psychiatric disorders are generally much higher in treatment settings (Helzer and Pryzbeck 1988). For example, Ross and colleagues (1988) found that two-thirds of women in inpatient addiction treatment were experiencing at least one current psychiatric disorder. Among the most common disorders for women are depression and anxiety (Helzer and Pryzbeck 1988) as well as posttraumatic stress disorder, the anxiety disorder diagnosis most directly related to traumatic experiences (Brown et al. 1995, Cottler et al. 1992). Although none of these studies identify the rates of psychiatric disorders among addicted mothers, given that most women in addiction treatment have children (Beckman and Amaro 1986, Marsh and Miller 1985), it is probably safe to assume that mothers in treatment generally have similar rates of mental health problems to women in general. In fact, findings from an implementation evaluation of substance abuse treatment programs for pregnant and parenting women indicated that many mothers had coexisting mental health problems and that program staff had the most difficulty treating those women who needed psychiatric care (Hermann et al. 1994).

The concurrence of psychiatric disorders and substance abuse, often called dual disorders, may affect parenting in two major ways, although these effects will vary with the nature and severity of both problems. First, women with dual disorders may face additional barriers to consistently completing daily activities. For example, depressed substance-abusing women will have more problems with fatigue, lack of motivation, and inability to concentrate than substance-abusing women without depression. This, in turn, can affect their ability to fulfill parenting tasks and other family roles.

Second, the presence of a concurrent psychiatric disorder can complicate substance abuse treatment and recovery (Evans and Sullivan 1990). This is especially true if only one of the dual disorders is recognized by treatment professionals. Clearly, women who have more difficulty in treatment and recovery will experience more difficulty fulfilling their roles as mothers.

> Recently Anna has started to experience severe difficulty sleeping. She reports waking frequently because of nightmares about the sexual abuse she experienced in childhood. In addition, she has been feeling more irritable, less interested in activities, detached from her life, and is having problems concentrating. She feels more overwhelmed and quick to anger than in the past and feels tense and "on edge" in the agency's treatment groups and in AA meetings (mixed gender groups).

Low Self-Esteem and Stigmatization

Substance-abusing women report more problems with low self-esteem and guilt than do other women (Colten 1979, Reed 1985). This is especially true for mothers with substance abuse problems, who often feel as though they have failed as nurturers and caregivers (Bepko 1989), a perception that is compounded by and perhaps a function of society's negative, punitive attitudes toward addicted mothers (Finkelstein 1994). When addicted mothers lose custody of their children, their shame and guilt are further intensified.

Davis (1990) observes that a healthy parental self-concept, necessary for effective parenting, consists of a combination of experiences from one's own childhood as well as current experiences with parenting. Both are often areas of difficulty for substance-abusing mothers.

Family System Issues

Parents with substance abuse problems often experience difficulties fulfilling the diverse requirements of parenting, a problem that can result in other members of the family (including children) assuming aspects of parental roles (Straussner 1994, Wallen 1993). As with parental substance abuse, many factors can affect the impact of a mother's addiction on her family. However, because substance-abusing women report heavy drinking or drug-using partners more often than do substance-abusing men (Gomberg and Nirenberg 1993, Tucker 1979), the impact of parental addiction is likely to be greater. When the high likelihood of partner violence is added to this picture (Downs et al. 1993), the impact on children becomes a greater concern. In addition, as children get older they also have potential to become violent with parents (e.g., Doueck et al. 1987), particularly since boys who have witnessed family violence are more aggressive than boys without that history (Jaffe et al. 1986). Blume (1991) identified the following problems as overrepresented among children of substance abusers: fetal alcohol syndrome, other fetal alcohol effects, fetal drug effects, child abuse and neglect, sexual abuse, behavioral/conduct disorders, attention-deficit/hyperactivity disorder, physical illnesses/injuries, depression, suicidal behavior, eating disorders, substance abuse, and antisocial behavior. As noted earlier, children also are at higher risk of abuse and neglect.

Substance Use during Pregnancy

Much attention has been focused on the effects on unborn children of alcohol and other drug use during pregnancy. While the increased risk of birth defects, low birth weight, and cognitive and motor impairments among the children of these women are of real concern, the risk of these problems also may serve as important motivators for women to seek treatment (Straussner 1994). The needs of children who are exposed to alcohol and other drugs during pregnancy can be varied. If they are born physically addicted they will experience withdrawal symptoms, such as irritability, frequent crying, and hyperactivity, making them much more difficult to parent (Straussner 1989). Children with birth defects resulting from fetal alcohol syndrome or fetal alcohol effects will have special needs that substance-abusing or recovering mothers will be ill-equipped to meet on their own.

Recognition of the special needs of pregnant addicted women has resulted in more programs targeting this population (Acuff et al. 1994). However, social policy directed at this problem has been inconsistent and conflicting. In some states, these women face prosecution under child abuse laws (Hawk 1994), thereby discouraging women from seeking addiction treatment and prenatal care (Hawk 1994, Merrick 1993). In her review of fetal abuse and criminalization, Farr (1995) raised numerous concerns about the inequity and ineffectiveness of this policy, specifically that both race and class affect the likelihood of arrest for fetal abuse and that incarceration of mothers destroys the family unit and introduces more family crisis. In this latter case, children will most likely end up in the foster care system.

Social and Economic Resource Deficits

Substance-abusing women tend to have fewer social and economic resources than their male counterparts (Beckman and Amaro 1986, Gomberg and Nirenberg 1993, Tucker 1979). This is not surprising given that substance-abusing women are more likely to be divorced than their male counterparts, a status more often associated with lower incomes and single-parent families (Beckman and Amaro 1984/1985, Gomberg and Nirenberg 1993).

Evaluation data from programs for pregnant and parenting addicted women indicate that women's multiple needs and lack of resources were major barriers to continuing in treatment. Lack of child care, lack of transportation, and lack of resources to meet basic needs such as food, clothing, and housing all were cited as common problems (Clayson et al. 1995, Hermann et al. 1994). One study found that lack of child care was cited by women as a major reason for leaving inpatient treatment (Zankowski 1987). Another study found that mothers in treatment for substance abuse had lower incomes and more problems with child care than nonaddicted Head Start mothers (Hawley et al. 1995). The addicted mothers also reported that their children had experienced more residence changes than the children of the Head Start mothers (Hawley et al. 1995). A comparison of addicted and nonaddicted pregnant women receiving obstetric services at an inner city clinic found that the addicted women had greater needs for health care, food, and housing (Marcenko et al. 1994).

Women who abuse illegal drugs often resort to prostitution or theft to maintain their habits (Vandor et al. 1991) and as a result may enter treatment through the criminal justice system or with charges pending. In addition, these women are at high risk of becoming infected with the HIV virus. Finally, these women may experience additional shame and stigma and are at greater risk of losing their children to foster care (Vandor et al. 1991).

In addition to deficits in concrete resources, substance-abusing women may have less social support for treatment than their male counterparts. One study found that women were more likely than men to experience opposition from friends and family about entering alcohol treatment (Beckman and Amaro 1986). For mothers relying on family and friends for child care or transportation, this lack of support can translate into concrete resource deficits. Single mothers, in particular, are vulnerable to higher levels of stress because of the numerous demands they face coupled with inadequate social support as well as resource deficits (Finkelstein and Derman 1991). When programs provide treatment for the family, single mothers are spared the difficult choice between their own recovery and caring for their children (Finkelstein and Derman 1991).

PRACTICE IMPLICATIONS

Assessment Issues

Effective practice with mothers with substance abuse problems requires a comprehensive approach that addresses the psychosocial characteristics identified above while simultaneously integrating content related to parenting. As exemplified in the case of Anna, there are many difficulties that can confront substance-abusing mothers. Her circumstances illustrate the intergenerational patterns of substance abuse and violence, the influence of her partner on her drug use, her inadequate financial and social resources, alcohol use during pregnancy, and concurrent psychiatric difficulties, most likely posttraumatic stress disorder related to childhood sexual abuse, as well as possible depression. Not unexpectedly, Anna is having difficulty in her role as parent: she lacks the skills to provide effective and consistent structure, and she uses methods of discipline that are excessive, harsh, and potentially abusive. In addition, her children are exhibiting problems frequently found among children growing up in addicted and violent families. Her son Kevin is exhibiting aggressiveness that is characteristic of boys raised in violent homes; he currently is at high risk of becoming a perpetrator of violence. Sarah's problems may stem from many possible sources, including the violent environment and chaotic family functioning. However, given the intergenerational patterns of victimization, it is possible that sexual abuse also is involved. All of the children should be carefully evaluated for signs of emotional, behavioral, and learning problems, including fetal alcohol effects, as well as possible physical and sexual abuse, and linked with appropriate services, including child protective services, when necessary.

Anna herself needs services for domestic violence, child care, mental health problems, a more supportive living environment, and parenting skills and support, in addition to her substance abuse. She has minimal social support. Her problematic relationship with Jack will need to be addressed. Her current relationship with her mother, coupled with her childhood history, suggests problems with assertiveness and self-esteem that are long standing. Her adult victimization experiences can only have exacerbated these problems. Although these issues often are interrelated, they usually require specific interventions. Multiple, competing concerns must be assessed and prioritized so as not to overwhelm the woman or her family.

Clinical work around parenting must begin with a careful assessment of the substance-abusing woman's functioning in the mothering role, as well as of the environmental resources and social supports that exist relative to parenting and child care. Although it often is assumed that all addicted women abuse or neglect their children, this is not the case (Davis 1990, Gomberg 1987); therefore, each woman and family deserves a careful, comprehensive assessment. Given the guilt and shame that women, and especially mothers, experience (Bepko 1989, Davis 1990, Gomberg 1987), women who are functioning well as mothers may still have a poor parental self-concept. Consequently, assessment should include a woman's perceptions of herself as parent as well as her actual behavior.

Ideally, assessment of parenting should include actual observation of the woman's behavior with her children. When this is not possible, open-ended questions specific to parenting can be used to gather information. For example, mothers can be asked about the rules in their households, how children are disciplined, where children go after they leave school, child care arrangements, how caregivers were selected, and what activities outside the house that children attend unsupervised. It is often useful to have a mother describe a typical day from the point that she and the children wake up to the time everyone goes to bed. There also are a range of assessment instruments that focus on family functioning as well as parenting that are easily utilized in clinical practice (Fischer and Corcoran 1994a).

The interrelationship of substance abuse problems and violence supports the need for careful assessment of the following: current partner violence, current child abuse and/or neglect, the presence/impact of past partner violence (on both mothers and their children), and the presence/impact of the mother's and her partner's history of childhood abuse or neglect. Assessment of sexual and physical violence is best approached by asking multiple questions about specific behaviors, such as, "Does your partner ever hit you?" or "Has anyone ever made you touch his or her genitals when you didn't want to?"—instead of a global question that applies a label, such as, "Were you ever sexually abused as a child?" Research indicates that multiple specific questions yield more reports of childhood sexual abuse than single general questions (Peters et al. 1986). Women are more likely to share information regarding sexual abuse in particular with women interviewers (Miller 1993). In addition, assessment instruments such as the Conflict Tactics Scale (Straus 1979) can be used to assess physical violence in partner or parent–child relationships (both present and past).

In addition to assessment of violent victimization, comprehensive screening for concurrent psychiatric problems also is essential. This should be done on an ongoing basis, not only at intake, because the clinical picture changes as people establish some sobriety (Brown et al. 1991, Davidson 1995, Sederer 1990). Evans and Sullivan (1990) identify the following as indicative of the presence of psychiatric disorders among people with substance abuse problems: (1) psychiatric symptoms present before heavy and/or problematic substance use started; (2) qualitative differences in the type, intensity, or pattern of psychiatric symptoms that are normally seen with only substance use; and (3) psychiatric problems persist after four weeks postdetoxification (or during similarly long periods of nonuse).

The severity and nature of psychiatric disorders can vary over time, as well as change through the course of recovery. For these reasons, the disorder may affect parenting ability differently at different times. Assessment of the relationship between psychiatric symptoms, substance use, and role functioning should include not only the present but also the time period that encompasses the duration of the psychiatric disorder. The following questions should be considered when drugs are being used: At its most severe, how did the psychiatric disorder affect your functioning as a parent? How did this relate to your substance use? At that time, were there environmental/social supports or stressors that affected the disorders and your functioning? At its best, how did the psychiatric disorder affect your functioning as a parent? How did this relate to your substance use? At that time, were there environmental/social supports or stressors that affected the disorders and your functioning? Questions to be asked during recovery/or nonusing periods should include all the questions asked during periods of use. In addition, the practitioner needs to assess the ways in which these answers change as the client acquires more substance-free time.

The answers to these questions can help practitioners identify the range of parent functioning as it relates to the psychiatric disorder for a given mother with dual disorders. This information can be used in turn to help mothers see the impact of their disorders on parenting and can help practitioners and clients plan for the future. In addition, questions regarding the environment draw attention to factors that may intensify dysfunction or enhance positive functioning.

Assessment of low self-esteem and poor parental self-concept can be accomplished in several different ways. Listening carefully to women as they talk about themselves often reveals many negative self-statements that are indicative of low self-esteem. Low self-confidence about parenting can be evident through the repeated expression of confusion about how to handle various child-rearing situations. Many times, nonverbal behaviors are important clues to strong feelings like shame and guilt. For example, a woman who suddenly speaks more softly and averts her eyes when she is talking about the impact of her substance abuse on her parenting may well be feeling shame and guilt. In other cases, the omission of information may suggest these same feelings. For instance, a mother who never discusses her ability to parent her children, even when other women discuss this topic, may be avoiding discussing what she knows is very painful material for her. Finally, there are several instruments that measure self-esteem in general (see Fischer and Corcoran 1994b) as well as attitudes and perceptions about parenting in particular (see Fischer and Corcoran 1994a), that can assist in the assessment process.

There are a range of issues related to the women's current family system that must be addressed. A comprehensive assessment of the family system is essential, with special attention given to roles, relationships, and other family members' substance use and abuse. Partners who continue to abuse substances can place a woman at higher risk of relapse. Even when family members are not abusing substances, other concerns can complicate recovery. For example, communication skills and boundaries may be poor, and family members who have assumed aspects of the mother's roles may be slow to relinquish these roles (Wallen 1993). Children need to be assessed for the full range of psychosocial problems that are associated with children of substance abusers.

When exploring a mother's substance abuse history, careful attention should be paid to patterns of use during pregnancy. Ideally, this information can be gathered in the context of a general substance abuse history, hence not drawing too much attention to this issue before she is emotionally ready to confront it. Children's health and development should be assessed with a particular eye to learning disabilities and other effects of exposure to alcohol and other drugs during pregnancy.

Finally, a thorough exploration of the environmental resources and deficits is necessary. Specifically, access to adequate housing, child care, health services, transportation, financial support, employment, education, and legal services must all be assessed. In addition, the extent and nature of a woman's social support network must be evaluated. Does she have sources of emotional support? Practical support (e.g., child care, transportation, money)? Does she have a partner, family, or friends who are supportive of her stopping substance use? Are there other parents in her support network? What strengths and weaknesses do these other parents possess? A comprehensive assessment of a mother's social and environmental resources will identify any needs for services or for advocacy on her behalf.

Treatment Issues

There are a range of treatment concerns that arise related to the psychosocial characteristics of substance-abusing women as well as parenting in particular. The treatment plan must be individualized to address any issues identified during assessment, and the treatment-planning process should be one that empowers women by involving them in the development of their treatment plans.

Psychosocial Concerns. Given the strong association between victimization and women's substance abuse, psychosocial education regarding the dynamics and consequences of violence should be incorporated into treatment programs for substance-abusing mothers. When current violence is identified as a problem, immediate safety issues should take precedence. When women are in violent situations, emergency safety plans should be developed and information about community domestic violence services offered. In planning for intervention for women with histories of victimization, it is important not to reestablish a patriarchical system of response. For example, removing the decision-making from the woman and not involving her in generating her own options can reinforce her role as a helpless woman with no control over her life. Presenting a realistic portrayal of dangers within the home setting can be important to helping the woman make informed choices. However, the line between realistic portrayals and threatening images can be difficult to maintain. In efforts to provide women some protection, it is important to ensure that the relationship between practitioner and client does not mirror the relationship between the woman and the perpetrator. Of particular importance to women is a reframing of their ability to survive violent and abusive situations. It is essential to help women recognize that their strengths and resiliency in the face of adversity provide a measure of their ability to survive and persevere in the world at large. These capabilities can then be used as a cornerstone for building a better future.

When children are victims of abuse or neglect, the situation must be reported to state child abuse hotlines, a process that often raises many concerns for practitioners, including violation of the mother's trust (Levine and Doueck 1995). For example, when the mother is both the agency client and the perpetrator, staff often have valid concerns that a child abuse report will cause the woman to leave treatment (Levine and Doueck 1995). Many programs address this concern by providing informed consent regarding the limits of confidentiality when mothers enter treatment and by encouraging mothers, in the presence of practitioners, to call child abuse hotlines themselves (Levine and Doueck 1995). Providing effective intervention for women who are abusive or neglectful of their own children is particularly fraught with concerns over balancing the rights of the child, the need to protect the child, and the mother's rights. Ultimately, there are conflicts inherent in providing services in the same program to both women and their families, since the interests of individual family members may be different. On the other hand, providing these services in the same program appears to be an important characteristic of agencies that serve large numbers of women (Beckman 1984). There are no easy ways to resolve this apparent contradiction, although the assignment of different practitioners to parents and children may mitigate the problem. There is also a range of other strategies that can be employed to help preserve the therapeutic relationship with the mother when a report must be made. Reporting by the supervisor instead of the clinician and encouraging women to report themselves in the presence of the therapist (followed by a report filed by the therapist) are two examples of such strategies (Levine and Doueck 1995).

For those women who grew up in substance-abusing families, the impact of this experience needs to be carefully assessed in light of the issues identified earlier. Treatment for adult children of alcoholics/addicts (ACOAA) is provided in many programs and may be appropriate for women at some time in recovery. However, women who are mothers will not be able to reflect on their own childhood experiences without simultaneously evaluating themselves as parents. It is the latter that often evokes feelings of guilt and shame for substance-abusing mothers (Finkelstein 1994). Practitioners working with mothers on ACOAA issues should continually monitor the impact of that work on women's feelings of guilt and shame about parenting their own children. Helping mothers understand their own path into substance abuse may help them alleviate their guilt and shame. By understanding the common pathways into addiction, the stigma of being different from everyone else can begin to dissipate. Women may need to reexamine their negative beliefs about themselves, beliefs that often originated in interactions with abusive or neglectful parents. Understanding the origins of guilt and shame can not only be constructive in helping women give up such feelings but can also increase the chances they will not repeat such behaviors with their own children. Treatment for childhood sexual and physical abuse survivors also should be made available. While some women may be able to defer addressing these issues until later in recovery, a subset will need to begin work in early recovery (Gorski 1989, Trotter and Gorski 1991).

The presence of a concurrent psychiatric problem will necessitate treatment that targets the psychiatric disorder. Addiction programs with mental health professionals on staff may well be able to meet clients' needs by individualizing treatment within the existing program; however, there will still be times that concurrent enrollment in a mental health program is required (Ries 1994). A comprehensive treatment program for mothers with dual disorders must include interventions that help women to explore the impact of both problems on their ability to parent effectively and consistently. This can be accomplished through both psychoeducation and support groups.

Low self-esteem issues can be addressed effectively through counseling that focuses on this concern and through skill-building activities (e.g., assertiveness training, coping skills) that allow women to experience success (Reed 1985). Support groups can be quite helpful in that they can give women feedback on their strengths as well as reduce the personal impact of stigmatization. Psychoeducation regarding substance abuse and the other issues with which women are coping (e.g., the impact of violent victimization) can help women normalize their experiences, reduce self-blame, and recognize their perpetrators' responsibility for abusive behavior. Issues regarding parental self-esteem and self-concept will be most effectively addressed in parenting groups.

Women who have lost custody of their children, either temporarily or permanently, will struggle with additional shame, guilt, and inadequacy as mothers. The intensity of these feelings may make it difficult for these women to openly acknowledge the feelings as well as the impact of their addiction; women in this situation may present with more resistance to treatment. They can benefit from empathy and compassion from practitioners as well as listening to other women who have experienced these losses. In addition, these women also will need to be helped through a grieving process related to these losses, especially when custody has been lost permanently.

The broader practice implications of stigmatization speak to the need for intervention that targets the social attitudes toward substance-abusing women. Public education can help to change attitudes. In addition, if done appropriately, the popular media (e.g., television shows and movies) may help to break down stereotypes by including stories about substance-abusing mothers.

As a result of the family system's problems discussed earlier (i.e., role reversal, communication problems, and poor boundaries), counseling for the couple or the entire family may be necessary. Individual family members, particularly children, may be in need of treatment (Logue and Rivinus 1991). The willingness of a program to treat children is important to many mothers with substance abuse problems. Beckman (1984) found that the percentage of women in addiction treatment was positively related to the provision of treatment for children. However, mothers often will feel much guilt and shame connected to their children's problems, particularly those that she perceives are related to her substance use (VanBremen and Chasnoff 1994). Programs that address children's problems must be sensitive to this issue.

Early prenatal care is essential for pregnant, addicted women, and the development of special programs targeting this population has resulted in more services to this population (Acuff et al. 1994). Engaging this group of women in treatment has, historically, been quite difficult, in part because of the added stigmatization they face (Center for Substance Abuse Treatment 1994) and because they face increased risk of incarceration or losing custody of their children (Hawk 1994, Merrick 1993). Recommended strategies for engaging pregnant addicted women include: (1) providing specialized services targeting this population that would include social services and child care; (2) ensuring that advertisements include information about the program's social and child care services; (3) conducting outreach activities in women, infants, and children (WIC) programs, department of social services offices, public health clinics, emergency rooms, Head Start programs, obstetricians' offices, and family-planning centers; and (4) educating health professionals about treatment resources and the identification of substance-abusing women (CSAT 1994). Finally, social policies are needed to encourage women to utilize community resources that will benefit their babies.

The concrete resource deficits experienced by this group of women suggest the need for strong linkages between women's addiction treat-

ment programs and a wide range of social, health, and community resources (Reed 1985, 1991) as well as the need for staff who will act as
brokers and advocates for clients. Many separated/divorced women and
women experiencing domestic violence, as well as women with legal
charges pending, will need legal services. In addition, the provision of
onsite child care, or at least access to a wide range of child care options,
is important.

Finally, resource deficits speak to the need for intervention at a social policy level. Women with substance abuse problems may be unable
to advocate on their own behalf for policies that support their interests.
Most practitioners direct their efforts toward helping individuals to
change, rather than by addressing the structural problems in communities. As professionals with expertise on social problems, we need a greater
commitment to promoting social change and to organizing women for
social action.

Social support deficits may be addressed in a variety of ways. The
most commonly utilized strategies are group treatment and self-help
groups. However, programs also should provide information on other
community resources, including those appropriate for special populations
such as lesbian women, women of color, women with disabilities, and
women infected with HIV. In addition, clinical work with individual clients should include careful assessment of their social networks and a
willingness, when warranted, to include significant others such as friends
and co-workers in treatment, in addition to family.

Parenting Intervention. Although by no means the norm, some substance abuse treatment programs now offer parenting groups (e.g., Plasse
1995). Parenting groups can provide safe places for women to express
feelings about parenting while exploring, in a safe environment, the ways
substance use has affected their families. This latter point often is a source
of much guilt for substance-abusing mothers (Gomberg 1987, VanBremen
and Chasnoff 1994) and therefore may not come up in parenting groups
that include parents without substance abuse problems. Because of these
feelings and the added stigmatization faced by substance-abusing mothers, it is recommended that parenting groups include only this population. While there has been some debate about whether women, including mothers, should be in women-specific versus mixed-gender groups
(McCrady and Raytek 1993, Vannicelli 1984), an evaluation of women-
only versus mixed-gender addiction groups found that women identified
several issues that they would discuss only in women's groups, including guilt regarding being an inadequate mother (Kauffman et al. 1995).
For this reason, particularly in light of the societal attitudes about mother-

hood that were discussed earlier, it is recommended that parenting groups include only women.

Typically, parenting programs in addiction treatment agencies provide information about children's development and needs (Lief 1985, Plasse 1995), communication skills (Plasse 1995), and limit setting (Lief 1985, Plasse 1995). While many of the communication skills apply to all parenting situations, they can be adapted to be recovery-specific, such as rebuilding trust with children and making amends (Plasse 1995). In addition, these groups should provide information on how to protect children from victimization (within and outside the family), to recognize signs of possible child sexual abuse, and to recognize signs of possible child alcohol and drug involvement. Many mothers who are mandated to treatment by the child welfare system often are simultaneously mandated to parenting classes. When these classes are provided outside the addiction treatment agency, parenting support groups within the treatment agency can provide a vital place for women to address parenting concerns that are unique to their addiction.

Mothers also need to be taught the difference between discipline and punishment (Lief 1985) and to be informed about alternatives to the use of corporal punishment. Research on the use of corporal punishment suggests that its use, particularly with older children, is associated with increased risk in adulthood of depression, suicidality, alcohol abuse, child abuse, and partner abuse (Straus and Kantor 1994). In addition, since low frustration tolerance is associated with child abuse (Davis 1990), mothers will need help strengthening their ability to manage frustration and anger.

Effective parenting intervention can go beyond providing parenting classes to include support groups, child–parent play groups, and family literacy activities (VanBremen and Chasnoff 1994). Potential techniques include role playing communication and discipline strategies (Plasse 1995), drawing genograms to provide insight into intergenerational cycles of abuse and neglect, and videotaping mother–child interactions to increase skills in self-evaluation and observation of children's behavior (VanBremen and Chasnoff 1994). Furthermore, parenting support groups can provide women with a chance to experience receiving nurturance and validation of their feelings, two experiences that may have been rare while they were growing up. This provides an opportunity for reparenting for the women and models for them on how to provide these experiences for their own children.

Finally, clinical work must include a focus on women's own perceived concerns about parenting and their own lives. Issues that may be of importance to women may vary or take on different meanings, depending on their lifestyle and previous life experiences. For example, impoverished minority women may express concerns about competency (e.g., their ability to do things for themselves), personal instability (e.g., losing hope in the future, not feeling safe), and survival (e.g., where the next meal is coming from) (Nyamathi and Flaskerud 1992). These realms can directly impact their ability to function as parents, even though the perceived concerns about parenting (e.g., health and safety of the children) may mirror women's concerns from higher socioeconomic groups.

CONCLUSION

There are many issues that can affect parenting for substance-abusing women, and a greater understanding of the impact of these issues on women's lives is necessary for developing effective intervention. Some of these issues, such as violent victimization and mental health problems, have their origins in the unique characteristics of substance-abusing women. Others, such as alcohol and other drug use during pregnancy and low parental self-esteem, apply to mothers only, not all women.

Treatment programs are only beginning to scratch the surface in addressing the needs of mothers, a factor that may be partially responsible for the underrepresentation of women in addiction treatment facilities. Practitioners in nonaddiction treatment settings often will best be able to identify mothers with substance-abuse problems. For this reason, in addition to providing specialized services for substance-abusing women, it is essential to integrate screening procedures and information about substance abuse into other services for women, such as battered women's shelters, rape crisis services, and women's centers, as well as general health, mental health, and child welfare settings (Beckman 1984, Bennett and Lawson 1994, Institute of Medicine 1990, Reed 1991, Roth 1991).

Effective intervention requires that we not look for quick fixes to complex problems. Providing assistance for substance-abusing mothers necessitates our consideration of the political and social climate that affects their lives and requires a professional appraisal of policies that have been implemented. In the long run, our ability to help mothers and their children will depend on the degree to which we can address the diverse needs of this population by developing relevant policies, programs, linkages among programs, and individualized treatment plans. Effective practice with addicted mothers will require intervention on all of these levels, individual, social, political, and structural, if we hope to interrupt the intergenerational cycle of addiction, violence, and mental health and behavior problems.

REFERENCES

Acuff, K., Spolarich, A. W., Andrulis, D. P., and Gerstein, S. (1994). *Vulnerable Women and Visionary Programs: Safety Net Programs for Drug-Involved Women and Their Children.* Washington, DC: The National Public Health and Hospital Institute.

Beckman, L. J. (1984). Analysis of the suitability of alcohol treatment resources for women. *Substance and Alcohol Actions/Misuse* 5:21-27.

Beckman, L. J., and Amaro, H. (1984/1985). Patterns of women's use of alcohol treatment agencies. *Alcohol Health and Research World* 9(2): 15-25.

———(1986). Personal and social difficulties faced by women and men entering alcoholism treatment. *Journal of Studies on Alcohol* 47:135-145.

Beitchman, J. H., Zucker, K. J., Hood, J. E., et al. (1992). A review of the long-term effects of child sexual abuse. *Child Abuse and Neglect* 16:101-118.

Bennett, L., and Lawson, M. (1994). Barriers to cooperation between domestic-violence and substance-abuse programs. *Families in Society: The Journal of Contemporary Human Services* 75(5):277- 286.

Bepko, C. (1989). Disorders of power: women and addiction in the family. In *Women in Families: A Framework for Family Therapy*, ed. M. McGoldrick, C. M. Anderson, and F. Walsh, pp. 406-426. New York: Norton.

Binion, V. J. (1979). A descriptive comparison of the families of origin of women heroin users and nonusers. In *Addicted Women: Family Dynamics, Self-Perceptions, and Support Systems*, pp. 77-113. Washington, DC: National Institute on Drug Abuse.

Black, C. (1982). *It Will Never Happen To Me*, 1st ed. Denver: M.A.C. Printing and Publications Division.

Black, M. M., Nair, P., Knight, C., et al. (1994). Parenting and early development among children of drug-abusing women: effects of home intervention. *Pediatrics* 94:440-448.

Blume, S. B. (1991). Children of alcoholic and drug-dependent parents. In *Alcohol and Drugs Are Women's Issues*, vol. 1, ed. P. Roth, pp. 166-172. Metuchen, NJ: Women's Action Alliance and Scarecrow.

Brown, P. J., Recupero, P. R., and Stout, R. (1995). PTSD substance abuse comorbidity and treatment utilization. *Addictive Behaviors* 20:251-254.

Brown, S. A., Irwin, M., and Schuckit, M. A. (1991). Changes in anxiety among abstinent male alcoholics. *Journal of Studies on Alcohol* 52:55-61.

Center for Substance Abuse Treatment (1994). *Practical Approaches in the Treatment of Women Who Abuse Alcohol and Other Drugs*. Rockville, MD: Department of Health and Human Services, Public Health Service.

Clayson, Z., Berkowitz, G., and Brindis, C. (1995). Themes and variations among seven comprehensive perinatal drug and alcohol abuse treatment models. *Health and Social Work* 20:234-238.

Cole, P. M., and Woolger, C. (1989). Incest survivors: the relation of their perceptions of their parents and their own parenting attitudes. *Child Abuse and Neglect* 13:409-416.

Cole, P. M., Woolger, C., Power, T. G., and Smith, K. D. (1992). Parenting difficulties among adult survivors of father–daughter incest. *Child Abuse and Neglect* 16:239-249.

Colten, M. E. (1979). A descriptive and comparative analysis of self-perceptions and attitudes of heroin-addicted women. In *Addicted Women: Family Dynamics, Self-Perceptions, and Support Systems*, pp. 7-36. Washington, DC: National Institute on Drug Abuse.

Cottler, L. B., Compton, W. M., III, Mager, D., et al. (1992). Posttraumatic stress disorder among substance users from the general population. *American Journal of Psychiatry* 149:664-670.

Davidson, K. M. (1995). Diagnosis of depression in alcohol dependence: changes in prevalence with drinking status. *British Journal of Psychiatry* 166:199-204.

Davis, S. K. (1990). Chemical dependency in women: a description of its effects and outcome on adequate parenting. *Journal of Substance Abuse Treatment* 7:225-232.

Doueck, H. J., Ishisaka, H. A., Sweany, S. L., and Gilchrist, L. D. (1987). Adolescent maltreatment: themes from the empirical literature. *Journal of Interpersonal Violence* 2:139-153.

Downs, W. R., Miller, B. A., and Panek, D. D. (1993). Differential patterns of partner-to-woman violence: a comparison of samples of community, alcohol-abusing, and battered women. *Journal of Family Violence* 8:113-135.

Evans, K., and Sullivan, J. M. (1990). *Dual Diagnosis: Counseling the Mentally Ill Substance Abuser*. New York: Guilford.

Faludi, S. (1991). *Backlash: The Undeclared War Against American Women*. New York: Crown.

Farr, K. A. (1995). Fetal abuse and the criminalization of behavior during pregnancy. *Crime and Delinquency* 41:235-245.

Finkelhor, D., and Browne, A. (1988). Assessing the long-term impact of child sexual abuse: a review and conceptualization. In *Family Abuse and Its Consequences*, ed. G. T. Hotaling, D. Finkelhor, J. T. Kirkpatrick, and M. A. Straus, pp. 270-284. Newbury Park, CA: Sage.

Finkelstein, N. (1994). Treatment issues for alcohol- and drug-dependent pregnant and parenting women. *Health and Social Work* 19:7-15.

Finkelstein, N., and Derman, L. (1991). Single-parent women: what a mother can do. In *Alcohol and Drugs Are Women's Issues*, vol. 1, ed.

P. Roth, pp. 78–84. Metuchen, NJ: Women's Action Alliance and Scarecrow.

Fischer, J., and Corcoran, K. (1994a). *Measures for Clinical Practice: A Sourcebook, Vol. 1, Couples, Families and Children.* New York: Free Press.

——(1994b). *Measures for Clinical Practice: A Sourcebook, Vol. 2: Adults.* New York: Free Press.

Gomberg, E. S. L. (1986). Women and alcoholism: psychosocial issues. In *Women and Alcohol: Health Related Issues.* Research Monograph 16 (DHHS Publication No. ADM 86–1139), pp. 78–120. Washington, DC: US Government Printing Office.

——(1987). Shame and guilt issues among women alcoholics. *Alcoholism Treatment Quarterly* 4:139–155.

Gomberg, E. S. L., and Nirenberg, T. D. (1993). Antecedents and consequences. In *Women and Substance Abuse*, ed. E. S. L. Gomberg, and T. D. Nirenberg, pp. 118–141. Norwood, NJ: Ablex.

Gorski, T. T. (1989). ACA recovery: How soon is too soon? *Alcoholism and Addiction* 9:25.

Hawk, M. A. N. (1994). How social policies make matters worse: the case of maternal substance abuse. *Journal of Drug Issues* 24:517–526.

Hawley, T. L., Halle, T. G., Drasin, R. E., and Thomas, N. G. (1995). Children of addicted mothers: effects of the "crack epidemic" on the caregiving environment and the development of preschoolers. *American Journal of Orthopsychiatry* 65:364–379.

Helzer, J. F., and Pryzbeck, T. R. (1988). The co-occurrence of alcoholism with other psychiatric disorders in the general population and its impact on treatment. *Journal of Studies on Alcohol* 49:219–224.

Hermann, J., Shur, G., McKinney, S., et al. (1994). *Implementation evaluation findings from substance abuse treatment programs for pregnant and parenting women.* Paper presented at the American Psychological Association's National Multidisciplinary Conference on Psychosocial and Behavioral Factors in Women's Health: Creating an Agenda for the 21st Century, Washington, DC, May.

Institute of Medicine (1990). *Broadening the Base of Treatment for Alcohol Problems.* Washington, DC: National Academy Press.

Jaffe, P., Wolfe, D., Wilson, S. K., and Zak, L. (1986). Family violence and child adjustment: a comparative analysis of girls' and boys' behavioral symptoms. *American Journal of Psychiatry* 143:74–77.

Jaudes, P. K., Ekwo, E., and Voorhis, J. V. (1995). Association of drug abuse and child abuse. *Child Abuse and Neglect* 19:1065–1075.

Johnson, J. L., and Rolf, J. E. (1990). When children change: research perspectives on children of alcoholics. In *Alcohol and the Family*, ed. R. L. Collins, K. E. Leonard, and J. S. Searles, pp. 162–193. New York: Guilford.

Kauffman, E., Dore, M. M., and Nelson-Zlupko, L. (1995). The role of women's therapy groups in the treatment of chemical dependence. *American Journal of Orthopsychiatry* 65:355–363.

Levine, M., and Doueck, H. J. (1995). *The Impact of Mandated Reporting on the Therapeutic Process: Picking up the Pieces.* Thousand Oaks, CA: Sage.

Lief, N. R. (1985). The drug user as a parent. *International Journal of the Addictions* 20:63–97.

Logue, M. E., and Rivinus, T. M. (1991). Young children of substance-abusing parents: a developmental view of risk and resiliency. In *Children of Chemically Dependent Parents: Multiperspectives from the Cutting Edge,* ed. T. M. Rivinus, pp. 55–73. New York: Brunner/Mazel.

Marcenko, M. O., Spence, M., and Rohweder, C. (1994). Psychosocial characteristics of pregnant women with and without a history of substance abuse. *Health and Social Work* 19:17–22.

Marsh, J. C., and Miller, N. A. (1985). Female clients in substance abuse treatment. *International Journal of the Addictions* 20:995–1019.

McCrady, B. S., and Raytek, H. (1993). Women and substance abuse: treatment modalities and outcomes. In *Women and Substance Abuse,* ed. E. S. L. Gomberg and T. D. Nirenberg, pp. 314–338. Norwood, NJ: Ablex.

Merrick, J. C. (1993). Maternal substance abuse during pregnancy: policy implications in the United States. *Journal of Legal Medicine* 14:57–71.

Miller, B. A. (1993). *Retrospective accounts of childhood victimization: methodological issues and considerations.* Presented at the annual meeting of the New York State Sociological Association, Potsdam, NY, October.

Miller, B. A., Downs, W. R., Gondoli, D. M., and Keil, A. (1987). The role of childhood sexual abuse in the development of alcoholism in women. *Violence and Victims* 2:157–172.

Miller, B. A., Downs, W. R., and Testa, M. (1993). Interrelationships between victimization experiences and women's alcohol use. *Journal of Studies on Alcohol* Supplement 11:109–117.

Miller, B. A., Smyth, N. J., and Mudar, P. (1995). Unpublished data, Research Institute on Addictions, Buffalo, NY. Study funded by the National Institute on Alcohol Abuse and Alcoholism (Grant No. R01AA07554).

Morell, C. M. (1994). *Unwomanly Conduct: The Challenges of Intentional Childlessness.* New York: Routledge.

Nyamathi, A. M., and Flaskerud, J. (1992). A community-based inventory of current concerns of impoverished homeless and drug-addicted minority women. *Research in Nursing and Health* 15:121–129.

Peters, S. D., Wyatt, G. E., and Finkelhor, D. (1986). Prevalence. In *A Sourcebook on Child Sexual Abuse,* ed. D. Finkelhor, pp. 15–59. Beverly Hills: Sage.

Plasse, B. R. (1995). Parenting groups for recovering addicts in a day treatment center. *Social Work* 40:65–74.

Reed, B. G. (1985). Drug misuse and dependency in women: the meaning and implications of being considered a special population or minority group. *International Journal of the Addictions* 20:13–62.

——(1991). Linkages: battering, sexual assault, incest, child sexual abuse, teen pregnancy, dropping out of school and the alcohol and drug connection. In *Alcohol and Drugs Are Women's Issues: Review of the Issues*, vol. 1, ed. P. Roth, pp. 130–149. Metuchen, NJ: Scarecrow.

Ries, R. (1994). *Assessment and treatment of patients with coexisting mental illness and alcohol and other drug abuse* (Treatment Improvement Protocol Series No. 9, DHHS Publication No. SMA-94– 2078). Rockville, MD: Center for Substance Abuse Treatment.

Roth, P. (1991). Program activities. In *Alcohol and Drugs Are Women's Issues: The Model Program Guide*, vol. 2, ed. P. Roth, pp. 21–31. Metuchen, NJ: Scarecrow.

Sederer, L. I. (1990). Mental disorders and substance abuse. In *Treatment Choices for Alcoholism and Substance Abuse*, ed. H. B. Milkman and L. I. Sederer, pp. 163–181. Lexington, MA: Lexington Books.

Seilhamer, R. A., and Jacob, T. (1990). Family factors and adjustment of children of alcoholics. In *Children of Alcoholics: Critical Perspectives*, ed. M. Windle and J. S. Searles, pp. 168–186. New York: Guilford.

Starr, R. H., Jr., MacLean, D. J., and Keating, D. P. (1991). Life-span developmental outcomes of child maltreatment. In *The Effects of Child Abuse and Neglect*, ed. R. H. Starr, Jr., and D. A. Wolfe, pp. 1–32. New York: Guilford.

Straus, M. (1979). Measuring intrafamily conflict and violence: the Conflict Tactics (CTS) Scale. *Journal of Marriage and the Family* 41:75–88.

Straus, M. A., and Kantor, G. K. (1994). Corporal punishment of adolescents by parents: a risk factor in the epidemiology of depression, suicide, alcohol abuse, child abuse, and wife beating. *Adolescence* 29:543–561.

Straussner, S. L. A. (1989). Intervention with maltreating parents who are alcohol and other drug abusers. In *Clinical Social Work with Maltreated Children and Their Families*, ed. S. M. Ehrenkranz, E. G. Goldstein, L. Goodman, and J. Seinfeld, pp. 149–177. New York: New York University Press.

——(1994). The impact of alcohol and other drug abuse on the American family. *Drug and Alcohol Review* 13:393–399.

Straussner, S. L. A., Kitman, C., Straussner, J., and Demos, E. S. (1980). The alcoholic housewife. *Focus on Women* 1:15–32.

Trotter, C., and Gorski, T. T. (1991). Relapse and the survivors of childhood abuse. *Focus* 13:30–39.

Tucker, M. B. (1979). A descriptive and comparative analysis of the social support structure of heroin-addicted women. In *Addicted Women: Family Dynamics, Self Perceptions, and Support Systems*, pp. 37–76. Washington, DC: National Institute on Drug Abuse.

VanBremen, J. R., and Chasnoff, I. J. (1994). Policy issues for integrating parenting interventions and addiction treatment for women. *Topics in Early Childhood Special Education* 14:254–274.

Vandor, M., Juliana, P., and Leone, R. (1991). Women and illegal drugs. In *Alcohol and Drugs Are Women's Issues*, vol. 1, ed. P. Roth, pp. 155–160. Metuchen, NJ: Women's Action Alliance and Scarecrow.

Vannicelli, M. (1984). Barriers to treatment of alcoholic women. *Substance and Alcohol Actions/Misuse* 5:29–37.

Wallen, J. (1993). *Addiction in Human Development: Developmental Perspectives on Addiction and Recovery*. New York: Haworth.

Wasserman, D. R., and Leventhal, J. M. (1993). Maltreatment of children born to cocaine-dependent mothers. *American Journal of Diseases of Children* 147:1324–1328.

Wegscheider, S. (1981). *Another Chance: Hope and Help for the Alcoholic Family*. Palo Alto, CA: Science & Behavior Books.

Wyatt, G. E., Guthrie, D., and Notgrass, C. M. (1992). Differential effects of women's child sexual abuse and subsequent revictimization. *Journal of Consulting and Clinical Psychology* 60:167–173.

Zankowski, G. L. (1987). Responsive programming: meeting the needs of chemically dependent women. *Alcoholism Treatment Quarterly* 4:53–66.

7

High-Achieving Women: Issues in Addiction and Recovery

Betsy Robin Spiegel

Donna Demetri Friedman

The French art critic Marius Ary-Leblond described the feminist of 1901.

The new woman, he wrote, lives *"a full life, a complete and powerful one, equal in intensity and output to that of a man."*

(New York Times Magazine, July 16, 1995)

Women and men are different. From early psychological development to the issues and conflicts of late adulthood, women's lives are informed by this difference. This chapter is concerned with women who have seized the opportunities resulting from the women's movement of the 1960s and 1970s to pursue careers in businesses staffed and managed by men. They have sought to enter the old boys network where they have clambered toward the top, to find not only a glass ceiling limiting their achievement but also a sense of emptiness and isolation. Some of these "successful" women have turned to alcohol and other substances.

This chapter will examine the workplace of today, women's relationship to success and power, and their need for connection. It will illuminate the kind of stressors potentially leading to substance abuse and address the dynamics of substance-abusing, high-achieving women and their recovery from addiction as it applies to their professional lives.

WOMEN'S JOURNEY TO THE WORKPLACE

American women of today live in a nation that was built on the pioneer spirit and on rugged individualism. "The overarching emphasis on individualism, the exercise of 'power over' others, creates divisive tensions throughout the society . . . and a tendency to take an aggressive, assaultive stance toward more vulnerable, marginalized groups" (Jordan 1996, p. 1). Vulnerability and the need for connection, so intrinsic to women, are not valued (Gilligan 1982).

Women's strivings for parity in the workplace have been an issue for decades. The dilemma of high-achieving women today reaches at least back to postwar America, the baby boom, and the compulsive domesticity of the late 1940s and 1950s. After World War II, women were shifted from the factory back to the kitchen. While most women complied, many silently grieved for their lost freedom and instilled in their daughters an internalized knowledge of their frustration (Friedan 1963). Some of these daughters who came of age in the 1960s formed the leadership of the women's movement.

Thus the late 1960s and early 1970s witnessed a reaction to the domesticity of the previous decades. Small groups raised the consciousness

Authors' note: Special thanks to Marjorie Hirsch, Dr. Anne Geller, Laura Smith, and Dr. Nancy Waite-O'Brien.

of many urban educated women who demanded economic and professional equality with men. The women's movement facilitated the entrance of thousands of women into the workplace. "In 1960, not even 20 percent of married women with children under six years of age were in the workplace. In 1991, almost 60 percent of married women with children under six years of age were working outside the home" (Lundy and Younger 1994, p. xvi).

The successful women of the late 1980s and 1990s have entered the corporate boardroom through a half-open door. They have been equipped with education, and many have had work experience. Yet after several years in business, and despite high incomes and promotions, many women believe they have failed. Having it all has not been enough; they have tried to thrive in a competitive, task-oriented, male-dominated culture. They have betrayed their intrinsic need for relationships (Gilligan 1982) and have gained success without authenticity and speech without voice.

THE RELATIONSHIP BETWEEN WOMEN'S EMPLOYMENT AND SUBSTANCE ABUSE

As women began to enter the workforce more aggressively in the 1970s, some researchers hypothesized that employment outside the home might negatively affect women's mental health (Johnson 1982). Studies in the late '70s and early '80s reported that the "married, working woman—the modern 'superwoman' trying to juggle both family and work responsibilities—was most likely to abuse alcohol" (Straussner 1985, p. 70). However, surveys done during the mid-to-late 1980s disputed the notion that employment for women leads to harmful drinking behavior. The findings did show that although working women were more likely to drink than other women, they did not drink more heavily or have more adverse drinking consequences than homemakers (Shore 1992). A 1981/1986 longitudinal study and a 1991 survey both found no significant relationship between women's full-time employment and alcohol-related problems (Wilsnack et al. 1991).

Currently, it is believed that multiple roles for women (such as family, marriage, and paid employment) reduce women's risk for mental health and drinking problems (Froberg et al. 1986). Working outside the home increases self-esteem and social support, and it provides responsibilities and performance demands, as well as increased social monitoring. These factors discourage excessive alcohol use. Moreover, studies of women ranging in ages from 20 to 60 years found that lack of defined social roles (e.g., being unmarried or without full-time employment) and loss of social roles are associated with higher rates of problem drinking in women of several age groups (Wilsnack and Cheloha 1987).

Further research informs us that increased drinking among working women depends on the level of employment: women working in non-traditional, male-dominated occupations are more likely to report increased drinking or adverse consequences of drinking. For example, LaRosa (1990) found that high-ranking women executives were more likely to be drinkers than women of comparable age and education but employed at lower-level jobs. According to Wilsnack and Wright (1991), women drinkers in occupations with more than 50 percent males scored higher on a problem-drinking index than women in female-dominated careers.

Wilsnack and Wilsnack (1992) emphasized that drinking patterns of employed women seem to be influenced by greater accessibility to alcohol and by complex issues surrounding the gender balance of a workplace or occupation. They hypothesize that women are influenced by their need for connection to their male peers and that they are imitating the male drinking model ("being one of the boys").

Not only are there more drinking opportunities in male-dominated businesses, but also the stress of having a minority status in the workplace can increase drinking behavior. Drinking can be used as a symbolic expression of power and gender equality. In addition to alcohol, high-achieving women tend to abuse prescription pills (Gordon 1989), cocaine, and more recently, intranasal heroin. For example, a recent news article described how a successful female stockbroker, who was married with children and lived in a prosperous area of Manhattan, overdosed on heroin while her husband and children were in the next room (Van Natta 1995).

THE PSYCHOLOGY OF WOMEN AND PROFESSIONAL SUCCESS

Professional success for women carries certain burdens and responsibilities as well as losses. Successful women can be the recipients of resentment, envy, financial expectations, and other stressful demands and a hidden loneliness that can hover like smoke: enticing, barely visible, and toxic. This loneliness and isolation are often medicated by alcohol and cocaine.

Earlier investigators such as Maccoby (1963) pointed out that a girl who maintains the qualities of independence and active strivings necessary for intellectual mastery defies the conventions of sex-appropriate behavior and must pay a price in anxiety. Matina Horner found a high incidence of fear of success among women: " . . . most women have a motive, that is a disposition to become anxious about achieving because they expect negative consequences (such as social rejection and/or feelings of being unfeminine) as a result of succeeding" (Horner 1972, p. 159). Highly competent women, when faced with the conflict between maintaining their feminine image on the one hand and expressing their competencies and developing their interests on the other, adjusted their behavior to their internalized sex-role stereotypes.

Carol Gilligan (1982) described the sadness and the pervasive ennui that descend upon young girls as they approach adolescence and realize that their role as women will keep them from full participation in the American dream:

> Young women feel under pressure from within and without to sacrifice or sequester themselves to hide what they most want and value. Girls at this time often protect an inner world that seemingly cannot be in the outer world, saying that the innermost part of themselves cannot survive the experience of not being listened to, not being taken seriously. [Gilligan 1996, p. 1]

Perhaps some of these girls will become the nurturers behind a great man. However, if they succeed on their own, the cost can be high, and maintaining the success can be impossible without annihilating authenticity.

Nancy Chodorow (1974) has attributed the differences between the sexes to the fact that women, universally, are largely responsible for early child care. Female identity formation takes place in a context of ongoing relationship since "mothers tend to experience their daughters as more like, and continuous with, themselves" (p. 7). Girls identify themselves as females and experience themselves as like their mothers, thus intertwining the experience of attachment with the process of identity formation. Mothers, on the other hand, experience their sons as different from themselves. Boys, in defining themselves as males, separate their mothers from themselves. According to Gilligan (1982), "The elusive mystery of women's development lies in its recognition of the continuing importance of attachment in the human life cycle" (p. 23). If those needs in women are disavowed or split off to adjust to a male-based workplace, women will pay an emotional price. For some, alcohol or drugs may be temporary solutions.

The attainment and maintenance of power in some corporate settings is based in a competitiveness and assertion that is not innate in women. Women and power may seem to some a contradiction in terms. Jean Baker Miller (1976) defined power as the capacity to produce change. She believes that in our culture, the myth that women do not and shall not have personal power on any dimension has been maintained. It is only in the service of others that women can exert power comfortably. High-achieving women in male-dominated businesses must contend with their own and society's ambiguity about women and power. They must adopt positions that are alien to mutuality and the need for connection. This process is usually unconscious.

According to the scholars of the Stone Center for Developmental Services and Studies (Jordan et al. 1991), "feminization" of the workplace is essential for women's success. Feminization of the workplace implies fostering a less competitive environment with emphasis on cooperation. Many women leave successful corporate positions to create their own feminized workplaces through entrepreneurial endeavors. This is true of high-achieving women in recovery who may abandon a career despite great success in order to find something more gratifying internally.

As depicted in the following case, women often struggle in a workplace which does not meet their needs.

> Lois, 30, was an assistant to a commodities broker on the New York Stock Exchange. She had loved her job. The excitement, the high stakes, the "big bucks" seemed to fill the emptiness and quiet the longing for a peace that she had never experienced yet yearned for. One morning she awoke in a strange room with an unknown man and no memory of how she got there. She had no memory of using cocaine heavily and drinking as well. Lois was lucky. She had a friend who drugged and drank with her who had gotten clean and sober and was more than willing to take her to the rooms of AA and refer her to the female therapist she had been seeing. Lois bonded immediately with the twelve-step program, got a sponsor, and got sober.
>
> As Lois experienced the first real support system and the first positive relationship with a woman in many years, she began to be resentful of her work, weary of the competitive milieu, and lonely for the companionship of other women. She also found the desperate hustle for money increasingly alien. As she had been nurtured, she wanted to nurture. She wanted to help others. She loved sponsoring people and her therapist suggested she begin an educational program to get her master's degree in social work. She entered a five-year program while she continued to work. Gradually the emptiness was replaced with wonderful relationships, professional and personal, and she gradually entered a profession where she could be of service to others.

If the workplace were feminized, that is, had values of connection and service, women like Lois would have other choices.

It is important to add that gender roles are a societal construct. The high-achieving, substance-abusing woman identified more with her father and took on a more "masculine" role. Through the process of recovery she becomes more "feminine." Modern analysts, such as Benjamin (1988), have suggested that the ideal would be for both men and women to be able to incorporate both the masculine and the feminine, hence identifying in part with both parents. This, however, is not presently accepted in American culture. Current cultural values result in women being nurturers and men wielding power.

NARCISSISM IN THE HIGH-ACHIEVING, SUBSTANCE-ABUSING WOMAN

An excessive amount of narcissism in the alcoholic's ego gives rise to feelings of omnipotence (Zimberg et al. 1987). Many successful women who turn to alcohol and drugs feel driven to achieve to satisfy an insatiable need for praise and power. These women are living with a sense of emptiness and a diffuse sensitivity and vulnerability to other people, in addition to intense ambitiousness. Their grandiose fantasies compensate for a feeling of inferiority and overdependence on external admiration and acclaim. Such women require constant or immediate feedback or applause; many are chronically fearful of being discovered as impostors (Krueger 1984).

As Horner (1968) suggested, many women may be afraid of becoming too successful and too powerful, of surpassing the mother who was viewed as weak and "only a woman." Ultimately, they may be too afraid of their own competitiveness (Krueger 1984).

Women who are unable to identify positively with their mothers may identify with their successful, often alcoholic fathers by default. Such women may initially feel more at ease in the male-dominated workplace. These women typically have difficulty relating to other women, equating them with the deficient mother. They try to be *not like mother*, which transitions into being *like father*. These women reject the mother role and want to be taken care of themselves. Many remain unmarried and become workaholics. Some use alcohol and other substances to medicate anxiety and depression.

Frequently these women feel very isolated in the workplace and in the rest of their lives. Women cannot be friends with male colleagues, and they have become alienated from female friends who have chosen a more domestic life.

For narcissistic, high-achieving women, sex can be a tool used to gain control, power, and physical affection. Sex and involvement with many lovers has often been a theme in the life of the alcoholic or cocaine-abusing woman. For successful women, the dilemma is even greater as sexual activity may enter the workplace. This can take the form of sleeping with men at work or even in some cases the boss. The shame and depression associated with sexual acting-out behavior can be only temporarily numbed by substances.

TREATMENT ISSUES AND APPROACHES

High-achieving, substance-abusing women are more visible than their domestic counterparts. They enter into treatment in a variety of ways. Some are identified through their Employee Assistance Program (EAP) in the workplace, others seek individual or group psychotherapy for depression and/or anxiety. Others are taken by a friend to the rooms of Alcoholics Anonymous (AA), while some may even be hospitalized for detoxification or physical or psychological complications of their substance abuse.

Beyond the treatment issues and approaches that are similar for all substance-abusing women, unique issues are dealt with in the treatment of high-achieving women. Regardless of the setting, the issues around success need to be addressed as they emerge. Although the women can be visible, successful, and responsible, internally they experience themselves as impostors. Like their male counterparts, their self-esteem can hinge on workplace achievement. Many have identified with their fathers and retreated from femininity, which leaves them lonely and depressed.

The Value of EAPs in Identifying and Getting High-Achieving Women into Treatment

The major techniques of intervention for employees with alcohol problems are largely designed for male employees and based on data and experience with male substance abusers. "For about fifteen years women professionals in both the Employee Assistance and the alcohol and drug addiction treatment fields have diligently pursued efforts to raise awareness in the workplace about the specific problems faced by women" (Reddy 1994, p. 1). The specific problems include: sexual harassment, lack of availability of child care, inequality in pay, lack of opportunities and training for advancement, and lack of recognition and respect for gender differences.

Historically, the pattern for women has been to quit a job before being identified by an EAP. Today, however, women are more likely to stay at their job and seek treatment. This is due to the reduction in stigma associated with substance abuse among women and to an increase in early intervention for women, particularly high-achieving women.

High-achieving women are identified through the EAP in two ways. The woman can be self-referred, in which case her job is not in jeopardy per se and her involvement in the EAP is voluntary. These women learn of the EAP in a variety of ways—through word of mouth, a brochure, a poster, or a mailing sent to the home. The human resource department, a supervisor, and the employee benefit manual are important avenues of referral as well. A woman can also be referred to the EAP because her job performance has declined and her supervisor, manager, or human resources professional is sufficiently concerned to alert the EAP.

In both circumstances the woman is evaluated by the employee assistance professional. The key to a successful intervention is motivating the woman to acknowledge a problem with addiction and to accept treatment. For the woman referred by her supervisor for definable deteriorating performance, the important leverage will be that her job is at stake. If the denial is indeed broken, she has taken the first step to recovery with the EAP. Often significant others are involved, which facilitates compliance with treatment recommendations. Since high-achieving women need others with whom they can identify, rehabilitation programs and twelve-step groups must be chosen carefully to ensure the opportunity for full identification.

Once the assessment and referral stage is complete, the EAP monitors the woman's progress while in treatment and during early recovery. The high-achieving woman is usually in a responsible and visible position. Her sudden departure and return may raise questions. If she is sent to a detox or treatment facility, her absence will not be elaborated on except to say that she will be out of the office. Strict confidentiality is an essential component of all EAPs.

The Role of Inpatient Rehabilitation

In today's managed care climate, a twenty-eight-day stay in an inpatient rehabilitation treatment facility is becoming highly unusual. However, many high-achieving women have the money or the insurance to pay for inpatient treatment.

Many rehabs combine group counseling, education, individual counseling, and twelve-step programs to address the needs of the very newly

sober. Interventions are usually behavioral, confrontational, and evoca-
tive of the process of recovery in twelve-step programs.

Many rehabs have been structured to meet the needs of the male
substance abusers who first utilized them. High-achieving women have
a need for connection, for immediate support. Because of the narcissistic injury of facing an addiction and seeking treatment, they reach the
rehab highly vulnerable and in desperate need of positive nurturing and
feedback. Mixed-gender therapy groups invariably inhibit this process.
As a consequence, many excellent rehabs have a separate track for women
or incorporate women's groups into the regular program. Here is the
beginning of the connection women so desire (Miller 1976).

Through the female counselor and the other female patients, these
women begin the important process of sexual identification for the second time. Thus the women's groups and the sober counselor model for a
different kind of femininity—femininity that involves resolve, warmth,
and self protection, as well as empathy and sexuality.

The reentry into the workplace and into society may be more complicated for high-achieving women, many of whom do not have families and must go through the process alone. The shame and silence
around the substance abuse also intensify the isolation. Therefore, an
important contact is a sober woman to introduce the newcomer to AA,
and a pre-scheduled appointment with a psychotherapist or counselor
is critical. Follow-up is crucial for this population in order to continue
on the path to recovery initiated in the rehab.

Group and Individual Psychotherapy

Many high-achieving, substance-abusing women do very well with the
structure and total immersion of the rehabilitation facility, only to slip
on the treacherous rocks of reentry to community, workplace, and family. Rarely do high-achieving women who abuse substances enter treatment through a community mental clinic. Usually such women seek treatment privately with a psychiatrist, psychologist, or clinical social worker.

Successful substance-abusing women are often hungry for contact,
for connection, for an end to their isolation and self-betrayal. Similar to
the benefit of the consciousness-raising groups that existed in the early
stages of the women's movement, the use of weekly small groups for high-
achieving women is highly valuable. The opportunity to learn, identify,
and seek intimacy with others is a profound and stimulating experience,
often resulting in real characterological change. For some women this is
the first real intimacy with other women.

Twelve-Step Programs

Twelve-step programs such as Alcoholics Anonymous (AA) are self-help fellowships based on the twelve steps described in *Twelve Steps and Twelve Traditions* (1952). The only requirement for membership is a desire to stop drinking. "Other facets of this organizational structure include: scheduled meetings, a twenty-four–hour telephone network for immediate intervention, outreach to other alcoholics and sponsorship, whereby a member with long-term sobriety provides voluntary guidance to a beginner" (Spiegel and Mulder 1986, p. 34).

The focus in twelve–step recovery programs is on the inner life, for example, the slogan "recovery is an inside job." Twelve-step programs function like Winnicott's (1975) "good enough mother" or a second-chance family where the damaged and inhibited maturational process can be reexperienced, healed, and integrated. By being held, educated, and cared for, the successful woman can take up the "abandoned bricks of self-actualization" and begin anew (Spiegel 1993, p. 154).

Twelve-step programs address the pervasive narcissism of high-achieving women. The constant opportunity to tell their story (or qualify) and to relate to a group offers the mirroring process that was so missing from the early development of the narcissist. The group norms of consistent and unconditional regard enable the woman to gradually fill the emptiness that indicated a camouflaged and therefore unknown self.

Unfortunately, power and success strivings are not consistent with the emphasis of self-actualization within the framework of a spiritual life. The addict will, through "working the program," access the authentic part of her personality and act on its needs.

Many high-achieving women thrive in the rooms of Alcoholics Anonymous. The flexibility and the anonymity of the twelve-step programs make them often the treatment of choice for these high-achieving women. AA functions on the principle of identifying and sharing the emotions that are compatible with the need for connection and the relational theory developed by Miller (1976). For women who have buried the words for their feelings, hearing the words and experiencing the feelings of others is essential. The sponsorship relationship with another woman (other high-achieving women as well) constitutes the first positive long-term relationship with another woman and is therefore reparative of the profoundly disappointing process of sexual identification. The confusion and ambivalence about being a woman dissipates. Through this process, a woman begins to identify more closely with some of the qualities most identified with women, that is, the need to nurture and enable others.

THE RECOVERY PROCESS

According to a slogan in Alcoholics Anonymous, "It takes two years to get your brains out of hock and three more to unscramble them." Usually early recovery lasts between two and five years. During this time, the woman regains her health and develops a new identity as a person in recovery and one whose commitment to abstinence has stood the stresses of life. Primitive defenses such as denial and projection are replaced with healthier defenses such as rationalization and sublimation. Psychotherapy, both individual and group, greatly enhances the successful resolution of these issues. The issues that commonly emerge are those around intimacy and success.

The following case example illustrates the process of recovery for a woman who was successful in a male-dominated career, who identified with her father by default, whose life became unmanageable because of substance abuse, and who found her way to treatment and eventually sobriety.

Cassandra is a 48-year-old divorced woman who had a very quick and eventually unsustainable professional success. Cassandra grew up in Canada on a farm north of Toronto. She was the third child of a stern and distant mother and an alcoholic father. While attending a well-known university, she met the brother of a publisher of a monthly literary magazine. "Come to New York," he said. "Meet my brother and go to work as a writer." And she did. She was a gifted writer and soon basked in praise, success, and easy money. There were fashion shows, museum openings, photography exhibits. She attended elegant dinners with famous people. What fueled it all was alcohol—alcohol at lunch on white linen tablecloths with the men with whom she worked, alcohol in the evening at dinners and parties, and alcohol on the bed table for lovemaking or sleep. She felt the pressure to keep up with the men with whom she worked. She was one of few women among many men. There was no woman in her professional life to whom she really felt connected.

Cassandra married an important writer twenty-three years her senior who worked on the magazine. He was a star and she was in his orbit. She worked on the magazine for ten years, and her drinking escalated each year. She did not remember the day that it crumbled; she was frequently drunk. Her husband left her for another woman and her boss, the editor, was fired. A new editor came in. She was no longer the favorite daughter, the special writer. Her alcoholic father had died several years ago. She had replaced him with her husband and then with her editor. Now all were gone. There was no understanding, no mourning. Her drinking robbed her of any opportunity for psychological growth.

The drinking had become out of control and was destroying her life. She had the shakes. She suffered the shame of waking up with the morning after hangover and ashamed of her previous night's sexual activities, much of which she could not remember. Finally, when a former friend who was in recovery reached out to her, she was ready to accept help. At the recommendation of her friend she entered a twenty-eight day rehab where she began the long and difficult road to recovery. It was there that she first noticed women. She experienced her counselor as warm and concerned. Power was not an issue. No one there knew that she was an important writer. They were interested in her as a person, not as a writer. She confided her feelings to her roommate and listened to her fellow patients. She was safe for the first time in years.

It was there that she first became introduced to the twelve-step programs. After discharge, she was referred to a psychotherapist in private practice and to AA. She fell in love with the program.

After almost two years of recovery, Cassandra reached a point where inner peace was more important than the glitter and the glamour. She began to slide in her career and question what she was doing. She no longer could write about the superficial things (the opening, the star, and the pretty bow on a frock). Gradually, she began to write for herself on serious topics about women and about art.

CONCLUSION

High-achieving women face myriad challenges as they face the world without substances. They live in an environment that encourages individualism and the attainment of power and devalues a concentration on communication and relationships. Turning to alcohol and drugs to resolve conflicts around gender and success camouflages the issues and numbs the pain and frustration.

The relationship between success for women and addiction is an issue that requires further investigation. Research around the issues of gender role and management style, workplace triggers for relapse, and communication issues will yield important information. How successful women fare over the long run as they try to maintain high-level jobs is a matter of further investigation and research.

How women can retain their unique and authentic selves in certain workplaces remains an unanswered question. Perhaps workplace adjustment to women's needs for connection is a partial response to this dilemma, allowing women to seek and find success with authenticity and speech with "voice."

REFERENCES

Alcoholics Anonymous (1939). New York: Alcoholics Anonymous World Services.

Benjamin, J. (1988). *The Bonds of Love*. New York: Pantheon.

Chodorow, N. (1974). Family structure and feminine personality. In *Woman, Culture and Society*, ed. M. Z. Rosaldo and L. Lamphere. Stanford, CA: University of California Press.

Friedan, B. (1963). *The Feminine Mystique*. New York: Norton.

Froberg, D., Gjerdingen, D., and Preston, M. (1986). Multiple roles and women's health: What have we learned? *Women and Health* 11(20): 79–96.

Gilligan, C. (1982). *In a Different Voice*. Cambridge, MA: Harvard University Press.

—— (1996). *Remembering Iphigenia: voice, resonance and a talking cure*. Paper presented at the Learning from Women Conference, April 26–27, Boston, MA.

Gordon, B. (1989). *I'm Dancing as Fast as I Can*. New York: HarperCollins.

Horner, M.S. (1972). Toward an understanding of achievement-related conflicts in women. *Journal of Social Issues* 28(2):157–175.

Johnson, P. B. (1982). Sex differences, women's role and alcohol use: preliminary national data. *Journal of Social Issues* 38(2):93–116.

Jordan, J. (1996). Relational therapy in a non-relational world. In *Learning from Women*. Conference, April 26–27, Boston, MA.

Jordan, J. V., Kaplan, A. G., Miller, J. B., et al. (1991). *Women's Growth in Connection*. New York: Guilford.

Krueger, D. W. (1984). *Success and the Fear of Success in Women*. Northvale, NJ: Jason Aronson.

LaRosa, J. H. (1990). Executive women and health: perceptions and practices. *American Journal of Public Health* 80:1450–1454.

Lundy, M., and Younger, B. (1994). Forward-women: the invisible majority. In *Empowering Women in the Workplace*, pp. xv–xxvi. New York: Haworth.

Maccoby, E. (1963). Women's intellect. In *The Potential of Women*, ed. S. M. Farber and R. H. L. Wilson, pp. 24–29.. New York: McGraw-Hill.

Miller, J. B. (1976). *Toward a New Psychology of Women*. Boston: Beacon.

Reddy, B. (1994). The emergence of women as a force for change in EAPs. In *Empowering Women in the Workplace*, ed. M. Lundy and B. Younger, pp. 1–9. New York: Haworth.

Shore, E. R. (1992). Drinking patterns and problems among women in paid employment. *Alcohol, Health and Research World* 16(2):160–163.

Spiegel, B. R. (1993). Twelve–step programs as a treatment modality. In *Clinical Work with Substance-Abusing Clients*, ed. S. L. A. Straussner, pp. 153–168. pp.153–168. New York: Guilford.

Spiegel, B., and Mulder, E. A. (1986). The anonymous program and ego functioning. *Issues in Ego Psychology* 9(10):34–42.

Straussner, S. L. A. (1985). Alcoholism in women: current knowledge and implications for treatment. In *Psychosocial Issues in the Treatment of Alcoholism*, ed. D. Cook, S. L. A. Straussner, and C. H. Fewell, pp. 61–77. New York: Haworth.

Twelve Steps and Twelve Traditions (1952). New York: Alcoholics Anonymous World Services.

Van Natta, D. (1995). Publisher arraigned after wife's drug death. *New York Times*, August 8, p. B3.

Wilsnack, R. W., and Cheloha, R. (1987). Women's roles and problem drinking across the lifespan. *Social Problems* 34(3):231–248.

Wilsnack, R. W., and Wilsnack, S. C. (1992). Women, work, and alcohol: failures of simple theories. *Alcoholism: Clinical and Experimental Research* 16(2):172–179.

Wilsnack, R. W., and Wright, S. I. (1991) *Women in predominantly male occupations: Relationships to problem drinking.* Paper presented at the annual meeting of the Society for the Study of Social Problems, Cincinnati, OH, August.

Wilsnack, S. C., Klassen, A. D., Schur, B. E., and Wilsnack, R. W. (1991). Predicting onset and chronicity of women's problem drinking: a five-year longitudinal analysis. *American Journal of Public Health* 81(3): 305–318.

Zimberg, S., Wallace, J., and Blume, S. B. (1987). *Practical Approaches to Alcoholism Psychotherapy*. New York: Plenum.

8

Lesbian Women and Substance Abuse

Eloise Rathbone-McCuan

Diana L. Stokke

There has been speculation that one in three in the lesbian female and gay male population has a problem with chemical dependency (Fifield 1975, Lewis et al. 1982, McKirnan and Peterson 1989a). Although this figure is repeated throughout the sparse literature and tends to be corroborated, at least for gay men, by addictions treatment specialists (Israelstam 1988), "reliable epidemiological estimates, requiring random samples and/or structured comparison groups, are not currently obtainable in stigmatized, hidden populations, such as sexual minorities" (Hall 1990b, p. 110). Therefore, if the assumption is made that in order to know something is true it must be documented by empirical research with large random samples, then the extent of chemical dependency in lesbian women is not known.

Research on possible antecedents to substance abuse has been discussed in the literature, until recently, in terms of what was true for men. Sandmaier (1980) noted that, historically, substance abuse research "barely acknowledges the presence of women" (p. xv). Although there have been a number of U.S. studies that compared consumption rates and drinking patterns of women and men, to date, there has never been a reliable national prevalence and incidence study of women's alcohol and drug use in America. Results of research done on alcoholic or problem-drinking males were generalized to women (as is often the case with medical and health research) without consideration that women have both a distinct biochemical makeup and different socialization from men (Wilke 1994). Even the few large surveys of the homosexual population were done almost exclusively with male subjects (Fifield 1975, Lohrenz et al. 1978, McKirnan and Peterson 1989a). "Women in general and lesbians specifically, even when included in the samples, were not usually taken into account in the conclusions" of research into substance-abusing behaviors (Lewis and Jordan 1989, p. 170).

Women's alcohol and other drug abuse has remained invisible, to a large extent, due to its greater social stigma (Blume 1991, Celentano and McQueen 1984). This minority bias in the alcohol and drug field includes not only gender but also racial/ethnic groups (see, for example, Fellios 1989, Wilsnack and Wilsnack 1991) and sexual orientation minority groups (Israelstam and Lambert 1989, McKirnan and Peterson 1989b, Mongeon and Ziebold 1982). It is only in the last twenty years or so that the multivariate nature of antecedents to chemical dependency have begun to be discussed in the literature *not* in terms of an almost exclusively white, heterosexual male focus.

Whatever the actual incidence of substance abuse might be in the lesbian population, the purpose of this chapter is to discuss issues particularly relevant to the provision of effective services and supports for lesbian women wanting to recover from chemical dependency. This chapter will address factors of etiology, treatment considerations, and perspectives on recovery, and will describe the types of treatment settings available to lesbian women. Lesbian-specific treatment protocols will be suggested.

ETIOLOGY OF SUBSTANCE ABUSE

"The origins of alcohol problems remain obscure. No single factor has been found to explain or predict why some people develop alcohol problems and others do not" (Mendelson and Mello 1985, p. 229). That statement remains true more than a decade later. Probably most substance abuse professionals feel that alcohol and drug abuse have a complex etiology which includes genetic/biochemical, psychological, and social/environmental factors interacting to create a probable cause-and-effect equation. The four or seven or eleven "causes" that lead to substance abuse by Mary, an agnostic, working class lesbian woman of color, are most likely *not* the same four or seven or eleven causes of substance abuse by Larry, a white, heterosexual, Christian, upper middle-class male. There may be many factors at work helping to create the desire or need to abuse chemicals, and "one-size" substance abuse treatment does *not* fit all. In order to address effectively the substance-abusing behaviors of an individual, it is important for the professional to begin to determine the social and historical context of that chemically dependent person's life.

American culture tends to take a simplistic, binary approach to all the major markers identifying individuals. Sex is either female or male (regardless of people who consider themselves transgendered or who have XXY or XYY chromosomes, for example). Sexual orientation is homosexual or heterosexual (despite a growing understanding of bisexuality). Race is thought of as white or people of color (regardless of the percentage of "nonwhite blood" in a person's lineage). Individuals are able-bodied or "handicapped"/differently abled. People are young or they are not.

Such constricted cultural views devalue and stigmatize those characteristics that do not belong to the dominant group. "These perceived differences are used to justify discrimination against, and oppression of, one group of people (women, homosexuals) by another (men, heterosexuals). The creation and exaggeration of difference provide an opportunity to increase the value of one group at the expense of others. Difference is used to create and maintain power" (Ellis and Murphy 1994, p. 48).

When diversity is used to polarize, alienating one person from another in order to foster a hierarchy of dominance, a highly detrimental sense of disconnection between people takes place. As Heyward (1992) noted: "Alienation is not, at root, a feeling. In fact, frequently we do not *feel* alienated at all, which is part of the problem. We learn not to feel, not to see, not to recognize our alienation from one another. But alienation does to our relationships and self-images much what polluted air does to our bodies: it wears us down and, over time, destroys us" (p. 6).

This disconnection from others may be the result of racism, sexism, classism, and other "structures of alienation" (Heyward 1992, p. 6) such as heterosexism[1] or homophobia,[2] as well as other problems or conditions in an individual's development. It is this disconnection or alienation that can be fundamental to a person's desire to numb the pain resulting from such a sense of isolation, thus incubating future chemical dependency in the marginalized individual. Lesbian women, as recipients of multiple forms of societal stigma, are therefore probably at greater risk for addiction as a coping or numbing mechanism.

Historical Link of Alcoholism and Homosexuality

Alcoholism and homosexuality began to be linked together with the rise of the new fields of psychoanalysis and sexology around the turn of the twentieth century, as "more and more behavior and personality characteristics were being related to sex, and theories proliferated based on one or at most a few studies" (Lewis and Jordan 1989, p. 166). These linkages were riddled with moralistic themes of sexual deviance and perversion as causally related to alcoholism. It was proposed that excessive use of "alcohol caused regression to various levels of psychosexual development: to a level of lewdness, to one where sadistic and masochistic tendencies are released, or to a stage where latent homosexuality is released" (pp. 166–167).

As usual, these psychoanalysts and others studying alcohol abuse in the general population focused primarily on men. Only a few studies included a small number of women, most of whom did not meet the re-

---

1. Heterosexism may be defined as "an ideological system that denies, denigrates, and stigmatizes any non-heterosexual form of behavior, identity, relationship, or community" (Herek 1990, p. 316).

2. Homophobia may be defined as "the prejudice, discrimination, and hostility directed at gay men and lesbian women because of their sexual orientation" (Ellis and Murphy 1994, p. 50).

searchers' rather loose criterion for defining homosexuality as "a tendency to associate with one's own sex to the exclusion of the opposite sex" when drinking (Lewis and Jordan 1989, p. 168). Women who overindulged in alcohol were thought to do so to compensate for sexual frigidity or to have gender role conflicts and hence a desire to indulge their masculine side. Clark, in a 1919 article, stated: "Women who have a strong desire for liquor are likely to prove homosexual" (quoted in Lewis and Jordan 1989, p. 170). Riggall, in his 1923 tract *Homosexuality and Alcoholism*, concurred: "Such women as drink [sic] will frequently show strong homosexual tendencies. Whereas men, however, drink to overcome the repression of natural homosexuality, women are more likely to drink to bring out the male side of their bisexuality" (quoted in Lewis and Jordan 1989, p. 170). Little, if any, empirical data supported these rather bizarre contentions rooted in sexist attitudes, but it was not until the 1960s that the supposed causal connection between homosexuality and alcoholism, as two diseases that might be cured by the medical profession, began to fade in popularity.

Homosexuality and Stigma

The pathologization of homosexuality itself began to be challenged with the rise of the gay liberation movement. Previously considered a psychiatric disorder, the classification of homosexuality was downgraded to an "orientation disturbance" in the 1973 American Psychiatric Association's (APA) *Diagnostic and Statistical Manual of Mental Disorders (DSM-II)*. Mental health professionals began to identify homophobia, which contributed to a negative sense of self, as the locus of distress for lesbian women and gay men, not homosexuality per se (Weinberg 1972). If there was any link between homosexuality and substance abuse, then, it was the narcotizing effect chemicals had to numb the feelings of "society's hatred becom[ing] internalized as self-hatred" (Nicoloff and Stiglitz 1987, p. 286).

DMS-III (1980) further modified its pathologization of homosexuality, and the current *DSM-IV* (1994) contains just a one-sentence reference to sexual orientation as a "sexual disorder not otherwise specified" only if there is a "persistent and marked distress about sexual orientation."

As gender-based theories began to emerge in social science research, feminist analysis voiced a radical alternative to the pathologizing explanations for all forms of "mental illness" among women such as chemical abuse, depression, and menopausal symptoms. Long-discussed popular concepts such as "sex [sic] role conflict" (i.e., women unable to accept societally determined "appropriate" behaviors of work, sexuality, demeanor, etc.) as possible precipitators of chemical dependence—which located the problem in the individual—slowly began to be replaced by a feminist understanding of structural gender oppression (Nichols 1985). The intrapsychic pain caused by the diminished opportunities and stigmatized identity of "woman" in a misogynist, male-dominated world could then be seen as a possible antecedent to substance abuse. Hence, lesbian women suffer, at the very least, a doubly stigmatized identity in this culture. Other personal characteristics that this society also devalues, such as race, age, victimization, or disability, also contribute to stigma.

Lesbians and Childhood Abuse

Many substance abuse professionals, as well as therapists and other counselors, anecdotally note the apparently high percentage of lesbians who have suffered childhood abuse and sexual victimization. Again, little empirical data is available to corroborate this observation. Perhaps the largest survey of lesbian women (N = 1566) to inquire about a history of childhood sexual victimization (Loulan 1987) revealed that 38 percent acknowledged such an abuse history. A nationwide survey by Grundlach (1977) revealed a much elevated percentage of sexual abuse survivors in the 225 lesbians participating in the study, as compared to a heterosexual control group. Several smaller studies (N = < 50) in the 1980s have found similarly high rates of sexual abuse survivors among lesbian women (Brady 1992). Small samples and other methodological problems prevent the extrapolation of these data, however.

A clinical issue that occasionally arises as a result of noting the large number of lesbians who have been sexually victimized is whether the sexual abuse (i.e., "a bad experience with a man") is responsible for turning a particular woman into a homosexual. It should be obvious that if it were that easy to make someone a lesbian, then perhaps most of the female population might be bisexual or lesbian. Indeed, the majority of women with a history of sexual victimization in childhood identify themselves as heterosexual. While many lesbian women see no correlation between their sexual orientation and a history of abuse, a significant number of lesbians do feel, however, that their early childhood abuse experiences may have affected the "choice" of their orientation to some extent (Brady 1992).

What is far more certain in the literature is the correlation between having a history of childhood sexual abuse and being a substance abuser (Barrett and Trepper 1991, Cohen and Densen-Gerber 1982, Hurley 1991, Janikowski and Glover 1994, Neisen and Sandall 1990, Rohsenow et al. 1988). Researchers have found it is a common phenomenon to use and abuse chemical substances to deaden the psychic pain resulting from sexual trauma. Professionals must be aware that in the process of treatment and recovery, abstinence/sobriety may uncover emotional, physical, and behavioral symptomatology of posttraumatic stress disorder (PTSD) previously masked through self-medication with drugs and alcohol.

Treatment Issues

Some of the environmental constraints that affect service delivery to lesbian women include heterosexist and homophobic attitudes, racism, absence of social supports, and resistance from significant others (Hall 1994). There are other constraints, also. Unfortunately, even when a lesbian woman is able to confront her chemical abuse and opt for recovery, she often experiences difficulty in finding an appropriate inpatient treatment center to fit her needs. To begin with, inadequate economic resources or health care coverage are frequently encountered by marginalized people such as lesbian women. "Unlike gay men, lesbians also face socioeconomic discrimination based on gender" (Underhill 1991, p. 73).

Mainstream treatment centers are designed to service a heterosexual, predominantly male population. These facilities are not compatible with the treatment needs of lesbian women for a variety of reasons. The majority of lesbian women who manage to gain access to inpatient substance abuse treatment will probably participate in programs that are dominated by male staff and male clients. The lesbian client not only encounters sexism but blatant homophobia that can quickly undermine treatment. The presence of other female clients and staff does not necessarily lessen or eliminate negative attitudes toward women who identify themselves as lesbians.

> Lesbian alcoholics are even more marginal and, therefore, more highly stigmatized as women alcoholics. They must cope with the standard stereotyping attitudes about alcoholics: that they are weak willed, irresponsible, immoral, and emotionally disturbed. Moreover, they bear the stigma of being women and being lesbians. Considering the negative social meanings traditionally attributed to lesbians' identity, taking on another stigma by identifying oneself as alcoholic and seeking treatment must be difficult indeed for many lesbian women. [Hall 1990a, pp. 94–95]

Treating Lesbians in Mainstream Programs

Many mainstream programs have limited space for women, and what space they do have often provides inadequate physical facilities or safety.

They often have little incentive to adapt their programs (out of ignorance or sexist assumptions) to meet the needs of women, let alone lesbian women, as a minority population, because of judgmental attitudes toward homosexuality. Hence there may be a general lack of interest in identifying lesbian clients through intake and assessment protocols, unless mandated in policy, because of both a sexist and heterosexist world view.

Mainstream treatment centers usually have few or no "out" lesbian or gay staff, unless they are in large cities with a significant lesbian and gay population and therefore may have created a special track in their program for this population. Mainstream treatment personnel often have limited, if any, knowledge of abstinence and community support resources for lesbian women. There is frequently little to no training regarding appropriate treatment needs of lesbian women because of that same heterosexist view which suggests that first, lesbian women do not exist, and secondly, if they do, they should be ashamed of themselves because of their deviant lifestyle and encouraged to become heterosexual. Unfortunately, such an attitude is much more common than many professionals might think. This attitude is especially pronounced with religious-affiliated treatment programs that are often located in private hospitals. Many of these programs directly discourage positive recognition of lesbian women in their facilities because of denominational dogma opposing homosexuality. As exemplified in the following case example, religious or sexual orientation conversion (called *reparative therapy*) sometimes becomes the focus of "treatment" rather than addressing the chemical dependence primarily.

Beth is a 37-year-old, white social science teacher at a university-affiliated high school. Her alcohol abuse peaked when she was being pressured by her partner to become more political and be an "out" lesbian. Beth feared she would suffer professional and social repercussions from being identified as a "dyke." Beth came to the conclusion she might have a problem with alcohol after one of a long history of holidays and weekends, often spent alone, in a binge and blackout spree. Beth contacted her school's counselor with whom she was friendly to ask for a referral to an alcoholism treatment center. The only program the counselor knew offhand was a religious-affiliated program in a local hospital.

Beth attempted to ward off her trepidation at taking this step by bringing some of her favorite mementos including a picture of her and her partner at their commitment ceremony, her favorite volume of lesbian love poems, and a book of lesbian fiction.

After Beth checked into the hospital unit and was assigned a detox monitoring bed, a nurse began to help her unpack. Beth recalled her first overt signal she was to encounter pervasive homophobia: "I put my personal possessions on the desk before unpacking my clothes. When I turned toward the dresser, I saw the nurse flipping through my short story collection as if it were pornography. I said 'I'm a lesbian' without really thinking about it first. The nurse dropped my book with disgust, and told me that *that* was perfectly obvious and she would be making a notation to that effect in the admittance summary that my primary counselor would read in the morning."

One of the major, mandatory treatment modules in this treatment program was to be "Group Sharing of Love from Loved Ones," where each patient was required to receive letters of love and support from family or friends that would be read by another patient with whom she was closest during a group therapy session. Beth recounted: "I felt a total sense of panic. I didn't think I could get any of my lesbian friends to write a 'straight'-sounding letter of sisterly affection, and I was too ashamed to tell my family I was in treatment for alcoholism. So I decided to write the letter myself and claim it had been sent by a 'loving friend.' I don't think I ever felt so isolated in my life—not even on my worst drunk. I felt a kind of oppressive terror rise up in me, and after that 'therapeutic love-in' I just walked out the front door of that place and took a cab back home. I was too ashamed to talk about what happened to me in that treatment center and too afraid to stay sober for long."

On reflection, Beth felt the most destructive part of her experience at this treatment center was her primary counselor's unrelenting attempts to have Beth seek help from the program's chaplain in order to overcome her "sexual deviance" through spiritual guidance.

Beth had two more years of painful drinking before she was able to access a more appropriate treatment center for her needs and achieve a stable sobriety.

Lesbians in Women's Treatment Facilities

Some lesbian women may be able to access an all-women's inpatient treatment setting. Some of the problems that any woman might encounter in mainstream programs (e.g., inability to accept pregnant clients because of liability insurance, no provision for child care and on-premise residence) are usually handled with greater ease in an all-women's treatment center. While there are a number of all-women's recovery centers that emphasize women's strengths and empowerment, the source of funding all too often dictates more limited policy parameters. Treatment guidelines are frequently set down, even in women's programs, by white, Christian, heterosexual men with a traditional Alcoholics Anonymous (AA) focus. Women's treatment environments may be supportive to women, but they may also exhibit the same heterosexist and homophobic bias as a mainstream program and thus are insensitive to the realities of a lesbian lifestyle.

Heterosexism still leads some people to think that lesbian women "can't have children," or if they do, they will be bad parents and possibly molest them because of their "perversion." Kelly and Jamie encountered these attitudes from clients *and* staff in their all-women's residential treatment program.

Kelly and Jamie entered an all-women's residential substance abuse treatment program as an "out" lesbian couple when Jamie was eight months pregnant. Jamie, an African-American woman in her late twenties, discovered that she was pregnant following a rape by a neighborhood drug dealer. She returned to heavy crack cocaine use mid-point in her pregnancy after several months of abstinence. Kelly was an Asian-Irish real estate broker in her early thirties. Both women had an extended history of alcohol abuse, accentuated with periodic drug binges. Both women had attempted to stay clean and sober at various times in their lives, but sobriety had been transitory, and neither had been in formal treatment before. The women decided they wished to keep Jamie's baby and co-parent, regardless of how it was conceived. In order to become better parents, they each pledged to get clean and sober.

Jamie, however, remained a resident only long enough to deliver her baby and abandon it into Kelly's care. She then disappeared completely. Kelly stayed in treatment and the aftercare program to see if she could maintain her sobriety and fight for custody of Jamie's infant son Shakeen. Kelly felt that Jamie either must have died of an overdose or been murdered by the drug dealer; otherwise, she would have returned.

"We were told at admissions that the staff had never seen a couple like us before. I guess that meant an interracial lesbian couple trying to get their act together before the baby was born. The staff—I don't know, they just seemed to have a hard time with the pregnancy of a dyke. The counselors, they just tried to ignore the basic truth about who we were, that's all, like they wanted to ignore my role in the kid's future."

Compartmentalizing by the staff was evident in difficulties over allowing Kelly to participate in off-site programs about the care of high-risk drug-dependent infants. Whenever topics of family or building a sober life with one's significant other were being discussed in group with residents, no staff would address the issues Jamie and Kelly might face in their relationship in early recovery.

"I guess I got pretty good treatment from the standpoint of my needs as an independent woman. The point is, I wasn't an independent woman—I was part of a lesbian *couple*, and that never really got recognized. The worst part of the whole thing, I think, for me anyway, was seeing Jamie get attacked by the other women there as unfit to be a mother because she was a lesbian. I mean, who are they? Addicts, poor, no education, battered or whatever, they still felt like they were more fit to be a parent than a dyke. The staff never stopped it or took our side. Maybe that's what sent Jamie back out. I don't know."

Gay-Specific Treatment

There are no lesbian-only residential treatment programs at this time, although a few inpatient substance abuse programs are dedicated to serving both the lesbian *and* gay male population. These programs are affirming of lesbian women and gay men. But even in these settings, lesbians often find themselves in a very small minority. The preeminent reason for this is economic. Lesbians, as women, tend to have lower socioeconomic status, and because of that, less comprehensive health insurance, so they are less likely to be able to access this type of program.

Because lesbians are in the minority in gay-affirming programs, they may find themselves, again, battling a male-dominated, often sexist world view that could negatively impinge on their vision of recovery. Gender and sexual orientation must be coequal issues for the lesbian woman to receive appropriate intervention. "Lesbians differ from gay men in many respects of their lives, just as men differ from women. From health care issues to the dynamics of intimacy in a couple, lesbian issues are by and large women's issues" (Underhill 1991, p. 73).

Suzanna, a 45-year-old, white, corporate middle manager, was convinced by her Employee Assistance Program (EAP) counselor to enter inpatient treatment. She made a decision to go to a lesbian- and gay-specific substance abuse treatment center covered by her insurance. Suzanna was sure that she could not get sober unless she was free to acknowledge and affirm her lesbian identity, since it was partly the dissonance between her public and private personae that was creating so much distress in her.

The inpatient population at the treatment facility was predominantly men. Two women clients who were there when Suzanna was admitted were discharged a few days later just as she was finishing her detox monitoring.

"I was assigned to the group with the most senior lesbian counselor. Even though I was the only woman patient, I felt some immediate rapport with a couple of men in my first group. We shared a lot of our ambivalence and fears about 'coming out' in our local communities in order to protect jobs, family members, and partners. We had a lot of common ground around struggling with 'the closet.'

"I'm a lesbian feminist politically, but not a separatist. I've always gotten along with gay men pretty well. But after awhile in these groups, I began to feel like these guys were always in my face. Everything began to feel like it was dominated by male presence, male issues, male histories. It felt like I was immersed in a hypermale culture, which, come to think of it, I was. None of them seemed very political. For me, a big motivation for getting sober was to stop being afraid and get more involved in the gay rights movement.

"One day we all attended a session on gay victimization. All the guys wanted to talk about was gay-bashing. I kept trying to talk about woman-hating and the sexual victimization that had been done to me because I was a female child and a woman. When I talked about being molested at age 4, I didn't feel as if any of those men were connecting to what I was saying at all. I tried to talk about how I used alcohol to blur the flashbacks, but I got no feedback, nothing but blankness and silence. Then later, some of these same guys from my group came up to me and started to tell me about their own sexual victimization as children.

"During the rest of my treatment, I became the safe place for lots of these men to dump their own sexual abuse histories. I *really resented* being placed in a position of woman comforting man as I listened to their stories. There were times I wanted to scream at them about all their anger at mothers who didn't protect them, or sisters who broke their secrets of early incest, instead of righteous rage at their male perpetrators. I became their 'mother confessor,' and I felt trapped in that old role of supportive, silent female . . . or maybe *silenced* would be a better word, because that's effectively what happened. Nobody, not even the lesbian counselors, seemed to know how to give me the space to be a woman. My lesbian being was treated in a genderless manner, and the female part of me was put on the back burner much of the time I was in treatment."

The case illustrations presented reflect common varieties of problems, needs, and strengths that lesbian women bring to treatment and recovery. Both blatant and more subtle sexism and homophobia suffuse the treatment options open to them. Mainstream, women-only, and gay-designated treatment programs all have some characteristics that may work against the full recovery potential of lesbian clients. Because of the attitudes and behaviors of some staff and other clients in treatment, lesbian women may feel forced to remain silent about a core part of their identity, diverting their energies from treatment participation to self-protection from aggressively hostile, demeaning statements. The presence of such behavior is intolerable and severely destructive to recovery if ignored or tacitly or openly condoned by treatment staff.

Outpatient Treatment

Major changes in how addictions are treated will occur as battles rage over health care modalities. Inpatient treatment for chemical dependency is less likely to be the paradigm of choice as insurance reimbursement shrinks and discussion of the medical perspectives of addiction as "illness" takes a moralizing turn towards criminalization (Andrews and Patterson 1995, Wilton 1991). Treatment, when available at all, will increasingly be on an outpatient basis.

Many of the issues for lesbians in residential treatment are true for outpatient treatment also. Perhaps the most salient difference for outpatients is that there is no built-in support system to assist in recovery as generally exists in residential treatment. When the lesbian woman does not have a strong gay community in her area for support, she is likely to be even more silenced about her lesbian status. Thus the issue of lesbian community social supports becomes even more important in the context of a heterosexist and homophobic culture.

One of the ways women's or community health care venues can address this seriously underserved population of lesbian women is to include articles targeted to lesbian health care, including substance abuse information and resources, in health care newsletters. An important yet often under-recognized health issue for lesbian substance abusers is their risk for acquiring the Human Immunodeficiency Virus (HIV). While lesbian women are considered to be among the lowest risk groups for HIV infection, it is not sexual identity but sexual practices and substance-abusing behaviors that are the most likely determinants for seropositivity. Studies have shown that drug abusers, including lesbians, are more likely to practice unsafe sex (Kravis et al. 1991) and thereby contract HIV or exacerbate HIV-related illness.

Health care providers and others in the lesbian and gay community must advocate for more balance in the range of lesbian women's health concerns that are discussed in gay community publications. Too often these publications are biased toward male issues because they are seen as the primary economic target of advertisers.

Lesbian Treatment Protocols

Appropriate substance abuse treatment for lesbian women, whether in-patient or outpatient, must first and foremost recognize the social context in which lesbians drink and use drugs (Deevey and Wall 1993) as a stigmatized class of individuals: as both women and homosexuals. Treatment must take place in an environment that is not just nonheterosexist, nonsexist, nonhomophobic, but *affirming* of the client's lesbian status (Neisen 1994). It should go without saying that the environment needs to be safe, physically and emotionally, with well-trained, empathic service providers. The environment should offer safeguards (i.e., adequate staffing, supervision, and training opportunities) to prevent the all-too-frequent problem of staff burnout.

Staff should have a feminist consciousness and be able to offer an analysis of the political factors invested in the continuing use and abuse of chemicals by lesbians, that is, "drugs and alcohol are provided in order to keep people under control. Addiction takes away the focus and power of minority individuals and communities, keeping them ineffective in the world" (Nicoloff and Stiglitz 1987, p. 286).

Holistic educational modules should be offered that not only address the damaging physical realities of addictive chemicals but also include work on self-image and pride in lesbian identity. One of the transformations that needs to take place in recovery is a movement toward a well-integrated, self-affirming understanding of lesbian status. "The process of recovery is one of 'de-shaming' a shame-based identity. . . . The tools used in the process of recovery help women de-shame their stigmatized identity" (McNally and Finnegan 1992, pp. 95–96). This is especially important for many lesbians living in rural or semirural communities who may not have been aware, until perhaps their adulthood, that other women like them existed. When options for various ways of being are not available to people in society, the sense of "otherness" that can develop for those who are different often creates internalized feelings of inferiority and unacceptability. Bibliotherapy addressing the *herstory* of important or famous women who are/were lesbian or bisexual and can become role models can act as an anchoring point from which lesbians can start to rebuild their own self-esteem and pride.

Marital status should not be overlooked for its relevance to lesbian women in chemical dependency treatment. A substantial number of lesbian women are involved in legal and sometimes emotionally committed marriages to gay or nongay men, relationships that may have been initiated originally as a denial of lesbian status. Others have formed marriages with or without legal sanction, or gone through commitment rituals with lesbian partners. As the lesbian client seeks to sort out matters relating to her marriage, which may include economic issues, motherhood, and child care concerns, as well as a range of social and psychological issues (including sexual intimacy), it is imperative for treatment staff to provide respectful support throughout this process. Practitioners need to be sensitive to these very complex relationships.

Moreover, practitioners need to recognize the reality of dual diagnosis for some lesbian women (Helfand 1993). Lesbians with treatable psychiatric conditions (e.g., depression, bipolar disorder, etc.), which may have been masked by substance abuse or ignored because of the addiction, may need psychopharmacological intervention. There is frequently a delicate balance to be learned by the addict who may have abused antipsychotic or other prescription drugs in the past, but who now needs similar drugs for healthy functioning.

Lesbians with a history of sexual traumatization must be identified by appropriate intake and assessment protocols (Janikowski and Glover 1994). Unaddressed sexual abuse and its sequelae can be instrumental in substance abuse treatment failure (Root 1989). Staff and counselors need to be aware that PTSD symptomology can become acute as the numbing effects of chemical dependency fade away. Clients must be reassured that they can survive the escalation of these symptoms without resorting to the use and abuse of chemicals, just as they obviously survived the abuse earlier in their lives. The important clinical issue of determining whether the client is able to confront her early abuse history simultaneously with her treatment for chemical dependency needs to be made between client and counselor or therapist. They also need to negotiate the direction, timetable, and modality her recovery should take in order to help empower this client, because control over her life was taken away at an early age by her perpetrator(s). Feeling as if she is the primary agent of her own recovery process is important to a woman disempowered by childhood victimization.

The diversity that is represented in the lesbian population (i.e., race, age, class, etc.) should be represented in the recovery experience. "It is difficult for many patients to recover from substance abuse without role models who demonstrate, through their day-to-day existence, that recovery is possible and perhaps even desirable. Clinical staff from unfamiliar ethnic groups cannot provide this kind of concrete example" (Westermeyer 1995, p. 596). Informal networking among clients can be as powerful an experience promoting recovery as the formal program of treatment. It is important for counselors and staff to affirm the personal insights and realities of each woman as she moves through the recovery process, as well as connect it to the experiences of other recovering women.

Effective treatment should incorporate the client's significant others. If there is a positive relationship between client and family-of-origin members, they should be invited to become a part of the client's recovery—with her consent, of course. Unfortunately, all too often there has been a rift between the client and her family of origin because of her sexual orientation and/or other reasons. The client may need support in exercising boundary control with these family members, possibly excluding them from the purposeful, positive experience she is attempting to create should the relationship continue to be toxic. Or she may need help in learning how to communicate with these family members. Members of the client's family of choice should also be encouraged to participate in the recovery process.

Both gender and sexual orientation oppression tend to limit the ability of lesbian women to access work commensurate with their talents. Therefore, the more limited economic resources of many lesbian women will tend to limit their access to the specialized treatment they need for optimal recovery potential. Financial flexibility is needed in programs addressing the treatment needs of this population through aggressive fundraising, special grants, and other financial supports.

Finally, post-discharge support systems must be in place and discussed with the client. Most treatment centers provide six months to a year of aftercare for their clients, with differential payment options. Other appropriate supports such as Women for Sobriety groups, Alcoholics Anonymous, or Rational Recovery groups should be strongly encouraged.

Women for Sobriety (WFS) is a single-gender self-help group with a primary goal of rebuilding women's self-esteem. Rather than the negative focus of AA (on past drinking and problematic behaviors), the founder of WFS, Jean Kirkpatrick, believes that "faulty thinking underlies destructive behavior and can be corrected by the power of positive thinking. WFS teaches that women have the power to change their way of thinking and that their very mental images, whether negative or positive, directly shape their actions. . . . WFS and AA meetings differ in structure, format, and program philosophy" (Kaskutas 1994, pp. 188–189). WFS groups are sometimes difficult to find because WFS views recovery as a finite process, unlike AA which considers that once persons are alcoholic they remain alcoholic all their lives and the recovery process is ongoing. Rational Recovery, another cognitive-behavioral sobriety support program, also considers recovery to have an endpoint. Women may combine WFS and AA or Narcotics Anonymous (NA) meetings the better to meet their needs (Kaskutas 1992).

Alcoholics Anonymous is the original twelve-step support group for alcoholics, started in the mid-1930s by two middle-class, Christian, white men. Narcotics Anonymous is a twelve-step program based on the same precepts as AA, but more specifically addressing drugs other than alcohol. Many lesbian women find AA or other twelve-step programs to have too much sexist, racist, homophobic, and otherwise insensitive language for their taste. They don't like the concept of *powerlessness* that is a seminal concept of these programs, feeling that lesbians are all too knowledgeable about the lack of actual power women have in this society. They prefer to think of women being empowered in their struggle against addiction. However, the near universality of AA and NA throughout the country, as well as the AA program's dictum—take what you like and leave the rest—allows many lesbian women to utilize these sources of sobriety maintenance as part of the bedrock of their abstinence.

In addition, many medium to larger size cities have lesbian-specific AA or NA groups. These groups can be a powerfully positive sobriety resource for lesbian women. However, in smaller communities, a lesbian AA/NA group can often become somewhat "incestuous" as lesbians look for romance and partners from the small group of clean and sober lesbian women they meet in recovery. The potential for relapse increases when a couple breaks up, and each woman may feel uncomfortable attending the lesbian AA/NA meeting so as not to continually encounter her ex-lover. Friends of the couple may feel they have to take sides in the relationship split, and one or both recovering women may lose an important source of sobriety support.

Harm-reduction theories of substance abuse which posit that complete abstinence from drugs may not be possible or even necessary for all addicts have little currency in mainstream chemical dependency treatment. Harm reduction suggests that for some addicted people, total abstinence will never become a reality, and therefore needle exchange programs, government controlled access to drugs like heroin, or increased availability of methadone will lessen the incidence of crime and diseases such as HIV that often result from addiction to illegal drugs. Treatment modalities such as methadone maintenance may offer substantial amelioration to an addict's life in that it reduces her exposure to the dangers inherent in accessing illegal drugs, as well as possibly reducing HIV seroprevalence (Nathan and Karan 1989). This intervention does not equate to recovery, however. There are recent initiatives among some clients of methadone maintenance treatment programs (MMTPs) to establish methadone twelve-step groups. These individuals perceive the use of medically dispensed methadone, used to block the craving for illegal opiates, as an important support in their pursuit of recovery through twelve-step methods.

RECOVERY PERSPECTIVES

Recovery is an evolving concept for many people. Some see it as a multidimensional change process that incorporates identification of addiction problems and participation in interactions that alter meanings, behaviors, self-images, and world views as a means to enhance life and growth (Hall 1994). It can be a long-term process of transformation that originates within and impacts upon a person's physical, spiritual, and sociocultural life (Hall 1990b). It involves internal and external change (Underhill 1991). This process helps people learn (or relearn) to love and respect their bodies, increase self-esteem, take pleasure in work and activities of daily living, while respecting and enjoying others simply for being who they are (Heyward 1992).

Recovery is also about owning individual responsibility and coming to understand the need for society's transformation from discrimination against lesbians to acceptance and affirmation of diverse expressions of sexuality. A feminist consciousness, "as applied to addiction issues, emphasizes that recovery is a paradoxical process that does not take place in a vacuum. It involves surrendering to the uncontrollable (the addiction) and empowering the controllable (responsibility to self). The challenge . . . is to design and deliver services that address the devastation of the addiction process in a way that empowers lesbians to make the internal and external changes necessary to recovery" (Underhill 1991, pp. 83–84).

There are many different ways that lesbian women view their healing process from alcoholism or drug addiction. Hall (1992) suggests that some may have an understanding of this process as one of conversion, similar to the concept presented by Alcoholics Anonymous "reflected in the format of telling one's story in AA: What it was like, what happened, and what it is like now. In religious terms this might be expressed as sin or moral decline, transformation, and then moral virtuousness" (p. 95).

Still others may have a variety of images of recovery, conceptualizations that encompass the totality of meanings relative to their recovery experience across the physical, metaphysical, mental, and emotional spectrum and that may fluctuate according to the temporal and experiential reference point in their recovery process.

Hall (1992) suggested a number of recovery images (i.e., recovery as physical transition, personal growth, struggle with compulsivity, reclaiming the self, connection and reconnection, empowerment, social transition) as areas in which lesbians often find transformation and sometimes transcendence in recovery. Other images of recovery that can be important to this process include cyclic/celebration, vocational change, and spiritual transformation.

Members of Alcoholics Anonymous often refer to alcoholism as a "disease of isolation." "Social isolation is a problem common to alcoholics. This problem for the lesbian alcoholic is doubled since it is also one of the most devastating aspects of lesbian life. Many lesbians are well into their adult lives before they meet other lesbian women or even recognize their own homosexuality" (Underhill 1991, pp. 77–78). Many of the images that Hall identifies have the outcome of reducing social isolation, a key issue in so many lesbian women's lives. But that may not be enough. "We cannot heal diseases of isolation, loneliness, and disconnection primarily by helping people feel more autonomous, separate and on their own. . . . We are interdependent and interactive" (Heyward 1992, p. 12). These images of recovery can help restore lesbian women's spirits damaged by addiction and oppression.

Recovery as Physical Transition

Years of substance abuse can do great harm to the physical well-being of lesbian women, disrupting their menstrual and reproductive cycles, exacerbating migraines, neurological problems, permanent disabilities and malnutrition, as well as precipitating accidental or intentional injuries and liver problems, to name a few. Many lesbian women, suspicious of the traditional Western medical establishment that has pathologized their existence in the past, may embrace holistic health care and alternative medical resources as they begin to honor and respect their bodies by terminating the abuse of chemicals. These approaches, sometimes including herbal remedies, many types of massage and body work, acupuncture, and the like, are available from feminist practitioners and female spiritualists who may attend to points of psychic stress and anxiety. These alternative sources of healing are highly valued in most nonlesbian and lesbian women's communities.

Recovery as Personal Growth

Once free from the self-destructive influences of drug or alcohol dependency, lesbian women begin to discover anew the infinite possibilities for personal development. Self-imposed isolation may become a lifestyle choice for a lesbian involved in addiction, so the destruction of that wall of isolation that is initiated by recovery must continue to eradication. Sometimes self-imposed isolation is a result of a generalized rage at perceived or actual social or personal injustices suffered by lesbian women in a society that hates and fears homosexuals. One of the tasks of recovery is the transformation of that anger and rage into assertive expression and actions that can help ameliorate, change, or transcend those injustices. Helping lesbian women find ways to apply assertiveness techniques and to explore their anger are important pieces in the recovery process.

Building a social network that can help a woman progress beyond her internal and interpersonal isolation will not occur without a concerted effort at engagement. In Alcoholics Anonymous, for instance, people with more sobriety become sponsors to newcomers and often act as social outreach coaches and facilitators for women attempting to establish new relationships in the early stages of recovery, in addition to providing a better understanding of how that program of recovery works. In larger cities, lesbian and gay community centers provide multiple opportunities to become engaged in activities and organizations for alcohol- and drug-free socializing.

Recovery as Struggle with Compulsivity

As a woman's freedom from chemicals becomes well established, she might begin to notice compulsivity in other areas of her life such as overeating, sex or relationships, or gambling. She may again have to examine her personal behaviors, conditions, or situations that have become a source of too much dissonance in her life. She may come to understand that addiction is not only a problem in itself but symptomatic of other problems in her life that she may not want to look at, such as a history of childhood sexual abuse. The successful modeling of other recovering lesbian women can help to inspire and sustain efforts to confront additional addictions, dependencies, or self-injuring behaviors.

Recovery as Reclaiming the Self

As previously noted, apparently a large percentage of lesbian women have suffered childhood abuse. As the anesthetizing effects of abused chemicals disappear, the long-suppressed or repressed pain and rage surrounding early traumatization may surface. This kind of emotional roller coaster puts women in some jeopardy for relapse as they seek to escape intense emotions and flashbacks. Although mutual aid alternatives do exist in some communities for healing from childhood damage, it is usually necessary and preferable to seek trained professional assistance to help manage and dissipate the ongoing and further damaging symptoms of chronic PTSD.

It is also important to note that some lesbian women may have been involved in physically abusive relationships with other women. A battering relationship, regardless of sexual orientation, is based on issues of power and control. As a stigmatized community, lesbian women do not often wish to acknowledge that battering occurs in some lesbian relationships, fearing that other people will see them as even more pathological than they might already. This tends to silence lesbian women about this kind of abuse, further isolating them and contributing to the internalization of guilt and shame about this issue. If not addressed, abusive relationships, current or past, can detrimentally affect recovery from substance abuse.

Recovery as Connection/Reconnection

Throughout the recovery process, lesbian women may find it necessary to engage in an inventory process (known in AA as the "Fourth Step") to assess the status of their life and relationships. This can include an appraisal of broken or dysfunctional family-of-origin relationships to see which, if any, of these intergenerational or multigenerational ties might be mended. Frequently, rifts occur between family-of-origin members and the lesbian woman if she has "come out" and disclosed her sexual orientation at some point in the past. Heterosexist prejudice can be so strong, often coupled with anti-gay religious dogma, that parents will reject and disown a child who declares her sexual identity to be lesbian. Parents and siblings may have taunted or abused the lesbian woman because of her sexual identity. Or the lesbian woman may have opted for preempting the rejection she felt surely awaited her if she were to declare herself and unilaterally separated herself from family. Or the rest of her family may still be in the throes of their own addictions, and the woman may wish to distance herself from the addicted family system as a self-protective measure for the sake of her own sobriety.

Whatever the circumstances in the past, with the passage of time, the recovering lesbian woman may feel freer to engage with her addicted or antigay family on various levels. Some aspects of family dysfunction may begin to be resolved through her own sober behavior modeling. But whether other family members enter recovery or not, the recovering lesbian woman must determine her own ground rules for interaction with her family and set clear boundaries in order to protect her sobriety. This selective process may also apply to friendships and other relationships formed during her "active" years. This may also include a reconnecting to cultural and ethnic heritage, rituals, and ceremonies, as well as pride. For example, for an African-American or Native American lesbian it may involve a reinvestment in extended families of choice and culture-based spirituality (Aguirre-Molina 1991, LaDue 1991, Mora and Gilbert 1991, Taha-Cisse 1991).

Recovery as Cyclic/Celebration

Special holidays, family-of-origin or family-of-choice celebrations, and annual events like birthdays, Gay Pride Day, etc., may be triggers to drink or drug because of remembered emotional highs or lows. These celebratory events frequently must be reframed within a clean and sober context. Christmas Day might be spent doing volunteer work at a shelter for the homeless or mentally ill as a reconstructed way of giving, devoid of "slippery" family traditions. Sobriety anniversaries can become new, important clean and sober celebrations. The annual anniversary of the founding of a lesbian AA group would be another opportunity for collective celebration. Attendance at one of the many annual gay AA "round-ups" (a conference for lesbian and gay AA and Al-Anon members to discuss issues of relevance about being lesbian or gay and in recovery), which take place in cities all over the country, offers feelings of reunion and the personal and collective recognition of recovery in the lesbian and gay community.

Recovery as a Vocational Change

One of the short- and long-range outcomes of recovery is the potential to restructure the role of work in women's lives in ways that make it a previously unknown source of meaning and reward. In addition to the devastating economic consequences that may be an outcome of addiction, it is also possible to have lost the ability to concentrate, retain information, enjoy physical dexterity, and sustain a belief in personal capabilities. The realization that change is possible and that hopes and dreams, long delayed or abandoned, might be realized comes with recovery. Joblessness can be replaced with employment, offering economic security and personal satisfaction. Old jobs can be left behind and new ones found. Career advancements become possible that were previously beyond reach, and capacities for new learning can be acted upon, whether in the workplace or in the pursuit of higher education.

Recovery as Empowerment

Recovery may bring a new desire and capability for becoming personally and politically integrated in sectors of lesbian and gay community life that were previously foreign or threatening. The growth of self, the beginnings of a new life of openness and pride, may start by throwing off the burden of internalized and externalized demoralization and stigma resulting from homophobia. Participation in voluntary social action or political involvement may lead to an inner and outer comfort with one's lesbian lifestyle. Personal pride from having entered into a recovery process from addiction may be a necessary but insufficient step in the vital process of self-acceptance and freedom from society's shaming of lesbian identity.

Recovery as Social Transition

Aloneness and isolation are so much a part of the addiction lifestyle that many lesbian women have to learn to rebuild social relationships from the most basic friendships to lover/partnerships. Often lesbian women find a new self-awareness and sense of confidence that allows them to make a closer inspection of their role in previous dysfunctional or codependent relationships with partners, friends or family, and in work situations. They may learn to replace outmoded ways of relating with an enduring sense of interdependency between self and others. Learning how to be with self, overcoming the fear and boredom of one's own company, may be the basic foundation in building life-enhancing social ties.

Recovery as Spiritual Transformation

Many lesbian women have turned away from traditional religions that might moralize against homosexuality and that tend to be dominated by men who refuse to share ecclesiastical power in their denomination with women. In so doing, addicted lesbians may descend into what some characterize as "spiritual bankruptcy," in that they lose their sense of the divine or a benevolent power in their lives. Many women feel a beginning of reconnection to the spirit as a result of recovery—that, indeed, it was a power greater than themselves that kept them from going completely into the abyss through addiction. For some, going back to a traditional, patriarchy-based religious denomination is not an option. They may choose to involve themselves in women's spirituality groups, such as Womynspirit, or become interested in Wicca, a benevolent "witchcraft" religion based in a love for nature and animals. They may develop their own religion or sense of spirituality which is not based on anyone else's dogma, but rooted in symbols imbued with personal significance to their lives and honored on home altars. Gargaétas (1995) asserts that "altar work is a transformative act which engenders personal wholeness, is certainly beneficial to women's mental health, and is a self-identified aspect of women's culture" (p. 99).

Others may choose to involve themselves in the lesbian/gay offshoots of traditional religions such as Catholicism's "Dignity," Episcopalian "Integrity," or "Lutherans Concerned," or to join the church specifically developed to address the needs of Christian lesbians and gays: Metropolitan Community Church (MCC). Large cities may also have a lesbian/gay Jewish synagogue. Whatever form it may take, recovery reconnects most lesbian women to a sense of the spirit that many thought they had lost or had abandoned them as a result of addiction.

CONCLUSION

Stigmatized sexual orientation, gender oppression, and chemical addiction in combination create devastating consequences for many lesbian women. Population estimates to measure the prevalence of alcohol and illicit and prescribed drug abuse among lesbian women in the United States have not been conducted, and process and outcome research on the substance abuse treatment experiences of lesbians is very limited.

Despite the severely limited research database, there is a growing body of practitioner experience and descriptive reports that indicate that heterosexist-homophobic and sexist conditions interconnected to economic and social conditions are both antecedents and intervening factors in the onset and continuation of, as well as recovery from, chemical abuse.

The application of feminist and empowerment paradigms to the provision of mental health and health care services to lesbian women has reduced the once-unquestioned pathologizing interpretation of a relationship between female sexual "deviance" and substance abuse. A feminist approach to needs assessment and service delivery has been proposed as a more effective and appropriate approach to intervention for lesbian women drug addicts and alcoholics. Unfortunately, heterosexist norms still prevail in many mainstream and women's treatment programs.

Managed care may detrimentally impact the modalities and participants in chemical dependency treatment (both staff and clients), as the variety of health care reimbursement options diminish and mainstream facilities may be seen as "good enough" for all. Experience has proven, however, that one-size-fits-all chemical dependency treatment does not work for special populations. This systemic availability limitation and reduced access because of marginalized employment options for many lesbian women loom as powerfully restrictive barriers to substance abuse recovery. Practitioners must be aware of and advocate for the services their clients need.

Recovery themes common among lesbian women who are able to progress into long term sobriety are ever-evolving and life-encompassing. Recovery usually demands transformations in vocational and educational areas, relations with partners, friends, and family-of-origin members, as well as spiritual or religious practices. Long-term recovery may be sustained with professional, personal, program, and community supports that can offset, mediate, and help to eradicate the influences of homophobia and sexism, as well as other "structures of alienation" suffered by lesbian women.

REFERENCES

Aguirre-Molina, M. (1991). Issues for Latinas: Puerto Rican women. In *Alcohol and Drugs Are Women's Issues*, ed. P. Roth, pp. 93–100. Metuchen, NJ: Women's Action Alliance and Scarecrow.

American Psychiatric Association. (1973). *Diagnostic and Statistical Manual of Mental Disorders, 2nd ed.* Washington, DC: American Psychiatric Association.

—— (1980). *Diagnostic and Statistical Manual of Mental Disorders, 3rd ed.* Washington, DC: American Psychiatric Association.

——(1994). *Diagnostic and Statistical Manual of Mental Disorders, 4th ed.* Washington, DC: Author.

Andrews, A. B., and Patterson, E. G. (1995). Searching for solutions to alcohol and other drug abuse during pregnancy: ethics, values, and constitutional principles. *Social Work* 40:55–64.

Barrett, B. J., and Trepper, T. S. (1991). Treating women drug abusers who were victims of childhood sexual abuse. In *Feminism and Addiction*, ed. C. Bepko, pp. 127–146. Binghamton, NY: Haworth.

Blume, S. B. (1991). Sexuality and stigma: the alcoholic woman. *Alcohol, Health, and Research World* 15:139–146.

Brady, E. (1992). Psychotherapy issues in working with the lesbian incest survivor. In *Counseling Gay Men and Lesbians: Journey to the End of the Rainbow*, ed. S. H. Dworkin and F. J. Gutierrez, pp. 203–218. Alexandria, VA: American Association for Counseling and Development.

Celentano, D. D., and McQueen, D. V. (1984). Multiple substance abuse among women with alcohol-related problems. In *Alcohol Problems in Women*, ed. S. C. Wilsnack and L. J. Beckman, pp. 97–116. New York: Grune & Stratton.

Cohen, F. S. and Densen-Gerber, J. (1982). A study of the relationship between child abuse and drug addiction in 178 patients: preliminary results. *Child Abuse and Neglect* 6:383–387.

Deevey, S., and Wall, L. J. (1993). How do lesbians develop serenity? In *Lesbian Health: What Are the Issues*, ed. P. N. Stern, pp. 109–118. Washington, DC: Taylor and Francis.

Ellis, P., and Murphy, B. L. (1994). The impact of misogyny and homophobia on therapy with women. In *Women in Context*, ed. M. P. Mirken, pp. 48–73. New York: Guilford.

Fellios, P. G. (1989). Alcoholism in women: causes, treatment and prevention. In *Alcoholism and Substance Abuse in Special Populations*, ed. G. W. Lawson and A. W. Lawson, pp. 11–36. Rockville MD: Aspen.

Fifield, L. (1975). *On My Way to Nowhere: Alienated, Isolated, Drunk.* Los Angeles: Gay Community Services Center and Department of Health.

Gargaetas, P. (1995). Altared states: lesbian altarmaking and the transformation of self. *Women and Therapy* 16:95–105.

Grundlach, R. (1977). Sexual molestation and rape reported by homosexual and heterosexual women. *Journal of Homosexuality* 2:367–384.

Hall, J. M. (1990a). Alcoholism in lesbians: developmental, symbolic interactionist, and critical perspectives. *Health Care for Women International* 11:89–107.

—— (1990b). Alcoholism recovery in lesbian women: a theory in development. *Scholarly Inquiry for Nursing Practice: An International Journal* 4:109–122.

—— (1992). An exploration of lesbians' images of recovery from alcohol problems. *Health Care for Women International* 13:181–198.

—— (1994). Lesbians recovering from alcohol problems: an ethnographic study of health care experiences. *Nursing Research* 43:238–243.

Helfand, K. L. (1993). Therapeutic considerations in structuring a support group for the mentally ill gay/lesbian population. *Journal of Gay and Lesbian Psychotherapy* 2:65–76.

Herek, G. M. (1990). The context of anti-gay violence: notes on cultural and psychological heterosexism. *Journal of Interpersonal Violence* 5:316–333.

Heyward, C. (1992). Healing addiction and homophobia: reflections on empowerment and liberation. *Journal of Chemical Dependency Treatment* 5:5–18.

Hurley, D. L. (1991). Women, alcohol, and incest: an analytical review. *Journal of Studies on Alcohol* 52:253–268.

Israelstam, S. (1988). Knowledge and opinions of alcohol intervention workers in Ontario, Canada, regarding issues affecting male gays and lesbians, parts I & II. *International Journal of Addictions* 23:227–252.

Israelstam, S., and Lambert, S. (1989). Homosexuals who indulge in excessive use of alcohol and drugs: psychosocial factors to be taken into account by community and intervention workers. *Journal of Alcohol and Drug Education* 34:54–69.

Janikowski, T. P., and Glover, N. M. (1994). Incest and substance abuse: implications for treatment professionals. *Journal of Substance Abuse Treatment* 11:185–195.

Kaskutas, L. A. (1992). Beliefs on the source of sobriety: interactions of membership in Women for Sobriety and Alcoholics Anonymous. *Contemporary Drug Problems* 19:631–641.

—— (1994). What do women get out of self-help? Their reasons for attending Women for Sobriety and Alcoholics Anonymous. *Contemporary Drug Problems* 11:185–195.

Kravis, N. M., Weiss, C. J., and Perry, S. W. (1991). Drug and alcohol addiction and AIDS. In *Comprehensive Handbook of Drug and Alcohol Addiction*, ed. N. S. Miller, pp. 891–904. New York: Marcel Dekker.

LaDue, A. (1991). Coyote returns: survival for Native American women. In *Alcohol and Drugs Are Women's Issues*, ed. P. Roth, pp. 23–31. Metuchen, NJ: Women's Action Alliance and Scarecrow.

Lewis, C. E., Saghir, M. T., and Robins, E. (1982). Drinking patterns in homosexual and heterosexual women. *Journal of Clinical Psychiatry* 43:277–279.

Lewis, G. R., and Jordan, S. M. (1989). Treatment of gay and lesbian alcoholics. In *Alcoholism and Substance Abuse in Special Populations*, ed. E. W. Lawson and A. W. Lawson, 2nd ed. pp. 165–203. Rockhill, MD: Aspen.

Lohrenz, L., Donnelly, J., Coyne, L., and Spare, L. (1978). Alcohol problems in several midwestern homosexual communities. *Journal of Studies on Alcohol* 39:1959–1963.

Loulan, J. (1987). *Lesbian Passion*. San Francisco: Spinsters/Aunt Lute.

McKirnan, D. J., and Peterson, P. L. (1989a). Alcohol and drug use among homosexual men and women: epidemiology and population characteristics. *Addictive Behaviors* 14:545–553.

——(1989b). Psychosocial and cultural factors in alcohol and drug abuse: an analysis of a homosexual community. *Addictive Behaviors* 14:555–563.

McNally, E. B., and Finnegan, D. G. (1992). Lesbian recovering alcoholics: a qualitative study of identity transformation—a report on research and applications to treatment. *Journal of Chemical Dependency Treatment* 5:93–103.

Mendelson, J. H., and Mello, N. K. (1985). *Alcohol: Use and Abuse in America*. Boston: Little, Brown.

Mongeon, J. E., and Ziebold, T. O. (1982). Preventing alcohol abuse in the gay community: toward a theory and model. *Journal of Homosexuality* 7:89–99.

Mora, J., and Gilbert, M. J. (1991). Issues for Latinas: Mexican-American women. In *Alcohol and Drugs Are Women's Issues*, ed. P. Roth, pp. 43–48. Metuchen, NJ: Women's Action Alliance and Scarecrow.

Nathan, J. A., and Karan, L. D. (1989). Substance abuse treatment modalities in the age of HIV spectrum disease. *Journal of Psychoactive Drugs* 21:423–429.

Neisen, J. H. (1994). *Counseling Lesbian, Gay, and Bisexual Persons with Alcohol and Drug Abuse Problems*. Arlington VA: NAADAC Education and Research Foundation.

Neisen, J. H., and Sandall, H. (1990). Alcohol and other drug abuse in a gay/lesbian population: Related to victimization? *Journal of Psychology and Human Sexuality* 3:151–168.

Nichols, M. (1985). Theoretical concerns in the clinical treatment of substance-abusing women: a feminist analysis. *Alcoholism Treatment Quarterly* 2:79–90.

Nicoloff, L. K., and Stiglitz, E. A. (1987). Lesbian alcoholism: etiology, treatment, and recovery. In *Lesbian Psychologies*, ed. Boston Lesbian Psychologies Collective, pp. 283–293. Chicago: University of Illinois Press.

Rohsenow, D. J., Corbett, R., and Devine, D. (1988). Molested as children:

A hidden contribution to substance abuse? *Journal of Substance Abuse Treatment* 5:13–18.

Root, M. P. P. (1989). Treatment failures: the role of sexual victimization in women's addictive behavior. *American Journal of Orthopsychiatry* 59:542–549.

Sandmaier, M. (1980). *The Invisible Alcoholic: Women and Alcohol Abuse in America*. New York: McGraw-Hill.

Taha-Cisse, A. H. (1991). Issues for African-American women. In *Alcohol and Drugs Are Women's Issues*, ed. P. Roth, pp. 54–60. Metuchen, NJ: Women's Action Alliance and Scarecrow.

Underhill, B. L. (1991). Recovery needs of lesbian alcoholics in treatment. In *Feminist Perspectives on Addiction*, ed. N. Van Den Bergh, pp. 73–123. New York: Springer.

Weinberg, G. (1972). *Society and the Healthy Homosexual*. New York: St. Martin's.

Westermeyer, J. (1995). Cultural aspects of substance abuse and alcoholism. *Psychiatric Clinics of North America* 18:589–605.

Wilke, D. (1994). Women and alcoholism: how a male-as-norm bias affects research, assessment and treatment. *Health and Social Work* 19:29–35.

Wilsnack, S. C., and Wilsnack, R. W. (1991). Epidemiology of women's drinking. *Journal of Substance Abuse* 3:133–157.

Wilton, J. M. (1991). Compelled hospitalization and treatment during pregnancy: mental health statutes as models for legislation to protect children from pre-natal drug and alcohol exposure. *Family Law Quarterly* 25:149–170.

9

The Impact of AIDS on the Lives of Women

Ellen Grace Friedman

The impact of the AIDS pandemic on the lives of women has been profound. "HIV infected women grieve every day for their multiple losses—of their health; sense of invulnerability; of their hopes and dreams for the future; of feeling physically desirable; of an unborn child they may have otherwise wanted; of the ability to bear more children; of financial security; and of friends, lovers, spouses, and children who have already died . . ." (Wiener 1991, p. 377).

AIDS is growing twice as fast among women as among men (Finnegan et al. 1994). Despite early widespread media attention to women as vectors of transmission to men and children, women are more likely to become infected by men than to transmit the AIDS virus to men (Padian et al. 1990). Substance abuse plays a crucial role in the lives of HIV-affected women. Not only does substance abuse greatly increase the risk of HIV infection through direct transmission of the virus, but the loss of judgment and impulse control associated with alcohol and other drug use exacerbates risk behaviors. In addition, the codependent role of women increases the chance of their failing to assert themselves successfully in avoiding risk behaviors. Codependency also reinforces the tendency of women to take the role of caregiver to those with AIDS to the point of neglecting their own needs.

The impact of gender on HIV-infected and at-risk women warrants attention and concern. Women, often rendered powerless by dint of poverty and social inequality, must be offered ways to prevent becoming infected and, if infected, to meet the many challenges imposed by their illness. This chapter will discuss the history of women and AIDS, review current information, and address ways of enhancing clinicians' practice with women affected by AIDS. It provides information about women who inject drugs, women who become infected via heterosexual and lesbian sexual behaviors, and women in relational roles as mothers and caregivers to family members with AIDS.

CURRENT EPIDEMIOLOGY OF AIDS AMONG WOMEN

By the end of December 1995, the Centers for Disease Control and Prevention reported 71,818 cases of women with AIDS (Centers for Disease

The author wishes to thank Stephanie Caloir, Wendy Chavkin, Diane Grodney, Diana Hartel, and Denise Paone for their insightful comments and suggestions.

Control and Prevention 1995). The importance of women's drug use as a route of HIV transmission cannot be overstated. By 1994, AIDS had become the fourth leading cause of death in women ages 25–44 in the United States, with injection drug use directly or indirectly accounting for 84 percent of the AIDS cases among women (Centers for Disease Control and Prevention 1994). Injection drug use remains the most frequent route of infection in American women (Hankins and Handley 1992). The lifestyles and social/sexual relationships of drug-abusing women make them particularly vulnerable to HIV infection and AIDS. In addition to direct transmission, women who inject drugs are also at greater risk than nonabusing women of contracting HIV infection through unprotected heterosexual contact with an infected male. There is every reason to believe that injection drug use as a direct or indirect route of HIV transmission to women will continue to be a significant problem.

Any woman who has unsafe sex with an infected partner is vulnerable to HIV infection. Male-to-female transmission of the virus is more efficient, raising the risk of infection for females (Padian et al. 1990). There are other ways of contracting HIV that continue to affect females. Among them are rape and incest by an HIV-positive male, unsafe sex with an infected woman, and infection by needle prick. Little has been written about females infected in these ways.

HISTORY OF WOMEN AND AIDS

The history of AIDS in the United States reveals the absence of clear information on women. Early in the pandemic, AIDS became known as a gay men's disease (Strom 1993). Initial studies mistakenly saw women primarily as givers rather than as recipients of HIV. Although the first reported case of a woman with AIDS was in 1981 (Wiener 1991), the extent and impact of AIDS on women was understated for many years. It was only after AIDS spread among gay men and injection drug users that national policymakers alerted women that they, too, might be a group at risk (Treichler 1988).

AIDS appeared in a society where both science and medicine have been recognized as male-centered (Rossner 1991). This androcentrism has "placed women at a disadvantage for diagnosis, treatment and care" (Rossner 1991, p. 231). Because of this, the health care concerns of women with AIDS remain significant but are typically neglected. Women have been consistently excluded from clinical trials and have had only limited access to experimental treatments. The original trials of azidothymidine (AZT) of 282 subjects included only 13 women (Fischl et al. 1987). Until recently, women comprised only 6–7 percent of the patients in antiviral drug clinical trials (Pizzi 1992). Participation of women in clinical trials remains very limited. Additionally, the early definition of AIDS excluded opportunistic infections clearly associated with women with AIDS, which deprived many women of needed services and entitlements.

As awareness of the growing number of women with AIDS increased, political activists and researchers insisted that policymakers address the plight of women with AIDS. Initially, research initiatives focused on issues of transmission of the virus by women to men and children. In response to continued advocacy, in 1993 the Centers for Disease Control and Prevention expanded its definition of AIDS to include some of the opportunistic infections unique to women. Research protocols and experimental drug trials that had formerly excluded women were mandated to include women, and recently the Federal Drug Administration revised its guidelines also to include women of childbearing potential in drug trials (Nightingale 1993). Nonetheless, despite requirements that women be included in clinical trials or that researchers give a specific reason for their exclusion, the effect of this requirement remains uncertain (Cotton et al. 1993).

IMPACT OF AIDS ON WOMEN

AIDS affects women who already suffer from unequal status. Miller (1986) has stated that women live in a state of permanent inequality. Inequality creates powerlessness. Women rendered unequal must rely on those who have power and dominance. In our society, this power and dominance is most often granted to men. The inequality of women significantly affects their ability to cope with the many challenges that AIDS presents. Among these challenges are coping with the alienation resulting from the stigmatizing nature of AIDS, the many illnesses that affect them, depleting their strength and resistance, the relational difficulties created by their inability to continue to function in their roles as partners and mothers, and the challenges to their emotional well-being as AIDS destroys the very fabric of their lives.

Women tend to be diagnosed and obtain health care at a later stage of AIDS than men (Rothenberg et al. 1987). There are many reasons for this. Gender affects economic status, creating a situation where more women than men live below the poverty level. Poverty requires that many women focus on getting through the day and delay seeking health care. Many women infected with HIV live in poor, drug-infested areas where health services are not readily available and preventive care is not accessible. Additionally, women are generally the caregivers of HIV families (Minkoff and DeHovitz 1991) and may not access health care for themselves because of their need to care for their children and/or partners (Newman and Martens 1994).

Diagnosis and treatment may also be impeded by the misdiagnosis of women presenting indications of HIV infection (Schoenbaum and Webber 1993). The failure of the medical profession to adequately research the reproductive and immune responses unique to women has created enormous difficulties for physicians in providing accurate diagnosis and treatment of women patients.

For women who contract the virus by unprotected sex or injecting drug use, or both, "coming out" as an injecting drug-user, partner of an injecting drug-user, or as a woman who had unprotected sex with an infected partner may be more frightening and shameful than the illness itself. Women who are HIV infected may realistically fear expulsion from family and community as their illness becomes apparent to others. Other factors that mitigate against early diagnosis and treatment for women include the fear of knowing their HIV status, the fear of sexual violence from a partner upon learning that the woman has been tested, and the fear that if HIV infection is found the woman may lose custody of her children.

WOMEN WHO INJECT DRUGS

The number of women who become HIV infected through injection drug use and by sexual contact with infected partners continues to rise (Amaro 1995). As indicated earlier, injection drug use is the most frequent route of HIV infection in women (Shiboski et al. 1994). A variety of activities associated with injection drug use have been identified as risk factors for HIV infection, including needle sharing, back loading (a sharing technique used to distribute drugs from one syringe to another), and renting unsterilized injecting equipment. Among the drugs that can be injected are heroin, cocaine, and amphetamines. Combining drugs ("speedballing") is common. Studies suggest that injecting drug users most often share injecting equipment primarily because of their difficulty in finding clean "works," as well as for social reasons (Barnard 1993).

Injection drug use patterns are bound to the relationships and lifestyles of addicted women. The sharing of injecting equipment follows lines of traditional male/female gender roles. In the context of a sexual relationship, many men supply drugs to women; women, more often than men, share needles with partners or friends (Barnard 1993). Often the male shoots first, raising the risk for the woman of receiving contaminated blood (Pivnick 1993).

In addition, frequency of shooting drugs has been related to HIV seropositivity (Marmor et al. 1987). The more often a woman injects drugs, the more likely she is to become HIV infected. This places women who inject cocaine at particular risk. Because cocaine is a shorter-acting drug, cocaine users may inject themselves more frequently than if they were using heroin alone (Gawin and Ellinwood 1988). Moreover, cocaine has been associated with high-risk sexual behavior. Crack, an inexpensive, highly addictive, and readily available form of cocaine, heightens the perception of sexual arousal that can result in decreased sexual inhibition and increased desire for drugs. Crack use in women also has been associated with high-risk, often degrading forms of trading sex for drugs and prostitution (Fullilove et al. 1992), increasing the risk for HIV infection via unsafe sex as well as spreading the virus to their partners. Women who abuse alcohol also place themselves at risk for HIV infection since alcohol is a disinhibitor and can contribute to a poor choice of partner and unsafe sexual practices while inebriated (Cunningham et al. 1994).

Injection drug use is also related to the transmission of the HIV virus to the fetus. Ninety percent of women who inject drugs are of childbearing ages (Bell 1989), and the virus can be transmitted to the fetus during pregnancy or delivery. Studies show that alcohol and other drug use have been related to less use of birth control and fewer HIV prevention measures (Leigh and Stall 1993). Moreover, drug use may produce amenorrhea (absence of menstrual cycles), or irregular cycles causing some addicted women to believe that they cannot become pregnant.

HETEROSEXUAL TRANSMISSION OF AIDS

Heterosexual contact is the only AIDS risk behavior in which women outnumber men (McCoy and Inciardi 1993). It is important for clinicians to understand the routes of sexual transmission of HIV infection in order to help women clients who unrealistically believe that their sexual behavior does not place them at risk of contracting the virus. As a group, female partners of injection drug-using men are at particular risk. Sexual behaviors known to transmit the virus include vaginal and anal intercourse and "rough sex" involving the sharing of blood. The number of women who participate in anal intercourse or rough sex is unknown.

Marjorie is a wealthy, single, 29-year-old Caucasian woman. Uncomfortable about relating to men, she drinks heavily before going out on dates and often has vaginal intercourse with the men she dates. She believes that the men she dates are heterosexual and clean, although she has sex during blackouts and does not always remember her partners. She does not discuss safer sex or insist on condom use with her partners because she feels it would be inappropriate and uncomfortable. Recently Marjorie began to lose weight and develop night sweats. Her physician suggested that she take the ELIZA test, which detects the presence of HIV. Marjorie tested positive.

Contrary to popular belief, the nonuse of condoms is not related to the absence of knowledge (Nyamathi et al. 1993). Marjorie's inability to insist that her partner use a condom was caused by her ideas of propriety and poor judgment resulting from her drinking. Additionally, many women believe that condom use represents a barrier to intimacy and that "the purest, most intimate expression of conjugal bonding is demonstrated through the non-use of condoms" (Pivnick 1993, p. 443).

Georgie is a 34-year-old African-American woman. She is in love with Ralph, a man with whom she has been involved for three years. Ralph uses heroin and cocaine by injection. Although Ralph is married, Georgie believes that he loves her more than he loves his wife. Ralph does not use condoms when they have sex. Georgie fears that if she insists, Ralph will leave her or believe that she is involved with other men. Georgie knows how HIV is transmitted and that she is placing herself at risk. She says that she is willing to "die for love."

Heterosexual contact is the second most common route of transmission of HIV (Ickovics and Rodin 1992). Like Georgie, women partners of injecting drug-using men are the most rapidly growing risk group in the United States (Miller et al. 1990). At particular risk ("double jeopardy") are women who both engage in sexual risk-taking with HIV-positive partners and inject drugs. Studies demonstrate that substance-abusing women are more likely than male substance abusers to be sexually and romantically involved with substance-abusing partners (Rosenbaum 1981a,b). This sexual relationship dramatically increases the possibility of contracting an HIV infection.

The difficulties that all heterosexual women have negotiating safer sex become more comprehensible when it is understood that many women, vulnerable to HIV infection, depend upon men for their emotional and economic survival (Kane 1990). Thus women may fear abandonment if they say no to unsafe sexual practices or if they step out of the societally prescribed role of docile female.

In most cultures, a woman's acquiescence to sex is both expected and enforced. Koss and colleagues (1994) report that women's greatest risk of assault is from male partners, with women more likely to be injured, raped, or killed by a male partner than by any other type of assailant. Therefore, for some women, "just saying no" to sex (or to unprotected sex) turns into a prescription for battering and other forms of abuse (Bacon 1987). Especially in cultural contexts where women are expected to be passive and compliant, demanding that male sexual partners use condoms will reasonably be faced with trepidation by some women.

The only female condom on the market is still undergoing safety and efficacy evaluation in the United States and is not readily available to many women who might use it. Moreover, because its presence is obvious, this form of protection remains problematic to those women who fear disclosure of HIV prevention measures to male partners. At this time there is no safer sexual device that does not involve the cooperation of men.

Heterosexual transmission via unsafe sexual practices associated with prostitution has been recognized as a route of transmission of HIV infection in the United States and other countries. Women working as prostitutes have been blamed for both infecting men and infecting women whose husbands were their clients (Anastos and Marte 1989). The targeting of prostitutes for blame is misguided because transmission of the virus is related to the number of unprotected sexual contacts, not whether women trade sex for money (Rossner 1991). Like other women, female prostitutes are more likely to get the AIDS virus than to give it. As also true of women who do not trade sex for money or drugs, prostitutes report being less able to insist on safer sexual practices in their intimate relationships than in their casual encounters. Not surprisingly, those prostitutes studied frequently reported that they felt unable to demand that their boyfriends use condoms (Cohen 1988). Like other women, prostitutes' infection rates are most often related to injecting drug use (Johnson 1988) rather than the prostitution per se.

WOMAN-TO-WOMAN TRANSMISSION OF AIDS

Marge is a 55-year-old Jewish woman who lives with her lover Donna, a 38-year-old Italian-American woman who had a history of injection drug use before meeting Marge. Although Marge has such symptoms as night sweats, weight loss, and gynecological problems, her doctor has not considered the possibility of HIV infection.

Current research indicates that most cases of AIDS among lesbians are related to injection drug use (Chu et al. 1990). There is also some anecdotal material indicating that lesbian women can get AIDS through sexual contact with an infected woman (Stevens 1993). As a group, lesbian women have been ignored by AIDS researchers and excluded from treatment protocols. One justification for the exclusion of lesbian women from studies was offered by a Centers for Disease Control (CDC) physician in the late 1980s, who said that it was not necessary to study lesbians because "lesbians don't have much sex" (Chiaramonte 1988). Until recently, the CDC defined lesbians as women who have had sexual contact only with women, ignoring the experience of many lesbian women who have had some or regular sexual contact with men (Hunter 1992). Using this rigid definition, the CDC estimated that only 0.8 percent of lesbians have AIDS.

Women who have sex with women suffer from the absence of knowledge and clear information about HIV infection as well as from discrimination by the health care industry. Further, Hunter (1992) noted that a false perception of security among lesbians themselves is a primary obstacle to prevention. Since HIV is present in vaginal and cervical secretions, these secretions should be considered infectious (Kennedy et al. 1995), and safer sexual practices, including the use of dental dams, should be taught to lesbians.

WOMEN AS MOTHERS

Laura discovered that she was HIV positive when she became pregnant and her entire pregnancy was clouded by the fear that her children would be born infected. She gave birth to twins: one twin was HIV positive while the other was not. The infected child was ill most of the short time that it lived and Laura had to cope with her infant's illness and death while caring for the other baby as well as caring for her own health and psychological needs.

In addition to caring for their own survival needs, many women infected with HIV care for children. Because women may passively infect their infants through "vertical transmission" in the delivery process and through breast-feeding (Mok 1993), HIV-infected women risk the life of their unborn children by becoming pregnant. When women give birth to

HIV-infected infants, they must contend with the responsibility of caring for an ill or dying child. Increased knowledge of safer delivery techniques and breast-feeding have reduced the risk of transmission of the virus from mother to infants. Significant, well-documented research has demonstrated the efficacy of AZT in reducing the transmission of HIV infection from mother to fetus (Saba 1995). However, questions remain regarding the long-term effect of AZT on both mothers and infants (CDC 1995).

Most of the children born to HIV-infected women will not carry the HIV virus when they develop their own immune systems. HIV infection rates via perinatal transmission are between 13–32 percent in developed countries (Mok 1993). Despite an initial concern that pregnancy for seropositive women compromised the mother's health, research continues to be done on the question of whether pregnancy for asymptomatic women is injurious to the mother (Carpenter et al. 1991).

In addition to the many children born infected with HIV, the AIDS pandemic is leaving a generation of "AIDS orphans" in its wake. Levine (1993) estimates that there will be between 72,000 and 125,000 AIDS orphans in the United States by the year 2000. Their mothers, who are HIV infected and often ill, must care for them and plan for their children's future before they die.

Motherhood creates particular stresses and responsibilities for HIV-infected women. HIV-infected and AIDS-diagnosed mothers of HIV-infected children have to contend with the many psychosocial issues related to being an ill or dying parent to an ill child while simultaneously struggling with their own survival needs. In addition to being immune compromised, many of these women live in poverty. Shayne and Kaplan (1991) report that almost three-fourths (73 percent) of the mothers of HIV-positive children they studied received public assistance.

In addition to poverty, the woman, often a single parent, has to handle the issue of stigma as it relates not only to herself but also to her children once it is known that she is HIV infected or has AIDS. She will need to contend with her child's shame with peers and at school as well as in the family and the community. At a time of deteriorating health and resources, a mother who is HIV infected or ill with the opportunistic infections caused by AIDS will need to cope with her children's anger and fear of abandonment as she becomes sicker and has frequent absences through hospitalizations.

Practical issues become paramount amid the chaos imposed by the illness (Zuckerman and Gordon 1988). Resolving custody issues and handling legal issues becomes overwhelming to ill and dying mothers. Since revealing one's HIV status is extraordinarily painful, many women fear telling their children and put off these discussions until it is too late.

ASSESSMENT AND TREATMENT
OF WOMEN AFFECTED BY AIDS

Assessment and treatment of women affected by AIDS presents both challenges and opportunities for clinicians. Clinical practice must be informed by a clear understanding of the physical and psychosocial factors and environmental stresses that impact on these women's lives.

Medical Issues

Knowledge of the illnesses women with AIDS commonly suffer will assist clinicians in encouraging at-risk women to seek early diagnosis and treatment. The opportunistic infections of women include some of the same illnesses and symptoms as those suffered by men, such as weight loss, persistent fevers and diarrhea, fatigue, night sweats, oral candidiasis, cytomegalovirus, toxoplasmosis, tuberculosis, mycobacterium avium, and PCP pneumonia. Women are less likely to be diagnosed with Kaposi's sarcoma than are men (Wofsy 1987). Gynecological infections that often present in HIV-infected women and women with AIDS include pelvic inflammatory disease, cervical dysplasia, vaginal candidiasis, and cervical carcinoma.

Cultural Issues

The majority of women with AIDS in the United States are women of color (Mays and Cochran 1988). While 52 percent of those cases are African-American women, 20 percent of the AIDS cases are Hispanic women (Ickovics and Rodin 1992). In order to work effectively with the many women of color affected by the AIDS pandemic, it is important for clinicians to understand the impact of culture as it informs their sexual practices and health care decision making.

Early studies revealed some difficulties women of color, particularly Hispanic women, have in encouraging safer sexual practices. These studies emphasized the power imbalance frequently seen in Latino/Latina relationships making assertiveness difficult and the general lack of sexual decision making among women in minority communities as contributing to unsafe sexual practices. Worth and Rodriguez (1987) have suggested that Latina women's dependency and deference in the Hispanic community to men, who are viewed as innately superior, may contribute to engaging in unsafe sexual practices. Additionally, the high value placed on fertility and mothering among Hispanic clients may discourage the use of safer sex devices (O'Leary 1994).

In addition to relationship issues, culture is important in defining how health-related services are utilized. Distrust may contribute to a delay in seeking services (Airhihenbuwa et al. 1992). Among African-American women who are HIV positive, the delay in seeking health care or emotional support may be because of their fear of backlash or racism (Hine and Wittenstein 1981). The cultural beliefs of some minority women in folk medicine and alternative healing, which define both the reason for illness and its cure, must be considered. Clinicians will need to assess how these beliefs may lead some women to reject experimental treatments or to delay in utilizing traditional mainstream health care services (Flaskerhud and Rush 1989, Suarez et al. 1993). The use of culturally congruent clinicians and paraprofessionals can assist these women in utilizing health care services. For some women, referral to alternative, nontraditional health care may be appropriate.

Many women are biracial or bicultural. The identities of African-American and Hispanic women will vary in relation to where they were born and the extent to which they identify with their culture. Therefore, clinicians must consider the meaning of culture as it relates to each woman and as it informs her individual values and behavior to ensure that clinical interventions are culturally sensitive and referrals are appropriate.

HIV Prevention and Safer Sexual Behavior

In order to assist women at risk for infection and HIV-infected women, clinicians need to engage in frank discussions of sexual behavior with women clients. While this is a difficult subject, it is the clinician's responsibility to help women to assume responsibility for their safety. HIV infection in and of itself is not apparent to others. The assumption that a partner who looks physically healthy or that a partner who is currently monogamous is not HIV infected is naive, and clinicians need to help women clients to understand the routes of transmission and manifestations of AIDS.

It is important that clinicians understand that HIV can be easily transmitted via unprotected heterosexual anal intercourse (DesJarlais 1996) and rough sex involving the exchange of blood products as well as via unprotected vaginal sex. Many women occasionally or frequently engage in anal intercourse (Seidman and Reider 1994), and clients are often unaware of their HIV risk. In addition, women can contract the HIV virus via unprotected sexual contact with an infected bisexual male. Behavior-ally, it is estimated that 14 percent of the men with AIDS are bisexual (Chu et al. 1992).

By suggesting safer sexual practices, which include abstinence and the use of condoms for protection against HIV infection, clinicians may be failing to respond to the religious values and lifestyles of many women. Additionally, the idea that experimentation with safer sexual practices can be "fun" and erotic may fail to address the meaning of sexuality for procreation for some women of color (Houston-Hamilton 1988). Clini-cians need to help women clients develop ways of discussing sex with their partners and find ways to negotiate sexual experiences to feel safe.

In order to help women protect themselves, clinicians need to find ways of enhancing their client's self-esteem. Research has demonstrated that women with higher self-esteem and a greater sense that life is mean-ingful are better able to practice more self-protective behaviors (Nyamathi et al. 1993). It has been demonstrated that skill-building groups that teach cognitive and behavioral skills in sexual negotiation and relapse preven-tion are useful in helping women with addiction histories to develop HIV-preventive behaviors (Schilling et al. 1991a,b).

Psychological Issues

Women of childbearing age, the ages of highest risk for HIV infection, are also at highest risk for depression (Orr et al. 1994). Injection drug-using women often present with histories of depression, anxiety, or sui-cide attempts. Therefore, the depression that commonly accompanies HIV infection makes them particularly vulnerable to profound emotional dis-tress. Moreover, women who live in poverty and have few social and economic supports are particularly prone to feeling hopeless when HIV infection strikes. Depression may lead to drug or alcohol relapse and to avoidance of necessary treatment. Women clients who are HIV positive or diagnosed with AIDS may benefit from psychiatric evaluations to as-sess their suicidal ideation and organic deterioration. Psychiatrists can also assist clients by providing appropriate psychotropic medication for anxiety and depression.

The inability to fulfill their roles and loss of physical desirability will have profound meaning for women clients. Physical attractiveness and the ability to function in roles as sexual partners and homemakers have historically been very important to women. As HIV infection progresses to AIDS, loss of sexuality, frequent illnesses, weight loss, and fatigue can make these women feel undesirable and worthless, which impacts on their self-esteem and their already vulnerable sense of security. Such self-perceptions can only serve to increase their isolation and fear of abandonment.

TREATMENT OF HIV-INFECTED WOMEN
AND WOMEN WITH AIDS

Clinicians need to individualize their treatment of women clients, providing treatment that is sensitive to the woman's culture and lifestyle. Based on the clinician's assessment, appropriate individual and group treatment can be offered and community resources be put in place.

When a woman is HIV positive or has AIDS, she needs a safe and confidential place to address her concerns and to receive support to handle the many tasks of caring for her physical and emotional needs. Clinicians need to encourage and assist women clients to express their feelings to avoid becoming overwhelmed. During sessions, clinicians can provide, as appropriate, support, education, sustainment, reflection, referrals for concrete services, and insight. During times of particular stress, clinicians should use the techniques of crisis intervention by reframing, partializing, prioritizing, and helping clients resolve their immediate situations.

Some issues that present as obstacles to treatment for injection drug-using women with AIDS have been outlined by Strom (1993). They include the reluctance to engage in treatment with the clinician because of a history of disappointing interpersonal relationships leading to a fear of rejection or criticism by the worker, a difficulty accepting medical treatment that requires regularity and the need to take prescribed medications consistently, and the powerful emotional reactions that are triggered by an AIDS diagnosis.

Clinicians need to become familiar with the rights of privacy governing HIV/AIDS information. Women clients will need to understand who they must allow to know their diagnosis and the contexts in which their HIV status may legally remain confidential. Clinicians also need to respect the numerous family responsibilities that many HIV-infected women carry. Missed appointments should not be seen as resistance to treatment until explored with the client. Practical considerations such as the provision of child care and transportation will assist women clients to engage in treatment.

Clinicians must help these women maintain a sense of equilibrium amidst the chaos imposed by their illness. Flexibility of care has become a cornerstone of effective practice. For clinicians who were trained to provide ongoing weekly sessions, the parameters of the treatment contract will need to change. Because the trajectory of AIDS is very uneven, with clients feeling healthy one day and seriously ill the next, it is important for clinicians not to be lulled into an artificial sense of well-being when the client is well or to become hopeless when the client becomes ill.

Clinicians will be called upon to provide treatment in various settings. It is appropriate for clinicians to go on home visits and to meet with clients in the hospital. When meeting with clients who are hospitalized, clinicians must be sensitive to the client's feelings about the clinician's presence within earshot of family members who may be visiting and try to arrange hospital visits outside of regular visiting hours. It is important to be sensitive to the client's weakened condition and keep sessions short. In general, hospital visits should be prearranged and coordinated with the inpatient treatment team. During visits, clinicians should focus on the client's adjustment to her hospitalization and her immediate needs. In addition, clinicians should be prepared to provide telephone sessions to offer support to clients during crisis periods or when clients are too ill to keep office appointments.

Clients need additional support to that of their primary therapists. Treatment offered to women should include both professional and paraprofessional supports. Primary clinicians also need to prepare clients for times when the clinician is not available. In planning for vacations and absences, clinicians should provide backup therapists and, wherever possible, consider working in teams for client support.

To expedite referrals clinicians must become knowledgeable about different substance abuse treatment options, including methadone maintenance, Alcoholics Anonymous (AA), Narcotics Anonymous (NA), residential treatment, detoxification, and outpatient programs. It is important to be aware that when under stress, some women may relapse or increase their use of drugs. For women with substance abuse histories, drug and alcohol use have been familiar ways of coping and relapse should be seen as a sign of distress rather than client failure. Clinicians working in substance abuse treatment settings need to continue to support drug and alcohol abstinence among their HIV-positive and AIDS-diagnosed clients and assist them in developing their repertoire of coping skills. Clinicians will need to evaluate the client's potential for relapse and make referrals as necessary in a nonjudgmental manner. If the clinician is not treating the client for her substance abuse problem, collegial contact with the woman's drug treatment providers, with properly executed release forms, will assist in case management and coordination.

Countertransference

While clinicians face many challenges in helping women clients affected by HIV, the most powerful may be the clinician's own countertransference. It is easy for clinicians to burn out and become immobilized. In the necessary identification with clients, clinicians will experience their clients' feelings of anger, despair, and helplessness. When working with women who are HIV infected, women diagnosed with AIDS-related illnesses, and women caregivers, clinicians must work hard to remain objective, empathic, and optimistic.

When working with women who are poor, women of color, and women whose lifestyle choices differ from their own, practitioners need to challenge their internalized sexism and heterosexism, which result in judgments about how women should be and how women should act. As in all work with the terminally ill, the clinician's own fear of mortality and unresolved losses will impede his or her effectiveness and should be recognized and addressed.

Work with Families

Since HIV affects the entire family, the clinician's work needs to include parents, children, and other important relationships. As the disease progresses, greater involvement of significant others becomes necessary. Family education in the health care and emotional needs of ill women can do much to promote the well-being and quality of life for both women and their loved ones.

Women with Children

For HIV-infected ill women with children, clinicians need to locate programs that recognize and respect the importance of their clients' mothering needs. Supports that allow women to continue to function in some aspects of their mothering role throughout their illness include the use of home care attendants, homemakers, and babysitters, as well as the creation of flexible guardianship arrangements. At-home services for ill women should include emotional and practical support as well as legal assistance in future planning and custody issues.

Caregivers

Women are relational (Miller 1986), and their identities are interwoven with the people in their lives. Because women are expected to provide care, their caregiving often goes unnoticed, unappreciated, and unreimbursed. The inequality and concomitant devaluation of tasks designated as "women's" serve to minimize and trivialize women's roles as care-givers for partners and family members with AIDS. For women in re-covery, the need to take care of others may interfere with their own recovery efforts.

> Maria is a 40-year-old Mexican-American woman who is enrolled in a training program for recovering alcoholics. She is at risk of being terminated from the training program because she is often late and sometimes falls asleep in class. What the program does not know is that every day Maria wakes up at 4 AM to care for her brother who is dying of AIDS and that she is late to class when-ever the homemaker does not show up on time.

Despite a perception that people with AIDS die alone in hospitals, most people with AIDS receive care from relatives (Schiller 1993). There are many women in this country who, like Maria, after a full day's work go home to tend to a family member or a friend with AIDS. Because AIDS remains a stigmatizing illness, many of these women cannot talk about what their lives are really like and emotional or financial support remains unavailable to them. The burden of caring for men and women with AIDS has fallen unequally on elderly women, particularly low income women of color. Elderly women often are called upon to care for their sons and daughters who are dying of AIDS-related illnesses and to raise their grand-children once their children die.

> Margaret is a 63-year-old African-American widowed grand-mother. She is a retired nurse. She has diabetes and hyperten-sion. When her drug-abusing son died of AIDS, Margaret took her son's three children to keep them out of foster care and because of love and loyalty to her son. At a time of life when elderly people must take care of themselves, Margaret, burdened by serious health problems and financial constraints, is also performing a demanding parenting task.

For women coping with a partner or family member's illness, group support, respite care, and financial assistance must be made available. Feelings of being overwhelmed, ambivalence, anger, fear, and loss need to be addressed. Caregiver groups can be very helpful and should be provided. Until greater societal recognition and support exists, the clinician's respect, compassion, and acknowledgment of the value of the caregiving work will be very healing.

Advocacy

Clinicians working with women affected by AIDS need to advocate for their clients in a variety of spheres. Wherever possible, clinicians working in substance abuse settings should seek to influence agency policies to ensure that relapse among AIDS-diagnosed women does not result in termination from treatment. There is also a need to advocate for humane treatment for women clients as they interface with social service providers, drug treatment programs, hospitals, and child care agencies. Professionals responsible for the care of HIV-infected women should use their understanding and status to demand respect and appropriate care for their women clients.

As well as advocating for individual women clients, clinicians can inform politicians and policymakers about the way AIDS and AIDS-related gender discrimination affect women and of the real life conditions under which their women clients suffer. Clinicians are in a good position to confront long-standing political and societal attitudes toward the women most stigmatized by AIDS: women of poverty, women of color, and women who inject drugs. They must protest laws that discriminate against HIV-infected women, such as mandatory drug testing, sterilization, and the prosecution of mothers who give birth to babies with AIDS.

Since injection drug use is the most frequent route of HIV infection, drug treatment programs that are adequate in number and services are needed to stem the tide of HIV infection and AIDS. Critically important in the prevention and treatment of HIV illness is the establishment and support of publicly funded drug treatment programs that are sensitive to the multifaceted needs of addicted women. Among the successful programs are methadone maintenance programs. Such programs provide an effective treatment for narcotic abuse (Horowitz 1996) and have a high retention rate, yet remain politically unpopular and underfunded. Residential programs designed for HIV-positive pregnant women and women with children, as well as expanded outpatient services, are necessary.

REFRAMING GENDER ROLES AND RESPONSIBILITIES

Larry is a widower. His wife died of AIDS last year, and the children were placed with their grandmother. Larry is lonely and regularly seeks sexual contact with prostitutes. He is HIV positive. Sometimes, when the prostitute insists, he uses condoms.

Otherwise he does not, believing that it is up to the women to ensure their own safety.

Traditionally, women have been held responsible for both reproductive decision making (Kandel et al. 1986) and sexual disease transmission. This responsibility has found its way into HIV prevention measures. Women are now being told that they are responsible for the sexual transmission of the virus. The message is that women are responsible for HIV infection and therefore responsible for its prevention (Pivnick 1993). Women are regularly being counseled about ways to convince or coerce men into using condoms. Condom use remains "embedded in the nature of culture-specific, socially mediated, unequal gender relations" (Pivnick 1993, p. 432). The idea that powerless, dependent women are able to convince or coerce men to use condoms remains uninformed by knowledge of the unequal status of women. The inequality inherent in holding women primarily responsible for something largely out of their control is rarely recognized and more rarely challenged.

If HIV infection in women is to be curtailed, it is critical that men become involved in the solution. Motives for having sex are gender related. Men attach much more importance than do women to sexual pleasure, conquest, and the relief of sexual tension as reasons for having sex. Women see emotional closeness as more important than do men (Leigh 1989). A study of condom use and sexual attitudes found that men were more likely than women to view condoms as interfering with their sexual pleasure (VanOss Marin et al. 1993). Treatment offered by clinicians must take these attitudes into account in developing effective treatment strategies to assist men in assuming greater responsibility toward women.

Addressing and changing male attitudes and behavior is imperative to stem the spread of AIDS infection in women. Clinicians need to get heterosexual and bisexual men actively involved in AIDS risk reduction and help them to assume responsibilty for the protection of their partners as well as themselves. Education and individual and group support to help heterosexual and bisexual men—aimed at fostering the use of condoms—needs to start to replace the "just say no" or "convince your man to do the right thing" mentality currently applied to women.

CONCLUSION

Clinicians have a key role in helping women to access services and to improve their quality of life. Every day throughout this country, clinicians counsel women affected by AIDS. They share their grief, loneliness, and pain and have learned of their resilience and courage. Knowing that they cannot heal them, clinicians nonetheless offer these women enormous support, sustainment, and constancy in their struggle to cope with the profound impact that AIDS has on their lives.

The increasing number of HIV-positive and AIDS-affected women adds an urgency to the need to provide them with appropriate medical and psychosocial care. Clinicians need to focus on the correlation between women's substance abuse and HIV, as well as the reinforcement of excessive caregiving in women affected by the substance abuse of loved ones. Ways of preventing and treating HIV infection in women, sensitive to the physiology and social standing of women, still need to be developed. Along with high-quality clinical treatment, gender-sensitive political activism will need to continue in order to help move the national agenda toward a greater regard for the impact of AIDS on women's lives.

REFERENCES

Airhihenbuwa, C. O., DiClemente, R. J., Wingood, G. M., and Lowe, A. (1992). HIV/AIDS education and prevention among African-Americans: a focus on culture. *AIDS Education and Prevention* 4:267–276.

Amaro, H. (1995). Love, sex and power: considering women's realities in HIV prevention. *American Psychologist* 50(6):437–447.

Anastos, K., and Marte, C. (1989). Women: the missing persons in the AIDS epidemic. In *The AIDS Reader*, ed. N. McKenzie, pp. 190–199. New York: Penguin.

Bacon, L. (1987). Lessons of AIDS: racism, homophobia are the real epidemics. *Listen Real Loud* 8(2):5–6.

Barnard, M. (1993). Needle sharing in context: patterns of sharing among men and women injectors and HIV risk. *Addiction* 88:805–812.

Bell, N. (1989). AIDS and women: remaining ethical issues. *AIDS Education and Prevention* 1(1):22–30.

Carpenter, C. J., Mayer, K. H., Stein, M. D., et al. (1991). Human immunodeficiency virus infection in North American women: experience with 200 cases and a review of the literature. *Medicine* 70(5):307–325.

Centers for Disease Control and Prevention (1994). *HIV/AIDS Prevention*. Atlanta, GA: U.S. Department of Health and Human Services.

—— (1995). *HIV/AIDS Surveillance Report*. Atlanta, GA: U.S. Department of Health and Human Services.

Chiaramonte, L. (1988). Lesbian safety and AIDS: the very last fairy tale. *Visibilities* pp. 6–8.

Chu, S. Y., Buehler, J. W., Flemming, P. L., and Berkelman, R. L. (1990). Epidemiology of reported cases of AIDS in lesbians, United States 1980–89. *American Journal of Public Health* 80(11):1380–1381.

Chu, S. Y., Peterman, J. A., Doll, L. S., et al. (1992). AIDS in bisexual men in the United States: epidemiology and transmission to women. *American Journal of Public Health* 82(2):220–224.

Cohen, J. B. (1991). Why women partners of drug users will continue to be at high risk for HIV infection. In *Cocaine, AIDS and Intravenous Drug Use*, pp. 99–109. New York: Haworth.

Cohen, J. B., Alexander, O., and Wofsy, C. (1988). Prostitutes and AIDS: public policy issues. *AIDS Public Policy Journal* 3:16–22.

Cotton, D., Finkelstein, D., He, W., et al. (1993). Determinants of accrual of women to a large multicenter clinical trials program of human immunodeficiency virus infection. *Journal of Acquired Immunodeficiency Syndromes* 6(12):1322–1328.

Cunningham, R., Stiffman, A. R., Dore, P., and Earls, F. (1994). The association of physical abuse with HIV risk behaviors in adolescence and young adulthood: implications for public health. *Child Abuse and Neglect* 18(3):233–245.

DesJarlais, D. (1996). Personal communication, May.

Finnegan, L. P., Sloboda, Z., Haverkos, H., Mello, N. K., et al. (1994). *Drug Abuse and the Health of Women in Problems of Drug Dependence 1994: Proceedings of the 56th Annual Scientific Meeting*. NIDA, vol. 1, 45–48. Rockville, MD: U.S. Department of Health and Human Services.

Fischl, M., Richman, D., Grieco, M., et al. (1987). The efficacy of Azidothymidine (AZT) in the treatment of patients with AIDS and AIDS-related complex: a double-blind placebo-controlled trial. *New England Journal of Medicine* 317(4):185–191.

Flaskerhud, J. H., and Rush, C. E. (1989). AIDS and traditional health beliefs and practices of Black women. *Nursing Research* 38:210–215.

Fullilove, M., Lown, A., and Fullilove, R. (1992). Crack 'Hos and Skeezers: traumatic experiences of women crack users. *The Journal of Sex Research* 29(2):275–287.

Gawin, F. H., and Ellinwood, E. (1988). Cocaine and other stimulants. *New England Journal of Medicine* 318(18):1173–1182.

Hankins, C., and Handley, M. (1992). HIV disease and women: current knowledge and a research agenda. *Journal of Acquired Immunodeficiency Syndromes* 5(1):957–971.

Hine, D., and Wittenstein, K. (1981). Female slave resistance: the economics of sex. In *The Black Woman Cross-Culturally*, ed. F. Steady, pp. 189–344. Cambridge: Schenkman.

Horowitz, C. (1996). The no win war. *New York Magazine* February 5, pp. 22–33.

Houston-Hamilton, A. (1988). *Implications of Sexual and Contraceptive Practices on Attitudes for Prevention of Heterosexual Transmission in Blacks.* Washington, DC: Paper presented at National Institute of Drug Abuse Technical Review.

Hunter, J. (July 1992). Sexual and substance abuse activities that place lesbians at risk for HIV. *International Conference on AIDS* 8:D421 (Abstract no. PoD 5205).

Ickovics, J., and Rodin, J. (1992). Women and AIDS in the United States: epidemiology, natural history, and mediating mechanisms. *Health Psychology* 11(1):1–16.

Johnson, A. M. (1988). Social and behaviourial aspects of the HIV epidemic: a review. *Journal of the Royal Statistical Society* A(151): 99–114.

Kandel, D. B., Davies, M., Karus, D., and Yamaguchi, K. (1986). The consequences in young adulthood of adolescent drug involvement. *Archives of General Psychiatry* 43:746–754.

Kane, S. (1990). AIDS: Addiction and condom use: sources of sexual risk for heterosexual women. *Journal of Sex Research* 27(3):427–444.

Kennedy, M., Scarlett, M., Duerr, A., and Chu, S. (1995). Assessing HIV risk among women who have sex with women: scientific and communication issues. *Journal of the American Medical Women's Association* 50(3&4):103–107.

Koss, M. P., Goodman, L. A., Browne, A., et al. (1994). *No Safe Haven: Male Violence Against Women at Home, at Work and in the Community.* Washington, DC: American Psychological Association.

Leigh, B. (1989). Reasons for having sex and avoiding sex: sexual orientation and relationship to sexual behavior. *Journal of Sex Research* 26(2): 199–209.

Leigh, B., and Stall, R. (1993). Substance use and risky sexual behavior for HIV: issues in methodology, interpretation and prevention. *American Psychologist* 48(10):1035–1045.

Levine, C. (1993). *A Death in the Family: Orphans of the HIV Epidemic.* New York: New York Hospital Fund.

Marmor, M., DesJarlais, D., Cohen, J., et al. (1987). Risk factors for the human immunodeficiency virus among intravenous drug users in New York City. *AIDS* 1(1):39–44.

Mays, V. M., and Cochran, S. D. (1988). Issues in the perception of AIDS risk and risk reduction activities by Black and Hispanic/Latina women. *American Psychologist* 43(11):949–957.

McCoy, V., and Inciardi, J. A. (1993). Women and AIDS: social determinants of sex-related activities. *Women and Health* 20(1):69–84.

Miller, H., Turner, C., and Moses, L. (eds). (1990). *AIDS: The Second Decade.* Washington, DC: National Academy Press.

Miller, J. B. (1986). *Toward a New Psychology of Women*. Boston, MA: Beacon.

Minkoff, H. L., and DeHovitz, J. A. (1991). Care of women infected with the human immunodeficiency virus. *Journal of the American Medical Association* 226(16):2253–2258.

Mok, J. (1993). Vertical transmission. In *HIV Infection in Women*, ed. Johnson and Johnstone, pp. 199–212. Edinburgh: Churchill Livingstone.

Newman, T., and Martens, M. (1994). Women and HIV. In *HIV Manual for Health Care Professionals*, ed. R. Muma, B. Lyons, M. Borucki, and R. Pollard, pp. 137–147. Norwalk, CT: Appleton and Lange.

Nightingale, S. (1993). From the Food and Drug Administration. *Journal of the American Medical Association* 270(11):1290.

Nyamathi, A., Bennett, C., Leake, B., et al. (1993). AIDS-related knowledge, perceptions, and behaviors among impoverished minority women. *American Journal of Public Health* 83(1):65–71.

O'Leary, A. (1994). Factors associated with sexual risk of AIDS in women. In *NIDA Research Monograph 143*, ed. R. J. Battjes, Z. Sjoboda, and W. Grace. Rockville, MD: U.S. Department of Health and Human Services:

Orr, S., Celentano, D., Santelli, J., and Burwell, L. (1994). Depressive symptoms and risk factors for HIV acquisition among Black women attending urban health centers in Baltimore. *AIDS Education and Prevention* 6(3):230–236.

Padian, N. S., Shiboski, S., and Jewell, N. (1990). The effect of the number of exposures on the risk of heterosexual HIV transmission. *Journal of Infectious Diseases* 161:883–887.

Pivnick, A. (1993). HIV Infection and the meaning of condoms. *Culture, Medicine and Psychiatry* 17:431–453.

Pizzi, M. (1992). Women, HIV infection and AIDS: tapestries of life, death and empowerment. *American Journal of Occupational Therapy* 46(11):1021–1027.

Rosenbaum, M. (1981a). Sex roles among deviants: the woman addict. *International Journal of the Addictions* 16(5):859–877.

—— (1981b). *Women on Heroin*. New Brunswick, NJ: Rutgers University Press.

Rossner, S. V. (1991). AIDS and women. *AIDS Education and Prevention* 3(3):230– 249.

Rothenberg, R., Woefel, M., Stoneburner, R., et al. (1987). Survival with the acquired immunodeficiency syndrome. *New England Journal of Medicine* 317(21):1297–1302.

Saba, J. (1995). Prevention of mother-to-child transmission of HIV. *International AIDS Society Newsletter*, July, no. 2, pp. 6–7.

Schiller, N. (1993). The invisible women: caregiving and the construction of AIDS health services. *Culture, Medicine and Psychiatry* 17:487–512.

Schilling, R. F., El-Bassel, N., Gilbert, L., and Schinke, S. (1991a). Correlates of drug use, sexual behavior, and attitudes toward safer sex among African–American and Hispanic women in methadone maintenance. *Journal of Drug Issues* 21(4):685–698.

Schilling, R. F., El-Bassel, N., Schinke, S., et al. (1991b). Building skills of recovering women drug users to reduce heterosexual AIDS transmission. *Public Health Report* 106:297–304.

Schoenbaum, E., and Webber, M. (1993). The underrecognition of HIV infection in women in an inner-city emergency room. *American Journal of Public Health* 83(3):363–368.

Seidman, S., and Reider, R. (1994). A review of sexual behavior in the United States. *American Journal of Psychiatry* 151(3):330–341.

Shayne, V. T., and Kaplan, B. T. (1991). Double victims: poor women with AIDS. *Women's Health* 17(1):21–37.

Shiboski, C. H., Hilton, J., Greenspan, D., et al. (1994). HIV-related oral manifestations in two cohorts of women in San Francisco. *Journal of Acquired Immunodeficiency Syndromes* 7:964–971.

Stevens, P. (1993). Lesbians and HIV: clinical, research, and policy issues. *American Journal of Orthopsychiatry* 63(2):289–294.

Strom, D. (1993). AIDS and intravenous drug users: issues and treatment implications. In *Clinical Work with Substance Abusing Clients*, ed. S. L. Straussner, pp. 330–350. New York: Guilford.

Suarez, M., Raffaelli, M., O'Leary, A., and LoConte, J. (1993). *Use of alternative healing practices among HIV-infected Hispanics*. Paper presented at the Ninth International Conference on AIDS, 9(2):899 PO-Dss-4089. Berlin, June 6–11.

Treichler, P. (1988). AIDS, gender and biomedical discourse: current contexts for meaning. In *AIDS: The Burdens of History*, ed. E. Fee and D. Fox, pp. 172–189. Berkeley, CA: University of California Press.

VanOss Marin, B., Tschann, J., Gomez, C., and Kegeles, S. (1993). Acculturation and gender differences in sexual attitudes and behaviors: Hispanic vs. non-Hispanic white unmarried adults. *American Journal of Public Health* 83(12):1759–1761.

Wiener, L. (1991). Women and human immunodeficiency virus: a historical and personal psychosocial perspective. *Social Work* 36(5):375–378.

Wofsy, C. (1987). Human immunodeficiency virus infection in women. *Journal of the American Medical Association* 257:2074–2076.

Worth, D., and Rodriguez, R. (1987). Latina women and AIDS. *Radical America* 20:63–67.

Zuckerman, C., and Gordon, L. (1988). Meeting the psychosocial and legal needs of women with AIDS and their families. *New York State Journal of Medicine* 88(12):619–620.

10

Women with Depression and Substance Abuse Problems

Carolyn Morell

The co-occurrence of depression and substance abuse creates a challenge for clinicians in the addictions field. We know that women are more likely than men to have depressive reactions connected to drinking and drugging, and also to have a history of depression that predates their abuse or dependence (Griffin et al. 1989, Turnbull 1988). We also know that if depressive symptoms are ignored, women in this population are likely to return to the abuse of substances to cope with depression's low mood (Sobell and Sobell 1993, Turnbull 1988). Simply put, unmanaged depression threatens recovery, and failed recovery leads to depression.

Since the concept of dual diagnosis is relatively new, little attention has been paid to treating women who are so defined (Blume 1992). Recovery means more than not drinking and/or drugging; it implies a reorientation to life that includes change as well as acceptance of self and others. Creative experimentation is needed to find meaningful interventions for women whose energies are doubly silenced by depressive and addictive conditions.

Silence, of course, is not always debilitating. The word signifies two very different potentialities: oblivion and stillness (Mish 1983). Feminists interested in spirituality often speak about the recuperative nature of contemplative silence, the practice of inner listening that promotes genuine self-knowledge and self-acceptance. In this view—which does *not* negate the need for changes in the gendered organization of social life but rather arouses engagement in such change—the well-being of an individual woman depends on periods of meditative solitude in order for her to experience her life in a larger and wiser way (Gross 1993, Hooks 1993).

This chapter makes a case for treating harmful silences with healing silence. Women in treatment need to attend to both inner and outer reality and to the connections between the two. Learning meditation skills within the context of a women's support group is one concrete strategy for assisting women who are traveling the road of recovery. After presenting a selective current review of information about women, depression, and substance abuse problems, with an emphasis on feminist writings, an extensive rationale for using mindfulness meditation to treat women with both maladies is introduced. Finally, guidelines for implementing an eight-week "One Moment at a Time" group in an addictions treatment context are offered. This approach is not recommended as a substitute for other woman-sensitive alcohol and drug treatment strategies but rather as one specific intervention that can be incorporated into a larger treatment plan where appropriate for the client.

WHAT WE KNOW: THE LITERATURE

Since not much has been written about women who are dually diagnosed with depression and addiction, it is necessary to discuss separately recent writings about women and depression and women with substance abuse problems, prior to reviewing the few articles that address both diagnoses among women.

Women and Depression

Feminist writers and researchers describe the unspoken suffering of women with depression. In the late 1950s, Sylvia Plath (1971) eloquently described her descent into depression as a bell jar descending down around her body and mind, quelling her relationship with the social world. More recently, clinician/researcher Dana Crowley Jack (1993) has described women's depression as a loss of one's voice and a stifling of one's very self.

Listening to the subjective experiences of women, Jack (1993) described the patterns associated with depression that women themselves identify. Such patterns include: self-condemnation, compliant relatedness, massive self-negation in order to secure relationships, fear of being wrong, inner division caused by self-silencing, and covert rebellion where a mix of anger and anxiety are present. Although women's behavior may *look* passive, dependent, and helpless, the silencing of self that the compliant role requires involves great cognitive and emotional activity in order to curb expression of negative feelings and perceptions. According to Jack, successful treatment of this condition involves exploration of those areas where a woman feels silenced and where she silences herself, and help in taking her own knowledge seriously. Group work is suggested as a context that supports this endeavor.

Psychologist and researcher Susan Nolen-Hoeksema (1990), while studying sex differences in depression, found that women's *responses* to depressive symptoms differ from those of men. Women are more likely to think and worry compulsively about their condition, which tends to increase the duration and intensity of the depressive episode. From the standpoint of treatment, a ruminative style may render ineffective behavioral interventions popularly prescribed. For instance, physical activity may be recommended, yet a woman can ruminate while walking or jogging. She may be encouraged to build a support system and end up with "ruminating partners." Nolen-Hoeksema (1990) concluded that "the specific foci and techniques of different types of therapies for depression may be less important than the extent to which these therapies give the ruminator a sense of control over her ruminations" (p. 176).

Focusing on the link between anger and depression, Lois P. Frankel (1992) reminds her readers that a depressed mood is more acceptable among women than the expression of negative feelings. Rather than acting out their anger, Frankel has suggested that women deny these feelings by participating in behaviors such as excessive sleeping, eating, drinking, or being depressed. "The depressed woman retreats to a place that is safe—inside herself. She is then filled with a brewing storm of emotions, none of which she can put a name to" (p. 15). Feeling a lack of control, the depressed woman may engage in compulsive behavior to try to experience control and to avoid painful feelings. Self-empowerment strategies recommended by Frankel include cognitive and behavioral changes that emphasize assertiveness skills.

The link between physical and sexual abuse and depression is discussed by Judith Lewis Herman (1992) in her study of survivors of trauma. Again the theme of silence appears. She found that certain violations are "too terrible to utter aloud: this is the meaning of the word *unspeakable*" (p. 1). Women's self-silencing in this case is not within the realm of intention and choice. Indeed, the "conflict between the will to deny horrible events and the will to proclaim them aloud is the central dialectic of psychological trauma" (p. 1). Women who are survivors of child abuse may become adults with a dazzling array of symptoms, including depression and alcohol and other drug addictions. The restoration of self and voice takes place during discrete stages of recovery. The central task of group treatment in stage one is the establishment of safety, in stage two, remembrance and mourning, and in stage three, reconnection with ordinary life.

Jane Ussher (1991) reminds us that there are many manifestations and routes to depression. There are also many responses. Different women may benefit from different interventions. Ussher argues that individual women need treatment to alleviate their pain, but such treatment must be part of a larger process of addressing the collective condition of women. She warns: "Any solution which treats the symptoms without looking to the cause of the problem is short-sighted, be it a physical, therapeutic or sociopolitical change" (Ussher 1991, p. 298). She calls for a feminist reeducation of women and of the "experts" who treat them.

Feminist Perspectives on Women and Substance Abuse Problems

Feminists writing about women and substance abuse and dependence also rely on the construct of silence when characterizing the impact of drugs on women's lives. In her classic work, Marian Sandmaier (1980) described alcohol abuse as a way for women to quiet the excruciating conflicts created by the female life condition. More recently, Elizabeth

Ettorre (1992) asserted that the goal of substance abuse treatment should be a woman's reclamation of her voice. Sexism, racism, classism, ageism, heterosexism, and "every other system of inequality" erode a woman's power and self-esteem and thus contribute to her abuse of substances, including alcohol, pills, heroin, nicotine, and food (Ettorre 1992, p. 37).

Critical of the disease model, Ettorre (1992) advocates the use of a more holistic notion of body-mind unity that does not separate the individual from her social context. She contends that substance abuse workers must not rely on psychiatric models that ignore cultural reality. Pointing out that women are often reluctant about connecting to professional treatment because of potential adverse consequences, including being stigmatized or losing their children, Ettorre calls for new components within existing services that are women-friendly and that will attract women to seek the services they need. All women need "more public and private space to explore what pleases them and to empower themselves as women" (Ettorre 1992, p. 136). Such liberation zones allow women to move towards self-definition.

In an extensive review of old and new data about alcoholism and women, with special reference to treatment issues, Edith Gomberg (1993) has summarized both the characteristics of women who abuse alcohol and a variety of treatment recommendations. In this review, she reported that it is not necessarily the *existence* of early life negative events that distinguishes women who become alcoholic from those who do not, but women's *affective response* in describing their early lives. In short, women's negative interpretations of negative life events is linked to alcoholic drinking. Selected other characteristics of women with alcohol abuse and dependency that appear in the scientific literature, summarized by Gomberg (1993), include inadequate coping mechanisms, self-destructive ways of managing anger, depression, and a high degree of guilt and shame.

The literature reviewed by Gomberg suggests that no special skills are needed to treat women, only "real sensitivity about women" (Gomberg 1993, p. 217). Since most women arrive at treatment depressed and with low self-esteem, women need reassurance about their abilities to make changes and relief from their heavy load of guilt and shame. All-women's groups are recommended, as are family therapy and resources for children. Gomberg concluded by asserting that "the most critical aspect of treatment for alcoholic women lies in therapists' attitude toward women in general and toward substance-abusing and alcoholic women in particular" (p. 217).

In another recent review of the literature on women with alcohol and other drug problems, Blume (1992) reported on the factors influencing chemical dependency. Although there is much uncertainty about the role played by psychological factors in the etiology of addictive disorders in general, women being treated for substance abuse have higher levels of anxiety and depressive symptoms and lower self-esteem than their male counterparts. Blume also reported that alcohol abuse and dependence in women correlates with a history of physical and sexual abuse.

Among the treatment recommendations summarized in Blume's work (1992) is the recommendation that special techniques should be employed to deal with women's low self-esteem and with sexism and its consequences as personally experienced. Therapeutic intervention should not aim to adjust women to societal norms, but to enlarge the range of women's conscious choices about their lives and their autonomous functioning.

Straussner (1985), addressing the special needs of women in treatment for alcoholism, asserted that it is crucial for workers to be knowledgeable about a woman's pill history as well as drinking history. A woman with a history of both pill and alcohol dependence may require a longer detoxification and treatment process. By the time a woman seeks treatment she frequently feels depressed and has a tremendous sense of shame and guilt. Straussner suggests a variety of techniques to help women learn "how to muster her resources to help herself" (Straussner 1985, p. 75).

Women who become dependent on psychotropic drugs affirm the social image of women as compliant and dependent. In a vivid account of her painful odyssey with Valium, Barbara Gordon (1979) referred to the drug as "a leveller . . . It evens things out silently, quietly. No rush, no thrill, no charge . . . the safe and sane drug" (p. 51). Most addictive substances are self-administered, but women's use of tranquilizers is commonly prescribed by a physician. Nairne and Smith (1984) point out that the reason that women abuse prescribed drugs is similar to the reasons that women get depressed—both responses help women escape oppressive aspects of the female role. Yet legal drug use can be a vicious cycle since dependence on tranquilizers may induce a sense of guilt and shame among users (Sterling 1989).

Because women's drug abuse has most often involved legal drugs, such as alcohol and prescription medication (Davis 1990), little attention has been given to understanding the characteristics and needs of women addicted to street drugs such as heroin and cocaine. The silences surrounding this group of chemically dependent women can be explained, in part, by the fact that many women never enter treatment, given the great stigma placed upon this group and the insensitivity of treatment programs to their needs (O'Connor et al. 1994). The few studies that have been conducted establish correlations between depressive symptoms and use of illicit substances (Beck et al. 1984, Boyd 1993, Griffin et al. 1989, Halikas et. al. 1994, O'Connor et al. 1994, Rounsaville et al. 1985).

For example, Boyd (1993), looking at a sample of predominantly African-American women who used crack cocaine, found that a significant number of the women had a history of sexual abuse and depressive symptoms. Griffin and colleagues (1989), using a convenience sample of 34 women and 95 men, found that women presenting for cocaine abuse treatment were more likely than men to be dually diagnosed with major depression. Griffin also reported that women in treatment experienced slower recovery from their depressive symptoms than did men. Griffin concluded that given the likelihood of depression and addiction co-existing in crack cocaine-using women, "centers that treat women for substance abuse must be prepared to employ a dual diagnostic model, concomitantly providing support and treatment for the addiction and the depression" (p. 427).

In a study conducted by Halikas and colleagues (1994) that determined psychiatric diagnoses in 207 cocaine abusers seeking outpatient treatment, women were found to have significantly higher rates of current and lifetime psychiatric disorders, including affective disorders.

O'Connor and colleagues (1994) studied shame, guilt, and depression in 130 men and women in recovery from addiction to a variety of substances, including cocaine, opiates, alcohol, marijuana, and amphetamines. They found women had significantly higher rates of shame and depression than men. The results of the study "support persistent anecdotal reports among chemical dependency professionals that women coming into treatment tend to suffer from a greater sense of shame, self-blame, and depression than do men" (O'Connor et al. 1994, pp. 506–507). The authors conclude that confrontational and shame-inducing methods of treatment developed to treat male addicts are contraindicated with chemically dependent women.

Schliebner (1994) summarized what all the previously mentioned researchers document: Women who are chemically dependent are underrepresented in treatment and thus undertreated. Gender-sensitive therapeutic approaches are necessary to deal with this fact. Such treatment must address women's special needs, sex-role socialization, and thus must be innovative.

The Coexistence of Substance Abuse Problems and Depression

There are few writings that deal with the interplay of depressive and addictive conditions in the general population and even fewer that deal with these dual conditions among women specifically. The majority of books and articles addressing the needs of dually disordered clients do not address gender issues (Cohen and Levy 1992, Evans and Sullivan 1990, Leibenluft et al. 1993, Schuckit and Monteiro 1988). No mention is made of the differing cultural context in which women and men reside. Thus the authors engage in what some feminists describe as context-stripping.

In 1969, Schuckit and colleagues used the concepts of primary and secondary alcoholism to distinguish between the presence of alcohol problems in the absence of a preexisting affective disorder and those that follow an affective disorder. These researchers found that women with secondary alcoholism are often younger, have a shorter period of alcoholism, and have a better treatment prognosis. In 1988, Turnbull, using these same categories, stated the view that secondary alcoholic women may use alcohol to medicate their low mood. Yet eventually, alcoholism becomes an independent problem and the "dysphoric symptoms of alcoholism are added to those of the preexisting depression" (Turnbull 1988, p. 291).

After a period of sobriety, the depressed mood associated with alcohol abuse may lift, making a diagnosis of primary or secondary alcoholism possible (McGrath et al. 1990). Turnbull (1988) suggested that women with secondary alcoholism need a treatment plan that effectively addresses two separate goals—an alcohol-free life and the alleviation of depressive symptoms. Women with chronic dysphoria require specialized treatment such as cognitive therapy. Turnbull concluded that many of the issues that are critical for women with secondary alcoholism are identical to those issues that are critical for depressed women, such as low self-esteem, guilt, and feelings of helplessness.

Although researchers have established the co-occurrence of depression with use of opiates, cocaine, marijuana, sedative-hypnotics, and benzodiazepines, equivalent studies in primary versus secondary substance abuse in women who suffer from drug dependencies other than alcohol are not available.

As this literature review makes clear, there is a great deal of overlap in the characteristics seen in women who are depressed and women who have substance abuse problems: compulsive behavior, low self-esteem, self-condemnation, guilt and shame, negative interpretations of life events, self-negation, anxiety, denial, suppression of feelings, and alienation from self and others.

Among the various treatment recommendations aimed at helping substance-abusing depressed women are: providing cognitive therapies; providing women-only treatment groups; helping women "rename" or redefine identity; increasing assertiveness and the subjective experience of choice; teaching constructive coping skills; helping women experi-

ence more pleasure and increase their sense of worth; and providing opportunities and skills for self-exploration and self-acceptance.

Treatment for women who are diagnosed with both conditions is
necessarily experimental because, as Blume (1991) reminds us, we do
not really know how to treat this population. One of the practice problems that needs to be addressed is the higher rates of relapse among
women with depressive symptoms (Turnbull and Gomberg 1990). The
remainder of this chapter presents an experimental intervention designed to help prevent relapse: a women-only mindfulness meditation
group for women diagnosed with depression and substance abuse or
dependence.

MINDFULNESS MEDITATION FOR WOMEN

Mindfulness meditation, also known as *Vippasana* or Insight Meditation,
teaches one how to scrutinize one's own perceptual processes with pre-
cision. One learns to watch the arising of thought and perception with
serene detachment (Gunaratana 1993). The meditator trains the mind
to watch thoughts and feelings come and go, without judging or rejecting them, without trying to change them, and without getting lost in
them. One learns not to be victimized by his or her thoughts and recognizes that a thought is only a thought.

This ability to observe thoughts is an extremely useful skill for women
in recovery for several reasons. First, women in groups commonly get
stuck in their own and each other's stories (interpretations of events) and
get lost in turbulent emotions. As Marsha Linehan (1993a) reminds us,
neither stories nor emotions should always be taken literally, as literal
reflections of environmental events. Thoughts ("I feel unloved") are confused with facts ("I am unloved"). Certain forms of meditative practice
provide an excellent opportunity for such testing, as the practitioner
learns to distinguish between interpretations of events and actual events.

Second, in feminist-oriented recovery groups, women are encouraged
to take an active stance and keep a focus on changing the circumstances
that trigger their reactions. This practice is essential but needs balancing, however, because in some circumstances taking action may be premature, unskillful, or diversionary. Sometimes the wiser response is the
one embodied in the phrase, "Don't just do something, sit there" (Kabat-
Zinn 1994). Furthermore, sometimes the pain women experience is connected to the human condition, not to gender conditions or conditioning. As Rita Gross (1993) has put it, "basic human suffering and existential
anxieties are not patriarchy's fault and will not be eliminated in post-
patriarchal social conditions" (p. 13). Developing equanimity in the face

of "the things I cannot change" is essential during the recovery process of all individuals.

During formal meditation practice sessions, the individual becomes an *observer* of the impact of mind on the body and emotions, a "silent witness" (Chopra 1990) or a "listening presence" (Kornfield 1993). A woman sits in silence and trains attention by focusing on the breath. She is invariably pulled away from the breath by thoughts, by emotions, by noises, by sensations. The meditator simply notes what is present and gently returns attention to the breath. The task is to remain keenly aware of what is actually happening from moment to moment, without wishing things to be different.

Rather than mechanically changing the content of interpretations and beliefs, a mindfulness meditative approach involves returning to the present moment whenever one becomes caught in mental distractions (Welwood 1992). Immediate experiencing stops the war within (Kornfield 1993).

Over time, a perceptual shift occurs. The woman meditating becomes anchored in a more spacious sense of self and is not tossed away by internal events. Her pain may be great, but the edge comes off as she observes the mind flailing about, interpreting and evaluating, and scripting stories. An extremely complex series of events may be summarized in one simple sentence. Cultural and personal conditioning is neutralized by the deepening of our momentary awareness (Feldman 1989).

The impact of regular meditation practice is summarized by Jack Kornfield (1993):

> When we take the one seat on our meditation cushion, we become our own monastery. We create the compassionate space that allows for the arising of all things: sorrows, loneliness, shame, desire, regret, frustration, happiness . . . In the monastery of our own sitting meditation, each of us experiences whatever arises again and again as we let go, saying, "Ah, this too." . . . [When taking] the one seat we discover that we are unshakable. We discover that we can face life fully, with all its suffering and joy, that our heart is great enough to encompass it all. [p. 36]

Underlying both Western cognitive approaches and Eastern meditative strategies to deal with substance abuse and depression is the knowledge that our interpretations of ourselves and our life circumstances are "the ropes that bind us to suffering" (Nhat Hanh 1990, p. 37). East and West diverge in their views on how to transform these troublesome interpretations. For the most part, Western cognitive interventions emphasize the *content* of consciousness. For example, negative self-statements or beliefs are replaced with positive self-statements and views, or illogical thoughts are challenged by logical ideas (Beck and Young 1985, Freeman et al. 1990). Meditation practice goes deeper to transform the *process* of consciousness. Framed in terms of cognitive science, meditation is "simply the sustained effort to retrain attentional, perceptual habits" (Goleman 1991, p. 95).

According to some researchers (Prochaska et al. 1992), successfully changing an addictive condition involves a progression through a series of changes: precontemplation, contemplation, preparation, action, and maintenance. Mindfulness meditation may be an effective intervention in any of the stages of change. In early recovery, a meditation practice involves internal cognitive change that can help move clients from precontemplation into the contemplation and preparation stages. A woman in denial may learn how important a drug (or drugs) has become in her life as she watches her thoughts and experiences her body. As previously mentioned, in the active stage, meditation offers the meditator a concrete tool for letting go of thoughts and physical urges to use mind-altering chemicals. Clients in later stages of recovery who are working to maintain sobriety can benefit from the counterconditioning effects that ongoing meditation practice offers.

Since meditation is not traditionally valued in this culture, how can such a skill be incorporated into dual diagnosis treatment programming? Who should be included and excluded? At what level of treatment should it be offered? How long should the group run and what is the content of the sessions? How can the group's effectiveness be evaluated? Who should teach it? How can staff be trained? Following are some guidelines for offering a mindfulness meditation group for women with depression and substance abuse problems within the context of an outpatient addiction treatment facility.

SETTING UP A "ONE MOMENT AT A TIME" GROUP

The goals of a mindfulness meditation group are threefold: first, to teach women a way of managing depression through nonjudgmental detachment from their thoughts and feelings; second, to increase their capacity for experiential living; and third, to prevent the return to alcohol and/or other drug use to deal with low mood. Women must be free from alcohol and other mood-altering drugs, other than prescribed antidepressants, before beginning in the group.

The group should meet for an extended period of time, long enough for participants to develop and appreciate a meditative habit. An eight-week group that meets twice a week for one and a half hours may be sufficient. A women-only group with female-identified leaders skilled in addressing women's issues allows participants to discuss openly painful issues that surface and to revise conditioned beliefs.

Who Is a Good Candidate for the Group?

Treatment matching is a critical issue to consider. No one treatment approach works for all people who experience substance abuse problems. Female clients who are experiencing both depressive and addictive conditions represent a large group of women in treatment. Careful assessment is needed to increase the likelihood of intervention effectiveness and to decrease the chances of doing harm. The guidelines suggested here should be considered flexible, since no rigid rule can supersede the need to individualize treatment.

The severity of depression may be more important to consider than whether it is primary or secondary. Women with active suicide plans, psychotic symptoms, or bipolar disorders may not be appropriate for the group, because severe psychiatric conditions could become magnified during meditation. The Beck Depression Inventory (Beck 1961) may be used to measure severity. Caution is required with women whose alcohol or other drug abuse or depression is related to a history of sexual abuse. Herman's (1992) book, *Trauma and Recovery*, may be a useful guide here. Because recovery occurs in stages, Herman has found, a form of therapy useful at one stage may actually cause harm if offered when a woman is at a different stage. Since the one-moment-at-a-time group is not a trauma-focused group, women in the final stage of trauma recovery, reconnection to ordinary life, may benefit the most.

For depressed women without a traumatic disorder, perhaps more salient than the stage of change is the depressed woman's interest in and energy level for a meditation group. During the entrance interview, the counselor can educate the client about the benefits of meditation and assess motivation. If a client chooses to enter the group, she should be expected to commit to the entire eight-week program, to attend twice a week, and to complete homework exercises.

What Happens in Each Session?

A variation on Kabat-Zinn's (1990) program of stress reduction could provide some initial structure. Kabat-Zinn incorporates body work using some yoga positions as a way of increasing mindfulness. Brief yoga exercises facilitate a body-mind receptive to silent meditation. Sessions should include a combination of instruction, practice, and discussion.

At the beginning of each session, information can be shared to motivate and guide the meditation practice. Many teaching tools are available that can be integrated into each session. A variety of audio and
videotapes are also available.[1] For example, the mindfulness skills training that Linehan (1993b) has developed for the treatment of borderline
personality disordered individuals can also be utilized in explaining
mindfulness practice. Her *Skills Training Manual for Treating Borderline
Personality Disorder* (1993b) includes an outline of her mindfulness skills
module, complete with handouts that may be freely reproduced for use
in clinical practice.

During the first session, a ten-minute meditation practice may be
followed by a discussion. Participants can share their experiences and
ask questions. Homework assignments should involve the practice of
formal sitting meditation and informal mindfulness (Kabat-Zinn 1990).
Audiotapes could be made available to help guide meditation at home.
Informal practice aimed at cultivating mindfulness in one's daily activities
might require women to pick an activity to do mindfully each day,
whether that activity is taking a shower, changing a diaper, eating a
meal, or going for a walk. This assignment requires the woman to stay
wholeheartedly focused on the immediate experience of her body and
the activity she is engaged in, rather than being lost in thought while
showering, diapering, eating, or walking. For example, being mindful
in the shower involves attending to how the soap and water look and
feel on the body, what sensations are experienced as the body is gently
stroked and cleaned, how one's feet feel touching the bottom of the tub,
what aromas are in the air, how the water tastes, and so forth. Staying
in the present is no small feat. Women need to practice staying present
consciously in order to experience the benefits of being alive. Showering can be a great pleasure when our minds are not making us miser-
able by dwelling on anxiety, pain, or anger related to the past or the
future.

Another homework assignment could involve keeping a calendar of
pleasant experiences. A calendar-of-events form can be given to members to record what the experiences are, whether or not they were aware

---

1. A series of tapes used by Kabat-Zinn, used in conjunction with his stress
reduction workshops, are listed with order form on pp. 271–275 of *Wherever
You Go, There You Are*. A catalog of highly recommended tapes and videos can
be secured from The Insight Meditation Society (IMS) by writing to Dharma
Seed Tape Library, Box 66, Wendell Depot, MA 01380. *Inquiring Mind*, a semi-
annual journal, with articles, listings of retreats, and locations of sitting groups
all over the United States, is available free from Box 9999, North Berkeley Station, Berkeley, CA 94709.

at the time of the experience, how their body felt, what feelings and thoughts were present, and what they are feeling as they record the event (Kabat-Zinn 1990). Such an exercise can help women get in touch with a range of experiencing and balance their tendency to focus with greater frequency on negative experiences.

Subsequent sessions follow a structure similar to the first, but with increasing time devoted to silent meditation. During the last week, the group participates in sitting meditation for 45 minutes during each session. Practice outside the sessions should also last 45 minutes.

Measuring Group Effectiveness

Health and mental health providers in the United States are beginning to draw on Eastern views for holistic ways of understanding and treating a wide variety of human ailments (Alexander 1989, Ash 1993, Cowley 1993, Kabat-Zinn 1990, Langer 1990). Related to this trend is a growing scientific literature indicating that psychological health may be developed through the systematic practice of various meditative skills (Bogart 1991, Gelderloos et al. 1989, Kabat-Zinn 1992, Linehan 1993a). Yet to date, there is no empirical justification of using such an approach with the population of women dually diagnosed with depression and substance abuse problems. Care with outcome evaluation procedures may document the usefulness of the specific approach outlined in this chapter and also contribute to the research on meditation and mental health more generally.

Three different methods of evaluation are suggested: The Beck Depression Inventory (BDI) to measure objectively changes in depressive symptomology, a participant questionnaire to measure subjective perceptions of change, and an exit interview with the same counselor who did the entrance interview for a professional assessment of change.

As noted earlier, the Beck Depression Inventory (BDI) should be administered before the group begins to provide a baseline for comparison. At the end of each week, the BDI could be administered and results plotted on an individual graph kept in the client's case folder (Miranda et al. 1992). This visual documentation of the client's progress, or lack thereof, can be shared during the exit interview as counselor and client evaluate the client's experience. The majority of clients should show improvement in managing depressive symptoms and thus experience a lighter mood. In the event that a member does not improve, counselors must take precautions not to frame the woman's experience as a failure. The counselor should reassure the client that there are many ways to deal with depression and that no one way works for all people. Together the counselor and client can use her participation in the group as a valuable learning experience, tease out what may have been helpful, and make a different treatment plan.

During the last session, participants could be asked to fill out a short-answer questionnaire to evaluate their experience, since important changes in a woman's behavior may not be reflected on the BDI. For example, women may continue to feel sad, discouraged, disappointed, and so on. What may have changed is their *relationship* to these feelings. Perhaps they deal with these emotions in a more skillful way. Or perhaps such emotions bother them less as they develop a more philosophical attitude about their lives. These changes in behavior and attitude might be missed if only the BDI is used to measure outcomes.

Examples of open-ended questions might be: "What was most helpful to you about this meditation workshop?" "Do you manage your low mood differently since you have attended this workshop? If so, how?" "Do you think you will continue a meditation practice after this group ends? Why or why not?" "Do you experience daily pleasures with more frequency now than you did before entering the group? If so, give examples." "Has mindfulness meditation helped you remain abstinent? If so, how?"

The exit interview serves two purposes. First, through conversation with the counselor, the client may come to a richer understanding and deeper evaluation of her experience with mindfulness meditation. Thus the interaction between counselor and client provides another measure of client outcomes. And second, the interview can be used to reinforce the client's learning and develop individualized strategies that enable continued mindfulness practice. For some women, joining an ongoing meditation group may be possible; for others, reading, listening to tapes, with an occasional sitting practice may suffice. What is important is that women find ways to reinforce mindfulness in their daily living.

Group Leadership

As presented above, key variables in women's treatment are women-only groups and gender-sensitive counselors. Interest in and sensitivity to women's issues as well as in mindfulness meditation are thus indicated for staff who lead this group. Although many women counselors are already knowledgeable about women's unique stressors and understand how social subordination is implicated in the lives of their clients, they may not be qualified to teach the workshop. On the other hand, it may be that some staff already are practitioners of meditation and interested in leading the group.

To get more staff interested and competent to run a mindfulness meditation group, an extensive in-service training may need to be set up, drawing on local resources if they exist. Alternatively, one or two interested staff members could be sent for training to one of the many meditation retreat centers that operate across the United States and Canada. For example, the Insight Meditation Center in Barre, Massachusetts, runs retreats year round. Unless counselors become practitioners able to experience the benefits of mindful meditation themselves, they will be in no position to become teachers to clients.

CONCLUSION

Helping women who are both depressed and addicted is a difficult process: no single intervention can possibly deal with all the variables that need to be addressed. Mindfulness meditation may, in conjunction with other interventions, prove invaluable because it simultaneously addresses the silences associated with being a woman, depressed and addicted. It is appropriate for women who are depressed as it helps women to stay connected to the present reality, develop compassion for self, and reconnect with ordinary pleasures. It also fits neatly into the philosophy of twelve-step recovery programs. Step Eleven of Alcoholics Anonymous (1976) reads: "Sought through prayer *and meditation* [emphasis added] . . ." Meditation is a route to three critical needs identified in the Serenity Prayer for the woman with a substance abuse problem: acceptance, change, and wisdom.

Further, it offers women a more spacious sense of identity than patriarchal conditioning promotes—an identity that expands beyond the small story of one's life to encompass the flow of momentary experience and the splendor of all life. Accordingly, using silence to help mend silence is an experiment worth pursuing.

REFERENCES

Alcoholics Anonymous. (1976). Third edition. New York: Alcoholics Anonymous World Services.

Alexander, S. (1989). Transcendental meditation, mindfulness and longevity: an experimental study with the elderly. *Journal of Personality and Social Psychology* 57:950–964.

Ash, M. (1993). *The Zen of Recovery*. New York: Tarcher/Perigee Books.

Beck, A., Steer, R., and Shaw, B. (1984). Hopelessness in alcohol- and heroin-dependent women. *Journal of Clinical Psychology* 40:602– 606.

Beck, A. T., and Young, J. E. (1985). Depression. In *Clinical Handbook of Psychological Disorders*, ed. D. H. Barlow, pp. 206–244. New York: Guilford.

Blume, S. B. (1991). *Clinical research on alcohol and women: gaps and opportunities*. Unpublished paper delivered at the National Academy of Sciences, Washington, DC, May 30–31.

——— (1992). Alcohol and other drug problems in women. In *Substance Abuse: A Comprehensive Textbook*, ed. J. H. Lowinson, P. Ruiz, and R. B. Millman, pp. 794–807. Baltimore: Williams & Wilkins.

Bogart, G. (1991). The use of meditation in psychotherapy: a review of the literature. *American Journal of Psychotherapy* 45(3):383–412.

Boyd, C. J. (1993). The antecedents of women's crack cocaine abuse: family substance abuse, sexual abuse, depression and illicit drug use. *Journal of Substance Abuse Treatment* 10:433–438.

Chopra, D. (1990). *Quantum Healing*. New York: Bantam.

Cohen, J., and Levy, S. J. (1992). *The Mentally Ill Chemical Abuser: Whose Client?* New York: Lexington Books.

Cowley, A. S. (1993). Transpersonal social work: a theory for the 1990s. *Social Work* 38:527–534.

Davis, D. J. (1990). Prevention issues in developing programs. In *Women: Alcohol and Drugs*, ed. R. C. Engs, pp. 71–77. New York: Kendall/ Hunt.

Ettorre, E. (1992). *Women and Substance Use*. New Brunswick, NJ: Rutgers University Press.

Evans, K., and Sullivan, M. J. (1990). *Dual Diagnosis: Counseling the Mentally Ill Substance Abuser*. New York: Guilford.

Feldman, C. (1989). *Woman Awake*. New York: Arkana.

Frankel, L. P. (1992). *Women, Anger and Depression: Strategies for Self-Empowerment*. Deerfield Beach, FL: Health Communications.

Freeman, A., Pretzer, J., Fleming, B., and Simon, K., eds. (1990). *Clinical Applications of Cognitive Therapy*. New York: Plenum.

Gelderloos, P., Hermans, H. J. M., Ahlscrom, H. H., and Jacoby, R. (1990). Transcendence and psychological health: studies with long-term participants of the transcendental meditation and tm-sidhi program. *The Journal of Psychology* 142(2):177–197.

Goleman, D. (1991). Tibetan and Western models of mental health. In *MindScience: An East-West Dialogue*, ed. D. Goleman and R. A. F. Thurman, pp. 89–102. Boston: Wisdom.

Gomberg, E. S. L. (1993). Women and alcohol: use and abuse. *Journal of Nervous and Mental Disease* 181(4):211–219.

Gordon, B. (1979). *I'm Dancing As Fast As I Can*. New York: Harper & Row.

Griffin, M., Weiss, R., Mirin, S., and Lange, U. (1989). A comparison of male and female cocaine abusers. *Archives of General Psychiatry* 46:122–126.

Gross, R. M. (1993). *Buddhism After Patriarchy*. Albany, NY: State University of New York Press.

Gunaratana, H. (1993). *Mindfulness in Plain English*. Boston: Wisdom Publications.

Halikas, J. A., Crosby, R. D., Pearson, V. L., et al. (1994). Psychiatric comorbidity in treatment-seeking cocaine abusers. *American Journal on Addictions* 3(1):25–35.

Herman, J. L. (1992). *Trauma and Recovery*. New York: Basic Books.

Hooks, B. (1993). *Sisters of the Yam: Black Women and Self-Recovery*. Boston: South End.

Jack, D. C. (1993). *Silencing the Self: Women and Depression*. New York: HarperCollins.

Kabat-Zinn, J. (1990). *Full Catastrophe Living*. New York: Delta.

—— (1992). Effectiveness of a meditation-based stress reduction program in the treatment of anxiety disorders. *American Journal of Psychiatry* 149(97):936–943.

—— (1994). *Wherever You Go, There You Are*. New York: Hyperion.

Kornfield, J. (1993). *A Path with Heart: A Guide through the Perils and Promises of Spiritual Life*. New York: Bantam.

Langer, E. J. (1990). *Mindfulness*. New York: Addison-Wesley.

Leibenluft, E., Fiero, P. L., Bartko, J. J., et al. (1993). Depressive symptoms and the self-reported use of alcohol, caffeine, and carbohydrates in normal volunteers and four groups of psychiatric outpatients. *American Journal of Psychiatry* 150(2):294–298.

Linehan, M. M. (1993a). *Cognitive-Behavioral Treatment of Borderline Personality Disorder*. New York: Guilford.

—— (1993b). *Skills Training Manual for Treating Borderline Personality Disorder*. New York: Guilford.

Mairs, N. (1989). Conspiracies of silence. *The Women's Review of Books* 6:10–11.

McGrath, E., Kieta, G. P., Strickland, B., and Russo, N. F. (1990). *Women and Depression: Risk Factors and Treatment Issues*. Washington, DC: American Psychological Association.

Miranda, J., Schreckengost, J., and Heine, L. (1992). Cognitive-behavioral treatment for depression. In *Focal Group Psychotherapy*, ed. M. McKay and K. Paleg, pp. 135–162. Oakland, CA: New Harbinger.

Mish, F. C., Gilman, E. W., Lowe, J. G., et al., eds. (1983). *Ninth New Collegiate Dictionary*. Springfield, MA: Merriam-Webster.

Nairne, K., and Smith, G. (1984). *Dealing with Depression*. London: Women's Press.

Nhat Hanh, T. (1990). *Transformation and Healing: Sutra on the Four Establishments of Mindfulness*. Berkeley, CA: Parallax.

Nolen-Hoeksema, S. (1990). *Sex Difference in Depression*. Stanford, CA: Stanford University Press.

O'Connor, L. E., Berry, J. W., Inaba, D., et al. (1994). Shame, guilt, and depression in men and women in recovery from addiction. *Journal of Substance Abuse Treatment* 11(6):503–510.

Plath, S. (1971). *The Bell Jar*. New York: Bantam Books.

Prochaska, J. O., DiClemente, C. C., and Norcross, J. C. (1992). In search of how people change: applications to addictive behaviors. *American Psychologist* 47(9):1102–1114.

Rounsaville, B. J., Kosten, T. R., Weissman, M. M., et al. (1985). Treatment research monograph: *Evaluating and treating depressive disorders in opiate addicts*. Rockville, MD: National Institute on Drug Abuse.

Sandmaier, M. (1980). *The Invisible Alcoholics: Women and Alcohol Abuse in America*. New York: McGraw-Hill.

Schleibner, C. T. (1994). Gender-sensitive therapy: an alternative for women in substance abuse treatment. *Journal of Substance Abuse Treatment* 11(6):511–515.

Schuckit, M. A., and Monteiro, M. G. (1988). Alcoholism, anxiety, and depression. *British Journal of Addiction* 83:1373–1380.

Schuckit, M. A., Pitts, F. N., Jr., Reich, T., et al. (1969). Alcoholism I: two types of alcoholism in women. *Archives of General Psychiatry* 20:301–306.

Sobell, M. B., and Sobell, L. C. (1993). *Problem Drinkers: Guided Self-Change Treatment*. New York: Guilford.

Sterling, S. (1989). Benzodiazepines. *SCODA Newsletter*, July–August, pp. 5–7.

Straussner, S. L. A. (1985). Alcoholism in women: current knowledge and implications for treatment. In *Psychosocial Issues in the Treatment of Alcoholism*, ed. D. Cook, S. L. A. Straussner, and C. Fewell, pp. 61–77. New York: Haworth.

Turnbull, J. E. (1988). Primary and secondary alcoholic women. *Social Casework* 69(5):290–297.

Turnbull, J. E., and Gomberg, E. S. L. (1990). The structure of depression in alcoholic women. *Journal of Studies on Alcohol* 51(2):148–155.

Ussher, J. (1991). *Women's Madness: Misogyny or Mental Illness?* Amherst, MA: University of Massachusetts Press.

Welwood, J., ed. (1992). *Ordinary Magic: Everyday Life as Spiritual Path*. Boston: Shambhala.

Substance-Abusing Women and Eating Disorders

Katherine van Wormer

Emily Askew

11

There are three major types of eating disorders: anorexia nervosa, bulimia, and compulsive eating. Ninety-five percent of clients suffering from these conditions are women (Kuba and Hanchey 1991). In recent years, concurrent with the intensified pursuit of a lean, fat-free body promoted in the mass media, the prevalence of eating disorders has increased by leaps and bounds (Seid 1994, Wolf 1991). While up to one percent of females in late adolescence and young adulthood meet the strict standards of the medically dangerous disorder of anorexia, one to three percent of the same age group have a serious problem with bulimia according to the American Psychiatric Association (APA 1994). Moreover, millions of women without clinical eating disorders mimic the behavior and mind-set of affected women by being obsessed with their weight and body size (Seid 1994).

The current research indicates that it is not uncommon for women to have an eating disorder in conjunction with other substance abuse. Eating disorders may also develop in response to parental substance abuse, particularly alcoholism. It is essential, therefore, for clinicians working in the field of addiction to have a working knowledge of the characteristics of the various eating disorders. From a preventive viewpoint as well as for treatment intervention, early identification of the illness is crucial. The purpose of this chapter is to provide an overview of eating disorders in women in terms of their interconnectedness with other substance abuse and to offer a holistic, gender-based, biopsychosocial approach to the treatment of eating-disordered women.

THE CONNECTION BETWEEN EATING DISORDERS AND CHEMICAL DEPENDENCY

In women, bulimia/anorexia and chemical dependency often coincide. The frequency of other substance abuse in eating-disordered populations has been studied far more extensively than the frequency of eating disorders in women who abuse alcohol and other substances. Moreover, many substance abuse treatment centers, often male focused, overlook the existence of eating disorders entirely.

In his summary of research studies in the field, Krahn (1991) reported that the development of eating disorders generally precedes the emergence of alcoholism. This finding is logical in light of the prevalence of anorexia and bulimia among very young females, while alcoholism, which takes a longer time to develop, is more common among mature women. Longitudinal studies summarized by Krahn bear this out: individuals who suffered eating disorders often experience later development of alcoholism. Moreover, alcohol is the most frequently abused drug by patients with eating disorders, with 50 percent of bulimic patients using alcohol excessively at some point in their lives (Krahn 1991). A history of disordered eating, especially of bulimia, therefore, should alert clinicians to the increased risk for alcoholism, as well as other substances, down the road.

In a rare study that measured the frequency of eating disorders in substance abusers, Hudson and colleagues (1992) studied 386 consecutive male and female patients hospitalized for alcohol and other drug problems. They found that 15 percent of 143 women had a lifetime diagnosis of anorexia or bulimia compared to only one percent of the men. These findings give some indication of a correlation for women between eating disorders and other addictions. Providers of either chemical dependency treatment or eating disorders treatment, therefore, must become adept at assessing and treating both disorders. In fact, a holistic clinical approach suited to individual needs can easily teach life-coping strategies (such as stress management techniques) that are relevant to a host of addictive-related afflictions (van Wormer 1995).

Many alcohol and other drug users, according to Ross (1993), turn to food as a substitute addiction. Some had been overeaters as children before turning to alcohol and possibly even stimulants to reduce their food cravings. Others overeat as compensatory behavior during the general malaise that accompanies early sobriety. They react to their new cravings for sweets and starches by bingeing, gaining weight, purging, undereating, overexercising, or relapsing to the drug of choice. The possibility of a biological component in this craving for sweets is explored by Krahn (1991). Deprivation of one reinforcer (alcohol) may increase the use of other reinforcers (sweets). However, more study in this area is needed. In the late 1980s, as Ross recounts, Alcoholics Anonymous (AA) members in Monterey, California formed several chapters of Anorectics and Bulimics Anonymous after discovering that half of the women in AA and one-third of the men in the local area were anorexic or bulimic.

The fact that multiple addictions coincide in one individual is indicative of a likely common organic predisposition toward compulsive involvement with a number of substances rather than an exclusive susceptibility to only one form of addiction (Kramer 1993, *Psychology Today* 1992). This tendency is suggestive of a biological factor in eating disorders.

The psychology of compulsive eating considers such factors as depression. Depression is highly correlated with *all* substance abuse problems in women (McNeece and DiNitto 1994) and with eating disorders in particular (Fisher et al. 1995). Suicidal ideation is also a concomitant of disordered eating (Gleaves and Eberenz 1993). Further psychological aspects of this disorder concern the feelings of shame, guilt, and self-disgust connected with the self-abuse related to food. Moreover, research in the area of sexual victimization indicates a correlation between early childhood sexual abuse and eating disorders (Wooley 1994).

The social component unique to eating disorders is the influence of media and other cultural images enforcing standards of slimness for women. The female propensity for weight obsession would seem to indicate a cultural dimension in the widespread concern among women in Western society about being fat (Wolf 1991). A lower prevalence of eating disorders among African-Americans compared to European-American women seems related to body-size ideals that are fairly congruent with the actual dimensions of black women (Rucker and Cash 1992).

Together, the biological, psychological, and social factors in the development and consequences of eating disorders are incorporated in the biopsychosocial conception of this illness. Such a biopsychosocial, or holistic, view is the theoretical framework of this discussion.

DEFINITION OF EATING DISORDERS

Anorexia, bulimia, and compulsive overeating are three manifestations of disturbances concerning food. In the fourth edition of the *Diagnostic and Statistical Manual* (APA 1994), *anorexia* is defined as refusal to maintain body weight over a minimal normal level for age and height; intense fear of gaining weight or becoming fat, even though underweight; a distorted body image; and amenorrhea (in females). *Bulimia* is defined in terms of recurrent episodes of binge eating; a sense of lack of control over eating behavior during the episodes; recurrent inappropriate compensatory behavior in order to prevent weight gain, such as self-induced vomiting, misuse of laxatives, diuretics, enemas, or other medication; fasting or excessive exercise; the binge and inappropriate behaviors both occur an average of at least twice a week for three months; and self-evaluation is unduly influenced by body shape and weight. Bulimia, further, may be associated with a tendency toward overweight in early adolescence. Anorexics are often described as perfectionists, "model children." Anorexia is a life-threatening condition.

Individuals with a combination of binge eating and anorexia are likely to have other impulse control problems and to abuse alcohol or other drugs (APA 1994). Those who have mild anorexia or bulimia are often rewarded by society for their efforts. "Why, you never have to worry about your weight!" the outsider exclaims. In fact, quite the opposite is the case. Pressure by society not to be fat may lead to food obsession by the individual.

Compulsive overeating alone is not identified in *DSM-IV* as a disorder. However, binge-eating disorder is discussed under the appendix heading "Criteria Sets and Axes Provided for Further Study." Compulsive overeating is described by Koontz (1988) as addictive eating—bingeing on food to the point of overdose. Strong biological and emotional components are thought to characterize this disorder. Anorexia and bulimia have in common an absence of control over food intake.

ETIOLOGY AND MAINTENANCE FACTORS

Eating disorders are multicausal, and causality differs for each woman. Before discussing the woman-centered, multifaceted treatment approach recommended here for optimum results, let us examine the etiology of compulsive eating problems. Biological, psychological, and social aspects will be addressed.

Biological Factors

A biological dimension is suggested in the finding of a relationship between bulimia in the daughter and alcoholism in the father (Mitchell et al. 1990). Lundholm (1989) confirms this association between eating disorders and substance abuse in close relatives. Anorexia, furthermore, is associated with major depression and bipolar disorder among close relatives (APA 1994). One-third of anorexics themselves manifest concurrent problems with alcohol or drugs (Mitchell et al. 1990). Also, among women in chemical dependency treatment, as we have seen, a high rate of bulimia is reported.

Disturbances in serotonin, a key neurotransmitter in the brain, are associated with a diminution in the natural highs or feelings of pleasure that people experience. Such biochemical disturbances occur with frequency among those diagnosed with eating disorders. The persistence of depressed mood and obsessional symptoms described in anorexic clients even following recovery may be due to impaired serotonin function (Zerbe 1993). The person suffering from a serotonin imbalance is predisposed to anxiety, obsessiveness, and inhibitions (van Wormer 1995). The fact that antidepressants reduce bingeing behavior is suggestive of a medical basis to this disorder.

Family history data, similarly, suggest some common underlying factors for drug abuse and eating disorders. A higher-than-expected prevalence of substance abuse is reported among the relatives of bulimic patients (Vandereycken 1990).

Food deprivation, a correlate of anorexia and often of bulimia, is one of the most potent environmental stimulants of drug self-administration in animals (Krahn 1991). Studies of rats as well as of rhesus monkeys reveal that the self-administration of a wide variety of drugs (including alcohol, pentobarbital, cocaine, heroin, and nicotine) increase with food deprivation.

The medical complications of anorexia, bulimia, and compulsive overeating are quite severe. Over 10 percent of all anorexic people eventually will die from the disorder, many at a relatively young age (APA 1994). Death most commonly results from starvation or suicide. Patients with bulimia nervosa, similarly, may remain burdened by the earlier physical effects of the problem including swelling of the hands and feet, fatigue, cardiac abnormalities, and serious dental problems (Zerbe 1993). The lifespan of the severely obese compulsive overeater also is apt to be shortened considerably. Hypertension, diabetes, and coronary disease are especially associated with upper body obesity or the accumulation of fat near the heart (see Logan 1995).

Psychological Factors

Included in the psychological dimension of disordered eating are such dynamics as personality traits and early childhood trauma, especially sexual abuse. Personality traits in a girl at risk for developing an eating disorder are perfectionism, absolute conformity to external criteria of success, and emotional isolation (Kuba and Hanchey 1991). Eating compulsiveness would clearly be reflected in other compulsive and rigid behaviors. Anorexics, especially, can be said to have a personality profile characterized by perfectionism, obsessive delusions, and severely poor self-esteem.

Although the exact relationship between personality disorders and eating disorders is unknown, most patients with eating disorders will meet *DSM-IV* criteria for at least one personality disorder, such as borderline, histrionic, or obsessive-compulsive personality (Zerbe 1993). The relationship between eating disorders, depression, self-mutilation, and suicidal tendencies is also widely reported in the literature (Kuba and Hanchey 1991).

Prior to the early 1980s, the literature revealed a lack of awareness of the role of childhood sexual abuse in the lives of persons with eating disorders (Wooley 1994). Recent research in the area of sexual victimization is providing a revised explanation of feelings of shame, guilt, and self-disgust that often accompany compulsive eating problems. In fact, reports of a history of sexual abuse in up to 60 percent of patients with eating disorders have been noted by clinicians for some time, according to Wooley (1994), but were largely ignored by the mainstream journals, which subscribed to a "defective mothering" explanation of eating disorders. In her summary of the scarce but convincing findings of a correlation between early abuse and a later diagnosis of an eating disorder, Wooley reported that sexual abuse may be more predictive of bulimic than of anorexic symptoms and related to severity of symptoms. Compulsive eating stimulates a rise in the levels of mood enhancers; studies have shown that endorphins, the natural opiates in the brain, are released through the bingeing, purging, and fasting cycle (Ross 1993). More research is needed on this aspect of compulsive eating, however, and a need for further research is also evident in order to clarify the intricate relationship between childhood sexual abuse and the later development of problems related to food.

Sociocultural Factors

The role of gender and the social norms defining gender role expectations are implicated in the etiology and treatment of eating disorders (Fallon et al. 1994). In light of the apparent biological and psychological predisposition for certain individuals to have an eating disorder, how does one explain its predominance among women in Western society and its relative absence in non-Westernized societies? Cooley's (1909) classic explanation for the social psychology of human behavior, "self and society are twin-born," clearly applies here (p. 5).

The society that middle-class European-American girls are born into and within which they are socialized creates pressures to grow into a certain body size and shape: to be thin. Female fat, according to Wolf (1991), is the subject of public passion and private guilt; hunger is a social concession exacted by the community. In certain sensitive, possibly obsessive individuals, then, these norms are internalized to a dangerous degree. Both adolescent girls and gay males (who are subject to the same cultural repugnance for fat) become highly susceptible to the anorexic response to the point of almost killing themselves through self-imposed starvation.

From a sociocultural standpoint, therefore, eating disorders may be conceptualized as largely a socially induced illness manufactured, in effect, by conflicting demands and images of the society. While the mass media promote the skinny, hard, long-legged look for females, manufacturers and advertisers promote fattening, processed foods and beverages (such as beer). There is also a big business in the low-fat diet products. Women who eat heavily without gaining weight are also praised, for example, in popular fiction. For women who lose weight, often perennially, there is praise and admiration; for the woman who does not "take care of herself," there is blame, labeling, and fat oppression. And then, finally, there are the treatment providers who only are called upon to begin their work years after the real damage has been done. Insurance companies, however, often fail to take the problems of disordered eating seriously, and coverage is minimal for all but those whose condition is clearly life threatening.

TREATMENT CONSIDERATIONS

Prognosis for recovery from an eating disorder was considered, until recently, to be very poor (Goode 1988). Some therapies seem to work better than others, however. For anorexia, the most effective treatment seems to be a combination of cognitive-based techniques, aimed at distorted body image and thoughts about food, and family counseling. Use of antidepressant medication has been promising, perhaps because it curbs the tendency toward obsessiveness, including food obsessiveness. In a review of the literature, Raymond and colleagues (1994) reported fairly dramatic reduction in binge eating and purging through use of appropriate medication in conjunction with other forms of therapy. However, additional research is needed to test the effectiveness of this approach. In his review of outcome effectiveness studies, Hsu (1990) finds room for cautious optimism: Most anorexics in treatment gain weight. Approximately 50 percent of bulimic patients in the effectiveness studies recover, at least in the short term.

The primary challenge in eating disorders treatment compared to other substance abuse treatment is that, because food, unlike alcohol and cocaine, is required for life, treatment protocols that involve a commitment to abstinence (successful with alcohol and cocaine) do not apply. Moderation must be learned by those with eating problems. As many cigarette smokers are aware, it is often easier to give up a substance altogether than to practice moderation. A second factor affecting recovery evaluation and outcome is the difficulty in defining or detecting a relapse of abnormal eating patterns. The binge/purge cycle, in fact, can go on for years undetected by family members as well as practitioners. Thirdly, as mentioned previously, the society rewards slimness far more than it rewards moderation. For instance, among fashion models and ballerinas, anorexia is endemic. In short, motivation for treatment of behaviors that are continually reinforced is problematic.

The complex etiology and potential entrenchment of eating disorders are best addressed by multimodal intervention (Fisher et al. 1995). Treatment of eating disorders can be roughly divided into four categories: medical considerations, nutritional counseling and monitoring, psychotherapy, and social awareness/activism. Ideally, professionals with specific expertise in each area will function as a team.

Medical Considerations

Initial medical concern identifies both the acute and the chronic physical damage resulting from eating disorder behaviors. All physiological systems may be impacted by self-starvation and bingeing and purging, but general examination focuses on blood chemistries, cardiac abnormalities, gastrointestinal distress, and symptoms of dehydration. The attending physician may prescribe and monitor medication for depression to inhibit bingeing or reduce anxiety. Dental health is also at risk for eating-disordered patients who may not be taking in enough calcium and are washing their teeth and gums with stomach acid because of frequent purges. Therefore, referral to a dentist who is aware of the manifestations of eating disorder behaviors is recommended.

Medical professionals may also monitor weight changes in the treatment process and treat gastrointestinal problems as they occur in the restoration of normal eating patterns. Those clients who have practiced eating disorder behaviors over an extended period or to great excess report significant gastrointestinal discomfort when they begin the refeeding process and if unattended will use that discomfort as a rationale for sabotaging treatment.

The degree of physical impairment significantly impacts the potential psychotherapeutic intervention (Vandereycken 1993). Memory, concentration, decision making, and rational thought are casualties of malnutrition and dehydration. As with any addictive behavior, the active substance abuse must be controlled and the physical symptoms dealt with before the client can make best use of therapy. Clinicians seeing a woman with an eating disorder may consider strongly encouraging that she have a physical examination by a medical professional sensitive to the needs of clients with eating disorders. Many physicians who are not knowledgeable about eating disorders will misinterpret symptoms associated with malnutrition—depression and preoccupation with food—as psychological rather than metabolic (Ross 1993). Another common mistake made by physicians is to focus on obesity but to ignore medically the presence of compulsive eating without obesity. Appropriate questions that health professionals should ask to detect and treat eating disorders are: Is there a family history of alcoholism? How often do you skip meals? Has there been dieting? What has been the pattern of dieting, that is, how often? How many calories per day? Was there overeating in childhood? Is there a history of depression? Of other substance abuse? Are there concerns about eating in public? Is there stimulant or diet pill use to control appetite? Such questions as these will clue medical practitioners to a pattern centered around weight and body image obsession accompanied by food obsession.

Nutritional Counseling

Nutritional care and counseling are important components of the comprehensive care of women with eating disorders (Fisher et al. 1995). Nutritional counseling is optimally done by a registered dietitian, or a suitable alternative or holistic practitioner, with experience in eating disorders. Persons with eating disorders are usually very well read in nutrition, keeping abreast of the most recent popular and scientific information on fat, calories, and exercise. However, because of the degree of their cognitive distortion, that information may be misunderstood and misused. For example, if lowering dietary fat is recommended for overall health and weight loss, a woman with anorexia might conclude that if less fat is better, then none must be best. She does not understand why her hair and nails become brittle and break off when she eliminates all fat from her diet.

The role of the nutritional counselor is to correct faulty nutritional assumptions and practices, promote regular eating habits (i.e., the inclusion of proteins, sugars, fats, and sodium), help individuals plan meals, and resensitize them to the feelings of hunger and satiety. To the degree possible all questions of calories, portion sizes, and fat grams are dealt with in nutritional counseling sessions, freeing the primary psychotherapist to focus on the crucial area of emotions.

Together with the health care provider, the nutritional counselor monitors weight changes and sets an appropriate weight range for the client. In an inpatient setting the dietitian may select all meals until the patient is able to make appropriate selections. Inclusion of a nutritional consultant as part of the treatment team is invaluable, providing an expert to address the persistent questions and misconceptions of the patient and freeing other professionals on the team to attend to their specialties.

Recent literature directed toward nutritionists working in the field of eating disorders addresses the need for the professional dietitian to separate counseling and dietary issues, as these issues are closely related in women with eating disorders (Lyon 1995). Too often, as in chemical dependency treatment, when the client begins work on food issues the pain suppressed by the eating disordered behavior surfaces, overwhelming both the client and the nutritional counselor. A team approach to eating disorders, involving frequent consultation among the members about the feelings that emerge can minimize that discomfort and allow the client to cope with the feelings.

Psychotherapy

Psychotherapy, in a combination of individual counseling, group, and family therapy, is the most extensive and comprehensive of the interventions for eating disorders. Long after the physical manifestations of anorexia or bulimia have been resolved, cognitive distortion, impairment in coping skills, and inaccurate affective identification continue to be causes for concern in the individual with an eating disorder. Studies indicate that one year of psychotherapeutic intervention increases the chances of symptomatic recovery up to 75 percent (Yeager 1995).

Cognitive-behavioral therapy is the treatment of choice in addressing the complex interplay of irrational thoughts that plague persons with eating disorders. The focus here is on the beliefs that power the distorted thoughts and the behavior based on those thoughts. Women's pursuit of the cultural stereotype of feminine beauty is characterized by thoughts such as "If I am fat then I am ugly, and if I am ugly, I am unlovable," or "Since I have eaten three cookies, I might as well eat the whole box." These self-defeating thoughts and the resultant actions serve to sabotage women's lives and perpetuate the eating disorder (Ellis et al. 1989).

According to Vandereycken (1990), the skilled cognitive-behavioral therapist will selectively address issues of weight phobia, distorted perceptions of the body, fear of loss of control over eating and weight, and negative perceptions of self. Cognitive-behavioral treatment is generally focused on the present, serving to identify the immediate behavioral consequences of irrational beliefs.

Affective work is critical in the treatment of persons with eating disorders. Inability to cope with early painful experiences such as rape, incest, an alcoholic family, or transitions from childhood to adolescence or from adolescence to adulthood are common underlying dynamics. Root and Fallon (1988) estimate that 60 to 66 percent of women with bulimia have experienced some degree of sexual, physical, or emotional abuse in their lives. Eating-disordered clients frequently express a very narrow spectrum of feeling and spend a great deal of energy creating an atmosphere in which everything is "all right." Because they may lack experience in identifying and expressing a broad range of feelings, counseling sessions may be initially oriented toward examination of affective states, with counselors modeling appropriate affect for given situations and practicing healthy modes of expression.

Family therapy, particularly for the adolescent girl, is an important first step in educating the family as a whole to the apparently strange behaviors of eating-disordered individuals. Parents need to be encouraged to set clear boundaries about appropriate behavior, such as insisting on some financial contribution to the household grocery bill from a daughter who regularly binges on "family" food. Family members also need a forum in which they can express the feelings of frustration, confusion, and mistrust that accompany life with an eating-disordered person, as well as a place to begin to explore the familial issues that encourage the dysfunctional eating.

Couples counseling with an eating-disordered woman and her spouse or partner shares elements with family work but adds the component of sexuality. The intense body hatred and shame characterizing eating disorders significantly interferes with positive sexual relations. Some therapists report that couples who present with concerns about their sexual relationship eventually reveal hidden eating disorders or body dysmorphia in one or both members.

Research indicates the efficacy of various types of group work with eating-disordered individuals (Krahn 1991, Kuba and Hanchey 1991, Tenzer 1989). The effectiveness of group treatment for women who are troubled with eating problems stems from the tremendous sharing and support that derive from a positive collective experience. Women's relationships become more open through the process of mutual decision making and feedback. Women can develop a sense of self in relation to others in a group setting. When a woman begins to build trust and empathy with others, she also develops these feelings for herself (Kuba and Hanchey 1991).

Case Study: The Group Process

This multifocused group met for twelve weeks and continued to meet informally following termination. Its membership was comprised of six women with a variety of body sizes; their weight ranged from 90 to 350 pounds. The discomfort caused by such diversity was often a potent therapeutic issue that served to help members connect with one another. Each of the women wrestled with cultural prescriptions for body size and shape. All six members had had some individual therapy, but only one had ever participated in a therapy group. Two members had participated in Overeaters Anonymous, and one had been going to Alcoholics Anonymous meetings for many years. Two other women had problems with alcohol abuse that paralleled the eating problems. Weekly discussions related to the issues the women experienced during the previous week. The group format was chosen because of the connecting support and honest confrontation provided by the peer process. In addition to group discussions, group members also occasionally were provided with clay. The molding of figures out of clay to represent significant others in their lives helped give women a physical means of expression. This excerpt from the fourth session reveals the magnitude of feeling elicited in this exercise:

> "I just want to tear down this wall between my mother and me . . ." Sandy says, smashing the clay barricade separating a small clay girl from her large, faceless clay mother, whose arms have been created to reach out in embrace to the distant child. As Sandy sobs at the recognition of her separateness that forty years of disordered eating could not take away, Leah, Beth, Jolene, Carolyn, and Kristin, the other members of this therapy group, some crying quietly, attend to the personal and very familiar scene played out before them. The story expressed is of women's separation from one another, mothers from daughters, sisters from sisters, and friends from friends.

Initially, these women considered the pain exclusively within a personal context. "There is something really ugly and disgusting about me and I can't see past that," Carolyn said in despair during one session. Variations of this were expressed by all group members in the early stages. Throughout the course of treatment, the therapist consistently brought those feelings into the social, cultural, and familial context that had helped cultivate this assumption of personal failure. Recognizing the powerful social forces against which they had been shaped quickly produced a great outpouring of anger and hurt, no longer directed at themselves:

- "I am so mad that I'm forced to shop at special shops for clothes that are ugly and expensive."
- "I don't go to the movies any more because the seats dig into my legs and it hurts! What am I supposed to think about my welcome at that theater?"

- "I'm sick of getting stared at every time I buy an ice cream cone. It's nobody's business but mine what I eat and when."
- "Every waking moment I'm worried that if I gain one pound people will think I'm a slob and I just can't live like this anymore. My life is making sure other people think I'm OK, not me."

Cognitively, group members began to examine collectively the sense of shame and other self-blaming attitudes they had internalized and personalized. By identifying the sources of the messages of worthlessness they had received—whether from the culture, family members, or both—individuals were enabled to work toward personal and social changes.

An important focus of discussion was the biological component in both depression and eating disorders. All six women disclosed that they took antidepressant medication with varying degrees of satisfaction. Leah and Beth felt very angry that they had been labeled "sick," a label they felt was implied by the prescription of medication for their "illness." The biological and genetic considerations of depression and binge eating made them feel less powerful and somehow doomed. Carolyn, Jolene, and Kristin felt medication was critical to their recovery and would not mind taking it for the rest of the their lives if necessary. Being diagnosed as mentally ill had provided them further relief from feeling personally flawed. "If it's biological, then I am not to blame," they reasoned. One point of consensus seemed to be that medication was a tool and that each woman could interpret the biological aspects of her eating disorder in a way that was useful for her, understanding that her opinions could change as she changed.

The physical aspect of their eating disorder was addressed in terms of external comfort. Chairs that had either no sides or had especially wide sides were chosen for the group room. Although not all group members felt completely comfortable with the furniture, fat women especially felt pleased that options had been provided because they felt that usually they did not have much of a choice in such things as clothing or furniture. From the beginning, emphasis was placed on attending group in comfortable clothing and shoes. Individuals discussed how they used clothing, make-up, hairstyle, fragrance, and tanning to disguise or change themselves to fit a perceived social image. Group members recognized that they often denied their own comfort and sometimes safety to appease an image that they did not inherently share. Still, acknowledging the disparity and changing their own grooming behaviors were two different things. Leah set the goal of using less makeup when she came to group and reported that she found this extremely difficult because of the great vulnerability she felt.

Frequently group members wanted to talk about their parents and issues that they had begun to struggle with as adults. As the majority of the group had been brought up in alcoholic families, early childhood issues were paramount. Issues tackled included survival strategies in a dysfunctional setting and how the roles played in childhood affect present day relationships. All group members came to the group with the concept of their families as dysfunctional, an extension of seeing themselves as dysfunctional. The mothers of all the members of this group were described as obese. There was intense fear of becoming like their mothers, but this gradually changed over the course of treatment. Members came to identify the pressures they felt to be "perfect" as those that had driven their mothers' unrealistic expectations of them as children. While no attempt was made on the part of the therapist to diminish feelings of anger or pain or to advocate forgiveness, the group members were encouraged to empathize with their mothers within the context of family/societal dynamics.

In all interactions, affect was stressed as a primary source of information. Identifying the feelings behind the thoughts and behavior served as a springboard for discussion. Because these women were estranged from their affective lives, encouragement to identify and learn from their feelings became a powerful tool. At the end of twelve weeks Cindy, who had told the group that she could not cry, asked to be held by another group member as she was racked with grief. The ability to connect at this deep level was the function of working past the shame of being fat, of feeling fat, working past the sense that they were sick and their families were sick, and coming to see that they were women who needed people and who could depend on each other.

A HOLISTIC TREATMENT APPROACH

An individualized but still holistic treatment approach is essential to meet the diverse needs of women with various forms of disordered eating and to address the susceptibility of women with eating disorders to multiple substance abuse problems. The holistic, biopsychosocial model provides an appropriately diversified clinical approach to address the biogenetic factors that may predispose women to difficulty with self-regulation of food consumption and the biological factors, such as depression, in the etiology of disordered eating and in its consequences. The psychology of compulsive eating needs to be addressed by helping women to face the pain of their earlier lives and to cope with the memory of this pain by cognitively substituting more positive thoughts for the negative ones. Working to prevent feelings of depression by taking a more positive attitude toward oneself and toward life itself is also a part of the psychological side of treatment. The social and environmental aspect of therapy work are addressed through the support system itself, of women helping women to recover and to counter the bombardment of "fat-is-ugly" messages in the society.

The approach offered in the case study cited is decidedly feminist: there was no emphasis on labeling worried families as overly protective and dysfunctional, fat oppression by society was addressed openly, and strong bonding among female group members was actively encouraged. In short, the biopsychosocial framework with a feminist slant combines the strengths of numerous approaches in one. A synthesis of various techniques, such as cognitive-behavioral therapy, relapse training, and psychodynamic therapy, is important in the treatment of women with eating disorders (Johnson et al. 1987).

A holistic approach also incorporates social awareness and activism during the treatment process. However, eating-disordered women need to have the cognitive and affective tools with which to understand the social and cultural influences on their eating behaviors and aesthetic beliefs. From giving away uncomfortable clothing, saved for "the day when . . . ," to analyzing the subtexts in advertising (thin, beautiful women and muscular men sell happiness and love, not diet soda), to confronting businesses that have structural barriers to large women, clients can make great personal use of their energy in making social change.

Primary prevention at the societal level is crucial in eliminating or at least minimizing eating disorders. Fundamental education in schools concerning biomedical factors in weight loss and gain would do much to prevent development of the kind of disorders described in this chapter. The stigma of obesity could be addressed in the same way that racism and sexism are now addressed—aggressively. The effects of the stigma of obesity could be described—graphically, and perhaps augmented with relevant media images projected upon the screen. Through such means of mass education, the social world might be a little kinder to women with non-normative body weight and shape.

CONCLUSION

Anorexia, bulimia, and compulsive overeating are the three major types of eating disorders. All are found disproportionately among substance-abusing women as compared to men, presumably due to society's more rigid standards for slimness in the female. Mass media images promoting exclusively thin body builds as most desirable for women create a climate conducive to much personal dissatisfaction. In certain vulnerable females who are inclined toward obsessiveness and perfectionism in general, weight obsession and compulsive dieting may occur, as well as the abuse of chemicals to control weight. When carried to the extreme, the adolescent or young woman may develop anorexia or bulimia or both. The third variety of eating disorder, compulsive overeating, bears a remarkable similarity to abuse of substances other than food (for example, alcohol). Compulsive overeating, which may involve the use of food to get a high, is correlated with depression, suicidal ideation, and early childhood sexual abuse. Eating disorders are also correlated with growing up in dysfunctional, substance-abusing families.

Because eating disorders vary in form as well as in their etiology, and because of the close link between eating disorders and other forms of substance abuse, a multidimensional approach to treatment is essential. Treatment should address the biological components, the psychological factors, as well as the social dimension. Medication for depression, nutritional counseling, and individual, group, and/or family therapy may be needed.

In short, an eating disorders treatment group of actively participating members can provide a woman-centered, holistic approach to treatment and help women achieve optimum results as they pursue their personal issues in a supportive and nurturant atmosphere.

REFERENCES

American Psychiatric Association (1994). *Diagnostic and Statistical Manual of Mental Disorders*, Fourth Edition. Washington, DC: Author.

Brown, C., and Jasper, K. (1993). *Consuming Passions: Feminist Approaches to Weight Preoccupation and Eating Disorders*. Toronto: Second Story Press.

Cooley, C. H. (1983). *Social Organization: A Study of the Larger Mind* (1909). New Brunswick, NJ: Transaction.

Ellis, A., McInerney, J. F., DiGiuseppe, R., and Yeager, R. J. (1989). *Rational-Emotive Therapy with Alcoholics and Substance Abusers*. New York: Pergamon.

Fallon, P., Katzman, M. A., and Wooley, S. C., eds. (1994). *Feminist Perspectives on Eating Disorders.* New York: Guilford.

Fisher, M., Golden, N. H., and Katzman, D. K. (1995). Eating disorders in adolescents: a background paper. *Journal of Adolescent Health* 16:420–437.

Gleaves, D. H., and Eberenz, K. P. (1993). Eating disorders and additional psychopathology in women: the role of prior sexual abuse. *Journal of Child Sexual Abuse* 2(3):71–80.

Goode, E. E. (1988). When dieting is all that counts. *U.S. News & World Report* May 9, pp. 74–75.

Hsu, L. K. (1990). *Eating Disorders.* New York: Guilford.

Hudson, J., Weiss, R., Pope, H., et al. (1992). Eating disorders in hospitalized substance abusers. *American Journal of Drug Alcohol Abuse* 18:75–85.

Johnson, C. L., Connors, M. E., and Tobin, D. L. (1987). Symptom management of bulimia. *Journal of Consulting and Clinical Psychology* 55(5): 668–676.

Kaplan, A., and Garfinkel, P. E. (1993). *Medical Issues and the Eating Disorders: An Interface.* New York: Brunner/Mazel.

Koontz, K. (1988). Women who love food too much. *Health* February, 40–42.

Krahn, D. D. (1991). The relationship of eating disorders and substance abuse. *Journal of Substance Abuse* 3:239–253.

Kramer, P. (1993). The transformation of personality. *Psychology Today* 26:42–47, 70–76.

Kuba, S. A., and Hanchey, S. G. (1991). Reclaiming women's bodies: a feminist perspective on eating disorders. In *Feminist Perspectives on Addiction,* ed. N. van den Bergh, pp. 125–138. New York: Springer.

Logan, S. L. (1995). Eating disorders and other compulsive behaviors. In *Encyclopedia of Social Work,* pp. 805–815. Washington DC: NASW Press.

Lundholm, J. (1989). Alcohol use among university females: relationship to eating disordered behavior. *Addictive Behaviors* 14:181–185.

Lyon, T. (1993). Patient education during nutrition intervention. *Eating Disorders Review* 4(6):8–9.

—— (1995). When a patient needs more than nutritional counseling. *Eating Disorders Review* 6(1):7.

McNeece, C. A., and DiNitto, D. M. (1994). *Chemical Dependency: A Systems Approach.* Englewood Cliffs, NJ: Prentice Hall.

Mitchell, J. E., Pyle, R. L., Eckert, E. D., and Hatsukami, D. (1990). The influence of prior alcohol and drug abuse problems in bulimia nervosa: treatment outcome. *Addictive Behaviors* 15:169–173.

Psychology Today (1992). Serotonin: neurotransmitter of the '90s. *Psychology Today* 25:16.

Raymond, N. C., Mitchell, J. D., Fallon, P., and Katzman, M. A. (1994). A collaborative approach to the use of medication. In *Feminist Perspectives on Eating Disorders*, ed. P. Fallon, M. A. Katzman, and S. C. Wooley, pp. 231–250. New York: Guilford.

Root, M. P., and Fallon, P. (1988). The incidence of victimization experiences in a bulimic sample. *Journal of Interpersonal Violence* 3(2):161–173.

Ross, J. (1993). Food addiction: a new look at the nature of craving. *Addiction and Recovery* 13:17–19.

Rucker, C. E., and Cash, T. F. (1992). Body images, body-size perceptions, and eating behaviors among African-American and white college women. *International Journal of Eating Disorders* 12:291–299.

Seid, R. A. (1994). Too "close to the bone": the historical context for women's obsession with slenderness. In *Feminist Perspectives on Eating Disorders*, ed. P. Fallon, M. A. Katzman, and S. C. Wooley, pp. 3–16. New York: Guilford.

Tenzer, S. (1989). Fat Acceptance Therapy (F.A.T.): a non-dieting group approach to physical wellness, insight and self-acceptance. *Women and Therapy* 8(3):39–47.

Vandereycken, W. (1990). The addiction model in eating disorders: some critical remarks and a selected bibliography. *International Journal of Eating Disorders* 9(1):95–101.

—— (1993). Therapists' reactions toward eating disordered patients. *Eating Disorders Review* 4(3):1–4.

van Wormer, K. S. (1994). "Hi, I'm Jane; I'm a compulsive overeater." In *Feminist Perspectives on Eating Disorders*, ed. P. Fallon, M. A. Katzman, and S. C. Wooley, pp. 287–298. New York: Guilford.

—— (1995). *Alcoholism Treatment: A Social Work Perspective*. Chicago: Nelson Hall.

Wolf, N. (1991). *The Beauty Myth*. New York: Morrow.

Wooley, S. C. (1994). Sexual abuse and eating disorders: the concealed debate. In *Feminist Perspectives on Eating Disorders*, ed. P. Fallon, M. Katzman, and S. Wooley, pp. 171– 211. New York: Guilford.

Yeager, J., ed. (1995). How much psychotherapy is enough? *Eating Disorders Review* 6:2.

Zerbe, K. J. (1993). *The Body Betrayed: Women, Eating Disorders, and Treatment*. Washington, DC: American Psychiatric Press.

Overcoming Sexism in AA: How Women Cope

Margaret Coker

12

Despite the existence of numerous rehabilitation centers, outpatient programs, and professional counselors and psychotherapists specializing in alcoholism, most alcoholics do not seek professional help for their drinking. This is particularly true for women, who are twice stigmatized, first by the double standard of a patriarchal society and then by the disease of alcoholism. Many of those who do want help choose to become members of Alcoholics Anonymous (AA), a self-help group whose primary purpose is to help alcoholics achieve sobriety (AA Grapevine, Inc. 1994a, Spiegel 1993).

A 1992 survey found that 35 percent of all AA members were women and that women accounted for 43 percent of all those under age 30 (Alcoholics Anonymous World Services 1993). Unfortunately, AA has been slow to respond to the needs of its female members. AA still remains a male-oriented and male-dominated organization. It is the intent of this chapter to examine the existence of sexism in AA and its impact on alcoholic women and to suggest some ways that women can use AA and other self-help modalities effectively to achieve sobriety.

A BRIEF HISTORY OF ALCOHOLICS ANONYMOUS

Alcoholics Anonymous has its roots in American Protestantism and the temperance movement. Its ancestry includes such organizations as the Seminal American Temperance Society, founded by a Lutheran minister named Justin Edwards, the Washingtonians, the Sons of Temperance, the Good Templars (who picked up backsliding Washingtonians), and the Oxford Group (Alcoholics Anonymous World Services, Inc. 1980). Originating in England, the Oxford Group was a nondenominational evangelical movement based on the "four absolutes" of honesty, purity, unselfishness, and love and the "five C's" of confidence, confession, conviction, conversion, and continuance. This moral script was coded into "five procedures" which read: (1) give in to God, (2) listen to God's direction, (3) check guidance, (4) restitution, and (5) sharing—for witness and confession (Alcoholics Anonymous World Services, Inc. 1980). The tenets of the Oxford Group are today reflected in the twelve steps of Alcoholics Anonymous.

Originally a Christian fellowship, AA broke away from the Oxford Group in 1939. Founded by Bill Wilson and Dr. Bob Smith in 1935, AA members (almost all men at that time) decided it was easier and more effective for drunks to work directly with each other, rather than to continue being the objects of reform of the more upstanding citizens of the Oxford Group.

At the onset, women who were involved in AA were wives of the confessed alcoholics. They generally met in the kitchen while their newly sober husbands met to discuss the challenges and pitfalls of sobriety. Women as alcoholics were not readily accepted and, in fact, were scorned. The double standard of the 1930s was even more rigid than today. In *Dr. Bob and the Good Oldtimers* it is said that, "Most of the women came in with the label 'nymphomaniacs'. The wives backed away and the men were leery of getting into a 'situation'" (Alcoholics Anonymous World Services, Inc. 1980, p. 241). Usually, the woman alcoholic was turned over to the wives of the male alcoholics for help.

Over the past 50 years, the proportion of female members of AA has steadily increased. Between 1968 and 1977, the rate of female members rose from 22 to 32 percent, and to 34 percent in 1986 (Galanter 1989). In its most recent membership survey (1992) of AA members from the U.S. and Canada, it was found that 35 percent of the more than 6,500 responding members were women (Alcoholics Anonymous World Services, Inc. 1993). Women have slowly penetrated the policymaking groups of the AA framework. The financial affairs, general inquiries, and publishing activities of AA are handled by an office in New York that is administered by the General Service Board. In an unpublished communication, the AA Liaison to the Professional Community reported that of the twenty-one member-elected representatives serving on this board, currently nine are women (AA General Service Office 1995).

Despite the increase in female membership, women have thus far had little influence over long-standing traditions and attitudes. Sexism is readily apparent in the literature put forth by the General Service Office (GSO), especially in the form of AA's basic text, *Alcoholics Anonymous*, or, "The Big Book."

THE BIG BOOK

Originally written in 1939, the book *Alcoholics Anonymous* virtually ignored the existence of alcoholic women. In the first half of the book the chapter entitled "To Wives" is directed toward the spouse of the male alcoholic. The chapter "To Employees" addresses employees of male alcoholics. All of the other eight chapters are written with the male alcoholic as the reader, the only exception being the first sentence of Chapter 2, which includes the phrase "thousands of men and women" (Stafford 1979, p. 249). Even though the book was updated to a third edition in 1976, little effort has been made to revise or amend these chapters.

The second half of the Big Book is composed of personal stories from those who have recovered in AA. In the first edition of 1939, only one out of the thirty stories was by a woman. In the second edition of 1955, eleven of the thirty-six stories were by, and for, women. In the most recent third edition of 1976, thirteen of the forty-two stories are about women alcoholics (Stafford 1979). Those who take exception to this are told to identify with the feelings in the stories instead of comparing events, the implication being that all alcoholics are the same despite their gender or socialization process.

Those who do take exception to this do so because it negates their own history and their own uniqueness as women. Adams and Ware (1989) noted that "one of the most intriguing characteristics of language is that it acts as a kind of social mirror, reflecting the organization and dynamics of the society of which it is a part" (p. 470). In addition to the male-oriented stories and usage of the generic term "fellowship," the usage of male pronouns is also subtly sexist. Throughout the Big Book, the consistent utilization of the pronouns "he," "him," and "his" reinforce the prevailing social opinion that the invisible alcoholic, who is woman, should remain invisible. One woman, Julie S., relates this story:

> In 1986, the General Service Office was considering the publication of a fourth edition to the book *Alcoholics Anonymous*. The intention was to alter the language of the book to nonsexist terms, that is, *he* would become *s/he*. It decided to put this proposal out to its member groups (over 24,000 in the U.S. and Canada alone) for a vote. I attended the business meeting of a large AA group to which I belong.
>
> By a large margin, this proposal was defeated at the local level, the reason being that it would make for cumbersome reading. As one might expect, the proposal was defeated nationwide, and at this time, no fourth edition is planned.

Another issue that is both sexist and religiously biased lies in the wording of the twelve steps. Found in Chapter 5 of the Big Book, and read aloud at the start of each meeting as a part of "How It Works," the steps are spiritual measures suggested in the program of recovery. Step 3 best illustrates this point: "Made a decision to turn our will and our lives over to the care of God *as we understood Him*" [emphasis original] (Alcoholics Anonymous World Services, Inc. 1976, p. 59).

The program itself takes great pains to describe the "Higher Power" as an entity greater than ourselves. "We do not need to consider another's concept of God. Our own conception, however inadequate, was sufficient to make the approach and to effect contact with *Him*" [emphasis mine]. (Alcoholics Anonymous World Services, Inc. 1976, p. 46). This statement belies its intent. It indicates that the Higher Power can be anything a person understands it to be (i.e., for some it might be Buddha or a deeper self, for others, the people at the meetings). Yet because of its Christian foundation, AA calls the Higher Power "God," and "He" is male. Sandy F., an avowed feminist and member of AA, gives this account:

> Not long ago, in 1988, as program chairman of my group, I asked a friend of mine to chair that night's meetings. She obliged, and proceeded to lead the meeting of over 100 people. As is tradition, she read aloud the preamble and then "How It Works." In the reading, however, she substituted the pronouns referring to God as 'Him' or 'He' with simply 'God' so that "God as we *understood Him*," would read "God as we understood God." This today is a common practice, particularly among women's groups or by those women (and few men) who align themselves with the feminist cause.
>
> After the readings and introduction she asked for a topic for discussion. Immediately a hand flew up with an urgency that demanded our attention. One of our male members proposed, with a certain edge of self-righteousness, that we discuss the reading of "How It Works" *as it is written* by the founders of the program! After many groans and a couple of polarized opinions, the chair deferred the issue to the next group business meeting.
>
> Now this member did have a point, that in order to reinterpret what was written, one must proceed through proper channels and not to take it upon themselves to change the basic text. In addition, he felt that by changing the words, we are changing the meaning of what those words represent. Our founders intended the Higher Power to be called God and that He is male.
>
> Nonetheless, the argument continued at the next business meeting. He proposed that we as a group instruct all future chairpersons, orally and in writing, that "How It Works" be read exactly as written. A vote was then taken and the proposal was defeated by a narrow margin—one small step for womankind.

The bias presented in the basic text of AA is a subtle but significant form of sexism that affects all female members, whether it offends or not. Yet one does not have to look far to see how pervasive it is, for AA is but an extension of the society from which its members come. It is for this reason that the more blatant and offensive forms of sexual harassment occur.

THE MEETINGS

Generally speaking, there are more men in attendance at AA meetings than women, and meetings are basically dominated by men. Men participate at a greater rate. They also assume greater leadership roles.

Women are also less inclined to share in a large group, especially if it is mixed. They generally suffer lower self-esteem than their male counterparts, and many have a history of sexual abuse (Institute of Medicine 1990). Adams and Ware (1989) add that women are more easily intimidated because men more naturally dominate conversations and sharings at meetings. Mary L. shares this experience:

> I recently attended a meeting of about 30 people. There were eight women there, and a man was chairing the meeting. Chairpersons generally run the meetings in one of two ways: they either ask for a show of hands, or they hand pick those who will participate in the discussion. At this meeting, the gentleman who was chairing selected those who would share. He didn't call on one woman for the entire hour. I was furious. I suppose I could have raised my hand, but that's not the way the meeting was being run. I didn't have a "burning desire" to share, I just wanted the women to be recognized. It happens all the time.

The ego-deflating principles of the program (i.e., a heavy emphasis on assessing one's character defects) can psychologically undermine an already low sense of self-esteem, particularly in women. Michele Clark (1986) has stressed this point when she stated:

> Bill W., one of the founders of AA, called the average alcoholic self-centered in the extreme, likely to think of himself as invulnerable, always right, always in control, a man who habitually thinks of his own good before the good of others. AA was started by men. Its particular mixture of support and confrontation developed to heal such self-centered men. But a woman alcoholic might be the opposite kind of person: overly solicitous of others, habitually putting herself last. Some of the self-critical aspects of AA might make a woman with low self-esteem feel even more worthless, and she would not be able to stay with the program. [p. 72]

AA has its limitations. Long-standing conservative attitudes towards cross-addiction, treatment programs, and mental illness tend to exclude those who are dealing with these issues. Traditionally, AA meetings have encouraged discussions to be limited to problems as they relate to alcohol. While no one is formally ejected for "illicit" sharing, an atmosphere of intolerance prevails, especially outside of large urban areas. AA is gradually evolving, however, since many members are referred directly from treatment centers and many participate in outside therapy. These members are demonstrating that working the twelve-step program can be integrated into dealing with many life problems.

While recent AA literature supports more open attitudes toward the use of psychiatric medications, their use is often subtly discouraged. The "hard-line" AA member can be quite vocal in proclaiming that medication stops a person from dealing with their emotional illness. It is assumed that recovering persons can solve their problems by working the program and using the twelve steps, implying that all alcoholics are the same and will respond to the same treatment. It is particularly difficult for women, more of whom suffer from preexisting affective disorders (Institute of Medicine 1990), to talk about their struggle with depression. By using antidepressant medication, they are often thought to be taking the "easier, softer way" (Alcoholics Anonymous 1976, p. 58). Persons who are taking prescribed medication can be encouraged to look for more progressive meetings, which support medication compliance.

In order to perceive the aforementioned forms of sexism within the AA program, one generally needs to be sensitive to, and aware of, women's issues. Oftentimes though, a meeting will expose more overt and blatant attitudes among some of its members as a part of the sharing of their experience, strength, and hope. Beth C. told me about this incident:

> I had the opportunity in the context of a rather large mixed group to respond to one of the more crude male members in this way: The topic was, "How life has changed since I stopped drinking." Most who shared were sincere and grateful for their sobriety. One young man, however, took the opportunity to make light of his drunken days at the expense of women. He said, "I no longer greet the day with my head in the porcelain, I no longer cut myself shaving, and I don't rape women anymore." He, of course, drew a good deal of amusement and laughter from the group, but not from all of us, particularly those of us women who had been sexually abused (more than a few). When it was my turn to speak, I glibly shared, "I no longer wake up with hangovers, I no longer borrow beer from my neighbors, and I don't rape men anymore!" A certain number among us applauded and thanked me afterwards.
>
> After the meeting I confronted this young man. I wanted to be sure that he understood that his kind of humor was offensive to many of us and so is the act of rape. I was understood . . . for sure.

Sexual harassment comes in many forms, according to Martin (1989), sometimes as a more covert form of prejudice, which creates an atmosphere of intimidation, and sometimes in more overt forms that include a variety of behaviors. These behaviors, such as touching, teasing, and making comments about a woman's appearance or sexuality, greet most female members of AA who enter the rooms. Generally, this behavior is unsolicited, nonreciprocal male behavior that asserts a woman's sex role over her functioning as a person, much less an alcoholic in need of help (Martin 1989). This most often occurs in the context of the socializing that takes place before and after the meetings.

SOCIALIZING WITH "FELLOW" ALCOHOLICS: THE THIRTEENTH STEP

Most alcoholics who initially enter the AA program are defeated, frightened, and vulnerable. This is particularly true of alcoholic women who, because of the stigma associated with women who drink, have a greater sense of shame. It is a perfect set-up for the opportunistic male alcoholic who is looking for a new relationship, short- or long-term, to boost his faltering ego. The newly sober woman is in need. She needs guidance, she needs reassurance, and she needs friends.

It is this scenario that is played out time and time again within AA. If a woman is single, she is prey to getting involved with a "more sober" male, who is more than willing to assist her (sometimes all the way to the bedroom). This is more prevalent if she is young and, of course, "provocative." This is what is known as *thirteenth stepping*, and most women who enter the program are warned by those who came before them to be careful. There are also the more common advances or commentaries that women become accustomed to as a result of their conditioning, but are nonetheless intrusive. Married or single, women alcoholics often become victims of rude and inappropriate behavior.

It is important for the new AA member to know that AA does not condone this behavior but that persons who come to AA are often lacking in impulse control and sober social interactions. The twelve steps are designed to help alcoholics examine their behaviors and change them accordingly. Unfortunately though, this does not prevent incidents from occurring. The following are examples of this type of harassment described by Jill S.:

> I am a married woman and do or say nothing to hide the fact. But even married women have to put up with crass comments like . . . "Boy, if you weren't married . . ."—the implication being that

he'd be after me in a flash. Another encounter involved a man twice my age and half my brains (I suspect he drank far too long), who insisted one night that "he knew I had a 'thing'" for him and always felt some special feelings toward me and that he understood why I "never said anything." I, of course, understood nothing and walked away totally bewildered, wondering what on earth he was talking about. Then there have been those few occasions on which I have worn a skirt, only to be followed by cat calls and whistling, men expressing their approval of my "great legs." I now rarely wear a skirt to meetings—the men can't handle it.

Nothing, though, bothers me quite so much as the practice of hugging in AA meetings. It is assumed that, because we are all victims of the same misfortune, we have an automatic bond that transcends that of other relationships. When I first arrived in the program, I was overwhelmed by the amounts of hugs I was given, mostly by overbearing men, all who seemed to be over 6 feet tall and 200 pounds, crushing me with their good intentions. More than annoyance, it is intrusive of my personal space, uninvited, but usually unavoidable without coming off as a "royal bitch." In my mind, hugs are reserved for very special people with whom I am close or even intimate. I am very selective for the most part, as is my right.

But not so long ago, one man (who I barely know) was greeting incoming people at the door. I saw him coming. I knew what to do. I was mentally prepared to react. So I offered him my hand and said, "Hi, Joe," and he immediately deflected my outstretched hand and wrapped his arms around me in a warm embrace! I wanted to scream, kick, and stamp my feet—why do they keep doing that?!! I really thought my message was pretty clear. One thing is clear, though, hugs are better than drugs only when asked for.

. . . and from Joanna T.:

Once I was approached by this guy who was a self-proclaimed stud who had been staring at me for the whole meeting. Afterwards he came up to me and said: "You know, I really love your hair. I keep thinking about what you must look like naked." At another time he told me that he was only in AA for the "broads."

. . . and from Peggy M.:

When I was new, I think I was only in AA for a month, this man came up to me to give me a hug, only this hug included a pelvic press! And at another meeting, I heard another man say to the group, "My wife doesn't understand me, and neither does my girlfriend."

It can be surmised that many women in AA have this kind of story, particularly if they are young and single.

New AA members are routinely encouraged to find a sponsor soon after entering the program. The AA sponsor is ideally a person who possesses a significant period of quality sobriety. "Quality" sobriety may be described as a clear commitment to the program while utilizing the principles of the twelve steps as a part of daily living. A sponsor assumes a certain degree of responsibility in helping the early recovering alcoholic attain sobriety. It is often a lifetime relationship. Generally, newcomers are advised to listen and observe other members before choosing a sponsor who would be compatible and helpful. Unfortunately, the relationship is not always a helpful one. Although it is usually recommended that the sponsor be of the same sex, sometimes seasoned AA members will offer their services to the rookie who unknowingly and eagerly accepts the help. One such woman, Pat B., shared her early experience with me:

> When I came into AA I was confused, defeated, and vulnerable. He was older, two and a half years sober (a long time for someone just coming around), and very willing to help me along the road to sobriety. At the time, I felt that he was just very caring and comforting, much like a father-figure who "embraced" me with his experience, strength, and hope. But then I became attracted to him and him to me. I later found out, after a good deal of time, that not only was he married, but his wife was in the program too! Here I was, all tangled up in a love triangle, and *I* was the "other" woman and barely sober enough to deal with the flood of emotions that came with it. I decided to distance myself, and I began to go to other meetings where he would not be. I tried very hard to avoid him (and his wife) and tried to concentrate on my own sobriety. Needless to say, he kept showing up. I had to alter my whole routine and meeting schedule to get away from him. I know I'm not the only one who's fallen prey to the thirteenth step. A friend of mine knows someone in the program who's pregnant because she fell in love with her sponsor, and he's been sober for twelve years!

Some are sicker than others. Women are encouraged to confront these situations as they occur, which, given most situations, is more trouble than it is worth, by going to another meeting where it could surely happen again (but unlikely if it is a women's group), or by abandoning AA altogether. It can be assumed that a good number of women whose initial contact with AA was met with some sort of sexual harassment have chosen the latter.

GENDER DIFFERENCES

Sandmaier (1980a,b) highlighted some of the factors differentiating alcoholic women from men: Women tend to be dependent on men; women are more likely to begin drinking in connection with depression, sex role conflicts, or as the result of life crisis such as divorce or children leaving home; alcoholic women suffer lower self-esteem, more anxiety, and more guilt about their drinking than men; women lack job skills and are often primarily responsible for child rearing; and alcoholic women are more likely to have a history of psychiatric care. Sandmaier's descriptions of alcoholic women are echoed in more recent literature (Covington 1994, Institute of Medicine 1990, Turnbull 1989, U.S. Department of Health and Human Services 1993).

The differences do not end here. Straussner (1985) presented a thorough exploration of current knowledge regarding women and alcoholism. She cited research conducted by Reich that "genetic factors outweigh environmental factors in producing alcoholism in men, but that the opposite is true in women" (p. 63). AA has long maintained that individual change is the solution to life's problems. "AA ideology does not encourage discussion of the social and political causative factors in alcoholism. For women, it may be that the environment contributed to the drinking and the environment prevents the recovery from occurring" (Covington 1991, p. 90).

To understand fully the dynamics of alcoholic women in AA, it is important to become familiar with the socialization process and psychological development of women in general. Early object relations theorists (e.g., Fairbairn 1952, Guntrip 1971, Kohut 1971, Mahler et al. 1975, Winnicott 1965) described how the relationship to the mothering figure forms a basis for future relationships and how disturbances in personality development can occur as a result of failures in early object relationships. Chodorow (1978) in *The Reproduction of Mothering* extended object relations theory to include gender-specific process. Her focus was on the influence of identity development in the separation-individuation process. Elise (1991) extended and elaborated theory in this area by bringing the mother's active efforts in the socialization of the child into relation with the process of self–other differentiation. In this regard, the male child, through gender socialization, is encouraged to move *away from* the mother to identify with the father and his maleness, while the girl child is encouraged to remain *connected with* the mother and her femaleness. The term *connected with* is the essence of the relational model developed by feminist theorists at The Stone Center (Jordan et al. 1991).

The relational model, simply put, posits that women's development centers on and evolves in relationship with others. Connectedness is considered a strength rather than a weakness. Miller (1976), in her pivotal work *Toward a New Psychology of Women*, emphasized the need to view characteristics such as "vulnerability, weakness, helplessness, emotions, participation in the development of others, cooperation and creativity" (p. 27) as essential to psychological health in both men and women.

The frequently seen dynamic of dependency in women also has been noted and reframed. Zelvin (1988) has described the changing theoretical underpinnings of women's psychological development and the meaning of dependency. She credits Eichenbaum and Orbach (1983) for emphasizing that, from a feminist psychoanalytic perspective, "dependency is not innately pathological but is rather a fundamental human need that is never adequately met for women" (Zelvin 1988, p. 100). It is therefore important to view these fundamental traits of women's psychology in a positive mind-set, when in the past even women themselves have internalized these assets in a negative way.

In keeping with the relational model, the problem of alcoholism in women, and of addictions in general, is a relationship problem, not a moral one. A primary reason that the woman alcoholic drinks is because she needs to be connected with her husband, her lover, her family, her friends. She uses substances to fill a void, an inner emptiness. The drink, the drug, the food become her primary object relationship with the world. AA and other self-help groups can serve to fill that inner emptiness. Covington (1991) explores the evolution of mutual help groups and the natural tendency of women to be drawn to one another in explaining women's attraction to AA:

> For centuries women have sought to teach and support themselves and each other by meeting in groups and pooling information and experiences. In traditional and modern societies alike, women continue to meet to wash clothes and sew quilts together, share stories around a cup of coffee, play cards and watch children. These activities have always and will always involve offers of solace and support that come in casual conversation with dependable and cherished sisters. [p. 85]

INTEGRATING AA INTO TREATMENT

Treatment professionals who work with women addicts need to be knowledgeable about both the benefits (Spiegel 1993) and the shortcomings of

AA and similar twelve-step groups. If a woman alcoholic complains about the meetings or some unhappy experience involving her participation in AA, her complaint need not be heard as a resistance to treatment. Rather, she needs to be listened to and validated. Turnbull (1989) stated that the "socialization of women as caretakers may compel some women to attend to men rather than their own problems in mixed groups, and others may feel uncomfortable if they have been victimized by male alcohol abusers" (p. 365). Turnbull further suggested that participation in a women's group may be advised early in treatment.

The importance of the role of the therapist as well as the one-to-one relationship with an AA sponsor cannot be overly emphasized. There is evidence to support the notion that women respond to individual relationships more positively than to group situations (Stafford 1979). It is at this dyadic level that a woman's need for connectedness is best met. In order to help women avoid getting involved with a sponsor who may have ulterior motives or poor sobriety, therapists should encourage the woman alcoholic to seek a female sponsor and support her efforts to question this person's quality of sobriety.

Clinicians need to carefully evaluate underlying problems that may hinder a successful recovery such as depression, a history of sexual abuse, and other family dysfunctions that contribute to the woman alcoholic's sense of shame (Kovach 1986). The professional must be prepared to counteract the ego-deflating principles of AA, both formal and informal, and to help rebuild a positive self-esteem. Terms frequently heard at AA meetings, such as *drunk, alkie*, etc., make it particularly hard for a woman to accept her alcoholism. In addition, recovering women need to learn to protect themselves from various forms of sexual harassment both in and out of AA. Clinicians can play a significant role by providing supportive therapy and assertiveness training. For example, the therapist may help the client claim ownership of her body and personal space by teaching her to say no to sexual advances and compromising situations. Role playing is a useful technique in this regard. Abuses of AA principles need to be recognized so that women can be assisted in applying the twelve-step program to further their recovery. In the book *A Woman's Way Through the 12 Steps*, Covington (1994) provides valued insight into helping women integrate these steps into their own lives.

Most importantly, it should not be assumed that all alcoholic women are the same. Options need to be seriously considered and presented to clients in order to respond to individual needs and belief systems. AA should not be viewed as a Utopia for recovery. A saying commonly heard among AA members is "take what you need and leave the rest." Treatment professionals should assist their clients in this effort.

Despite its shortcomings, a great amount of diversity can be found within the AA framework. Specialized meetings for women only, for lesbians, for nonsmokers, for persons affected by HIV, and so forth, can be found in most areas. These meetings generally adhere to the principles of the twelve-step program, but offer additional support for other issues affecting a person's recovery. Members are encouraged to shop around for meetings where they can be comfortable. Then too, if support exists, new meetings can be created by any AA member to respond to specific needs. Clinicians may need to encourage women to establish new meetings to meet their unique needs.

AA has the potential to be a vital source of healing. It has the potential for forming new, sober relationships, for belonging, and for being connected. As Covington (1991) has noted, there are many advantages to recovery in mutual help groups. First, the meetings are free and can offer different things for different people. In most communities, meetings are available throughout the day or night, accommodating most women's schedules and needs. In addition, meetings tend to take on their own "personality," offering a wide variety of group styles. There are meetings for everyone.

Secondly, sharing is not dependent on hierarchy or status. Even the newcomer has something to offer the group. Input from all members is considered valuable, which can lead to increased self-esteem. There are no "bosses" in AA, but rather a group of peers helping each other to stay sober.

Third, AA provides an opportunity for alcohol- and drug-free social activities. Meetings can be fun and a way to make new friends. Members often gather together before or after the meetings for coffee and are encouraged to maintain phone contact between meetings. Groups also sponsor organized social events such as picnics, dances, and bus trips. Indeed, the benefits are many. The need for connection and a sense of belonging is of primary importance to women alcoholics, and the meetings they attend need to address and satisfy this need.

Women in recovery can be encouraged to consider alternative self-help programs. Perhaps Save Our Selves (SOS), Rational Recovery, Support Together for Emotional and Mental Serenity and Sobriety (STEMSS), or Women for Sobriety (WFS) will be better suited to some women than AA or NA. WFS, founded in 1972, offers women a feminist perspective on sobriety, affirming the value and worth of each woman. In place of the twelve steps are thirteen statements of affirmation or acceptance. Though fewer in number than AA, WFS meetings can be found in many metropolitan areas. SOS was begun in 1984, designed to "specifically address the needs of agnostics, atheistic, and humanist alcoholics who were dissatisfied with AA" (Covington 1991, p. 90). More recently, Rational Recovery has emerged as a self-help group to support those persons for whom the concept of a Higher Power is unacceptable. It uses cognitive-behavior therapy along with rational emotive therapy (RET). Rational Recovery teaches members "unconditional acceptance of themselves and others, how to evaluate their thoughts, feelings and actions but not to measure or devalue their self or personhood" (Bowen 1988, p. 561). It teaches participants how to think, feel, and act more appropriately in order to achieve their goals.

For those persons who are experiencing problems with addictions as well as mental illness, (STEMSS) is a program in which issues surrounding medications and sobriety can be openly discussed without feeling stigmatized or censored. This program can be particularly helpful to women, many of whom are dually diagnosed.

While these alternative programs for recovery are available, it is important to recognize that no other single treatment has done so much for so many thousands of alcoholic people as AA. In spite of its shortcomings, many of which have to do with the larger society from which it comes, AA offers new friends, new hope, and a new life for those asking for help. Whenever anyone reaches out, no matter who they are or where they come from, "the hand of AA is always there" (Alcoholics Anonymous Grapevine, Inc., 1994b).

For most, it is the end of the line. But they soon find that it is the beginning of a new freedom. Part of that freedom comes in discovering who they are. The women in AA are courageous in that they continue to survive and overcome their own history. They, in turn, help other women to overcome theirs. As survivors, they consciously choose to take the action and initiative that is needed for change, first in themselves, then in the world around them. It is with that vision that the women of AA commit themselves to their own sobriety, to each other as women, and to the community of Alcoholics Anonymous.

Part of reclaiming their own power is not by abandoning AA, but by remaining a part of it. Only through education, awareness, and time will attitudes and prejudices toward women change. Most meetings continue to grow in membership. More and more women are a part of this number. More and more women are taking an active role in the running of individual groups. At the same time, more women's AA meetings are being formed, and more weekend retreats for AA women can be found. These incremental measures, along with the confrontation of situations or individuals that are offensive, will continue to provide the impetus for change. In this way women can overcome their past and lead the way for those to follow, to share their experience, strength, and hope—a day at a time—for as long as it takes.

WHERE TO GET INFORMATION ABOUT SELF-HELP GROUPS

National Clearinghouse for
Alcohol and Drug Information
PO Box 2345
Rockville, MD 20852
(301) 468–2600

The Augustine Fellowship, Sex
and Love Addicts Anonymous
PO Box 88
New Town Branch
Boston, MA 02258

Alcoholics Anonymous
PO Box 459
Grand Central Station
New York, NY 10163–1100
(212) 686–1100

Save Our Selves (National Organi-
zation for Secular Sobriety)
PO Box 15781
North Hollywood, CA 91615–5781

Overeaters Anonymous
2190 190th Street
Torrance, CA 90504

Al-Anon/Alateen Family Group
Headquarters, Inc.
PO Box 862
Midtown Station
New York, NY 10018–0862

Women for Sobriety, Inc.
PO Box 618
Quakertown, PA 18951
1 (800) 333–1606

Adult Children of Alcoholics
6381 Hollywood Boulevard,
Suite 685
Hollywood, CA 90028
(212) 464–4423

Narcotics Anonymous
PO Box 9999
Van Nuys, CA 91409

National Association for Children
of Alcoholics
31706 Coast Highway Suite 201
Laguna, CA 92667
(714) 499–3889

Support Together
for Emotional and
Mental Serenity and Sobriety
322 Main Street (Newburg)
West Bend, WI 53095

REFERENCES

Adams, K. L., and Ware, N. C. (1989). Sexism and the English language: the linguistic implications of being a woman. In *Women: A Feminist Perspective*, ed. J. Freeman, pp. 470–484. Mountainview, CA: Mayfield.

Alcoholics Anonymous (1995). Unpublished communication. New York: General Service Office.

Alcoholics Anonymous World Services, Inc. (1976). *Alcoholics Anonymous.* New York: Author.

—— (1980). *Dr. Bob and the Good Oldtimers.* New York: Author.

—— (1993). *Membership Survey.* New York: Author.

Alcoholics Anonymous Grapevine, Inc. (1994a). *Preamble.* New York: General Service Office.

—— (1994b). *I am responsible.* New York: General Service Office.

Bowen, G. R. (1988). Raising public awareness about the extent of alcohol-related problems: an overview. *Public Health Reports* 103:559–563.

Chodorow, N. (1978). *The Reproduction of Mothering.* Berkeley, California: University of California Press.

Clark, M. (1986). Alcoholism first. *Women in Therapy* 5(1):72.

Copeland, J., Hall, W., Didcott, P., and Biggs, V. (1993). Comparison of a specialist woman's alcohol and other drug treatment service with two traditional mixed-sex services: client characteristics and treatment outcome. *Drug and Alcohol Dependence* 32:81–92.

Covington, S. S. (1991). Sororities of helping and healing: women and mutual help groups. In *Alcohol and Drugs Are Women's Issues,* ed. P. Roth, pp. 85–93. Metuchen, NJ: Women's Action Alliance and Scarecrow.

—— (1994). *A Woman's Way through the 12 Steps.* Center City, MN: Hazelden.

Eichenbaum, L., and Orbach, S. (1983). *What Do Women Want: Exploding the Myth of Dependency.* New York: Coward-McCann.

Elise, D. (1991). An analysis of gender difference in separation-individuation. *Psychoanalytic Study of the Child* 46:51–67. New Haven, CT: Yale University Press.

Fairbairn, W. R. D. (1952). *An Object Relations Theory of Personality.* New York: Basic Books.

Galanter, M., ed. (1989). *Recent Developments in Alcoholism,* vol. 7. New York: Plenum.

Guntrip, H. J. (1971). *Psychoanalytic Theory, Therapy, and the Self.* New York: Basic Books.

Institute of Medicine (1990). *Broadening the Base of Treatment for Alcohol Problems.* Washington, DC: Academy.

Jordan, J. V., Kaplan, A. G., Miller, J. B., et al. (1991). *Women's Growth in Connection.* New York: Guilford.

Kohut, H. (1971). *The Analysis of the Self.* New York: International Universities Press.

Kovach, J. A. (1986). Incest as a treatment issue for alcoholic women. *Alcoholism Treatment Quarterly* 3(1):143.

Mahler, M. S., Pine, F., and Bergman, A. (1975). *The Psychological Birth of the Human Infant.* New York: Basic Books.

Martin, S. E. (1989). Sexual harassment: the link joining gender stratification, sexuality and women's economic status. In *Women: A Feminist Perspective*, ed. J. Freeman, pp. 57–75. Mountainview, CA: Mayfield.

Miller, J. B. (1976). *Toward a New Psychology of Women*. Boston: Beacon.

Sandmaier, M. (1980a). *The Invisible Alcoholics*. New York: McGraw-Hill.

——(1980b). Women helping women: opening the door to treatment. In *Alcoholism in Women*, ed. C. C. Eddy and J. L. Ford, pp. 161–170. Dubuque, IA: Kendall-Hunt.

Spiegel, B. R. (1993). Twelve-step programs as a treatment modality. In *Clinical Work with Substance-Abusing Clients*, ed. S. L. A. Straussner, pp. 153–168. New York: Guilford.

Stafford, R. (1979). Alcoholics Anonymous and the woman alcoholic. In *Women Who Drink*, ed. V. Burtle, pp. 248–269. Springfield, Illinois: Charles C Thomas.

Straussner, S. L. A. (1985). Alcoholism in women: current knowledge and implications for treatment. In *Psychological Issues in the Treatment of Alcoholism*, ed. D. Cook, S. L. A. Straussner, and C. H. Fewell, pp. 61–77. New York: Haworth.

Turnbull, J. E. (1989). Treatment issues for alcoholic women. *Social Casework: The Journal of Contemporary Social Work* 70(6):364–369.

U.S. Department of Health and Human Services (1993). *Alcohol and Health: Eighth Special Report to the U.S. Congress*. Rockville, MD: Author.

Winnicott, D. W. (1965). *The Maturational Processes and the Facilitating Environment*. New York: International Universities Press.

Zelvin, E. (1988). Dependence and denial in coalcoholic women. *Alcoholism Treatment Quarterly* 5(3/4):97–115.

III

Men's Issues in Addiction Treatment

13

Psychodynamic Perspectives on Substance-Abusing Men

Jerome D. Levin

PSYCHODYNAMIC PERSPECTIVES ON SUBSTANCE-ABUSING MEN

Although the vast majority of the research and theorizing on addiction is on addiction in men, there is something gender-specific about the way men drink and drug that is worth elucidating. The emergence of a literature on female addiction during the past decade has sharpened our awareness of this gender specificity and made us realize that there is a connection between maleness and the way that men use and abuse drugs. This chapter will elucidate this connection using the theoretical insights of a variety of psychodynamic thinkers.

As we survey some of the major psychodynamic theories of addiction, it is important to remember that addicted men come from diverse cultural backgrounds and have different childhood experiences, peer groups, values, economic situations, and accessibility to drugs. No one rubric is going to fit them all. We need also remember that the pharmacology of the various drugs is extremely powerful and can override emotional, psychological, dynamic, and interpersonal factors in determining the behavior of the addict.

EARLY THEORIES OF ADDICTION IN MEN

Early dynamic theorists contributed unique insights into the psychodynamics of male addiction.

Thomas Trotter

Thomas Trotter (Jellinek 1994) was a British naval physician who wrote a dissertation on inebriety. In 1804, Trotter postulated that alcoholism was a disease having two causes: heredity and premature weaning. This combination of predisposition and early environmental trauma as etiological in the development of addiction has a strikingly modern ring, as exemplified by the case of a brilliant college professor who stupefied himself on a daily basis. During treatment, he spontaneously related his behavior and generally high anxiety level and tendency toward depression to the fact that upon his birth, he was unable to accept his mother's milk and had almost died before they found a formula that he was able to tolerate. Though there was certainly some post-hoc rationalization in his account of what predisposed him to compulsive drinking, he was somehow convincing. Ultimately recovering by becoming as compulsive a member of AA as he had been a consumer of gin, he found a more adaptive way to feed himself in his belated attempt to avert starvation.

Sigmund Freud

Almost a hundred years after Trotter, Sigmund Freud (1897/1985) wrote to his friend, Wilhelm Fliess, "It has occurred to me that masturbation is the one great habit that is a 'primary addiction,' and that the other addictions to alcohol, morphine, etc., only enter into life as a substitute and replacement for it" (p. 287). Thus, masturbation is the "model" addiction among men. According to Freud, infantile masturbation is both compelling and guilt-inducing. Forbidden by parents, the child comes to internalize the prohibition. A struggle ensues between a wish for instinctual gratification and the internalized prohibition. The struggle not to masturbate is almost always lost; however, the return to masturbation is accompanied by guilt and a fall in self-esteem. Masturbation can then be used as a way of assuaging the anxiety, and a vicious cycle is set up. This is indeed the pattern of much addictive behavior. Later addictions are not only replacements and reenactments of the original addiction to masturbation, they are also attempts to master, through repetition, the traumatic loss of self-esteem that follows the failure to live up to the resolution not to masturbate.

Freud returned to this theory of addiction many years later in *Dostoevsky and Parricide* (1928). There he analyzed the great Russian novelist's compulsive gambling. Freud traced Dostoevsky's compulsion back to an addiction to masturbation, but he added the insight that the addiction also served as a means of self-punishment for the original forbidden wish. The payoff, for Dostoevsky, was losing. There was a condensation of guilts: masturbatory, oedipal, and for the addiction itself, all of which are "punished" by the negative consequences of the addiction.

Freud's theory has the merit of highlighting the narcissistic nature of addiction. In masturbation one's love object is oneself. The love object of the addict becomes the abused substance itself. Freud's theory also highlights another aspect of the narcissistic pathology inherent in addictions: the loss of self-esteem that the addict experiences when he "slips." This loss of self-esteem in turn requires more of the addictive substance or activity to raise the lowered self-esteem, and an addictive cycle is established.

Freud's (1920) theory of the repetition compulsion also sheds light on addictions. In it he postulates an innate death instinct (Thanatos) with which the life instinct (Eros) struggles. Freud thought that some sort of innate destructive drive had to exist to account for such phenomena as self-mutilation, suicide, and addiction. Most analysts have rejected Freud's theory of an innate self-destructive drive, but they have thought him correct descriptively: human beings do hold on to and repeat the familiar no matter how pernicious it may be. This built-in resistance to change plays a large role in maintaining addictions.

Karl Abraham

Karl Abraham (1908) published the first psychoanalytic paper on addiction. In it he stated that "alcoholism is a nervous and sexual perversion" (p. 87). By perversion he meant oral regressive and homoerotic tendencies. Abraham based his theory on an analysis of male alcoholics and on his observation that homophobic men become openly physically affectionate in the camaraderie of the beer hall. He inferred that heavy drinking allows the expression of forbidden homosexual wishes and postulated that alcohol addicts have especially intense conflicts about repressed homosexuality. In emphasizing the regression to orality in alcoholism, he not only calls attention to the oral ingestion of the drink but also points out the parallel between drunken stupor and the warmth and security felt by the satiated infant.

Abraham highlights the psychological and emotional regression brought about by the drinking itself. Historical changes in attitudes toward homosexuality notwithstanding, it is surprisingly common to encounter men who drink or drug in order to express forbidden homosexual wishes. Other repudiated sexual desires also find expression while men are high. For example, a young artist got "coked up" in order to masturbate to sadistic videos. He then punished himself for this "indulgence" by continuing his "run" until he became paranoid and terrified.

Edward Glover

Edward Glover (1928) emphasized the aggression in addiction. He spoke of "oral rage" and "anal sadism," expressed by drinking or drugging *at* somebody. Addictive rage is partly in defense of the addiction, partly self-hatred projected outward, partly a response to narcissistic vulnerability, partly pharmacologically induced, and partly repressed childhood rage.

Most "slips" are rage responses. Glover also cites the use of drugs to quell castration anxiety, the fear of retaliation by the father for murderous wishes toward him.

Sandor Rado

Sandor Rado (1933) was the first to point to the similarity between addiction and manic-depressive psychosis. Rado related both the mood alterations of manic-depressive illness and the addictive pattern of highs and lows to the cycle of infantile hunger and satiation. He movingly captured the addict's futile attempt to relieve "tense depression" chemically and turn it into elation, only to fall into an even deeper depression, necessitating more intake. As the addiction proceeds, the periods of elation become progressively briefer, and in the end there is nothing but unrelieved depression.

Rado saw the key issue in addictions as a disturbance in the regulation of self-esteem. What the user seeks in the chemically induced elation is the elevation of self-esteem.

Robert Knight

Robert Knight (1937, 1938), emphasized the depressive aspects of the addictive dynamic. Frustrated orality results in repressed rage that in turn results in depression characterized by rage turned against the self.

Knight observed two types of male addicts. *Essential addicts* never established themselves in life and were financially and emotionally dependent on their families. Knight described these patients as oral characters who had not reached the "mastery of the object" characteristic of the anal stage of psychosexual development. Oral character disorder is characterized by angry dependency, impulsivity, and lack of frustration tolerance. The essentials had a borderline character structure. Many borderlines become substance abusers, although most substance abusers are not borderline.

The *reactive addicts*, on the contrary, were those who had managed some life successes. They had achieved economic independence. They had generally succeeded in marrying and establishing families. The quality of their object relations had once been fairly adequate. Knight saw their addiction as a reaction to life stresses or losses. From his description of these men, they seem to be a mix of "normals" with drinking or drug problems and men with narcissistic personality disorders, characterized by low self-esteem, feelings of entitlement, manipulative interpersonal relations, and psychological deficits in such areas as the ability to modulate anxiety.

Knight also described the family dynamics of his addicted patients. He found that the fathers of his reactives were frequently highly success- ful, powerful, erratic, inconsistently punitive men whom their sons ambi- valently hated. Unable either to live up to their fathers' expectations or to rebel openly against them, they turned to drink (or drugs) as a form of passive-aggressive rebellion.

Otto Fenichel

Otto Fenichel (1945) also thought that oral dependence and frustration result in chronic depression in addicted men. He saw addiction as a maladaptive defense mechanism used to resolve neurotic conflicts, especially conflict between dependence and the expression of anger. It is to Fenichel that we owe the observation that "the superego has been defined as that part of the mind which is soluble in alcohol" (p. 387), thereby making it possible for the drinker to indulge in forbidden impulses and resolve id-superego conflicts in favor of the id.

Karl Menninger

Karl Menninger (1938) called alcoholism and drug addiction forms of *chronic suicide*. There is no question that addicts engage in self-destructive behav- ior. The question is whether such self-destruction is sought on an uncon- scious level. Analytic writers like Menninger cite clinical evidence that addicts do seek self-destruction, while behaviorally oriented clinicians tend to believe that addicts initially seek positive affect (elation) and only later, after the drug itself has produced dysphoria, use to alleviate negative af- fect (tense depression) and that the self-destruction is a side effect. It is likely that both pleasure seeking, with self-destruction as a byproduct, and unconsciously motivated self-destruction, operate simultaneously.

Harry Tiebout

Harry Tiebout (1949, 1957), who was AA founder Bill Wilson's analyst, saw the operative dynamic in alcoholic men as grandiosity—ego inflation of such proportions that reality is lost and a near psychotic condition results. Tiebout alluded to "His Majesty the Baby," a phrase from Freud's 1914 essay "On Narcissism" which Wilson incorporated into AA literature.

He saw archaic, infantile narcissism as driving addiction and treatment as what he called "ego deflation."

EGO PSYCHOLOGY AND SELF PSYCHOLOGY APPROACHES TO ADDICTION

More recent psychoanalytic theorists, including Szasz (1958), Hartocollis (1968), Krystal and Raskin (1970), Wurmser (1978), Kohut (1977a,b), Khantzian (1981), and Levin (1987, 1991), have stressed the adaptive function of the addiction and emphasize impairments in ego functioning, lack of affect tolerance, and the use of primitive defense mechanisms.

Thomas Szasz

Thomas Szasz (1958) viewed addictions as counterphobic activities. The addict uses drugs to confront and master intolerable fears, including the fear of being addicted. The user's basic motivation is to prove that he is in control. A defiance of fate is implicit in this counterphobic behavior. The underlying problem is a fear of psychic annihilation and oblivion, of both regressive fragmentation of the self and engulfment of the self by the symbiotic mother. Experientially, both outcomes are death. Addicts therefore self-inflict death in order to master their fear of death. Seen in this way, addicts are mythic heroes who descend to the underworld and emerge intact—at least that is their hope. The addict's defensive grandiosity is fed by participation in this unconscious drama.

Henry Krystal and Herbert Raskin

Henry Krystal and Herbert Raskin (1970) offer a theory of affect development in which the infant starts out with global, undifferentiated feelings, including a primitive dysphoria, which will later differentiate into anxiety, tension, and depression. They postulate that addicts suffer *affect regression* and experience feelings as massive, primitive, and overwhelming. Many addicts have been deprived of the experience of labeling of affects by loving parents. The addict literally doesn't know what he is feeling.

Krystal and Raskin's theory has important clinical implications. Since verbalization is a crucial developmental task, the therapist must facilitate affect progression by giving the addict words for what he is feeling.

This provides cognitive structure, starts the process of affect (re)differentiation, and reduces the terror of the experientially primitive, unfamiliar, and chaotic emerging feelings. Affect labeling is a way station on the road from feelings experienced as mysterious happenings inflicted on the addict to feelings experienced as consciously owned aspects of the self.

Edward Khantzian

Edward Khantzian (1981) emphasized ego and self-deficits in the areas of self-care and regulation of feelings. He saw addictive self-destruction as resulting from a deficit rather than as a self-punishment. This deficit precludes normal affect regulation and tolerance.

Leon Wurmser

Leon Wurmser (1978) proposed a powerful psychodynamic model in which the addict is caught in a seven-stage vicious circle. In stage one, there is a sudden plummeting of already tenuous self-esteem, usually following a disappointment in reality or in fantasy, which leads to a narcissistic crisis (stage two). This crisis leads to a breakdown of affect defense (stage three) in which feelings become overwhelming, global, generalized, archaic, and incapable of being expressed in words. This experience is intolerable and leads to repression and denial of inner reality, leaving only a vague tension and restlessness (stage four). In the process, the self is split and depersonalized. The addict experiences an urgent need to act; because the inner world is denied and externalized, it is logical to look for the answer externally and concretely in the drug. At this point aggression is mobilized which may be turned against the self (stage five). In stage six, the superego is split so that it will not be an impediment to action, and feelings of entitlement and grandiosity lead to a consummation in the binge. The narcissistic crisis ends in short-lived pleasure. Wurmser quoted Rado (1933): "The elation had augmented the ego to gigantic dimensions and had almost eliminated reality; now just the reverse state appears, sharpened by the contrast. The ego is shrunken, and reality appears exaggerated in its dimensions" (Wurmser 1978, p. 10). The addict is in worse shape than ever, with even lower self-esteem (stage seven). Wurmser's emphasis was on maladaptive defenses—particularly the defenses of splitting of self, superego, and reality into incommunicable parts; of denial, not only of the addiction but of the inner world of fantasy and feelings; and of externalization of inner deficit, conflict, and possibility of resolution. The socialization of most men lends cultural support to these defenses, making their interpretation and working through difficult.

Peter Hartocollis

Peter Hartocollis (1968) stressed the use of drugs to bolster defenses. The defense most in need of bolstering is denial, which Hartocollis saw as repudiation of the need for help. In a later paper (Hartocollis and Hartocollis 1980), he presented clinical evidence that this denial originates in a disturbed mother–infant relationship, postulating that the difficulty starts in the rapprochement substage of the separation-individuation process. Hartocollis hypothesized that these developmental problems predispose men to borderline and narcissistic personality disorders as well as to addiction. To account for reports of lack of psychopathology antecedent to addiction, he pointed to the relatively smooth surface functioning of narcissists who compensate for inner emptiness and emotional shallowness by acting "as if" all is well. He suggested that as this compensation falters, they turn to drugs to maintain their "as-if personalities" (Deutsch 1965). The counterdependency that Hartocollis focused upon is one of the most powerful and most frequently encountered dynamics in addicted men.

Erich Fromm

Erich Fromm synthesized Freudian and Marxist thought into a unique amalgam. In his exploration into the intersection of the political and the personal, Fromm (1941) tangentially elucidated one of the most powerful dynamics driving addictive behavior: escape from freedom. Fromm convincingly demonstrated that one of the social dynamics behind the rise of fascism and other forms of totalitarianism is a desire to escape from anxiety, concomitant with the realization that the individual is responsible for his choices. Twelve-step programs intuitively address this anxiety and help recovering addicts deal with this form of dread by providing them with meaningful activities, goals, values, and social supports. Fromm saw not only social but individual psychopathology as derived from a desire to flee the anxiety of being free. A neurosis, a psychosis, or an addiction is a constriction, a narrowing of possibility. Addiction with its progressive impoverishment of the self and loss of potentiality is clearly an escape from freedom. The achievement of sobriety is a reclamation of freedom. Fear is always concomitant with this newfound freedom, with its choices, decisions, and responsibilities. What Kierkegaard (1849) called "the dizziness of freedom" has caused many a relapse (p. 55).

Heinz Kohut

Heinz Kohut (1971/1977b) conceptualized narcissistic pathology, including addiction, as a deficit state—something is missing inside. It is missing inside because something went wrong developmentally. Thus it makes perfect sense to take something, alcohol for instance, to remedy such an internal lack. The only trouble is that what is missing can only come from people, not from a chemical, so the treatment of addiction must be a replacement of rum with relationship. Kohut compared an addiction to a futile attempt to cure a gastric fistula by eating. The food may taste good, but it falls right out the hole without either nourishing or repairing the hole.

Kohut distinguished between two kinds of narcissistic transferences: *mirror transferences* and *idealizing transferences*. In the mirror transference, the analyst's only function is to reflect back (mirror) the patient's wonderfulness. What the patient seeks is affirmation of archaic (infantile) grandiosity. In the idealizing transference, the patient puts all the wonderfulness—omnipotence and omniscience—in the analyst and then fuses with him. The addict's relationship to drugs can usefully be understood as a combined mirror and idealizing transference.

The Kohutian notion of *narcissistic rage* further illuminates much addictive behavior. Narcissistic rage, unlike mature aggression, is not instrumental in the service of a reality-based goal; rather, it is the response of the unmirrored self to narcissistic injury (see Levin 1993) characterized by deep pain, intense feelings of shame, precipitous fall in self-esteem, and an unquenchable desire for revenge. Most "slips" are narcissistic rage responses. Such a dynamic is particularly true of men who, more typically than women, use acting-out defenses to mask their inner pain and emptiness. Helping the recovering man to recognize, contain, and appropriately express rather than act out rage and anger is vital.

DEPENDENCY CONFLICT AND POWER THEORIES

The dependency conflict theory of addiction states that male addicts are people who have not succeeded in establishing healthy patterns of interdependence. This theory also states that their failure to establish such forms of adult mutuality is the principal etiological factor behind their addition. In its naïve form, the theory states that addicts are socially, psychologically, and often economically dependent people. Proponents of this view cite the openly dependent behavior of many addicts. Some addicts, however, are not openly dependent. Additionally, the open dependence of some addicts may be a consequence, not a cause, of their disease.

The more sophisticated form of this theory (Blane 1968, Child et al. 1965, Knight 1937, 1938, McCord and McCord 1960, Menninger 1938) states that addicts are people who suffer particularly acute conflict over how to meet their dependency needs and who have turned to drugs in an attempt to resolve this largely unconscious conflict. Important support for the dependency conflict theory comes from a cross-cultural anthropological study by Child and colleagues (1965). They studied 138 preliterate societies and demonstrated that drunkenness was positively correlated with the punishment of open expression of dependency needs. Societies that demand independence, individual achievement, and self-reliance, while frustrating the meeting of dependency needs, have higher rates of drunkenness. For men, ours is such a society.

Additional support for the dependency conflict theory comes from a longitudinal study by McCord and McCord (1960). The McCords (1960) described the childhood personalities of men who later became alcoholic as "outwardly self-confident, undisturbed by abnormal fears, indifferent toward their siblings, and disapproving of their mothers. . . . [They] evidenced unrestrained aggression, sadism, sexual anxiety, and activity rather than passivity" (p. 427). The McCords found that these active and aggressive boys became dependent, passive, self-pitying, and grandiose after they developed alcoholism. A combination of *aggressivity and shyness* made for the greatest risk of alcoholism. The researchers theorized that this childhood pattern is a reaction formation to an intense unresolved dependency conflict resulting from inconsistent, erratic satisfaction of childhood dependency needs. Men who suppress or repress their dependency needs are prone to meet those needs in a veiled manner through drug use. From this perspective, male addiction is a form of pseudoself-sufficiency.

Blane's Dependency Types

Howard Blane (1968) developed a system of classifying male alcoholics by dividing them into openly dependent, counterdependent, and dependent–counterdependent types.

Openly dependent alcoholics want to be cared for by others. They are similar to Knight's essential alcoholics. Blane believed that their prognosis is poor.

Counterdependents handle their dependency needs by denial and reaction formation. They are the "two-fisted drinkers" who "don't need anybody." They are the men prone to break up the bar and give similar evidence of their "independence." Some counterdependent men are overtly sociopathic; many are addicted to street drugs. Blane believed that their prognosis also is poor.

The third group, the *dependent-counterdependents*, are those alcoholics and drug addicts for whom the conflict around dependency is most active and intense. They are in the most pain and therefore are the most amenable to treatment.

Need-for-Power Theory

McClelland and colleagues (1972) theorized that men drink to feel powerful and that the kind of power men seek in alcohol is personal (egoistic) and not social. Using the Thematic Apperception Test (TAT) to study why men drink, the researchers found that men who told TAT stories of personalized power while sober were men who drank the most. Moreover, consumption of alcohol increased the incidence of themes of personal power. On the basis of this evidence, McClelland and colleagues concluded that the dependency conflict theory of alcoholism is wrong, and they proposed a countertheory that men drink to feel personally powerful and that alcoholics are men with a particularly strong need to feel powerful.

McClelland and colleagues also analyzed folktales as if they were TAT stories and found a correlation between tribal cultures that drink heavily and cultures that tell stories with personal power themes. In the cultures that had high levels of drunkenness, they found that tribesmen experienced conflict between obedience and achievement or autonomy and that the enhanced feelings of personal power induced by alcohol allowed them to resolve this conflict.

McClelland's power theory and the dependency conflict theory are not so far apart. The intense need to feel powerful suggests underlying feelings of powerlessness, and to be powerless is necessarily to be dependent. It is of some interest that Bill Wilson, co-founder of AA, in discussing the "proper form of dependence" used the example of being dependent on electrical *power* as an example of healthy dependence. It is also noteworthy that the twelve-step recovery turns on the admission of powerlessness, which would seem to undercut the power motivation that McClelland hypothesized.

PRIMARY AND SECONDARY ADDICTION

There are two important ways of dividing addictive populations into subgroups. The first is between primary addiction and secondary addiction (Winokur et al. 1971); the second, proposed by Cloninger (1983), is between early onset male addiction (type 2) and late onset male and female addiction (type 1).

Winokur and associates (1971) make an important distinction between primary and secondary addiction. Writing about alcoholism, Winokur described *primary alcoholics* as those whose alcoholism is not preceded by a major psychiatric illness. *Secondary alcoholics* are those whose alcoholism follows or is concomitant with a major psychiatric illness. In women, the major psychiatric illness was usually affective disorder; in men, it was antisocial personality disorder. Primary addicts, who may display some sociopathic behavior while under the influence of a substance, are not sociopaths; sociopaths, however, are often heavy users without necessarily being addicted. Winokur's alcoholism as secondary to sociopathy overlaps with Blane's counterdependent alcoholism. Both are generally male phenomena; both are difficult to treat. This form of male addiction secondary to antisocial personality disorder is thought to comprise 20 percent of the male alcoholic population and 30 percent of the male drug addict population.

C. Robert Cloninger (1983) investigated the heritability of alcoholism. The alcoholics in his 1983 study who manifested early-onset severe alcoholism, characterized by inability to abstain, fighting, arrests, and little or no guilt about their drinking, had a type of alcoholism that is heavily influenced by heredity and is limited to men. He called this *male-limited* or *type 2* alcoholism. The other group of alcoholics in his study showed late onset, progression, psychological dependence, and guilt about that dependence. This type of alcoholism occurs in men and women, and although Cloninger believed that genetic factors are involved here too, they do not manifest themselves without environmental provocation. He called this *milieu-limited* or *type 1* alcoholism.

EMPIRICAL PSYCHOLOGICAL FINDINGS

There are few consistent empirical psychological findings in addicted male populations. The well-replicated findings include elevated psychopathic deviance scores on the Minnesota Multiphasic Personality Inventory (Loper et al. 1973), field dependency (Goldstein 1976, Witkin et al. 1959), ego weakness, and impoverished self-concept. There is also considerable evidence of tendencies toward confused identity, including sexual identity, in male addicts (Irgens-Jensen 1971).

Tarter and colleagues (1988) found that learning difficulties and poor school performance are overrepresented in male alcoholic populations. They argue for a cluster of problems: hyperactivity, attention deficit disorder, and childhood conduct disorder being antecedent to some forms of addiction.

Cox (1985), reviewing the empirical psychological findings, concluded that there is compelling evidence of a male preaddictive personality characterized by nonconformity, impulsivity, and reward-seeking characteristics. There is even more compelling evidence that clinical addicts are characterized by negative affect (depression and anxiety) and low self-esteem, as well as by a cognitive perceptual style that includes field dependence, external locus of control, and stimulus augmentation (Petrie 1978).

SUBSTANCE ABUSE AS A DEVELOPMENTAL STAGE

Another dynamic with a sociocultural tinge is the degree to which heavy drug use may simply be a developmental stage for the male members of some subcultures. Jessor (1987) in his discussion of problem behavior in adolescence suggested that for some adolescents heavy drug use is a rite of passage into adulthood. In the 1960s, being "stoned" was a political statement in parts of the counterculture. Currently, for some disadvantaged men, drinking and drugging is still a form, however self-defeating, of protest and rebellion. Without romanticizing a potentially deadly behavior, it is illuminating to factor in the developmental and generational aspects of the dynamics of addiction.

IDENTIFICATION WITH THE FATHER

One of the most commonly seen dynamics in male addiction, particularly to alcohol, is identification with the father, or sometimes with older brothers. Often drinking or smoking marijuana together is the one strong common bond and shared activity between sons and fathers or between brothers. The object-hunger of the boy seeking to bond with a distant or absent father cannot be overestimated. The bliss of finally getting close to father as an adolescent or young adult, when the boy starts drinking with him, is intense. Here the identification is both interpersonal and intrapsychic. The intensity of the longing and identification seems to be directly proportional to the distance and/or abusiveness of the father. For example:

> Jack came into therapy after he received his fourth citation for drunk driving (DWI). An intelligent, capable technician, his goal in life was to be "a successful alcoholic" like his father, who had never been picked up for DWI (possibly because he lived in a large city and did not drive much) and who made a great deal of money. The father had beaten him often; otherwise, he did not pay too much attention to Jack. Now the father was "supportive"—went to court with Jack and then took him out to lunch with, needless to say, drinks. All Jack could see was that his father "was there for me." To stop drinking would be to "lose" father, and there was no way Jack would let that happen.

In addition to identification, there is also hatred of the father. Thus, the alcohol/drug orgies of bands of young men can be viewed as enactments of the murder of the father as elaborated in Freud's "Totem and Taboo" (1913–1914). The substance can be seen as symbolic of the mutilated, dismembered body of the murdered father. With each member of the gang having, in his mind, murdered his own father, the shared crime and shared guilt forges strong bonds between the drinkers/druggers. The "sons" then consume the father's remains, thereby gaining control over him and assimilating his strength; they consummate their "devouring affection" for the father. Here identification becomes literal incorporation. This modern version of the band of primitive brothers killing the primal father can also be enacted by the solitary drug consumer, with the sharing of guilt with brothers being purely psychical. One wonders if this unconscious dynamic plays a role in the extraordinary curative potency of guilt sharing at twelve-step meetings.

THE PATHOLOGIZING OF MALENESS

The various theories previously discussed raise a number of questions. Are there multiple dynamics of male addiction? Do the supposedly pathological traits of the male pre-addict simply reflect maleness? Are we dealing here with a pathologization of maleness in which high activity levels, physicality, high levels of aggression, and stimulus seeking are redefined as negative and pathological, setting up a secondary conflict that in turn may be self-medicated, leading to addiction? While feminists also complain about the pathologizing of femalessness, "feminine virtues" such as empathy, nurturance, and emotional sensitivity are increasingly seen as essential to mental health. In other words, the sex-role conflicts endemic to our rapidly changing culture affect men as well as women, engendering anxiety and insecurity that predisposes to addiction. It is possible that some men find that their native endowments are now dysfunctional, and finding it beyond their capabilities to change, turn to drugs. For example:

Bill, a recovering alcoholic and pothead in his forties with seven years of stable sobriety, was seen in marital therapy with his wife. Bill was highly involved with AA, and working at the same difficult, dangerous, technically demanding job for twenty years. He seemed to be a limited, likable guy who was pretty content with his sobriety. Never much of a student, he described a childhood of roaming the woods and getting in minor scrapes: Like Huck Finn, he was always ready to "light out for the territories." While the therapist found nothing pathological in his exploratory, adventurous, physically active childhood, his wife, Joan, was convinced that he had attention deficit disorder, citing as evidence the fact that he didn't listen to her. The therapist wondered how Bill, who had worked with dangerous equipment for years, could be alive if his attention was so deficient.

Joan proved to be an unremittingly critical monologist. Her main theme was her feelings: "He doesn't care about my feelings." The therapist found his attention constantly wandering. Frustrated, the therapist finally said to her, "I don't particularly care about your feelings," an intervention which surprisingly—after her initial outrage—led to a real breakthrough and renegotiation of their relationship.

Bill, although he contributed his share to the marital difficulties, can be seen as a victim of the pathologization of maleness as he had been in his family of origin. His involvement with alcohol and drugs had given him a sense of male solidarity, acceptance, and belongingness that he had not otherwise found.

PATHOLOGICAL NARCISSISM AS AN INTEGRATING PSYCHODYNAMIC MODEL OF MALE ADDICTION

Pathological narcissism is the regression or fixation to the stage of the archaic self (Kohut 1971,1977b). It is characterized by the presence of a cohesive, but insecure, self that is threatened by regressive fragmentation and grandiosity of less than psychotic proportions, which manifests itself in the form of arrogance, isolation, and unrealistic goals. Feelings of entitlement, the need for omnipotent control, poor differentiation of self and object, and deficits in the self-regulating capacities of the ego are also characteristics of pathological narcissism. Further, affect tolerance is poor. The tenuousness of the cohesion of the self makes the narcissistically regressed individual subject to massive anxiety, which is, in reality, fear of annihilation (that is, fear of fragmentation of the self). Pathological narcissists are also subject to empty depression, which reflects the emptiness of the self. These manifestations of the archaic self may be blatantly apparent or deeply repressed or denied, with a resulting facade of pseudoself-sufficiency so often seen in male addicts. The idea that addicts experience regression or fixation to the stage of the archaic nuclear self provides an explanation of the previously discussed findings regarding the psychological correlatives of addiction (elevated scores on the "psychopathic deviate" scales, field dependency, ego weakness, and stimulus augmentation). It also integrates competing psychodynamic theories.

It is noteworthy that according to the twelve-step literature (Alcoholics Anonymous World Services 1952), which is based on the experiences of male addicts, "Alcoholism (addiction) is a disease of the attitudes." This view of addiction and various slogans such as "Alcoholism is self-will run wild"; "Get out of the driver's seat"; "Let go and let God", further support the dynamic view of addiction as related to pathological narcissism.

TREATMENT IMPLICATIONS

The view of pathological narcissism as the cornerstone of male addiction suggests a number of interventions for men who are struggling to recover from addiction as well as those in early recovery.

In their respective ways, these interventions address the patients' narcissistic deficits and narcissistic injury and the attempted self-cure through drug use. They also attempt to fill the patients' inner emptiness and halt the acting-out of and turning against the self of the narcissistic rage, address the idealizing and mirror transferences to drugs (that is, experiencing drugs as ideal objects or as a source of affirmation of one's grandiosity or both), focus on the patients' attempts at omnipotent control and efforts to boost their abysmally low self-esteem through the use of drugs, and acknowledge the shame experiences that are both antecedents to and consequences of drug abuse.

Dealing with Narcissistic Deficits and Narcissistic Injury

It is important for the therapist to address the narcissistic wound inflicted by not being able to drink or drug "like other people." The admission that one is "powerless," as AA puts it, or that one cannot use without losing control, is extremely painful. It is experienced as a defect in the self, which is intolerable. To be able to "drink (or drug) like a man" is a central component of the addict's self-concept—his identity. This is particularly so for "macho" men. The therapist must recognize and articulate the conflict between the patient's wish to stop and the patient's feeling that to do so entails admitting that he is fundamentally flawed. The therapist does this by saying, "You don't so much want *to* drink/use as you do not want *not* to be able to drink/use." Such intervention makes the patient conscious of the conflict in an empathic way and allows him to struggle with this issue.

Addictions result in one long experience of narcissistic injury and failure. As one patient put it, "When I drink, everything turns to shit." So it does: career setbacks, job losses, rejection by loved ones, humiliations of various sorts, ill health, economic decline, accidental injury, and enduring "bad luck" are the all too frequent concomitants of addiction. Each negative experience is a narcissistic wound. Cumulatively, they constitute one massive narcissistic wound. Even if the outward blows have not yet come, the inner blows—self-hatred and low self-regard—are always there. The addict has all too frequently heard, "It's all your fault." The therapist must empathize with the suffering. "Your addiction has cost you so much," "You have lost so much," and "Your self-respect is gone," are some of the ways to make contact with the user's pain and facilitate his experiencing this pain instead of denying, acting out, or anesthetizing it.

Dealing with Chronic Emptiness and Lack of Identity

Addicts feel empty. Either they have never had much "good stuff" inside or they have long ago flushed their positive feelings, ability to connect, virtues, and spiritual spark out with drugs. "You drink (or drug) so much because you feel empty" makes the connection as well as brings into awareness the horrible experience of an inner void. After sobriety has been achieved, the historical, or childhood, determinants of the paucity of psychic structure that is experienced as emptiness need to be interpreted.

Addicts lack a firm sense of identity. How can you know who you are if your experience of self is tenuous and its partially unconscious inner representation lacks consistent cohesion? The therapist can comment on this and point out that being an addict is at least something definite—having an identity of sorts. When an AA member says, "My name is —— and I am an alcoholic," he is affirming that he exists and has at least one attribute. With sobriety many more attributes will accrue; the self will enrich and cohere. A way of conveying this to the patient is to say, "You are confused and not quite sure who you are. This is partly because of your drug use. Acknowledging your addiction will lessen your confusion as to who you are and give you a base on which to build a firm and positive identity."

Building the Capacity to Be Alone

Many men use drugs because they cannot stand to be alone. They have not developed what Winnicott (1958) called *the capacity to be alone*. Winnicott believed that this ability comes from the experience of being alone in the presence of another—from having been a small child in the presence of an empathic, nonimpinging other, whom one has internalized so that one is not really alone when one is by oneself.

Being alone in this sense is very different from defensive isolation driven by fear. Presumably, those who drink or drug for companionship have never acquired the capacity to be alone. This, too, should be interpreted. "You drink so much because you can't bear to be alone and drinking gives you the illusion of having company, of being with a friend. After you stop drinking, it will be important for us to discover why it is so painful for you to be alone."

Addressing the Idealizing and Mirror Transferences to Drugs

Addicts form idealizing and mirror transferences to drugs. The image of the archaic idealized parent is projected onto the drug, which is regarded as an all-powerful, all-good object with which the user merges in order to participate in this omnipotence. The user's unconscious fantasy is that "cocaine will deliver the goods and give me love, power, and whatever else I desire." The therapist should interpret, "Cocaine has felt like a good, wise, and powerful parent who protected you and made you feel wonderful, and that is why you have loved it so much. In reality, it is an unreliable drug, not all the things you thought it was." The therapist can go on to say, "Now that getting high isn't working for you anymore, you are disillusioned, furious, and afraid. Let's talk about those feelings."

One of the reasons that addicts are so devoted to using their drug of choice is that it confirms their grandiosity. In other words, they form a mirror transference to it. One alcoholic patient told the therapist that he felt thrilled when he read that a sixth Nobel Prize was to be added to the original five. He read this while drinking in a bar at 8:00 A.M. His fantasy was to win all six.

The therapist can make the mirror transference conscious by interpreting it. "When you get high, you feel that you can do anything, be anything, achieve anything, and that feels wonderful. No wonder you don't want to give it up."

Addicts have a pathological need for omnipotent control. Their drug is simultaneously experienced as an object they believe they can totally control and coerce into doing their will and as an object that they believe gives them total control of their subjective states and of the environment. This can be seen as a manifestation of their mirror and idealizing transferences to substances. Addicts frequently treat people, including the therapist, as extensions of themselves. Therapists should interpret this need to control the substance, other people, and the therapist. For example, "You think that when you drink, you can feel any way you wish," "You go into a rage and get high whenever your wife doesn't do as you wish," or "You thought of smoking because you were upset with me when I didn't respond as you thought I would."

Dealing with Low Self-Esteem and Grandiosity

Addicts, without exception, have abysmally low self-esteem. Men are ashamed of this and cover it up with bluster and bravado. Low self-esteem persists well into sobriety. At some point, the therapist needs to say, "You feel like shit, and that you are shit, and all your claims to greatness are ways to avoid knowing that you feel that way." The particular reasons, whether they be antecedents to or consequences of the addiction, that the patient values himself so little need to be elucidated and worked through.

Sometimes the patient's crazy grandiosity is simultaneously a defense against and an acting out of the narcissistic cathexis of the patient by a parent. In other words, the patient is attempting to fulfill the parent's dreams in fantasy while making sure not to fulfill them in reality. Heavy drinking or drugging makes such an acting-out defense easy. If the recovering man's grandiosity seems to be a response to being treated by either parent as an extension of himself, the therapist can say, "One reason you feel so rotten about yourself is that you're always doing it for

Mom or Dad and not for yourself. You resent this and spite them by undermining yourself by drinking (or drugging)."

Addressing Shame

Addicts suffer greatly from shame experiences. Addicted patients are ashamed of having been shamed and often use drugs to obliterate their feelings of shame. Men, far more commonly than women, will do almost anything to avoid feeling shame. Therapists need to help addicts experience rather than repress these feelings. One way to do this is to identify feelings of shame and the patient's attempts to anesthetize them. For example, the therapist can say , "You felt so much shame when you realized that you were a junkie that you kept on getting high so you wouldn't feel your shame."

CONCLUSION

Addiction in men is driven by many social, biological, and psychological dynamics. As Freud would put it, addiction is overdetermined. In one clinical situation or another, each of the dynamics discussed in this chapter will be evident and interpretable, and all of them contribute to our understanding of male addiction and should be addressed by the therapist.

REFERENCES

Abraham, K. (1908). The psychological relations between sexuality and alcoholism. In *Selected Papers on Psychoanalysis*, pp. 80–90. New York: Brunner/Mazel, 1979.

Alcoholics Anonymous World Services (1952). *Twelve Steps and Twelve Traditions*. New York: Author.

Blane, H. T. (1968). *The Personality of the Alcoholic: Guises of Dependency*. New York: Harper & Row.

Child, I., Bacon, M., and Barry, H. (1965). A cross-cultural study of drinking. *Quarterly Journal of Studies on Alcohol* Suppl. 3:5–96.

Cloninger, C. R. (1983). Genetic and environmental factors in the development of alcoholism. *Journal of Psychiatric Treatment and Evaluation* 5:487–496.

Cox, W. M. (1985). Personality correlates of substance abuse. In *Determinants of Substance Abuse: Biological, Psychological, and Environmental*

Factors, ed. M. Galizio and S. A. Mausto, pp. 209–246. New York: Plenum.

Deutsch, H. (1965). Some forms of emotional disturbance and their relationship to schizophrenia. In *Neuroses and Character Types*, pp. 262–281. New York: International Universities Press.

Fenichel, O. (1945). *The Psychoanalytic Theory of the Neurosis*. New York: Norton.

Freud, S. (1897/1985). *The Complete Letters of Sigmund Freud to Wilhelm Fliess*, ed. and trans. J. M. Masson. Cambridge, MA: Harvard University Press.

—— (1913/1914). Totem and taboo. *Standard Edition* 13:1–162.

—— (1914). On narcissism: an introduction. *Standard Edition* 14:67–104.

—— (1920). Beyond the pleasure principle. *Standard Edition* 18:1–64.

—— (1928). Dostoevsky and parricide. *Standard Edition* 21:173–196.

Fromm, E. (1941). *Escape from Freedom*. New York: Rinehart.

Glover, E. (1928). The etiology of alcoholism. *Proceedings of the Royal Society of Medicine* 21:1351–1355.

Goldstein, G. (1976). Perceptual and cognitive deficit in alcoholics. In *Empirical Studies of Alcoholism*, ed. G. Goldstein and C. Neuringer, pp. 115–152. Cambridge, MA: Bollinger.

Hartocollis, P. (1968). A dynamic view of alcoholism: drinking in the service of denial. *Dynamic Psychiatry* 2:173–182.

Hartocollis, P., and Hartocollis, P. (1980). Alcoholism, borderline, and narcissistic disorders: a psychoanalytic overview. In *Phenomenology and Treatment of Alcoholism*, ed. W. G. Fann, I. Haracan, A. D. Pokovny, and R. L. Williams, pp. 93–110. New York: SP Medical & Scientific.

Irgens-Jensen, O. (1971). *Problem Drinking and Personality: A Study Based on the Draw-a-Person Test*. New Brunswick, NJ: Rutgers Center for Alcohol Studies.

Jellinek, E. M. (1994). Heredity and premature weaning: a discussion of the work of Thomas Trotter, British naval physician. In *The Dynamics and Treatment of Alcoholism: Essential papers*, ed. J. Levin and R. Weiss, pp. 28–34. Northvale, NJ: Jason Aronson. (Trotter's original work published 1804, Jellinek's article, 1943)

Jessor, R. (1987). Problem-behavior theory, psychosocial development, and adolescent problem drinking. *British Journal of Addictions* 82:331–342.

Khantzian, E. J. (1981). Some treatment implications of ego and self-disturbances in alcoholism. In *Dynamic Approaches to the Understanding and Treatment of Alcoholism*, ed. M. H. Bean and N. E. Zinberg, pp. 163–188. New York: Free Press.

Kierkegaard, S. (1849). *The Concept of Dread*, trans. W. Lowrie. Princeton, NJ: Princeton University Press, 1944.

Knight, R. P. (1937). The dynamics and treatment of chronic alcohol addiction. *Bulletin of the Menninger Clinic* 1:233–250.

—— (1938). The psychoanalytic treatment in a sanitarium of chronic addiction to alcohol. *Journal of the American Medical Association* 111: 1443–1448.

Kohut, H. (1971). *The Analysis of the Self: A Systematic Approach to the Psychoanalytic Treatment of Narcissistic Personality Disorders*. New York: International Universities Press.

—— (1977a). *The Restoration of the Self*. New York: International Universities Press.

—— (1977b). *Psychodynamics of Drug Dependence* (National Institute on Drug Abuse Monograph 12, pp. vii–ix). Washington, DC: US Government Printing Office.

Krystal, H., and Raskin, H. (1970). *Drug Dependence: Aspects of Ego Function*. Detroit: Wayne State University Press.

Levin, J. D. (1987). *Treatment of Alcoholism and Other Addictions: A Self-Psychology Approach*. Northvale, NJ: Jason Aronson.

—— (1991). *Recovery from Alcoholism: Beyond Your Wildest Dreams*. Northvale, NJ: Jason Aronson.

—— (1993). *Slings and Arrows: Narcissistic Injury and Its Treatment*. Northvale, NJ: Jason Aronson.

Levin, J., and Weiss, R., eds. (1995). *Dynamics and Treatment of Alcoholism: Essential Papers*. Northvale, NJ: Jason Aronson.

Loper, R. G., Kammeier, M. L., and Hoffman, H. (1973). MMPI characteristics of college freshmen males who later became alcoholics. *Journal of Abnormal Psychology* 82:159–162.

MacAndrew, C. (1965). The differentiation of male alcoholic outpatients from non-alcoholic psychiatric outpatients by means of the MMPI. *Quarterly Journal of Studies on Alcohol* 26:238–246.

McClelland, D. C., Davis, W., Kalin, R., and Wanner, E. (1972). *The Drinking Man: Alcohol and Human Motivation*. New York: Free Press.

McCord, W., and McCord, J., with Gudeman, J. (1960). *Origins of Alcoholism*. Stanford, CA: Stanford University Press.

Menninger, K. (1938). *Man Against Himself*. New York: Harcourt Brace.

Petrie, A. (1978). *Individuality in Pain and Suffering*, 2nd ed. Chicago: University of Chicago Press.

Rado, S. (1933). The psychoanalysis of pharmacothymia. *Psychoanalytic Quarterly* 2:2–23.

Rohsenow, D. J. (1983). Alcoholics' perceptions of control. In *Identifying and Measuring Alcoholic Personality Characteristics*, ed. W. M. Cox, pp. 37–48. San Francisco: Jossey-Bass.

Szasz, T. (1958). The role of the counterphobic mechanism in addiction. *Journal of the American Psychoanalytic Association* 6:309–325.

Tarter, R. E., Alterman, A. I., and Edwards, K. L. (1988). Neurobehavioral theory of alcoholism etiology. In *Theories of Alcoholism*, ed. C. D. Chaudron and D. A. Wilkinson, pp. 73–102. Toronto: Addiction Research Foundation.

Tiebout, H. M. (1949). The act of surrender in the therapeutic process. *Quarterly Journal of Studies on Alcohol* 10:48–58.

—— (1957). The ego factor in surrender to alcoholism. *Quarterly Journal of Studies on Alcohol* 15:610–621.

Winnicott, D. W. (1958). The capacity to be alone. In *The Maturational Processes and the Facilitating Environment*, pp. 29–36. New York: International Universities Press, 1965.

Winokur, G., Rimmer, J., and Reich, T. (1971). Alcoholism IV: Is there more than one type of alcoholism? *British Journal of Psychiatry* 18: 525–531.

Witkin, H. A., Karp, S. A., and Goodenough, D. A. (1959). Dependence in alcoholics. *Quarterly Journal of Studies on Alcohol* 20:493–504.

Wurmser, L. (1978). *The Hidden Dimension: Psychodynamics in Compulsive Drug Use*. New York: Jason Aronson.

14

Incorporating Men's Values into Substance Abuse Treatment

Jeffrey Zeth

Whi. alcoholism treatment first became professionalized, emphasis seemed to be on the universality of experience among alcoholics. Patients were herded into groups and encouraged to talk about what they all had in common. Differences in socioeconomic background, ethnicity, gender, and sexual orientation were minimized; the emphasis was on how much everyone shared the disease of addiction. This strategy was important at the time, since the disease concept was relatively new. As the field of addiction treatment matured it began to examine variations in the experience of addiction and recovery among various groups of people. One of the groups to which treatment professionals have turned their attention has been women (Pape 1993).

The growth of special treatment programs for women has been valuable and necessary. However, as more women are placed in special groups or women-only treatment centers, the remaining men find themselves, by default, in men-only groups, with the old "cookie cutter" approach to treatment. Yet, men, like women, do have special needs in treatment, and the men's movements have the potential to provide more effective treatment for men. The purpose of this chapter is to take a brief look at the history of men's movements and explore how they can be applied to addiction counseling. By developing a conscious understanding of masculine core issues and values, treatment providers will be better able to offer more appropriate, individualized treatment plans and remove, or minimize, some of the obstacles to compliance.

EVOLUTION OF THE MEN'S MOVEMENTS

There is not one men's movement, but many. Space considerations do not allow for a complete discussion of all these groups; however, a look at some of the major groups may provide appropriate background for a larger discussion of gender-specific substance abuse treatment.

The Feminist Men's Movement

The seeds of the contemporary men's movements were sown during the early days of the women's movement, from the 1840s through the early part of this century. These groups were mostly established in reaction to the drive toward legislative and social changes promoted by women's suffrage groups. The Men's League for Women's Suffrage and the Greenwich Village "Sex Radicals," organized during the teens and 1920s, were both organizations where men worked alongside women to promote a pro-feminist agenda (National Organization of Men Against Sexism [NOMAS] 1996).

The second wave of pro-feminist men's groups emerged in the 1970s with the advent of the "sensitive man." Reacting to the social changes catalyzed by the women's movement of that time, the men in these groups accepted feminists' invitation to get in touch with their sensitive sides. Author Herb Goldberg (1979) exemplified this new point of view. His emphasis was on discarding old sets of defenses—the "macho" behavior that fell out of favor in the 1960s—and on supporting women's efforts to revise sexist policies among institutions. This new focus tended to make sweeping generalizations about men's experiences and often to place extremely condemning value judgments on men, as exemplified in the following comments:

> It is my interpretation that on the deepest archetypal level the feminist movement is partially fueled by an intuitive sensing of the decay and demise of the male. Women are rushing in to take men's places, as much for survival's sake as for any sociological or philosophical reasons. He has become a hyperactive, hyper-cerebral, hyper-mechanical, rigid, self-destructive machine out of control. [Goldberg 1979, p. 8]

Goldberg saw addiction as one of many problems in men that result from rigid and compulsive personality styles that are the product of socialization into narrow and stereotyped roles.

Contemporary outgrowths of the pro-feminist men's movement have tempered the severe criticism of men. They espouse a desire for positive personal change for men without giving up their commitment to equal rights for women. The most visible of these groups is the National Organization for Men Against Sexism (NOMAS). A product of pro-feminist consciousness-raising efforts in the mid-1970s, and originally calling itself the National Organization of Changing Men, NOMAS engages in feminist, antisexist, gay-affirmative activism, education, and publishing, and has active members in many parts of North America.

Currently, some theorists and clinicians, influenced by the views just mentioned, see rigid male gender roles as contributing to, though not the sole cause of, the development of addictive disease in men (Nowinski 1993). Such views, however, may simply reflect a preference for typically feminine modes of intimacy and communication over masculine ones. For example, advocates of these views often devalue shared, task-focused activities (such as team sports), seeing them as an avoidance of group intimacy rather than as a particularly male style of fostering intimacy.

Men's Rights Groups

Other men's organizations, reacting to the legal rights gained by women, are the various groups of fathers, battered men, and male survivors of female-perpetrated sexual abuse. Most of the groups in this movement, such as Men's Rights, Inc., are sponsored by individuals directly involved in child custody and support cases as well as alimony suits. They provide legal counsel, information, networking, and support groups for men involved in various types of family court cases. They also advocate to change men-only draft laws. Most of these men believe that women's rights groups promote a one-sided agenda that seeks to eradicate sex discrimination when women stand to benefit and impedes it when they do not. While they support some of the legislative and policy changes wrought by feminists, they believe there is a need to balance these changes with radical initiatives aimed at ending gender discrimination against men. They call attention to interests specific to men as a group, as shown by this excerpt from a speech delivered at a men's rights rally:

> Why aren't you as angry that you will live 8 years *less* than she, as she is that she will make 59% of what you will make? Personally, I'd rather have the 8 years. . . . Women may make 59% of what men make, but you would be naive to think that women live at 59% of the male standard of living—receive 59% of the health care, eat at 59% of the nutritional level, wear 59% of the wardrobe. . . . Let us be willing to talk about it—*all* of it. [Hayward 1981]

To this author's knowledge, no representative of the men's rights perspective has ever addressed any possible connection between the legal issues affecting some of these men, such as child and spousal abuse, and the abuse of alcohol and other drugs.

Mythopoetic Groups

The most recent development in men's consciousness has been the mythopoetic thread, literally the "myth-making" aspect of the movement. Mythopoetic groups (sometimes called "councils" or "lodges") draw their inspiration from preagricultural hunter-gatherer societies and what they believe were men's roles in them. This recent men's movement places value on the intuitive aspects of historical men—such as assertiveness, inner (as opposed to external) authority, physical fitness, community spirit, and a sense of humor. Writer and spokesman Robert Bly (1990) has called such combination of values "Zeus energy"; men's movement leaders such as Shepherd Bliss (1988) have referred to it variously as "earthy masculinity," "the deep masculine," and simply "recovery work." The mythopoetic movement looks for such masculine values among various cultures and attempts to restore them through storytelling, mask-making, drumming, dancing, and psychodrama. Though skeptics see these efforts as artificial or contrived, they have served as vehicles for genuine intimacy that participants find useful.

The concept and practice of initiation is a primary element of these groups. Initiation in hunter-gatherer societies emphasized the importance of various stages of the life cycle, such as birth, puberty, marriage, midlife, and old age. Men and women were seen as having something unique to offer their communities at each of these stages (Meade 1993). In most cultures, these rites of passage tended to be gender-exclusive; they took place in restricted gatherings of men (or women) only. The development of modern Western civilization has seen the gradual elimination of this aspect of life. At the same time as initiatory practices have decreased, addictive problems have increased.

Many advocates of the mythopoetic men's movement view addiction as a direct product of civilization itself (Diamond 1994). They point out that addiction was completely absent in early hunter-gatherer cultures that took an initiatory approach to life. Consequently, they seek to restore an understanding of the importance of initiatory practices (though not necessarily in a literal fashion) as part of a recovery program that includes a reverence for the environment as well as oneself. Although they do not advocate a return to the hunter-gatherer lifestyle, they believe that a renewal of one's sense of life's passages is an important aspect in recovery. At the same time, there is an added feeling of responsibility to protect the environment, which also goes through processes that parallel the human life cycle. "Recovery" thus acquires the larger meaning of renewal of the earth and protection of its other species.

Addiction/Recovery Groups

The evolution of addiction-focused men's groups has paralleled that of the mythopoetic movement. The best known of these groups, Alcoholics Anonymous (AA), began in 1935. During its early years, AA, the first organization that directly addressed alcohol problems, was comprised primarily of men (Diamond 1994). Although AA has since welcomed women into its ranks, there is still a wide variety of men-only meetings.

In many ways, AA, with its written and oral traditions, its rituals, its emphasis on telling one's own story, as well as stories of its founders and heroes, and its tradition of mentorship (as seen in the relationship between sponsor and new member) provides a kind of mythology and initiatory context for its members. Recovery takes place in an atmosphere that encourages interdependence, rather than autonomy and self-reliance, and that emphasizes a move from a hierarchical, or positional, sense of self to a relational one (Nowinski 1993).

More recent addiction/recovery men's groups have expanded their view of addiction to include sex and love addiction, codependency, and adult children of alcoholics (ACOA) issues. Many have taken a view of recovery similar to that of the mythopoetic groups. Often, in fact, it is hard to tell the difference between the two. They view recovery as similar to initiation and often see their approach as extensions of twelve-step work. According to Jed Diamond (1994), a leading authority in this area:

> In a society that has lost its rituals of initiation, recovery is one of the few passages available that men can use to cut away the dead wood of their civilized prison and return to the wild path of the warrior. Addiction can be seen as both a refusal to be "a good little boy" and a misguided attempt to find an authentic ground of being. Just as addiction is the disease of lost selfhood, recovery gives us the opportunity to journey home. [p. 29]

Aaron Kipnis, the author of *Knights without Armor* (1991), described the evolution of a men's group that provided the inspiration for his book. He and several other men began meeting as an informal early recovery group looking to each other for support around abstinence from alcohol and drugs. As time progressed and the men grew accustomed to sobriety, other long-term issues came to the surface. What developed as a result was a list of twelve tasks that the men felt they needed to accomplish in order to continue their personal growth in recovery. These tasks were a combination of personal, social, and educational goals and, though Kipnis did not phrase it this way, amounted to a modern "men's twelve steps."

Part of the recovery process for men in such groups includes not only the re-establishment of initiatory modes of thought but also the seeking of archetypal images of masculinity from many different cultures. For example, Kipnis (1991) as well as Edinger (1985) and others relate alcoholism to possession by the archetypal figure of Dionysus, the ancient god of ecstasy, drunkenness, and violence. To the Greeks, Dionysian rituals represented a temporary break with civilization, a culturally sanctioned revolt against social convention. Much more than simply a "wine god," Dionysus is a complicated figure representing a wide range of aspects of the human psyche (Bolen 1989). However, he also can be seen quite literally as the personification of alcoholism. Many of the physical characteristics attributed to Dionysus are similar to the physiological effects of long-term alcohol abuse in men. These characteristics include ruddy cheeks and feminine features—the symptoms of high blood pressure and increased production of estrogen caused by high levels of alcohol use (Metzger 1988). One challenge for men in recovery is to reestablish connection with this archetype and to experience ecstasy and passion without relying on the use of alcohol or drugs (Kipnis 1991).

HEROIC MALE VALUES

A truism of the chemical dependency treatment field is that we should educate and treat addicts, rather than prosecute them. This argument is often heard applied to adolescents and to women—particularly when a mother loses custody of her children because of child abuse or neglect due to her drug use. Yet somehow, the image of a man exercising poor judgment during an alcoholic blackout stirs less sympathy in the eyes of many people. Those in the men's movement would say this is because men and women have been socialized to "heroic" male values. These values teach men to bury strong emotions and not to show physical or emotional pain. Further, they teach women to expect this behavior in men (Kipnis 1991). If we are less sympathetic toward impaired men, it may be because we see them as stronger and more capable of exercising good judgment. We see male addicts as failures in the realm of self-control and willpower. If a man is assumed to have good judgment and he is obviously not using it, he will more easily be seen as a moral failure. Along these lines, the use of denial by men can be seen as one manifestation of heroic values:

> We cheer the sports hero who, after being clobbered and smashed on the playing field, gets up and plays even though he is hurt. Little is said about those who do not recover and are maimed for life. Pressure to play while they're hurt is also a major contributor to drug abuse among professional athletes as they attempt to numb the pain. This epidemic problem reflects the broader state of the entire speeded-up culture, in which almost every man is *playing hurt*, to some degree. [Kipnis 1991, p. 28]

Such idealization of the defensive function of denial can be seen as a direct contributor to many cases of substance abuse (Nowinski 1993). The men's movement asks us to confront denial socially as well as personally and to give up basic cultural assumptions about men *always* needing to be strong and in control.

However, men also are raised with other values—values that may be utilized to help male addicts during their recovery from addiction. One task of men's movements is to foster the healthy application of these values, by both men individually and society in general. Approaching men in treatment with an understanding of the basic assumptions, communication styles, and expectations that men bring to the recovery process will help us build more effective working relationships with them. It may also improve treatment outcomes.

The discussion of values that follows is based on anecdotal and experiential observations. There is, at this time, little empirical evidence to validate these views. The values and assumptions that men bring to treatment and their relationship to those of treatment centers represent a fruitful area for further investigation and clarification.

INCORPORATING MASCULINE VALUES INTO SUBSTANCE ABUSE TREATMENT

Many of the values brought by men into substance abuse treatment have been established during their early life and form the basis of their gender identity. These culturally defined masculine values affect how a man views himself, his feelings about participating with other men in an alcohol or drug treatment program, and his attitude toward his relationship with substances. In turn, treatment settings have their own institutional values. At times, an institution's values and resulting expectations of clients may run counter to what men expect from themselves. Such conflict of values and expectations lends itself to struggles that are easily labeled *resistance* by treatment providers. At other times, however, shared values between a treatment setting and its male clients can lead to unhealthy collusion between them. Thus it is crucial that both male and female clinicians become aware of the various values that may result in conflict as well as collusion during the treatment process.

Masculine Values in Conflict with Traditional Treatment

Despite the large numbers of men seen in alcohol and drug treatment programs, treatment programs generally prefer feeling-oriented, stereotypically feminine modes of relating as opposed to more traditionally masculine, action-oriented activities. Consequently, if a man finds it difficult to ask for help in the first place, and if, once he does seek help, he is confronted with values he sees as feminine, immediate conflict can be expected. Such potential conflict needs to be recognized and addressed openly during the beginning treatment process.

Other areas where conflicts are particularly likely to arise relate to: (1) face-to-face versus shoulder-to-shoulder contact; (2) surrender versus failure; (3) process versus result-oriented activities; (4) work and home versus work, home, and "hangout"; (5) a tendency to conceal medical problems out of embarrassment at perceived weakness; and (6) relational versus positional stance in group therapy. These areas are discussed below.

Face-to-face versus shoulder-to-shoulder contact. Face-to-face communication with direct eye contact is the preferred form of intimate communication in most forms of psychotherapy, including substance abuse counseling. But for many men, such a stance suggests confrontation or competition. In high school, boys become used to "squaring off" or "facing off," with each other or with a sports team, and use eye contact as a form of intimidation. For men who embrace these values, face-to-face psychotherapy with a male therapist can be seen as intimidating, while with a female therapist, extended eye contact may be misconstrued as flirtatious or provocative. Instead, many men prefer shoulder-to-shoulder contact in which they face each other at an angle (Kipnis 1991).

Shoulder-to-shoulder contact implies participation in a shared activity, and it is through this shared action that intimacy may often develop in groups of men. It may be partly because of some intuitive espousal of this value that many men question whether they will receive help from "just talking." Taking action, not talking, is seen as a primary way to address problems (Diamond 1994). Thus a man influenced by action-oriented values may have difficulty sitting with feelings and not acting on them. In their urge to do something about a particular feeling, such men often put themselves at risk of relapse. This particular male tendency needs to be addressed during relapse prevention counseling.

Conversely, men who reject this action-oriented value in favor of the feeling-oriented, face-to-face posturing and direct eye contact may be quite comfortable with traditional treatment values and processes. However, they may find it difficult to engage with other men in a group and thus feel more isolated.

Distinguishing between surrender and failure. Men entering a traditional substance abuse treatment program usually run up against values that go counter to theirs as soon as they are told that "surrender" is essential for their recovery. The notion of powerlessness and surrender comes easily to women—some would say too easily—but it is difficult for men to admit powerlessness over alcohol or drugs. Often surrender is equated with failure. For example, the view that a man "can't hold his liquor" is likely to be viewed as a negative judgment and a confession of weakness.

An alcoholic's self-concept includes his gender identification as well as his relationship to alcohol. Many active alcoholics define themselves with such statements as "I'm not an alcoholic" and "I can control my drinking." The phrase "I am a man" may be closely connected with these statements. If being a man means being in control of alcohol, then acknowledging loss of control may mean an accompanying loss of masculinity. Furthermore, if being a man is viewed as closely connected with being an alcoholic (as it may be for a male adult child whose father was an alcoholic), masculinity and alcoholism may become linked together. Consequently, clinicians need to help their male clients to differentiate between surrender and failure and to reexamine their definition of masculinity. They may also need to help clients to integrate the sentiments "I am an alcoholic" and "I can't control my drinking" into their new definition of self (Brown 1985).

Process versus results-oriented activities. The masculine focus on results-oriented activities may lead to pressures to produce, to "do it right." Such a value can interfere with a man's ability to recover from a relapse. Men often have difficulty with the notion that relapse may be a part of recovery and that recovery is a process. They may respond to relapse-prevention counseling as if they are being scolded for failing at the task of recovery. The male client may therefore revert to earlier defensive functions, such as denial. Or, he may again give credence to the unrealistic belief that he has control over alcohol or drugs.

The role of the "third place hangout." In alcohol and drug treatment, particularly in outpatient settings, the counselor is interested as much in what takes place between sessions as in what happens in the counseling session itself. The usual focus of this interest is home and work. But another setting to which men seem especially drawn is what Ray Oldenburg refers to as the "third place" (Rheingold 1995). The third place is a public place, neither home nor work, where men have traditionally gathered for games, gossip, and other conversation. The third place satisfies the need for play, for having fun, for engaging in light conversation, and at times, for sharing physical activity. In the early part of this century, men had their own places to congregate, such as barbershops and bars. But today, most barbershops have become unisex hair stylists and almost all of the bars allow women. Even the bars to which women choose not to go are off-limits to alcoholics in early recovery.

As a rule, twelve-step meetings cannot assume the role of the third place because they are serious, talk-oriented settings. Although many speakers at meetings use humor, the emphasis during meetings is on sharing feelings and on speaking along the lines of a particular structure, rather than on action, light conversation, and fun. The need to discharge energy through constructive channels is met by verbalizing emotions and telling one's story. Their locations and constituencies are interchangeable: anyone can go to any meeting at any time. The bonding takes place through a sense of the universality that comes from everyone sharing the same problem and through a common understanding that addictive disease is stronger and smarter than any single individual. By contrast, third places offer a routine that includes smaller groups and more stable locations and members. Bonding takes place through shared activities. Usually, for recovering men, third places are destinations following a meeting, such as coffeehouses, diners, or bowling alleys.

Third places, then, are not, for the most part, to be found within twelve-step meetings. Access to a stable third place, though, greatly improves the quality of recovery. Clinically, it is useful to assess early in treatment if such a "third place hangout" was once a part of a client's life. A man whose third place during his drinking and drugging phase was filled with relapse triggers may need to give up such a place during early recovery. Subsequently, he needs to be helped to deal with the loss of such a third place and find a replacement hangout.

When a man feels grief about a third place he has lost, he may respond in a variety of ways. Often, and particularly if the client is a young adult, he may respond with some physical acting out. If the client is middle-aged or older, there may be other symptoms such as somatization, depression, or anxiety. It is important to separate grief over the loss of alcohol or drugs from one's life from the grief felt over the loss of a third place.

> John, a 27-year-old African-American man in inpatient treatment for cocaine and alcohol abuse, enjoyed going out to play basketball every Friday afternoon with some of the other men on the unit. One Friday after another patient was injured while playing, the administrator decided against allowing the men to go out to the court. In group the following Monday, John was unusually fidgety. He had always had some trouble staying seated in group, but on that particular day he was especially quiet and yet full of nervous energy. When the counselor passed around a handout, John absent-mindedly made small rips in the paper, occasionally tossing the paper aside in obvious disgust. When asked what was wrong, he made some complaints concerning the conditions on the unit. Only later when asked directly about Friday's "hangout activity" was he able to verbalize the disappointment he felt upon losing that important and special activity.

When a client has never had a third place as part of his life, he may still feel its absence and experience this as a void long before coming to treatment. However, unlike clients who lose access to a third place, clients who never had one may be unable to articulate this absence in any meaningful way. A close look at the overall content of a client's individual sessions may reveal a hunger for a third place. While the client may have felt a need for a third place before recovery, such a need becomes even more urgent during recovery. Despite attending twelve-step meetings, the client may be having feelings of isolation. He may never talk about other people in his life, or he may talk about how much work it takes to go to meetings. He experiences twelve-step meetings as places where he "drops off" rather than "picks up" energy. Such a client may lack a sense of humor (outside of sarcasm), be unable to relax, and paradoxically, have an unusually low energy level.

> Frank, a 40-year-old white lawyer, presented for outpatient treatment for alcohol and benzodiazepine dependence following his discharge from detox. Most of his leisure time was spent with his wife. In the diagnostic interview it emerged that it had been many years since he had had a place to spend his time outside of work and home. He had formerly used alcohol in a solitary manner and, more rarely, to relax at parties. He soon developed a "stiffness" in early recovery, manifesting in a loss of spontaneity, and his sense of humor turned to sarcasm. A weight problem, which had always been present, became worse.
>
> Although nominally interested in going to meetings, he had trouble attending on a regular basis, saying he was too tired to go in the evenings after he got off work. Instead of feeling energized by the meetings he did attend, his energy level after leaving a meeting was the same or reduced. Although encouraged by his counselor and by his wife, he never managed to go out with others for coffee after a meeting. Only after his wife, who had complained of being unable to function as his entire support system, threatened to leave him did he agree to go to a weekly get-together with his sponsor and a couple of other men from AA.

Tendency to minimize medical problems.   Another issue to which counselors need to be alert is the tendency of men to minimize or conceal medical problems, especially those that are a result of long-term drinking. For women, disclosure of a medical problem may not be considered a sign of weakness, or if it is, it is not in conflict with their identity as women. However, for men embracing traditional values, an ability to function in spite of severe pain is considered a sign of strength and is one measure of their masculinity (Kipnis 1991). For many men, the use of alcohol or opiates may be closely connected to their need to avoid feeling physical as well as emotional pain. Consequently, in order to help their male clients to recover, clinicians need to pay attention to clients' medical problems and to help them deal with their pain in healthier ways.

Relational versus positional perspective toward other men. Relating to other men as equals is another potential point of dissonance between male clients and treatment programs. Intimacy with others requires a relational orientation, something alien to most men.

> The self-esteem that emanates from [a relational] identity is considerably less conditional than are positional identity and self-esteem. It is not dependent on performance, or on maintaining some position in the hierarchy. It is based instead on maintaining the relationship itself, in affirming the attachment that bonds two people together . . . [Men] speak very little about their attachments to other men, and may not even be able to make much sense of that concept. In contrast, they readily relate to such concepts as being allies, teammates, colleagues, or competitors, all of which have a positional connotation. [Nowinski 1993, p. 68]

Nowinski believed that a man's relationship with his father has an important influence over whether he will develop a positional or relational perspective toward other men. Father–son relationships have been much discussed in the men's movement literature, and for good reason. If a positional, hierarchical orientation is established early in childhood, a man will adopt a similar attitude toward other adults later in life. His self-esteem will also be determined from his "place on the totem pole" with respect to other men and from his feelings about it (Nowinski 1993).

There are many ways in which a positional orientation, learned during childhood, can play a role in adult chemical abuse. One example is the case of William.

> William was a 45-year-old white man, raised by a father who prided himself on his high standards. His oldest brother, James, however, did poorly in school and was constantly criticized by the father for neglecting the chores and for getting into fights with older neighborhood kids. His second brother, Michael, by contrast, was the model son, excelling in school and taking on much responsibility around the house. William, the third son, quickly learned to avoid attracting too much attention. Wanting to be loved and accepted by both his father and his brothers, he did just well enough in school to avoid his father's criticism, but not well enough to threaten his brother's place as the family's standard-bearer. As an adult, William found work in a union shop, where roles were highly stratified and clearly defined. He did

his job adequately, in a way that earned some moderate approval from his bosses but that avoided drawing the attention of other workers.

His positional orientation had a direct influence on his abuse of alcohol. "I thought that no one would notice me and that I could do whatever I wanted," he said. "I thought I was invisible." The feeling of being invisible, while isolating, also gave him a sense of power and control. Eventually, three charges of driving while intoxicated drew the attention of the authorities. Recovery for William meant dealing with his conflicting feelings of wanting to be noticed and looking at the dysfunctional ways in which he had been expressing them.

Engaging this type of client in group therapy may be a much slower process than it is for many women, who are raised with a relational orientation and who may feel more comfortable discussing problems in a group. It may mean educating a male client to experiment with new behaviors and relationships. Men who are comfortable with intimacy and emotional expression from the beginning of their treatment are relatively rare, and so the challenge for therapists is to help them develop these qualities. On the other hand, clinicians may want to explore how a client's positional orientation can be utilized during treatment to expedite the recovery process of their male clients.

The preceding discussion focuses on problems that arise when a client's assumptions conflict with those of the therapist or the treatment program. Therapists often expect face-to-face contact, with which men are sometimes uncomfortable. They talk about surrender as if it were a positive thing, when for men it may mean a loss of power and diminished masculinity. They try to focus on the process of recovery, rather than the end result, as men do. They exclude the role of the hangout from recovery, an important place for many men. They also hope that men will promptly reveal embarrassing medical problems, which male clients often want to conceal. Finally, they believe that male clients should engage in a relational orientation with others without ever having been taught this. In order to provide good clinical treatment to male clients, such potential areas of conflict need to be recognized and addressed.

Masculine Values Congruent with Treatment

Some values become problematic when they encourage collusion between the male client and the therapist or treatment program. Rather than generate conflict or slow down the treatment, they offer the illusion that treatment is proceeding quickly and without complications. However, these shared values and assumptions, when unexamined, may interfere with long-term recovery. Such shared assumptions may relate to: (1) a belief that middle-aged men abuse only alcohol, (2) emphasis on the work ethic, (3) a belief that expression of strong feelings is unsafe for men, and (4) dealing with men who reject action-oriented values.

Middle Aged Men and Alcohol Abuse

Middle-aged men who present for alcohol-related problems may not initially discuss a secondary problem with narcotics or other drugs. Often a problem with cocaine, heroin, or another substance may come to light later—sometimes much later—after a positive urinalysis or some other signs become evident. Such minimization or denial of their drug problems may be fostered by clinicians used to dealing with middle-aged men who have used only alcohol. For example:

> Jose, a 47-year-old Hispanic man, told his counselor that he was determined not only to stop drinking but also to stop swearing so much. He also planned to start going to church more and to exercise. Most especially, though, he was determined to stop smoking. Without exploring further, the counselor encouraged Jose to take on one problem behavior at a time. Jose was unreceptive to this. He felt that smoking was his main issue: He really should stop because it was ruining his health. The counselor came back with his stock admonition against taking on nicotine too soon: it was a harder habit to break than alcohol, it was too soon in his recovery, etc. The client stopped him, made direct eye contact, and said, "I'm not speaking about cigarettes, you know."
>
> "Well, what are you talking about?"
>
> He gave a fatherly smile. "Crack," he said.

Men and the Work Ethic

The work ethic is another value that needs to be examined in order to avoid colluding with the client. Often, and especially in early phases of treatment, clients express a desire to return to work. Work is usually a place where men draw much of their identity. Yet it is also a place increasingly plagued with substance abuse (Wallace 1985). In addition, the pressures of staying clean and sober are sometimes best handled before adding job pressures. For this reason, some clients do well to avoid returning to work, job hunting, or participating in vocational rehabilitation counseling programs too soon.

Because men are traditionally the "breadwinners" of the household, they may face numerous pressures to return to work. Pressure may come from the client himself, his family, his employers, and increasingly, from governmental mandates. A client's job concerns may be manifested indirectly through questions about the length of time he will be expected to stay in treatment, agency policies regarding employment, and requests for referral to vocational rehabilitation counseling.

If a man still has his job, he may be anxious about reestablishing contact with his employer and co-workers. If he has not worked for some time, or if he has recently lost his job, there may be an underlying sense of shame that could jeopardize his sobriety. He may also be worried about looking for work. Because work is so closely connected with their identity as men, men who are involved in physical labor, and especially day laborers, are particularly sensitive about being out of work (Metzger 1988). Moreover, if the client's spouse is not working, or if she is not earning much, pressure may also come from the family as well as society at large expecting a man to support his family. Finally, if the client was referred by an employee assistance program (EAP), the EAP and the employer may have their own priorities, which may or may not coincide with the best interests of the client.

It is all too easy for a therapist or treatment program to help a client cave in to these pressures based on unexamined ideas about the role of men and work. One contribution of the men's movement has been to show how men have been socialized to continue to attempt to function even when it is inappropriate or unhealthy. A challenge for therapists is to help men in early recovery gain an understanding of their own limitations in functioning; this may mean returning to work later than they are comfortable doing. No matter how much men may clamor about their need to earn a living, therapists need to keep in mind that they are dealing, as always, with impaired individuals.

One way therapists can approach this problem is to frame recovery and participation in treatment as a job in itself. Treatment plans that include written assignments or other clearly defined tasks give clients the impression that they are expected to do more than attend meetings and refrain from drinking or drug use. Often, a detailed daily schedule with time allotted for "work" that focuses on treatment goals adds to the desired message that a client is not expected to be passive or inactive in recovery. Working with a client on a daily schedule can also have the added benefit that comes with shared participation in a task. If the client sees this work as important and not patronizing, it is an opportunity to build intimacy with the client along his own value system.

Expression of strong feelings. Expression of strong feelings is another area where shared assumptions between the client and the therapist and/ or treatment program may work to the client's disadvantage. The women's movement has encouraged women to show their emotions, especially anger. But open expression of feelings remains taboo for most men. "You go walking in a grocery store, down at Safeway, say, and if you see a woman taking Cheer and Pepsi off the shelf with tears running down her cheeks, you don't think much of it. Maybe you think, 'She probably feels better for crying.' But if you see a man crying in the same situation you think, 'Uh-oh, danger. Better tell the store people so they can call the guys with the nets'" (Lee 1990, p. 7).

Grief and anger are two emotions that are often viewed as inappropriate when expressed by men, although these do emerge in gender-exclusive meetings or groups (Kipnis 1991). Additionally, for some men, any expression of anger is associated with loss of control over emotions and situations, and therefore, with weakness (Kipnis 1991). Therapists need to take care that they do not carry over this societal taboo into their treatment sessions.

For some men, their anger can only be expressed under the influence of substances, particularly alcohol. For such men with "rageaholic personality," anger really does become more dangerous when it is expressed. They tend to express their anger by acting it out physically with other men or by battering their partners or children. A treatment priority for these men is to learn to contain their anger, rather than express it (Lee 1993).

Men who reject action-oriented values. When a man in treatment has rejected the whole range of action-oriented values, he may be easier to engage in treatment, but his relationship to other men in the treatment program may be problematic. Certain characteristics will call attention to him: He will be the first to form a therapeutic relationship with the counselor, and he is more likely to identify primarily with the women in his group. Moreover, he will be less likely to focus on his sexuality, or even verbalized feelings of sexual attraction to women. Sometimes he will brag about how most of his friends in AA or NA are women and will denigrate those other men he sees who practice "thirteenth stepping" (i.e., using meetings as places to meet women). There may be unstated homosexual urges, but more often there are no questions as to the client's heterosexual orientation (for gay men, there is the added problem of whether, or when, to come out to the group). However, devaluation of other men who discuss their sexual activities may be a sign that the client is uncomfortable with his own sexuality. Sexual assertiveness and desire for women may be projected onto other men, whom he then belittles.

While such men are often viewed as "perfect" clients, their rejection of action-oriented values needs to be explored further. Such values and behaviors may indicate problem areas that may interfere with their long-term recovery.

Tony was a 34-year-old white salesman who originally came in for outpatient treatment with his wife, Jean. He worked at a company where he was quickly becoming successful and earning a high salary; she had been caring for their children until recently, but the children were currently in foster care due to her drug use.

During childhood, Tony had a distant relationship with his father, whom he perceived as controlling, severe, and making frequent use of corporal punishment. His relationship with his mother was comfortable, though enmeshed. Tony was frank in his assertion that, even to this day, he found women easier to talk to than men. After graduating from high school, he went into sales and has worked in this field ever since. At age 28 he was initiated into the world of high-priced cocaine by an erotic dancer he met in a nightclub; three years later, he met his wife, who introduced him to crack cocaine. Both he and his wife were mandated to treatment because of two unrelated court cases. Both presented for treatment at the same treatment center and were intentionally placed in separate therapeutic groups.

From the beginning, Tony took pains to make it clear to the therapist that he was taking his treatment seriously. He sat close to the counselor and often addressed his remarks to him. At first skeptical of his motives, as treatment progressed, the counselor gradually became aware that Tony, who was highly articulate and insightful, in many ways represented the ideal, motivated client. It was easy to understand why he was so successful at his job, which involved a great deal of direct customer contact. Much of his interaction in the group, however, was with other women, mostly around their problems. His style was basically to "sell" them on recovery, in much the same way as he sold products to his customers. Yet, he also consciously avoided direct competition with the (male) counselor. He would often defer to him in discussing a problem and, when asked to talk about his own recovery, he asked questions of the counselor about what abstinence-related activities were appropriate.

The group eventually became aware of a certain naïveté in Tony that, it turned out, was closely connected with his drug use, his codependency issues, and his wife's increasing inability to make good use of outpatient treatment. In spite of having formed friendships with the women in group, the real woman to whom he was trying to sell recovery was his wife. He would extract promises from her and then become dejected when they were broken. He would make arrangements for her to enter inpatient treatment, only to see her sabotage them at the last minute. His sincere but somewhat unsophisticated attempts to manipulate her into taking her recovery seriously soon became the major focal point around which his own recovery turned.

Although many of the women in the group provided empathy and advice (often with a variety of motives of their own), it was the confrontational stance of other men, both in and out of the group, that finally influenced Tony to separate himself from his wife. During talks with male friends, Tony was finally able to see how his focus on helping other women was a quite purposeful method of avoiding dealing with his own issues.

Albeit ostensibly committed to his wife, Tony's addiction to a dysfunctional relationship had nothing to do with commitment or relationship. He had confused intimacy with intensity and involvement with entanglement (Diamond 1994). Staying with a woman who was consistently unavailable to him was his unconscious way of simultaneously acting out deep-seated fears of abandonment and providing him with a sense of competence. His need for connection and his more masculine need to take action were thus satisfied, though in a dysfunctional way.

It was only after he was able to overcome his initial resistance to spending time with other men that Tony was able to begin his recovery process. Particularly helpful was another man in the group who helped him to personify his addictive disease by using the metaphor of "the General." "The General" eventually became Tony's image for his compulsive behavior and dysfunctional thinking that led to his acting out of both his codependency and drug-seeking urges. It took another man to help him view his addiction as a toxic masculine introject, with origins in his relationship with his father. Thus, both his addiction and his recovery were each accompanied by an initiation: His initiation into addiction, born of a superficial relationship with a woman, was paralleled by his initiation into recovery through intimate relationships with other men.

One final chapter to Tony's story needs to be written—his need to eventually cultivate healthy relationships with women. He has identified this, as well as his need to extend and deepen his relationships with men, as a primary aftercare issue. An increased ability to experience emotions and sexual urges without acting them out will be the "cutting edge" issue in his long-term recovery.

CONCLUSION

The men's movements and the authors cited in this chapter have articulated a new vision of masculinity that has challenged both men and women to reexamine stereotyped gender roles. This vision can bring a fresh awareness to substance abuse counseling. Values that help perpetuate unhealthy living and development of addictive disease need to discarded. However, there is no need to throw out the baby along with the bathwater. We can separate dysfunctional, outmoded male values from neutral or helpful values in recovery, and "take what we like" even as we "leave the rest." Nevertheless, men as a group have for the time being been influenced by all the various values. Some of them may conflict with helping professionals' values and expectations, and a failure to address them may inhibit the building of a working alliance and the process of recovery. Other values may coincide with therapists' prejudices and give the false impression that treatment is moving quickly.

Therapists owe it to men to look for creative ways to capitalize on neutral or helpful values even as they attempt to minimize the impact of dysfunctional ones. Treatment programs should pay attention to how male clients have been socialized and to develop a respect for men's values that would make it easier for them to stay in treatment. Though we still lack a full understanding of the needs of men in treatment, hopefully this situation will change as the substance abuse treatment field continues to mature and change.

REFERENCES

Bliss, S. (1988). What happens on a men's mythopoetic weekend. *Wingspan*, Summer.

Bly, R. (1990). *Iron John: A Book about Men*. Reading, MA: Addison-Wesley.

Bolen, J. S. (1989). *Gods in Everyman*. New York: Harper & Row.

Brown, S. (1985). *Treating the Alcoholic: A Developmental Model of Recovery*. New York: Wiley.

Diamond, J. (1994). *The Warrior's Journey Home: Healing Men, Healing the Planet*. Oakland, CA: New Harbinger.

Edinger, E. F. (1985). *Anatomy of the Psyche: Alchemical Symbolism in Psychotherapy*. La Salle, IL: Open Court.

Goldberg, H. (1979). *The New Male*. New York: Signet Books.

Hayward, F. (1981). Opening Address to the National Congress for Men, June 13.

Kipnis, A. (1991). *Knights without Armor*. New York: Jeremy Tarcher/ Pedigree.

Lee, J. (1990). *Recovery: Plain and Simple*. Deerfield Beach, FL: Health Communications.

——(1993). *Facing the Fire: Experiencing and Expressing Anger Appropriately*. New York: Bantam.

Meade, M. (1993). *Men and the Water of Life*. San Francisco: HarperSan-Francisco.

Metzger, L. (1988). *From Denial to Recovery: Counseling Problem Drinkers, Alcoholics, and Their Families*. San Francisco: Jossey-Bass.

National Organization of Men Against Sexism (1996). Homepage on World Wide Web.

Nowinski, J. (1993). *Hungry Hearts: On Men, Intimacy, Self-Esteem, and Addiction*. New York: Lexington Books.

Pape, P. (1993). Issues in assessment and intervention with alcohol and drug-abusing women. In *Clinical Work with Substance-Abusing Clients*, ed. S. L. A. Straussner, pp. 251–269. New York: Guilford.

Rheingold, H. (1995). The virtual community. *Utne Reader* 68:61–64.

Wallace, J. (1985). *Alcoholism: New Light on the Disease*. Newport, RI: Edgehill Publications.

15

Alcoholic Fathers and Substance-Abusing Sons

Paul Mulinski

It has long been recognized that substance abuse runs in families and that sons of alcoholic fathers comprise the highest risk group for the development of substance abuse problems (Penick et al. 1978). There is mounting evidence that some types of substance abuse, such as alcoholism, may be inherited in the sense that individuals are genetically predisposed (Cloninger et al. 1981). Other forms of substance abuse may be passed on from parent to child in the form of learned behavior. Consequently, it is important for clinicians to consider what impact growing up in a substance-abusing family had on the use and abuse of substances and on the recovery process.

Male substance abusers in treatment often describe their fathers as alcoholic and express deep-seated resentments toward fathers, whom they experienced as neglectful or abusive when drinking. In discussing their relationships with their fathers, it appears that sons may consciously reject their fathers' substance abuse. For example, it is not uncommon to hear them say that while growing up they swore they would never be like their fathers. Yet, like their fathers, they developed serious substance abuse problems. Underlying the conscious rejection of their fathers' substance abuse is an unconscious identification with the abuse of mood-altering substances. Many substance-abusing men are unable to come to terms with what is essentially an ambivalent identification with their fathers. Clients' identification with understanding of parental behavior can deeply affect their decision to stop using drugs and alcohol and their motivation to remain free of substances. The focus of this chapter is on the perceptions and impact of fathers' substance abuse on substance-abusing sons and how these perceptions affect the clients' recovery.

THEORIES OF ETIOLOGY OF SUBSTANCE ABUSE

Research in the field supports the existence of a genetic predisposition to alcoholism among sons of alcoholics (Schuckit 1994). Therefore we should not conclude that psychological factors alone can explain the high incidence of alcoholism among fathers and sons. Nevertheless, in a complex disorder like substance abuse, psychological issues should not be dismissed. In alcoholic families, there are often memories of several generations of alcoholic males. This is significant in itself, beyond the issue of genetic transmission, because the son's relationship with an alcoholic father may contribute to the development of substance abuse in the son.

An individual's personality can be understood as the result of inter-play between genetically determined temperament and environment. The environmental component emphasizes interactions between parent and child and interactions with other psychologically important individuals. It is therefore natural to look at the issue of father and son substance abuse from the combined perspective of genetic predisposition and learned behavior when considering etiology. Role modeling and, specifically, identification between father and son may contribute to the transmission of learned addictive behaviors.

Developmental Theories

Ego psychological approaches to the treatment and understanding of substance abuse integrate perspectives from object relations theory and self psychology. For example, drugs can be used to soothe and calm when anxiety is not maintained or experienced at tolerable levels. Some have labeled substance abuse as a basic failure at self-care or self-governance (Mack 1981). In contrast, adaptive methods for coping with anxiety or aggression are behaviors that result from identification with a role model with developmentally sound coping skills (Vaillant 1976). The substance-abusing father fails to provide such a role model.

An additional dynamic is the degree to which the father is able to nurture in response to the son's dependency. A multitude of determinants influence emotional development; of special significance are those related to the dependency situation and parental nurturance (Blum 1966). In this context, it is possible to understand psychological explanations of substance abuse from the perspective of developmental failure. Boys are apt to identify with their fathers when fathers are perceived as highly nurturant and rewarding. It is closeness with father and trust in him that allows the son to temper his aggression. Expressions of aggression by the son are neutralized by the father's expressions of affection. Healthy paternal nurturing includes the father's ability to create a safe psychological environment for the son in which the son perceives the father as having an important role in his life. Closeness to father expands the boy's concept of manhood to encompass a range of affects and attitudes that might otherwise be associated only with mother, and therefore eschewed by the son as womanly. Drugs may be abused when dependency needs are not met appropriately through internalization and identification with a nurturing father. It is not difficult to understand why a father's alcoholism would diminish his ability to meet his son's dependency needs. An alcoholic father does not provide a safe environment for his son because father's alcoholism compromises his ability to be physically and psychologically present for his son. This is in marked contrast to what we have come to accept as contemporary notions of good male parenting (Cath et al. 1982).

Family Perspectives

A significant number of substance abusers were raised in alcoholic families (Penick 1978). Comparatively, sons of alcoholic fathers comprise the highest risk group for the development of substance abuse problems. This is especially evident among younger males whose alcohol use is strongly determined by the use and attitudes of the same-sex parent (Johnson and Pandina 1991). For the client in recovery, this means having the opportunity to talk about being raised by a father who was alcoholic. Men in treatment for substance abuse often discuss their family's abuse of alcohol and other drugs. Sometimes they make comparisons between their fathers' substance abuse and their own. Because of generational and age differences, clients in treatment for polysubstance abuse usually describe fathers who used or abused alcohol. Younger men in treatment are much more apt to report the abuse of other drugs along with alcohol. In their fathers' generation the use of illicit drugs was not prevalent to the degree it is today, so their fathers' substance abuse was limited to alcohol. Growing up in an alcohol- or drug-dependent family is a reality that can have a significant impact on the recovery process. Not to take drugs or not to drink may be considered an act of disloyalty (Brown 1988). In these families, drinking together is experienced as a family activity; not to drink is to turn away from family.

As evident in the following representative vignette from a group therapy session composed of men in treatment for drug and alcohol problems, some men experienced feelings of camaraderie based on episodes of drinking together with their fathers, while others report that their fathers were verbally or physically abusive when intoxicated.

CLIENT A
My first job was in a steel mill where my father worked. We used to go to the bar across the street after work and have five or six beers; we would talk and joke with the other guys. Most of the guys did that. We would go home, eat supper, and go to sleep because we had to get up at 4:00 in the morning. On weekends we started drinking beer at noon. It's how we spent time together. It was a way of life.

CLIENT B
My father did the same thing, but after five or six beers he would get nasty and there was no way you could talk to him. The kids learned

to stay out of his way, but he and my mother would always get into an argument. One of the reasons I decided to stop drinking was because I realized I was doing exactly what my father did. I would get drunk and get abusive to my wife. When I saw how it was affecting my kids, I remembered how it felt when my father did it to me. That's when I made the decision to get sober.

CLIENT C

My father didn't drink at all. I mean once in a while he would have a beer with his meals but that was it. The other men in my family did drink. All my uncles in both my mother's and father's family were heavy drinkers, and I used to drink with them at family parties.

In common with their fathers, many clients viewed heavy drinking as acceptable masculine behavior. Consuming alcohol was viewed as a recreational activity that was a reward for work that was usually physically demanding. Like their fathers, they spent time after work and on weekends drinking; minimal time was spent in family-centered activities, and comments from wives or mothers were dismissed as nagging.

When thinking about these families, systems approaches to understanding familial alcoholism help to integrate complex and sometimes contradictory data on family interactions (Steinglass et al. 1971). It is a framework for addressing a family's adaptive and coping skills. These coping skills may be severely compromised in the alcoholic family, resulting in the disruption of family tasks involving parental coalitions, nurturance, and the provision of appropriate role models. Studies using large samples of children from alcoholic homes indicate that these children are likely to have many more problems than children raised in nonalcoholic families (Miller and Jong 1977). In both poor, multiproblem families and economically stable ones, father's alcoholism is likely to increase the children's risk for the development of social and emotional problems (Nylander and Rydelius 1982). Even when compared to psychiatrically disturbed families, alcoholic families have higher rates of marital problems, separation, and financial difficulties (Chafetz et al. 1971). Children of fathers who abuse alcohol and other drugs also differ significantly from children whose parents do not use drugs on measures of depression and attributional style (Perez-Bouchard et al. 1993). The negative impact of an alcoholic father can be mediated by other crucial social-familial variables. Of special importance is the role of the nonalcoholic mother in relation to the alcoholic father. Some mothers are able to protect the family from major disruption by setting limits around the behavior of the alcoholic partner. In other cases members of an extended family, or family-like network, help sustain a consistent safe environment to foster the children's adaptive development.

Although it is not possible to define a unified model for intergenerational transmission, descriptive studies have indirectly helped to refine variables involved in a number of possible psychosocial models. Studies of the impact of paternal alcoholism on children's psychological development from adolescence to adulthood have described the effect in terms of an earlier age at first intoxication, more rapid progression from first intoxication to treatment, more numerous pretreatment behavioral problems (including school suspension, alcohol related arrests, days spent in jail), and reports of markedly aggressive behavior. In comparing the variable of paternal versus nonpaternal alcoholism, paternal alcoholism was directly related to elevations of psychopathology, especially aggression, among alcoholic subjects (McKenna and Pickens 1983).

Role Theory

A limited number of studies have examined the possible developmental ramifications of paternal alcoholism on the child using a role-theoretical perspective (Nardi 1981). Families where the father is alcoholic are a classic example of role reversal that compromises appropriate role identifications, and boys with alcoholic fathers show more disturbances than do girls with alcoholic fathers (El-Guebaly and Offord 1977). As fathers become increasingly passive in their interactions with the family, mothers are forced to make executive decisions on their own. In cases where the father actually abandons the family, mothers must provide financial support. From the son's perspective, father is seen as weak and ineffective in contrast to mother's dominance.

In families where the father is alcoholic, it has sometimes been the case that parents separate at mother's insistence that father leave. In other cases the separation is the result of father's abandoning the family emotionally and/or financially. These absences may be permanent or intermittent, depending on the father's attempts to get sober and reunite with the family. In situations where the father is not present, the son is apt to produce idealistic, affectionate, and nonaggressive father fantasies. These fantasies may reflect a personality organization influenced by the increased role of the mother as a major social stimulus (Socarides 1982). In situations where the parents remain together, mother's overinvolvement with the son is an attempt to compensate for father's emotional distance.

As fathers retreat from participating in family life, mothers make more and more executive decisions. As mothers assume more responsibility for discipline of the children, struggles around control ensue, especially between mothers and adolescent sons. This is a no-win situation for both. Mother's dominance as the major parental influence intensifies the son's perceptions that mothers are overcontrolling and fathers ineffective. Mother's anger toward father leads to open expressions of resentment and, in some cases, demeaning comments about men in general. For the son, the result can be intense confusion and conflict in relating to both parents. As a male, the boy knows at some level that he should behave differently than mother; but to behave like father means being ineffective. From one perspective, the substance abuse can be understood as the son's attempt to deal with an ongoing sense of identity diffusion; however, the substance abuse ultimately exacerbates these conflicts and interferes with maturation.

Identification

Boys are more apt to identify strongly with their fathers when the fathers are perceived as highly nurturing and rewarding. It is the son's perception of his father's importance in his life. In contemporary terms, identification can be thought of as an ongoing rather than fixed process that is open to modification even in adulthood. It can include the components of emotional alliance, modeling, and unconscious defensive functions (Shafer 1968). In the simplest of terms, how we view ourselves can be modified over time by interactions with others. Developmentally there are multiple opportunities for identity to be modified in interpersonal relationships with relatives, teachers, employers, spouses, significant others, and of course, psychotherapists.

Adolescent males with conflicts in identification are less likely to perceive their fathers as like themselves when compared to less conflicted adolescents (Esman 1982). Developmentally, boys model their expressions of aggression after their fathers; the more highly identified the boy is with his father, the more apt he is to replicate expressions of aggressive behavior (Levin and Sears 1956). It is the context of the father–son relationship that determines the degree to which expressions of aggression are neutralized by affection and nurturance. Aggression and conduct disorders that are indicators of weak impulse control are potential predictors of problem drinking in boys (Pulkkinen and Pitkanen 1994). Perhaps this is related to the finding that there is a high incidence of sociopathy among adult alcoholics (Hill 1992).

For the substance-abusing son, ambivalence toward the alcoholic father needs to be addressed in recovery, because at a conscious level the son may reject the concept of father's drunkenness but at an unconscious level maintain an affinity for alcohol (Mik 1970). Sons of alcoholic fathers are less likely to see themselves as like their alcoholic fathers when compared to male alcoholics whose fathers were not alcoholic (Mulinski 1989). This presents an interesting clinical dichotomy. On the one hand these men are identified with an alcoholic style of coping, while on the other, they are not consciously identified with their alcoholic fathers. They do not describe themselves as like their fathers and do not see their fathers as having had an important positive role in their lives. A significant percentage of these men also describe their fathers as being verbally or physically abusive. Thus, the perception of the father as abusive may contribute to the conflicted identification.

If not described as violent, fathers are frequently described by clients, and described in the professional literature, as either physically or emotionally absent (Koller and Castanos 1969, McKay 1961, Schneider et al. 1977). Some professionals have interpreted the high incidence of substance abuse in sons of alcoholic fathers to support the conclusion that the son's substance abuse is the product of identification with an inadequate role model (Aronson and Gilbert 1963, Higgins 1953, Levy 1958).

A focus on identification can increase our understanding of psychodynamic factors that influence recovery. For males, identification with an alcoholic father may include identification with an alcoholic style of dealing with conflict and the outside world. Alcohol and other drugs like marijuana are used to calm intense feelings generated in relation to intrapersonal and interpersonal dynamics (Mack 1981). Confrontations are avoided, and psychological retreat becomes a mode of functioning.

Perceptions of Father

In the clinical setting, identification is often talked about indirectly in the context of clients' perceptions of the quality of their relationships with their fathers. Therefore, in substance abuse treatment, clinicians should consider how male clients' identifications with their fathers influence recovery based on what clients say about their fathers. The clinician will hear a number of repetitive themes that clients share in common when talking about their substance abuse in the context of family relationships.

Some clients talk about drinking as a way to escape what they experienced as intolerable home situations involving violent expressions of aggression by their fathers. It appears that the father's physical acting out and resulting family violence significantly damage the son's ability to perceive the father as nurturing, irrespective of the father's substance abuse. In other words, the fact that the parent is a substance abuser can be less important than how the parent behaves. For example, negative parental affect is a predictor of early adolescent alcohol abuse in children of both alcoholic and nonalcoholic parents. Teenagers may resort to using alcohol in response to stressors at home, irrespective of whether or not a parent or both parents abuse alcohol (Molina et al. 1994).

Often when male substance abusers describe their fathers as heavy drinkers, they also describe their mothers as abstainers. These men have been exposed to alcohol use—especially heavy drinking—by their fathers, so in some sense, to be like father means to be a heavy drinker. Differences in parental drinking habits can reinforce the perception for boys that heavy drinking is a masculine behavior; not drinking is perceived as feminine. These learned roles significantly influence the development of individual identity as adult males.

As outlined in the clinical vignettes that follow, identification with father can serve as one of a number of possible organizing principles to help the abstinent substance abuser better understand his substance abuse and its role in his own psychological development. For example, a common theme is the perception of the alcoholic father as emotionally distant. To counter this sense of distance, some men relied on recollections of time spent with father in drinking-related activities. Closeness to father was equated with time drinking together. As adults, the elation secondary to intoxication could be understood as an attempt to regain a wished-for but never genuinely achieved relationship. For example, one client described his interactions with his father:

> If I had something to ask him, he would give me a quick simple answer. He always seemed to be in a rush—maybe because he had two jobs. But even when he wasn't working he would be in a rush, a rush to spend time by himself. His evening job was cleaning a diner that belonged to my aunt and uncle. When I was 16 I started working with him at night after the diner closed. My aunt and uncle didn't pay him much but he could drink all the beer he wanted. That was the only time we talked. Not that he was ever a big talker, but I felt at least there was some communication, some connection. We did that until I was 18 and went into the service. The whole time we kept the drinking together a secret from my mother. He didn't know that I was also smoking grass with my friends. When I went to Vietnam I stayed drunk and stoned as much as possible. When I was home on leave I knew my father was worrying about my being in Vietnam but he couldn't say it. We would get drunk together and it would be OK.

The preceding comments illustrate the point that for some men, drinking with father is recalled in either positive or benign terms and as a behavior that did not include mother. Also typical is the client's report that he started drinking as a teenager. Separation from family, characteristic of adolescence, is compromised by the use of alcohol and marijuana. Because his alcohol and drug use rapidly escalated to abuse, this client reached young adulthood developmentally arrested in an adolescent mode of relating to family and others. The client served in the military in Vietnam. This was his first separation from his family. Father was concerned about his son's safety in Vietnam but unable to verbalize it. Whatever feelings were shared between the two occurred in the context of getting drunk. Alcohol provided the only opportunity for some sense of connection between father and son, and subsequently between the son and other men.

One client, whose father had died from alcoholism, reported that his father began taking him to bars when he was 8. These outings with his father were a totally new experience that filled him with anxiety and excitement. Together they would take a bus to his father's favorite "gin mill." The bus trip with his father was considered something special since his mother and younger siblings were left at home. In the bar his father would seat him at a corner table and buy him soda and potato chips. He would sit quietly and wait for his father, never showing any signs of impatience. Sometimes these visits would last for an hour or two. At times he would be frightened by men who would try to speak to him. He experienced their intoxicated friendliness as aggressive since he could not escape the foul smell of beer and liquor on their breath. On the bus trip home he and his father would always agree to keep their visit to the bar a secret. At home his father would occasionally allow him to drink small amounts of beer from his glass. The sharing of beer was also something they agreed to keep a secret.

After a year of sobriety, the same client was able to share some very intense and poignant feelings about his father:

CLIENT

Sometimes when I see a wino on the street, I feel like beating him up.

THERAPIST

What is that about?

CLIENT

It's obvious, it's like a father figure.

THERAPIST

You would really like to beat your father?

CLIENT

Maybe not him, but the alcohol.

THERAPIST

Seeing these men reminds you of your father?

CLIENT

He was never that deteriorated. He always kept up his appearance. His appearance was important to him. He was sort of a rakish character, but he did terribly humiliating things when he was drunk. He used to drink cheap wine. I remember once going to see him after my mother threw him out of the house. I brought him some good wine, but he wouldn't drink it. He took one or two gulps and spat it out. So I drank it.

THERAPIST

You used to drink with him?

CLIENT

Sometimes I would go and visit him when I was really feeling down.

THERAPIST

What about these visits?

CLIENT

I used to hate myself afterwards.

THERAPIST

Then why did you visit?

CLIENT

I thought it would make me feel better. It did because I used to drink his wine and take his Valium.

THERAPIST

Is that why you would visit?

CLIENT

No, I wanted to show him that someone in the family still cared about him.

THERAPIST

Because your mother didn't?

CLIENT

I can't blame her for throwing him out. She had to do what she did. There was no money, no food. Do you know what it's like not to have enough to eat, to be really hungry or really cold? Not just a passing condition, but to be cold all the time because the paycheck got drunk up. Today when I see people who mocked me as a kid because my father was drunk, I think I'm better than them. I feel stronger.

Many substance-abusing men talk about their fathers in the context of their relationships with their own sons. They are concerned about their adequacy as parents and the impact of their substance abuse on their children. Such concerns about their sons can be used as a natural bridge to explore perceptions of their relationships with their fathers. For example:

CLIENT

I think the problem is that I feel guilty about my drinking and guilty that I've demanded too much of my son. I always felt that my father had pushed me to grow up too fast. I remember saying to myself that I would never do that to my son. One of the reasons I'm depressed is that I realize I've treated my son just like my father treated me.

THERAPIST

Can you give an example of what you mean?

CLIENT

When I was very young, my father used to take me for rides and he would always ask me if I wanted a soda. He would stop at a bar and leave me in the car. Eventually he would come out with my soda after he had a chance to have a few drinks. I still remember that bar; it was called the Top Hat. I must have been very young, because I wondered why my father bought so many hats. I used to think he must have a lot of hats. As I look back on my drinking, I realize that I did the same soda routine with my son, except I would stop off at a package store. When I was really down and had the money I would do cocaine, and that scared me—drinking and drugging with my son in the car.

THERAPIST

What was it that scared you?

CLIENT

I realized I didn't know what it meant to be a good father. I don't know how to bridge the distance between myself and my son. Once, one of my counselors asked me to rate myself as a father. On a scale of one to ten, I gave myself a five.

THERAPIST

How would you have rated your father when you were 8 years old?

CLIENT

I couldn't have given him a rating; he was never there. I couldn't talk to him. Even now I can't have a logical conversation with him. He doesn't talk about feelings. He doesn't have feelings. *(Client pauses)*

I shouldn't say that. He has feelings; he just can't talk about them. I guess I'm angry with him. I was proud of him when he got sober, and I think that affected my decision to get sober myself. I don't know how to feel about the fact that he's drinking again.

Perceptions of Mother

It is important to understand that images and recollections of father are influenced by perceptions of mother. The issue of keeping the drinking a secret from mother is indicative of another theme involving the complexity of these men's relationships with their mothers. The emotionally unavailable alcoholic father does not facilitate the son's separation from mother. In functional families, fathers help both daughters and sons appropriately separate and gain independence from mother. In alcoholic families, the father's drinking is a constant source of tension for the wives, which is frequently interpreted as purposeful and defiant. Imitating their fathers, male substance abusers may use alcohol or other drugs as a means of obtaining distance from their mothers. The mother's anger over the drinking reinforces the image that the mothers are hypercritical of men. In treatment, this issue was often expressed in conflicts with their wives or other women perceived to be in authority. What is needed is positive symbolic representation of father for the satisfactory resolution of ambivalent feelings toward mother (Abelin 1971).

CLIENT

I can remember a time in my early teens when I went to my father about my mother. She was always angry with me because I was challenging her rules which were way too restrictive for a teenage boy. On one occasion she was so angry she poked me with a fork. I said to my father, "Look, she's gone off the deep end, and we have to do something about her." I was really looking for his help. He turned to me and glared and told me never to refer to her as "she" and never to speak about her like that again. It makes me furious just to think about it.

THERAPIST

Do you think you were more angry with your mother or your father?

CLIENT

(Before answering the client smirks.) Well, I had a wonderful mother who always sacrificed for her family because of my alcoholic father, so logic would have it that I should be angry with my father. But I know that's not right. It just doesn't feel right.

THERAPIST

It's interesting that you developed a problem with alcohol like your father.

CLIENT

It makes sense to me. My father was alcoholic and depressed, and I'm alcoholic and depressed. But I'm starting to see some qualities in him that I admire. I would like to think that I have some of those qualities. Now that I'm straight I can try to understand him. I realize that he can be warm and that he can be aware of other people's feelings.

Verbal and Physical Abuse by Fathers

In many substance-abusing families there is a significant correlation between drug behavior and child abuse (Kelleher et al. 1994, Murphy et al. 1991, Zeitlin 1994). Some researchers have concluded that there is an association between alcohol abuse and physical mistreatment and between cocaine abuse and sexual maltreatment (Famularo et al. 1992). Many men in treatment recount that their fathers were verbally or physically abusive. Male substance abusers who describe their fathers as alcoholic are three times more likely also to describe their fathers as abusive when compared to male substance abusers who do not describe their fathers as alcoholic (Mulinski 1989). Verbal or physical abuse further compromises the quality of the relationship to father (Henderson et al. 1994). It interferes with the son's own ability to modulate aggressive feelings. Some men report fathers who were abusive only when drinking, while others describe their fathers as abusive whether sober or intoxicated. All experienced the anxiety secondary to the unpredictable behavior of their fathers when drunk. The sustained trauma of having lived with an alcoholic, physically abusive father contributes to problems with impulse control and violent acting out. From a developmental perspective, good and bad fathers represent discrepant models of masculinity (Ross 1982). Closeness with father tempers the aggressiveness of the son's curiosity and assertiveness. When the only model is a bad father, it is much harder for the boy to modulate aggression in the service of discovery and industry. "The restless, angry, shouting father serves as a poor role model for the latency bound youngster. Beatings, seduction and excited behavior on the part of the father, maul the state of latency" (Sarnoff 1982, p. 260). The father's availability as a mentor needs to continue throughout the son's adolescence. When this is missing, males enter adulthood with a sense of longing for this lost relationship:

CLIENT

I used to fantasize that my father would sober up and get back together with my mother. Then I could have a father like other boys.

THERAPIST

Then your father could have given you advice.

CLIENT

Sometimes he did.

THERAPIST

About what?

CLIENT

He told me not to drink and use drugs. He wasn't a stupid man. He knew what his alcoholism was about. At the end he was addicted to alcohol and Valium the way I was. His drug addiction killed him, and I felt he abandoned me. My mother tried to make up for it, but it's not the same. Kids need love. No one ever loved me.

THERAPIST

No one loved you? Your mother didn't love you?

CLIENT

She's a nag.

THERAPIST

Your father?

CLIENT

He told me he loved me, but I never believed him. I was always suspicious.

THERAPIST

Suspicious?

CLIENT

How could I believe he loved me when he would abuse my mother and tear up the house and then tell me he loved me? The bottle was the only thing he loved, not me, not his family. Nothing mattered to him, not the house, the heat, food, nothing!

THERAPIST

Is it possible your father could have loved you even though at times he was abusive and violent?

CLIENT

No.

THERAPIST
Maybe he loved you the best he could.

TREATMENT IMPLICATIONS

Treatment is focused on helping the client establish a drug-free identity by exploring how perceptions of father influence the decision to use, or not use, drugs and alcohol. Traditional approaches to substance abuse treatment have ignored developmental issues and treatment has indiscriminately employed confrontational techniques which may be contraindicated for many clients (O'Connor et al. 1994). Confrontation can be appropriate with clients who deny their substance abuse; however, once they acknowledge it and make attempts to get help, confrontation can be counterproductive. Substance abuse eventually produces a negative effect—guilt, anxiety, physical ill feelings, and the breakdown of social functioning. The majority of clients experience a combination of depression and shame during recovery that is best responded to by empathy from therapists. This approach can be conceptualized as ego oriented and ego supportive. For the substance-abusing client, the learning of new behaviors is based on ego psychological principles and includes increasing frustration tolerance, delay of gratification, anticipation through cognition, and differentiation and regulation of affect (Khantzian 1981). For male substance abusers to sustain recovery, this means identifying with role models that support a drug free identity. Treatment is directed toward facilitating more adaptive modes of ego functioning that alter or eliminate maladaptive and dysfunctional behavior. For the male substance abuser whose father was alcoholic, this means understanding how perceptions of father affect his own drug free identity. Therapeutic intervention can range from intensive individual treatment to participation in self-help groups like Alcoholics Anonymous or Narcotics Anonymous. The human relationship in which the internalization occurs can vary from an intensive therapeutic contact with an individual therapist to broad-based group support. The therapeutic principles involving internalization and object relations are similar, irrespective of the treatment modality.

In the following, a client describes the impact of his father's behavior on his ability to stay free of drugs:

CLIENT
My father started drinking again and ended up in the hospital. I knew this would happen. Last week we went to my parents' house for din-

ner on Sunday. My mother brought out a bottle of wine and four glasses. My wife and I refused, my father drank the wine. After dinner I asked my mother why she had served the wine since I had asked her not to serve alcohol. She told me she wasn't going to deprive herself of something just because the men in the family had a problem. She said my father was a grown man and could make his own decisions. She went on to say that anyone with any will power should be able to control his drinking. So it's two weeks later and he's in the hospital. I went to see him yesterday. When I walked into his room my mother was there. An intern came in and asked my mother a few questions about his medical history, including a question about his drinking. My mother told him that he drank moderately. My father just smiled at the intern in agreement. I couldn't believe it. My father is drinking a quart of whiskey a day. They put this poor doctor through this long runaround about what they think is the problem with his stomach. I wanted to walk out of the room and not come back.

THERAPIST

Why?

CLIENT

It was too much like the past. It reminded me of how we all used to ignore my father's drinking and pretend it wasn't happening. I didn't want to be a part of it anymore.

THERAPIST

Why not?

CLIENT

Because it's destructive to my father and to me. He's going to kill himself with alcohol and I could have killed myself from drugs and alcohol. What frightens me is wondering if that is what my mother wants.

THERAPIST

Do you really think that's what she wants?

CLIENT

I don't really know. I don't think so. I don't want to think about it right now. I want to take some distance from it.

THERAPIST

What makes it hard to take distance?

CLIENT

I don't know. I just can't let go of it.

THERAPIST
Maybe there are some other feelings involved.

CLIENT
I guess it makes me angry. Yes, it makes me furious!

THERAPIST
Any other feelings?

CLIENT
It makes me feel crazy. My parents were sitting there telling this intern a story that had no relation to reality whatsoever. What was worse is that they just dismissed the fact that I was standing there listening. I mean, do they believe that I believe them, or was I supposed to go along with the story? I don't think it made any difference to them what I thought. That was their reality and I just had to accept it.

THERAPIST
How do you feel about their reality?

CLIENT
At first I felt anger, and then I guess I felt overwhelmed, like there was nothing that I could do.

THERAPIST
Tell me more about feeling overwhelmed.

CLIENT
At first I felt hopeless, then I got depressed.

THERAPIST
Are you depressed now?

CLIENT
I've been depressed ever since the day I stopped using drugs, actually since the day I decided to stop using drugs. It makes me want to go back to the cocaine and vodka.

This vignette illustrates a number of important themes that the therapist can use to guide interventions. The most obvious is ambivalence toward father. The client expresses sadness and anger and concludes that he doesn't know how to feel now that his father is drinking again. In helping the client remain drug free, information about father's drinking behavior can have a powerful positive or negative influence on the client's motivation. An in-depth exploration of feelings around father's drinking can help the client prevent an impulsive return to drug use. Substance abusers do not readily recognize their use of alcohol and other drugs as an attempt to escape unpleasant feelings. Helping them recognize the connection between feelings and drug use is essential. In the clinical vignette just cited, ambivalence toward father can interfere with the conscious recognition that father's drinking behavior evokes a powerful emotional response.

Also of clinical importance is that perceptions of one parent are always influenced by perceptions of the other. Perceptions of father, or identification with father, can be more fully understood in the context of the relationship to both parents. What is essential to treatment is that perceptions of father can be modified over time. The key to the process is an extended period of sobriety that provides an opportunity for the sober and drug free substance abuser to explore important relationships. Timing is important. The first concern should always be helping the client change behavior to support and maintain abstinence. Exploration of important relationships and specifically discussions of father come when, and if, the client is ready. They can occur in the context of either individual or group treatment and are best accomplished when the client feels safe to reveal feelings about father. Some clients have fixed images of their parents that they don't want challenged in therapy. These relatively fixed images can be either highly idealized or extremely negative. Clinicians must respect a client's defenses around such material. It is the client who will let the therapist know whether or not looking more closely at perceptions of father is helpful.

Identifications are open to modification through the process of internalization, which spans the entire developmental continuum (Shafer 1968). Throughout life interactions in important relationships are internalized and modify our self-image. Perceptions of other positive role models such as teachers, employers, counselors, or AA sponsors can facilitate the process by providing new opportunities for identification. Fixed internalizations can be modified. For example, a man may identify with a father he perceived as inadequate and therefore feel inadequate himself. If, as an adult, he develops a more accepting or positive image of his father, this can result in a more positive image of himself. In treatment, clients talking about being fathers themselves is an opening to explore their perceptions of their fathers. Often identification with father is addressed indirectly, as in the following example of a client talking about his son in group therapy.

CLIENT A

It bothers me that my son still worries about me drinking.

THERAPIST

How do you know he's worried?

CLIENT A

Whenever a beer commercial comes on television he looks at me for reassurance. I can see it in his face. I wonder what other effect my drinking has had on him. Is he going to be screwed up as an adult?

CLIENT B

I think it's just your typical alcoholic guilt. We all spend a lot of time worrying and feeling guilty about our families.

THERAPIST

No, I think you're not understanding what he's trying to say.

CLIENT C

Do you spend time with him?

CLIENT A

That's the problem. I don't know how to spend time with him.

THERAPIST

How did your father spend time with you?

CLIENT A

My father had no patience with me, especially when he was drunk. I was the same way with my son. What really bothers me is that now I know how much I frightened him when I lost my temper. One of the things I've learned from my sponsor is the importance of keeping my cool. It actually feels good not to lose my temper.

Role of Mentor

In many ways treatment for substance abuse incorporates the concept of a mentor in the role of counselor-therapist or sponsor. That is, someone is identified in the substance abuser's life who is available, knowledgeable, and willing to give advice. In recovery there may be many opportunities for mentoring from the therapist, AA sponsor, twelve-step members, or from other group members. The philosophy underlying the twelve-step method of Alcoholics Anonymous has been criticized as "grounded in patriarchal thinking" (Nelson-Zlupko et al. 1995). However, it is effective for some male substance abusers. The mentor function can contribute to strengthening identification with a male role model, as in the following example where a client discusses his relationship with his sponsor.

CLIENT

There was a certain kind of security I thought I could get from taking drugs, but I don't think I've ever felt secure.

THERAPIST

What do you think it would be like to feel secure?

CLIENT

Like when I'm with Larry, my sponsor. He's 55 years old. When I'm in his car and he's driving, I can just sit there and feel secure. I guess that's what I missed by not having a father. That's what a father must give you—a sense of security.

Later in the session:

CLIENT

I think a big problem for me is that I don't know how to calm myself down. I think I'm learning, but I worry too much about things. If I hadn't gotten into drugs I would have had more options in life.

CONCLUSION

A central developmental principle is that a child's interactions with his parents are metabolized into psychic structure. Traditionally, developmental theory focused on the mother–child interaction. Recently more attention has been focused on the father's role, not only in the child's early development but on his impact during adolescence and adulthood. Indeed, some have proposed that it is not until young adulthood that men are able to come to terms with a range of intense feelings toward their fathers (Blos 1984). Substance abuse in father and son confounds the process. This is especially true in regard to how men learn to deal with anger and hostility. "The parent whose modes of functioning are relatively highly neutralized is one who also conveys modes of neutralizing" (Shafer 1968, p. 175). Social skills of the young adult must be considered in conjunction with specific types of family communication (Jones and Houts 1992). A father's substance abuse can contribute to the unleashing of aggressive impulses characterized by abusive and violent acting out. The result is a son who is developmentally stuck and unable to mature in his use of higher-level defenses and coping styles (Vaillant 1980). In order to achieve successful recovery, these issues must be addressed during the treatment process of male substance abusers.

REFERENCES

Abelin, E. (1971). The role of the father in the separation-individuation process. In *Separation-Individuation*, ed. J. B. McDevitt and C. F. Settlage, pp. 229–252. New York: International Universities Press.

Aronson, H., and Gilbert A. (1963). Preadolescent sons of male alcoholics. *Archives of General Psychiatry* 8:235–241.

Blos, P. (1984). Son and father. *Journal of the American Psychoanalytic Association* 32(2):301–324.

Blum, E. (1966). Psychoanalytic views of alcoholism: a review. *Quarterly Journal of Studies on Alcohol* 27:259–299.

Brown, S. (1988). *Treating Adult Children of Alcoholics.* New York: Wiley.

Cath, S. H., Gurwitt, A. R., and Ross, J. M. (1982). *Father and Child: Developmental and Clinical Perspectives.* Boston: Little, Brown.

Chafetz, M., Blane, H., and Hill, M. (1971). Children of alcoholics: observations in a child guidance clinic. *Quarterly Journal of Studies on Alcohol* 32:687–698.

Cloninger, R., Bohman, M., and Sigvardsson, S. (1981). Inheritance of alcohol abuse: cross-fostering analysis of adopted men. *Archives of General Psychiatry* 38:861–867.

El-Guebaly, N., and Offord, D. R. (1977). The offspring of alcoholics: a critical review. *American Journal of Psychiatry* 134(4):357–365.

Esman, A. H. (1982). Fathers and adolescent sons. In *Father and Child: Developmental and Clinical Perspectives,* ed. S. H. Cath, A. R. Gurwitt, and J. M. Ross, pp. 265–274. Boston: Little, Brown.

Famularo, R., Kinscherff, R., and Fenton, T. (1992). Parental substance abuse and child maltreatment. *Child Abuse and Neglect* 16(4):475–483.

Goodwin, D. W. (1953). Alcoholism and heredity: a review and hypothesis. *Archives of Psychiatry* 36:57–61.

Henderson, M. C., Albright, J. S., Kalichman, S. C., and Dugoni, B. (1994). Personality characteristics of young adult offspring of substance abusers: a study highlighting methodological issues. *Journal of Personality Assessment* 63(1):117–134.

Higgins, J. W. (1953). Psychodynamics in the excessive drinking of alcohol. *Archives of Neurology and Psychiatry* 69:713–726.

Hill, S. (1992). Absence of paternal sociopathy in etiology of severe alcoholism: Is there a Type III alcoholism? *Journal of Studies on Alcohol* 53(2):161–169.

Johnson, V., and Pandina, R. J. (1991). Effects of the family environment on adolescent substance use, delinquency, and coping styles. *American Journal of Drug and Alcohol Abuse* 17(1):71–88.

Jones, D. C., and Houts, R. (1992). Parental drinking, parent–child communication, and social skills in young adults. *Journal of Studies on Alcohol* 53(1):48–56.

Kelleher, K., Chaffin, M., Hollenberg, J., and Fischer, E. (1994). Alcohol and drug disorders among physically abusive and neglectful parents in a community-based sample. *American Journal of Public Health* 84(10):1586–1590.

Khantzian, E. J. (1981). Some treatment implications of the ego and self-disturbances in alcoholism. In *Dynamic Approaches to the Understanding and Treatment of Alcoholism*, ed. N. Zinberg and M. Bean, pp. 97–127. New York: Free Press.

Koller, K. M., and Castanos, J. N. (1969). Family background and life situation in alcoholics: a comparative study of parental deprivation and other features in Australians. *Archives of General Psychiatry* 21(5): 602–610.

Levin, S., and Sears, R. (1956). Identification with parents as a determinant of doll play aggression. *Child Development* 27(2):135–153.

Levy, R. J. (1958). The psychodynamic functions of alcohol. *Quarterly Journal of Studies on Alcohol* 19:649–659.

Mack, J. (1981). Alcoholism: A. A. and the governance of the self. In *Dynamic Approaches to the Understanding and Treatment of Alcoholism*, ed. N. Zinberg and M. Bean, pp. 128–162. New York: Free Press.

McKay, J. R. (1961). Clinical observations on adolescent problem drinkers. *Quarterly Journal of Studies on Alcohol* 22:124–134.

McKenna, T., and Pickens, R. (1983). Personality characteristics of alcoholic children of alcoholics. *Journal of Studies on Alcohol* 44(4):688–700.

Mik, G. (1970). Sons of alcoholic fathers. *British Journal of Addiction* 65:308–315.

Miller, D., and Jong, M. (1977). Children of alcoholics: a 20-year longitudinal study. *Social Work Research and Abstracts* 13(4):23–29.

Molina, B., Chassin, L., and Curran, P. (1994). A comparison of mechanisms underlying substance use for early adolescent children of alcoholics and controls. *Journal of Studies on Alcohol* 55(3):269–275.

Mulinski, P. (1989). Male alcoholics' perceptions of their fathers. *Journal of Nervous and Mental Disease* 177(2):101–104.

Murphy, J. M., Jellinek, M., Quinn, D., et al. (1991). Substance abuse and serious child maltreatment: prevalence, risk and outcome in a court sample. *Child Abuse and Neglect* 15(3):197–211.

Nardi, P. (1981). Children of alcoholics: a role theoretical perspective. *Journal of Abnormal Social Psychology* 115:237–245.

Nelson-Zlupko, L., Kauffman, E., and Dore, M. (1995). Gender differences in drug addiction and treatment: implications for social work intervention with substance-abusing women. *Social Work* 40(1):45–54.

Nylander, I., and Rydelius, P. A. (1982). A comparison between children of alcoholic fathers from excellent versus poor conditions. *Acta Paediatrica Scandinavica* 71:809–813.

O'Connor, L., Berry, J., Inaba, D., et al. (1994). Shame, guilt and depression in men and women in recovery from addiction. *Journal of Substance Abuse Treatment* 2(6):503–508.

Penick, E., Read, M., Crowley, P., and Powell, B. (1978). Differentiation of alcoholics by family history. *Journal of Studies on Alcohol* 39(11): 1944–1948.

Perez-Bouchard, L., Johnson, J., and Aherns, A. (1993). Attributional style of children of substance abusers. *American Journal of Drug and Alcohol Abuse* 20(3):341–354.

Pulkkinen, L., and Pitkanen, T. (1994). A prospective study of precursors to problem drinking in young adulthood. *Journal of Studies on Alcohol* 55(5):578–587.

Ross, J. M. (1982). Mentorship in middle childhood. In *Father and Child: Developmental and Clinical Perspectives*, ed. S. H. Cath, A. R. Gurwitt, and J. M. Ross, pp. 243–252. Boston: Little, Brown.

Sarnoff, C. A. (1982). The father's role in latency. In *Father and Child: Developmental and Clinical Perspectives*, ed. S. H. Cath, A. R. Gurwitt, and J. M. Ross, pp. 253–263. Boston: Little, Brown.

Schneider, R. J., Kojak, G., and Ressdorf, H. (1977). Father distance and drug abuse in young men. *Journal of Nervous and Mental Disease* 165(4):269–274.

Schuckit, M. (1994). A clinical model of genetic influences in alcohol dependence. *Journal of Studies on Alcohol* 55(1):5–17.

Shafer, R. (1968). *Aspects of Internalization.* New York: International Universities Press.

Socarides, C. W. (1982). Abdicating fathers, homosexual sons: psychoanalytic observations on the contribution of the father to the development of male homosexuality. In *Father and Child: Developmental and Clinical Perspectives*, ed. S. H. Cath, A. R. Gurwitt, and J. M. Ross, pp. 509–522. Boston: Little, Brown.

Steinglass, P., Weiner, S., Mendelson, J., and Chase, C. (1971). A systems approach to alcoholism: a model and its clinical application. *Archives of General Psychiatry* 24:401–408.

Vaillant, G. (1976). Natural history of male psychological health—V: the relation of ego mechanisms of defense to adult adjustment. *Archives of General Psychiatry* 33:535–545.

——(1980). Natural history of male psychological health—VIII: antecedents of alcoholism and orality. *American Journal of Psychiatry* 137(2): 181–186.

Zeitlin, H. (1994). Children with alcohol misusing parents. *British Medical Bulletin* 50(1):139–151.

16

Sexual Dependence among Recovering Substance-Abusing Men

Douglas K. Braun-Harvey

Men recovering from a history of substance abuse sometimes face the disappointing reality that chemical sobriety is not the end of their problematic sexual behavior. They may find themselves able to abstain from alcohol and drugs, yet continue sexual behavior that is a source of confusion, secrecy, and distress. Addiction treatment professionals may also find their client's sexual behavior a source of consternation and frustration. Therapists may be perplexed about how to continue treatment and may find themselves personally ambivalent about addressing the sexual problems of their client.

This chapter will address the issue of recovering men who are disturbed by their preoccupation with excessive or unacceptable sexual behavior. It will review the theoretical conceptualizations of compulsive sexual behavior, sexual addiction, and hyperphilia/paraphilia and address the interactive influences between substance abuse and sexually dependent behavior among both gay and heterosexual men. Using the models of motivational interviewing (Miller and Rollnick 1991) and the change process (Prochaska and DiClemente 1982) as a foundation, this chapter will discuss a variety of treatment approaches for men with sexual dependency.

SEXUAL PROBLEMS AND MEN

Sexual problems such as compulsive sexual behaviors, sexual addictions, and hyperphilia are much more prevalent among men than women in treatment (Carnes et al. 1991, Coleman 1992, Money 1984). Various explanations are postulated for this gender difference, including the greater propensity for men to self-identify or to be diagnosed with having sexual problems. Gender differences have also been noted in other forms of problematic sexual behavior. Carnes and colleagues (1991) found that men engage more frequently in excessive behaviors that objectify their partners and require little emotional involvement, whereas women tend toward excessive behaviors that distort power. Carnes also found that men with sexual dependency problems intensify sexual behavioral trends already existing in the general male population, whereas women with such problems break general social conventions about women. According to Coleman (1992) men more commonly suffer from compulsive sexual behavior involving cruising and multiple partners than from multiple sexual relationships involving emotional connections.

Research literature seems to support connections between disturbed and traumatic psychological wounds in early life, failed gender expectations, and sexual addiction, compulsion or hyperphilia in men (Coleman 1990, Earle and Earle 1995, Money 1984). For example, the experience of physical or sexual abuse in childhood may force a young male to experience a gender expectation failure (i.e., not being in control, being victimized by an aggressor, and being forced into a passive role during sexual contact). This painful experience becomes deeply shameful as the boy learns through socialization that this experience may call his maleness into question.

Some men may develop sexual rituals that allow them secretly to cross their socially presented gender selves and explore alternative means of expression. For example, a heterosexual single man may spend hundreds of dollars a month hiring dominatrix prostitutes, which allows him to cross traditional male gender conventions without risking public social shame. Acknowledging the stress associated with male gender expectations, and helping the client understand his psychological response in not meeting these mandates, is an important component of treating sexually dependent men.

THE HISTORICAL CONCEPTUALIZATIONS OF SEXUAL DEPENDENCY

The cultural and historical relativity of sexual behaviors and the cultural-specific definitions of "controlled" and "uncontrolled" sexual behavior have been used to argue against the very notion of sexual deviancy. "What one society regards as being sexually out of control or deviant may or may not be viewed as such in another" (Levine and Troiden 1988, p. 351). Currently, the United States has three normative, yet competing, "erotic codes" of sexual behavior. Sexual behavior can be *procreational*, *relational*, or *recreational*. This means that for some, sexual pleasure can be valued only when limited to the context of procreation within a heterosexual marriage. For others, sexual contact can also be a means of expressing and reinforcing one's emotional and psychological intimacy within any committed relationship. Still others view erotic feelings and sexual expressions between mutually consenting adults, even between strangers, without emotional commitment as acceptable behavior. These conflicting views create an underlying tension in the conceptualization and treatment of sexual dependency. They are reflected in the many historical labels used to describe excessive sexual behavior among men, such as: the Casanova type, compulsive promiscuity, compulsive sexuality, Don

Juanism or the Don Juan syndrome/complex, erotomania, hyperaesthesia, hypereroticism, hyperlibido, hypersensuality, hypersexuality, idiopathic sexual precocity, oversexuality, pansexual promiscuity, pathologic multipartnerism, pathologic promiscuity, satyriasis, sexual hyperversion, and urethromania (Orford 1978).

CURRENT CONCEPTUALIZATIONS FOR OUT-OF-CONTROL SEXUAL BEHAVIOR

The key diagnostic terms currently used to label excessive sexual behavior are: *compulsive sexual behavior, sexual addiction,* and *hyperphilia*. None of these three contemporary terms is used in the *DSM-IV* (1994) as a recognized diagnostic category, and no consensus exists whether excessive sexual behavior can be described as an addictive disorder, impulsive behavior, obsessive-compulsive behavior, or a psychosexual disorder. Some attempts were made to include a category of a psychosexual disorder called "Hyperactive Sexual Desire Disorder" in *DSM-III* (1980); however, these attempts were abandoned (Coleman 1986). The terms reviewed in this chapter are associated with the original researchers who have written extensively to promote their particular theories.

Compulsive Sexual Behavior

The concept of compulsive sexual behavior is most closely associated with Eli Coleman (1990). Coleman defined compulsive sexual behavior as behavior driven by anxiety reduction mechanisms rather than by sexual desire. The obsessive sexual thoughts and compulsive behaviors serve the function of temporarily reducing anxiety and distress. However, these thoughts and behaviors create a self-perpetuating cycle since the temporary relief that they provide is followed by further psychological distress (Coleman 1990).

Coleman saw compulsive sexual behavior as a symptom of a more pervasive obsessive-compulsive disorder (OCD) in which the "anxiety driven behavior happens to be sexual in nature" (Coleman 1990, p. 12). Some experts believe compulsive sexual behavior does not meet the diagnostic criteria for OCD because sexual behavior involves pleasurable behavior and feelings. According to Coleman, however, persons with compulsive sexual behavior "rarely report pleasure in their obsessions or compulsive behavior . . . their recurrent thoughts or behaviors are senseless or distasteful"(Coleman 1990, p. 12).

Compulsive sexual behavior is exemplified by the married man who insists upon sexual intercourse with his wife several times a day. Varying the type of sexual contact, such as mutual masturbation, oral sex, or simply masturbating himself, is simply unacceptable. He needs the specific ritual or "fix" to avoid feeling depressed, nervous, or irritated. Another example is that of a gay man in a committed relationship who spends hours cruising gay chat lines on computer bulletin boards. He may spend all day looking for opportunities to hook up with a sex partner or engage in phone sex and then rush to complete home or work duties that will cover up the evidence of this compulsive ritual. The anxiety and stress of this cover-up plus living on the edge of discovery may lead to further compulsive sexual episodes.

Sexual Addiction

The term *addiction* began to be loosely applied to destructive forms of sexual behavior during the 1970s. This term may have been first used because the lack of behavioral control associated with men's sexual behavior resembled the behavior of alcohol and drug addicts (Carnes 1990, Coleman 1990). Published in 1983 by Patrick Carnes, *The Sexual Addiction* resulted in the popularization and recognition that sexual addiction is a clinically identifiable illness. Carnes provides an operational definition of *sexual addiction* as "a pathological relationship with a mood-altering experience. . . . The sex addict relies on sex for comfort from pain, nurturing, or relief from stress, etc., the way an alcoholic relies on alcohol, or a drug addict on drugs" (Carnes 1989, pp. 4–5). The sexual addiction becomes the primary driving force in the addict's life. Persons suffering from sexual addiction are called sex addicts in much the same way a person suffering with alcoholism is called an alcoholic. According to Carnes, a sex addict "transforms sex into the primary relationship or need, for which all else may be sacrificed, including family, friends, values, health, safety, and work" (1989, p. 5).

Sexual addiction differs from sexual compulsion in that in sexual compulsion, the sexual behavior is a means to reduce anxiety inherent in an underlying obsessive-compulsive disorder. In sexual addiction, sexual behavior is out of control and is relied upon for coping, nurturing, or stress relief that transforms sex into the central organizing principle of one's life. With compulsive sexual behavior, the sexual behavior is a serious symptom of an untreated disorder, whereas in sexual addiction the sexual behavior *is* the problem.

Sexual addiction may escalate, resulting in a progressive decline in psychological functioning for some, while others may remain constant in their behavior over many years. For example, a single heterosexual man spends his rent and food money on prostitutes, phone sex, and pornography. He promises himself he will not let this happen again, only to resume the same behavior three months later. Or, a gay man recovering from crystal methamphetamine addiction may have anonymous sex five to ten times a week, sometimes with crystal using partners, eventually risking his drug recovery to maintain his sexual addiction. Other sex addicts may substitute one addictive behavior for another. For example, an alcoholic man may have been arrested for anonymous public restroom sex while drinking. While in sobriety he may begin calling 976 phone lines to talk with other men while masturbating himself.

The sex addict has developed a system of faulty beliefs, impaired thinking, and a repetitive addictive cycle that can be influenced by family, culture, and other addictions. For example, he may hold the belief that his sex drive is just more intense than others', or if people were not so hung up on sex and just loosened up, there would not be a problem. The addict views the concern of others about his sexual behavior as a symptom of their problem, not his. He may also view each sexual activity as a separate experience and not look at the larger pattern of behavior. He will promise himself he will not go back to a particular video/book store or nude beach, but not connect this promise with the ten previous times he has made similar bargains with himself.

This addictive system repeats itself through a series of phases: initiation, establishment, contingent-escalation, contingent-deescalation, acute, and chronic (Carnes 1989). The first two phases describe the beginning of an addiction with the remaining phases addressing the growth process of a sexual addiction. In the contingent-escalation phase the addictive system is fully established and fluctuates in intensity depending upon certain environmental or emotional events. Most sexual addicts progress to the acute phase in which a break with reality occurs and the preoccupation with sexual thoughts and behavior is almost constant. At this point, either the addict gets help or proceeds to the chronic phase. In this phase, according to Carnes, the addiction is irreversible and no longer responsive to treatment, and the only way to stop the behavior is to limit opportunities through institutionalization.

These phases can occur within a variety of sexual behaviors. Carnes (1989) categorized all sexual addiction into three levels of addictive behavior. These three levels of acuity depend on the actual behavior and its consequences within the culture, under the law, for other persons, and in public opinion. Level one behavior includes behavior that is usually considered acceptable within the culture and is widely practiced. Masturbation, same/opposite-gender sexual relationships, pornography, computer chat line activity, and prostitution are examples of level one behavior. Nuisance behavior is the common factor in level two behaviors that include exhibitionism, voyeurism, bestiality, indecent phone calls, and indecent liberties. Such activities are not considered acceptable, are usually judged as sick behaviors, and may involve serious legal consequences. Level three always involves dangerous and victimizing sexual behavior and includes incest, child molestation, rape, and other forms of coercion and forced sexual contact.

Paraphilia and Hyperphilia

An alternative model proposed by John Money (1988a) involves neither an obsessive-compulsive nor an addictive disorder conceptualization. Money has investigated "paraphilias" or what are typically called sexual perversions or kinky and bizarre behavior. He identified more than 50 paraphilias that individuals may exhibit to achieve a state of erotic arousal or to achieve orgasm (Money 1988a). Some more common paraphilias include: exhibitionism, voyeurism, fetishism, pedophilia, and frotteurism (sexual arousal contingent upon rubbing the genital area against the body of a stranger in a densely packed crowd).

According to Money (1988a), sexual behaviors that are in conformity with standards dictated by custom, religion, or legal authorities are *normophilic*. An excessively dominant, prevalent, or frequent normophilic sexual behavior is called *hyperphilia*. Hyperphilia, as postulated by Money, is a pathology in which lust displaces love and lovebonding. This displacement results in the genitalia functioning in the service of lust, typically with multiple partners and with compulsive frequency (Money 1986). "The hyperphilic solution is one in which the lovemap defies defacement, so that the sex organs, in adulthood, are used with exaggerated defiance, frequency, and compulsiveness, and/or with great multiplicity of partners, in pairs or in groups" (Money 1984, p. 165). One consequence of a defaced or incomplete lovemap is hyperphilia (Money 1984). *Lovemap*, a term originated by Money, is an individual's specific template depicting his idealized lover and idealized romantic and erotic relationship with the lover. It includes a person's erotic fantasies and behaviors. Defaced lovemaps, which result from interference with normal childhood sexual rehearsal and development, lead to distortions in sexual fantasies and practices and are responsible for the various paraphilias (Money 1986).

Money proposed that some men with sexual dependency may be dealing with a paraphilic addiction. "In the language of common sense, an addiction always has a predicate: one is addicted to something. . . . The sexual addict is always addicted to something sexually specific" (Money 1988b, p. 261). The paraphilic sexual addiction is to something or someone specifically in the context of sexual arousal. Therefore, the person does not have an addiction to sex itself. Because the addiction is to a specific sexual object or experience, not sex, Money (1988b) concluded there is no such entity as sexual addiction.

Coleman made distinctions between paraphilic and nonparaphilic compulsive sexual behavior (Coleman 1992). When the sexual behavior used in a compulsive way to relieve anxiety is paraphilic, Coleman has labeled this *paraphilic compulsive sexual behavior* (CSB). Normative sexual behavior taken to a compulsive extreme is considered *nonparaphilic* CSB (Coleman 1992). Money has described a certain overlap between paraphilia and hyperphilia. He believed that the existence of paraphilic imagery and ideation may be masked by the hyperphilic behavior. For example, compulsive cruising and picking up of casual sex partners may be part of a person's paraphilia for having oral sex with the biggest penises. Money (1988a) also states, "It is not necessary to equate all hyperphilia with paraphilia" (p. 176). While diagnostically important, not much research or detailed clinical studies of hyperphilia have been conducted. Hyperphilia is partially addressed in the behavioral symptoms of sexual addiction concerning frequency, loss of control, and increasing preoccupation with sexual thoughts and acts. Paraphilia is partially addressed in the model of level one, two, and three behaviors discussed earlier. Together, these three conceptualizations—compulsive sexual behavior, sexual addiction, and hyperphilia—create a useful and potent clinical treatment approach to treat an individual with out-of-control sexual behavior.

SEXUAL DEPENDENCY

The term *sexual dependency* is used by this author as a general term to describe sexual behaviors that involve problems of sexual control and excessive, intrusive sexual preoccupation leading to psychological distress. It is assumed that any sexual behavior can become a source of harmful dependence, rather than just certain sexual preferences or object choices. Sexual dependency will be used throughout this chapter to describe problematic sexual behaviors, while ideas such as compulsive sexual behavior, sexual addiction, and hyperphilia will be used only in their specific theoretical orientations. All three conceptualizations see sexual dependency as a ritualistic, repetitive, rigid set of behaviors that require professional treatment and compassionate understanding from well-informed clinicians.

Etiology of Sexual Dependency

Much has been researched and postulated about the etiology of sexual dependency (Carnes 1989, Coleman 1986, Money 1986). Researchers agree that childhood trauma, an abusive and restrictive family milieu, and sociological and cultural influences contribute to a predisposition for sexual dependency. Some have also hypothesized genetic, neurological, and/or biochemical explanations for this problem (Coleman et al. 1992). Others have studied mood disorders in nonparaphilic male sex addicts (Kafka 1991), while Carnes (1989) examined the childhood family systems of adult sexual addicts using the circumplex model of marital and family systems. The circumplex model describes several possible extremes a family can reach in its functioning while providing a means and a vocabulary for examining dynamics in understanding the family system of a sex addict.

The inability of a person with compulsive sexual behavior to control behavior may be due to abnormalities in the basal ganglia and/or the prefrontal cortex of the brain (Coleman 1990). It is believed the compulsive sexual behavior is in part explained by neurotransmitter dysfunction that can be treated with serotonergic medications in combination with psychotherapy (Coleman 1992).

Both heterosexual and homosexual men can suffer from sexual dependency. Straight and gay sex addicts intensify already existing trends in male heterosexual and homosexual sexual behavior. Rarely will a gay male sex addict become preoccupied with the opposite sex. While heterosexually identified sexually dependent men may report experiencing same-sex contact, they are usually involved in this activity because of circumstances in which male partners are more readily available than females.

Gay men must deal with the added oppression that the very act of their lovemaking is illegal in some states, let alone considered perverse, deviant, sinful, and sick by many. Consequently, gay men with sexual dependency walk an additional tightrope in defining their own sexual health in a culture that relegates their entire sexual self to the margins of society. A sexually dependent gay man who is in the developmental stages of coming out may face additional stressors in his diagnosis and recovery from sexual dependency. For example, a 33-year-old single devout Mormon requests an assessment for sexual compulsion because he goes to pornographic bookstores to watch videos and receive oral sex from anonymous men. He is trying to honor the church's expectation of no premarital sex but of course is sinning even more deeply by being sexual with men. An extensive understanding of the forces of homophobia, religion, sexual orientation, and sexual dependency is required to understand this man's behavior and to establish appropriate treatment goals.

Substance Abuse and Sexual Dependency

Research and clinical experience support the likelihood of a higher incidence of sexual dependency among substance-abusing men (Coleman 1987). The issue of undeveloped or dysfunctional sexuality has long been a significant focus of substance abuse treatment and recovery. Yet only recently has the addiction treatment community been distinguishing between sexual dysfunction secondary to alcohol and drug abuse and sexual dependency that requires separate treatment from substance abuse treatment.

Sadly, the professional addiction treatment community does not have a reputation for effectively addressing sexuality issues. The spread of HIV and other sexually transmitted diseases has required chemical dependency counselors to confront these limitations. However, understanding issues surrounding sexually transmitted diseases does not constitute sufficient knowledge and training for therapists treating substance-abusing men with sexual dependency problems. Specific emphasis on sexual dependency assessment and treatment is a necessary part of a multidisciplinary treatment plan to address the unique clinical needs of a dually diagnosed substance-abusing and sexually dependent man.

The reasons for the strong correlation between substance abuse and sexual dependency are manifold. Many chemically dependent adults have rarely, if ever, been sexual without being under the influence of chemicals. The use of chemicals as a disinhibitor to begin exploring sexuality is a commonplace practice for American youth, and drugs are commonly thought of as a reliable resource for managing sexual response. Stimulants such as cocaine and methamphetamine have long been associated with intensifying sexual thoughts, feelings, and fantasies (Hoffman et al. 1994). Some cocaine users only use the drug in sexual situations while others may pursue or engage in sexual activity because of the heightened arousal. One study found that 60 percent of clients entering an outpatient cocaine treatment program describe a pattern of sexual compulsivity (Hoffman et al. 1994). Carnes (1989) has noted how alcoholism can interact with sexual addiction in a mutually supportive way. The alcoholic may rationalize his sexual behavior because of having drunk too much. Men who may be anxious about having sex may use a drink or another drug to help themselves relax or worry less about getting an erection or having an orgasm either too fast or not at all (Coleman 1987).

TREATMENT ISSUES

Many recovering addicts and their therapists are surprised to find that chemical sobriety does not result in stopping out-of-control sexual behavior. Equally distressing are chemical use relapses resulting from the abuse of alcohol or other drugs in order to continue the untreated sexual dependency cycle. A therapist's assessment skills and intervention methods are very important in helping clients maintain chemical sobriety while looking at the possibility of sexual dependency.

The theoretical and personal beliefs of the therapist can be a significant barrier for the client concerned about his sexual behavior. Prematurely using diagnostic language such as "sexual addiction" or "sexual compulsion" can send a client fleeing from treatment. Just as worrisome, these labels can send someone into yet another full program of addiction recovery before an adequate assessment and understanding of the sexual problem is completed. The premature referral to one of the various twelve-step programs (such as Sex Addicts Anonymous, Sex and Love Addicts Anonymous, Sexaholics Anonymous, or Sexual Compulsives Anonymous) may be motivated by the therapist's anxiety or discomfort with detailed discussion of a client's sexual world or lack of information and experience in treating sexual dependency. An added complication in such referrals is that these fellowships go by different names, are not unified nationally, and do not operate quite the same even if the groups have the same name in the same city.

MODELS FOR TREATMENT

A variety of treatment approaches have been proposed and carried out for the treatment of sexual compulsive disorders, sexual addiction, and hyperphilia. Treatment approaches are closely linked to the specific theoretical conceptualization. Men who suffer from compulsive sexual behavior are helped through a combination of psychotherapy and pharmacotherapy (Coleman 1992). For paraphilia and hyperphilia, the ideal treatment is one in which hormonal and talk therapies are combined (Money 1986). Sexual addiction is treated through a combination of twelve-step programs and psychotherapy (Carnes 1989). Missing from the literature are studies that address factors that motivate a sexually dependent man to seek and remain in treatment (Garland and Dougher 1991). While motivation is widely recognized as a key issue in the treatment of sex offenders, studies specific to motivation and sexual dependency are nonexistent. The remainder of this chapter will provide a model for treatment of sexual dependency that focuses on motivating the client toward change and helps the therapist to process the cyclical nature of change with his client.

The Change Model

James Prochaska and Carlo DiClemente (1984) developed a model for behavioral change based on six stages through which people pass to change their problems. Beginning with precontemplation, and moving from contemplation and determination to action, maintenance and relapse, these six stages describe the progression of change. A person's readiness for change or motivation to change is stage dependent. People must sometimes experience a cyclical repeating of these stages before establishing a pattern of lasting change. These stages are represented by a "wheel of change" that reflects the practice and repetitive nature of changing human behavior. It also incorporates relapses as a normal occurrence in change. Because of the universal human desire for sexual relating and the lifetime sexual history clients bring to the counseling room, a model that incorporates slips and relapses as normal, expected occurrences is essential for maintaining motivation for change.

This model requires clinicians to use different approaches and skills with each client, depending upon where he is in the change process. When using motivational interviewing techniques in a professional therapy setting, it is the therapist's responsibility to use stage-appropriate counseling strategies to motivate the client to the next stage of change.

A therapist committed to motivating the client toward sexual health will provide a conceptualization that motivates the client at a specific stage of change to move to the next level of change. For example, a heterosexual male with a three-year recovery from cocaine addiction comes to therapy with his wife. The wife reports that her husband masturbates in front of her every morning before work. The husband sees nothing wrong with his masturbation and accuses the wife of being uptight about sex. Although he is willing to attend the therapy session, it is important for the therapist to approach the husband in the context of the precontemplative stage for change. Treatment interactions that raise the husband's doubts about his current behavior and that increase his perception of the risks and problems associated with his current behavior will be more valuable than focusing on diagnosis for sexual dependency. In another example, a recovering alcoholic will consider treating a sexual problem only if his treatment includes an assessment for sexual addiction. Providing the assessment or referring the client to someone who can meet this need is very important.

Prochaska and DiClemente's change model is useful when treating sexually dependent behavior. Each phase from the precontemplative to the relapse stage is the backdrop for considering timely clinical treatment strategies that build on the premise of client and therapist mutually negotiating for change. Traditional clinical addiction treatment protocols emphasize teaching the recovering addict how to change, using a skill building approach, that is, "Do this now," "Do not do that yet." These protocols underemphasize how the therapist, by actively creating discomfort within the client, enhances motivation for change and resolves the client's painful personal ambivalence. The emotional and cognitive process of resolving ambivalence empowers the client to experience his own intrinsic motivation for change. Thus the principle for treatment is to have change arise from within rather than be imposed from without. Treatment sessions ideally will have the client, rather than the therapist, presenting arguments for change.

The development of the notion of motivational interviewing is based on the work of Miller and Rollnick (1991). They drew upon strategies from client-centered counseling, cognitive therapy, systems theory, and the social psychology of persuasion to design an approach that helps clients build commitment and reach a decision to change. While most therapists working in the field of addiction are armed with a treasure chest full of actions that clients may take to change their behavior, taking action is the fourth stage in the change model. Presenting action-oriented options when a client is still contemplating whether he is sexually dependent will not lead to increased motivation for change. It will also not help the client resolve the underlying central issue in front of him, namely, his ambivalence.

Precontemplation: Getting to Ambivalence

Men with sexual compulsion, addiction, or hyperphilia may appear for treatment at this stage in response to a recent arrest, a threat of separation or divorce from their spouse, or a workplace-related disciplinary action. In other words, the motivation for being in the therapist's office is due to the motivation and needs of someone other than the client. The community wants him to stop breaking the law and victimizing citizens, or the family or employer can no longer tolerate the behavior. The treatment goal is to move the client to the contemplative stage. This is accomplished by raising the client's doubts about his sexual behavior and increasing his reality-based perceptions regarding the risks and problems with his current behavior. In other words, the therapist fosters the client's ambivalence about his sexual behavior. Primarily, the goal is to have the client understand his internal conflict in a more conscious way. The client is "caught in an approach–avoidance conflict" (Miller and Rollnick 1991, p. 40) in which he needs to become increasingly aware of the costs and benefits of his unique individual situation.

Effective strategies are those that help the client see his ambivalence and articulate reasons for change. If the client revealed over the phone that he had a recent arrest or personal crisis, the therapist may ask: "You told me on the phone that you had recently been arrested. Will you fill me in on what happened?" or "What concerns have you had that you decided to give me a call?" These very elementary beginnings can convey that the therapist is interested in understanding the client's perception of his life, not the perception of the source of his motivation.

Listening reflectively is the distinct art of conveying a response that attempts to summarize what the client said. The reflective part invites the client to either clarify or confirm the therapist's assumption. This skill is especially important for working with sexually dependent clients who feel shame and defensiveness about their sexual behavior and anxiety when talking to a total stranger about sex. As sexually active as many sexually dependent men are, they can be extremely uncomfortable in speaking honestly to anyone about sex.

When the court orders a client to schedule an appointment, the therapist can praise the client for making the call, being on time, and speaking openly. For another client, affirming reactions from the therapist about the client's difficulty in revealing this part of himself and having finally accomplished taking a step toward honest self-disclosure can be an important reinforcer.

Summarizing the clinical session at intervals throughout the initial sessions as well at the end of each session can be very useful for sexual dependents. If the client is sexually compulsive and managing an untreated anxiety disorder, the summation can act as an organizing and calming experience for the client. It provides time to put several ideas together, since his anxiety may be interrupting his ability to reflect and review. For the sexual addict, a summation is a means of interrupting or slowing down an impulsive spilling of his psychological internal self. Without time for summation, the client may become so focused and dissociated during the session that he may leave the office in a mental blackout not unlike that experienced after a sexual binge. Summarizing can also be an effective tool to address a possible hyperphilia. The verbal review can begin externalizing the distorted perceptions that accompany the client's lovemap. The summary may be the first time the client has heard or experienced his lovemap from somewhere other that his own thoughts.

A crucial strategy in motivational interviewing, according to Miller and Rollnick (1991), is to elicit from the client self-motivational statements. The goal is to have the sexually dependent client verbally express his own recognition of the problem and voice concern about his sexual behavior. He might state a direct desire to change his sexual behavior. He may also express some optimism and ability to make a change (self-efficacy) in his sexual behavior. It is essential that these statements are made in response to the client's deliberating about his own ambivalent thoughts, not in response to a confrontation or a convincing argument the therapist may have offered. Self-motivational statements lie at the heart of motivational interviewing.

Miller and Rollnick (1991) review several strategies for eliciting self-motivational statements. These strategies include a variety of questions that invite the client to look more closely at himself without being burdened with judgments, conclusions, or decisions. Examples of these strategies include: "What else do you do that concerns you?" "What else are you tired of not being able to stop?" "What do you like about your sexual behavior?" "What would you miss the most if you were to change your sexual behavior?" The strategy here is to acknowledge the loss and the gain resulting from changing one's behavior. This is particularly important when dealing with the powerful feelings and sensations associated with sexual contact. Reviewing the positives of his behavior can also provide a window into the future challenges the client may face in maintaining his motivation for continued recovery.

Questions that invite the client to discuss the worst or most painful aspect of his behavior are also useful in altering motivation. For example, "What is the most frightening sexual situation you have ever been in?" or "What are you most worried will happen to you?" The therapist must not expect that the client will focus on the same issues that might most concern the therapist. It is very important for the therapist to know what worries the client the most, because that is the source of potential motivation for change in future stages.

If a therapist engages in a premature debate with clients, the result will be defensiveness from the client. Sometimes this is what a therapist calls denial or client resistance. Rarely does a therapist conclude after an intense exchange with a client that the conflict is a direct result of the therapist using a clinical skill that does not match with the client's current motivational level. Nevertheless, this is in fact what often happens.

Asking the client to reflect on larger issues beyond his sexual behavior will allow both client and therapist to meet the part of the client that has aspirations, ideals, and values that he holds dear. This information will be valuable in pointing out the discrepancy between the sexual behavior and these higher ideals. The trick is not to get prematurely focused on these contradictions. Allowing the client to express these ideals can help motivate him to contemplate his sexual behavior in more detail. Exploring these contradictions will be done at a later motivational stage.

The clinical circumstance of the initial contact is another factor that influences the precontemplative stage. Inpatient hospital programs specifically designed for sexual compulsive or addictive behaviors are rare. In an acute setting such as a hospital or intensive outpatient chemical dependency treatment setting, establishing the patient's motivation for being in a time-limited acute treatment setting is very important. "There is a tendency to think that when time is limited (as it generally is), you just have to confront people and tell them what to do. The problem, however, is that people's reactions to such strategies tend to be the same, whether or not time is limited" (Miller and Rollnick 1991, p. 133). The stages and phases for motivating change must still be experienced by the patient and worked through. The time to accomplish this work, however, may be compressed.

Contemplation: Tolerating Ambivalence

When the client is simultaneously considering and rejecting change, he has moved from precontemplation to contemplation. Contemplation may be the stage in which a person suffering with sexual dependency most frequently presents for treatment. For many clients, the therapy room is the only safe place to discuss their ambivalence about change. A spouse, friend, or even fellow twelve-step group member may quickly engage in a debate rather than listening to the internal conflict that may be surfacing. The pervasive ignorance in the general population regarding sexual dependence plus the lack of nonjudgmental resources to discuss "perversions" make the confidentiality of the therapy room an important resource. The most common mistake therapists make when meeting with a client at this stage is prematurely focusing on client actions. By focusing on resolving the client's ambivalence, the therapist moves the client closer to being ready for change and teaches him the most important skill he will need after any future relapses. The client begins to tolerate diverse feelings and motives, learning to evaluate these internal conflicts without remaining in the relapse state. To move beyond the discouragement or demoralization following a relapse, clients need to become very skilled at observing ambivalence and be empowered to process the ambivalence. Taking this step allows the client to move on to determining a plan of action to get back on his feet. Normalizing ambivalence as a necessary part of the change process provides the client one of the most powerful sources of hope he will need throughout his treatment for compulsive sexual behavior, sexual addiction, or hyperphilia.

A structured assessment process is an essential resource for the client to resolve ambivalence. Before beginning an assessment process, the client should verbalize to the therapist what he hopes to gain from the assessment. Male sexual dependents who identify as gay in orientation or consistently complete their sexual ritual primarily with male partners may be looking for a diagnosis of sexual dependency to confirm their own homophobic beliefs about their orientation. They may think their desires for men are sick and view treatment for sexual dependency as a way to end their homosexual desire or behavior. The client's goals and plans for using the assessment information provide insight into how he feels about his overall sexuality.

During the assessment process the clinician is faced with sorting out the disparate theoretical conceptualizations discussed earlier. Typically, assessment should include "a complete clinical history and psychosocial history, a thorough sexual history, objective and projective personality testing, sexual behavior inventories, and a family interview if possible" (Harnell 1995, p. 91). For adults in treatment for sexual-related offenses, a clinical polygraph examination and a penile plethysmography may be mandated (Earle and Earle 1995). A physical exam by a urologist will explore any internal or external damage to the genitalia. Personality inventories and other mood disorder evaluation measures can be of assistance. Assessing the interaction between sexual behavior and dependency on drugs, alcohol, gambling, and/or eating disorders is essential to revealing the coping function of the anxiety avoidant or compulsive addictive sexual behavior. Determining the extent of the patterned sexual behavior plus the individual's ideal sexual scenario is extremely important in the assessment process (Carnes 1989). Carnes has developed the Sexual Addiction Screening Test (SAST) and more recently the Gay Sexual Addiction Screening Test [G-SAST] (Carnes 1995). Given the recent success of pharmacological therapies, a psychiatric assessment for potential use of lithium carbonate, fluoxetine, and other psychotropic medications is recommended (Coleman 1992, Kafka 1991). An assessment of the client's motivation is another important component of a comprehensive assessment. This can be addressed by having the client create a decisional balance sheet that summarizes the perceived positive versus negative effects of the client's sexual behavior (Miller and Rollnick 1991).

Successfully navigating the normal resistances presented by ambivalent clients is essential to moving clients into the determination stage. Motivational interviewing suggests several strategies for dealing with resistance. They include using reflection, shifting focus, emphasizing personal choice and control, reframing, and using therapeutic paradoxes. No matter what form of resistance a client presents, from arguing or interrupting to denying or ignoring, these motivational techniques interrupt a verbal dance that the client has been repeating either in his mind or in his relationships. For example, a client may report he hired a prostitute the day after his last therapy appointment. Reframing the behavior by asking him what needs was he trying to meet through this behavior rather than letting the client focus on judgments or disappointments can increase contemplation regarding the behavior and increase the probability for a more determined course of action.

Determination: Toward Action

Recognizing when a sexually dependent man is ready for change is an important and sometimes difficult clinical skill. Important clues may include his complete cooperation with the assessment process and a genuine interest in the information and what personal relevance it may have for himself. Timely arrival for appointments and maintaining focus on goals without the need for therapist imposed limits is another clue that the client may be more determined to prepare for change. A general lessening of the urgency and anguish may occur when the client no longer verbalizes impatience regarding the recovery process or uses the therapy hour for constant reassurance. The client may initiate discussion of self-observations regarding his sexual behavior or thoughts that previously went undetected or were kept to himself. The client may have begun to experiment with initiating his own ideas for addressing his problem.

Setting limits on clients who are too eager to get going on their recovery is important. For some clients this rush into sexual health may be motivated by seeking approval or getting a spouse or partner off their back. For others it may be a response to feelings of anxiety or another symptom of an impulsive style. It is important that the treatment plan be a joint effort planned in a clearly articulated procedure that allows the client to ask questions and to understand why the therapist is recommending certain courses of action.

Another area crucial to maintaining client motivation is the actual assessment review and treatment recommendation meeting. It is recommended that therapists do not discuss any behavior changes during the assessment phase unless the behavior is seen by the client and the therapist as having grave consequences for himself or another person. Because behaviors such as exhibitionism, voyeurism, and sexual assault always have a victim, specific behavioral contracts or consideration of inpatient treatment may be required as part of the initial assessment. The specific details of what these boundaries may entail should be clearly reviewed with the client in the initial session.

To help with establishing a course for treatment, the client should write a personal sex plan. A sex plan is a written document that specifies which behaviors the client determines are no longer acceptable and those that may be high-risk activities. High-risk behaviors may make a sexually dependent man vulnerable to engaging in unacceptable sexual behavior. The plan also outlines the treatment and recovery activities he will pursue in support of his sexual recovery. This list may include individual and group therapy and telephoning other recovering men for support when thinking about engaging in unacceptable behavior. Daily ritual self-care like getting enough sleep, having daily meditations, being honest with others, and reading inspirational books are other examples of recovery sex plan activities. The clinician must remind the client that these are only initial objectives and that abstinent behaviors will change as he learns more about his recovery.

Certain twelve-step recovery programs define abstinence for their members. Sexaholics Anonymous (SA) is one such program. SA defines sobriety for the married sexaholic as having no form of sex with self or with persons other than the spouse (Sexaholics Anonymous 1989). For the unmarried sexaholic, sexual sobriety means freedom from sex of any kind, that is, abstinence. For single and married alike, sexual sobriety also includes "progressive victory over lust" (Sexaholics Anonymous 1989). The anonymous authors of the publication *Hope and Recovery* (1987) found that "compulsive abstinence from sex was just as unnatural to us as compulsive sexual behavior had been . . . [and] that behaviors such as having a sexual relationship with someone of the same sex, or having sex before marriage is not necessarily acting-out behavior" (p. 77). They go on to state that "whatever it is that motivates us to masturbate, not the act of masturbation itself, determines whether the activity should be considered acting-out behavior" (p. 77). According to Coleman (1992), "Treatment of compulsive sexual behavior does not involve eradicating all sexual behavior. Sexual expression is an important ingredient of sexual health. Patients need to set limits or boundaries around certain patterns of sexual expression" (pp. 324–325).

To increase the frequency of self-motivational behavior, defining acceptable and attainable goals that increase the client's determination toward recovery is important. If a client wants to end all sexual activity outside heterosexual marriage, then establishing a sex plan that reflects this behavior will be likely to result in increased motivation of the client.

If the therapist is concerned that the client's initial definition of sexual recovery may be unattainable, then the therapist can ask the client to anticipate the consequences of these possibly unreasonable objectives. When the client expresses the positives and negatives of achieving these initial abstinence goals, he may find a more reasonable starting place to define his abstinent boundaries.

The high-risk aspect of a sex plan contains a list of behaviors plus thoughts, obsessions, or preoccupations that put the recovering person at risk for crossing his abstinence line. From a compulsive sexual perspective, this occurs when anxiety triggers illicit rehearsal behaviors that prepare the sexual compulsive to slip into a relapse incident. Examples include driving by the adult bookstore when an alterative route is available, keeping phone numbers for past sexual one-night stands, and keeping the phone connected to 900 number services. For others, high risk may be failing to comply with prescription medication treatment recommendations or changing dosage or frequency without first consulting the prescribing physician. High-risk mental activities on this list include dissociative states, which are frequently experienced during sexual arousal, intense preoccupation with seeing most people as potential sex partners or as sex objects, or considerable time spent imagining erotic sexual contact with strangers met throughout the day. The more specific the written description of the thoughts or behavior, the more helpful the sex plan will be to the client.

The recovery list reviews the actions that the client will take to maintain his abstinence goals and begin the healing process. This is the area of treatment that seems to have the most agreement within the various theoretical conceptualizations. It is also the area where using self-motivational principles has significant benefits. With current treatment options for sexual dependency creating hope for recovery, presenting clients with a variety of recovery activities to choose from may increase their motivation. The primary task for the therapist is to help clients match treatment approaches with treatment goals.

Several factors must be taken into consideration when planning the recovery activities. First, a starting place must be identified. Overwhelming the client with too many treatment modalities and psychological issues is an error. Secondly, some combination of professional psychotherapy with self-help measures will need to be explored for each client. Also, a combination of individual, group, and family-based treatment modalities is generally seen as a necessary triad for resolution of sexual dependence.

Coleman recommends focusing on family-of-origin issues via individual, group, and family therapy. "Intensive treatment is best accomplished in a group therapy format with adjunctive family or relationship therapy. The spouses or partners should also be involved in the treatment process given that they are often similarly afflicted or need assistance because of the damaging effects of the patient's compulsive sexual behavior on the relationship" (Coleman 1992, p. 324).

Given the vast array and availability of options for treatment, how is a client to decide what recovery activities to include in his plan? This is where the therapist's clinical judgment, based on the notion of matching the person to the optimal treatment strategy, may work to the client's benefit.

Recent research supports an integrated treatment approach using self-help with psychological and psychopharmacological approaches (Earle and Earle 1995, Harnell 1995). Lennon (1994) has described how the Integrated Treatment Program for Paraphiliacs (ITPP) program combines a strong cognitive-behavioral component, a relapse prevention approach plus a treatment modality that is highly accountable and oriented to outcome research, while integrating the twelve-steps into the treatment regime. Mark Schwartz (1994) has pointed out that therapeutic programs that limit their treatment options to reductionistic and mechanistic views of sexual compulsivity are not sufficient to bring total rehabilitation to an individual. He has found that these methods are more successful when integrated within a comprehensive framework that draws upon many treatment philosophies, including systemic, trauma-based, addictionology, psychodynamic, gestalt, and feminist-humanistic conceptualizations.

Action Stage: Do It

This is the stage of treatment psychotherapists and addiction counselors are usually most comfortable in addressing. Setting priorities for action is an important function of therapy at this time. Having the client initiate group therapy or group contact is essential. The limitations of individual therapy will become obvious as the client begins to integrate sexual dependence recovery into his day-to-day life. This kind of significant life change needs to be discussed, processed, and supported. Whether in twelve-step groups, group psychotherapy for sexual dependency, or a psychoeducational program, contact with other people who are also motivated for recovery will be a significant source of support for the client.

Setting an expectation for group therapy early in the contemplative stage can simplify the client's later acquiescence to this treatment modality. By the time a person has reached the action stage, any ambivalence regarding group therapy should have been explored. It is suggested that clients in group therapy have a separate individual therapist. Individual therapy allows group participants to process significant issues in the privacy of individual therapy before bringing them to a group session.

Maintenance and Relapse: Ongoing Management of Recovery

The skills required to maintain any changes in the action stage may be different from the skills required to make the change initially. For example, a sexually compulsive man who achieves abstinence for two continuous months for the first time in his fifteen-year history of sexually compulsive behavior may experience many unaccustomed emotions. The excited feelings of success in response to his extended sexual sobriety are counterbalanced with feelings of boredom, irritability, and increasing anxiety. He must now learn to recognize and manage many new feelings. He may also begin to reveal the symptoms of an untreated anxiety disorder that has been driving his compulsion all these years. Although he may eventually relapse, the insight gained during this abstinence serves to solidify his determination for continued recovery.

In ongoing treatment, the important factor in a relapse is the response by the client and the therapist to the relapse. Relapses require the client to contemplate what led up to relapse and become determined to work to return to a maintenance level of functioning. This cycle will be repeated often as healing progresses. New treatment options may be added. Early treatment issues may become resolved, and the client may expand his definition of abstinence. Certain behaviors that were once high risk may now be seen as abstinence-breaking behaviors. A client who continues to masturbate but struggles with using mental memories of previous compulsive sexual situations as erotic imagery may decide that this is now a slip in his abstinence. Men taking psychotropic medications could decide to stop their prescription after consultation with their physician. Even if these choices lead to relapse, the important treatment goal is to help the client avoid discouragement and demoralization in response to this temporary setback. The therapist helps the client by normalizing the relapse and reframing it as an educational event in recovery.

Most treatment for sexual dependency takes time. Many clients are actively involved in therapy and self-help support for five or more years to maintain enduring periods of abstinence and recovery. For the recovering substance abuser who has already achieved years of chemical sobriety, finding the motivation to sustain that kind of commitment to healing his sexual life takes a great deal of patience and support. Additionally, the recovering substance abuser may have adjusted to a certain degree of pride in his recovery and find it painful to run into the judgmental and dismissive social context that currently exists for sexual dependents in most communities.

CONCLUSION

Treatment of substance-abusing men with sexual dependency is still an emerging clinical specialty. The paradigms for understanding these behaviors are still openly debated. Varying theories can result in particularly complex treatment considerations when a recovering addict or alcoholic committed to the twelve-step model for chemical addiction now must address sexual dependency. Motivational interviewing strategies are a useful way to help a client with sexual dependency issues. The change model also helps the clinician avert potential pitfalls associated with a rigid adherence to a narrowly defined course for treatment. This chapter reviewed therapeutic techniques for engaging the newly diagnosed sexually dependent male client. It is hoped that focusing on the early stages of treatment will empower clinicians who may currently be avoiding or dismissing symptoms of sexual dependency in their substance-abusing clients.

REFERENCES

American Psychiatric Association (1980). *Diagnostic and Statistical Manual of Mental Disorders, Third Edition*. Washington, DC: APA.

—— (1994). *Diagnostic and Statistical Manual of Mental Disorders, Fourth Edition*. Washington, DC: APA.

Anonymous. (1987). *Hope and Recovery: A Twelve-Step Guide for Healing from Compulsive Sexual Behavior*. Minneapolis, MN: CompCare.

Carnes, P. J. (1988). *The Sexual Addiction*. Minneapolis, MN: CompCare.

—— (1989). *Contrary to Love: Helping the Sexual Addict*. Minneapolis, MN: CompCare.

—— (1990). Sexual addiction: progress, criticism, and challenges. *American Journal of Preventive Psychiatry & Neurology* 2(3):1–8.

—— (1995). New screening test: G-SAST. *The Carnes Update: Sexual Disorders Program at Del Amo Hospital*, Spring, insert.

Carnes, P. J., Nonemaker, D., and Skilling, N. (1991). Gender differences in normal and sexually-addicted populations. *American Journal of Preventive Psychiatry & Neurology* 3(1):16–23.

Coleman, E. (1986). Sexual compulsion vs. sexual addiction: the debate continues. *SIECUS Report*, July, pp. 7–11.

—— (1987). Sexual compulsivity: definition, etiology, and treatment considerations. In *Chemical Dependency and Intimacy Dysfunction*, pp. 189–204. New York: Haworth.

—— (1990). The obsessive-compulsive model for describing compulsive sexual behavior. *American Journal of Preventive Psychiatry and Neurology* 2(3):9–14.

——(1992). Is your patient suffering from compulsive sexual behavior? *Psychiatric Annals* 22(6):320–325.

Coleman, E., Cesnik, J., Moore, A., and Dwyer, S. M. (1992). An exploratory study of the role of psychotropic medications in the treatment of sex offenders. *Journal of Offender Rehabilitation* 18(3/4):75–88.

Earle, R. H., and Earle, M. R. (1995). *Sex Addiction: Case Studies and Management.* New York: Brunner/Mazel.

Garland, R. J., and Dougher, M. J. (1991). Motivational intervention in the treatment of sex offenders. In *Motivational Interviewing: Preparing People to Change Addictive Behavior,* ed. W. R. Miller and S. Rollnick, pp. 303–313. New York: Guilford.

Harnell, W. (1995). Issues in the assessment and treatment of the sex addict/offender. *Sexual Addiction and Compulsivity* 2(2):89–97.

Hoffman, J. A., Mayo, D. W., Koman, J. J., and Caudill, B. D. (1994). Description and initial use of the cocaine and sexuality questionnaire. *Sexual Addiction and Compulsivity* 1(4):293–305.

Kafka, M. P. (1991). Successful antidepressant treatment of nonparaphilic sexual addictions and paraphilias in men. *Journal of Clinical Psychiatry* 52(2):60–64.

Lennon, B. (1994). An integrated treatment program for paraphiliacs, including a 12-step approach. *Sexual Addiction and Compulsivity* 1(3): 227–241.

Levine, M. P., and Troiden, R. R. (1988). The myth of sexual compulsivity. *The Journal of Sex Research* 25(3):347–363.

Miller, W. R., and Rollnick, S. (1991). *Motivational Interviewing: Preparing People to Change Addictive Behavior.* New York: Guilford.

Money, J. (1984). Paraphilias: phenomenology and classification. *American Journal of Psychotherapy* 38(2):164–179.

——(1986). *Lovemaps: Clinical Concepts of Sexual/Erotic Health and Pathology, Paraphilia, and Gender Transposition in Childhood, Adolescence, and Maturity.* New York: Irvington.

——(1988a). *Gay, Straight and In-Between: The Sexology of Erotic Orientation.* New York: Oxford University Press.

——(1988b). Paraphilia: motivation and nonjudgmentalism. *American Journal of Psychotherapy* 42(2):260–262.

Orford, J. (1978). Hypersexuality: implications for a theory of dependence. *British Journal of Addiction* 73:299–310.

Prochaska, J. O., and DiClemente, C. C. (1984). Transtheoretical therapy: toward a more integrative model of change. *Psychotherapy: Theory, Research, and Practice* 19:276–288.

Schwartz, M. F. (1994). The Masters and Johnson treatment program for sex offenders: intimacy, empathy, and trauma resolution. *Sexual Addiction and Compulsivity* 1(3):261–277.

Schwartz, M. F., and Masters, W. H. (1994). Integration of trauma-based, cognitive, behavioral, systemic and addiction approaches for treatment of hypersexual pair-bonding disorder. *Sexual Addiction and Compulsivity* 1(1):57–76.

Sexaholics Anonymous (1989). Simi Valley, CA: SA Literature.

17

Recovery
Issues
of
Substance-Abusing
Gay
Men

Douglas J. Warn

Alcohol and drugs have a significant presence in the gay community. Gay bars and clubs where alcohol and other drugs are consumed have traditionally been places for gay people to meet and socialize. The bars and clubs remain central to the social fabric of gay life, especially among gay men, and alcohol consumption continues to be one of the most visible behaviors of the gay male community. Other substances—cocaine, methamphetamines, and the so-called designer drugs such as Ecstasy and Special K—are readily available in dance and after-hours clubs frequented by gay men.

Addiction has long been a notable problem in the gay community. Researchers generally agree that approximately 30 percent of gay men and women experience substance abuse; the incidence among the studies ranges between 20 and 35 percent (Bickelhaupt 1995, Cabaj 1996, Finnegan and McNally 1987, Weinberg 1994), compared to 10 to 12 percent in the general population (Cabaj 1996). It is important to note the methodological problems inherent to incidence studies: there is no standard definition of substance abuse or, significantly, homosexuality itself. Moreover, the studies' designs are marred by skewed samples and poor or absent control groups. Further, most studies undertaken to date have focused on the incidence of alcohol abuse; only a few studies document the incidence of other drug abuse within the gay community (Bickelhaupt 1995). Nonetheless, the remarkable uniformity of results suggests the magnitude of addiction among gay people.

Although some principles of treatment apply to both gay men and lesbians, the biopsychosocial realities of homosexual men and women differ enough to warrant separate consideration. Male-dominated political, economic, and religious forces shape male and female experiences differently. In addition, socially constructed gender roles and expectations, coupled with the impact of homophobia and misogyny, create sharply differing life problems for gay men and lesbians. Therefore, this chapter will focus exclusively on treatment issues that typically emerge with substance-abusing gay men.

Note must also be made at the outset that homosexuality itself is not a pathology requiring treatment. Rather, the focus is on the addiction. It is important to understand the relationships between addiction, the gay male's perception of his homosexuality, and the diverse biopsychosocial forces of his life, so that the goal of helping him attain and sustain sobriety can be achieved.

Human sexuality is best understood on a continuum. Homosexuality, bisexuality, and heterosexuality are not discrete categories but are convenient referents to describe sexual orientations. For purposes of this chapter, the term *gay men* refers to men who identify their sexual orientation as either exclusively or predominantly homoerotic (Lewis and Jordan 1989).

ETIOLOGIES OF ADDICTION AMONG GAY MEN

The high incidence of addiction in the gay community has been attributed to many factors. However, theoretical paradigms describing etiologies of addiction among homosexuals must be reviewed critically: the existing literature has too often been flawed by the theoretical biases of the writers. In the psychoanalytic literature, homosexuality itself was thought, at one time, to cause alcoholism. Indeed, Freudian thinkers linked alcoholism to repressed homosexuality. While such psychoanalytic theories are no longer widely accepted and are even dismissed (Israelstam and Lambert 1983, Nardi 1982), bias is often subtly present in other approaches. For example, recent biological-genetic research into the origins of substance abuse and the growing evidence that homosexuality may have some biochemical or genetic component have led some researchers to postulate a genetic link between homosexuality and addiction. (See Pillard 1996 for a complete review of genetic studies on homosexuality and Byne 1996 for a review of neuroendocrinological and neuroanatomical studies of homosexuality.) Nardi (1982) has warned that such hypotheses are based on assumptions about normality and abnormality that mask bias (i.e., heterosexuality is "normal," but homosexuality is "abnormal"). According to Cabaj (1996), such a biological-genetic link is unlikely to be the sole determinant of addiction in gay people. He noted that the incidence of addiction is equal among gay men and lesbians, although male and female homosexuality appear to be different phenomena.

Other theorists suggest that cultural forces, social and psychodynamic factors, and behavioral rewards impact the development of addictions in gay men. Societal prejudices and stigmatization, cultural homophobia, internalized homophobia, social and legal discriminations, disruptions in familial patterns, social isolation and alienation, and many other biopsychosocial factors have all been cited as contributing to addiction in gay men. Clearly, addiction and homosexuality are phenomena with complex origins, developmental paths, and manifestations. (The reader is referred to Cabaj 1996, Nardi 1982, and Weinberg 1994 for a more complete review of the theoretical literature.)

CLINICAL CONSIDERATIONS

In many ways, treating substance-abusing gay men is no different from treating substance-abusing heterosexual men: establishing and sustaining sobriety is the primary goal. Sobriety must be established and concrete needs must be met before deeper issues can be addressed. Sober support systems must be identified and utilized; sober socialization must be encouraged and practiced. Moreover, the therapist must take an active stance in developing treatment contracts, setting goals, and monitoring sobriety.

Clinical experience shows that solid recovery from substance abuse cannot be achieved in gay men without carefully identifying and working through homophobia in all its subtle manifestations (Cabaj 1996, Colcher 1982, D'Augelli 1996, Finnegan and McNally 1987, Kominars 1995, Kus 1988, Kus and Latcovich 1989, Lewis and Jordan 1989). Indeed, other issues that typically emerge during treatment of gay men are impacted by homophobia: identity development and other life cycle issues, problems in socialization, body image, sexual behaviors, dysfunctional relational patterns, intimacy, and HIV/AIDS. Thus, treatment must be dually focused: recovery from substance abuse and recovery from homophobia.

HOMOPHOBIA

Homophobia is one of the most insidious and pervasive realities affecting all gay men. Weinberg (1973) has defined homophobia as the irrational fear, hatred, and intolerance of homosexuals. However, it is also important to understand that homophobia is closely related to misogyny. Indeed, this relationship is made clear upon examining common pejoratives aimed at gay men. Epithets such as "sissy," "fairy," and "fag" conflate sexual orientation and gender identity, calling into question the male's masculinity and virility as well as his conformity to socially prescribed gender roles and expectations. Antigay pejoratives frequently imply a "fear of the feminine" (Isay 1989, 1996) and equate homosexuality with stereotypically feminine roles: lack of interest in athletics, heightened sensitivity, aesthetic interests, and, significantly, passive/receptive sexual roles.

Socioculturally, homophobia manifests itself in many ways: "fag jokes" heard on the street, on television, and in the movies; rejection by the biological family; exclusion from legal protections; exclusion from participation in institutional communities (e.g., the church, the military); discrimination and harassment in the workplace or in housing; denial of equal opportunity; nonrecognition of gay partnerships and families; and "gay-bashing."

The persistence and ubiquity of homophobia affects all gay men. From birth onward, homoerotically oriented males are exposed to society's negative attitudes about homosexuality and homosexuals. Many homophobic messages are internalized by homosexual men, thereby setting up intrapsychic conflict about their desires, identities, and relationships. Homophobia becomes an internal oppressor that rigidly regulates and proscribes the homosexual's beliefs and behaviors (Malyon 1982, Margolies et al. 1987). Internalized homophobia induces shame, the feeling that one's very being is bad or corrupt.

Internalized homophobia becomes an aspect of the ego (Malyon 1982). It interrupts psychosocial development as identity formation and ego integrity become foreclosed. Patterns of cognition, object relations, and the configuration of defenses are also affected. Psychological integrity becomes impossible as the ego fragments and the psychic structures that define self-concept and provide the foundation for intimacy are suppressed. Internalized homophobia also impacts superego functioning, further contributing to the gay male's sense of shame and guilt (Malyon 1982). Self-hatred along with self-punitive beliefs and behaviors may emerge. In some cases, self-destructive patterns of behavior—including substance abuse and other addictions—may develop. A tenuous false self may develop to protect the homoerotically oriented male from social disapproval and enable him to pass as heterosexual. Consequently, social relationships become truncated, and the homoerotically oriented male can become socially isolated, playing heterosexual roles that are inevitably shallow and inauthentic.

The Impact of Homophobia on Substance Abuse

Homophobia certainly contributes to the persistence of substance abuse among homosexual men. Alcohol and drugs may be used to ameliorate the tension created by environmental and internalized homophobia. ("I get high to stop feeling bad.") Further, use of substances may loosen inhibitions so that the homoerotically oriented male can engage in activities he would otherwise find unacceptable. Here, homosexual impulses and activities are disassociated from the self and attributed to the effects of the drugs or alcohol. ("I didn't know what I was doing: I was high. I'm not gay.") Subsequently, internalized homophobia induces shame that overwhelms the client who then resorts to further substance use to reduce the negative feelings.

Similarly, alcohol and drugs may be used to relieve stresses created by stereotypically rigid notions of masculinity. Use of substances may ameliorate tensions that evolve when the client does not conform to socially prescribed gender expectations or roles. Alcohol and drug use may also disinhibit gay men, enabling them to adopt atypical gender roles in defiance of social norms.

Homophobia is an obstacle to sustained sobriety since self-acceptance of sexual orientation is critical to recovery. Unfortunately, internalized homophobia is not always easy to identify. While many gay men begin to identify environmental and internalized homophobia during the coming out process, the insidious nature of homophobia requires persistent therapeutic exploration, identification, and processing. Claiming an identity as a gay man does not mean that the client is free from internalized homophobia or that the impact of environmental homophobia is reduced. Quite the contrary: the client must identify the subtle manifestations of internalized homophobia, particularly as they emerge around social interactions, body images, sexual behaviors and patterns, intimate relationships, and familial issues. The client must work through the complexities of internalized homophobia and develop sober coping mechanisms so that sobriety can be sustained.

As with any client, the early stages of treatment must be devoted to establishing a safe forum in which to work. The therapist is challenged to identify, with the client, how homophobia has been internalized. Similarly, the therapist must assess the extent and depth to which homophobia persists within the client. The therapeutic relationship is critical to this process. The therapist must project a warm, accepting, nonjudgmental stance while also firmly supporting abstinence. A gay-affirming posture is particularly important for the substance-abusing gay client who is highly attuned to subtle judgments about his substance abuse as well as to environmental homophobia.

Lawrence is a 47-year-old white college instructor with a twenty-five-year history of alcohol abuse who entered treatment following a two-month period of binge drinking. During the initial assessment, he revealed that his sobriety had been sporadic and that he had been in treatment with several therapists over a period of six years. He expressed skepticism about entering treatment again. Lawrence revealed that he is gay, but was unwilling to discuss his homosexuality. Additional exploration revealed that Lawrence typically left treatment after three to four months because he did not feel comfortable discussing his homosexuality with his therapists. He stated that he felt "pressured" by his therapists to discuss his homosexuality when he did not feel ready. He also stated: "I feel judged because I'm gay, and I feel judged because I can't talk about it." He reported that he usually relapses within thirty days of termination. Aware of this pattern, the therapist chose to focus the early phases of treatment on helping Lawrence stabilize and sustain his sobriety. Sexuality and sexual behavior were addressed only insofar as they related to relapse cravings and urges. As treatment progressed and Lawrence's sobriety stabilized, the therapist began to explore the meaning of Lawrence's sexuality and its relationship to his addiction.

The pace of treatment and timing of questions are crucial. A probing question asked too soon may create such anxiety in the client that he may flee treatment. Careful attention to the client's language and behavioral patterns—especially sexual patterns—is warranted. Reaching for feelings and probing for the meanings of sexuality and sexual behaviors can be extremely useful. Exploring the client's self-descriptive metaphors is also helpful.

Finnegan and McNally (1987) have provided a useful guide for identifying and assessing the impact of homophobia. They noted that the emotional symptoms and effects of homophobia parallel those of addiction: denial, fear and anxiety, anger and rage, paranoia, hopelessness and powerlessness, depression, self-pity, guilt, shame, development of a false self, low self-esteem, self-loathing, isolation and alienation, passivity and victimization, and feeling uniquely misunderstood. As the therapist listens for and explores these signs with the client, homophobia can be identified and worked through.

ASSESSING GAY IDENTITY DEVELOPMENT: THE COMING-OUT PROCESS

Beginning "where the client is" is one of the central tenets of good clinical practice. This is especially true when working with substance-abusing homoerotically oriented men for whom a number of issues related to identity formation impact treatment. Consequently, understanding the developmental processes unique to gay men is crucial. The formation of a gay identity is a long and often difficult process, and homoerotic behavior must not be equated with the consolidation of a gay identity. The therapist must ask several questions: At what stage is the client in the coming-out process? (Coming out refers to the process of accepting one's sexual orientation and incorporating that orientation into one's identity.)

What does the client's gender mean to him? What does the client's sexuality mean to him? What has been the client's coming-out experience? Several theorists have studied the coming-out process and have developed useful paradigms for understanding it (Cass 1979, 1996, Coleman 1982). Although the number of stages differs with each paradigm, theorists generally agree about the sequence of events. Cass's (1979, 1996) is typical:

Pre-stage 1. Men or boys at this stage have a vague awareness of difference. They consider themselves part of the heterosexual majority. They understand that heterosexuality is desirable and acceptable, and that homosexuality is not. Gay men often recall feeling different at very young ages: while a few can remember feeling vaguely different at the ages of 4 or 5, most gay men first identified the feeling when they were 9 or 10 years old.

Stage 1: Identity Confusion. "Does having these feelings mean I am gay?" "Does having sex with another man mean I'm gay?" Men at this stage recognize homoerotic feelings and behaviors but experience confusion about their meaning.

Stage 2: Identity Comparison. "I may or may not be homosexual." Men at this stage tentatively acknowledge the implications of their homoerotic feelings and behaviors with respect to identity. Recognition that one may be a member of a negatively valued minority group creates feelings of loss and alienation. However, as previous feelings of being different are clarified in light of emerging self-understanding, the client may also experience relief.

Stage 3: Identity Tolerance. "I am probably homosexual." The meaning of homoerotic feelings and behaviors is becoming clarified. This is typically a stage of exploration and sexual experimentation. Men at this stage begin to focus on meeting their emotional, sexual, and social needs. Many consider disclosing their self-understanding to others. However, awareness of societal disapprobation typically tempers self-understanding so that the homosexual self is merely tolerated. The awareness of social disapproval also limits social interactions with and disclosure to the heterosexual majority. However, social contacts are made with other gay men.

Stage 4: Identity Acceptance. "I am a gay man." The self is clearly understood to be homosexual, but the inner sense of self as gay remains tenuous. The therapist must be careful to assess the degree of self-acceptance because the inner sense of self is still emerging. Many gay men experience their first sexual relationship at this stage. Gay men increase their social contacts with the gay community, and disclosures are made to carefully selected heterosexuals. Gay men at this stage often speak about a feeling of inner peace: "I feel like I'm finally at home."

Stage 5: Identity Pride. "I affirm that I am different from heterosexuals; I am proud of this difference." Gay men recognize the difficulties of expressing their identities in the heterosexual context. Heterosexuality is devalued. Pride and anger empower gay men at this stage as they abandon "passing" strategies.

Stage 6: Identity Synthesis. "I belong to the world as a gay man and am in control of my life." Devaluation strategies are reevaluated and abandoned; anger is diminished. Gay men at this stage express feelings of wholeness; feelings of frustration and defensiveness diminish. Gay identity is integrated into a whole self. Gay men at this stage are clear about their relationships to the larger community.

It is important to note that gay men do not progress uniformly through these stages. Identity development often occurs in fits and starts; regression to earlier stages may occur. Further, gay identity formation is not bound to any age. While identity development typically begins during adolescence, the development of sexual identity can be delayed until young adulthood or later.

Identity foreclosure (i.e., the failure to acquire understanding of one's self as a gay person) can occur at any point in the process (Cass 1979, 1996). Homophobia is often a factor in identity foreclosure. Similarly, substance abuse hinders identity formation because it reduces self-awareness. Rigid ego defenses associated with addiction (denial, rationalization, projection, and splitting) are typically used to suppress awareness of homoerotic feelings. Moreover, substance abuse numbs feelings and physical sensations. Finally, substance abuse diminishes the individual's capacity for taking personal responsibility: substance abuse enables the client to dissociate behavior from identity.

Awareness of the client's progress with identity development is critical when working with substance-abusing gay men and the therapist must be very careful to use language that is stage-appropriate. A common error is made when a client discloses sexual involvement with other men and the therapist labels the client as gay, compounding the error further by subsequently using gay referents in sessions. It is an even more serious error for the therapist to use pejorative slang in an effort to demonstrate comfort or solidarity with the gay client.

Alex is a 22-year-old, polysubstance-abusing Hispanic male who was referred to outpatient treatment following an arrest for possession of crack-cocaine. During the psychosocial assessment, he revealed that he sleeps with his male roommate, also a poly-substance abuser; he stated that he had been doing so for several months. Alex stated that he and his roommate share a bed because the apartment is too small. Further exploration revealed that Alex occasionally had sex with his roommate, but Alex stated that the relationship is presently platonic. The therapist asked Alex if he had "other gay relationships." Alex became agitated and quickly denied that he is gay. He abruptly concluded the session and did not return to treatment.

Engaging in homosexual behavior and viewing oneself as *being* gay are two different phenomena. Many substance abusers make ambiguous or impulsive sexual choices while they are actively using substances. Others engage in relationships that are largely dictated by the limitations imposed by their social context (e.g., prison). The therapist must carefully explore the client's relational patterns within their context and help the client resolve any identity confusion. Probing for meaning will also reveal the client's progress with the tasks of identity formation. Similarly, the therapist must be careful to accept the stage at which the client is, not where the therapist wants him to be (Cass 1996). Identity development is a process that unfolds uniquely with each individual; the pace and timing of development varies. Moreover, self-identified gay men should not be viewed identically. The label *gay* is loaded with connotations, and the therapist must probe for information and meaning.

ASSESSING OTHER LIFE CYCLE ISSUES

Of course, gay male identity development does not occur in isolation from other developmental processes or life events. Coming out is not a process unique to adolescents or young gay men. Indeed, many gay men do not fully enter the process of gay identity development until middle age or later. Therefore, it is vital to understand and assess other life cycle processes when working with the substance-abusing gay man. The issues concerning gay adolescents, young gay men, middle-aged gay men, and elderly gay men differ significantly. Because identity formation is the central task of adolescence, youth and young adulthood are particularly vulnerable periods for homoerotically oriented males who have not yet developed adequate skills for coping with homophobia and other social pressures. Gay youth are at high risk for not only substance abuse but suicide and a host of other mental health problems as well (D'Augelli 1996). In contrast, older gay men face many losses concomitant to age:

declining health, loss of social networks, social isolation. Losses must be processed and absorbed into identity. Depression is common among the elderly, and substance abuse may become a means of medicating depression (Berger and Kelly 1996). Middle-aged gay men may be struggling with generativity and creating legacies for themselves (Kertzner and Sved 1996). Substance abuse may be a response to the exigencies of changing health, aging, and changes in work identity. Middle-aged gay men are also disproportionately affected by the HIV/AIDS epidemic. Men who have the virus are challenged to reconceptualize themselves in relation to time as they face their own mortality. Bereavement is a powerful experience for gay men in mid-life for whom friendship networks and families of choice may be severely decimated by AIDS. Again, substance abuse may develop in response to the grief and fear related to AIDS.

The experience of being gay varies among the generations. Significantly, the impact of homophobia differs among the generations, and awareness of these differences is important when treating self-identified substance-abusing gay men. Older gay men have experienced overt hostility and homophobia over the course of their lives. They will often disclose their sexual orientation with great hesitation, and then only through the use of subcultural words and phrases (e.g., "being in the life"). In contrast, middle-aged men who came of age during the advent of Gay Liberation in the late '60s and early '70s view themselves as groundbreakers. They have developed strategies for using gay identity for political gain and to confront homophobia. However, middle-aged gay men have also sustained the heaviest losses to AIDS and have had to cope with a resurgence of homophobia. The youngest generation of gay men (i.e., those 20 to 35 years of age) have come of age during a period of increasing social awareness of and tolerance for gay people. Nonetheless, homophobia also impacts these men. In response, younger gay men will often defiantly appropriate homophobic pejoratives (i.e., "queer") to empower themselves and assert their identities.

The client's developmental position within the life cycle can guide the therapist to use the client's life experience to constructively support sobriety. This is especially true with middle-aged and older substance-abusing gay men who have developed lifelong strategies for coping with stigmatization and loss. The therapist is challenged to help the client creatively adapt those strategies to coping with the loss of the substance.

BODY IMAGE

Body image is a prevalent concern for many gay men. Self-esteem is frequently founded on body image and feelings of attractiveness. Indeed, images of youthful, athletic men abound in the gay media, and many gay men spend hours working out in gyms to attain that ideal. Much attention has been given to the oppressiveness of "ideal beauty" images, and astute observers note that pursuit of "ideal beauty" may be a manifestation of internalized homophobia.

Negative self-image and low self-esteem are highly related to the body images held by gay men. Clients may report feeling inferior when they cannot achieve "ideal beauty" because of their body type. Here, the therapist must be alert to the shame that often underlies body image concerns. Similarly, anxiety over "inadequate" body parts—especially penis size—correlates with low self-esteem and may affect the client's ability to have sober sex. Aging also provokes anxiety in many gay men who, as they age and are increasingly unable to sustain youthful appearances, believe that they will become ugly and unable to attract sexual partners (Berger and Kelly 1996, Kertzner and Sved 1996). Too often, these beliefs produce social isolation and feelings of despair, both of which trigger substance use.

Substance abuse compounds negative body image and low self-esteem. The gay substance abuser often feels unattractive. In exploring body image issues with the client, the therapist can point out that drug abuse and alcoholism diminish hygiene and physical attractiveness. Physical attractiveness, which depends on mood, health, and personality, will develop in sobriety. Feeling well correlates with looking good.

Mark is a 28-year-old cocaine abuser who is eight months sober. At 6 feet 4 inches, he is taller than most of his peers and has a slender build. Although he has put on weight since abstaining from cocaine, he remains slim. He joined a gym after achieving three months' sobriety and works out seven days a week for two to three hours per day. He states he does not enjoy working out but feels compelled to develop a more muscular body in order to attract men. He further states that he feels ashamed of his body when he watches other men work out at the gym. Consequently, he keeps to himself and avoids any social interaction while at the gym. Treatment involved exploring Mark's feelings related to his body image. The therapist challenged Mark's negative self-images and supported Mark's awareness that he could not change his body type. The therapist also explored the relationship between Mark's body image and the body-building activities in which he engaged. As Mark began to develop a more positive body image and accepted the limitations of his body type, he stopped going to the gym in favor of joining a gay men's volleyball team where he could exercise and feel comfortable socializing with other gay men.

The relationships between body image and addiction, body image and homophobia, and body image and self-esteem must be examined through an actively supportive yet directive approach. The therapist can challenge a negatively distorted self-image while giving the client information about body types and helping the client realistically assess the limitations of his own body. The therapist may also intervene by helping the client acknowledge and feel positive about nonphysical attributes, thereby shifting the base of self-esteem away from body image.

SOBER SOCIALIZATION

Clinicians agree that a stable sober social support network is critical to sustaining sobriety. Similarly, a gay-affirming support network is vital to ameliorating the effects of homophobia and consolidating a positive gay identity. Developing sober support networks and finding sober places to socialize is one of the greatest challenges facing gay men in recovery.

Many gay men have strong desires to form close friendships with other gay men. Bars and clubs have traditionally been central to developing social networks. Indeed, gay bars and clubs serve several important functions. Up until recently, gay bars and clubs have been the only places where gay men could gather and freely socialize, and in many parts of the country, particularly in small communities, this remains true. Many gay men make their first and only contacts with the gay community at bars and dance clubs. In addition, bars are places where gay men often meet sexual partners. Thus, the importance of bars and clubs must not be minimized, and the client's use of them must be carefully explored and understood.

While many gay men emphasize the centrality of the bars to developing social networks, substance-abusing gay men often reveal that the relationships formed in gay bars are tenuous and unsatisfying. Indeed, many gay recovering alcoholics and drug abusers complain of having no friends. Others complain of having difficulty developing and sustaining personal relationships. Therefore, it is important that the therapist not take a client's statements about his relationships at face value. Rather, exploration of the client's social network—its membership, its meaning for him, his fantasies about his social life, his fantasies about intimacy— is in order (Smith 1985).

The client's set of social skills is often a neglected treatment issue that may affect his ability to develop sober relationships. Substance-abusing gay men often develop a unique repertoire of coping skills and social behaviors. These behaviors serve to protect the gay man from environmental hostility while enabling him to meet his social and sexual needs. Many gay men acquire social skills that allow them to move within the gay bar subculture. However, they may not have adequately developed their social skills for use in other social situations. Treatment must address social skills deficits: self-confidence, sober assertiveness, the ability to engage in and enjoy sober activities. Role playing is particularly effective for helping clients acquire sober social skills. Group work is also helpful: the safety of the group allows clients to experiment with various social roles, practice and master social skills—especially assertiveness—and receive feedback about themselves.

Community resources may also help the client develop and practice social skills while simultaneously building social networks. Significantly, gay twelve-step meetings provide the gay substance abuser with forums in which to develop sober support networks. Gay twelve-step groups developed out of the perception that gay men bring special issues to recovery. Many gay men feel uncomfortable disclosing their sexual orientation and life problems in twelve-step meetings dominated by heterosexuals. These gay men may feel more comfortable sharing their issues in gay meetings; many recovering gay substance abusers report feeling supported in gay-positive meetings, in contrast to feeling different and peripheral in meetings with heterosexuals. The therapist should develop awareness of gay twelve-step resources and explore their utility with the client. Where clinically appropriate, the therapist should encourage attendance at gay twelve-step meetings.

Kus and Latcovich (1995) document ten aspects of gay twelve-step groups that help recovering gay men sustain their sobriety. Gay twelve-step groups:

1. help clients develop trust in others,
2. help clients share life experiences,
3. support clients as they work through homophobia,
4. help clients develop sober support systems,
5. help clients adapt and integrate twelve-step philosophies and principles to gay life,
6. help recovering gay men develop a sense of spirituality,
7. help clients develop a service ethic and leadership capabilities,
8. help clients develop social awareness and a sense of relatedness to the larger social community,
9. celebrate possibilities within clients' lives,
10. reduce negative feelings toward heterosexuals, especially heterosexual males.

It is important to point out that gay twelve-step meetings can be important means for helping the gay male work through identity development issues. Many of the issues that arise in the course of gay identity formation will emerge in gay twelve-step meetings. Identification with recovering gay men can reduce the confusion concomitant to the coming-out process.

Although gay twelve-step meetings can be an important source of sober social support, they may also be a source of conflict for substance-abusing gay men with coexisting sexual compulsive disorders.

> Richard, a 38-year-old alcoholic, was referred by his therapist to a gay AA meeting at a gay and lesbian community center. After his first meeting he reported that he enjoyed the meetings and found them supportive. He stated that he intended to return. Several weeks later, he reported that he had been attending meetings nightly and mentioned that he found gay meetings to be good places to "cruise" other men. He further reported that he had been picking up men and having sex with them after meetings. Further exploration revealed that Richard had long been engaged in sexually compulsive behavior. Although Richard did not believe that his behavior was problematic, he acknowledged that he relapsed several times because he picked up someone who had wanted to "get high." Treatment focused on educating Richard about sexual compulsions and their relationship to substance abuse. Group therapy and cognitive-behavioral techniques helped Richard identify and cope with triggers for both substance abuse and his sexual impulses.

The therapist must be sensitive to sexual issues as they impact the client's ability to socialize. Assessment and exploration of the relationship between substance abuse and sexual addictions is particularly critical. In cases where substance and sexual addictions coexist, group therapy may be appropriate. Limit setting and other cognitive-behavioral techniques may help the client develop skills for coping with inappropriate sexual impulses. Referral to Sexual Compulsives Anonymous may also be appropriate.

Colcher (1982) pointed out that the centrality of gay bars for socializing can impact the recovery of substance-abusing gay men. It is not uncommon for gay men to continue to go to gay bars once sobriety has been achieved. In fact, many gay men in recovery will often go to the bars for dancing, meeting sexual partners, and conversation after their twelve-step meetings. However, clinical experience shows that attending bars during early sobriety is counterproductive. Sobriety is too tenuous, and the client needs to distance himself from the bars in order to develop self-awareness and learn new recovery skills. While Colcher (1982) asserted that socializing at bars need not be a obstacle to recovery, both therapist and client must develop awareness of relapse triggers, cravings, and urges that are likely to be stimulated in the bars and ways of dealing with them.

Metropolitan areas offer many other opportunities for socialization. Gay social groups, political organizations, sporting clubs, and other groups exist, providing opportunities to meet men and develop sober interests and social support networks. In very large cities such as New York and Los Angeles, lesbian and gay community centers provide opportunities for interacting with a wide array of gay people. Therapists can encourage their clients to explore these venues in support of recovery. While urban centers offer other opportunities for sober socialization, gay men who live in suburban and rural areas may be unable to find places to meet and socialize with other gay men. Here, the therapist will be challenged to seek resources that will diminish the client's sense of isolation and affirm the client's identity in recovery.

SEX AND INTIMACY

The issues of sober sex and intimacy will inevitably arise during the course of treatment (Colcher 1982, Smith 1985). Sex and intimacy are subjects about which both client and therapist hold strong feelings and values and which must be approached with great sensitivity. The clinician must be aware of transference dynamics and, more important, his or her own countertransference feelings. The therapist must be careful not to impart moral judgments upon the client's sexuality or his sexual behavior and avoid equating the client's behavior with the client's being. The therapist must respect and accept the meanings sexual activities have for the client. Support for the client's sobriety, the illumination of the dysfunctional relationships between substance abuse and patterns of sexual behavior, and the development of a sober sex life are paramount treatment concerns.

Most substance-abusing gay men engage in sexual activity while intoxicated or high, and many express concerns about sex once they are abstinent. For some gay men, substance abuse coexists with sexual dependence or sexual compulsive disorders. Sober sex and discussions about sex are often undertaken with great fear and trepidation. Anxieties about sexual potency, changing libido, and male-male intimacy are common.

Many gay men experience sexual problems while abusing substances. Alcoholics and opiate abusers experience decreased sexual desires and feelings as well as diminished erections and orgasms. Cocaine and methamphetamine abusers experience heightened libido, which can lead to compulsive sex. Substance abuse affects hormonal balance and damages nerves, leading to problems with motor control and ejaculation. On an emotional level, substance abusers universally express anxiety about the ability to experience satisfactory sober sex. Smith (1985) has noted that many gay men assert that they can only have sex when they are high or intoxicated. Clinical work here must focus on helping the client engage in and enjoy sober sex. Masturbation and other self-pleasuring activities, nonorgasmic sex with others, conjoint sexual exercises, self-affirmations, and other sex therapy techniques can help the individual develop a satisfactory sex life (Lewis and Jordan 1989, Smith 1985).

Compulsive sexual behavior is common among substance abusers, and the clinician must be careful to discriminate between sexual compulsiveness and high-frequency casual sex. Smith (1985) has pointed out that sexual compulsiveness is driven behavior that gives no sense of satisfaction; in contrast, casual sex may be highly satisfying and filled with intimate conversation. The therapist must explore the meaning of sexual activities to determine whether they are problematic for the client and his sobriety.

Similarly, it is critical for the therapist to explicitly explore the client's sexual behaviors. What does the client know about safe and unsafe sex? Is the client practicing safer sex? Does the client know how to use condoms and dental dams? Does he use them? A review of the concept of risk, identification of risky sexual activities, identification of safer sex practices, and a review of condom and dental dam use is always worthwhile, regardless of the client's level of awareness. The therapist must also be alert to more subtle issues.

> Paul is a 42-year-old black businessman who entered treatment for alcoholism. He stated that he enjoyed cruising the bars in search of sexual partners. Although he stopped cruising the bars when he became sober, he began cruising gay AA meetings. He stated that he often picked up men, brought them home, and had sex with them. Paul stated that he used condoms and "usually" practiced safer sex. The therapist asked Paul to elaborate on what "usually" meant. Paul responded that he didn't always insist that his partner use a condom and that he did not feel comfortable setting behavioral limits with his partners. Further questioning revealed that Paul frequently engaged in risky sexual activities. Paul was given HIV/AIDS educational materials, and condom use was reviewed. The therapist also explored Paul's discomfort and provided assertiveness training through role-playing exercises.

The client may be well informed about safer sex practices but be unable to insist on engaging in safe sex activities with his partners. Similarly, the client who is unable to talk about his sexual behavior with the therapist may also be unable to set limits or insist upon engaging only in safer sex. The therapist must assess the client's ability to assert himself, especially during highly charged sexual encounters.

Developing and sustaining intimate relationships is a challenge for the recovering gay substance abuser. Many gay men express powerful desires for intimate relationships. Although the client may have had numerous sexual experiences with many partners, he may never have experienced intimacy. Here again, homophobia is an underlying factor. Many gay men have spent years hiding their sexuality from others. While they may have come out and openly affirm their identity, intimacy often awakens early memories of homophobic family experiences and feelings of shame. Overwhelmed by shame and guilt and/or lacking in strong coping skills, the client may flee the relationship or relapse.

Exploration of relational patterns is crucial to helping the client develop intimate relationships. The intimacy of the therapist–client relationship will be critical in helping the client develop the ability to tolerate intimacy. Framing the therapeutic relationship as a form of sober intimacy that the client is able to tolerate—albeit one with clear boundaries—can empower the client to seek other intimate sober relationships.

HIV/AIDS AMONG SUBSTANCE-ABUSING GAY MEN

No discussion about clinical issues with substance-abusing gay men would be complete without examining the impact of HIV/AIDS. The gay male community experienced the first casualties of HIV/AIDS and has continued to bear heavy losses. Although the incidence of HIV/AIDS among gay men has leveled off and even diminished in recent years, the numbers affected by the epidemic are legion. Through 1995, over 300,000 people have died from AIDS-related complications; gay and bisexual men represent 50 percent of the AIDS cases in the United States (Centers for Disease Control and Prevention 1995). Even those who are uninfected with the virus are affected by it: the very act of male-male sex has become imbued with caution, and gay men are routinely reminded of the risks unprotected sex now involves.

Substance-abusing gay men are especially vulnerable to exposure and infection. It is not uncommon for gay men to engage in sex while intoxicated or high. Alcohol and illicit mood-altering substances impair thinking, perception, impulse control, motor control, and judgment. Consequently, the client may engage in dangerously impulsive, unprotected sexual encounters. As the number of unsafe, drug-related sexual activities increases, the risk for infection also increases. Moreover, the clinician must not assume that the client will cease to engage in unprotected sex upon sobriety. Many gay men in recovery continue to engage in sexual behaviors that put them at risk for HIV infection.

Assessing the client's knowledge about and understanding of HIV/AIDS is imperative. Shame may prevent the client from acknowledging that he does not know enough about HIV/AIDS and its transmission. Moreover, myths and misinformation abound. A good rule of thumb is to assume that the client knows nothing about HIV and its transmission and to teach accordingly. The relationship between substance abuse and HIV/AIDS must be firmly and explicitly addressed. Information about self-protection must be provided. Periodic review of safe and unsafe sexual practices and condom/dental dam use are important harm-reduction activities. Similarly, intravenous drug-using clients must be taught about cleaning needles and the dangers of shared needles. There can never be too much teaching.

In addition, gathering information about the client's addiction and sexual history, past and current sexual practices, including their relationship to substance use, and relational patterns is extremely helpful. Compulsive, substance-related sexual encounters may also indicate such deeper problems as the compulsion for risk-laden activities and self-destructive impulses. Time and attention must be given to exploring the feelings that drive addiction-related sexual behaviors.

HIV Testing

The issue of HIV testing will need to be addressed during treatment. As the client establishes sobriety, he will typically recognize that he is at risk for infection. The client's anxiety about his unknown serostatus can be a trigger to relapse, testing itself can be a trigger, and obtaining the result—be it positive or negative—can also be a trigger. Since the goal of treatment is to establish and support stable sobriety, the therapist should recommend that, unless there are compelling reasons, testing should be delayed during the earliest stages of sobriety. During that time, the therapist should provide AIDS education while also exploring the meaning of testing with the client. Particular attention should be paid to the concept of seroconversion and the "window period" between infection and testing positive. This information usually helps the client recognize the ambiguity inherent in early testing and helps the client strengthen his impulse control. The therapist and client must also anticipate the impact of a positive or negative result before undertaking the HIV test. (Negative results can trigger relapse, as when the client feels compelled to celebrate his infection-free status.) Ideally, testing should be integrated into treatment planning. To that end, the therapist must approach the subject of testing with great sensitivity to ensure that the client feels supported. In any event, the therapist must always prepare to respond to crises concomitant to positive results.

The HIV-Seropositive Client

The HIV-seropositive substance-abusing gay man presents a number of treatment challenges. The newly diagnosed HIV-seropositive client may respond to the news of his seropositive status with rage, depression, relapse, suicidality, or homicidality. Relapse is common among newly diagnosed clients who rationalize: "Why not get high? I'm going to die anyway." Relapse prevention strategies coupled with supportive interventions that address the client's concerns about the future and his mortality are obvious therapeutic responses.

The newly sober HIV-seropositive client who has been living with the knowledge of his serostatus presents other challenges. The HIV-seropositive gay male may experience further stigmatization because of his HIV status. Consequently, he may be ostracized by his gay peers or, if he is in a relationship, abandoned by his partner. Indeed, relational networks often undergo dramatic shifts as the client copes with the realities of infection and illnesses. The HIV-seropositive client may seek to develop relationships with other HIV-affected people while the intensity of relationships with HIV-seronegative men diminishes. Further, the HIV-seropositive client will experience profound and terrifyingly sudden changes in his health. These changes are particularly startling when they appear after long periods of medical stasis. The potential for relapse is great, especially during the period that immediately follows the emergency. Finally, the HIV-seropositive client will express fears about death and dying. It is vital to provide a safe, accepting milieu in which to air these issues. Failure to do so denies a central reality of the client's life and may trigger relapse or other acting-out behaviors. However, focus must be kept on sobriety while support is given around medical issues.

HIV-seronegative gay men are also affected by HIV/AIDS. These men often assume caregiving roles for their ill partners and friends. The stresses of these roles coupled with the uncertainties of the disease can be overwhelming. Further, the impact of AIDS on the gay community has been enormous, as many gay men have absorbed multiple losses. The cumulative impact of multiple deaths can trigger powerful grief responses that can in turn trigger relapse or return to other compulsive behaviors—particularly sexual compulsions. In addition, many HIV-seronegative gay men experience survivor guilt, which can impair the process of grief resolution as well as the recovery process.

Issues for Clinicians

Substance abuse and the existence of HIV/AIDS present complex treatment demands and challenges for clinicians working with gay men. The therapist needs to develop a knowledge about HIV/AIDS, the diseases commonly associated with it, the disease's trajectory, and treatment protocols. Since the HIV-seropositive gay male will typically take a number of medications during the course of his illness, the therapist needs to be aware of their medical effects and their impact on psychosocial functioning. Further, the therapist may need to teach the client about the differences between taking addictive substances and prescribed medications. It is useful to monitor the client's health, medication compliance, and functional capacities in order to anticipate and respond to changes during the course of substance abuse treatment.

Above all, however, the clinician must take care of him/herself. Powerful countertransference feelings will be stirred up as the client experiences medical emergencies and increasingly debilitating illnesses. Equally strong countertransference feelings may be aroused by the client's attitudes toward HIV testing, safer sex, illness, and death. Countertransference feelings may affect professional boundaries; the clinician may unconsciously adopt a co-dependent role with HIV-affected clients. Burnout is also a danger. Supervision is critical for any clinician working with HIV-affected clients. In addition, a number of support groups for clinicians are available, and the therapist would be wise to seek out such peer support when working with HIV-affected clients.

GAY COUPLES

Many partnered gay substance abusers enter treatment. Indeed, the impact of addiction on a relationship may propel many substance-abusing gay men and their partners into treatment.

> Bruce is a 55-year-old attorney who entered treatment after his
> lover of twenty years threatened to leave him. Bruce acknowl-

edged that he drank "more than I should" but denied that he had a problem. He felt Robert, his partner, was overreacting to a recent fight during which Bruce had struck Robert and given him a black eye. Bruce stated that both men had been drinking at the time. Bruce did not believe that Robert had an alcohol problem and stated that alcohol had always been part of their relationship. Indeed, Bruce felt that alcohol was a normal part of his social world. Further exploration revealed that the couple quarreled frequently, but their fights had never become physical until now. Bruce reported that the couple's fights would often end with sex. The relationship between Bruce's drinking and the couple's fights was explored. The therapist challenged Bruce's view that his drinking did not contribute to the couple's problems and encouraged Bruce to abstain from drinking. Bruce agreed to abstain and was eventually able to discern that the couple's drinking patterns contributed to their difficulties. He then began to encourage Robert to enter treatment. When Robert agreed to seek a therapeutic consultation, the therapist provided a referral for Robert.

Clearly, the therapist must assess the nature of the relationship: Do both men use substances? What role does the substance play in the relationship? What is the partner's sobriety status? What has been the impact of the client's addiction on his partner? What is the function of sex in the relationship? Has the partner sought help for himself? While the therapist must keep focused on the identified client, some attention must be paid to the partner, if only for purposes of education and referral. Substance abuse affects not only the abuser but those around him. One or two sessions devoted to treatment for the couple is often useful. The therapist can develop a deeper awareness of the relational structures, boundaries, and stressors affecting the client. The partner can be educated about addiction and encouraged to seek help for himself, and the client's sobriety can be supported.

Other questions must be asked of clients involved in intimate relationships. Have both come out? Are both comfortable with their identities as gay men? What are the levels of internalized homophobia in each partner? Are both comfortable with the level of their sexual intimacy? Relationship conflicts are often rooted in developmental differences between the partners (Cabaj and Klinger 1996). For example, if the client is out but the partner is not (or vice versa), relational dynamics will be dysfunctional and become potential triggers for relapse. Relational expectations must be explored in couples therapy with a therapist who is sensitive to the special concerns of gay couples.

RESOURCES AND REFERRAL SOURCES
FOR SUBSTANCE-ABUSING GAY MEN

Knowledge of community resources is critical for therapists working with substance-abusing gay men. There are thousands of gay organizations (political groups, religious groups, social groups, sporting clubs), gay bookstores, gay twelve-step meetings, gay-affirming therapists, gay hotlines and switchboards, gay community centers, gay-positive doctors, and HIV/AIDS services throughout the country. National publications such as *The Advocate*, *Out*, and *Genre* are readily available. Weekly gay newspapers can be found in most major metropolitan areas. The *Gayellow Pages* is published annually and is distributed nationally in many major bookstores. Arranged by state and city, it provides a comprehensive list of gay resources and services in communities across the United States and Canada. Familiarity with these resources can provide invaluable support for clinical work.*

CONCLUSION

Substance-abusing gay men are challenged to recover from addiction and homophobia. Therapeutic interventions must thus be dually focused to establish and support sobriety. Such interventions must also affirm the validity of the client's identity and experience. Both recoveries must be concurrent if sobriety is to be sustained. Awareness of the issues faced by substance-abusing gay men, self-awareness on the part of the therapist, and an approach that balances firmness with flexibility will create a therapeutic milieu that supports recovery and growth.

REFERENCES

Berger, R.,M., and Kelly, J. J. (1996). Gay men and lesbians grown older. In *Textbook of Homosexuality and Mental Health*, ed. R. P. Cabaj and T. S. Stein, pp. 305–316. Washington, DC: American Psychiatric Press.

---

*There are a number of resources available to support the clinician working with gay clients, including: The National Association of Social Workers Committee on Gay and Lesbian Issues (750 First Street, N.E., Washington DC 20002-4241) and the National Association of Lesbian and Gay Alcoholism Professionals (Telephone: 213-381-8524).

Bickelhaupt, E. E. (1995). Alcoholism and drug abuse in gay and lesbian persons: a review of incidence studies. *Journal of Gay and Lesbian Social Services* 2(1):5–14.

Byne, W. (1996). Biology and homosexuality: implications of neuroendocrinological and neuroanatomical studies. In *Textbook of Homosexuality and Mental Health*, ed. R. P. Cabaj and T. S. Stein, pp. 129–146. Washington, DC: American Psychiatric Press.

Cabaj, R. P. (1996). Substance abuse in gay men, lesbians, and bisexuals. In *Textbook of Homosexuality and Mental Health*, ed. R. P. Cabaj and T. S. Stein, pp. 783–800. Washington, DC: American Psychiatric Press.

Cabaj, R. P., and Klinger, R. L. (1996). Psychotherapeutic interventions with lesbian and gay couples. In *Textbook of Homosexuality and Mental Health*, ed. R. P. Cabaj and T. S. Stein, pp. 485–501. Washington, DC: American Psychiatric Press.

Cass, V. C. (1979). Homosexual identity formation: a theoretical model. *Journal of Homosexuality* 4:219–235.

—— (1996). Sexual orientation identity formation: a Western phenomenon. In *Textbook of Homosexuality and Mental Health*, ed. R. P. Cabaj and T. S. Stein, pp. 227–251. Washington, DC: American Psychiatric Press.

Centers for Disease Control and Prevention (1995). *HIV/AIDS Surveillance Report* 7:1–18. Atlanta, GA.

Colcher, R. (1982). Counseling the homosexual alcoholic. *Journal of Homosexuality* 7(4):43–52.

Coleman, E. (1982). The developmental stages of the coming out process. In *Homosexuality and Psychotherapy: A Practitioner's Handbook of Affirmative Models*, ed. J. C. Gonsiorek, pp. 31–42. New York: Haworth.

D'Augelli, A. R. (1996). Lesbian, gay, and bisexual development during adolescence and young adulthood. In *Textbook of Homosexuality and Mental Health*, ed. R. P. Cabaj and T. S. Stein, pp. 267–288. Washington, DC: American Psychiatric Press.

Finnegan, D. G., and McNally, E. B. (1987). *Dual Identities: Counseling Chemically Dependent Gays and Lesbians*. Center City, MN: Hazelden.

Isay, R. A. (1989). *Being Homosexual: Gay Men and Their Development*. New York: Farrar, Straus & Giroux.

—— (1996). *Becoming Gay: The Journey to Self-Acceptance*. New York: Pantheon Books.

Israelstam, S., and Lambert, S. (1983). Homosexuality as a cause of alcoholism: a historical review. *International Journal of Addiction* 18(8): 1085–1107.

Kertzner, R. M., and Sved, M. (1996). Midlife men and lesbians: adult development and mental health. In *Textbook of Homosexuality and Men-*

tal Health, ed. R. P. Cabaj and T. S. Stein, pp. 289–304. Washington, DC: American Psychiatric Press.

Kominars, S. B. (1995). Homophobia: the heart of darkness. *Journal of Gay and Lesbian Social Services* 2(1):29–40.

Kus, R. J. (1988). Alcoholism and non-acceptance of gay self: the critical link. *Journal of Homosexuality* 15(1–2):25–41.

Kus, R. J., and Latcovich (1995). Special interest groups in Alcoholics Anonymous: a focus on gay men's groups. *Journal of Gay and Lesbian Social Services* 2(1):67–82.

Lewis, G. R., and Jordan, S.M. (1989). Treatment of the gay or lesbian alcoholic. In *Alcoholism and Substance Abuse in Special Populations,* ed. G. Lawson and A. Lawson, pp. 165–190. Gaithersburg, MD: Aspen.

Malyon, A. K. (1982). Psychotherapeutic implications of internalized homophobia in gay men. In *Homosexuality and Psychotherapy: A Practitioner's Handbook of Affirmative Models,* ed. J. C. Gonsiorek, pp. 59–69. New York: Haworth.

Margolies, L., Becker, M., and Jackson-Brewer, K. (1987). Internalized homophobia: identifying and treating the oppressor within. In *Lesbian Psychologies: Explorations and Challenges,* ed. Boston Lesbian Psychologies Collective, pp. 229–241. Chicago: University of Illinois Press.

Nardi, P. (1982). Alcoholism and homosexuality: a theoretical perspective. *Journal of Homosexuality* 7(4):9–25.

Pillard, R. C. (1996). Homosexuality from a familial and genetic perspective. In *Textbook of Homosexuality and Mental Health,* ed. R. P. Cabaj and T. S. Stein, pp. 155–128. Washington, DC: American Psychiatric Press.

Smith, T. M. (1985). Specific approaches and techniques in the treatment of gay male alcohol abusers. In *Gay and Sober: Directions for Counseling and Therapy,* ed. T. O. Ziebold and J. E. Mongeon, pp. 53–70. New York: Harrington Park.

Weinberg, G. (1973). *Society and the Healthy Homosexual.* New York: Anchor/Doubleday.

Weinberg, T. S. (1994). *Gay Men, Drinking, and Alcoholism.* Carbondale and Edwardsville, IL: Southern Illinois University Press.

18

Substance-Abusing Male Executives

M a r k   C o h e n

The abuse of alcohol and other drugs is prevalent throughout all socio-economic strata of American society, including business executives. As pointed out in a 1994 article in *The New York Times*: "Wardell R. Lazard, a prominent Wall Street executive died from an accidental drug overdose, and Larry Kudlow, a top Wall Street economist, owned up to a drug and alcohol habit (as) the nation remembered (that) drugs and alcohol are as big a problem in business as they are everywhere else" (Cohen and Solomon 1994, p. F11).

According to Summers (1990), in a moderate size company of 5,000 employees, chances are that 15 out of the 250 top executives are alcoholics. Stimmel (1984), examining chemical use among the affluent, concluded that 26 percent of the drug abusers studied held significant professional or managerial jobs, while Flax (1985) estimated that up to 10 percent of highly placed executives are drug or alcohol impaired or both. This proportion is not very different from that found in the overall workforce.

The overwhelming majority of executives are male. These men function within a subculture that is based upon traditional male values. The distinction between substance-abusing executives and other substance-abusing men lies in the broad impact that the executives' illness has on the lives of many others. There are also differences in the way their illness manifests itself. Gender-specific treatment that acknowledges the male executive's special role helps to maximize the chance for recovery. The purpose of this chapter is to describe substance-abusing male executives and how their role impacts on their condition and affects their own self-perceptions and the functioning of the organizations that they lead. It will also focus on treatment issues and approaches when helping male executives.

MALE QUALITIES IN THE BUSINESS WORLD

Much has been written recently about the increased stress in today's business environment (Harris and Cohen 1994). Highly successful executives, like other people, are vulnerable to stress and will seek out a means of reducing it when it becomes burdensome. Yet as described by Kipnis (1992), "Our predominant male self-image is tough, strong, optimistic and cool" (p. 30), and American men frequently deny their vulnerability because they grew up in a warrior culture. The American business culture sees the entrepreneur, the takeover warrior, and the inexhaustible team player as heroic ideals and discourages behaviors that conflict with this value base, such as acknowledging and reacting to stress. Since such perceived weakness compromises the business executive's public image, he will often go to great lengths to avoid being seen as stressed.

Drinking alcohol provides an acceptable and, at times, an encouraged, valued means of functioning in a stressful business environment. It is an expected and readily accepted part of our business culture. Although the majority of business executives function well in such a drinking culture, some are unable to do so. As their addiction progresses, their performance becomes increasingly impaired. Their inability to be culturally appropriate is viewed as a liability and a weakness.

The qualities traditionally associated with male executives are strength, clarity, decisiveness, intelligence, endurance, skill, and a highly competitive spirit. Men with those qualities are afforded respect and status in our society. They are clearly viewed as leaders and as authorities. As this perception builds, both the male executive and those around him become increasingly secure with his authoritative role. Consequently, he is less likely to be challenged when his use of chemicals compromises his performance. Rather, it is rationalized as "he's just having a bad day." A high-profile corporate life style and accompanying image create an appearance of invulnerability to drug and drinking problems. How could a self-achieving, bright, and successful businessman not be in control of his need for chemicals when he has already demonstrated the abilities to be a winner in the world of business? The perception that has been formed of the executive as one who has made it, has come through in times of crisis, a man who is able to handle the stresses associated with the daily challenges in business all seem to promote the image of a man who is the opposite of the mental picture people have of a substance abuser.

When an executive has authority he also has power. He is expected to have the power to accomplish difficult tasks and to achieve against the odds. This assumes a capacity to adapt, to effect change, and to control events that may be inconsistent with successful outcomes. As a result, corporate leaders assume that the executive who is abusing alcohol or other chemicals will be able to change himself. He is expected to have the willpower to control his alcohol or drug use and continue to perform well for his company. Barbara McCrady (1989) has pointed out that when drug or alcohol abuse leads to inability to cover up the impairment, mounting anxiety contributes further to decreased effectiveness in business practice. The overall deterioration in performance increases as the substance abuse progresses. When the ability to function of corporate leaders is impaired because of stress or their maladapted methodologies for coping with it, the organizations that they lead suffer.

IMPACT OF SUBSTANCE ABUSING EXECUTIVES

Speaking from a managerial point of view, Speller (1989) stated that "although alcoholism . . . can strike anyone, the potential effect . . . [of alcoholism] on an upper-level or senior executive is much greater than that on an hourly employee, supervisory manager, or middle manager. Alcoholic . . . senior executives are very costly to all organizations, whether private or public, large or small" (p. xiii). Since the top 5 percent of any organization formulates and operationalizes its strategic plan and provides the necessary leadership to achieve its business objectives, the future of the remaining 95 percent of the workforce is potentially compromised by the impaired performance of alcohol- or drug-abusing executives.

A CEO, president, or executive vice president provides direction, guidance, and overall leadership while engaging in a wide range of activities that enable a business organization to function and succeed. When impaired, the executive's ability to consistently perform these functions is greatly compromised. Behavior becomes erratic and inconsistent. Decision making and the use of sound judgment are skewed. There are even times when no decision is made for fear of making the wrong one. Reliability diminishes with an increased loss of control and a declining consciousness of the overall mission. Other key executives are often left to function more independently than would otherwise be the case. They are also forced to pick up the slack—to do more in the impaired executive's "functional absence." And if they, too, happen to be impaired, the organization's health and growth potential declines in a geometric progression.

Even when the CEO is healthy, impairment in key executives and department heads may have this same adverse impact, as their department's performance suffers even though the organization as a whole may still be able to prosper. "Complicating this picture is the fact that many seriously impaired senior executives as well as subordinates will still have periods when their behavior and performance appear quite normal, appropriate, and acceptable" (Speller 1989, p. 7). Given the skill, expertise, and overall ability of most executives, they occasionally perform admirably while on a specific project. Some executives are able to stop drinking at times or to drink less for several weeks and thus are still able to do their job. Unfortunately, this ultimately serves to reinforce the notion that everything is fine and increases their denial. Only when the project is concluded and the executive continues to drink or drug does the adverse impact of his substance abuse take an increasing toll on his co-workers and subordinates.

When leaders become less effective, the organizations that they lead deteriorate. There may be a gradual loss of coordination between key divisions, a decline in clarity of objectives, an increase in conflicting priorities, an increase in intradepartmental conflict or competition, patterns of unsound resource allocation, and an inability to "stay the course." Solutions to these problems are either focused on the external business environment or on a particular internal issue or division, seldom on the leader. Denying the executive's impaired performance, rationalizing the reasons for the organization's decline, and clinging to a delusional belief system that everything will be fine if just one variable is quickly changed simply serves to reinforce the impaired executive's defenses and enables his self-defeating and organizational disabling behavior to continue. Impulsive decision making ("the quick fix") becomes a way of doing business. The impaired CEO's grandiosity and narcissistic view of himself and his company are combined with the traditional defenses of the chemically dependent person to form a tightly knit and skewed alibi system to explain the many difficulties that the organization now faces.

It is only when the ultimate indicator of corporate well-being—the bottom line—decreases that the company's progressive decline from health to impaired functioning becomes visible. Consequently, the CEO may increasingly blame someone or something else for the decline in profits. Ultimately, competition and tension among the CEO's inner circle develops as team players scramble to survive, each attempting to formulate solutions while simultaneously vying for the CEO's ear. The organization's future becomes bleaker as the internal chaos continues to escalate. Mark Stevens' book *Sudden Death: The Rise and Fall of E. F. Hutton*, published in 1989, describes the progressive deterioration of the company's chairman and CEO that resulted in an adverse outcome for thousands of people and highlights the executive's unique role. Stevens stated that "the CEO's obsession with the liquor bottle finally caught up to him. The man who had once been the gutsiest leader on Wall Street was now frozen in place" (p. 139). He couldn't make a decision. "While he was twiddling his thumbs, the organization was out of control . . . he was a drunken stumblebum" (Stevens 1989, pp. 138, 140).

Corporate culture can help to maintain a support system for the impaired executive that perpetuates his assumption that only external events are in need of change. Drinking alcohol can be interwoven in this culture and, as such, can ensure the continuation of the executive's illness. The corporate culture can serve to insulate the impaired executive from the realities and consequences of his disease by providing people and support systems who cover up mistakes, screen telephone calls, diminish exposure, and provide everything from information to reports that support the image that business is proceeding as usual.

As the executive's functioning deteriorates, those around him frequently view his alcohol or drug consumption as the symptom rather than the cause of the enveloping stress. His executive team members may make excuses for him, cover up missed appointments, fabricate inappropriate responses, and justify outright mistakes while attempting to explain away his behavior through external events. Although everyone suspects that something is wrong, rarely will anyone attribute the decline in performance and organizational disarray to the executive's alcohol or other drug abuse. Ironically, the executive's success in business and his accompanying status and compensation directly contribute to his exceptionally strong defense system, which supports the executive's perception that he cannot have a drinking or drug abuse problem.

Such behavior by business subordinates is not surprising. The futures of these key players are perceived as being tied to the team's leader. Their vested interests dictate trying to help the impaired executive implement business strategies. Even when aware of the cause of the executive's dysfunction, telling their boss that he drinks too much may be accompanied by a fear of dire consequences. Also, if they themselves drink extensively, they may rationalize that it is just part of doing business.

Studying patterns of executive impairment, Charles Shirley (quoted in O'Connell 1986) found that 76 percent of newly sober executives reported that their secretaries conducted elaborate cover-up operations, and 60 percent said their fellow executives had protected them while they were drinking. One telling statistic was that more than 90 percent of the alcoholic executives had found it necessary to come in early, stay late, and work on weekends to compensate for an inability to get work done during normal hours.

GETTING THE EXECUTIVE TO TREATMENT

The day-to-day realities of business executives, especially men, serve to reinforce the notion of their having immunity from alcohol and other drug problems. Their defenses, most notably their denial, are continually validated by their position and by those with whom they interact. Colleagues and superiors, as well as the organization for which they work, often unwittingly contribute to the executive's illness by perpetuating the idea that everything is fine and that the executive's problems are not related to his drinking or drugging. Since executives have more power and autonomy than other workers, workplace intervention or confrontation, which can ultimately result in treatment, rarely occurs unless there is a major workplace crisis with extreme and clear negative consequences for the work organization.

Someone or something eventually has to change the pattern. On occasion, a corporate crisis will serve this end—a takeover attempt or a drastic error with potentially catastrophic results. However, most often, it is a family member, a friend, or colleague who confronts the impaired executive in a firm but caring manner (Casolaro and Smith 1993, O'Connell 1986). This is exemplified in the case of a well-known chairman of an insurance company who, over a decade ago, described on a nationally televised program how a business associate stated that he no longer wanted to do business with him because of his drinking. He went on to say how surprised, angry, and defensive he became but how this event served as a turning point in changing his life and his career for the better.

Job-based confrontation for executives differs somewhat from the more typical response when a lower-level employee is impaired. One major reason for this difference is that the responsibilities of lower-level employees are more narrowly defined, making their declining performance easier to observe and document. Such lower-level employees are usually held accountable for their declining job performance and are referred for help. Their impending job jeopardy status serves as the motivation to follow professional recommendations. However, high-level executives are rarely held accountable for performance in this same manner. When they are working longer hours ("putting in the effort") and continually demonstrating concern for the company's future ("merging the organization's life with one's own") they are seemingly addressing the appropriate standards for accountability of top-level executives. From an operational point of view, the CEO does not even have a boss. Although he is accountable to the company's board of directors, ongoing familiarity with the CEO's day-to-day functioning and performance is not possible. Consequently, the process of getting the impaired executive to obtain substance abuse treatment through traditional means is greatly diminished.

EXECUTIVE INTERVENTION

Although statements from co-workers, family members, or friends may eventually serve as the impetus for an impaired executive to seek help, this approach leaves much to chance. A proactive attempt at remedying the situation by engaging in an intervention process is almost always preferable. An intervention is a structured process that provides the opportunity for the alcoholic or other drug dependent person to get well. Its specific purpose is to help the impaired executive face the negative consequences of his chemical use and help him see that *only* through following a professionally prescribed course of treatment can these consequences be reversed (Casolaro and Smith 1993).

During the intervention the impaired executive is confronted by the group of people who have been most affected by his illness. The group is composed of those who are closest to the executive professionally and/or personally and who also have some leverage (both formal and informal authority) in his life. At the corporate office, they explain how they have been hurt by his actions, what the consequences of his not changing will be, and that they care about him and want him to get well. The message is conveyed with compassion, clarity, and unwavering resolve (Johnson 1987).

The intervention process is led by a specially trained professional (called an interventionist) who has met with, coached, and prepared each of the three or four executive members of the intervention team. They plan to meet with the impaired executive on a morning when they are assured that he will be present in the corporate office. Mornings are preferred because the impaired executive is more likely to be relatively sober and coherent (Casolaro and Smith 1993). Since most executives see company sponsored employee assistance programs (EAPs) as more appropriate for the average employee than for themselves, the interventionist is almost always an external consultant whose focus is to help the impaired executive function well once again.

Immediately following the intervention, the professional meets alone with the impaired executive in order to implement an individualized designated plan for his recovery that is based upon the clinical determinations made during the interventionist's evaluation. Should the intervention fail to accomplish its objectives, the interventionist continues to coach the members of the group in order help them initiate the consequences associated with noncompliance.

The following case example highlights the impact of a senior executive's use of chemicals and the value and process of intervention:

Bill is a CEO of a major company whose revenues exceed 450 million dollars a year. Before his promotion, he served as president of the company for four of its most exciting years. During his tenure, he was consistently admired. Energetic and creative, Bill "made things happen." He had vision, purpose, and ability to finesse a deal. As his star rose, so did the company's: revenues increased more than 20 percent each year of his presidency, while competitors were being adversely affected by the recession.

Not only was Bill a revered corporate leader, he "really knew how to have a good time." Clients enjoyed watching him get loose and become gregarious after a few drinks at a business dinner or corporate gala. However, a few of his staff wondered if, at times, he went too far. But no one was surprised that Bill was tapped to be the new CEO when the former chief retired.

After an apparently smooth transition, something changed. Bill could sometimes pull off his usual "superstar" performance, but at other times his behavior was erratic. He began to make costly, impulsive decisions. He misjudged the motives of adversaries as well as friends. Once he threatened to sweep out his entire executive committee, then blamed tough economic times for the company's recent decline in profits.

Even as he attempted to reassure a skittish board of directors that a turnaround in growth was imminent and the company's future bright, Bill became increasingly less involved with day-to-day operations. Staff found him elusive and unpredictable. Eventually they stopped seeking his direction altogether and began functioning like individual entrepreneurs. Divisional conflict sprang up and profits continued to decline. The company's future, once so promising, was now being questioned by industry analysts.

One day a member of the board (and longtime family friend) got a call from Bill's wife. She was desperate for help, she said. Bill had reportedly come home at 4:00 AM, fresh from a three-day drinking binge. When she confronted him, he lost control, hurling insults and finally a desk clock at her. She had to be stitched up at the local emergency room. Clearly at the end of her rope, Bill's wife even threatened to sue the company and make a fuss with the press if something wasn't done about her husband.

The board member contacted an interventionist who consulted with several other members of the board. Gathering together the key players in Bill's life, including the family friend and the chairman of the board, the consultant guided participants through an intervention with him. Bill was given an ultimatum to follow professional recommendations for treatment or leave the company. He agreed to attend a well-known inpatient treatment facility that specialized in treating renowned individuals and high-level executives.

TREATING THE EXECUTIVE

The main barrier during the treatment of an executive is the rigid use of defenses that perpetuate his perception that his drinking or drugging is not a problem and that his difficulties in life are the result of other people or circumstance. Typically, the alcohol and drug abuser's opportunity to bottom out can be the result of a major financial, familial, interpersonal, legal, medical, or job-related crisis. Alcoholic executives are often insulated from many of these realities because they are protected, financially secure, powerful, respected (although they may not be admired), feared, and desired individuals. Consequently, their capacity not to experience directly the troubles associated with their addiction is much greater than it is for others. This enables their defense system to remain intact and significantly decreases their opportunities to bottom out. When executives see themselves as so different and distinct from other patients entering treatment, they can become more resistant and convinced that a mistake has been made.

According to Flax (1985), executives succeed better at recovery than the average impaired employee once they bottom out. Flax states that "once they commit themselves to treatment, executives have about the best prognoses of all addicts . . . , the initial challenge is getting them to undertake treatment" (p. 27). Because this is exceedingly difficult given the extensive defense system that the executive addict (particularly when he is the CEO) has devised and that those around him often reinforce, an individualized strategy is needed to break down his defenses.

As described earlier, many factors that comprise the executive's role directly contribute to keeping his defenses in place. In essence, his role works against his treatment success. The key to recovery is breaking down his powerful, authoritative image. Only then can the qualities that allowed him to become an executive become assets in his quest to recover. The essence of treatment is providing information about alcohol and drug abuse while helping the impaired person apply it to himself as he struggles to get "painfully honest." The executive's intelligence, insightfulness, perseverance, endurance, and competitive spirit are valuable characteristics in the pursuit of recovery.

Male executives are best served under the following circumstances:

1. When their intervention and treatment process includes some individualized care: They are extremely comfortable with being coached. Consistent with their corporate position, executives are familiar with public-speaking tutors, speech-writing mentors, golf coaches, technology teachers, foreign language instructors, and so forth, to name but a few.
2. When necessary resources are made readily available: Executives will expect self-help groups to be easily accessible. Specific information about and directions to Alcoholics Anonymous (AA) meetings are essential in reducing the executive's frustration in accessing support.
3. When an educational opportunity has clear applicability in their daily lives: Executives appear comforted by alternative interpretations of

events to which they can apply their superior intellect in making them most relevant to themselves.

4. When they are challenged to tackle a problem: They are aided by identifying an achievable and clearly defined objective along with a self-fulfilling reward.
5. When they feel they can rely on someone with expertise: Both the interventionist and an AA sponsor who can easily identify with an executive's way of life are valuable assets.
6. When they are clearly told how things work: Executives readily comprehend the application of principles to practice, as in business, but are uncomfortable with being told what they must do.

Addressing the executive's particular treatment needs with some individualized attention works well in conjunction with standardized treatment. Clearly, treatment components such as using groups, undertaking defined tasks, identifying with others who suffer from alcoholism or drug addiction, becoming familiar with and accepting the twelve steps are also essential in helping male executives maximize their recovery opportunity.

The author has found that a systematic, organized, and professional approach maximizes the chance for success for the executive alcoholic to recover estimated at above 80 percent (as measured by one year of uninterrupted sobriety). This approach includes using an interventionist, planning and orchestrating the confrontation with the intervention team prior to their meeting with the impaired executive, clearly delineating and receiving a commitment to consequences of noncompliance with the interventionist's recommendations, and providing for extensive individualized assistance and support once the primary phase of treatment has been completed. The interventionist's work is completed only after the impaired executive has achieved a first anniversary of sobriety.

RETURNING TO WORK

The executive's return to work after undergoing inpatient treatment, an option still available to executives given their fiscal resources, presents several challenges that can be potential obstacles to long-term sobriety and require professional attention in the early stages of the recovery process.

The initial challenge in returning to work is centered upon the pace and expectations associated with the job. After being completely divorced from a corporate setting with little or no communication for several weeks, many co-workers, subordinates, and senior managers expect the executive to return to work in full stride and be "all better." Attempting to catch up can derail recovery because the executive can prioritize his work responsibilities over his need for regularly scheduled treatment appointments and self-help. Business travel accentuates this dilemma further. The recovering executive oftentimes requires coaching to ease back into his world of work and to resist his impulse to make up for lost time.

Another challenge concerns the fact that people in his company may have become aware of his situation. Although previously he may have had some success in hiding his problem, he may not be able to keep many colleagues and subordinates as well as senior management from quickly learning that he was in treatment. He is so "public" that his absence is readily noticed. This high visibility potentially interferes with his reentry into work by altering his relationships with colleagues who now view him differently than previously.

Some co-workers will relate to the returning impaired executive as "damaged goods." Their view of the alcoholic or chemically dependent individual will often conform with the stereotype of late-stage disease personified in the media. Colleagues may feel that they cannot count on the recovering executive to deliver when the pressure is on. The recovering executive may be labeled by some co-workers who are afraid of pushing him over the edge—of causing a relapse—so they tend to shy away from him. The responsibility is squarely on the alcoholic in early recovery to reestablish solid working relationships based on his expertise and business acumen, and oftentimes it takes considerable time to regain workplace status and liberation from the stigma associated with the executive's illness.

The recovering executive must engage in a process of rebuilding trust in his business dealings. Clients and co-workers whose trust in the executive has eroded will similarly require considerable time to rebuild enough trust to foster ongoing reengagement in a business relationship. Business associates will be focused on the recovering alcoholic executive, and his behavior can easily be misinterpreted. Yet he must be patient and skilled in dealing with frustration while avoiding the temptation to invest all of his energies in proving himself. Rather, the recovering executive needs to be consistent, thoughtful, focused, and truthful, as well as team-oriented to slowly but continually rebuild confidence and trust.

Returning executives also need to secure a support system of "allies in sobriety." Most executives are accustomed to functioning in a highly independent, self-determined, individualistic manner. Securing an AA sponsor, beginning as a novice in sobriety, finding a home group, regularly asking for help, and connecting to other recovering people who are not of one's social status can all prove quite difficult. The following case example highlights these obstacles:

> Jack, a 49-year-old senior vice president in an investment firm, completed a twenty-eight-day inpatient alcoholism treatment program. He worked hard to understand his disease, to accept his powerlessness over chemicals, and to honestly acknowledge how unmanageable his life had become. His wife participated in the family program offered by the rehabilitation facility. Although she had previously aided Jack's resistance to treatment, she was now supportive of his efforts to recover. The interventionist who collaborated with Jack and his company recommended that Jack take an additional week before returning to his job in order to begin his aftercare program and get familiar with a few AA meetings near his home and worksite.
>
> Jack's boss, an executive vice president (EVP), supported Jack's pursuit of treatment; however, he attempted to call Jack at the rehab center on several occasions to discuss business. Prior to discharge, Jack discussed with the inpatient treatment staff and with the interventionist how insecure he felt about going back to work. His feelings were strongly reinforced when the EVP met with him on the morning of his return, presented Jack with work objectives for the next quarter, and gave him an extensive list of potential business opportunities to pursue. During the next few weeks, Jack felt that his co-workers and support staff were avoiding him. He felt alienated from his colleagues, uncertain as to what they thought of his return and unclear of what they knew about where he had been. Jack felt exposed and vulnerable and increasingly stressed at work. He thought about drinking, became increasingly depressed, and felt that he didn't want to work for his company any longer.

Jack's return to work would have been easier if his EVP had helped to establish realistic performance expectations with a reintegration schedule and the executives who participated in Jack's intervention had kept the nature of Jack's whereabouts to themselves. Jack's boss should have been coached on Jack's need to establish supports for his recovery with time allocated for AA attendance. Likewise, his return to work would have been easier had Jack been introduced to other recovering executives in the financial services district. Such initiatives can help to formulate a balance between recovery and work and are the direct responsibility of the interventionist.

CONCLUSION

Male executives are not immune from substance abuse problems. Yet their role can have a negative impact on early assessment of their problems and on their utilization of treatment. In spite of the challenges that can derail recovery, substance-abusing executives can do well because of their heightened abilities to overcome obstacles—some of the same abilities that they can once again use to achieve success in the world of work. These qualities, when coupled with the work of the professional interventionist and other clinicians who counsel and consult with the impaired executive for an entire year after inpatient treatment, increase the odds for a successful recovery from alcohol and drug addiction.

REFERENCES

Casolaro, V., and Smith, R. J. (1993). The process of intervention: getting alcoholics and drug abusers to treatment. In *Clinical Work with Substance Abusing Clients*, ed. S. Straussner, pp. 105–118. New York: Guilford.

Cohen, M., and Solomon, J. (1994). Drugs at the top: risks and remedies. *The New York Times*, p. F11, June 26.

Flax, S. (1985). The executive addict. *Fortune* 3(13):24–31.

Harris, B. (1991). The politics of decision making. Internal memos from Harris Rothenberg International, 2.

Harris, B., and Cohen, M. (1994). Executive stress. *Employee Assistance* 6(10):23–26.

Johnson, V. E. (1987). *How to Use Intervention in Your Professional Practice.* Minneapolis, MN: Johnson Institute Books.

Kipnis, A. R. (1992). Caution: heroes at work. *Employee Assistance* 4:30–33.

McCrady, B. S. (1989). The distressed or impaired professional: from retribution to rehabilitation. *The Journal of Drug Issues* 19(3):337–349.

O'Connell, T. (1986). Alcoholic executives: EAP access limited. *U.S. Journal of Drug and Alcohol Dependence* 10(10):21.

Speller, J. L. (1989). *Executives in Crises: Recognizing and Managing the Alcoholic, Drug-Addicted or Mentally Ill Executive.* San Francisco, CA: Jossey-Bass.

Stevens, M. (1989). *Sudden Death: The Rise and Fall of E. F. Hutton.* New York: New American Library.

Stimmel, B., ed. (1984). *Alcohol and Drug Abuse in the Affluent.* New York: Haworth.

Summers, L. (1990). Book review of *Executives in Crises: Recognizing and Managing the Alcoholic Drug-Addicted or Mentally Ill Executive* by J. L. Speller. *Personnel Psychology* 4(4):871–875.

19

Assessment and Treatment of Male Substance Abusers with Learning Disabilities and Attention-Deficit/ Hyperactivity Disorder

Christianne DeWitt-Downey and Karen Spinelli-Falberg

During the past twenty years, the related conditions of attention-deficit hyperactivity disorder (ADHD) and learning disabilities have become closely correlated with substance abuse in men. Approximately 8 to 11 percent of boys with ADHD will have symptoms that persist into adulthood. Of that group, some 20 to 30 percent will experience difficulties related to drug and alcohol abuse (Hallowell and Ratey 1994). Although there are fewer studies that substantiate a link between learning disabilities and substance abuse, empirical support for their relationship does exist (Karacostas and Fisher 1993, Rhodes and Jasinski 1990).

Because males are at increased risk for learning disabilities and ADHD (Gualtieri 1985, Klein and Wender 1995), it is critical that professionals aggressively endeavor to assess and treat substance-abusing men for these disorders. This chapter provides an overview of learning disabilities and ADHD, emphasizing their relationships to male drug and alcohol abuse. Moreover, the relationship between antisocial personality disorder (and conduct disorder among children and adolescents) and ADHD will be addressed, since this particular combination has been found to be highly prevalent among male substance abusers. Suggested assessment and treatment interventions are presented.

DEFINITION AND ASSESSMENT OF LEARNING DISABILITIES

Learning disabilities are specific developmental disorders, usually first evident in infancy, childhood, or adolescence (APA 1994). These disorders are separated into three categories: academic skills disorders (arithmetic, expressive writing, and reading), language and speech disorders (articulation, expressive language, and receptive language), and motor skills disorder (coordination). Probably the most commonly accepted definition of the term *learning disability* is "a disorder in one or more of the basic psychological processes involved in understanding or in using language, spoken or written, which may manifest itself in an imperfect ability to listen, think, speak, read, write, spell or do mathematical calculations. The term includes such conditions as perceptual handicaps, brain injury, minimal brain dysfunction, dyslexia and developmental aphasia" (Federal Register 1977, p. 65083). In addition, the disorder must interfere significantly with the ability to function academically, which is reflected by a discrepancy between the person's intellectual capacity as measured by a standardized IQ test and the individual's academic performance (Ralph and Barr 1989).

Learning disabilities encompass a wide array of developmental, cognitive, and behavioral problems (Dane 1990). Dozens of different disorders affect one or more aspects of the learning process. For example, Bob, an 8-year-old, may have problems with visual perception; he confuses up and down and left and right, and so he has great difficulty learning how to read and do arithmetic. On the other hand, 12-year-old Juan may have problems with auditory perception, unable to grasp what the teacher is saying when he stands up in front of the room, while 5-year-old Steve may have limited fine motor coordination and may not be able to color inside the lines or draw and write clearly (Hallahan and Kauffman 1994).

Unfortunately, many of these childhood symptoms will persist into adolescence and adulthood, affecting not only academic functioning but also emotional, social, and vocational adjustment. Learning-disabled adults may experience literacy problems and difficulties in processing, comprehending, or retaining information, despite average IQs. As a result, many learning-disabled men avoid written work and reading at all costs. They may also have difficulty with time management and lateness, if they are able to remember appointments at all. Not only does the learning-disabled individual have to deal with repeated failures resulting from his symptoms, he is also likely to experience low self-esteem, anxiety, depression, unsuccessful social relationships, and poor interpersonal skills, increasing his susceptibility to abuse of alcohol and other substances.

Because of the general stigma associated with learning disabilities, many men spend a substantial amount of time and energy hiding their dysfunction from others. Hence, it is crucial that clinicians probe further when a learning disability is suspected, even if the client does not report one. The following are indicators of undiagnosed learning disabilities in adults (Kaplan and Shachter 1991): significant discrepancies between intellectual ability and school or work performance; significant poverty of social judgment; cognitive distortions; specific avoidance of selected tasks; hatred of reading; problematic school history; impulsivity, explosiveness, and concentration problems; poor self-esteem; a pervasive sense of badness; feelings of intellectual inferiority; impaired interpersonal relationships; and gender-identity confusion.

The characteristics of an individual with a learning disorder are similar to those of a substance abuser. Consequently, symptoms of learning disabilities may be overlooked, denying the client complete rehabilitation. A careful review of a client's educational and behavioral history may offer clues to the nature of his problem. For instance, an average or even a high level of academic achievement early in the educational history, followed by a sudden decline, could indicate a substance abuse problem that interferes with learning. However, a history of consistently below average grades followed by a sudden and dramatic change in behavior may be indicative of a learning disability that precedes the substance abuse (Fox and Forbing 1991). In short, the clinician's complete understanding of both learning disabilities and substance abuse is vital to ensuring appropriate treatment.

DEFINITION AND ASSESSMENT OF ATTENTION-DEFICIT HYPERACTIVITY DISORDER

Attention-deficit/hyperactivity disorder (ADHD), once believed to be a childhood psychiatric syndrome that diminished with age, is now known to be a common psychiatric disorder that affects nearly ten million adults (Wender 1995). Originally termed *minimal brain dysfunction, minimal cerebral brain dysfunction, hyperkinesis,* and *hyperactive child syndrome,* ADHD is a neurological disorder characterized by developmentally inappropriate inattention, impulsivity, distractibility, and hyperactivity or excess energy (Weiss and Hechtman 1993, Wender 1995).

For many individuals with ADHD, the symptoms of hyperactivity fade with age, although the deficits in attention may remain. In fact, currently the term *attention-deficit disorder* (ADD), rather than ADHD, is often used to describe adults whose disorders present without hyperactivity. These adults continue to struggle with inattention and impulsivity and are also likely to experience serious educational and social deficits, vocational disadvantages, and a negative self-image (Weiss and Hechtman 1993).

According to the *DSM-IV* (1994, pp. 83–85), a diagnosis of ADHD is assigned if an individual has persistently displayed six or more symptoms of inattention or hyperactivity-impulsivity for at least six months to a degree that is maladaptive. (The following list is reprinted with permission from the *Diagnostic and Statistical Manual of Mental Disorders. Fourth Edition.* Copyright © 1994 American Psychiatric Association.)

Inattention
(a) often fails to give close attention to details or makes careless mistakes in schoolwork, work, or other activities
(b) often has difficulty sustaining attention in tasks or play activities
(c) often does not seem to listen when spoken to directly
(d) often does not follow through on instructions and fails to finish schoolwork, chores, or duties in the workplace (not due to oppositional defiant disorder or failure to understand directions)
(e) often has difficulty organizing tasks and activities
(f) often avoids, dislikes, or is reluctant to engage in tasks that require sustained mental effort (such as schoolwork or homework)

(g) often loses things necessary for tasks or activities (e.g., toys, school assignments, pencils, books, or tools)
(h) is often easily distracted by extraneous stimuli
(i) is often forgetful in daily activities

Hyperactivity
(a) often fidgets with hands or feet or squirms in seat
(b) often leaves seat in classroom or in other situations in which remaining seated is expected
(c) often runs about or climbs excessively in situations in which it is inappropriate (in adolescents or adults, may be limited to subjective feelings of restlessness)
(d) often has difficulty playing or engaging in leisure activities quietly
(e) is often "on the go" or often acts as if "driven by a motor"
(f) often talks excessively

Impulsivity
(a) often blurts out answers before questions have been completed
(b) often has difficulty awaiting turn
(c) often interrupts or intrudes on others (e.g., butts into conversations or games)

Individuals must have demonstrated the preceding symptoms to the point of impairment prior to the age of 7 and must presently exhibit symptoms in two or more settings, such as work, school, or home.

While there is no single instrument or procedure that ensures an accurate diagnosis of ADHD, one of the most widely used assessments in the identification of adult ADHD is the Wender Utah Rating Scale (WURS), a sixty-item questionnaire that elicits information about childhood behaviors that fit the criteria for ADHD. Despite the extensive use of the WURS in assessing adult ADHD, it is not standardized, and the cutoff score required for a diagnosis is somewhat ambiguous (Weiss and Hechtman 1993). In addition, some of the questions may elicit information that is indicative of other psychiatric disorders or psychosocial problems, such as antisocial or borderline personality disorders.

Another drawback to relying on retrospective information stems from the fact that the results depend entirely on the recollections of those assessed. It is not unusual for a client to have a recollection of his behavior that is quite different from that of his parents or teachers. For example, Henry, a 24-year-old man in treatment for cocaine abuse, reported that his school marks were so exemplary that he was advanced several grades. Reports later obtained from his elementary school indicated that he received below average grades and that his teachers reported that his daydreaming suppressed his academic potential.

Additional tests that have been used to diagnose ADHD include the Conners Rating Scale, Beck Depression Inventory, Garfinkle Attention Battery, IQ tests such as the Wechsler Adult Intelligence Scale (WAIS), psychiatric assessments, and tests that measure math and reading levels. When administered together in varying combinations as test batteries, these instruments enable the clinician to obtain diverse information about the client without having to depend on the reliability and validity of a single tool. As a result, they should comprise a significant portion of any assessment for ADHD.

The medical field has also started to include more exacting technology, including positron emission topography (PET) and magnetic resonance imaging (MRI), in assessments for ADHD. Hauser and colleagues (1993) found a strong correlation between a thyroid dysfunction called generalized resistance to thyroid hormone (GRTH) and ADD. They found that 70 percent of subjects with GRTH also fit the criterion for ADD. Similarly, Giedd and colleagues (1994) reported abnormal frontal lobe development and functioning in ADD subjects, while another study revealed that glucose metabolism was 8 percent lower in ADHD adults than in a normal comparison group (Zametkin et al. 1990).

In summary, the most accurate diagnosis for ADHD will result from a combination of psychological and neurological tests, a thorough medical examination, data from schools and family members regarding childhood behavior, interviews with co-workers (where appropriate), and client self-reports, such as the WURS (Hallowell and Ratey 1994). Moreover, because substance abusers with ADHD frequently suffer from other disorders, including anxiety, depression, learning disorders, agitation or mania, borderline personality disorder, conduct disorder, oppositional defiant disorder or antisocial personality disorder, and obsessive compulsive disorder (Hallowell and Ratey 1994), these disorders have to be carefully assessed.

GENDER DIFFERENCES

Research by Nass (1993) reveals that males are more likely than females to have learning disabilities and ADHD at ratios of 4:1 and 3:1 respectively. The prevalence of learning disabilities among males is thought to be related to early developmental differences between the sexes. It has been suggested that males are more physically vulnerable than females, particularly during the first few years of development. Many more males than females die before birth or are born with birth defects (Jacklin-Nagy 1989). Jacklin-Nagy postulated that the male fetus elicits an inhospitable uterine environment, resulting from a disparate hormonal makeup from its mother's. This deviant environment causes the mother to produce antibodies that directly or indirectly inflict fetal damage upon the male fetus (Gualtieri and Hicks 1985). The female fetus is not subjected to these antibodies and subsequent fetal damage because her hormonal makeup is aligned with that of her mother.

Another reason why males may be more likely to have learning disabilities pertains to the hormone androgen, which is produced only by the male fetus. Androgen causes slower maturation of the left hemisphere of the brain (Geschwind and Behan 1982, 1984), thus prolonging the critical period of brain development. This results in decreased tolerance to seizures, which heightens the risk for major brain injury (Taylor and Ounsted 1971) and, subsequently, learning disabilities.

Attempts to decipher the reasons behind the increased incidence of ADHD in males have been less successful. While it is possible that the same biological vulnerabilities that influence the development of learning disabilities also impact ADHD development, this theory has not been substantiated. Recent interest in brain and thyroid abnormalities associated with ADHD (Giedd et al. 1994, Hauser et al. 1993) and genetic transmission theories (Wender 1995) may spur future research on this topic.

It is important to note that some researchers do not subscribe to the theory of male preponderance in ADHD and, instead, suggest that females may be underdiagnosed (Dane 1990). Tauber (1979) has alleged that boys with ADHD have more difficulty than females in tolerating impulses and, as such, may be more hyperactive and more likely viewed as disordered. In addition, because females are often discouraged from engaging in aggressive behavior, their ADHD symptoms may become increasingly disguised over time (Hechtman et al. 1984), again decreasing the likelihood of this diagnosis.

THE LINK BETWEEN SUBSTANCE ABUSE, ADHD, AND LD

The link between ADHD and alcohol and drug abuse, particularly among males, has been well established (Greenfield et al. 1988, Kellam et al. 1989, Weiss et al. 1985). One of the better known earlier studies, conducted by Blouin and colleagues (1978), revealed a higher incidence of alcohol consumption among previously diagnosed hyperactive, mostly male, adolescents compared to same-age controls. A later study of individuals applying for treatment for opiate addiction found that over 20 percent of the primarily male participants were retrospectively diagnosed as hyperactive (Eyre et al. 1982). A ten-year follow-up study on a 90 percent male high school population found that significantly more hyperactive youngsters than controls had a history of marijuana use (Hechtman et al. 1984).

Similarly, Mannuzza (1993) found males with at least one persisting ADHD symptom were seven times more likely than those whose symptoms had dissipated to have an ongoing drug abuse problem. Similar results have been found by researchers investigating substance abuse and learning disabilities without ADHD. Karacostas and Fisher (1993), for example, discovered that a higher proportion of adolescents with learning disabilities were classified as chemically dependent than those without learning disabilities.

Evidence of the relationship between ADHD and drug abuse spurred researchers to investigate the etiology of their connection. Some clinicians concluded that boys with ADHD are at greater risk for substance abuse as adolescents and adults because their ADHD symptoms are also the risk factors for drug and alcohol addictions. Among these symptoms and related risk factors are impulsivity, low self-esteem, noncompliance with authority, poor school performance, elevated activity levels, susceptibility to peer pressure, and related behavioral and social problems, as well as anxiety and depression (Kress and Elias 1993, Loney et al. 1981, Manly 1990).

An individual's self-concept is largely contingent upon the way others react to his achievements and failures (Dane 1990). Students with learning disabilities score lower on measures of personal adjustment and self-esteem than do nonlearning-disabled students (LeGreca and Stone 1990). Similarly, boys with ADHD are often subjected to repeated failures and called names like "dumb" or "daydreamer," further decreasing their self-esteem. They may be scapegoated and blamed for classroom turmoil in which they had no involvement merely because of their symptoms (Hallowell and Ratey 1994). Such boys may turn to substance abuse in efforts to cope with their low self-esteem and feelings of anger.

Studies on individuals with ADHD who abuse alcohol and cocaine also bolster the self-medication hypothesis. Hallowell and Ratey (1994) found that 15 percent of individuals with ADHD tend to feel more focused, rather than energized or "high," when they use cocaine and are probably self-medicating their symptoms. The authors also believe that these individuals use alcohol to alleviate the internal confusion and suppress the anxiety that may accompany their ADHD disorder. Other researchers assert that individuals who are learning disabled abuse substances in order to avoid experiencing the psychological symptoms, such as anxiety and depression, that often accompany their disabilities (Kaplan 1980).

Furthermore, researchers are now looking at the role of environmental influences, particularly in the home, in the transmission of ADHD (Faraone et al. 1992) and subsequent substance abuse. Children with ADHD have been known to come from homes characterized by disorganization, conflict, and parental psychopathology (Biederman et al. 1992).

Wender (1995) posited that psychiatric abnormality present in the parents of children with ADHD could indicate not only genetic transmission but also deviant child-rearing practices as factors in the development of this disorder. Barkley and co-authors (1992) reported that mothers of adolescents with ADHD exhibited anomalous relationships with their children and displayed more negative communication patterns, increased conflict, and a greater intensity of anger than control mothers. Siblings of children with ADHD may also display psychiatric abnormalities because of the same adverse parenting styles (Wender 1995).

COMORBIDITY OF CONDUCT AND ANTISOCIAL PERSONALITY DISORDERS IN CLIENTS WITH ADHD OR LD AND SUBSTANCE ABUSE

According to *DSM-IV* (APA 1994), the diagnosis of conduct disorder (CD) is given to youngsters whose pattern of behavior violates the basic rights of others or who repetitively and persistently break societal norms or rules. Those over the age of 18 whose behavior shows "a pervasive pattern of disregard for and violation of the rights of others" (APA 1994, p. 649), tend to be diagnosed with antisocial personality disorder (ASPD). Both of these diagnoses are more common in males than females, and both are frequently comorbid with ADHD and with substance abuse (Barkley 1990, Gittleman et al. 1985, Satterfield et al. 1982). One study that followed ADHD children into early adulthood found that 50 percent of the ADHD subjects, compared to 1.6 percent of controls, were conduct disordered (Fischer et al. 1990). In fact, according to Wender (1995), pure CD without ADHD is rare.

Relatives of individuals with ADHD are not only at greater risk for acquiring ADHD but are also at greater risk for having antisocial personality disorder (ASPD) (Faraone et al. 1981) and substance abuse disorder (Biederman et al. 1992). In fact, several researchers (Lahey et al. 1988, Wender 1995) have suggested that ADHD, ASPD, and substance abuse may actually be genetically transmitted as an intact triad or, perhaps, even as a single gene (Faraone et al. 1992). This is especially true in cases in which one or both of the biological parents had ADHD or conduct disorder as children. This was confirmed by Morrison and Stewart (1971), who found that 20 percent of hyperactive children versus only 5 percent of controls had a parent who was hyperactive in childhood. Furthermore, half of the parents who displayed hyperactivity in childhood also fit the adult diagnosis for alcoholism, sociopathy, or hysteria.

Studies found that ADHD, CD or ASPD, and substance abuse are strongly correlated (Gittleman et al. 1985, Greenfield et al. 1988, Kellam et al. 1989, Weiss et al. 1985). Goodwin and colleagues (1975) found that between 20 and 30 percent of the alcoholics studied, versus only 4 percent of the controls, were diagnosed as having frequently been truant, antisocial, or disobedient in childhood. Such results have led some researchers to conclude that substance abuse may be less common in individuals with only ADHD than it is in individuals with simultaneous conduct disorder and ADHD (Gittleman et al. 1985).

Researchers have directed similar attention to a possible relationship between learning disabilities, conduct disorder, and substance abuse. A connection between learning disabilities and juvenile delinquency was made by Keilitz and Dunivant (1986), who studied 970 adolescents with juvenile court conviction and 970 controls. They found that 36 percent of adjudicated adolescents were learning disabled as compared to 16 percent of the controls. In addition, 9 percent of the learning-disabled juveniles were found to have been convicted of some crime as opposed to 4 percent of controls. These authors believe that failure in school may foster a negative self-image. This in turn causes students to detach from authority and rules and engage in criminal behavior, which may lead to the abuse of alcohol and other substances.

Given these findings, mental health professionals and special educators need to emphasize substance abuse prevention in the schools. Traditionally, special education students have been left out of prevention programs because of their learning and behavioral problems. However, it is the very nature of these dysfunctions that places these students at high risk for substance abuse and should make them primary targets of drug abuse prevention efforts (Kress and Elias 1993). Fox and Forbing (1991) have suggested that drug prevention programs should emphasize the development of recreational skills. Because disabilities play a major role in the development of self-concept (Kaplan and Shachter 1991), increasing social, recreational, and educational skills will heighten self-esteem and encourage involvement in activities other than substance abuse.

TREATMENT

A large problem for substance abusers with a learning disability or ADHD is not only that of being identified but also that of receiving proper treatment (Moore 1990). For example, David, a 27-year-old client who was diagnosed with developmental dyslexia, was not accepted to a residential alcohol rehabilitation center after the medical director discovered he was illiterate. It appeared that the facility could not accommodate him because the program, which was based on the twelve steps of recovery, involved a substantial amount of reading and writing.

Thus, mental health professionals need to deal with a variety of issues when they devise a treatment plan for an individual who has both a learning disability and a substance abuse problem. It is not enough to evaluate the severity of the substance abuse disorder. The extent of the client's ADD or learning disability must be assessed, and factors such as reading level and IQ, attention span, and ability to process written and oral information must be carefully considered. In most instances, dually diagnosed clients will require a combination of different treatment methods to address their complex and unique needs. For example, David might benefit from audio and video instructional aids since he is not able to read or write. In essence, clinicians must remain flexible, rather than regimented in traditional treatment models.

Multimodel Treatment Approach

When treating substance-abusing men with ADHD, a multimodel approach that combines education, structure, psychotherapy, and "coaching" works best (Evans and Sullivan 1990, Hallowell and Ratey 1994). It is recommended that those with ADD learn as much as they can about the disorder and, in turn, educate their spouses, bosses, teachers, and other significant people in their lives about how it affects them (Wender 1995). Hallowell and Ratey (1994) also advocate the client's restructuring his life with external controls to compensate for unreliable internal controls. For example, clinicians may need to help clients develop reminder lists, appointment books, schedules, "in" and "out" boxes, and similar devices. Such tools help maintain routines or systems that become a source of calm for the person with ADHD; not only does the person start to function better, he may also experience a boost in self-esteem.

Psychotherapy has received mixed reviews with regard to its efficacy in the clinical management of ADHD. One of the impediments to implementing psychotherapy in the treatment of this disorder is that these clients often have poor follow-through, a characteristic required of most therapies (Weiss and Hechtman 1993). This is why the use of behavioral interventions combined with extensive psychotherapy tends to have more success (Evans and Sullivan 1990). Similarly, in treating substance abuse, behavioral interventions promoting abstinence must precede and accompany psychotherapeutic work.

Psychotherapy has proved helpful for mediating impaired interpersonal relationships, depression, and weakened impulse control that often accompany learning disabilities, ADHD, and substance abuse (Evans and Sullivan 1990). Hallowell and Ratey (1994) have stressed the need for such clients to bond with a therapist who can listen and offer understanding, yet caution against traditional psychoanalysis and similar unstructured approaches that make it easier for the client to go off on a tangent. Support groups may also be helpful, including groups such as Children and Adults with Attention-Deficit Disorder (CHADD), which is designed to meet the specific needs of family members of those with ADD.

A coach is often employed in the treatment of adult ADHD and may also prove effective in the treatment of male substance abusers with this disorder (Hallowell and Ratey 1994). A coach may be the person's therapist, but can also be a family member, friend, or co-worker. The coach must have a basic understanding of the disorder and must be willing to dedicate at least fifteen minutes a day to providing encouragement, directions, and reminders to the ADD adult. He or she also plays a critical role in preventing a reversion to old habits, such as procrastination and negative thinking. The coaching session is comprised of four components: help, obligation, plans, and encouragement (termed HOPE). Consider the following example of a typical coaching intervention:

> Andy, a 26-year-old Caucasian male who was dually diagnosed with cocaine addiction and ADD, selected his brother, Mark, to be his coach as part of his treatment plan. Applying the components of HOPE on a daily basis, Mark asks Andy if he needs help with better organizing his daily routine, including ensuring that he attends his treatment program and similar appointments on time. Next, Mark inquires about upcoming obligations, such as homework assignments required by his treatment program, and asks Andy what he is doing to prepare for them. Third, Mark asks Andy questions about ongoing plans toward achievement of his goals and helps define goals if Andy has forgotten them. Finally, Mark offers encouragement and affirms Andy's progress. This last step is particularly important in counteracting the feelings of negativity that frequently accompany ADD and may lead to substance abuse relapse.

Behavioral/Cognitive Treatment

Cognitive therapy is a treatment approach that is increasing in popularity and often has aided in the rehabilitation of substance abusers, especially when combined with behavioral therapy. Such a treatment may be useful with clients who are those dually diagnosed with substance abuse and ADD or a learning disorder. However, the clinician must be aware of the nature and extent of a client's ADD or learning disabilities, otherwise this kind of intellectual work may not be effective (Moore 1990). All material must remain simple and concrete, and information must be repeated and reviewed frequently. Tasks should be built upon only when the client is successful. As the clinician provides opportunities for success, the client will begin to take risks, and in doing so will achieve greater independence, autonomy, and self-confidence (Van Conas 1990).

A related form of treatment that is becoming more widely accepted is the psychosocial skills training model designed by Marsha M. Linehan (1993). Termed dialectical behavior therapy (DBT), it consists of a broad-based cognitive-behavioral treatment approach that combines psychotherapy with skills training. Although this model was first found effective for treating individuals diagnosed with borderline personality disorder (BPD), it is also a useful approach for helping clients who are learning disabled as well as substance abusers.

DBT teaches the client four specific skills: interpersonal effectiveness that focuses on helping clients learn to deal with conflicting situations effectively, emotion regulation training that addresses how to control intense emotions, distress tolerance training that focuses on learning how to tolerate stress, and core mindfulness that teaches clients to become self-observant. The DBT approach encourages the connection of the themes discussed in the client's individual therapy with the skills that are being taught in the cognitive skills group. For instance, a client who threatens to leave treatment after being confronted with his impulsive or negative behaviors in individual session may be encouraged to practice his distress tolerance skills in the group (Linehan 1993). The following case depicts a client involved in cognitive-behavioral therapy:

> Carlos, 34-year-old male born in the Dominican Republic, has been in treatment for the last four years for cocaine and marijuana addictions. Raised by relatives in the United States, Carlos has had limited contact with his biological parents, although he reports his father to be alcoholic and his mother has been in psychiatric care for an unspecified disorder. Growing up, Carlos experienced tremendous difficulty in school. Although he devoted hours to his studies, it was rarely reflected in his grades. He recalls being called "dumb" and "lazy" by other children, and his teachers often reprimanded him for daydreaming in class. After the ninth grade, Carlos dropped out of school and spent most of his time "hanging out" with other dropouts, many of whom used drugs. He began to use marijuana to "mellow out" and later developed an addiction to cocaine, which relaxed him and helped him to "slow down."

As a young adult, Carlos had difficulty maintaining employment because of his academic deficiencies, inability to sustain concentration, and continued drug abuse. He turned to public assistance for support and, without any structure in his day, spent even more time on the street. He fathered six children with several women, but rarely saw them because of intense problems in getting along with their mothers. He also spent time in jail following convictions for drug sales and assault. In both instances he reports that he acted without thinking and wishes he had considered the possible consequences first.

At age 30, as a condition of his parole, Carlos entered an outpatient, drug-free treatment program for his now chronic cocaine habit. He was first referred to the staff psychiatrist for recurrent suicidal thoughts, chronic feelings of emptiness, difficulty controlling anger, and unstable interpersonal relationships. After a thorough assessment, which included lab work (to rule out physical disorders), staff observations, a psychosocial history, school records and related information, and the administration of the WURS, he was diagnosed with ADD in addition to cocaine dependence.

Carlos now attends a structured day treatment program based on the concepts of Linehan's (1993) dialectical behavior therapy (DBT) program. His treatment plan focuses most specifically on his recurrent suicidal ideation and intense emotional reactions. Carlos participates in a distress tolerance training group to learn to better tolerate the stressors of daily living that lead him to impulsive behaviors, such as cocaine abuse and attempts to harm himself. Because of Carlos's ADD, the DBT program had to be modified. Carlos was assigned a "buddy" who sits next to him and helps him to stay focused during group sessions. In addition, he has an individual session with the group facilitator in order to review information presented during the group and to help him organize a plan for completing the required homework assignments.

Use of Twelve-Step Programs

In order to help clients achieve complete abstinence from alcohol and illicit substances, attendance in twelve-step programs should also be encouraged for the substance abuser with a learning disability or ADHD. In order to address the attention or learning disability, however, modifications may be warranted. For example, much like Hallowell and Ratey's "coach," a client might benefit from having a twelve-step "support per-son" (Evans and Sullivan 1990) who could remind him of the meeting, the time it begins, and where it will take place. Clients with a limited attention span also may need to plan to take a break or attend only part of the meeting. This may prevent these individuals from acting on their impulsive behaviors and making disorganized comments that ensue from an inability to stay focused. The support person may even need to attend the meeting with the client in order to help prevent him from rambling and to ensure he stays attentive during the session.

Use of Medication

Stimulant medications have long been successful in suppressing ADHD symptoms in children and, more recently, in adults (Wender 1995). The most popular of these is Ritalin (methylphenidate hydrochloride), which has had unparalleled success in the remission of childhood ADHD (Elia et al. 1991, Rapport et al. 1994). When administered to adults, it is gen-erally recommended that Ritalin be started at low doses and gradually increased until the maximum therapeutic benefit is achieved, unless the patient experiences negative side effects. Other stimulants that have been employed with some success in the clinical management of adult ADHD include amphetamines and methylphenidate. Pemoline, the newest stimulant used in ADHD treatment, has also been found effec-tive because of its long-lasting action and low abuse potential (Sallee et al. 1992).

The following vignette returns to the case of Carlos:

> In addition to attending the DBT-based program, Carlos was pre-scribed Ritalin and later Pemoline. The Pemoline was more ef-fective for Carlos because he only had to remember to take it one time a day, as opposed to the Ritalin which he had to take up to three times a day. Carlos's ADD symptoms have markedly decreased, and he has not used cocaine in almost a year. Carlos has also become more involved with his children. Recently, one of his sons, Michael, was diagnosed with ADHD following an extensive evaluation that included a history of Carlos's ADD. Michael was put on Ritalin and offered academic tutoring to help him succeed in school and minimize his chances of turning to drugs.

In the past, clinicians expressed concerns about the abuse potential of Ritalin because of its pharmacological similarity to cocaine, and many medical professionals are still resistant to prescribing stimulant medications to adult substance abusers, particularly those with a history of amphetamine or cocaine abuse. They believe that substance abusers are incapable of utilizing stimulant medication as prescribed and will use it to get high. However, such claims have never been backed by empirical evidence (Henker et al. 1981, Klein and Wender 1995, Laufer 1971). In fact, some researchers believe that the persistence of Ritalin in the brain, as opposed to the rapid brain consumption of other stimulants such as cocaine, renders it less likely to be abused (Volkow et al. 1995). Furthermore, administering Ritalin and other stimulants to cocaine abusers with a history of persistent ADHD has actually been known to reduce their cocaine cravings (Weiss and Mirin 1986, Wender 1995). The Ritalin simultaneously alleviates ADHD symptoms and stress associated with this disorder, thus decreasing vulnerability to substance abuse (Loney et al. 1981). In addition, the reduction of stress may result in improved interpersonal relationships, enabling the adult with ADHD to gain much needed support (Wender 1995).

Successful pharmacotherapy has also been accredited with bolstering the effectiveness of twelve-step groups such as Alcoholics Anonymous (AA) or Narcotics Anonymous (NA), as well as other drug treatment groups. By mediating symptoms, the medication not only decreases drug cravings but also enables the individual to better focus on the content of the meeting (Wender 1995). Yet, despite these findings, many twelve-step groups still discourage the use of any type of drug, including prescription stimulants such as Ritalin. Clinicians may need to help clients taking Ritalin or similar medication find alternative twelve-step groups that accept and value pharmacotherapy for such men.

Antidepressants and mood-stabilizing drugs represent another category of medications that have achieved some success in mediating ADHD symptoms. In addition, these types of medications generally meet with less criticism than stimulants in the substance abuse treatment field. In particular, monoamine oxidase inhibitors (Zametkin et al. 1985) and buproprion may prove helpful in treating this disorder because of their long-acting, nonaddictive properties. Tricyclic antidepressants may prove promising but they are still under evaluation (Wender 1995).

The following case exemplifies many of the dynamics and treatment issues discussed previously:

Bernard, a 38-year-old African-American male, was a self-referral to an outpatient drug treatment program for heroin abuse. He has never been married, lives with his girlfriend, and has no children. The youngest of three siblings, he was raised by both natural parents, but he reports that his mother and father never gave him any attention, especially in the academic area. His father often drank after work and is described by Bernard as illiterate.

Bernard reports having difficulties in school as early as second grade. He was afraid to read because he thought he would pronounce the words incorrectly. He was extremely nervous, terrified that the teacher would call on him to read aloud. Whenever he made a mistake the other children would laugh at him.

Bernard's sister introduced him to marijuana at age 12 and heroin at age 14. He states that the drugs changed the way he felt. It took the "fear, hurt, and pain" he experienced and replaced them with "numbness and confidence." He dropped out of school in the 10th grade and never went back. He first became involved with the legal system when he was 15 years old, jumping a turnstile in a subway station. His legal involvement continued at age 21 when he was arrested for possession of drugs, at age 23 when he was arrested for theft, and age 28 when he was arrested a second time for possession of drugs. It was at this point that the judge mandated him to attend drug treatment. While attending the drug treatment program he was assessed and diagnosed with dyslexia.

Bernard left treatment after achieving abstinence but relapsed soon after. His drug use continued, and he was eventually fired from his job for chronic lateness and absenteeism. Bernard is now involved in an intensive day treatment program, which focuses on individual therapy, academic skills remediation, vocational training, and pharmacotherapy for depression. He has been abstinent for four months but still struggles with issues of success, identity, and self-esteem.

CONCLUSION

Training mental health professionals and school personnel to detect the symptoms of substance abuse, learning disabilities, and ADHD is the key to prevention. It is also vital in ensuring appropriate treatment and remedial assistance for substance-abusing clients with co-occurring learning disabilities and/or ADHD. Many treatment professionals are unaware that these disorders may afflict adults and thus do not assess for them. This is particularly noticeable in the treatment of adult male substance abusers whose treatment providers often become so focused on the drug abuse behaviors that they fail to explore the possibility of learning disabilities and ADHD. However, overlooking the impact of these disorders can sabotage even the best treatment efforts. In order to provide effective treatment for substance abusers, it is crucial that clinicians be able to identify learning disabilities and ADHD and make sure that their clients receive proper treatment for all of their disorders.

REFERENCES

American Psychiatric Association. (1995). *Diagnostic and Statistical Manual of Mental Disorders*. 4th ed. Washington, DC: Author.

Barkley, R. A. (1990). *Attention-Deficit Hyperactivity Disorder: A Handbook for Diagnosis and Treatment*. New York: Guilford.

Barkley, R. A., Anastopoulos, A. D., Guevremont, D. L., and Fletcher, K. E. (1992). Adolescents with attention-deficit hyperactivity: mother–adolescent interactions, family beliefs and conflicts, and maternal psychopathology. *Journal of Abnormal Child Psychiatry* 20:263–288.

Biederman, J., Faraone, S. V., Keenan, K., et al. (1992). Further evidence for family-genetic risk factors in attention-deficit hyperactivity disorder. Patterns of comorbidity in probands and relatives, I: psychiatrically and pediatrically referred samples. *Archives of General Psychiatry* 49:728–738.

Blouin, A. G. A., Bornstein, R., and Trites, R. (1978). Teen-age alcohol use among hyperactive children: a five-year follow-up study. *Journal of Pediatric Psychology* 3:188–194.

Dane, E. (1990). *Painful Passages*. Washington, DC: National Association of Social Workers.

Elia, J., Borcherding, B. J., Rapport, J. L., and Keysor, C. S. (1991). Methylphenidate and dextroamphetamine treatment of hyperactivity: Are there true non-responders? *Psychiatry Research* 36:141–155.

Evans, K., and Sullivan, J. M. (1990). *Dual Diagnosis: Counseling the Mentally Ill Substance Abuser*. New York: Guilford.

Faraone, S. V., Biederman, J., Chen, W. J., et al. (1992). Segregation analysis of attention-deficit hyperactivity disorder. *Psychiatric Genetics* 2:257–275.

Federal Register (1977). *Procedures for Evaluating Specific Learning Disabilities*. Washington, DC: Department of Health, Education, and Welfare.

Fischer, M., Barkley, R. A., Edelbrock, C. S., et al. (1990). The adolescent outcome of hyperactive children diagnosed by research criteria, II: academic, attention, and neuropsychological status. *Journal of Consulting and Clinical Psychology* 58:580–588.

Fox, C. L., and Forbing, S. E. (1991). Overlapping symptoms of substance abuse and learning handicaps: implications for educators. *Journal of Learning Disabilities* 24:24–31.

Geschwind, N., and Behan, P. (1982). Left-handedness: association with immune disease, migraine, and developmental learning disorder. *Proceedings of the National Academy of Sciences* 79:5097–5100.

——(1984). Laterality, hormones, and immunity. In *Cerebral Dominance: The Biological Foundations*, ed. N. Geschwind and A. M. Galaburda, pp. 211–224. Cambridge, MA: Harvard University Press.

Giedd, J. N., Castellanos, X., Casey, B. J., et al. (1994). Quantitative morphology of the corpus callosum in attention-deficit hyperactivity disorder. *American Journal of Psychiatry* 151:665–669.

Gittleman, R., Mannuzza, S., Shenker, R., and Bonagura, N. (1985). Hyperactive boys almost grown up, I: psychiatric status. *Archives of General Psychiatry* 42:937–947.

Goodwin, D. W., Schulsinger, F., Hermansen, L., et al. (1975). Alcohol problems in adoptees raised apart from alcoholic biological parents. *Archives of General Psychiatry* 28:238–243.

Greenfield, B., Hechtman, L., and Weiss, G. (1988). Two subgroups of hyperactives as adults: correlations of outcome. *Canadian Journal of Psychiatry* 33:505–508.

Gualtieri, T., and Hicks, R. (1985). The immunoreactivity theory of selective male affliction. *Behavioral and Brain Sciences* 8:427–470.

Hallahan, D., and Kauffman, J. (1994). *Exceptional Children*, 6th ed. Boston: Allyn and Bacon.

Hallowell, E. M., and Ratey, J. J. (1994). *Drive to Distraction*. New York: Pantheon.

Hauser, P., Zametkin, A. J., Martinez, P., et al. (1993). Attention-deficit hyperactivity in people with generalized resistance to thyroid hormone. *New England Journal of Medicine* 828:997–1001.

Hechtman, L., Weiss, G., and Perlman, T. (1984). Hyperactives as young adults: past and current substance and antisocial behavior. *American Journal of Orthopsychiatry* 54:415–425.

Henker, B., Whalen, C., Bugental, D. B., and Barker, C. (1981). Licit and illicit substance use patterns in stimulant-treated children and their peers. In *Psychosocial Aspects of Drug Treatment for Hyperactivity*, ed. K. Gadow and J. Loney. Boulder, CO: Westview.

Jacklin-Nagy, C. (1989). Female and male: issues of gender. *American Psychologist* 44(2):127–133.

Kaplan, C. P., and Shachter, E. (1991). Adults with undiagnosed learning disabilities: practice considerations. *Families in Society: The Journal of Contemporary Human Services* 72:195–201.

Kaplan, H. (1980). Self-esteem and self-derogation theory of drug abuse. In *Theories on Drug Abuse: Selected Contemporary Perspectives*, ed. D. Lettieri, M. Sayers, and H. Pearson. NIDA monograph 30, DHHS 80-967. Rockville, MD: US Government Printing Office.

Karacostas, D. D., and Fisher, G. L. (1993). Chemical dependency in students with and without learning disabilities. *Journal of Learning Disabilities* 26(7):491–495.

Keilitz, I., and Dunivant, N. (1986). The relationship between learning disability and juvenile delinquency: current state of knowledge. *Remedial and Special Education* 7(3):18–26.

Kellam, S., Ialongo, N., Brown, H., et al. (1989). Attention problems in first grade and shy and aggressive behaviors as antecedents to later heavy or inhibited substance use. In *NIDA Research Monograph 95: The Committee on Problems of Drug Dependence*, ed. L. S. Harris, pp. 368–369. Rockville, MD: National Institute of Drug Abuse.

Klein, R. G., and Wender, P. H. (1995). The role of methylphenidate in psychiatry. *Archives of General Psychiatry* 52:429–432.

Kress, J. S., and Elias, M. J. (1993). Substance abuse prevention in special education populations: review and recommendations. *The Journal of Special Education* 27(1):35–51.

Lahey, B. B., Piacentini, J. C., McBurnett, K., et al. (1988). Psychopathology in the parents of children with conduct disorder and hyperactivity. *Journal of the American Academy of Child and Adolescent Psychiatry* 27:163–170.

Laufer, M. W. (1971). Long-term management and some follow-up findings on the use of drugs with minimal cerebral syndromes. *Journal of Learning Disabilities* 4:55–58.

LeGreca, A. M., and Stone, W. L. (1990). Learning disability status and achievement: confounding variables in the study of children's social status, self-esteem, and behavioral functioning. *Journal of Learning Disabilities* 23:483–490.

Linehan, M. M. (1993). *Skills Training Manual for Treating BPD*. New York: Guilford.

Loney, J., Kramer, J., and Milich, R. S. (1981). The hyperactive child grows up: predictors of symptoms, delinquency, and achievement at follow-up. In *Psychological Aspects of Drug Treatment for Hyperactivity*, AAS Selected Symposium 44, ed. K. D. Gadow and J. Loney, pp. 381–415. Boulder, CO: Westview Press.

Manly, H. (1990). Environmental impact. In *Alcohol and Other Drug Abuse: Implications for Mental Retardation and Learning Disabilities*, ed. J. S. Lechowicz. New York: Hofstra University Press.

Mannuzza, S., Klein, R. G., Bessler, A., et al. (1993). Adult outcome of hyperactive boys: educational achievement, occupational rank, and psychiatric status. *Archives of General Psychiatry* 50:565–576.

Moore, D. (1990). The magnitude of the problem: the scope of prevention and treatment issues for persons with mental retardation or learning disabilities. In *Alcohol and Other Drug Abuse: Implications for*

Mental Retardation and Learning Disabilities, ed. J. S. Lechowicz. New York: Hofstra University Press.

Morrison, J. R., and Steward, M. A. (1971). A family study of the hyperactive child syndrome. *Biological Psychiatry* 3:189–195.

Nass, R. D. (1993). Sex differences in learning abilities and disabilities. *Annals of Dyslexia* 43:61–77.

Ralph, N., and Barr, M. (1989). Diagnosing attention-deficit hyperactivity disorder and learning disabilities with chemically dependent adolescents. *Journal of Psychoactive Drugs* 21(2):203–214.

Rapport, M. D., Denney, C., DuPaul, C. J., and Gardner, M. J. (1994). Attention-deficit disorder and methylphenidate: normalization rates, clinical effectiveness, and response prediction in 76 children. *Journal of the American Academy of Child and Adolescent Psychiatry* 33:882–893.

Rhodes, S. S., and Jasinski, D. R. (1990). Learning disabilities in alcohol-dependent adults: a preliminary study. *Journal of Learning Disabilities* 23(9):551–556.

Sallee, F. R., Stiller, R. L., and Perel, J. M. (1992). Pharmacodynamics of pemoline in attention-deficit disorder with hyperactivity. *Journal of the American Academy of Child and Adolescent Psychiatry* 31:2.

Satterfield, J. H., Hoppe, C. M., and Schell, A. M. (1982). A prospective study of delinquency in 100 adolescent boys with attention-deficit disorder and 88 normal adolescent boys. *American Journal of Psychiatry* 139:797–798.

Tauber, M. A. (1979). Parent socialization techniques and sex differences in children's play. *Child Development* 50:225–234.

Taylor, D., and Ounsted, C. (1971). Biological mechanisms influencing outcome of seizures in response to fever. *Epilipsia* 12:33–46.

Van Conas, C. (1990). Implications of learning disabilities. In *Alcohol and Other Drug Abuse: Implications for Mental Retardation and Learning Disabilities*, ed. J. S. Lechowicz. New York: Hofstra University.

Volkow, N. D., Ding, Y. S., Fowler, J. S., et al. (1995). Is methylphenidate like cocaine? Studies on the pharmokinetics and distribution in the human brain. *Archives of General Psychiatry* 52:456–463.

Weiss, G., and Hechtman, L. (1993). *Hyperactive Children Grown Up*, 2nd ed. New York: Guilford.

Weiss, G., Hechtman, L., Milroy, T., and Perlman, T. (1985). Psychiatric status of hyperactives as adults: a controlled prospective 15-year follow-up of 63 hyperactive children. *Journal of the American Academy of Child Psychiatry* 24(2):211–220.

Weiss, G., Hechtman, L., Perlman, T., et al. (1979). Hyperactives as young adults: a controlled prospective ten-year follow-up study of 75 children. *Archives of General Psychiatry* 36:675–681.

Weiss, R. D., and Mirin, S. M. (1986). Subtypes of cocaine abusers. *Psychiatric Clinics of North America* 9:491–501.

Wender, P. H. (1995). *Attention-Deficit Hyperactivity Disorder in Adults*. New York: Oxford University Press.

Zametkin, A. J., Nordahl, T. E., Gross, M., et al. (1990). Cerebral glucose metabolism in adults with hyperactivity of childhood onset. *New England Journal of Medicine* 323:1361–1366.

Zametkin, A., Rapoport, J. L., Murphy, D. L., et al. (1985). Treatment of hyperactive children with monoamine oxidase inhibitors. *Archives of General Psychiatry* 42:962–966.

20

Hispanic Substance-Abusing Men and Machismo

Elisa Valladares Goldberg

Given the increasing number of Hispanic men in the United States and their reflection in the composition of client caseloads, clinicians may find themselves providing services to substance-abusing clients whose culture may be relatively unfamiliar to them (Castex 1994). Cultural competence, an integral part of professional training and competence in addiction treatment, requires that clinicians understand both the client as an individual and what the client brings from his culture. According to Bernal and Gutierrez (1988), culture must be understood as a process linked to time and conditioned by the evolving social and economic context of each particular cultural group. It follows that the role of acculturation is an important aspect of assessment and treatment. It is a particularly crucial element when assessing clients' issues of identity, of stressors, such as value dissonance in the host environment, adaptation, and intergenerational conflict.

This chapter will focus on the implications of cultural values and the process of acculturation in the clinical treatment of Hispanic substance-abusing men. Such knowledge can assist the clinician in establishing a therapeutic relationship, in using culture therapeutically, and in the service and support of recovery.

WHO ARE THE HISPANICS?

The "Hispanic" grouping was created by the United States government in 1978 (Castex 1994) and reflects the North American custom of viewing Spanish-speaking people, known interchangeably as Latinos, Spanish Americans, Chicanos, and Hispanics, as a homogeneous mass. The label may imply racial make-up or ethnicity, but the amalgam known as Hispanic includes people of more than 20 nationalities.

According to the 1993 U.S. Bureau of the Census report for the 1990 census, Hispanic Americans number 22.4 million, one in every ten Americans. This may increase to one in every five by the year 2050 (McLaughlin 1993). Persons of Mexican origin formed the largest group, nearly 13.5 million. Puerto Ricans were the second largest group, with over 2.7 million. The third largest were Cubans, with slightly over 1 million.

The male Hispanic labor force is more likely to be engaged in low paying, less steady occupations. Unemployment rates are consistently higher (11.3 percent) than for non-Hispanics (7.5 percent). Median family income is consistently lower: over 26 percent of Hispanic families live below the poverty level. Of all Hispanic children, 39.9 percent live in poverty (Castex 1994).

Hispanic racial identity is a product of the intermarriage of Spaniards with the native peoples of the Americas, Indian tribal groups, blacks from Africa, Northern Europeans, Asians, mestizos, and their descendants by intermarriage. If we define race as a term denoting possession of identifiable, distinguishing phenotypic characteristics, the value of race as a category for distinguishing Hispanics is questionable. With Hispanics, racial identity is based less on phenotype and more on cultural experience or personal choice. When asked to identify themselves racially, Puerto Ricans—the offspring of black, Spanish, and Caribbean Indian progenitors—rightfully label themselves as any one of the three.

The Spanish language is a common means of communication among Hispanics. However, clear evidence of differences in national or regional origin, history, and experience are noted in differences in syntax, sound, articulation, and vocabulary. Neither are all Hispanics fluent or literate in Spanish. Some may be bilingual, but are literate only in English. Millions of Hispanics speak Native American languages such as Mayan Quechua or Aymara, or any of a number of Creole or regional Spanish dialects. For them, Spanish may be a second language.

Examining Hispanic ethnicity in the United States, we see that the myth of the melting pot has obscured the degree to which Hispanics have retained an ethnocultural identity through active preservation of traditions, values, patterns of thinking, feeling, and behaving. Ethnicity is more than preservation of aspects of culture. Ethnicity results when a group is singled out or identifies itself as different from another in a we–they dichotomy. Cubans who have settled in the United States may or may not have observable cultural or biological traits. Salvadorans form that ethnic category because they self-identify as Salvadorans, as do Dominicans, Hondurans, or Colombians, and they differ from Anglo-Americans, who form the majority of mainstream American society. Hispanic subgroups maintain a visibly distinguishable autonomy, once the observer has developed an eye for those subtle yet distinctive culturally determined shadings and configurations. The Cuban-ness, Puerto Rican-ness, or Mexican-ness of each group is visible in both verbal and nonverbal behaviors.

Insufficient attention has been paid to the many differences—in lifestyle, social context, language, thinking, behavior, specific strengths, and weaknesses—among and within Hispanic subgroups. The literature makes frequent reference to Hispanics as a very diverse group, but there is little discussion of actual differences (Castex 1994).

When examining cultural differences, we see that national origin plays a key role in socialization, beliefs, and behaviors. However, specific differences within Hispanic subgroups are based on social class, immigrant/residential status, extent of acculturation, and diverse histories. In any given substance abuse treatment facility or caseload group, there can be a wide diversity of Hispanic men. For example, a Cuban client may come from a family that arrived in the late 1960s wave of upper middle-class Cubans who were given extensive assistance by the American government, while another can come from a working class poor family, or the so-called criminal underclass expelled in 1982 (Marielitos), and who upon arrival in the United States were sent directly to internment camps and psychiatric hospitals. Puerto Rican men in that same treatment group can come from very diverse mores and experiences. Some Puerto Ricans raised in the mainland United States are bilingual and bicultural. Although raised and educated in urban American settings, they often hold to very traditional Hispanic thinking and values. Some may have lived in an inner city neighborhood since childhood, yet speak little or no English, with little or no adaptation to the host culture.

The use of the term *Hispanic* to group people as diverse as Mexicans, Chileans, Cubans, and Salvadorans cannot be dismissed as simple use of a label. This label has cultural impact. It has a profound influence on identity and sense of self in reference to the ways Hispanics self-identify as bearers of their own specific culture, experience, values and mores, how the members of different Hispanic subgroups relate to one another, and more important, how non-Hispanic treatment providers see them.

ALCOHOLISM, DRUG ABUSE, AND HISPANIC MEN

According to Mayers and Kail (1993), Hispanic men drink more heavily and frequently than the general population, and their drinking decreases after middle age. The typical pattern is one of drinking infrequently to the point of intoxication. With acculturation, drinking patterns change. Puerto Rican men tend to retain a pattern of drinking to intoxication, while Mexican-American men abstain more, but those who drink do so more heavily than other Hispanics. With more acculturation, both Cubans and Dominicans stress moderation in drinking (Sanchez et al. 1993).

Mexican-American men tend to self-medicate with alcohol in the expectation that it will relieve depressive symptoms. It is also pointed out that the right to use alcohol is reciprocally linked with the male provider role, that is, as reward or entitlement (Martinez 1988). There is little research on alcohol or drug-related cognition among Puerto Ricans and Cubans (Sanchez et al. 1993).

Drug use among Hispanics resembles that found in the general population (Mayers and Kail 1993). Disparities in patterns of drug use among

Hispanics reflect the varied patterns of substance use in the general drug culture of the United States. This includes the regional preferences of the host culture. For example, on the West Coast where glue sniffing may be prevalent, Hispanic users show a preference for glue sniffing, as they may for crack use in Eastern urban areas.

CULTURAL DYNAMICS OF HISPANIC MEN

When looking at the source and unifying aspects of Hispanic culture, we see that Hispanic men share the heritage of Spanish conquest and consequently of Spanish culture. Hispanics share a largely similar common language, as well as the core values of cooperative interdependence and reliance upon the strength and support of the family, recognition of an individual's dignity and the giving of respect regardless of societal rank, conferring status and social esteem based on who a person is rather than what he has achieved, the valuing of interpersonal relationships, and the interpersonal sharing of the emotional aspects of life (Arce 1979). These real and reliable commonalities are what lead us to group and label Hispanics, despite the potential danger of inaccuracy and stereotyping. Placing emphasis on differences while ignoring similarities leads to another inaccuracy—that of "excessive empiricism" (Melville 1988).

CULTURAL VALUES

Familism, sense of hierarchy, fatalism, spiritualism, personalism (which includes *respeto* and *dignidad*), and machismo are unifying cultural concepts that distinguish Hispanics from the dominant society and form the foundation of Hispanic-American family structure and relationships (Ho 1987). Awareness and appreciation of these values are essential components of accurate empathy and vital to the process of engaging the Hispanic substance-abusing man in treatment.

Machismo is a broad Hispanic cultural term that is associated with sexual prowess, influence, and power over women that is reflected in vigorous romanticism and the jealous guarding of sweetheart or wife along with premarital and extramarital relationships. Unfortunately, this term has been frequently maligned and misunderstood, taken by non-Hispanics as equivalent to a brutal hypermasculinity, male chauvinism, physical aggression, entitlement, and promiscuity.

In Spanish, the use and meaning of this concept is quite different, and the term has many positive connotations. It suggests a personal behavior style—a kind of daring and control where the male meets challenge, risks, or threats with coolness and self-composure. Machismo holds the value of personal attraction, where others are positively influenced and will follow someone as a leader (Dillard 1983). The hierarchical role of male dominance and female submission (rightfully brought into question by feminists) is rooted in Spanish tradition and defines the husband-and-wife relationship, with husband in the role of provider and protector. He is expected to be dignified, hardworking, and macho, that is, a desirable combination of virility, virtue, romanticism, and courage (Ho 1987). Researchers (Dillard 1983, Ho 1987, Mirande 1988, Sanchez et al. 1993) agree that compliance with the cultural ideal of machismo may be more social fiction than actuality. As in Ho's (1987) examination of the literature, Hispanic families may include husbands who are domineering and patriarchal, who are submissive and dependent on their wives for major decisions, or who engage in a more egalitarian power struggle. Adherence to this cultural ideal is greatly influenced and altered by acculturation and adaptation.

There is no argument that sexism and chauvinism exist among Hispanics, but these are not the same things as machismo in the Hispanic context. Assumptions of male supremacy should not be made when establishing a treatment relationship with male Hispanic substance-abusing clients. They, like men of all cultures, subscribe to varying degrees of sexist stances, beliefs, and behaviors.

With a group as diverse as Hispanics, adherence to a cultural ideal and its influence on etiology in chemical dependency is not easily quantified. When clinicians confront, work with, or refer to sexism, the term machismo should not be used. It detracts from the term's positive connotation.

Machismo is the cultural concept most closely associated with Hispanic men and substance abuse issues. It is associated with the ability to use and abuse alcohol and substances without losing control. However, the influence of the concept of machismo on substance abuse patterns and etiology has not received great attention in the literature. Ramos-McKay and colleagues (1988) have cited a single study that asserts that alcoholism among Puerto Rican males is intertwined with machismo. According to those authors, Puerto Ricans are subjected to intensifying degrees of stress in their attempts to achieve an ideal macho self-image throughout their developmental span. They propose that inconsistencies in child-rearing patterns, coupled with overindulgence, tend to foster dependency and low frustration tolerance. When Puerto Ricans migrate to the mainland, acculturation threatens self-esteem and produces high levels of frustration. The authors have posited that Puerto Rican males may turn to alcohol as a source of dependency gratification, for release of anxiety and tension, or as a means of fantasizing macho characteristics in themselves.

Familism cuts across class lines and is a concept that requires the understanding that descriptions of "traditional" Mexican, Puerto Rican, or Cuban family values and normative rules are abstractions, broadly generalized, and sometimes exaggerated. It has been noted that a Hispanic male's self-confidence, worth, security, and identity are often determined by his relationship to other family members. Most studies of the extended kinship system of the Puerto Rican family stress loyalty and interdependence, reinforcing cooperation over competition. In Mexican and Puerto Rican families, each member has a deep sense of family obligation and family needs may supersede individual needs. Cubans tend to endorse individualistic responses in family problem-solving situations more often than do other Hispanics. Familism studies confirm that family disruption and lack of extended family may predispose adolescent boys to drug use. Conversely, strong familial ties may actually enable and permit the maintenance of drug and alcohol dependence, as Mexican-American, Puerto Rican, and Cuban families are likely to protect members who are "in trouble" from public recognition and censure (Sanchez et al. 1993).

Personalism is a concept describing how a Hispanic male defines self-worth in terms of the inner qualities that give him self-respect and earn respect from others. As described by Ho (1987), the Hispanic male feels an inner dignity (*dignidad*) and expects others to show respect (*respeto*) for that dignity and the inner qualities that constitute his uniqueness and internal goodness. In showing respect, he demands respect. Among Puerto Ricans, *respeto* toward the elderly and other figures of authority mitigates against the direct expression of anger, autonomy, and assertiveness, and may induce drinking as an outlet for frustrations (Ramos-McKay et al. 1988).

Personalism reflects a distaste for the impersonal aspect of situations (Queralt 1984) and can refer to preference for individualized treatment rather than rules. Clients will often identify and align with a particular counselor or therapist rather than with the agency or institution.

Sense of hierarchy governs interaction based on a role structure determined by age, sex, and professional authority. Because of the authoritative role of the treatment provider, clients may find it impolite to disagree during group or individual sessions. Being *simpatico* emphasizes maintaining a pleasant demeanor, lowering conflict, and promoting agreement. Many Hispanics come to treatment with the belief that anger must not be expressed overtly.

Fatalism is the Hispanic tendency to think in transcendent terms of the qualities of justice, loyalty, and destiny. Fatalistic thinking leads to the acceptance of tragic and unfortunate events as inevitable. It is reflected in the often heard expression "*si Dios quiere*" (if God wills it). Hispanic male substance abusers may use fatalism to support denial and to view chemical dependency and its consequential losses as destiny or divine providence rather than the product of progressive drug addiction or alcoholism.

Spiritualism is the belief that the visible world is surrounded by an invisible world inhabited by good and evil spirits that influence human behavior (Ho 1987). In Cuban communities, *Santeros* are faith healers. *Espiritismo* is the faith-healing system that predominates in both Cuba and Puerto Rico. Mexican-Americans often consider spiritual or religious factors important in explaining the cause or resolution of a problem, and many have strong devotion to the *Virgen de Guadalupe.*

THERAPEUTIC USES OF CULTURE

No matter what the clinician's theoretical stance or preferred treatment modality—be it psychosocial casework, group work, gestalt, psychoanalysis, object relations, self psychology, disease model, harm reduction, or any eclectic combination—treatment must take into account the client's acculturation level.

Acculturation is defined as the process whereby a cultural group learns, acquires, and integrates both the overt and covert cultural characteristics of a host culture, that is, the integration of the affective, cognitive, and behavioral cultural traits of the predominant culture (Mendoza and Martinez 1981).

Although Hispanics share many similarities, chemically dependent Hispanics come from many walks of life and have a wide range of personality dynamics. Because acculturation occurs at a different rate and depth for each individual, the clinician needs to assess the level of acculturation and incorporate this information into any interventions made. (See Valdez et al. 1987 for a listing of acculturation measurement tools.)

Machismo in Recovery

The concept of machismo can be used in the service of recovery and the protection of sobriety. Therapeutic use of this cultural value leads to exploration of recovery and the rewards of sobriety couched in terms of regaining strength of character and social control. Use of this cultural value assists the clinician to look for and work with client strengths.

What can emerge is a positive male identity utilizing machismo in the Hispanic sense of prized characteristics such as attractiveness, charm, and courage. The role of the client as a reliable, responsible provider, and protector can be noted, commended, and reinforced in the design of empowering psychological interventions. Positive cultural characteristics of machismo—respect, honesty, loyalty, fairness, responsibility, and trustworthiness—are attained by the recovering drug addict and alcoholic as he strives to maintain honor and integrity in treatment, in his twelve-step groups, in the family, and in the community.

> Manuel A. was a 35-year-old Puerto Rican male with four months of recovery from alcohol and cocaine dependence. As his wife neared release from prison, having served a term for drug sales and possession, he found the situation so stressful that it precipitated what looked like paranoid personality disorder. He obsessed and worried about her vulnerability. He obsessively feared that she would respond to sexual advances made by the drug-using and predatory men she might meet in the parole office, welfare lines, or on the streets. He also feared her using drugs with them. He became extremely suspicious and controlling around his wife's sobriety. His therapist did not talk about codependency (i.e. his attempts to control or direct her recovery), but focused on his role as sober husband and father. Since machismo values the role of the "man-in-control," the therapist used the positive aspects of machismo as a guide. He helped Mr. A. to test reality around "the ability of anyone to control an addict" (his wife). The therapist reinforced the view that each partner in a relationship is responsible for controlling his or her own recovery. Through controlling and maintaining his own recovery, Mr. A. could then be the man-in-control: the equitable, clear-thinking leader, protector, and provider he wanted to be.

Marin (1990) suggests machismo can be used in prevention efforts aimed at intravenous drug abusers, given that machismo incorporates the idea that the male has the serious responsibility of protecting his family and loved ones. Machismo is used to convey the message that preventive methods will protect family members from acquiring the HIV virus. This is particularly relevant when we see, as Soriano (1993) reported, that Hispanics are overrepresented among AIDS cases, and over half of all Hispanic AIDS cases are associated with intravenous drug use.

Control

Control is an important and valued aspect of the male role, the sense of self, and self-efficacy. If the male Hispanic client is currently chemically dependent, the issue of personal control will often be important to him.

According to Eden and Aguilar (1989), when the feeling of loss of social control in the new or host culture is combined with a more personal control issue, the Hispanic's psychological problems and chemical dependency difficulties are complicated even further.

A universally accepted component of the therapeutic work with male substance abusers is the exploration and processing of loss of control (i.e., chemical dependency) and loss of the ability to use drugs and alcohol recreationally or moderately. This is an issue that cuts across ethnic, racial, cultural, and class lines. The therapeutic work includes the exploration and processing of the corollary losses of work and the role of provider and protector, blows to pride and self-esteem, shame and guilt around the hurt and damage inflicted upon family members, and the consequential loss of trust and need to regain that trust.

With more traditional or recently arrived Hispanic men, these issues may be especially poignant, given the importance of male identity and control and the distinguishing cultural values of familism, *respeto* and *dignidad.* Loss of control over substances may be exacerbated by the real or perceived loss of control over social situations because of language and cultural differences between themselves and mainstream American culture.

The spiritual approach and concept of surrender is particularly helpful when giving up control is presented in the light of "surrendering our wills to a Higher Power" (the therapy group, clinic, twelve-step group, and for many Hispanics, God). There is a two-fold result. First, in surrendering, the Hispanic man is better able to bear the emotional pain of facing, accepting, and letting go of the loss, and ceasing the stress of battling the impossible in a hopeless struggle. Second, in surrendering his will to God, he behaves as he believes God would want him to and finds ease in accepting whatever happens as a result. This is an example of the productive utilization of fatalism.

Fatalism

Fatalism may explain or can be used to overcome resistance to entering treatment. To support or reframe mandated treatment, the clinician might say, for example, "You are here for a reason. You were meant to be helped." Fatalism may also have the adaptive effect of softening a sense of despair or personal failure with the statement, "It couldn't have been any other way."

The social worker wished Mr. R. a good weekend, and said, "I'll see you on Monday." Mr. R. answered, *"Si Dios quiere."* (If God wills it.) The social worker, knowing Mr. R.'s habit of weekend risk-taking behaviors, did not think Mr. R. was being religious. The worker refused to collude with the client's probable denial by responding, "Yes, *si Dios quiere*, and if Mr. R. stays away from people, places, and things!"

Personalism

When treating Hispanic substance-abusing men, utilizing personalism is essential in establishing the therapeutic relationship. Personalism includes a chat about the weather, baseball, the clinic, or a client's questions or comments about the clinician before the session. In the building of trust (*confianza*) with male Hispanic substance abusers, the clinician must act in a trustworthy manner. Asking many "personal" questions, especially of a sexual nature, is not productive (for example, in a psychosocial interview that looks for sexual abuse histories). These questions are better left until a therapeutic relationship has been established. Writing notes during early interviews is better left until after the session has ended and the client has gone. The limits and specifics of confidentiality must be clarified, with disclaimers of association with child welfare, criminal justice, and public assistance systems.

Hispanics feel an inner dignity (*dignidad*) and expect others to show respect (*respeto*) for that dignity and the inner qualities that constitute the client's uniqueness and "internal goodness."

Ernesto P. was an anxious, hypomanic, dually diagnosed client in an outpatient alcoholism treatment program. His eccentricity and thought disorder made him vulnerable to scapegoating behavior by other clients in the clinic. During group treatment, staff often intervened to model *respeto* by reframing his statements for the purpose of assisting and facilitating group members' understanding of and relating to the *content* of his contributions.

Sense of Hierarchy

In alcohol and drug abuse treatment, which often requires a directive and more confrontative approach, it is more effective to maintain a complementary relationship. The clinician should be less direct, more business-like, using *usted* (the formal pronoun for "you"), employing humor and diminutives to soften directiveness. It can be helpful when confronting a client to announce that the exchange that is occurring is a confrontation, along with an expression of regret that includes the explanation of the counselor's responsibility to assist and protect the client's recovery.

For many Hispanic clients, a therapeutic relationship is one in which the client comes to the practitioner for advice, as they might do with the *curandero*, priest, or *espiritista*. The clinician must be very careful in these circumstances, and if advice is given, it must be well thought out, consistent with clients' cultural values, and supportive of client empowerment.

> Mr. J. came to his clinic appointment where he showed *respeto* for his counselor by wearing a suit. She returned *respeto* by complimenting his appearance. He told her he had come because he trusted her (*confianza*) because she had always given him good advice, mentioning that his mother agreed it was always good advice. The fact was that the counselor's interventions were rarely "advice" but were generally a reframing that acted to steer Mr. J. toward his own decisions. His perception of the counselor, however, was that she was an authority who advised him. On one occasion he told the counselor he "listened to her even though she was a woman." Rather than confront the perceived male supremacy of such a statement, the counselor chose to support the behavior (*confianza*) that supported recovery and thanked him for his trust.

Spiritualism

All of the "spirit" and healer systems can be employed as potent supports that can augment substance abuse treatment with powerful therapeutic effects. It must be made clear, however, that they are helpful adjuncts, not replacements for treatment.

Hispanic clients may find it reassuring and fortifying to call on the guardian spirits, or *vejitas*, of childhood memories or to pray to hometown saints.

Familism

Culture can similarly be used to protect recovery, especially when dealing with the vulnerabilities that characterize early recovery. The longing to reestablish contact and regain lost trust with family can be very strong among Hispanics. In times of stress, Puerto Ricans may return to their old neighborhood to be with family or chat with friends (Ramos-McKay et al. 1988). The clinician must be careful not to dismiss this behavior as a return to "people, places, and things" and indicating resistance to sobriety. However, if a client's friends or family drink alcohol or use drugs, the clinician can reframe the client's strategic retreat from fearful or "un-macho" flight from personal challenge to the *need* to walk away. The distancing from family and friends can be supported culturally by reframing the need to pull away as a "correct response" if family or friends use alcohol or other substances in the client's presence or if they offer him alcohol or drugs. The lack of "respect" for the recovering client's sobriety by such friends or family members should be pointed out to the client.

CODEPENDENCY

Codependency has been defined as a relationship between two or more people who rely on each other to meet and provide for reciprocal needs, particularly unhealthy emotional ones (Barker 1991). Addressing codependency issues has been found to be useful in the provision of services to different addicted populations (Treadway 1990). Inclan and Hernandez (1992) have argued, however, that focusing on codependency reflects a value-laden Anglo-cultural narrative whose applicability to Hispanic clients needs to be examined further.

In the treatment of codependency, the goal is to assist the client to change self-defeating, dysfunctional patterns in a process that encourages separateness and individuation. The client's attention is redirected to the development of the client's own self. The clinical application of this model conflicts with the vital Hispanic value of familism in that it supports the Anglo value of individualism, which is not necessarily congruent with Hispanic culture. Inclan and Hernandez (1992) have pointed out that although growth through individuation is a universal developmental concept, there is evidence that individuation is expressed differently and at different phases of the life cycle in different cultures (see Inclan and Heron 1989). If the clinician organizes interventions or defines a client's recovery based on assumptions that the client has already incorporated the values, beliefs, and behaviors of the host culture, the clinician will encounter resistance and treatment failure caused by lack of cultural fit of an Anglo model to a Hispanic client.

It can be frustrating to clinicians to hear a Hispanic battered woman talk about her respect for the batterer "because he is the father of my children." This is especially problematic when the batterer is actively using alcohol or drugs. Nonetheless, it will be more productive to examine and modify the woman's behaviors that support the addiction and abuse in a culturally permissible way rather than intrusively pushing the client to acquire mainstream or host culture family values, norms, roles, and belief systems.

During family intervention with a Hispanic family, a child should not be asked to confront a parent or elder. A father's role as authority figure should not be challenged by the clinician, but reframed, for example, as the father's "concern for the well-being of his family." Moreover, recommending to the family that they should stop enabling the addiction and lock out or deny sustenance and financial aid to a substance-abusing family member, especially a parent or older relative, will be rejected by many Hispanic families. The more appropriate objective might be to assist the family to explore and modify those behaviors that support the member's addiction, while avoiding any resistance-provoking suggestion that the family values might have caused the problem.

CONCLUSION

Cultural competence is an integral aspect of good clinical training and practice. For Hispanic men, familism, sense of hierarchy, fatalism, spiritualism, personalism, and *machismo* are unifying cultural concepts. The understanding of these concepts is essential in the engagement process, is a vital element in development of accurate empathy, and can be employed in the service and support of recovery from substance abuse. Such understanding also serves to deflect the stereotypes, assumptions, and presuppositions that comprise the quality of both treatment and outcome. Cultural consciousness without an investigation of each client's actual history and level of acculturation leads to faulty assumptions about the client's value system and life experiences. When treating the Hispanic male substance-abusing client, having basic information about various Hispanic cultures, knowing what it means to be a man in these cultures, and evaluating the client's acculturation level will assist the clinician in defining what may be cultural dynamics and what may be specific to that particular client.

On a programmatic level, it is important that an adequate number of staff should both speak Spanish and be sensitive to the cultural aspects of treatment. When this is not feasible, an experienced and well-trained Spanish-speaking clinician should be available during the intake process to ensure correct assessment of a client's ability to comprehend and interact in a primary English-speaking environment and to make an accurate diagnosis. Hispanic clients may benefit from an open-ended support group where discussion of cultural aspects of recovery and the relapse process, cultural values, and historical themes can lead to an improvement of the members' competence, mastery, and self-esteem.

When the distinctive sociocultural needs of the Hispanic substance-abusing man and the rich diversity and sociocultural resources of the Hispanic people are not recognized or used as extensively as they might be, the result may be a treatment failure. Chemical dependency professionals must continue to strive for cultural competence and culturally specific guidelines that assist them in meeting the challenge offered by cross-cultural clinical encounters.

REFERENCES

Arce, A. (1979). *Discussion: Cultural Aspects of Mental Health Care for Hispanic Americans.* Paper from a workshop held in April, Boston, MA.

Barker, R. L. (1991). *Codependency: The Social Work Dictionary.* Washington, DC: National Association of Social Workers Press.

Bernal, G., and Gutierrez, M. (1988). Cubans. In *Clinical Guidelines in Cross-Cultural Mental Health,* ed. L. Comas-Diaz and E. E. H. Griffith, pp. 233–261. New York: Wiley.

Castex, G. M. (1994). Providing services to Hispanic/Latino populations: profiles in diversity. *Social Work* 39:288–296.

Dillard, J. (1983). *Multicultural Counseling.* Chicago: Nelson-Hall.

Eden, S. L., and Aguilar, R. J. (1989). The Hispanic chemically dependent client: considerations for diagnosis and treatment. In *Alcoholism and Substance Abuse in Special Populations,* ed. G. W. Lawson and A. Lawson, pp. 205–222. Rockville, MD: Aspen.

Ho, M. H. (1987). *Family Therapy with Ethnic Minorities.* Newbury Park, CA: Sage.

Inclan, J., and Hernandez, M. (1992). Cross-cultural perspectives and codependence: the case of poor Hispanics. *American Journal of Orthopsychiatry* 62:245–255.

Inclan, J., and Heron, G. (1989). Ecologically oriented therapy with Puerto Rican adolescents and their families. In *Psychological Treatment of Minority Children and Adolescents,* ed. J. T. Gibbs and L. N. Hung, pp. 251–277. San Francisco: Jossey-Bass.

Marin, B. (1990). Drug abuse treatment for Hispanics: a culturally appropriate, community-oriented approach. In *Prevention and Treatment of Drug and Alcohol Abuse,* ed. R. Watson, pp. 185–205. New York: Humana.

Martinez, C. (1988). Mexican Americans. In *Clinical Guidelines in Cross-Cultural Mental Health,* ed. L. Comas-Diaz and E. E. H. Griffith, pp. 182–202. New York: Wiley.

Mayers, R. S., and Kail, B. L. (1993). Prevention of Hispanic substance abuse: a workplace perspective. In *Hispanic Substance Abuse*, ed. T. D. Watts, pp. 175–186. Springfield, IL: Charles C Thomas.

McLaughlin, J. (1993). Judge rebuffs cities on altering census. *The New York Times*, April 14, p. 1.

Melville, M. B. (1988). Hispanics: race, class, or ethnicity? *The Journal of Ethnic Studies* 16:67–83.

Mendoza, R. H., and Martinez, J. L. (1981). The measurement of acculturation. In *Explorations in Chicano Psychology*, ed. A. Baron, pp. 157–173. New York: Holt.

Mirande, A. (1988). Chicano fathers: traditional perceptions and current realities. In *Fatherhood Today: Men's Changing Role in the Family*, ed. P. Bronstein and C. Cowan, pp. 93–105. New York: Wiley.

Queralt, M. (1984). Understanding Cuban immigrants: a cultural perspective. *Social Work* March–April:115–121.

Ramos-McKay, J., Comas-Dias, L., and Rivera, L. (1988). Puerto Ricans. In *Clinical Guidelines in Cross-Cultural Mental Health*, ed. L. Comas-Diaz and E. E. H. Griffith, pp. 205–231. New York: Wiley.

Sanchez Mayers, R., Kail, B., and Watts, T., eds. (1993). *Hispanic Substance Abuse*. Springfield, IL: Charles C Thomas.

Soriano, F. (1993). AIDS and intravenous drug use among Hispanics in the U.S.: considerations for prevention efforts. In *Hispanic Substance Abuse*, ed. R. Sanchez Mayers, B. Kail, and T. Watts, pp. 130–145. Springfield, IL: Charles C Thomas.

Treadway, D. (1990). Codependency: Disease, metaphor, or fad? *Family Therapy Networker* January–February, pp. 38–42.

U.S. Bureau of the Census (1993). *Current population reports: Hispanic Americans today*, pp. 23–183. Washington, DC: U.S. Government Printing Office.

Valdez, L., Baron, A., and Ponce, F. (1987). Counseling Hispanic men. In *Handbook of Counseling Psychotherapy with Men*, ed. M. Scher, M. Stevens, G. Good, and G. Eichenfield, pp. 203–217. Newbury Park, CA: Sage.

21

Men
and
Gambling

Rick LairRobinson

Games of chance have been described in every society where historical records exist (Cialella 1984). Civilization has recorded gambling activity for at least 40,000 years in all parts of the world, including ancient China, Egypt, Greece, and Rome (Wykes 1964). Some early accounts of gambling have been described in religious documents. For example, one can find references to the "casting of lots" in both Judeo-Christian and Muslim texts (Brenner and Brenner 1991, Rosenthal 1975). The Koran asserts gambling is Satan's way of spreading dissension and instructs Muslims to abstain (McGowan 1994). Ancient Jewish societies believed gamblers' debts left them vulnerable to corruption and therefore barred them from testifying in Jewish courts. Jews who won money from other Jews were instructed to return double the money (Fleming 1978).

Though primarily a leisure activity, forms of gambling have served different functions over time. Casting lots enabled priests and judges to answer questions of public concern, determine guilt or innocence of individuals charged with crimes, and select rulers of the day. The current legalization of gambling is often opposed on religious or moral grounds, but ancient religious leaders often opposed the use of lots in situations where their advice was not being sought (Brenner and Brenner 1991). Thus it appears that historically, religious leaders were more concerned with the social and political power of gambling, not the moral consequences that concern us today.

Gambling has also served as a source of "voluntary" funding for government activity, public interest projects, and construction of educational institutions. Currently, the growing competition for gambling dollars has led to legislation with little consideration for social and individual consequences. Rarely has there been an assessment of potential harm to participants before instituting legal games—only Texas and Minnesota are known to have funded a baseline prevalence study of gambling habits before the legalization of gambling (Volberg 1996). While estimates of the number of compulsive gamblers in the United States are unreliable in the absence of a national study, there is little doubt that the number of pathological gamblers has grown. It is estimated that the number of compulsive (or pathological) gamblers has increased from 1.1 million during the mid-1970s to between 3 to 10 million today (National Council on Prob-

---

Special acknowledgment to Randall Brooks for his valuable contribution to this chapter.

lem Gambling 1993, Volberg 1996). Prevalence studies in fifteen states indicate that rates of pathological gambling range from 1.5 percent to 4.4 percent (Laundergan et al. 1990, Volberg 1993). These estimates would be higher if those who are considered as "problem" and "probable pathological" gamblers were combined. These studies suggest that states with more legalized gambling have nearly double the rates of problem and pathological gambling compared to states with less legalized gambling (Volberg 1991, 1992, 1993b, Volberg and Steadman 1988, Volberg and Stuefen 1991).

Pathological gambling is twice as common among males as it is among females (Volberg and Steadman 1988, 1989), and men represent the majority of gamblers found in treatment and Gamblers Anonymous (Ciarrocchi and Richardson 1989, Lesieur 1988, Volberg and Steadman 1988). Many of the men experience serious financial, marital, vocational, and emotional problems. Although there are more pathological gamblers needing help than ever before, research for this new field is still limited and has primarily focused on men in treatment or Gamblers Anonymous. There are few treatment programs for pathological gamblers and a limited understanding of how best to help these individuals and their families. This chapter provides an overview of what is known about men and pathological gambling and discusses treatment issues and suggested interventions. It concludes with a description of the impact of pathological gambling on the family.

GAMBLING AS POLICY

Since the arrival of the first colonists, there have been three periods or "waves" of legalized gambling in the United States—we are currently experiencing the third wave (Rose 1995). The availability of gambling has reflected the political and economic influences of the times.

The Spread of Legalized Gambling

Throughout American history, legalized gambling provided funds for local communities. For instance, in 1611, shortly after founding the Virginia Colony in Jamestown, the Virginia Company of London found itself in serious financial straits. Officials applied for and received a franchise from the government to conduct lotteries and ensure the colony's continuation (Rosecrance 1988). The Puritans objected to gambling, but colonists found lottery revenues useful for building educational institutions and public interest projects. In fact, the history of gambling suggests that our dislike of taxes and the government's willingness to use gambling revenues as a tax alternative is a frequent policy response to economic need. Social and moral objections to gambling have historically given way to social and economic need.

Since the 1970s, legalized gambling has spread across the United States in unprecedented fashion. Economic need, political feasibility, change in public attitude, and modern technology are the primary forces behind the current growth of legalized gambling. Unlike the previous generations, Americans today seem to be less opposed to gambling on moral grounds, and politicians have come to view it as a means to generate handsome revenues without raising taxes (Rose 1991). Consequently, legal gambling is more accessible than ever. Most states have legalized some form of gambling, and obtaining credit is becoming easier. Currently, some form of gambling can be found in all states except Utah and Hawaii, and the individual states continue to expand the number of games offered to citizens. Legal wagers in the United States reached $330 billion, an 1800 percent increase since 1976 (Christiansen 1993). Finally, technology allows states to provide players with faster and easier games, which can be more satisfying than rub-off tickets or table games—video poker machines are often referred to as the "crack-cocaine" of gambling. Gambling is now accessible through the Internet, and in a short time we will be able to wager through interactive television.

The Indian Gaming Regulatory Act of 1988

One other factor that has contributed greatly to the rapid spread of gambling has been the Indian Gaming Regulatory Act of 1988. This act resulted from the fact that many Native American tribes have decided to invest in gambling as a means of raising revenue. Such Indian facilities were resisted by states that found themselves in competition for gambling revenues. In 1987, a California high court decided the case of *California v. Cabazon Band of Mission Indians* (Rose 1990), stating that once a state legalized any form of gambling, tribes in that state had the right to offer the same game, but without governmental restrictions. This had tremendous political and economic ramifications for all states and tribes, and Congress was forced to respond to the issue.

Congress devised a three-part solution to the question of government control of gambling. The solution identifies three distinct classes of gambling: Class I gaming consists of social games or traditional Indian games and is under Indian control. Class II gaming includes activities such as bingo and poker. These games became subject to regulation by a new National Indian Gaming Commission. Of the three members on the Commission, two must be Native American. Class III gaming includes casino games, parimutuel betting, and lotteries. Tribes may operate such games, but only if they reach an agreement, also known as a compact, with the state. Essentially, Congress decided both tribes and states were sovereigns and legally allowed to negotiate with one another.

The act was felt to favor the rights of the tribes to develop gambling revenues, but the spread of Indian gaming has prompted the states to escalate their competition for gambling monies. To date, there are 327 tribes offering some form of legalized gambling—130 tribes have opened Class III gaming operations, which includes casino gambling (Trina Fox, personal communication Feb. 11, 1997, National Indian Gaming Association). Other forms of casino gambling, such as riverboat gambling, became legal in six states. Since the act was passed in 1988, several states have refused to negotiate compacts. In April of 1996, the United States Supreme Court ruled that tribes cannot force states to negotiate gambling agreements by suing them. While states and tribes can still negotiate compacts if they so choose, this ruling has removed a key remedy for tribes that want to open casinos.

MEN AND GAMBLING

Men, more so than women, are socialized to be competitors and risk takers. This certainly fits the stereotype of the gambler—a big-talking high roller with flashy jewelry and beautiful women hanging on his arm. Men are more likely than women to believe they can win big through gambling and believe they are smarter than the average "sucker." Above all, men enjoy the sense of personal power that comes from winning the competition, whether it be from cards, sports betting, or the stock market.

Unlike many activities, almost any man can gamble, no matter what his size or physical condition. Gambling involves some type of competition (against machines, the house, or other gamblers) and has the goal of winning. Competitive games allow men to test and enhance their character and sense of self. Winning can produce an incredible feeling of power and control, and one should not underestimate its function in the development of a gambling problem. Gambling, particularly those games that combine skill and chance, offer men an ideal way to act on these needs in a culturally approved manner.

Professionals who treat pathological gamblers often speak of them as better educated or more intelligent than other addicted clients, but this perception is misleading. Although men who seek treatment for gambling problems tend to be better educated, they represent only a small portion of all men who have gambling problems. Addiction professionals, on the other hand, see a far broader representation of individuals with other dependencies; thus, one cannot easily compare other addicted clients with pathological gamblers.

THE CONTINUUM OF GAMBLING ACTIVITY

While most men gamble in a recreational fashion, there are some who are unable to control their gambling activity or the consequences of their gambling consistently. Many men experience serious financial, marital, vocational, and emotional problems as a result of their gambling. As with other addictions, gambling is rarely identified as the problem; instead, lack of money or bad breaks tend to be the culprit. In order to further discuss the issues related to men with gambling problems, it is important to understand the continuum of gambling activities.

Social Gambling

Most people gamble in a recreational fashion and have few of the characteristics that define disordered gambling (National Council on Problem Gambling 1993). These individuals gamble for entertainment and rarely risk more than they can afford. While there may be some short-term "chasing" (trying to win back losses), it does not have the progressive nature found in pathological gambling (Lesieur 1984). Social gamblers find losing to be part of the activity and do not experience the social, family, or economic consequences of pathological gambling.

Professional Gambling

Professional gamblers take limited risks, and discipline is absolutely central to the activity. Professional gambling might be thought of as a vocation that one studies and consists of a small number of gamblers (Abt et al. 1984). Some of these men may experience problems with their gambling and engage in short-term chasing (Lesieur 1984) but will not engage in such behavior for prolonged periods.

Problem Gambling

The term *problem gambling* is often used in confusing and contradictory ways. Sometimes it is used to describe individuals in early stages of pathological gambling. Other times, it is used to describe potential pathological gamblers. It is also used as an all-inclusive term for the whole spectrum of disordered gambling. Rosenthal (1989) and Lesieur and Rosenthal (1991) have recently used the term to describe gamblers who experience problems with their gambling but who tend to lack signs of progression or preoccupation with long-term gambling. The confusion over terms may reflect a need for more refined classifications of individuals with gambling problems. For the purpose of this chapter, *problem gambling* will be used to represent a continuum of disordered gambling unless otherwise specified.

Compulsive Gambling

The term *compulsive gambler* was used even before its recognition as a mental disorder by the American Psychiatric Association in 1980. However, unlike most early-stage pathological gambling activities, compulsions are not generally pleasurable and compulsive behavior is thought to be involuntary, much like repetitive hand washing (Moran 1970). Although the term *compulsive gambler* is still used by many professionals and by members of Gamblers Anonymous, in the field of gambling studies and treatment it has given way to the term *pathological gambling*.

Pathological Gambling

While most people are able to gamble in a recreational fashion, there are those individuals who seem incapable of controlling the compulsion to gamble, despite adverse consequences. According to the American Psychiatric Association (1994), pathological gambling is a "persistent and recurrent maladaptive gambling behavior that disrupts personal, family, or vocational pursuits" (p. 615).

In order for an individual to be diagnosed as a pathological gambler, at least five out of ten criteria must be met. These criteria include: loss of control; tolerance; withdrawal; increasing preoccupation; gambling to escape problems and dysphoric feelings; chasing one's losses in an effort to get even; lying about one's gambling; jeopardizing family, education, job, or career; serious financial difficulties requiring a bailout; and illegal activities to finance gambling or pay gambling debts (American Psychiatric Association 1994).

Surveys of problem and pathological male gamblers among the general population in five states (Montana, North Dakota, South Dakota, Texas, and Washington) found that they differ significantly from nonproblem gamblers or those who are found in treatment facilities (Volberg

1996). Problem and pathological gamblers in the community are more likely to be nonwhite, unmarried, young males under the age of 30. Additionally, they are less likely to have finished high school and tend to start gambling at an earlier age than nonproblem gamblers (Volberg 1992, 1993b,c, Volberg and Stuefen 1991, Wallisch 1993). The majority of individuals who enter treatment for gambling problems, on the other hand, are white, middle-aged men (Ciarrocchi and Richardson 1989, Volberg and Steadman 1988). This difference may be due to economics since gambling is seldom covered by insurance and white, middle-class men are more likely to be able to pay for treatment on their own.

Pathological gamblers may engage in illegal behaviors as they lose legal options to pay their debts. Typically, crimes committed by pathological gamblers are nonviolent, involving some form of embezzlement or fraud, and may include check forgery, embezzlement, larceny, loan fraud, bookmaking, hustling, and fencing goods (Lesieur 1984). A survey of Gamblers Anonymous members have found that a significant number have engaged in some form of insurance fraud, the average amount being $55,000 (Lesieur and Puig 1987). It has been estimated that pathological gamblers generate $1.3 billion in insurance fraud each year. Late-stage pathological gambling can also lead to workplace problems similar to those manifested by substance abusers. These include decreased productivity, absenteeism, embezzlement, and employee theft (Lesieur 1984). Some gamblers become desperate enough to commit armed robbery (Lesieur 1984). As many as 30 percent of prison inmates could be classified as probable pathological gamblers (Lesieur 1987, Lesieur and Klein 1987). Adolescents with gambling problems may deal drugs or commit other illegal acts in order to gamble or pay debts (Ladouceur and Mireault 1988, Lesieur and Klein 1987).

PHASES OF PATHOLOGICAL GAMBLING

There are many theories regarding the causes of pathological gambling and many efforts have been made to distinguish different types of pathological gamblers. While there is disagreement in these areas, there appears to be three phases in the career of most pathological gamblers: winning, losing, and desperation (Custer and Custer 1978, Lesieur and Rosenthal 1991). Phase one is a winning period in which gambling is fun and enjoyable. Initially, winning and losing are part of the excitement, and many gamblers report a big win at this point in their career. Winnings may be due to luck or simply employing a certain amount of skill, but this may bring about a false sense of confidence. Once a gambler begins to lose, he may develop irrational beliefs such as being dealt "cold hands." Winnings may be used for more gambling or to enhance his budding grandiosity. At this early stage, gamblers may begin to borrow money or take out short-term loans in order to continue the "action." It is the action that first hooks the pathological gambler.

Phase two is characterized by losing. The gambler may be gambling more often and increasing the size of his bets. The increased risk not only heightens the sense of action but becomes a dominant force in the gambler's life. The need to continue the action leads the pathological gambler to begin chasing his losses in order to get even (Lesieur 1984). A gambler in this phase chases not only to recoup losses but to maintain and regain his diminishing sense of self-worth.

As the gambler's finances become depleted, he may chase with borrowed money or money normally used for family finances. The gambler often convinces others that he is in need of money to pay debts or escape threats from banks or loan sharks. Such losses and loans are typically hidden from spouse, family, and friends. It is not unusual for gamblers to swear off gambling, but this promise is generally broken once they have the necessary bail-out money. Because of the increased gambling activity and loss, work and social relationships begin to suffer.

As the losing phase continues, the gambler might increase his loan debt and/or become involved in fraudulent activities, such as lies on loan applications or forgery of a spouse's signature. The rationalization and delusion continues as the gambler believes he will be able to pay back the money once he makes the big win. The gambler may lose jobs because of his absences, and family problems continue to mount.

Desperation is the third phase of the pathological gambler's career. A large bail-out may have occurred by now though the gambler continues to lose. Family and friends become tired and angry at the ongoing lies and deception. The gambler may embezzle from his workplace or drain his own business in an attempt to relieve the pressure. Losses and debt increase uncontrollably as the gambler makes reckless bets without regard to consequence.

Panic and increased risk-taking lead to physical and emotional exhaustion. Gamblers may become agitated, hypersensitive, and sleep-deprived. Many gamblers face divorce and arrest. A growing sense of hopelessness contributes to deep depression, suicidal thoughts, and suicide attempts. At this juncture, many pathological gamblers face four options: suicide, incarceration, running away, or seeking help. The case of Bert reflects many of the dynamics discussed above.

Bert is a 52-year-old male who works as a buyer for an Air Force base in California. He is a recovering alcoholic with ten years of sobriety, although he no longer attends meetings of Alcoholics

Anonymous. Gambling has been a part of Bert's life since he was child growing up in New York City. He first played typical children's games like marbles and pitching pennies. He also remembers playing "nickel, dime, and quarter" card games at family gatherings, but does not feel gambling was a problem until later in life.

Bert entered the Air Force at the age of 22 after graduating from one of the top universities in the country. It was during his stay in the service that Bert became concerned about his drinking. He found himself experiencing blackouts and fighting with his friends. Once he left the service, he was quickly arrested for driving under the influence and public intoxication. He was unable to hold a job and subsequently lost contact with his family. After a particularly severe fight in which he received a concussion, Bert began attending meetings of Alcoholics Anonymous. He claims to have stayed sober since that time, although he quit attending meetings five years ago since he "no longer drinks and doesn't need to go."

Bert began gambling after being sober for a few years. He had obtained a job as an engineer and found himself financially secure but somewhat bored and lonely. Bert was introduced to casinos by AA friends who occasionally played slots or a little blackjack on the weekends. He enjoyed the atmosphere and excitement of the various games, but it was his first win at the blackjack table that captured his devotion. At first he was winning $50 hands and never seemed to lose much. Bert began to fantasize about winning big and one night he decided to "push the envelope." He had been working on a system for blackjack in which he would triple his bet every time he lost. Without being conscious of the time, Bert gambled for hours and by the next morning was $38,000 richer. That was the moment he decided to give up his job and become a professional gambler.

Bert moved to New Jersey and claims to have been a successful gambler for many years, although he is somewhat vague on this issue. He tells anyone who will listen that he won and lost millions over the next few years, and was eventually barred from all the casinos on the boardwalk. From there, Bert moved to Colorado but continued to lose badly. According to Bert, this was because he was prevented from using his "system" under Colorado rules. He continued to play blackjack but was dissatisfied with placing such small bets. He loved to brag about playing hands for hundreds, even thousands, while he was in New Jersey. Hungry for action, Bert often played the slot machines, but this only contributed to his ongoing losses. It is unclear why Bert suddenly left Colorado, but it is believed he borrowed a great deal of money and was unable to pay it back.

Bert moved to San Diego in the hopes he would not gamble away his money as he did in Colorado. He found a good job at a local Air Force base and even began dating, but his newfound prosperity only seemed to fuel his desire to gamble. Before long, Bert had returned to the casinos with no more luck than before. He spent long nights and large sums of money chasing his losses and was soon missing work in order to continue playing. Bert claimed to be calling on customers when he was actually in the casino and was soon falsifying expense reports for extra money. His girlfriend tired of lending him money that was never repaid and left him. Bert moved into a cheap motel and borrowed more than $25,000 from loan sharks who were pressing him for the money. Depressed, fearful, and alone, he attempted suicide and was brought to a local hospital after being found unconscious by a maid at the motel.

PATHOLOGICAL GAMBLING, ADDICTION, AND MENTAL DISORDERS

Although differences exist between pathological gamblers and other addicts, there are also a number of similarities, particularly with substance abusers (Lesieur et al. 1986). Researchers have found that pathological gamblers seek euphoric states (National Council on Problem Gambling 1993). They experience cravings and tolerance so that they increase the size of bets or risks to produce greater highs. They undergo withdrawal symptoms and an intensified high in anticipation of gambling (Rosenthal and Lesieur 1992, Wray and Dickerson 1981). There is also a preoccupation with the behavior and repeated attempts to cut down or stop the activity.

Pathological gambling and substance abuse often coexist. In fact, as many as 50 percent of pathological gamblers experience substance problems at some point in their life (Lesieur 1987, Linden et al. 1986). As seen in the case of Bert, one addiction can be followed by another. Dually addicted individuals will face their own unique relapse issues. An intensely stimulating environment, cheap drinks, and a losing streak can present very real problems for a recovering substance abuser who gambles. Consequently, a careful assessment for all other addictions is essential.

In addition to chemical dependency, studies also find evidence of other coexisting diagnoses such as depression, bipolar disorder, schizoaffective disorder, and panic disorders (Linden et al. 1986, McCormick et al. 1984). A study of hospitalized psychiatric patients utilizing the South Oaks Gambling Screen (SOGS) has shown that as many as 6.7 percent of these patients met the criteria for pathological gambling—a rate that is two to five times higher than the general population (Lesieur and Blume 1990). In that same study, 10 percent of the entire sample believed their parents to be problem gamblers. This would be two or three times the estimated rate in the general population.

THE TREATMENT OF PATHOLOGICAL GAMBLERS

Like other addicts, pathological gamblers deny their problem and tend to seek help only after experiencing a significant crisis. Since gambling is generally viewed as a pleasurable experience, the need for help is commonly recognized only after a man is threatened with divorce, job loss, or by loan sharks. If the gambler is fortunate, his self-destructive cycle may be interrupted earlier through intervention by family, friends, or an informed employer.

Unfortunately, even if he is willing, the current treatment options available to the pathological gambler are very limited. Although legalized gambling has come to be seen as an answer for states and tribes that wish to fund education and reduce unemployment, there are few attempts to use some of the revenues from gambling activities to evaluate and treat the social and individual repercussions of legalized gambling. Of the forty-eight states that have legalized gambling, only seventeen states use gambling revenues for prevention or treatment efforts (Volberg 1996). Monies for gambling-related programs average about $100,000 and range from $20,000 to $2 million per state (Volberg et al. 1996). In some states, such funds have to be renegotiated yearly.

Essentially, there are two forms of help available to the pathological gambler: twelve-step support groups such as Gamblers Anonymous and professional treatment programs. Currently, there are fewer than 100 outpatient and a dozen inpatient treatment centers designed solely for pathological gamblers in the United States. Insurance rarely covers treatment when the primary diagnosis is pathological gambling.

Gamblers Anonymous

Gamblers Anonymous (GA) is a twelve-step group patterned after Alcoholics Anonymous, which shares the same goals of abstinence, restitution, and inner change. GA provides a source of fellowship for men and women who need to replace gambling as a source of friends and social activity. Members are encouraged to admit their powerlessness over gambling and avoid the people and places that are associated with gambling. Compulsive gambling is viewed as a progressive disease, and members must avoid placing bets a day at a time.

Compulsive gamblers, the term commonly used by GA members, find others like themselves who are able to understand and empathize. Newcomers will find little support in the meetings for their rationalizations and excuses. Older members, as measured by recovery time, share their experience and strength with newcomers. By taking responsibility for their behavior, compulsive gamblers stop blaming others for their problem and no longer rely on gambling to build their self-esteem. GA members become accountable for their debts and are encouraged to make financial restitution.

Therapists who treat gamblers should strongly consider the use of GA as part of their treatment process. At the very least, pathological gamblers should be encouraged to attend a few GA meetings so that they can find a constant source of support and understanding.

Treatment Programs

There is no consensus as to whether pathological gambling is a learned behavior, a physiological abnormality, a result of economic influences, or an interactive relationship of biological, psychological, and sociological forces. Not surprisingly, then, there is little agreement on the most effective treatment programs and clinical interventions for treating pathological gamblers. Much of the current treatment for pathological gambling is modeled after the disease and medical model utilized in the treatment of drug and alcohol addictions (Blume 1988). There is some evidence that certain pathological gamblers can be taught to moderate their gambling behavior. However, many gamblers prefer to abstain completely because decreasing the intensity of wagering eliminates the pleasure from the activity.

Although inpatient treatment for gambling problems is not always possible, it is the treatment of choice for individuals who are suicidal or experiencing concomitant disorders such as depression, anxiety, or substance abuse. During their stay, gamblers are carefully monitored during the early withdrawal period and are provided with lectures and group and individual therapy. Some treatment programs provide assistance in working out repayment of debts. GA attendance is often required as a part of therapy.

While inpatient and outpatient programs dedicated strictly to the treatment of pathological gambling may be preferable, such programs are limited in number and availability. Alternatively, there are many drug and alcohol programs that utilize a multiaddiction modality, and there are indications that gamblers can be successfully treated in such settings (Lesieur and Blume 1991). Given the lack of a national policy toward gambling problems and the current trend toward cutting health care, incorporating pathological gamblers into existing treatment programs for substance abusers may be a necessary option for now.

Treatment Issues and Approaches

As with any client, gamblers should be given a thorough screening at the time of admission. A detailed social history will help collect information on a client's emotional, marital, legal, financial, and employment situation. It is absolutely vital to collect a history of gambling practices. Professionals should utilize a valid and reliable instrument such as the South Oaks Gambling Screen (SOGS) when assessing clients (Lesieur and Blume 1987). Gamblers are asked about the type of games played, frequency of gambling activity, and their gambling practices, such as how often a gambler chases losses, whether anyone has criticized the gambler's activities, and how gambling debts have been covered. Some clinicians use the Gamblers Anonymous Twenty Questions with the SOGS. Because denial and minimization is part of the disease, it is helpful to obtain collateral information from spouses, significant others, and referral sources.

Treatment staff should be aware that some gamblers who have recently stopped gambling may experience headaches, diarrhea, sweats, and tremors. The exact cause of these symptoms—whether they are due to withdrawal or sleep deprivation—is not known. Nonetheless, clients seem to respond to structured routine, sleep, exercise, and opportunities to discuss their feelings in a supportive atmosphere. Because pathological gamblers tend to seek assistance late in their disease, many are physically exhausted, emotionally spent, and without family support. By the time a gambler enters treatment, he is often facing serious debt, deteriorating family relationships, work problems, and even legal problems. The result is often an overwhelming sense of guilt and shame; therefore, special care should be given to evaluating depression and suicidal ideation. *One out of five pathological gamblers attempts suicide*—a rate higher than that for other addictions (Custer and Custer 1978, Lesieur and Blume 1991). Although many programs administer paper and pencil instruments to measure depression, clients should always be interviewed directly about past suicidal behavior and present feelings. One should always be concerned about gamblers who have lost all family support and face serious financial debt or legal problems.

Treatment personnel must be prepared to deal with individuals who are defensive and controlling. As pathological gamblers lose control over their life, they become obsessed with regaining control. A gambler in this downward spiral becomes increasingly secretive in his behavior and, as a result, becomes distrustful and alienated from others. Although pathological gamblers mistakenly focus on money as *the* problem, they need to be helped to realize that they are hooked on the action.

The type of game a gambler plays tells much about the individual. In general, when developing a treatment plan, clinicians should distinguish escape gamblers from action gamblers. Escape gamblers prefer games like bingo, lottery, and slot machines. They are more likely to be isolated, lonely men or women who are depressed or trying to cope with problem marriages. Most men tend to use escape gambling as a response to the problems created by the gambling itself. Interventions such as skill training or relapse prevention can assist escape gamblers in strengthening their coping strategies and problem-solving skills. Action gamblers are often men who prefer games of "skill" such as cards, racing, sports betting, and the stock market. They are competitive, narcissistic, and gamble for excitement and power. Action gamblers need to confront their delusions of power and control. GA may be particularly useful in treating such individuals. There are many recovering gamblers in these meetings who can confront the newcomer's grandiose fantasies.

Cognitive-behavioral therapy (Marlatt and Gordon 1985) may prove to be an effective treatment approach with pathological gamblers. Such strategies address the thinking errors and behaviors that reinforce gambling behavior. Like many addicts in denial, pathological gamblers are subject to selective memory and illusions of control, as well as superstitious thoughts and rituals. Cognitive interventions help clients become aware of their distorted thoughts and beliefs. Clients can be taught to identify and record those thoughts that influence the desire to gamble and the situations in which such thoughts occur.

Clients also can be helped to identify those situations and relationships that are most likely to lead them to relapse. They can then role play or discuss methods by which they can successfully manage such situations. Clients might also use visual imagery and imagine themselves successfully passing up the opportunity to gamble. In this manner, gamblers can prepare themselves for future encounters with gambling stimuli and hopefully prevent a relapse.

It is likely that gamblers who receive treatment experience relapse problems much like substance abusers. Relapse is a "failure to maintain behavior change, rather than a failure to initiate change" (Annis and Davis 1989, p. 170). Because the techniques that produce change may not be the same ones that maintain change, follow-up care should involve process-focused strategies to assist individuals in maintaining change over time. Pathological gamblers may respond well to skills training, relapse prevention, and/or self-efficacy training (Annis and Davis 1989, Marlatt and Gordon 1985).

Whenever possible, group therapy is strongly suggested. While individual therapy is invaluable for building a relationship with a client, gamblers, like other addicts, carry feelings of shame and a sense of being "different" or "worse than" others. A group setting provides an immediate means for identifying with others in a similar situation and lessens the feeling of being alone. Additionally, group members who are further in recovery can help the newcomer address his denial and blame. Other gamblers and addicts bring a credibility that therapists have to work for. Their "success" in therapy shows the newcomer that he can also address the many problems his gambling has caused.

A frequent goal in the treatment of pathological gamblers is abstinence from all forms of gambling. Therapists in outpatient settings may want to be cautious in their insistence on immediate abstinence from gambling. An early and rigid insistence on abstinence may result in an unnecessary struggle between client and therapist. While abstinence should remain a long-range goal, gamblers in an outpatient setting may need to be encouraged to gradually decrease their gambling activities while they form a trusting relationship with the clinician.

Restitution of debt is a common feature of both GA and treatment programs. Gamblers are often overwhelmed by their debts and pressures from creditors and loan sharks. Once gamblers have had an opportunity to alleviate some of their concerns and anxiety, it is possible to discuss alternatives such as credit counseling. In general, gamblers are competitive, resourceful, and independent men. Therapists can easily reframe all these attributes as strengths to be used during the rehabilitation and restitution process.

IMPACT ON THE FAMILY

There are a number of effects on family members of pathological gamblers, with many spouses and children exhibiting substantial emotional disturbances, high rates of abuse, physical illnesses, depression, and suicidal behavior (Jacobs 1989, Lesieur and Rothschild 1989, Lorenz 1981). Thus it is important that clinicians become aware of the impact of pathological gamblers on the family.

Spouses of Pathological Gamblers

Spouses report they are ridiculed, demeaned, or insulted by their gambling spouse in front of the children, often being blamed for the gambler's problems. Additionally, many wives report they have to contend with bill collectors and demands for payments of cosigned loans, adding to the considerable stress. Obviously, gamblers face serious marital and family disruption.

Professionals should be prepared to help wives with their own concerns. Significant numbers of spouses report they are physically abusive toward their children, perhaps in response to the stress of their situation. In a study by Lorenz (1981), at least 11 percent of spouses (wives) reported they had been physically abused by their pathological gambler husbands, while 37 percent of the spouses admitted to physically abusing their children. This suggests a cycle of stress and abuse within the family that must be addressed.

Not surprisingly, wives of pathological gamblers report serious psychosomatic, emotional, and marital difficulties within the relationship. When comparing female Gam-Anon members with female hospital patients, researchers found a high incidence of chronic or severe headaches, bowel problems, and asthma (Lesieur and Rosenthal 1991). There was also a higher incidence of depression and suicide attempts. Wives of pathological gamblers are three times more likely to attempt suicide than the general population (Lesieur and Rosenthal 1991).

> Pat was attracted to her husband from the day she met him. She was shy and unsure where John was exciting and confident. He worked hard and seemed destined to go places in life. They seemed so different from one another, but no one was surprised when they married a year later.
>
> Pat knew her husband gambled, but he had enjoyed visiting the racetrack since he was a teenager, so she did not feel she could object. She could not understand the attraction and rarely accompanied him; besides, it was something he liked to do with his friends. John often came home with exciting stories of his big wins and they would go out for a night of dining and dancing.
>
> She's unsure of when things began to change. John was fairly successful in his business, so when he become a little more withdrawn and preoccupied, she assumed it was his work that drew him away. She barely noticed the time he spent reading racing forms and talking on the phone. She certainly knew he was spending more time at the track, but surely a man who worked so hard needed to have some fun. Pat did not know he had been losing

big money and was visiting the track during work hours. John had begun to juggle accounts at the store and sometimes left work early to bet that day's receipts. Naturally, he intended to pay it back, but sometimes he had to take money from their checking and savings accounts in order to do it. When Pat began to notice the missing funds, John always seemed to have a reason and would become angry if she pushed him for more information.

Pat assumed that whatever was causing John to become secretive and moody was her fault. She tried to become more attentive and take an interest in his work. Pat tried losing weight, changing her hair color, and they even talked of having another child, but life continued to feel crazy. Money kept disappearing from their accounts and she began to receive calls from creditors for past due bills. Worse, she was receiving calls from people she didn't know, insisting that John call or send money immediately. John refused to talk to her about it and their fights were getting worse.

Pat was worried for the kids and how they were coping with the constant arguments. She was angry with John and was scared every time the phone rang. Nothing seemed to make sense. She only knew she felt sick to her stomach and just wished she could go to sleep and not wake up. How did life ever get to be like this?

One source of help for the wives of pathological gamblers is Gam-Anon. Gam-Anon is a twelve-step support group for spouses, family members, and friends of pathological gamblers. Gam-Anon meetings frequently take place at the same time and place as GA meetings. Members learn to address their own issues and meet their own needs, while allowing the gambler to take responsibility for his own life.

Children of Pathological Gamblers

Relatively little is known about the children of pathological gamblers. Jacobs (1989) discovered that children whose parents are compulsive gamblers are more likely to use tobacco, alcohol, and drugs. They are also more likely to display overeating and gambling behaviors and to gamble at earlier ages than their peers. These children are more likely to report having an unhappy childhood, having almost twice the incidence of broken homes by death of a parent or through divorce. Most telling was the higher incidence of poor mental state and depression: children of compulsive gamblers attempt suicide at twice the rate of their peers.

Lesieur and Rothschild (1989) also studied children of Gamblers Anonymous members and found many of the psychosocial issues mentioned by Jacobs to be more true of children whose parents were experiencing problems that coexisted with the pathological gambling. It is also important to note that children of pathological gamblers are more likely than the general population to have a gambling problem themselves (Lesieur and Klein 1987, Lesieur et al. 1991).

WOMEN AND GAMBLING

Certainly women gamble; in fact, they may comprise one of the fastest growing groups of gamblers and problem gamblers. Unfortunately, there is little gambling research that focuses on women. They are significantly underrepresented in surveys of gamblers in treatment (Volberg 1991, 1993a,c) and represent only 2 to 4 percent of Gamblers Anonymous members (American Psychiatric Association 1994). This may suggest there is a greater stigma for women who have gambling problems, making them less likely to seek help. It may also reflect a lack of outreach, education, and financial assistance focused on women with gambling issues. Finally, there is some suggestion that health care professionals misdiagnose women with gambling problems or fail to offer appropriate treatment interventions (Lesieur 1987).

We have only begun to understand the differences between men and women gamblers. They seem to gamble for different reasons. Women may begin gambling later in life than men and are more likely to gamble as a response to depression or marital difficulties (Lesieur 1987). Escape behavior by male gamblers, on the other hand, tends to be centered around problems created by gambling (Lesieur 1987). Both men and women gamblers demonstrate distortions in thinking as evidenced by illusions of power and control (Rosenthal 1986), but women could have a somewhat different pattern of progression as they tend to use gambling as an escape mechanism and are more passive in their gambling activity.

CONCLUSION

The rapid spread of legalized gambling has produced a number of economic benefits for individual states and Native American tribes. At the same time, the spread of gambling may have created significant individual, family, and social problems. Pathological gambling is a devastating illness that affects the gambler and everyone who has a significant relationship with him.

Research data suggests that men suffering from pathological gambling are found in drug and alcohol treatment programs (Lesieur and Rosenthal 1991, Lesieur et al. 1986), in psychiatric units (Lesieur and Blume 1990), and are likely to seek assistance for concomitant disorders from hospitals, mental health centers, self-help groups, and professionals in private practice. Knowingly or unknowingly, problem gamblers are being encountered in a broad range of health care settings. Health care professionals need more training in identifying pathological gamblers and how best to approach such clients. Further research is needed to better determine the true scope of problem and pathological gambling and the clinical implications of gender, race, and age differences.

It is time to conduct another national study on the incidence and consequences of gambling. Health care professionals should advocate for funds to study the impact of legalized gambling. The total money set aside for education, outreach, and treatment represents a minuscule proportion of gambling revenues and varies greatly among states. Professional associations should encourage state legislators to give greater consideration to the social and individual harm created by pathological gambling and to encourage further treatment initiatives. A national policy statement is needed to acknowledge the seriousness of gambling problems and afford pathological gamblers the same protections, such as insurance coverage, as substance abusers.

REFERENCES

Abt, V., Smith, J. F., and Christiansen, E. M. (1984). *An explanation of gambling behavior.* Paper presented at the Sixth National Conference on Gambling, Atlantic City, December.

American Psychiatric Association (1980). *Diagnostic and Statistical Manual of Mental Disorders*, third edition. Washington, DC: APA.

—— (1994). *Diagnostic and Statistical Manual of Mental Disorders*, fourth edition. Washington, DC: APA.

Annis, H., and Davis, C. (1989). Relapse prevention. In *Handbook of Alcoholism Treatment Approaches: Effective Alternatives*, ed. R. Hester and W. Miller, pp. 170–182. Elmsford, NY: Pergamon.

Blume, S. (1988). Compulsive gambling and the medical model. *Journal of Gambling Behavior* 3:237–247.

Brenner, G. A., and Brenner, R. (1991). Gambling: shaping an opinion. In *Gambling and Public Policy: International Perspectives*, ed. W. R. Eadington and J. A. Cornelius, pp. 481–498. Reno, NV: University of Nevada Press.

Christiansen, E. M. (1993). 1992 gross annual wager: industry rebounds with 8.4% handle gain. *Gaming and Wagering Business* 14(7):12–35.

Cialella, E. C. (1984). *Casino gambling in New Jersey: a case study of predictions*. Dissertation. Philadelphia: Temple University.

Ciarrocchi, J., and Richardson, R. (1989). Profile of compulsive gamblers in treatment: update and comparisons. *Journal of Gambling Behavior* 5:53–65.

Custer, R. L., and Custer, L. F. (1978). *Characteristics of the recovering compulsive gambler: a survey of 150 members of Gamblers Anonymous*. Paper presented at the Fourth Annual Conference on Gambling, Reno, Nevada.

Fleming, A. (1978). *Something for Nothing*. New York: Delacorte.

Jacobs, D. F. (1989). Illegal and undocumented: a review of teenage gambling and the plight of children of problem gamblers in America. In *Compulsive Gambling: Theory, Research and Practice*, ed. H. J. Shaffer, S. A. Stein, B. Gambino, and T. N. Cummings, pp. 249–292. Lexington, MA: Lexington Books.

Ladouceur, R., and Mireault, C. (1988). Gambling behaviors among high school students in the Quebec area. *Journal of Gambling Behavior* 4:3–12.

Laundergan, J. C., Schaefer, J. M., Eckhoff, K. F., and Pirie, P. L. (1990). *Adult survey of Minnesota gambling behavior: a benchmark*. Report to the Minnesota Department of Human Services, Mental Health Division.

Lesieur, H. R. (1984). *The Chase: Career of the Compulsive Gambler*. Cambridge: Scherbman Books.

—— (1988). The female pathological gambler. In *Gambling Studies: Proceedings of the 7th International Conference on Gambling and Risk Taking*, ed. W. R. Eadington, pp. 230–258. Reno: University of Nevada Press.

Lesieur, H. R., and Blume, S. B. (1987). The South Oaks Gambling Screen (SOGS): A new instrument for the identification of pathological gamblers. *American Journal of Psychiatry* 144(9):1184–1188.

—— (1990). Characteristics of pathological gamblers identified among patients on a psychiatric admissions service. *Hospital and Community Psychiatry* 41(9):1009–1012.

—— (1991). Evaluation of patients treated for pathological gambling in a combined alcohol, substance abuse and pathological gambling treatment unit using the Addiction Severity Index. *British Journal of Addictions* 86:1017–1028.

Lesieur, H. R., Blume, S. B., and Zoppa, R. M. (1986). Alcoholism, drug abuse, and gambling. *Alcoholism: Clinical and Experimental Research* 10:33–38.

Lesieur, H. R., Cross, J., Frank, M., et al. (1991). Gambling and pathological gambling among university students. *Addictive Behaviors* 16:517–527.

Lesieur, H. R., and Klein, R. (1987). Pathological gambling among high school students. *Addictive Behaviors* 12:129–135.

Lesieur, H. R., and Puig, K. (1987). Insurance problems and pathological gambling. *Journal of Gambling Behavior* 3:123–136.

Lesieur, H. R., and Rosenthal, R. J. (1991). Pathological gambling: a review of the literature (Prepared for the American Psychiatric Association Task Force on *DSM-IV* Committee on Disorders of Impulse Control Not Elsewhere Classified). *Journal of Gambling Studies* 7:5–40.

Lesieur, H. R., and Rothschild, R. J. (1989). Children of Gamblers Anonymous members. *Journal of Gambling Behavior* 5:269–282.

Linden, R. D., Pope, H. G., and Jonas, J. M. (1986). Pathological gambling and major affective disorder: preliminary findings. *Journal of Clinical Psychiatry* 47:201–203.

Lorenz, V. (1981). *Differences found among Catholic, Protestant and Jewish families of pathological gamblers.* Paper presented at the Fifth National Conference on Gambling and Risk Taking, Lake Tahoe, NV, October.

Marlatt, G. A., and Gordon, J. R. (1985). *Relapse Prevention.* New York: Guilford.

McCormick, R. A., Russo, A. M., Ramirez, L. F., and Taber, J. I. (1984). Affective disorders among pathological gamblers seeking treatment. *American Journal of Psychiatry* 141:215–218.

McGowan, R. (1994). *State Lotteries and Legalized Gambling.* Westport, CT: Quorum Books.

Moran, E. (1969). Taking the final risk. *Mental Health* (London) 21–22.

——(1970). Varieties of pathological gambling. *British Journal of Psychiatry* 116:593–597.

National Council on Problem Gambling, Inc. (1993). *The Need for a National Policy on Problem and Pathological Gambling in America.* New York: Author.

Rose, I. N. (1990). The Indian Gaming Act and the political process. In *Indian Gaming and the Law: Proceedings of the North American Conference on the Status of Indian Gaming,* ed. W. R. Eadington, pp. 3–14. Reno: University of Nevada-Reno.

——(1991). The rise and fall of the third wave: gambling will be outlawed in forty years. In *Gambling and Public Policy: International Perspectives,* ed. W. R. Eadington and J. A. Cornelius, pp. 65–86. Reno: University of Nevada Press.

——(1995). Gambling and the law: endless fields of dreams. *Journal of Gambling Studies* 11(1):15–33.

Rosecrance, J. (1988). *Gambling without Guilt: The Legitimation of an American Pastime.* Pacific Grove, CA: Brooks/Cole.

Rosenthal, R. J. (1975). *Gambling in Islam*. Leiden: Brill.

—— (1986). The pathological gamblers system for self-deception. *Journal of Gambling Behavior* 2:108–120.

—— (1989). Pathological gambling and problem gambling: problems in definition and diagnosis. In *Compulsive Gambling: Theory, Research and Practice*, ed. H. J. Shaffer, S. A. Stein, B. Gambino, and T. N. Cummings, pp. 101–125. Lexington, MA: Lexington Books.

Rosenthal, R. J., and Lesieur, H. R. (1992). Self-reported withdrawal symptoms and pathological gambling. *American Journal on Addiction* 1:150–154.

Volberg, R. A. (1991). *A study of legal gaming in Connecticut: problem gambling*. Report to the Connecticut Division of Special Revenue.

—— (1992). *Gambling involvement and problem gambling in Montana*. Report to the Montana Department of Corrections and Human Services.

—— (1993a). Estimating the prevalence of pathological gambling in the United States. In *Gambling Behavior and Problem Gambling*, ed. W. R. Eadington and J. A. Cornelius. Reno: University of Nevada Press.

—— (1993b). *Gambling and problem gambling in Washington state*. Report to the Washington State Lottery.

—— (1993c). The prevalence and demographics of pathological gamblers: implications for public health. *American Journal of Public Health* 84:237–241.

—— (1996). Prevalence studies of problem gambling in the United States. *Journal of Gambling Studies* 12:111–128.

Volberg, R. A., and Steadman, H. J. (1988). Refining prevalence estimates of pathological gambling in New Jersey and Maryland. *American Journal of Psychiatry* 146:1618–1619.

Volberg, R. A., and Stuefen, R. M. (1991). *Gambling and problem gambling in South Dakota*. Report to the Governor's Office of South Dakota.

Wallisch, L. (1993). *The 1992 Texas survey of adult gambling behavior*. Report to the Texas Commission on Alcohol and Drug Abuse.

Wray, I., and Dickerson, M. G. (1981). Cessation of high frequency gambling and withdrawal symptoms. *British Journal of Addiction* 76:401–405.

Wykes, A. (1964). *The Complete Illustrated Guide to Gambling*. Garden City, NY: Doubleday.

Index

Abelin, E., 346
Abraham, K., 289
Abstinence, achievement of,
    codependency issues and,
    59–61
Abt, V., 475
Access, treatment, codependency
    issues and, 58–59
Acuff, K., 141
Adams, K. L., 267, 269
Addiction
    gender and, 12–19
    biophysiology, 16–17
    dual diagnosis, 14–15
    epidemiology, 13–14
    etiology, 15–16
    outcomes, 19
    psychosocial and family
        consequences, 17–18
    referrals, 18–19

men
    fathers and sons, 333–357. See
        also Father's and sons
    gambling, 469–492. See also
        Gambling
    Hispanic men, 451–467. See also
        Hispanic men
    homosexual men, 385–410. See
        also Homosexuality
    learning disabilities and
        attention-deficit/hyperactivity
        disorder, 427–449. See also
        Learning disabilities and
        attention-deficit/hyperactivity
        disorder
    male executives, 411–425. See
        also Male executives
    psychodynamic perspective on,
        285–309. See also Men and
        psychodynamic therapy

Addiction
  men (*continued*)
    sexual dependence and, 359–384.
      See also Sexually dependent
      men
    values of, 311–332. *See also* Men's
      values
  women
    Alcoholics Anonymous and, 263–
      281. *See also* Women and
      Alcoholics Anonymous
    codependency issues, 47–69. *See*
      also Codependency issues
    depression and, 223–242. *See also*
      Women and depression
    eating disorders, 243–262. *See*
      also Eating disorders
    high-achieving women, 151–166.
      See also High-achieving
      women
    HIV/AIDS infection, 197–221.
      See also Women and AIDS
    lesbian women, 167–196. *See also*
      Lesbian women
    mothering, 123–150. *See also*
      Mothering
    relational theory and, 33–46. *See*
      also Relational theory
    sexual abuse and, 97–122. *See*
      also Sexual abuse
    sexuality and, 73–95. *See also*
      Sexuality (female)
Aguilar, R. J., 461
Aguirre-Molina, M., 189
AIDS infection. *See* HIV/AIDS
  infection
Airhihenbuwa, C. O., 209
Alcoholics Anonymous (AA), 58
  men and, 316–318
  women and, 263–281. *See also*
    Women and Alcoholics
    Anonymous
Alcoholism. *See also* Addiction
  fathers and sons, 333–357. *See also*
    Fathers and sons
  homosexuality and, 171–172

Alexander, M. J., 14, 15, 16, 17, 19
Alexander, S., 237
Amaro, H., 34, 125, 131, 133, 202
American Psychiatric Association,
  245, 247, 248, 249, 429, 436, 476,
  488
Anastos, K., 205
Anderson, S. C., 53
Andrews, A. B., 180
Annis, H., 485
Annon, J., 81, 82
Anorexia nervosa, defined, 247–248.
  See also Eating disorders
Antisocial personality disorder,
  learning disabilities and
  attention-deficit/hyperactivity
  disorder, 436–437
Arce, A., 456
Aronson, H., 341
Ash, M., 237
Assessment
  gender differences and, 19–22
  mothering, 134–138
  sexual abuse, 102–105
Attention-deficit/hyperactivity
  disorder. *See* Learning disabilities
  and attention-deficit/
  hyperactivity disorder

Bacon, L., 205
Barker, R. L., 464
Barkley, R. A., 436
Barnard, M., 202
Barr, M., 429
Barrett, B. J., 173
Barrett, M. J., 44
Beck, A. T., 229, 234, 235
Beckett, L., 74
Beckman, L. J., 12, 125, 131, 133, 139,
  141, 144
Behan, P., 434
Beitchman, J. H., 127, 128
Bell, N., 203
Belle, D., 34
Benedek, T., 21
Benjamin, J., 158

Bennett, L., 144
Bepko, C., 16, 43, 44, 53, 99, 131, 135
Berger, R. M., 396, 397
Bernal, G., 453
Bernstein, M. A., 113
Beschner, G. M., 99
Bickelhaupt, E. E., 387
Biederman, J., 435
Binion, V. J., 15, 129
Biophysiology
  eating disorders, 248–249
  substance abuse and gender,
      16–17
Black, C., 130
Black, R., 34
Blane, H. T., 296–297, 298
Bliss, S., 315
Blouin, A. G. A., 434
Blume, S. B., 12, 76, 132, 169, 228,
    229, 232, 481, 482, 483, 489
Bly, R., 315
Body image, homosexual men, 396–
    498
Bogart, G., 237
Bolen, J. S., 317
Bollerud, K., 99
Bowen, G. R., 278
Bowen, M., 90
Boyd, C. J., 229, 230
Brady, E., 173
Brannon, L., 7, 9, 11
Bratter, T. E., 36
Brenner, C., 6
Brenner, G. A., 471
Brenner, R., 471
Broverman, I., 12
Brown, D., 104
Brown, P. J., 131
Brown, S., 321, 337
Brown, S. A., 136
Browne, A., 128
Bryer, J. B., 99
Bulimia, defined, 247–248. *See also*
    Eating disorders
Byington, D. B., 35
Byne, W., 388

Cabaj, R. P., 387, 388, 389, 407
Calao, F., 99, 100
Campbell, D. L., 76
Carmen, E. H., 99
Carnes, P. J., 361, 364, 365, 368, 369,
    370
Carpenter, C. J., 207
Cash, T. F., 247
Casolaro, V., 418, 419
Cass, V. C., 393, 394, 395
Castanos, J. N., 341
Castex, G. M., 453, 454
Cath, S. H., 337
Celentano, D. D., 169
Center for Substance Abuse
    Treatment, 18, 22, 141
Centers for Disease Control and
    Prevention, 199–200, 201, 206,
    207, 403
Cermak, T. L., 50
Chafetz, M., 338
Chasnoff, I. J., 141, 142, 143
Chaucer, G., 74
Cheloha, R., 42, 155
Chiaramonte, L., 206
Child, I., 296
Child abuse, fathers and sons, 347–
    349. *See also* Sexual abuse
Chodorow, N., 7, 8, 35, 52, 54, 156,
    274
Chopra, D., 233
Christiansen, E. M., 473
Chu, S. Y., 206, 210
Cialella, E. C., 471
Ciarrocchi, J., 472, 477
Clark, M., 269
Clark, W. B., 79
Clayson, Z., 126, 133
Cloninger, C. R., 15, 298
Cloninger, R., 335
Cochran, S. D., 208
Codependency issues, 47–69
  critique of concept, 53
  definitions, 49–50
  etiology, 50–51
  gender-specific factors, 55–56

Codependency issues (*continued*)
  Hispanic men, 464–465
  relational voice and, 54–55
  socialization of women, 51–53
  treatment and, 57–65
    abstinence achievement, 59–61
    access and persistence, 58–59
    denial, 57–58
    integrative approaches, 65–67
    recovery quality, 63
    settings, 63–65
    sobriety maintenance, 61–63
  utility of concept, 54
Codependents Anonymous, 50
Coghill, N. H., 74
Cohen, F. S., 173
Cohen, J. B., 205, 231
Cohen, M., 413
Coker, M., 42
Colcher, R., 389, 400, 401
Cole, P. M., 127
Coleman, E., 361, 362, 363, 364, 367,
    368, 369, 370, 376, 378, 379, 380,
    393
Colten, M. E., 131
Compulsive behavior
  gambling, 476
  homosexual men, 402
  sexually dependent men, 363–364
Conduct disorder, learning
    disabilities and attention-deficit/
    hyperactivity disorder, 436–
    437
Cooley, C. H., 250
Corcoran, K., 135, 137
Corrigan, E. M., 34
Cottler, L. B., 131
Cotton, D., 201
Countertransference
  codependency issues, 67
  gender differences and, 22
  women and AIDS, 212–213
Covington, S. S., 51, 54, 56, 74, 75, 76,
    77, 78, 79, 80, 81, 82, 83, 85, 87,
    274, 275, 276, 277, 278
Cowley, A., 237

Cox, W. M., 299
Culture
  eating disorders, 250–251
  gender differences, 9
  Hispanic men, 456–459
  women and AIDS, 209
Cunningham, R., 203
Custer, L. F., 477, 483
Custer, R. L., 477, 483

Dane, E., 430, 434, 435
D'Augelli, A. R., 389, 395
Davidson, K. M., 136
Davis, C., 485
Davis, D. J., 229
Davis, L. E., 5, 10, 12, 20, 22
Davis, S. K., 132, 135, 143
Deevey, S., 181
DeHovitz, J. A., 202
De Lange, J., 10
Densen-Gerber, J., 173
Dependency conflict, men and
    psychodynamic therapy,
    295–298
Depersonalization, sexual abuse,
    106
Depression, sexual abuse, 106
Derman, L., 134
DesJarlais, D., 209
Deutsch, H., 294
Developmental factors
  fathers and sons, 336–337
  men and psychodynamic therapy,
    299
*Diagnostic and Statistical Manual of
    Mental Disorders (DSM-IV)*
  attention-deficit/hyperactivity
    disorder, 431, 436
  eating disorders, 247–248
  homosexuality, 172
  sexual abuse, 100, 101
  sexually dependent men, 363
Diamond, J., 316, 320
DiClemente, C., 371, 372
Dillard, J., 457
DiNitto, D. M., 247

Dissociation
  sexual abuse, 105
  substance abuse and sexual abuse,
    110–111
Dore, J., 18, 20
Doueck, H. J., 132, 139
Dougher, M. J., 370
Downs, W. R., 127, 132
Dual diagnosis, substance abuse and
  gender, 14–15
Duck, S., 35
Duffy, T. K., 41
Dunivant, N., 437
Dweck, C. S., 9
Dysfunctional relationships, sexual
  abuse, 107

Earle, M. R., 362, 380
Earle, R. H., 362, 380
Eating disorders, 243–262
  definition, 247–248
  etiology, 248–251
  overview, 245
  substance abuse and, 245–247
  treatment, 251–259
Eberenz, K. P., 247
Eden, S. L., 461
Edinger, E. F., 317
Education. See Psychoeducation
Ego psychology, men and
  psychodynamic therapy,
  292–295
Eichenbaum, L., 275
El-Guebaly, N., 339
Elia, J., 442
Elias, M. J., 435, 437
Ellinwood, E., 203
Ellis, A., 254
Ellis, P., 170
Emotional problems, gender and, 10–12
Employee Assistance Program (EAP)
  high-achieving women, 159–160
  men's values, 327
Epidemiology, substance abuse and
  gender, 13–14
Erikson, E. H., 52

Esman, A. H., 340
Etiology
  codependency issues, 50–51
  substance abuse and gender, 15–16
Ettorre, E., 227–228
Evans, K., 131, 136, 438, 442

Fairbairn, W. R. D., 274
Fallon, P., 250, 254
Faludi, S., 125
Family
  fathers and sons, 337–339
  gambling, 485–488
  Hispanic men, 458, 463–464
  mothering, 132
  substance abuse and gender,
    17–18
Famularo, R., 347
Faraone, S. V., 435, 436
Farr, K. A., 133
Fathers and sons, 333–357
  etiological theory, 335–349
    abuse, 347–349
    developmental factors, 336–337
    family dynamics, 337–339
    identification, 340–341
    perceptions of father, 341–346
    perceptions of mother, 346–347
    role theory, 339–340
  overview, 335
  treatment, 349–354
Federal Register, 429
Feldman, C., 233
Fellios, P. G., 169
Female sexuality. See Sexuality
  (female)
Feminism. See also Women
  codependency issues, relational
    voice and, 54–55
  gender differences, 7–8
  lesbian women, 173
  men's movement and, 313–314
  pathologizing of maleness,
    300–301
  substance abuse and, 227–230
Fenichel, O., 291

Fifield, L., 169
Finkelhor, D., 128
Finkelstein, N., 125, 132, 134, 140
Finnegan, D. G., 181, 387, 389, 392
Finnegan, L. P., 199
Fischer, J., 135, 137
Fischer, M., 436
Fischl, M., 200
Fisher, G. L., 429, 435
Fisher, M., 247, 252, 253
Flaskerud, J. H., 144, 209
Flax, S., 413, 421
Fleming, A., 471
Forbing, S. E., 431, 437
Forrest, G. G., 36, 56
Forth-Finegan, J., 99
Fox, C. L., 431, 437
Fox, T., 474
Frankel, L. P., 227
Freeman, A., 234
Freeman, E. M., 80
Freud, S., 6, 7, 288–289, 300
Freudian perspective, gender
    differences, 6–7
Friedan, B., 153
Froberg, D., 154
Fromm, E., 294–295
Fullilove, M., 203

Galanter, M., 266
Gambling, 469–492
  continuum of activity, 475–477
  family impact, 485–488
  men and, 474–475
  overview, 471–472
  pathological
      mental disorders and, 480–481
      phases of, 477–480
      treatment, 481–485
  pubic policy, 472–474
  women and, 488
Gargaetas, P., 191
Garland, R. J., 370
Gawin, F. H., 203
Gelderloos, P., 237
Gelinas, D. J., 99, 100, 102

Gender
  assessment and treatment issues,
      19–22
  concept of, 5–6
  emotional problems and, 10–12
  substance abuse and, 12–19
    biophysiology, 16–17
    dual diagnosis, 14–15
    epidemiology, 13–14
    etiology, 15–16
    outcomes, 19
    psychosocial and family
        consequences, 17–18
    referrals, 18–19
Gender differences, 6–10
  current research, 8–10
  feminist perspective, 7–8
  Freudian perspective, 6–7
  learning disabilities and
      attention-deficit/hyperactivity
      disorder, 433–434
  socialization, 74–75
  women and Alcoholics
      Anonymous, 274–275
Gender identification
  concept of, 5–6
  female sexuality, 92
  feminist perspective, 7–8
  women and AIDS, 215–216
George, W. H., 75, 76
Geschwind, N., 434
Giedd, J. N., 433, 434
Gilbert, A., 341
Gilbert, M. J., 189
Gilligan, C., 8, 19, 35, 52, 54, 55, 153,
    154, 156
Gilmour, R., 35
Gittleman, R., 436, 437
Gleaves, D. H., 247
Glover, E., 289–290
Glover, N. M., 173, 182
Goldberg, H., 314
Goldstein, G., 299
Goleman, D., 9, 17, 234
Gomberg, E. S. L., 34, 129, 132, 133,
    135, 142, 228, 232

Good, C., 19, 21
Goode, E. E., 251
Goodwin, D. W., 81, 437
Gordon, B., 155, 229
Gordon, J. R., 484, 485
Gordon, L., 207
Gorney, B., 34
Gorski, T. T., 140
Grandiosity, men and
    psychodynamic therapy,
    305–306
Greenfield, B., 434, 436
Griffin, M. L., 12, 19, 225, 229, 230
Gross, R. M., 225, 232
Group psychotherapy, high-achieving
    women, 161
Grundlach, R., 173
Gualtieri, T., 429, 434
Guanaratana, H., 232
Guntrip, H. J., 274
Gutierrez, M., 453

Halikas, J. A., 230
Hall, J. M., 169, 174, 185, 186
Hallahan, D., 430
Hallowell, E. M., 429, 433, 435, 438,
    439, 441
Hamilton, G., 99
Hammen, C. L., 11
Hanchey, S. G., 245, 249, 255
Handley, M., 200
Hankins, C., 200
Harnell, W., 376, 380
Harris, B., 413
Harrison, D. F., 75
Hartocollis, P., 292, 294
Hauser, P., 433
Hawk, M. A. N., 133, 141
Hawley, T. L., 133
Hayward, F., 315
Healing, relational theory and, 38–40
Hechtman, L., 431, 432, 434, 438
Helfand, K. L., 182
Helzer, J. F., 13, 14, 130
Henderson, M. C., 347
Henker, B., 443

Herman, J. L., 78, 99, 100, 108, 110,
    227, 235
Hermann, J., 131, 133
Hernandez, M., 464
Heroic figures, men's values,
    318–319
Heron, G., 464
Heywood, C., 171, 185
Hicks, R., 434
Higgins, J. W., 341
High-achieving women, 151–166. *See
    also* Male executives
    historical perspective, 153–154
    narcissism in, 158–159
    professional success, 155–158
    recovery process, 163–164
    substance abuse and, 154–155
    treatment, 159–162
        EAP and, 159–160
        inpatient rehabilitation, 160–161
        psychotherapy (individual and
            group), 161
        twelve-step programs, 162
Hill, S., 340
Hine, D., 209
Hispanic men, 451–467
    codependency, 464–465
    culture, 456–459
    definitions, 453–455
    overview, 453
    substance abuse, 344–456
    treatment, 459–464
Hite, S., 75, 85
HIV/AIDS infection
    Hispanic men, 460
    homosexual men, 396, 402, 403–406
    lesbian women, 180–181
    mothering and, 134
    sexually dependent men, 369
    substance abuse and gender, 17
    testing, 404–405
    women, 34, 80, 197–221. *See also*
        Women and AIDS
Ho, M. H., 456, 457, 458, 459
Hocking, S. J., 117
Hoffman, J. A., 369

Holistic treatment, eating disorders, 258–259
Homophobia, homosexual men, 389–392
Homosexuality, 385–410. *See also* Lesbian women
  alcoholism and, 171–172
  assessment and treatment issues, 21
  body image, 396–498
  clinical considerations, 389
  couples, 406–407
  etiology, 388
  HIV/AIDS infection, 403–406
  homophobia, 389–392
  identity development, 392–395
  life cycle issues, 395–396
  men's values, 328
  overview, 387–388
  resources and referral sources, 408
  sex and intimacy, 401–403
  sexual addiction, 365
  sexually dependent men, 368
  sober socialization, 398–401
  stigma, 172–173
Hooks, B., 225
Horner, M. S., 155, 156
Horney, K., 7
Horowitz, M. J., 104
Houston-Hamilton, A., 210
Hsu, L. K., 251
Hudson, J., 246
Hunter, J., 206
Hurley, D. L., 173
Hyperphilia, sexually dependent men, 366–367

Ickovics, J., 204, 208
Identification, fathers and sons, 340–341
Identity development, homosexual men, 392–395
Impulsivity, sexual abuse, 106
Inciardi, J. A., 203
Inclan, J., 464
Inpatient rehabilitation, high-achieving women, 160–161

Institute of Medicine, 144, 269, 274
Interpersonal relationships, dysfunctional, sexual abuse, 107
Intravenous drug use, women and AIDS, 202–203
Irgens-Jensen, O., 299
Isay, R. A., 389
Israelstam, S., 169, 388

Jack, D. C., 226
Jacklin, C. N., 9
Jacklin-Nagy, C., 433
Jacob, T., 130
Jacobs, D. F., 485, 487, 488
Jacobson, A., 99
Jaffe, P., 132
Janet, P., 110
Janikowski, T. P., 173, 182
Jasinski, D. R., 429
Jaudes, P. K., 129
Jellinek, E. M., 74, 287
Jessor, R., 299
Johnson, C. L., 259
Johnson, J. L., 130
Johnson, N. P., 34
Johnson, P. B., 154
Johnson, V. E., 337, 419
Jong, M., 338
Jordan, J. V., 8, 34, 157, 275
Jordan, S. M., 169, 171, 172, 388, 389, 402

Kabat-Zinn, J., 232, 235, 237
Kafka, M. P., 368, 376
Kail, B. L., 455
Kandel, D. B., 216
Kane, S., 204
Kantor, G. K., 143
Kaplan, B. T., 207
Kaplan, C. P., 430, 435, 437
Kaplan, H. I., 11, 13, 14
Kaplan, H. S., 73, 82
Karacostas, D. D., 429, 435
Karan, L. D., 185
Kaskutas, L. A., 184
Kasl, C. D., 42
Kauffman, E., 142

Kauffman, J., 430
Kaufman, E., 13, 14, 20
Keilitz, I., 437
Kellam, S., 434, 436
Kelleher, K., 347
Kelley, A. M., 34, 35
Kelly, J. J., 396, 397
Kemper, J., 418
Kennedy, M., 206
Kertzner, R. M., 396, 397
Khantzian, E. J., 101, 292, 293, 349
Kierkegaard, S., 295
Kilbourne, J., 74, 81
Kinney, J., 18
Kinsey, A. C., 85
Kipnis, A. R., 15, 317, 318, 320, 323, 413
Kirkpatrick, J., 183
Klassen, A. D., 34
Klein, M., 7
Klein, R. G., 429, 443, 477, 488
Klinger, R. L., 407
Kluft, R. P., 100, 113
Knight, R. P., 290–291, 296
Kohen, J., 56, 76, 78, 79, 80, 87
Kohut, H., 274, 292, 295, 301
Kolata, G., 56
Koller, K. M., 341
Kominars, S. B., 389
Koontz, K., 248
Kornfield, J., 233
Koss, M. P., 205
Kovach, J. A., 276
Krahn, D. D., 245, 246, 248, 255
Kramer, P., 246
Kravis, N. M., 181
Kress, J. S., 435, 437
Krestan, J. A., 16, 43, 53, 99
Krueger, D. W., 158
Krystal, H., 292–293
Kuba, S. A., 245, 249, 255
Kübler-Ross, E., 41
Kus, R. J., 389, 399

LaDue, A., 189
Lahey, B. B., 436
Lambert, S., 169, 388

Landesman, T., 80
Langer, E. J., 237
LaRosa, J. H., 155
Latcovich, 389, 399
Laufer, M. W., 443
Laundergan, J. C., 472
Lawson, M., 144
Lazard, W. R., 413
Learning disabilities and
    attention-deficit/hyperactivity
        disorder, 427–449
    conduct and antisocial personality
        disorders, 436–437
    definitions and assessment, 429–433
    gender differences, 433–434
    overview, 429
    substance abuse, 434–436
    treatment, 437–444
Lee, J., 328
LeGreca, A. M., 435
Leigh, B. C., 86, 203, 216
Lennon, B., 380
Lerner, H. G., 42
Lesbian women, 167–196. *See also*
    Homosexuality
    AIDS, homosexual transmission,
        205–206
    etiology, 170–174
        alcoholism and homosexuality,
            171–172
        child abuse and, 173–174
        generally, 170–171
        stigma and, 172–173
    overview, 169–170
    recovery, 185–191
    treatment, 174–185
        gay-specific, 178–180
        generally, 174
        mainstream programs, 174–176
        outpatient treatment, 180–181
        protocols, 181–185
        women's facilities, 176–178
Leshner, A., 17
Lesieur, H. R., 475, 476, 477, 478,
    480, 481, 483, 485, 486, 488,
    489
Leventhal, J. M., 129

Levin, J. D., 292, 295
Levin, S., 340
Levine, C., 207
Levine, M. P., 139, 362
Levy, R. J., 341
Levy, S. J., 231
Lewis, C. E., 169
Lewis, G. R., 169, 171, 172, 388, 389,
    402
Lex, B. W., 10, 12, 15, 16
Lief, N. R., 143
Life cycle issues, homosexual men,
    395–396
Linden, R. D., 480, 481
Linehan, M. M., 232, 235, 440
Loftus, E. F., 104
Logan, S. L., 249
Logue, M. E., 141
Lohrenz, L., 169
Loney, J., 435, 443
Loper, R. G., 299
Lorenz, V., 485, 486
Loulan, J., 173
Lundholm, J., 248
Lundy, M., 154
Lyon, T., 254

Maccoby, E., 5, 155
Machismo. *See* Hispanic men
Mack, J., 336, 341
Mahler, M., 274
Maintenance, sexually dependent
    men, 381
Male executives, 411–425. *See also*
    High-achieving women
    male qualities, 413–414
    overview, 413
    return to work, 422–424
    substance abuse, 415–417
    treatment motivation, 417–418
Manly, H., 435
Mannuzza, S., 435
Marcenko, M. O., 134
Margolies, L., 390
Marin, B., 460
Marlatt, G. A., 484, 485
Marmor, M., 203

Marsh, J. C., 125, 131
Marte, C., 205
Martens, M., 202
Martin, S. E., 271
Martinez, C., 455
Martinez, J. L., 459
Mason, M., 37
Masturbation, female sexuality, 86
Mayer, J., 34
Mayers, R. S., 455
Maylon, A. K., 390
Mays, V. M., 208
McAuliffe, M. B., 37
McAuliffe, R. M., 37
McClelland, D. C., 16, 297, 298
McCord, J., 296
McCord, W., 296
McCormick, R. A., 481
McCoy, V., 203
McCrady, B. S., 142, 414
McGowan, R., 471
McGrath, E., 231
McKay, J. R., 341
McKenna, T., 339
McKirnan, D. J., 169
McLaughlin, J., 453
McNally, E. B., 181, 387, 389, 392
McNeece, C. A., 247
McQueen, D. V., 169
Meade, M., 316
Medication
    learning disabilities and
        attention-deficit/hyperactivity
        disorder, 442–444
    sexual abuse and substance abuse,
        117–118
Meditation, women and depression,
    232–234
Mello, N. K., 170
Melville, M. B., 456
Men
    fathers and sons. *See also* Fathers
        and sons
    gambling, 469–492. *See also*
        Gambling
    Hispanic men, 451–467. *See also*
        Hispanic men

homosexual men, 385–410. *See also* Homosexuality

learning disabilities and attention-deficit/hyperactivity disorder, 427–449. *See also* Learning disabilities and attention-deficit/hyperactivity disorder

male executives, 411–425. *See also* Male executives

psychodynamic perspective on, 285–309. *See also* Men and psychodynamic therapy

sexual dependence and, 359–384. *See also* Sexually dependent men

values of, 311–332. *See also* Men's values

Men and psychodynamic therapy, 285–309

dependency conflict and power theories, 295–298

developmental factors, 299

early theories, 287–292

ego psychology and self psychology, 292–295

empirical findings, 298–299

father identification, 299–300

narcissism, 301–302

overview, 287

pathologizing of maleness, 300–301

primary and secondary addiction, 298

treatment, 302–306

Mendelson, J. H., 170

Mendoza, R. H., 459

Menninger, K., 291

Men's values, 311–332

heroic figures, 318–319

men's movement, 313–318

overview, 313

treatment, 319–331

Mental health problems, mothering, 130–131

Merrick, J. C., 133, 141

Metzger, L., 318

Midanick, L. T., 79

Mik, G., 340

Miller, B. A., 18, 126, 127, 128, 136

Miller, D., 338

Miller, H., 204

Miller, J. B., 35, 54, 156, 161, 162, 201, 213, 275

Miller, K. J., 53

Miller, N. A., 125, 131

Miller, W. R., 361, 372, 373, 374, 375, 376

Mindfulness meditation, women and depression, 232–234

Minkhoff, H. L., 202

Minority groups, sexual orientation and, 169

Miranda, J., 237

Mirande, A., 457

Mirin, S. M., 443

Mish, F. C., 225

Mitchell, J. E., 248

Mok, J., 206, 207

Molina, B., 342

Money, J., 362, 366, 367

Monteiro, M. G., 231

Moore, D., 437, 440

Mora, J., 189

Moran, E., 476

Morell, C. M., 125

Morgan, S. M., 18

Morrison, J. R., 436

Mothering, 123–150

AIDS and, 206–207

assessment, 134–138

fathers and sons, 346–347

mother characteristics, 125–134

case example, 125–126

child maltreatment, 129

family system issues, 132

mental health problems, 130–131

parental substance abuse, 129–130

pregnancy, 132–133

self-esteem and stigmatization, 131–132

socioeconomic deficits, 133–134

victimization, 126–129

overview, 125

treatment, 138–144

Mulder, E. A., 162
Mulinski, P., 341, 347
Murphy, B. L., 170
Murphy, J. M., 347
Murphy, S., 34
Mythopoetic groups, men's
    movement and, 315–316

Narcissism
  high-achieving women, 158–159
  men and psychodynamic therapy,
    301–302
Nardi, P., 339, 388
Nass, R. D., 433
Nathan, J. A., 185
National Council on Problem
    Gambling, 471–472, 475, 480
National Institute on Alcohol Abuse
    and Alcoholism (NIAAA), 16, 81
National Institute on Drug Abuse
    (NIDA), 13, 22
National Organization of Men Against
    Sexism, 314
Need-for-power theory, men and
    psychodynamic therapy,
    297–298
Neisen, J. H., 173, 181
Nelson-Zlupko, L., 51, 52
Newman, T., 202
Nhat Hanh, T., 233
Nichols, S., 173
Nicoloff, L. K., 181
Nightingale, S., 201
Nirenberg, T. D., 132, 133
Nolen-Hoeksema, S., 226
Norris, J., 77, 80
Nowinski, J., 314, 317, 318, 324
Numbing, substance abuse and
    sexual abuse, 108–109
Nyamathi, A. M., 144, 210
Nylander, I., 338

O'Connell, T., 417, 418
O'Connor, L. E., 229, 230, 349
Oedipus complex, gender
    differences, 6–10

Offord, D. R., 339
Ofshe, R., 104
O'Hare, T., 11
Oldenburg, R., 321
O'Leary, A., 209
Olson, M., 21
"One moment at a time" group,
    women and depression, 234–239
Orbach, S., 275
Orford, J., 363
Orr, S., 210
Ounsted, C., 434
Outcomes
  codependency issues and, 58–59
  substance abuse and gender, 19

Padesky, C. A., 11
Padian, N. S., 199, 200
Pandina, R. J., 337
Pape, P. A., 12, 16, 55, 56, 313
Paraphilia, sexually dependent men,
    366–367
Patterson, E. G., 180
Peller, J., 22
Penick, E., 335, 337
Pennell, C. R., 75
Perez-Bouchard, L., 338
Persistence, treatment,
    codependency issues and, 58–59
Peterson, P. L., 169
Petrie, A., 299
Pickens, R., 339
Pillard, R. C., 388
Pitkanan, T., 340
Pivnick, A., 203, 204, 216
Pizzi, M., 201
Plasse, B. R., 142, 143
Plath, S., 226
PLISSIT model, described, 81–83
Posttraumatic stress disorder (PTSD),
    sexual abuse, 100, 102, 105, 107,
    174
Power theories, men and
    psychodynamic therapy, 295–298
Pregnancy, substance abuse during,
    132–133

Primary addiction, men and psychodynamic therapy, 298
Prochaska, J. O., 234, 371, 372
Proctor, E. K., 5, 10, 12, 20, 22
Professional women. *See* High-achieving women
Pryzbeck, T. R., 13, 14, 130
Psychoeducation, sexual abuse and substance abuse, 113–114
Psychopathology, gender and, 10–12
Psychosocial consequences, substance abuse and gender, 17–18
Psychotherapy
  eating disorders, 254–258
  group, high-achieving women, 161
  men and psychodynamic therapy, 285–309. *See also* Men and psychodynamic therapy
Public policy, gambling, 472–474
Puig, K., 477
Pulkkinen, L., 340
Putnam, F. W., 113

Queralt, M., 458

Rado, S., 290, 293
Ralph, N., 429
Ramos-McKay, J., 457, 458, 463
Rape, sexuality (female), stereotypes, 76
Rapport, M. D., 442
Raskin, H., 292–293
Ratey, J. J., 429, 433, 435, 438, 439, 441
Rational Emotive Therapy (RET), Alcoholics Anonymous and women, 278
Ravndal, E., 112
Raymond, C., 11
Raymond, N. C., 251
Raytek, H., 142
Recovery
  high-achieving women, 163–164
  lesbian women, 185–191

quality of, codependency issues and, 63
substance abuse and gender, 19
Reddy, B., 159
Reed, B. G., 125, 131, 140, 142, 144
Referrals
  homosexual men, 408
  substance abuse and gender, 18–19
Reidbord, S. P., 104
Reider, R., 209
Relapse
  codependency issues and, 58–59
  sexually dependent men, 381
  substance abuse and gender, 19
Relational theory, 33–46
  addiction and, 33–34
  addictions and, 35–38
  described, 34–35
  healing and, 38–40
  treatment approaches, 40–44
  women and AA, 274–275
Rheingold, H., 321
Rhodes, S. S., 429
Richardson, D., 76
Richardson, R., 472, 477
Richmond-Abbot, M., 75
Ries, R., 140
Rivinus, T. M., 141
Robbins, C., 17
Rodin, J., 204, 208
Rodriguez, R., 208
Rohsenow, D. J., 99, 173
Role theory, fathers and sons, 339–340
Rolf, J. E., 130
Rollnick, S., 361, 372, 373, 374, 375, 376
Root, M. P., 182, 254
Rose, I. N., 472, 473
Rosecrance, J., 472
Rosenbaum, M., 34, 204
Rosenthal, R. J., 476, 477, 488
Ross, J., 130, 246, 252, 347
Rossner, S. V., 200, 205
Roth, P., 144

Rothenberg, R., 201
Rothschild, R. J., 485, 486, 488, 489
Rounsaville, B. J., 230
Rucker, C. E., 247
Rush, C. E., 209
Russel, D., 99
Russell, S. A., 42
Russo, N. F., 12
Rydelius, P. A., 338

Saba, J., 207
Safety, sexual abuse and substance
    abuse, 112–113
Sakheim, D. K., 113
Sallee, F. R., 442
Sanchez Mayers, R., 455, 457, 458
Sandall, H., 173
Sandmaier, M., 12, 169, 227, 274
Sarnoff, C. A., 347
Satterfield, J. H., 436
Schaef, A. W., 50
Schafer, J. C., 86
Schilit, R., 34
Schilling, R. F., 210
Schliebner, C. T., 230
Schmidt, L., 12
Schneider, R. J., 341
Schoenbaum, E., 202
Schuckit, M. A., 231, 335
Schwartz, M., 380
Sears, R., 340
Secondary addiction, men and
    psychodynamic therapy, 298
Sederer, L. I., 136
Seid, R. A., 245
Seidman, S., 209
Seilhamer, R. A., 130
Self-esteem
    men and psychodynamic therapy,
      305–306
    mothering, 131–132
Self-harm, substance abuse and
    sexual abuse, 109–110
Self psychology, men and
    psychodynamic therapy,
    292–295

Self-soothing, substance abuse and
    sexual abuse, 108–109
Sexaholics Anonymous, 378
Sexism, Alcoholics Anonymous and,
    263–281. *See also* Women and
    Alcoholics Anonymous
Sexual abuse, 97–122. *See also* Child
    abuse
    assessment of abuse, 102–105
    assessment of substance abuse,
      107–108
    indicators of, 105–107
    lesbian women, 173–174
    mothering and, 129. *See also*
      Mothering
    overview, 99
    recovery process issues, 115–119
    sequelae of, 99–101
    substance abuse and, 101–102,
      108–111
    treatment goals, 119–120
    treatment of substance abuse, 111–
      115
Sexual addiction, sexually dependent
    men, 364–366
Sexuality (female), 73–95
    distortions, 78–81
    overview, 73–74
    socialization, 74–75
    stereotypes, 75–76
    treatment and, 81–92
    victimization, 76–78
Sexually dependent men, 359–384
    current concepts, 363–367
      compulsive behavior, 363–364
      paraphilia and hyperphilia, 366–
        367
      sexual addiction, 364–366
    dependency definition, 367
    etiology, 368–369
    historical perspective, 362–363
    maintenance and relapse, 381
    overview, 361
    sexual problems, 361–362
    substance abuse, 369
    treatment issues, 370–380

Shachter, E., 430, 437
Shafer, R., 340
Shaffer, K., 75
Shame, men and psychodynamic
     therapy, 306
Shayne, V. T., 207
Shiboski, C. H., 202
Shirley, C., 417
Shore, E. R., 154
Smith, R. J., 418, 419
Smith, R. M., 398, 401, 402
Sobel, S., 12
Sobell, L. C., 225
Sobell, M. B., 225
Sobriety, maintenance of,
     codependency issues and, 61–63
Socarides, C. W., 339
Socialization
     gender differences, 74–75
     of women, codependency issues,
         51–53
Socioeconomic deficits
     eating disorders, 250–251
     mothering, 133–134
Sokolow, L., 19
Solomon, J., 413
Soriano, F., 460
Speller, J. L., 415
Spiegel, B. R., 162, 265, 275
Stafford, R., 266, 267, 276
Stall, R., 203
Starr, R. H., Jr., 127
Steadman, H. J., 472, 477
Steinglass, P., 338
Stereotypes, sexuality (female), 75–
     76
Sterling, S., 229
Stevens, M., 416
Stevens, P., 206
Stewart, M. A., 436
Stiglitz, E. A., 181
Stigma, homosexuality, 172–173
Stigmatization, mothering, 131–132
Stimmel, B., 413
Stone, W. L., 435
Straus, M., 136, 143

Straussner, S. L. A., 12, 13, 15, 16, 18,
     19, 20, 107, 129, 132, 133, 154,
     229, 274
Strom, D., 200, 211
Stuefen, R. M., 472, 477
Suarez, M., 209
Sullivan, J. M., 131, 136, 438, 442
Summers, L., 413
Surrey, J. L., 51, 56, 77, 80, 85
Sved, M., 396, 397
Svikis, D. S., 15
Szasz, T., 292

Taha-Cisse, A. H., 189
Tannen, D., 10
Tarter, R. E., 299
Tauber, M. A., 434
Taylor, D., 434
Temple, M. T., 86
Therapeutic alliance, sexual abuse
     and substance abuse, 111
Tiebout, H., 291–292
Titration, sexual abuse and substance
     abuse, 114–115
Transference, codependency issues,
     67
Treadway, D., 464
Treatment
     Alcoholics Anonymous and
         women, 275–278
     codependency issues and, 57–65.
         See also Codependency issues
     eating disorders, 251–259
     fathers and sons, 349–354
     gambling, 481–485
     gender differences and, 19–22
     high-achieving women, 159–162
     Hispanic men, 459–464
     learning disabilities and
         attention-deficit/hyperactivity
         disorder, 437–444
     lesbian women, 174–185. *See also*
         Lesbian women
     male executives, 417–422
     men and psychodynamic therapy,
         302–306

Treatment (*continued*)
  men's values, 319–331. *See also*
    Men's values
    congruent values, 325–326
    middle aged men, 326
    traditional treatment versus,
      319–325
    work ethic, 326–331
  mothering, 138–144
  sexual abuse and substance abuse,
    111–115. *See also* Sexual abuse
  sexuality (female), 81–92. *See also*
    Sexuality (female)
  sexually dependent men,
    370–380
  women and AIDS, 211–215
  women and depression, 234–239
Treichler, P., 200
Trepper, T. S., 44, 173
Troiden, R. R., 362
Trotter, C., 140
Trotter, T., 287–288
Tucker, M. B., 132, 133
Turnbull, J. E., 34, 225, 231, 232, 274,
  276
Turner, S., 99, 100
Twelve-step programs
  high-achieving women, 162
  learning disabilities and
    attention-deficit/hyperactivity
    disorder, 441–442
  lesbian women, 184

Underhill, B. L., 174, 178, 185,
  186
Unger, R. K., 5
U.S. Department of Health and
  Human Services, 274
Ussher, J., 227

Vaglum, P., 112
Vaillant, G., 336, 354
Valdez, L., 459
Values, of men, 311–322. *See also*
  Men's values
VanBremen, J. R., 141, 142, 143

Van Conas, C., 440
Van Den Bergh, N., 22
Vandereycken, W., 248, 252, 254
Vandor, M., 134
Van Natta, D., 155
Vannicelli, M., 142
VanOss Marin, B., 216
Van Wormer, K. S., 16, 246, 248
Victimization
  mother characteristics, 126–129
  sexuality (female), 76–78
Volberg, R. A., 471, 472, 476, 477,
  481, 488
Volkow, N. D., 443
Volpe, J., 99

Waldorf, D., 33
Wall, L. J., 181
Wallace, J., 326
Wallen, J., 132, 137
Wallisch, L., 477
Walter, J., 22
Ware, N. C., 267, 269
Wasserman, D. R., 129
Watters, E., 104
Webber, M., 202
Wegscheider, S., 51, 130
Weil, A., 36
Weinberg, G., 388, 389
Weisner, C., 12
Weiss, G., 431, 432, 434, 437, 438
Weiss, R. D., 443
Welwood, J., 233
Wender, P. H., 429, 431, 434, 436,
  438, 442, 443
Westermeyer, J., 183
Wiener, L., 199, 200
Wilke, D., 169
Wilsnack, R. W., 13, 42, 155, 169
Wilsnack, S. C., 12, 13, 34, 42, 79,
  154, 155, 169
Wilton, J. M., 180
Winnicott, D. W., 162, 274, 304
Winokur, G., 298
Witenstein, K., 209
Wofsy, C., 208

Wolf, N., 245, 247, 250
Women. *See also* Feminism
  Alcoholics Anonymous and, 263–
    281. *See also* Women and
    Alcoholics Anonymous
  codependency issues, 47–69. *See*
    also Codependency issues
  depression and, 223–242. *See also*
    Women and depression
  eating disorders, 243–262. *See also*
    Eating disorders
  gambling and, 488
  high-achieving women, 151–166.
    See also High-achieving women
  HIV/AIDS infection, 197–221. *See*
    also Women and AIDS
  lesbian women, 167–196. *See also*
    Lesbian women
  mothering, 123–150. *See also*
    Mothering
  relational theory and, 33–46. *See*
    also Relational theory
  sexual abuse and, 97–122. *See also*
    Sexual abuse
  sexuality and, 73–95. *See also*
    Sexuality (female)
Women and AIDS, 197–221
  assessment, 208–211
  epidemiology, 199–200
  gender roles and responsibilities,
    215–216
  heterosexual transmission, 203–205
  historical perspective, 200–201
  homosexual transmission, 205–206
  impacts, 201–202
  intravenous drug use, 202–203
  motherhood, 206–207

  overview, 199
  treatment, 211–215
Women and Alcoholics Anonymous,
  263–281
  Big Book and, 266–268
  gender differences, 274–275
  historical perspective, 265–266
  meetings, 269–271
  overview, 265
  socialization, 271–274
  treatment integration, 275–278
Women and depression, 223–242
  literature review, 226–232
  mindfulness meditation, 232–234
  "one moment at a time" group,
    234–239
  overview, 225
Wooley, S. C., 247, 250
Woolger, C., 127
Work ethic, men's values, 326–331
Worth, D., 208
Wright, S. I., 155
Wurmser, L., 292, 293–294
Wykes, A., 471

Yandow, V., 99
Yeager, J., 254
Young, J. E., 234
Younger, B., 154

Zametkin, A. J., 433, 443
Zankowski, G. L., 99, 133
Zeitlin, H., 347
Zelvin, E., 50, 275
Zerbe, K. J., 248, 249
Zimberg, S., 158
Zuckerman, C., 207